WELSH SAILORS
OF THE SECOND WORLD WAR

Welsh Sailors

of the

Second World War

by

Phil Carradice

and

Terry Breverton

ISBN 1-903529-19-0
ISBN 978-1-903529-19-0

Published in 2007 by Glyndŵr Publishing,
PO Box 68, Cowbridge CF71 9AY

Cover Design by the Welsh Books Council

The publication was assisted by a grant from the Welsh Books Council

Printed in Wales by J&P Davison, Trefforest

ACKNOWLEDGEMENTS

Phil Carradice

Above all, sincere and heartfelt thanks to the men and women who so impressively and ably told their stories. Without their willing co-operation this book would not have been possible. Any errors or mistakes are entirely my own and do not reflect upon their recollections or judgements in any way. For those whose stories I have not been able to use, thanks for your interest and sincere apologies – it was just not possible to use all the material.

Many of the photographs in the book come from the author's own collection. The more personal ones, however, were provided by the sailors themselves. Thanks to them for giving a different perspective to the stories. Particular thanks need to go to George Akerman whose photographic collection has provided an invaluable resource.

Thanks to anyone who assisted in any way, with leads, stories, advice or criticism. Particular thanks must go to John Harrop of Newport, an invaluable source of information, and to the staff of the various libraries I have used.

Thanks to Margaret Stimson, Community Library Manager, Chepstow, and to Roy James, Secretary of the Submarine Old Comrades Association (No 1 Branch, South Wales).

And finally, thanks yet again to Trudy, my long-suffering and supportive wife. Without your encouragement, not to mention your forbearance at seeing the table disappear once again under mounds of paper, the book would still be only an idea.

EDITOR'S PREFACE

Terry Breverton

Both Phil and I come from ports – Phil from Pembroke Dock and myself from Barry. We are both of that fortunate first generation in British history who never had to go to war. Yet, we have grown up with our parents' and families' memories of World War II. We have known torpedoed uncles and relatives, and the relatives of friends and neighbours who died at sea.

In the great south Wales ports of Milford, Swansea, Barry, Cardiff and Newport, the sea was the natural vocation. Nearly everyone I knew of my father's generation went to sea from my home town of Barry. It was a town built upon the rise of its docks, and people were drawn either to work there or to go to sea. My father's generation participated in the great events of World War Two, one of the very, very few 'just' wars in man's history.

And it has been humbling to realise in the course of research and interviews, the true bravery of the survivors of the war at sea, especially the 'unsung service', the Merchant Navy. As Churchill rightly acknowledged, it was the Merchant Navy, more than any other service, which allowed Britain to win the war. One reads of a teenager trying to lift his friend out of the water, only to find that his legs are missing. One discovers men going mad from thirst on open boats. Men slipping quietly over the side when they can take no more pain. One learns of 15 year-old boys dying at sea, men hiding the extent of their terrible injuries so others can be helped.

The book began with the idea of trying to garner the memories of those Welsh survivors of the war at sea, before they are lost to us, as a memorial to real heroism – the heroism that seeks no reward. However, this is unfair to the memory of those who died at sea, and in the years afterwards, so it was also decided to choose one Welsh port and analyse how and where these brave men died. Barry was chosen, mainly because of the ground-breaking work of the late Fred Hortop, but it is hoped that such work can be completed upon the other Welsh ports.

I am extremely fortunate to know one of our best Welsh writers and broadcasters, Phil Carradice, who was equally enthusiastic that we should preserve these memories of bravery and selflessness for all time, for our heritage. We would welcome other stories from the sea, and hopefully they can be printed in the future. At present we are also collecting memories from Welsh airmen and soldiers and would welcome any contributions.

> Unrecognized, you put us in your debt;
> Unthanked, you enter, or escape, the grave;
> Whether your land remember or forget
> You saved the land, or died to try and save.
>
> (from 'For All Seafarers' by John Masefield)

CONTENTS

INTRODUCTION

During the Second World War there were many pivotal moments when the conflict swung, first one way and then the other. These ranged from events such as the Dunkirk evacuation and the Battle of Britain to the Japanese attack on Pearl Harbour and the German surrender at Stalingrad. For Britain, the war at sea was not just a pivotal moment; it was a long drawn-out conflict, the resolution of which was crucial to the survival of the nation. If the lumbering vessels of the Merchant Marine had failed to arrive in British ports, then the people would have starved and its forces could not have been supplied. If the Royal Navy had not maintained overall command of the sea then the country, and its far-flung Dominions, would have withered and perished.

During the war at sea there were successes and failures, moments of glorious triumph and of humiliating defeat. Ultimately, there was a hard-fought and deserved victory. That victory would have been impossible without the incredible bravery and sheer dogged persistence of Britain's sailors. Their story has been told many times. What makes this book different is the fact that, here, their voices, their views on battles, actions and life at sea, are recorded and presented in their own words.

While the focus of the book is on Wales and Welsh sailors, in many respects these stories could so easily have been told by men and women from Northern Ireland, Scotland or England. Their experiences were, broadly speaking, the same. The hidden enemy was certainly the same and, above all, what the writer Nicholas Monsarrat has so memorably called "the cruel sea" was also the same. All that is different is the way in which the sailors viewed their experiences - in this case in that particular and specific Welsh way that has, over the centuries, created a nation of story-tellers and poets.

The book is presented in three main sections. To begin with there is an overview of the sea war between 1939 and 1945, important if the sailors' stories are to be put into perspective. Then there is a brief look at the war around the Welsh coast. And finally – and most importantly – there are the stories of the sailors themselves. It was not the initial intention of the authors to add the subsequent chapters, but they are important and specific instances of heroism at sea; underline the contribution of Welsh ports and their seamen; and add information upon Welsh shipping losses and on a particular enemy – the U boat.

The stories are a representative selection but here you will find the recollections of Merchant and Royal Navy seamen, Wrens and dock workers. There are memories from men who served on the Russian and Atlantic convoys, tales from submariners and destroyer men. Men were hit and sunk by German, Italian and Japanese submarines, Axis planes and capital ships, and lost through the 'normal' perils of the sea. There is even one account from a Coastal Command flyer – after all, air power was one of the decisive factors in finally defeating the U Boat menace. From the Far East to the Home Fleet and the Mediterranean, the sailors have willingly and honestly told their stories. The importance of the Atlantic convoys is told in Part Fifteen – far more than any other factor in the war (which Churchill freely admitted) – this was its greatest, and longest, battle.

And what incredible stories they are. Courage and bravery run through all of them, although the sailors themselves would undoubtedly deny that they were doing anything out of the ordinary. Yet there is no doubt that without their contributions the war would not have been won. That is probably the best tribute anyone could give these incredibly brave men and women.

Read the book, enjoy the stories. They are a record of difficult and dangerous times. Above all they are a record of how ordinary people responded to those times and to the threat of total annihilation. They are a record of gallantry and sacrifice. They are history at its very best.

PART ONE

The War At Sea

'The Battle of the Atlantic was the dominating factor all through the war. Never for one moment could we forget that everything happening elsewhere, on land, at sea, or in the air depended ultimately on its outcome, and amid all other cares we viewed its changing fortunes day by day with hope or apprehension. The tale of hard and unremitting toil, often under conditions of acute discomfort and frustration and always in the presence of unseen danger, is lighted by incident and drama. But for the individual sailor or airman in the u-boat war there were few moments of exhilarating action to break the monotony of an endless succession of anxious, uneventful days. Vigilance could never be relaxed. Dire crisis might at any moment flash upon the scene with brilliant fortune or glare with mortal tragedy. Many gallant actions and incredible feats of endurance are recorded, but the deeds of those who perished may never be known. Our merchant seamen displayed their highest qualities, and the brotherhood of the sea was never more strikingly shown than in their determination to defeat the U-boat.

(Winston Churchill, The Second World War, Vol. V: The Closing Ring.)

The seeds of antagonism and aggression that eventually erupted into the Second World War owe their origins to the ill-judged, vindictive and, ultimately, destructive Treaties of Versailles and St Germain in 1919. These were the peace treaties that formally ended the First World War, the war to end all wars as it was universally known.

The two treaties saw Germany disarmed and humiliated in the eyes of the world, labelled as the major instigator of the conflict and therefore guilty of the deaths of ten million soldiers, sailors and airmen. Germany might have been beaten, her economy ruined by the crippling reparations she was forced to pay, but her people were far from cowed. The myth of "the stab in the back," later so successfully perpetuated by the Nazi Party, suggested that the

The advent of the Nazi Party in Germany during the 1920s and 30s meant that war was inevitable, sooner or later.

German armed forces had not been defeated in battle, simply betrayed by profiteers and politicians at home. Fallacy it may have been, yet the myth was an essential part of the character of the German people at this time, a character and spirit best exemplified by the behaviour of her sailors.

Seven months after the end of the war the "Friedrich der Grosse," flagship of the German High Seas Fleet at the Battle of Jutland, hoisted her battle ensigns in a signal that was quickly picked up by the other captive German ships moored in Scapa Flow. German flags rose to the mastheads of over seventy vessels – and then they began to sink. The "Friedrich der Grosse," the "Konig," the "Von der Tann," battleships and battle cruisers that had been the pride of the Kriegsmarine, slowly settled at their moorings and disappeared

Hitler enters the Sudetenland, the start of the slide to war.

beneath the waves. The name Kriegsmarine, or 'War Navy' existed from 1935 to 1945, replacing Reichsmarine.

Scuttling the ships that had been demanded by the allies as part of the punishment of defeated Germany might well have made the sailors feel a great deal better. Yet it did nothing to alleviate the situation in which the German Navy found itself. The Treaty of Versailles limited the Kriegsmarine to just six old battleships, six light cruisers, twelve destroyers and a number of smaller light craft. Significantly, no submarines were to be retained, Britain being only too aware that the U Boats had nearly succeeded where Admiral Hipper's giant dreadnoughts had failed and, in 1917 and early 1918, come as close to bringing Britain to her knees as at any time during the whole war.

The mood within Germany, as economic sanctions and world depression began to bite, turned rapidly towards the political extremes. The Weimar Republic, created after the abdication of the Kaiser in 1918, was always doomed to disaster. Riots and rebellions followed quickly on the heels of attempted coups d'etat, with pitched battles fought on the streets between political groups in order to gain ascendancy. Suffice to say, history records that Adolf Hitler's Nazi Party achieved the final victory when the Austrian corporal became Chancellor of Germany in January 1933.

After that it was simply a matter of gradual re-armament. A second world-wide conflict was inevitable, particularly after Hitler openly broke the conditions of the Treaty of Versailles in March 1935 by announcing the creation of an air force under Herman Goering. While the British, French and American governments did nothing, the German navy, like the country's army and embryo air force, was ready for the war that was now only a few years away.

From the early 1920s the hidden hand of the Kriegsmarine had been behind the building of several fast banana freighters for possible use as armed auxiliary cruisers at some stage in the future. The deception worked and no-one picked up on these potentially dangerous commerce raiders until they were at sea, scouring the sea lanes for victims in the early years of the next war. As early as 1922 the navy had also obtained a substantial interest in a Dutch design company where the leading German submarine engineers were employed, designing prototype vessels allegedly for foreign governments but, in reality, waiting and planning for the day when someone like Hitler would order a full U Boat building programme once more.

The 1930s, after Hitler's accession to power, saw the creation of the famous pocket battleships, vessels like the "Deutschland" and "Graf Spee," supposedly built within the limitations of the armaments treaties of the time but, in reality, heavily armed and armoured warships that were revolutionary in design. They were followed by huge battleships and battle cruisers such as the "Bismark," "Tirpitz," "Scharnhorst" and "Gneisenau." More importantly – and much more sinister – the spectre of the U Boat now reared its head once more.

Despite the signing of an Anglo-German Naval Treaty in June 1935, limiting the size and strength of the respective British and German fleets, it was only eleven days after the formalities that the sleek cigar-shape of the U1 slid easily and elegantly into the waters of Kiel dockyard. She had been laid down many months previously, long before the decision was taken to allow Germany to build a submarine fleet again, and by January 1936 a further eleven submarines were already in commission. The most potent and dangerous arm of the German navy was, therefore, in existence long before the war began and its sailors were ready and eager for the conflict.

For the British, however, it was all a rather different matter. With hindsight, it is difficult to understand quite how the controllers of Britain's naval strategy allowed the country to be brought within an inch of defeat by an attack against the commerce on which the country so clearly depended – not once, but twice within the space of thirty years! Yet this is exactly what happened.

Since the days of Nelson, defending merchant shipping had always been one of the main functions of the Royal Navy. It was an essential task when so much of the country's food supplies came in from abroad, from the different parts of the Empire and from trading countries like Argentina and the USA. However, following the carnage of the First World War, when a whole generation perished in the mud of Flanders, there grew in Britain a real desire never to go to war again. And as a result the Royal Navy was allowed to diminish and dwindle.

When war broke out on 3rd September 1939 the Royal Navy had only 150 destroyers in commission and almost no aircraft to provide escort for merchant ships. When compared to the figures for 1918 – 257 escorts, 490 aircraft and 75

HMS "Exeter," a typical "Treaty" cruiser, beautiful to look at but under armoured and under gunned.

airships, along with a further 500 vessels that could be deployed when necessary – the rundown of this particular arm of the Royal Navy can be clearly seen, if not understood. It was done despite the bitter experience of 1917 and 1918, when it had been clearly demonstrated that fast escort vessels armed with depth charges were the most effective way of dealing with the U Boat threat. Unfortunately, the success of the convoy system, combined with the invention, late on in the war, of a device that enabled the detection of submerged U Boats – ASDIC, called after the initials of the Allied Submarine Detection Investigation Committee - had led to a degree of misplaced optimism. The day of the submarine, many people felt, was over.

There was also an unjustified belief that, in the future, submarines would operate under the normal Rules of War. Such optimism was a total fallacy, as the U Boat fleet was soon to prove. Germany may well have had only 57 operational U Boats at the outbreak of war but that was more than enough to cause an immediate threat to the British lifeline.

As far as larger surface craft were concerned Britain had been one of the few major powers to adhere to the various treaties of the 1920s and 30s that limited the size of such warships. It meant that the Royal Navy was, perhaps, over burdened with capital ships dating from World War One and with "treaty cruisers" like HMS "Exeter". A beautiful ship to look at, "Exeter" with her limited weaponry was no match for the 11-inch guns of the "Graf Spee" and was duly pummelled at the Battle of the River Plate. A programme of building more capital ships had been set in motion once Hitler's real intentions became clear, but these new ships would take several years to become fully operational.

For the men of Britain's Merchant Navy the outbreak of war was met with resignation and an understanding that, as always, the supply of food to the civilian population and transport of military supplies for the armed forces would depend on them. Men of the merchant marine had faced the rigours of life afloat, battling against the elements and even the sea itself, for thousands of years. In time of war their job involved even greater danger. Now, in 1939, they were to face a challenge such as they had never encountered before, taking on a vicious and dedicated

*Britain's battleships, bulwark of the Empire and the country, although in 1939 too many of
them were First World War vintage.*

enemy which was equipped and ready to try and strangle the life out of Britain and
her Empire.

If the Royal Navy had suffered at the hands of those in power in the years
between 1918 and 1939, the Merchant Navy had endured similar treatment, if not
worse. There had been little improvement in the working conditions of the sailors
during this time. The basic working week of 64 hours, before overtime was paid, was
far longer than that of almost any other trade. Pay was poor and conditions on
board British ships were invariably uncomfortable, unhygienic and demanding.

In 1938 the death rate amongst merchant seamen was 47% higher than the
national average, tuberculosis being particularly rife. Cockroaches, bugs and filth
were common on many ships. Seamen had little or no privacy, living crammed
together in the most arduous of conditions. And that was for those sailors who
actually managed to find a berth. Many shipping companies went out of business in
the years after the Depression and unemployment in the Merchant Navy rarely fell
below 20% during this period.

Despite this, in 1939 there were still almost 3000 cargo ships and tankers
registered in Britain, along with 1000 coasters, giving a total of 21 million tons of
shipping. The average number of British ships at sea on any one day was 2500. In
1938 alone, cargoes weighing more than 67 million tons were brought into the
country by country's ships. The cargoes consisted of food and drink, oil and raw
materials for industry and a wide range of manufactured goods. Small wonder, then,
that the Kriegsmarine placed such emphasis on its submarine arm.

Wales had always maintained strong links with the sea. Nelson's fleet at the
Battle of Trafalgar had sailors from every Welsh county in its ranks while the stories
of the "Cape Horners" from the Cardigan Bay and North Wales coasts are too well
known to recount here. With the growth of the coal trade in the nineteenth
century, a plethora of shipping firms was quickly established in important ports like
Cardiff and Barry. By 1914 there were more than 120 separate shipping companies

Britain's merchant sailors were used to harsh conditions in the tramp steamers of the time.

with their head offices in Cardiff alone, most of them grouped around the Bute Street area of the city. By the end of the thirties, as the coming conflict loomed ever closer, that figure had been reduced to just 77, but shipping still represented a major employer in Wales. And that meant, once war came to the world, that the Welsh community of sailors was likely to be very hard hit indeed.

* * * * * *

Prime Minister Neville Chamberlain made his momentous broadcast, announcing that the country was at war with Germany, at 11 o' clock on the morning of Sunday 3rd September 1939. The U Boats were already at sea. Early on the morning of 4th September, barely 12 hours after war was declared, Kapitan-Leutnant Fritz-Julius Lemp sighted the 13,581 ton liner "Athena" crossing the bows of his submarine U30, some 250 miles to the north-west of Ireland. The "Athena" was blacked out, carrying 1400 passengers, many of them women and children who were being evacuated to the USA. Lemp later claimed that he mistook the "Athena" for an armed merchant cruiser and that is, indeed, quite possible.

However, the sinking, and the subsequent deaths of 112 passengers and crew, caused such bad publicity from all quarters of the world that the Germans first blamed the British for attacking one of their own ships and subsequently caused the entry about the sinking to be deleted from the U Boat's log. Whether the sinking was an accident or a deliberate act of war will never be known but the event marked the beginning of a long and vicious campaign in the North Atlantic.

Further U Boat successes were not long in coming. On 5th September Gunter Prien's U 47 sank the steamer "Bosnia," the first British freighter to be lost during the war, and later on the same day the armed merchant cruiser "Royal Sceptre" also went to the bottom.

The Royal Navy was certainly not immune during these early months of war. On 10th September the submarine "Triton" sighted and rammed another submarine before realising that it was actually another British vessel, HMS

"Oxley." Shortly afterwards the aircraft carrier "Ark Royal" was narrowly missed by three torpedoes from U 39 and, although the U Boat was destroyed by escorts, three days later, on 17th September, the carrier "Courageous" was sunk off the Irish coast with heavy loss of life.

The greatest blow to British prestige, however, came on 14th October in this first year of war. With amazing skill and courage Gunter Prien threaded U 47 through the boom defence nets of Scapa Flow and calmly put several torpedoes into the belly of the battleship "Royal Oak." The giant battleship was torn apart by internal explosions and 883 members of the crew were lost. In the confusion that followed the attack, Prien and his U Boat made it safely back to Germany where he was decorated with the Knight's Cross of the Iron Cross by Hitler himself. The sinking of the "Royal Oak" was a major blow to the morale of the British people who found it difficult to believe that a German submarine could unleash such mayhem in the centre of the country's most prestigious naval base.

Meanwhile, the pocket battleship "Graf Spee" was loose in the South Atlantic. Having sailed before war was declared; the "Graf Spee" constituted a serious threat to British shipping which, in these early days, was still engaged on a pattern of independent sailing rather than grouping together in convoys. She claimed her first victim, the SS "Clement," on 30th September and so began a brief but highly destructive career that saw her sink over 50,000 tons of allied shipping.

Other German surface raiders were also at work. As early as 6th October the "Deutschland" – soon to be renamed "Lutzow" to avoid the potential loss of any ship named after the German homeland – was sinking the British merchantman "Stonegate" within the US Neutrality Zone while on 23rd November the "Scharnhorst" and "Gneisenau" engaged and sank the armed merchant cruiser "Rawalpindi" north of the Faeroe Islands. It was an unequal contest, the "Rawalpindi" being heavily out-gunned but the action has gone down in the annals of the Royal Navy as a glorious and magnificent defeat.

Already, however, Hitler and Admirals Raeder and Donitz were conscious of the enormous strategic value of their submarine fleet. Despite having, initially,

The merchant ships of Britain were vital to keeping the country supplied and therefore an obvious target for German raiders and U Boats.

operated according to the Geneva Convention, on 17th November the U Boats were given permission to attack, without warning, any British or French merchant vessels they encountered. Just over a week later Hitler ordered the U Boat arm to pursue a strategy that would cut off Britain's contact with other nations – in other words the creation of a blockade.

The first real British success of the war came at the Battle of the River Plate in December 1939 when Commodore Henry Harwood and his cruiser squadron finally ran the "Graf Spee" to earth off the coast of South America. Heavily outgunned - but showing incredible bravery - the "Ajax," "Achilles" and "Exeter" engaged and closed on the German pocket battleship. As huge columns of spray and spume erupted from the sea alongside them, the British ships harried the German battleship for over two hours, damaging her and finally forcing her to seek the safety of neutral Montevideo harbour. "Exeter" was seriously damaged and all of the British cruisers suffered casualties. Once he had bottled up his enemy inside Montevideo, however, Harwood was happy to keep the "Graf Spee" there while he awaited reinforcements in the shape of the "Ark Royal" and the battle cruiser "Renown."

The end of the pocket battleship "Graf Spee," scuttled in shallow waters off South America.

Kapitan Hans Langsdorff believed he was trapped in Montevideo, BBC broadcasts suggesting to him that the British reinforcements were already waiting outside the harbour. In fact, only the heavy cruiser "Cumberland" had arrived to swell Harwood's force while the badly damaged "Exeter" had been forced to make for the Falkland Islands for repairs. Langsdorff could see no way out and, on 17th December, scuttled his mighty warship at the entrance to the harbour. The news was greeted by rapturous acclaim in Britain. Langsdorff shot himself three days later, possibly because he had disobeyed orders and, thinking of the safety of his crew rather than glorious defeat, had chosen not to fight his way out of Montevideo.

While convoy losses were, for the first few months of the war, fairly low – most Merchant Navy losses coming in the shape of single, unprotected ships - by February 1940 they had risen sharply. Too many escort vessels were being used to sweep the oceans in a vain attempt to locate U Boats while the convoys were often left with just a single sloop or destroyer for protection. It was misguided strategy. Wherever the convoys were, that was where you would find the U Boats.

Shades of Nelson's navy surfaced once more in February 1940 when the German Auxiliary vessel "Altmark" tried slipping down the Norwegian coast on her way back to Germany. In her holds she carried nearly 400 British prisoners, many of them merchant seamen taken by the "Graf Spee" in the South Atlantic. Despite the fact that she was in (what was then still neutral) Norwegian territorial waters, Captain Vian in the destroyer "Cossack" skilfully and courageously put his ship alongside the German vessel. A boarding party, armed with cutlasses, clambered across the railings onto the deck of the German supply ship. In a short but violent scuffle several of the "Altmark's" crew were killed but Vian had managed to rescue all the prisoners.

With the fall of France in the summer of 1940 the story of the war at sea began to take on a far more menacing turn, as the French Atlantic ports suddenly became available to the U Boat fleet. Germany's first Atlantic U Boat base came into operation at Lorient on the Bay of Biscay in July 1940 and almost immediately, the patrol distances of the deadly hunters were increased by 500 miles.

For ships operating in the North Sea or attempting to make the perilous passage down the English Channel the threat came not just from submarines but also from destroyers and, in particular, from E Boats. These fast and heavily armed motor launches were based in the Low Countries or France, and developed lightning raids on convoys or light support craft into a fine art. The British countered this threat

Britain's trawler fleets were an easy target for the U Boats.

9

with their own fast Motor Torpedo Boats, and the battles off the coast of France and Belgium were usually short lived but furious and costly in both lives and in the inevitable toll on ships.

Mines were laid off the coast of Britain, by submarines, surface craft and by aircraft, in the first few months of the war and these also caused severe losses. Newly designed acoustic and magnetic mines accounted for almost 13% of all sinkings in 1940 before counter measures could be devised and put into operation. German aircraft caused more problems, particularly after the fall of France, and of course the E Boats continued their raids on the English coast almost to the end of the war.

Trawlers continued to fish throughout the war years, many of them being sunk by German U Boats.

With fish becoming increasingly important as a food supply, it was essential to keep the fishing grounds as clear as possible. Britain's fishing fleets suffered severe losses during the war, many of the casualties coming from the guns of surfaced U Boats, particularly off the north and north-western coasts of Ireland. After the fall of France air attacks also accounted for many fishing boats while others were lost to mines. Still more were sunk because of extra wartime hazards such as the removal of light ships and the dimming of navigation lights.

As members of the fishing crews were called up for active service, their places were taken by older men who returned to sea to fill the gaps and a great many of the long-established fishing families suffered grievous losses. Eventually a total of 136 fishing boats were lost during the war, almost 900 fishermen going to their deaths.

Several members of the lighthouse service also lost their lives during the war. In attacking coastal craft in British waters the Germans did not hesitate to turn their guns onto the lightships and their tenders. On 9th January 1940 the Trinity House ship "Reculver" was bombed and machine gunned while relieving lightship crews. The East Dudgeon Light Vessel was subjected to a similar attack a few weeks later – there was only one survivor. These were just two of several such unexpected and deadly attacks.

The Pilot Service also saw a number of casualties, particularly in the early years of the war and the names of sixteen pilots who lost their lives during the conflict were later commemorated on the Tower Hill Memorial to Merchant Seamen who have no known graves. >From a German point of view it was a logical extension to the conflict. After all, ships with no pilots could not easily enter port and in a "total war" situation the pilots were considered fair game.

Out in the Atlantic the U Boat commanders quickly resumed the tactics of their predecessors from World War One and, whenever possible, attacked by night, on the surface. This gave them valuable extra speed as, on the surface, they could travel at a rate of around 18 knots. When submerged, the need to conserve batteries meant that the U Boats could, at best, make only four or five knots. As the war went on, larger and longer range U Boats were developed and put into service but the standard vessel, used throughout the conflict, was the Type V11. With a range of around 6500 miles they were the main killing machines of the U Boat fleet.

During the early stages of the war the battle against the submarines was always an unequal one. The low, slim shapes of the U Boats, wallowing in the Atlantic troughs, were hard to pick out against the dark sea while, in contrast, the rearing bulk of the freighters and their escorts invariably stood out starkly against the sky. For the U Boat commanders the merchantmen were easy pickings.

Between the outbreak of war in September 1939 and May 1940, British Merchant Marine losses, not counting the ships of foreign navies, amounted to 177 vessels – and this in a period before the U Boats began their work in earnest. From May 1940 onwards, and for the next six years, barely a day went by without the loss of at least one merchant ship. It was a long and brutal campaign with sailors knowing they risked their lives every time they left port. It was a campaign that Britain had to win – and one that she came very close to losing. Winston Churchill himself was later to write:-

"Battles might be won or lost - - - territories might be gained or quitted, but dominating all our power to carry on the war, or even keep ourselves alive, lay our mastery of the ocean routes and the free approach and entry to our ports - - - The only thing that ever really frightened me during the war was the U Boat peril."

In some respects the Battle of the Atlantic, as Churchill dubbed it, can be viewed as a contest between Karl Donitz, head of the U Boat arm and a legendary figure in the Kriegsmarine, and Max Horton, C in C of the Western Approaches, himself a renowned sub-mariner in World War One. They plotted and planned the battle but to attribute such acclaim simply to the two commanders is to devalue the contribution of the thousands of ordinary sailors who fought, lived and died in the most significant campaign in the whole war.

In these early years there was a "gap" of nearly 2000 miles in the mid Atlantic Ocean. It was an area of immense weakness, something about which Max Horton was very aware. Yet he was powerless to defend the area. The mid-Atlantic gap was beyond the range of escorts from either side of the ocean and, to begin with, outside the patrol range of Coastal Command aircraft. There were, anyway, too few of them to make much difference. And it was in this mid-Atlantic gap that most of the slaughter was to take place.

By the end of 1940 the hard pressed Flower Class corvettes, which made up the

Hunting for the hidden enemy, a depth charge is dropped.

bulk of the convoy escorts, were fighting a losing battle to keep the convoys running and Britain supplied. Armed with just one 4 inch gun and a supply of depth charges, capable of a top speed of around 15 knots, the corvettes had little chance against U Boats on the surface. Already over 1000 merchant vessels had been sent to the bottom and by the summer of 1941 more than seven million tons of allied shipping had been sunk. All too often the crews died, either trapped in their sinking vessels, drowned while abandoning ship or killed by exposure to the elements in fragile lifeboats.

Welsh shipping companies suffered like everyone else. The first Welsh ship to be sunk was the "Winkleigh," lost just five days after the outbreak of war. Thereafter, the ships of companies like Reardon Smith, Tatems and Evan, Thomas, Radcliffe & Co went to their watery graves with increasing regularity. By the time that the "Filleigh" was torpedoed by U 245 on 18th April 1945 in the North Sea, the last Welsh registered ship to be sunk during the war, total devastation had been wreaked on the Welsh merchant fleet. Out of a total fleet of 164 ships at the beginning of the war, no fewer than 123 were sunk. It was a body blow from which the Welsh shipping trade never recovered.

* * * * * *

The German invasion of Norway in the early part of 1940 saw considerable naval activity, the most significant moment coming when British H Class destroyers sank eight German destroyers, much larger and more heavily armed, at the Battle of Narvik. During the campaign, in a famous but foolhardy action, the hopelessly outgunned destroyer "Glow-worm" rammed and damaged the heavy cruiser "Admiral Hipper" before bursting into flames and sinking. German losses continued to be significant, the cruisers "Blucher" and "Konigsberg" being sunk by shore battery and by air attack respectively while the "Lutzow" was torpedoed and seriously damaged by the submarine "Spearfish."

Despite their losses the Norway campaign resulted in an almost inevitable German victory. During the subsequent evacuation of British troops the "Scharnhorst" and "Gneisenau" seized the moment and put to sea, hoping to encounter the evacuation convoy. Instead they came across the aircraft carrier "Glorious" and promptly sank the sitting duck, and her escorting destroyers, from a range of over 12 miles. More than 1500 sailors and airmen were lost but a torpedo from the destroyer "Acasta" seriously damaged the "Scharnhorst" and forced her to return to port, thus saving the evacuation convoy.

The German navy was not much in evidence during the Dunkirk evacuation but air attack still caused the loss of several destroyers and other craft during the "miracle of the little ships." It was a skilful enterprise, carried out with great courage by thousands of volunteers and by men of the Royal Navy. However, despite Churchill's rhetoric, Dunkirk was still a defeat and the surrender of France meant that the powerful French navy was now at the disposal of the Germans. Indeed, by the terms of the peace treaty France was obliged to hand over all its warships to the Kriegsmarine.

Several actions by Force H, under Vice Admiral Somerville, were planned and executed in order to eliminate this threat. While the French were clear that their ships would not be used by the Germans, Churchill had decided he could take no chances. None of the actions, which included a bombardment of the French fleet in Oran and torpedo plane attacks on the battleship "Dunkerque," was particularly successful but, at the same time, units of the French fleet moored in British Channel ports were seized by the British in case their crews ever felt inclined to hand them over. The naval actions and the seizure of the French ships caused incredible bitterness from the already badly humiliated French. Indeed, French officers refused to wear British medals for many years after the affair.

In August 1940 the battleship "Bismark" entered service but, for the moment, it was the U Boat threat that was causing Britain the greatest problems. In August 1940 alone, the submarines of the Kriegsmarine sent more than 260,000 tons of allied shipping to the bottom and with Donitz already experimenting with his wolf pack tactics things were not likely to get any easier. In the words of the U Boat commanders this was "the happy time" when it seemed as if the submarines could win the war on their own. With Focke-Wulf Kondor long range bombers and reconnaissance aircraft posted to Bordeaux a new threat, this time from the air, also now faced the British convoys. The bombers first success came on 26th October when the luxury liner "Empress of Britain" was attacked and seriously damaged, the stricken vessel being finished off by torpedoes from U 32 a few days later.

On 20th September a wolf pack located Convoy HX-72 and in the first really co-ordinated attack of the war twelve of the convoy's 41 ships were sunk. The escorts were powerless and, in the confusion, Commander Schepke of U 100 was able to cause chaos before slipping away, his torpedoes exhausted. Luckily, the autumn bad weather soon set in and the U Boat commanders like Prien, Kretschmer and Schepke were forced to return to their bases. It meant a short breathing space for the men of the Royal and Merchant navies.

Convoys, the safest way across the Atlantic.

While the Battle of the Atlantic was raging, in the Mediterranean there were notable British successes where the ships of Admiral Cunningham scored several morale boosting victories over the Italian navy. Most notable of these was the attack by aircraft of the Fleet Air Arm on the port of Taranto on 11th November 1940. The Swordfish, operating from zero height, sank three Italian battleships and the balance of power in the Mediterranean was totally altered. Four months later a British victory at the Battle of Cape Matapan saw the Italian fleet suffer the loss of five heavy warships and over 3000 men. British losses were just one Swordfish aircraft.

It was not all success, however, as German land forces moved into North Africa. The island of Malta began to assume significant strategic importance as the campaigns in Africa and Greece gathered pace, and the Kriegsmarine soon realised they would have to bolster the efforts of the flagging Italian navy. The cruisers "Southampton" and "Gloucester" were attacked by Stuka dive bombers on 11th January, "Southampton" being lost, despite attempts to tow her to the safety of harbour. Five days later the carrier "Illustrious" was damaged in an attack by over 80 Stukas whilst at anchor in Malta, having already been hit by bombs from Heinkel 111 aircraft while engaged on convoy duties.

Campaigning in the Mediterranean continued for many months, much of it centring on the North African campaign and the need to keep Malta supplied. The convoy battles to relieve and support the island were amongst the most hard-fought campaigns of the whole war, rivalling the Atlantic and Russian convoys in their ferocity as the Germans and Italians attacked the lumbering merchant ships with U Boats, surface vessels and aircraft. Meanwhile, the island itself was subjected to daily bombing raids. For a brief period Malta's only air defence lay in the shape of three ancient Gloucester Gladiator aircraft – "Faith," "Hope" and "Charity." Merchant Navy losses were high, sometimes only half the ships getting through. The Royal Navy also suffered heavy losses. For example, on 23rd July 1941 the destroyer "Fearless" was sunk by enemy planes while on convoy duties. She was just one of several Royal Navy casualties in the campaign.

On 14th November 1941 the carrier "Ark Royal," so long a symbol of hope and endurance for the British people, sank after having been torpedoed the previous day. She had been engaged in ferrying aircraft to Malta. The carrier was not the only capital ship to be lost in the Mediterranean. In November HMS "Barham" exploded after being struck by torpedoes from U331, the only British battleship to be sunk in open seas during the entire war.

The "Ark Royal," Britain's most famous aircraft carrier.

German U Boats had been operating in the Mediterranean from September 1941. Yet the shallow waters of the "inland sea" did not aid their efforts and the submarines were often easily seen, even when submerged. Additionally, very few parts of the sea could not be covered by aircraft and the Mediterranean, despite successes like the sinking of the "Ark Royal" and "Barham," certainly did not prove to be a "happy hunting ground" for the U Boats.

Despite everything the Germans and Italians threw at them, the convoys always managed to get through – somehow! And Malta and its people survived the intensive bombing, earning for themselves the award of a George Cross from the King.

Early in 1941, the commerce raider "Pinguin" was involved in one of the more bizarre episodes of the war. She was one of the fast cargo vessels ordered by the Reichsmarine and Kriegsmarine in the 1920s and 1930s and, roaming the seas in search of victims, in January carried out an action that can only be described as pure piracy. The Arctic whaling fleet, always previously left unmolested, was attacked and fourteen vessels taken as prizes. One of them held 22,000 tons of valuable whale oil.

Nine converted German freighters, vessels such as the "Pinguin," operated as commerce raiders until the autumn of 1943 with varying degrees of success. Heavily armed, the raiders prayed largely on solitary merchantmen but were also capable of handling themselves when they encountered allied warships. Between them they sank more than 800,000 tons of allied shipping, accounting for 130 different vessels.

The "Atlantis" was easily the most successful of these raiders, sinking 22 ships in a career of just under two years. She was eventually destroyed by the cruiser "Devonshire" off the coast of West Africa. The "Kormoran" was lost in a head-to-head encounter with the Australian cruiser "Sydney" in November 1941, an action that saw the Australian ship also sunk, lost with all hands. Importantly, quite apart from the vessels they destroyed, the commerce raiders tied up allied warships, distracting them from other important tasks.

Meanwhile, units of the Kriegsmarine's surface fleet were still active in the North Atlantic. In early February Admiral Lutjens led out the "Scharnhorst" and "Gneisenau" to seek and destroy British convoys. After an abortive attack on Convoy HX 106, when the battle cruisers realised at the last minute that the merchantmen were protected by the battleship HMS "Ramillies," they soon managed to encounter a dispersed convoy and sink five ships. A month later they sank a further sixteen ships from another dispersed convoy. Avoiding the searching units of Force H, "Scharnhorst" and "Gneisenau" eventually regained the safety of French waters, having destroyed a total of 115,600 tons of shipping in what was, for the German navy, a highly successful and morale boosting cruise.

Gunter Prien's U 47 sank three ships from Convoy OB 290 at the end of February and, the very next day, surfaced to call in Focke-Wulf Kondors to finish off the helpless merchantmen. Eleven ships were sunk, the most successful attack so far on allied shipping.

Time was running out for the hidden killers, however, and Prien, the idol of the U Boat fleet, did not last much longer. On 7th March 1941, while closing on yet another convoy, U 47 was depth-charged and sunk with all hands by HMS "Wolverine." The other U Boat aces, Kretschner and Schepke, were also victims of the war later in the same month, Kretschner being taken prisoner when his seriously damaged U Boat was forced to the surface.

One of the most famous campaigns of the war began on 18th May 1941 when Admiral Lutjens left port, flying his flag in the giant battleship "Bismark." He was

The enemy claims another victim.

Hunting for the "Bismark."

accompanied by the cruiser "Prinz Eugen." Lutjen's aim was to destroy as much commerce as he could locate out in the Atlantic – scouting vessels were already at sea, searching out suitable victims.

British intelligence alerted the Admiralty that the "Bismark" was at sea and the hunt was on. The German ships were located by scouting cruisers and the "Hood" and "Prince of Wales" raced to intercept the German ships in the Denmark Strait. On 24th May, in a short and violent battle, the newly completed "Prince of Wales" was damaged and "Hood" exploded in a mass of flames. Only three of her 1416-man crew were saved, the lack of sufficient deck armour making the old battle cruiser vulnerable to high trajectory, plunging shells. It was a tragic design flaw that meant HMS "Hood," the most famous and best-loved ship in the Royal Navy, had been destroyed in less than half an hour.

The "Bismark" had not gone unscathed, however, and Lutjens decided to head for Brest to undergo repairs. Fuelled both by the strategic need to destroy the "Bismark" and by an understandable desire for revenge on the ship that had sunk the "Hood," the Royal Navy began to hunt down the battleship in a tireless and desperate campaign. Despite horrendous weather, Swordfish from the "Ark Royal" managed to score two hits on the battleship, one of them seriously affecting her steerage gear. Wallowing helplessly in the Atlantic swell, the "Bismark" was now a sitting duck. Shells from the "Rodney" and "King George V" reduced her to a total wreck before torpedoes from the cruisers "Norfolk" and "Dorsetshire" ripped into her hull – forcing her crew to scuttle the vessel before going over the side. Sadly, many of the German sailors drowned or froze to death in the bitter Atlantic waves, when a submarine alert forced the British ships to abandon their rescue attempts.

At about the same time, the combined land and sea campaigns around Greece and the island of Crete were taking place. The Royal Navy lost nine ships during the invasion and evacuation of Crete, including the cruiser "York" and destroyers "Kelly" and "Kashmir." The Cretan adventure was wasteful and misguided and the Mediterranean fleet was deprived of several ships it could ill-afford to lose during the subsequent evacuation and defeat.

The "Channel Dash" of February 1942 saw the "Scharnhorst" and "Gneisenau" make a successful run from Brest up the Channel within sight of the English coast, despite the best efforts of the Royal Navy to stop them. Shielded by many escort vessels and 170 aircraft, news of the German's "dash" did not reach the British until it was half completed but the episode still caused considerable embarrassment – despite the fact that the Admiralty much preferred to see the two battle cruisers in German harbours where access to the Atlantic was not nearly as easy as it was from the more dangerous ports on the French coast.

It was an attempt to find a new "happy hunting ground" that led the "Scharnhorst" to disaster at the Battle of the North Cape on 26th December 1943. By then she was the last remaining German battle cruiser and, in pursuit of Convoy JW 55B, was unaware that the battleship "Duke of York" had been alerted to her presence. Damaged by the guns of British heavy cruisers, the "Scharnhorst" was eventually sunk after a three hour bombardment by the "Duke of York." There were only 36 survivors. The sinking effectively marked the end of Germany's High Seas Fleet, so many of the heavy cruisers like "Prinz Eugen" and even battle cruisers such as the "Gneisenau" having been destroyed in harbour by allied bombers.

The U Boats, however, had continued their deadly attacks. By now the British, thanks in large degree to the breaking of the German Enigma Code – thereby giving escorts advance notice of the gathering wolf packs - were achieving a degree of success in the battle. In a large escort-versus-U Boat action on 29th June 1941 five ships from Convoy HX 133 were sunk but, significantly, two U Boats were destroyed. When Convoy HG 76 sailed from Gibraltar that December it ran into an ambush by twelve U Boats. Five of the submarines were sunk, as well as two German bombers being brought down – for a loss of only two merchant vessels and the escort carrier "Audacity." It was a pattern that was beginning to be repeated.

On 15th April 1941 Coastal Command passed from the RAF into the operational control of the Admiralty. This was a significant move as the co-ordination of air support for convoy protection was made significantly easier. The

The sinking of the "Scharnhorst," December 1943.

use of Coastal Command aircraft duly became one of the most crucial factors in the defeat of the U Boat fleet.

CAM ships, merchant vessels that had been fitted with catapult mechanisms to launch the fighters they now carried in an attempt to provide some degree of aircraft cover, claimed their first success in early August 1941 when a Hurricane fighter from the "Maplin" shot down a Focke-Wulf Kondor. Pilots of these CAM aircraft had no way of getting back on board their ships. They were faced with the choice of heading for land, if it was close enough, or ditching alongside the mother craft – surely the ultimate in bravery!

Aircraft were a crucial element in the Battle of the Atlantic, in particular the giant Sunderland flying boats.

However, two significant events soon began to have a major effect on the course of the sea war – the Japanese attack on Pearl Harbour and the entry of Russia into the conflict. While Pearl Harbour brought the USA into the war, for British sailors, members of the Merchant and Royal Navies alike, Hitler's decision to fight on two fronts meant the advent of one of the most brutal and chilling of all campaigns – the Russian or Arctic Convoys.

The first Russian Convoy sailed from Iceland on 21st August 1941, carrying supplies and armaments to aid Stalin's hard pressed troops in their fight against the German invaders. It reached Archangel at the end of the month, having encountered no enemy submarines or surface raiders. Despite this "dry run," the threat from the mighty "Tirpitz," sister ship of the "Bismark," was significant and very real at this time. The Germans had recently formed the Baltic Fleet, based in the Norwegian fiords and centred on the "Tirpitz" and "Admiral Scheer," and including dozens of heavy destroyers, cruisers, escort craft and U Boats. Fear of the "Tirpitz" was never very far from the minds of naval planners and merchant seamen for virtually the rest of the war.

Two routes were used to supply Russia, one by way of the Persian Gulf, the other around North Cape of Norway. The northern route was the most direct but it was also the most vulnerable, both to the vagaries of the weather and, because of the proximity of the route to the Scandinavian coast, to attack from German ships.

Destroyers and cruisers at work.

The easy passage or "dry run" of the first convoy was not to be repeated. Before long U Boats and the ever-present Kondors were taking their toll on merchant ships and escort vessels alike. In all, 40 convoys totalling 775 ships made the arduous journey to Murmansk and Archangel by the North Cape route and no fewer than 57 vessels were lost. A further 21 were sunk on the return voyage. Such figures cannot even begin to do justice to the courage of the sailors involved in the Russian Convoys when the enemy included not just the threat of U Boats and the "Tirpitz" but also the icy sea which would kill a man in less than a minute.

Convoy PQ 16, for example, lost seven freighters from its total strength but that was nothing compared to the disaster waiting for the next Russian Convoy, PQ 17, in July 1942. Despite being escorted by a number of capital ships, the supposed threat of strong German surface raiders – including the "Tirpitz," "Hipper" and "Admiral Scheer" – led Admiral Dudley Pound, the First Sea Lord, to order the convoy to scatter. It was a fateful decision. Admiral Tovey in the "Duke of York" was later to comment: "Scattering the convoy was nothing more than sheer bloody murder."

With the escorts gone, the wolves closed in. In an orgy of destruction, thirteen ships from PQ 17 were sunk on 5th July alone, a further eight a few days later. Although the "Tirpitz" was still skulking in her Norwegian fiord, the Germans had been able to deploy nine U Boats and over 200 aircraft against the helpless merchantmen. When the last ships of the convoy reached Russia it became clear that 24 ships out of a total of 57 had been lost, a total of 3350 vehicles, including 430 tanks, having gone to the bottom of the sea. From PQ 17, Captain Sissingh of the Paulus Potter had abandoned his ship – it was later sighted and boarded by men from U 255. The boarding party retrieved a complete set of Admiralty codes and signal books, the sailing instructions for PQ 17 and routes to be taken through minefields around Iceland and in the approaches to Archangel.

The entry of the USA into the war meant that, ultimately, victory would rest with the allies. But it was likely to take time and, to begin with, Britain was faced

*HMS "Curacoa," built at Pembroke Dockyard and cut in half by the
"Queen Mary" in 1942.*

with another implacable enemy – Japan. The battleship "Prince of Wales," the battle cruiser "Repulse" and heavy cruisers "Dorsetshire" and "Cornwall" were all hunted down and sunk by enemy bombers in the early days of war with Japan, proof positive – as if any was really needed – that large surface vessels could no longer operate without the support of aircraft. With the sinking of the two capital ships the significant British naval presence in the Far East was, temporarily, reduced to zero.

In a bizarre but tragic incident in 1942, off the coast of Ireland, the cruiser "Curacao" – built at Pembroke Dockyard during the First World War – was cut in half by the liner "Queen Mary." The giant Cunard liner normally operated as an independent troop ship, her fast speed meaning that she operated separate from convoys and escort vessels. She was unused to the intricacies of zigzagging and the "Curacao" found herself in the wrong place at the wrong time.

It is a generalisation, maybe, but maritime activity during the last three years of the war tended to consist, in the main, of convoy actions, where the war of terror went on and on, and support activity in aid of invasion fleets. In the Pacific the Americans began to gradually plan and wage a number of costly but effective campaigns against the Japanese. There were setbacks and losses but it was a gradual war of attrition that, ultimately, could have only one result.

In the Atlantic there were setbacks, too. On 2nd February 1943 twenty U Boats attacked Convoy SC 118 and sank 13 merchant vessels for the loss of three submarines. Barely two weeks later, fourteen merchant ships from Convoy ON 166 were sent to the bottom. Most tragic of all was the attack on Convoy HX 229 on the night of 16th March. No fewer than 37 U Boats attacked the convoy, sinking 21 of them for the loss of just one submarine. This seeming disaster, however, marked something of a turning point. It was not the last success for the U Boats but never again would they achieve such mastery in the Atlantic. From March 1943 onwards carrier support groups and the use of long-range aircraft effectively closed the mid-Atlantic gap and began to take an increasingly heavier toll on the wolf packs.

In early May Convoy ONS 5 was attacked by 60 U Boats, operating in four distinct groups. The battle stretched over three consecutive nights and thirteen merchantmen were lost. Significantly, however, the escort vessels managed to sink six U Boats and badly damage four others while two more enemy submarines were sunk in a collision. Between April and the middle of May fourteen of the twenty two convoys across the Atlantic made the journey without a single loss. In the first three weeks of May thirty U Boats were sunk by allied escort vessels and Coastal Command aircraft. Surely but slowly, the battle was being won.

Destroyers, the work horses of the war.

RAF bombing raids on Hamburg caused mayhem to the U Boat building programme at this time and many partially completed submarines, some of them the new Type V11 boats, were destroyed while still on the stocks. With the escort vessels sinking more and more vessels out in the Atlantic, it was a series of losses that Germany could ill-afford.

Hundreds of Welsh men, and women too, had volunteered for service in the Royal Navy or WRNS as soon as war had been declared. Thousands more were called up or enlisted as the conflict progressed. They served in battleships and cruisers, corvettes and destroyers, in every theatre of war, right across the globe, many of them paying the ultimate price for their courage and commitment to defend their country. There probably wasn't one ship in the entire navy that did not have its "Taffy" or Dai somewhere in the crew. It was the continuation of a tradition that stretched back centuries. The Welsh had always made good sailors; after all there wasn't one part of the country that was more than 100 miles from the coast. The "essential calling of the sea," as the King had called it, was strong in Wales and during the Second World War the Welsh people had answered that calling with a vengeance.

* * * * * *

The allied landings in Sicily in the summer of 1943 saw over 200 warships involved in the operation. In addition there were some 2000 landing craft and 300 transports working and waiting off the beaches. Following the successful landings the battleships "Valient" and "Warspite" sailed on to bombard the Italian coast and when, on 10th September, the Italian fleet arrived in Malta to surrender, it marked the end of the Mediterranean conflict.

Admiral Cunningham, the architect of that victory, went on to succeed Dudley Pound as First Sea Lord. Pound, always a tireless worker, had made a tragic mistake over Convoy PQ 17 and there is little doubt that the disaster hurried him on to an untimely death in October 1943.

Action during the Mediterranean sea war.

The most serious threat to the Mediterranean fleet in the last months of the campaign had come from Italian midget submarines, several ships having been damaged by the intrepid submariners. And midget submarines were also used by the British in September 1943 to attack the "Tirpitz" in Altafiord. Submarines X6 and X7 managed to clear the torpedo nets around the battleship and attach limpet mines to her hull. The "Tirpitz" was severely damaged and put out of action for six months.

Aircraft from the carriers "Victorious" and "Furious" bombed the battleship in April 1944, damaging her and killing over a hundred of her crew. Conscious of the strategic value of the giant warship Donitz promptly ordered her repaired but forbade her to go to sea, thereby limiting her effectiveness to being a threat only.

Carrier born aircraft, a crucial element in the war.

German E Boats were busy in the Channel during 1944 as the build up to the invasion of Europe began to gather momentum. In April they attacked a poorly escorted convoy containing American servicemen en route for a training exercise on the beaches of Devon. It was easy pickings for the E Boats and total carnage ensued. A total of 749 Americans were lost.

A month later, on 14th May, the E Boats were again deployed, this time against allied landing craft off the Isle of Wight. In the encounter, Klaus Donitz, son of the U Boat Admiral, was killed when his boat was sunk by the Free French destroyer "La Combattante." Donitz had already lost his eldest son Peter twelve months before when U 954 was sunk with all hands by an RAF Liberator bomber of Coastal Command.

The D Day landings on 6th June 1944 were the largest combined operations ever conceived. Battleships and cruisers pounded the invasion beaches in a mighty naval bombardment while landing craft disgorged thousands of British, American and Dominion forces onto the five invasion beaches. After the bridgehead was established naval forces were involved in running convoys and supply missions to the French coast. They also towed the huge Mulberry harbours, purpose-built concrete jetties, across the Channel where they were moored to help vehicles to disembark.

With the success of the allied landings many German naval vessels were pulled back, either to Germany or to territories that remained occupied. The last pocket of Nazi strength in the Channel was destroyed when the port of Le Havre was raided by Lancaster bombers on the night of 14th June. Over 30 small vessels, E Boats and supply ships were sunk in the raid.

The Le Havre raid was not the end of the war in the Channel, however. During July German "manned torpedoes" were particularly active in the estuary around Villers-sur-Mer in Normandy. Hits were scored on allied ships, including several minesweepers and the destroyer HMS "Isis." Radio-controlled assault boats were also used against allied shipping. These 'Linsen boats', packed with upwards of 600 lbs of high explosives, were highly successful and managed to sink several small vessels, including the destroyer "Quorn."

It was a desperate time for German naval forces and in August the Kriegsmarine began to order the scuttling of any U Boats that had become trapped in French ports. The U 123 and U 129 were destroyed by their crews at Lorient while U 78 and U 188 went to the bottom in the port of Bordeaux – it was a far cry from the heady days of 1940 and 1941.

In the Pacific and Far East the war against Japan continued. At the end of July American forces landed on Guam and Tinian. During the latter landings napalm was used for the first time. On 25th of the same month the British Eastern Fleet attacked Sabang, aircraft from the carriers "Illustrious" and "Victorious" bombing the airfields while capital ships bombarded the harbour installations and oil depots.

In October the "Tirpitz" was moved from Altafiord into the shallower Tromsofiord. Significantly, it meant that the giant battleship, which had survived many air raids by British and Russian bombers, was now 100 miles closer to RAF airfields. It was inevitable that further attacks would be made and on 12th November she was hit by three Tallboy bombs dropped by British Lancasters. The ship capsized in a matter of moments and over 1000 of the crew went down with her. The destruction of the "Tirpitz" marked the end of the most sustained series of assaults against any German target during the Second World War.

On 9th February 1945 a remarkable "first" occurred when HMS "Venturer" fired her torpedoes at U 864. It would not have been unusual except for the fact that both vessels were submerged! U864 was hit by the torpedoes and quickly broke up, the first instance of any submarine successfully attacking and sinking another while both ships were under water.

As the war in Europe came to an end, the last remnants of the German surface fleet were bombed and destroyed by the RAF, many of them while isolated or tied up alongside their jetties in harbour. The pocket battleship "Admiral Scheer" was sunk in Kiel while the cruiser "Emden" and several smaller vessels were critically damaged. The "Admiral Hipper" went down in Kiel Bay while "Lutzow" was sunk on 16th April but re-floated before being, finally, scuttled by her crew on 4th May, just a few days before the war ended.

In a bizarre twist of fate Admiral Donitz, rather than Herman Goering, was named as Hitler's successor on 29th April, the day before the Dictator committed suicide. With his great fleets now in tatters, Donitz knew that his task was to secure peace and save as many German lives as possible. This he attempted to do with his usual skill and efficiency. He was not present when the formal surrender was signed on 7th May, the German signatories being General Jodl and Admiral Freideburg. VE Day was duly celebrated on 8th May.

The war against Japan continued, however. On 10th July American and British carriers began a campaign against the main Japanese islands, despatching bombers to attack the Japanese homeland on a daily basis. By the middle months of 1945 there were 34 Royal Navy aircraft carriers serving in the Pacific.

The threat of Kamikaze bombers was significant at this time, several British and US ships being hit and seriously damaged. Amongst these was the carrier

"Formidable" which was hit by a Kamikaze raider late in the war. The minesweeper HMS "Vestal" was also struck by a Kamikaze on 26th July and, being considered beyond help, was later sunk by gunfire from an escorting destroyer. The "Vestal" thus has the dubious distinction of being the last British warship casualty of the war.

When the submarines "Tiptoe" and "Trump" attacked a Japanese convoy in the Java Sea on 3rd August it was another memorable moment. "Tiptoe's" torpedoes tore into a 4000 ton freighter, marking the last effective torpedo fired by a British submarine against a "live" target in the war.

After the dropping of the two atom bombs on Hiroshima and Nagasaki in August the Japanese had no option but to ask for peace. Hostilities ceased and VJ Day was celebrated on 15th August, even though some engagements did take place over the next few days before news of the Japanese surrender seeped through to individual units. Tongue firmly in his cheek but also making sure his sailors remained alert, the Commander in Chief of the Fifth Fleet made the following signal to his ships:-

"The war with Japan will end at 12.00 on 15th August. It is likely that Kamikazes will attack the fleet after this time as a final fling. Any ex-enemy aircraft attacking the fleet is to be shot down in a friendly manner."

And that was it, the end of hostilities. A formal peace was signed on the deck of the USS "Missouri" on 2nd September. The Second World War had come to a close six years and one day after it had begun.

* * * * * *

Thousands of sailors lost their lives during the Second World War. The men of the Merchant Navy suffered particularly badly, most of the casualties being lost to U Boat attack. While most of those deaths occurred in the months and years before the mid-summer of 1943, the Merchant Navy continued to incur losses almost up

From the middle of 1943 onwards the shipyards of Britain and America were building ships at an incredible rate.

to the day that peace was declared. Indeed, even after the conflict had ended there were still recorded instances of merchant ships being damaged and sunk by mines. Three days after the German surrender the U 2336 torpedoed and sank the Canadian merchant ship "Avondale Park" off the coast of Scotland. Her captain claimed that he had not received the notification to cease hostilities that had been sent out by U Boat headquarters.

From June 1943 onwards, however, merchant ships were being built in allied shipyards, mainly in Britain and the USA, quicker than the U Boats could sink them. That might not have given much comfort to the hard-pressed men of the Merchant Navy but it did mean that the Battle of the Atlantic had, effectively, been won by the end of 1943.

Statistics or figures mean little and are often confusing. However, it would seem that the number of merchant sailors working at sea on any given day during the war was about 144,000 – not including members of the fishing fleets. As far as the ships were concerned, 2524 British Merchant Navy vessels were sunk by enemy action during the war while 29 foundered from other causes. No fewer than 912 were damaged. Of the losses, 1359 were sunk by U Boats, 291 by mines, 477 by aircraft, 76 by E Boats and 89 from other causes. A huge number of seamen died, 30,248 being killed with a further 4654 posted as missing. Over 5000 became prisoners of war and 4707 were injured while carrying out their duties.

When one considers the ships and men of all allied nations – and it must be remembered that, viewed through the periscopes of the hidden U Boats, there would have been no difference between the ships of the various nations - the figure for lost vessels rises to 4786, a total gross tonnage of 21 million tons. Those are staggering figures that do not begin to take account of Royal Naval ships and personnel. They do not include the men and ships of the US Navy or of the fighting ships of France. Neither do they include the men of the Kriegsmarine or the Italian Navy.

A battleship at sea.

The U Boats sank 148 Royal Navy ships during the war, including three aircraft carriers and two battleships. Most of their victims, however, were destroyers and corvettes, over 150 of them being sunk while trying to escort their convoys across the Atlantic. Other warships were, obviously, lost to the guns of surface ships, mines and air attack. The sinking of ships like the "Hood," "Repulse" and "Prince of Wales" led to the deaths of thousands of British sailors while still more lost their lives when serving as DEMS gunners on merchant vessels. In total, 49,305 Royal Naval sailors died during the war, quite apart from those who were reported as missing.

Out of 1131 U Boats commissioned during the war, no fewer than 785 were lost. The nature of the conflict meant that, when detected or under attack, U Boats dived as deep as they could go. If they were then hunted down by escorts and damaged by depth charges, the crews had little or no chance of survival. Not for nothing did the U Boat crews call their vessels "iron coffins." The U Boat Memorial near Kiel records the names of 27,491 German submariners who died.

Clearly, then, the Second World War was a significant event in naval history. A more brutal and destructive conflict had never been seen with British sailors serving and, in many cases, dying in all corners of the globe. In particular, the struggle to get the Atlantic convoys through was the single longest running battle of the whole war.

Probably more than any other single component of the war, the story of those convoys, not just across the Atlantic but also from Gibraltar to Malta and through the cold Arctic waters to Russia, is something that catches at the heartstrings. The story of the convoys is a story of bravery and dedication to duty, of men pushed to the limits of endurance. It is a story that needs to be told.

The story of sailors in the Second World War does not stop with those convoys, however. The real story of what went on in those tempestuous years cannot be told in mere facts and figures. That story can only come from the words and the memories of the men themselves.

PART TWO

The War Around The Welsh Coast

While most of the U Boat action between 1939 and 1945 took place hundreds of miles out in the Atlantic, the coastal waters around Wales – like all the coastal regions of Britain - saw numerous life and death struggles during the Second World War. It was inevitable, with dozens of heavily laden cargo ships regularly making for ports like Liverpool, Holyhead, Milford, Swansea, Newport, Cardiff and Barry, that sooner or later the enemy would target both the south and north shipping routes around Wales.

The sea lanes and approaches into the strategically vital port of Liverpool were invariably around the coast of Northern Ireland. It is important not to under-estimate the significance of Liverpool as an artery into Britain during this period. Over 140 million tons of shipping came into the Mersey during the Second World War, along with nearly five million soldiers who passed through the port. However, it was in the relative safety of deep water to the north and west of Ireland, beyond the range of aircraft and escort vessels, that the U Boats would strike, rather than in the areas closer to the North Wales coast. Vessels were, obviously, lost off the North Wales coast but the U Boats did not, generally speaking, come too close as the shallow waters of the coastal areas made it difficult for submarines to operate safely. Only as the war drew to its end did the U Boats venture closer to the North Wales coast, desperation forcing them to come nearer to the land in an attempt to find stragglers or unescorted merchant vessels.

In the early part of the war losses along the North Wales coast, when they occurred, tended to be from mines and aircraft attack – or from accident caused by the removal of navigational aids.

At the end of 1940 two vessels were lost within days of each other, thanks to the removal of navigational aids. The "Eaglescliffe Hall" ran aground

Patriotic postcard intended to keep up morale.

just north of Llanddwyn on 12th November while the "Watkins F Nisbet" came ashore in the same area on 6th December. Coastguards from Holyhead took off both crews by breeches buoy and while the "Eaglescliffe Hall" was soon re-floated, the second vessel was abandoned and cut in half. The after part was then sealed and towed to Birkenhead where her vital machinery was soon put to good use.

Further north, the motor vessel "Gleneden" had been damaged by enemy action in January 1940 and put into Conwy Bay looking for a suitable place to beach. She grounded on the north-western corner of Dutchman's Bank, however, and quickly broke up. The tug "St Olaves" was similarly lost – although she was later salvaged and repaired – in the Bay in the spring of 1941.

After the fall of France the northern coastal waters were within easy reach of German aircraft and, of course, mines dropped by these aeroplanes, submarines or by surface craft were always likely to cause casualties. Several losses occurred where it was impossible to say whether they were from submarine attack or mine.

In September 1940 the Coast Artillery School moved from Shoeburyness in Essex to Llandudno, taking up positions below the Little Orme. The unit fired thousands of shells during the war years but on 15th October 1943 they were too accurate for their own good. On that day they succeeded in sinking "one of their own" when shells struck the target ship "Ghambria", four miles off Puffin Island. She sank but remained a navigational hazard for some years in the shallow water.

A little-known claim to fame for the North Wales coast came in the shape of a secret operation at Morfa, near Conwy. Between 1942 and the end of 1944 prototypes and final components for the Mulberry Harbours, used to land troops in Normandy after D Day, were built. Working under the direction of Huw Iorys Hughes, a Civil Engineer from Bangor, thousands of construction and building workers were employed on the project in an operation that has never been really acknowledged.

The sea off Anglesey was considerably deeper than the waters to the east and the area witnessed several significant incidents during the war years. On 22nd July 1940 the 290-ton trawler HMS "Campania" struck a mine and sank just a few hundred yards off Holyhead's New Lighthouse. Less than a month later the SS "Meath" was mined close to the end of the breakwater. The patrol boat "Manx Lad" went to her rescue but struck another mine and sank at the entrance to the New Harbour.

The ferry "Cambria" was attacked by a German bomber on 19th December 1940 but she managed to beat off the attack. The "Cambria" was attacked by a U Boat the following year but again managed to gallantly fight off the enemy. U Boats were active around the coast of Anglesey for most of the war. As late as April 1945 an inward bound convoy was attacked by U 1024. The freighter "James W Nesmith" was torpedoed but was lashed to the side of a Canadian corvette and successfully brought into Holyhead harbour.

On 26th January 1945 the escort vessels "Aylmer," "Bentinck," "Calder" and "Manners" sank U 1051 in a combined operation 21 miles to the west of Anglesey. The "Manners" was damaged in the attack and had to be towed to Barrow-in –Furness for repair.

Accident and shipwreck continued to cause loss of life on the Anglesey coast throughout the war. Due to the blackout regulations the liner "Castillian" ploughed onto the Skerries on 12th February 1943 and only a heroic rescue by the Holyhead lifeboat managed to save the crew of 47.

In the final weeks of the war two U Boats were sunk close to Anglesey. First, the U 1024, which had recently torpedoed the "James W Nesmith," was forced to the surface after a depth charge attack from the "Loch Glendhu." She was boarded and taken in tow by the frigate "Loch More." Before they could reach port, however, the towline parted and U Boat sank quietly to the bottom. Next, a combined attack from Sunderland flying boat H/201 and the destroyers "Havelock" and "Hesperus" accounted for U 242 on 30th April.

Caernarfon Bay also saw considerable action, particularly after the Dunkirk evacuation had opened up French airfields to the Germans. The 19,900 ton "Orford" was bombed by a Focke-

Humour was important, even during the deadly days of the Battle of the Atlantic, as this postcard from the time testifies.

Wulf Kondor on 20th August 1940 while early the following year the SS "Iris" was machine gunned by enemy aircraft off Bardsey Island.

The oil tanker "Lucellum" was bombed and abandoned off Bardsey on 19th December 1941. She had left Belfast, in convoy, only the previous day but was attacked by a Dornier bomber and was hit by two bombs forward of the bridge. With several of the crew dead or dying and fires raging the captain ordered "Abandon ship." The survivors eventually reached Holyhead in their lifeboats, nine of the crew having died in the attack.

The "Lucellum" did not sink, however, and in a desperate attempt to save a valuable vessel, a small group of firemen sailed out on board the naval trawler "Libra" to investigate. They found the drifting tanker and quickly came to the decision that she could be saved. Eventually, 57 firemen in an odd assortment of vessels put to sea, boarded the tanker and got the fire under control. She was towed to Holyhead where she was moored and allowed to cool off until early in the New Year. She was then towed to Liverpool to discharge what remained of her vital cargo of oil and kerosene. For their incredible bravery and devotion to duty, the North Wales Fire Service was rewarded by the presentation of two OBEs, one MBE and two BEMs.

* * * * * *

The Pembrokeshire coast suffered particularly badly during the war. The area had been virtually beyond the reach of German aircraft in the early days of the conflict but, after the fall of France in 1940, the coastal regions of the county were suddenly within range of the enemy. The first recorded U Boat incident in the area did not come until December 1940 but the threat of air raids and mines had been present for several months. In one of the earliest air attacks, the trawler "Valeria" was sunk off the Smalls in August 1940 while a few days later the steamship "Thorold" was attacked by three bombers, lying helpless and disabled while the enemy aircraft circled and machine-gunned the crew. Only fifteen of them survived.

The first magnetic mine attack on Milford Haven, already an important convoy mustering area, occurred early in July 1940. The 6426-ton "Dakotian" was the first known victim to the mines, sinking in Dale Roads on 21st November and lying, for many years, just 10 feet below the surface at low tide. The same day as the "Dakotian" went down the steamship "Pikepool" struck a mine a few miles off Linney Head. Captain Atkinson and a few survivors were picked up from their life rafts after being adrift at sea for 48 hours. Mines and air attack soon accounted for several other vessels such as the steamer "Behar," the salvage vessel "Preserver" and the Holland-America Line "Beemsterdyke," all sunk within a dozen miles of the Pembrokeshire coast.

In the early days of the war only two trawlers were available for minesweeping duties in the Milford Haven area. This small fleet gradually grew in size and strength but the Dutch trawler/mine sweeper "Johanna Caroline" fell victim to one of the mines for which she was hunting on 18th February 1941.Other naval vessels based in Milford went to the bottom during these years, including the trawler "Tankerton Towers" and a small examination ship mined off the entrance to the Haven in June of the same year.

One of the county's blackest days occurred on 13th June 1941. The cross channel ferryboat "St Patrick" was en route from Rosslare to Fishguard and was just 12 miles off Strumble Head when she was spotted by German bombers. The ferry had already been attacked, twelve months before but on that occasion she had managed to evade the attention of the bombers and find safety in Fishguard Bay. This time, however, there was to be no escape.

The first bomb struck the "St Patrick" between her funnel and bridge, piercing the ship's oil tanks and setting them on fire. Within five minutes the ferry had disappeared beneath the waves. By the time the Fishguard lifeboat arrived on the scene all that was left were a few bubbles of oil and telltale wreckage. Seventeen crewmen and twelve passengers had drowned, including the ship's captain Jim Faraday and his son Jack, a Merchant Navy cadet who had decided to accompany his father on the trip.

Mine-laying by German aircraft continued well into the war. In July 1942 a three-night attack was launched and 42 mines were dropped in the waters of Milford Haven. It was the only occasion during the whole war that the port was closed to shipping for more than just a few hours.

HMS "Rosemary," the sloop that attempted a rescue during the disaster off the beach of Freshwater West in 1943.

Freshwater West beach was the scene of a terrible tragedy in April 1943 when LCGs (Landing Craft Guns) 15 and 16 sank just a few hundred yards off the beach. The unwieldy craft were bound for Falmouth, before heading off to the Mediterranean to take part in the Sicily landings, when they were overwhelmed by mountainous seas. With their partly-open decks the landing craft filled up with water quicker than the pumps could push it out. The ships sterns were soon out of the water, their rudders and screws churning wildly and helplessly at the air. The two vessels were virtually uncontrollable. They could not have run for the safety of Milford Haven, no matter how hard they tried.

LCG 15 sank within sight of the hundreds of watchers on the beach, dozens of young marines drowning or being dashed to death on the nearby rocks. LCG 16 foundered later in the night. The sloop "Rosemary" attempted a rescue but she was unable to get a line across to LCG 16. Six sailors volunteered to take the line in a whaler but the boat was swamped almost as soon as it was launched and the brave sailors drowned. There were only three survivors from the landing craft. Seventy two men had been drowned, the largest loss of life, excluding enemy action, in the entire war.

As the war began to draw to a close, the U Boat menace at last started to make itself felt in the waters around Pembrokeshire. The Luftwaffe bases in western France had begun to fall to advancing allied troops and the Kriegsmarine had no option but to turn once more to their submarine fleet.

On 10th December 1944 the Liberty Ship "Dan Beard" was torpedoed seven miles off Strumble Head. The ship broke in two and, while the aft portion quickly sank, the bow section drifted ashore. Twelve sailors were rescued by the Fishguard lifeboat. There were several other losses to U Boats, notably the "King Edgar," a 5000 ton motor vessel which was sunk by U 1302 off St David's Head on 2nd March 1945.

The next time the people of Pembrokeshire saw or heard anything about the dreaded U Boats was when U 861 slipped quietly up the waters of the Haven, bound for the dockyard town of Pembroke Dock. But that was after the war had ended and the submarine was on its way up river to go on public show in the town.

The port of Milford Haven had played a momentous part in the conflict. Over 17,000 convoys sailed from the Haven, carrying troops and supplies, returning with vital food stuffs that would help to keep Britain in the fight. That fact cannot and should not, ever, be forgotten or denied.

* * * * * *

The Bristol Channel was a crucially important cog in the battle for survival. The Welsh ports of Cardiff and Newport, Swansea and Barry, were all coal ports but, perhaps more importantly in these war years, they were the hubs through which vital supplies were imported and distributed. Thousands of American servicemen also came into Britain through the South Wales ports. It was obvious to naval planners and humble seamen alike that, sooner or later, the Germans would attempt to block or disable these vital harbours.

At least 30 merchant vessels were sunk in the Channel in the period from 1939 to 1945, the first known victim being the "Stanholme," a small tramp steamer that struck a mine six miles off Nash Point on 25th December 1939.

Several ships were lost after collisions with other vessels in the narrow waterway, lacking lightships and hugely dangerous in wartime conditions. HMS "Princess," originally a privately owned motor yacht but requisitioned by the Admiralty as an Anti-Submarine vessel at the beginning of the war, was lost on 11th January 1940 when she collided with the steamship "Blairmoor" off the North Foreland Point light.

On the very same day as the "Princess" disaster, the "Leonard Pierce," a tramp steamer carrying a cargo of coal from Barry to London, was in collision with the "Queen Adelaide" close to Lundy Island. She went down in a matter of minutes. However, most of the sinkings in the Bristol Channel came about through merchant ships, often travelling alone, striking mines that had been laid by enemy aircraft.

Losses by mines included the "Cato," a small cargo ship on her way from Dublin to Bristol. She was mined off Nash Point, fifteen of her crew being lost. The "Strombus" was mined in October 1940 but a tow line was got across to the stricken vessel and she was brought into Swansea and beached. Two years later she left Swansea, being towed to Briton Ferry for breaking. However, during the operation there was a sudden roar and the "Strombus'" forecastle broke away from the rest of the ship and sank.

The "Tafelberg" was a 13,640 ton oil tanker, en route to the USA when she struck a magnetic mine in the Channel in early 1944. The ship broke into two halves, both sections becoming beached on the Welsh coast. The two halves were promptly towed to Whitmore Bay, Barry. In due course she was welded back together and put back into service, now renamed "Empire Heritage." Sadly the vessel did not survive for long as she was torpedoed and was lost off Malin Head on 8th September of the same year.

Air attacks also accounted for several ships in the Bristol Channel. The

The "Tafelberg," in two halves after hitting a mine in the Bristol Chgannel.

"Tenerifa," "Meg Merrilees" and "Mill Isle" were all sunk by German bombers in the first few years of the war, before adequate air cover could be provided for coastal shipping. Several vessels simply disappeared. They sailed from port and were never heard from again. Whether these ships were lost to mine, aircraft or submarine attack may never be known.

And together again – the "Tafelberg" is now welded together and ready for sea once more.

U Boats did operate in the Bristol Channel but successes were not common. The waters of the estuary were, in general, far too shallow for safe hunting to take place and the Kriegsmarine preferred to risk its U Boats out in the Atlantic where pickings were richer and the risk of detection far less.

One of the few submarine victims was the brand new merchantman "Riverton" which was attacked by U 1023 off the Cornish coast on 23rd April 1945. Seriously damaged, she was towed to St Ives for temporary repairs before being taken to Swansea. Just as she arrived in Swansea Bay the "Riverton" broke in two. The stern section sank but the forward part was beached at Oystermouth. It was later taken to Tyneside where a 90 feet stern section was added and the ship was put back into service. She continued to operate until March 1969.

Over twenty merchant ships were attacked and damaged in the Bristol Channel or Pembrokeshire area during the war. Most of the damage was inflicted in the early part of the conflict, in the years before Coastal Command was able to establish an effective system of air patrols that provided protection for the merchant ships. Even then the threat of mines, sewn indiscriminately in the waterway, remained strong.

Even when ships were in port the threat from enemy action remained strong. The "Loch Dee," unloading a cargo of timber and grain at Queen Alexandra Dock in Cardiff, was seriously damaged when German bombers attacked the town and port. A delayed action bomb penetrated her deck and exploded at 1.30 on the morning of 3rd January 1940. One crew member was killed.

The ports of South Wales suffered particularly badly, both in terms of the damage they sustained from enemy bombers and in the numbers of sailors they lost. Cardiff was bombed on a number of occasions while the famous "three night blitz" of Swansea took place between 19th and 21st February 1941. Hundreds were killed. The face of Swansea was changed forever, the bombs wiping out buildings that had been landmarks for years and reducing the centre of the town to rubble.

The oil storage depot at Pembroke Dock was hit by a single bomb from a Junkers 88 on the morning of 19th August 1940. Within minutes the tank farm was on fire, millions of tons of valuable fuel oil going up in smoke. The blaze lasted for eighteen days, the largest fire seen in Britain since the Great Fire of London in 1666, while five firemen died trying to quell the blaze.

There were many other attacks on Pembroke Dock. These were partly carried out in an attempt to damage or destroy the Sunderland flying boats of Coastal Command which were based in the town. However, it was also partly due to faulty intelligence work that led the Germans to believe the dockyard was still building warships. Pembroke Dockyard had closed in 1926! Whatever the reason for the attacks the town and its people suffered badly during these years.

The towns along the Bristol Channel coast had always provided sailors for the ships that regularly sailed from their jetties and harbours. During the Second World War things were no different. In Cardiff there was not one street in the Tiger Bay/Bute Street area that did not have merchant navy fatalities while Barry sustained more casualties than any other port of comparable size in Britain. Newport, often overlooked as a port, had 454 sailor deaths during the war – the total number of armed service casualties from Newport was 755 people. A high price indeed.

* * * * * *

When one considers the hundreds of young men and women from Wales who enlisted in the Royal Navy once war was declared, it is clear that the connection between the Principality and the sea remained strong during these tempestuous years. The tradition of Wales turning out sailors in times of crisis was well established, something that had gone on since the days of the Spanish Armada and Trafalgar. It was a tradition of which the Welsh people were justifiably proud. And, in 1939, it continued.

Interestingly, the very first Victoria Cross of the Second World War was won by a Welsh sailor when Captain Bernard Warburton-Lee was awarded the VC for his actions at the Battle of Narvik. Warburton-Lee, who received his medal posthumously, came from Maelor in Flintshire.

For most Welsh sailors, however, it was not a case of heroic gestures or individual acts of gallantry. For most of them it was a case of burying their heads and getting on with the job in hand. They did not consider themselves particularly brave, simply viewing themselves as men – and women – with a job to do. That, in itself, is an altogether different type of heroism. And now it is time to tell their stories.

PART THREE

The Sailors' Stories

The stories told by the sailors are not presented in any particular order. To rank them in "importance" or according to whether the sailors served in the Royal or Merchant Navies, on trawlers or tankers, liners or armed merchant cruisers, battleships or submarines, would be invidious. Therefore they are offered here in alphabetical order of individual names.

Neither are the stories all uniform in length. Some are short, sharp accounts, others more detailed or extended. They vary according to the style, interest and memory of the people concerned. Yet they are all invaluable and they all give an amazing insight into the time, the people involved and into events as they occurred.

These are personal accounts that do not attempt, in any way, to chart the history of the sea war. For the majority of these sailors it was a war that was fought in isolation, away from the politicians and planners, naval commanders like Max Horton who directed the Battle of the Atlantic. For most of these men and women their world was contained within, and limited to, the steel walls of their ships or the concrete boundaries of their bases – they did their jobs, as they were expected to do, and let the planners, Horton and the rest, get on with theirs.

More often than not, the tales recounted here are of the ordinary, day to day life of sailors at war. They do not all tell of famous battles – although some, obviously, do exactly that – but speak of friendships and feelings, new and unique experiences, as men and women tried to come to terms with the strange world in which they had suddenly found themselves. They are infused with a compelling and low-key sense of duty and honour. None of the sailors whose lives and war are told here regarded themselves as being particularly brave or courageous. Yet there is a quiet courage that runs through all of the stories. That is what makes them special.

In some instances the stories are told by the children or other relatives, even by friends, of the sailors concerned, perhaps where the man has died or has been otherwise unable to tell his story personally. It does not matter. What is important is that the stories have been told. They are first hand accounts and wherever possible the exact words of the sailors have been quoted. After all, they are the people who were there. These are their memories. And that is what makes them an invaluable and fascinating account of the war at sea during the period 1939 to 1945.

George William Akerman - Royal Fleet Air Arm
("Ark Royal" – sinking the "Bismark" – in the Pacific)

George Akerman joined the RAF after leaving school in 1937. He trained as an Air Artificer and was one of the earliest servicemen to be involved in the setting up of the new Fleet Air Arm:-

We were asked if we wanted to join the Fleet Air Arm, to transfer over from the RAF. I was happy to get involved – well, it was something new and interesting. There were 82 of us in that first batch. Now there are only four of us left.

I was with 767 Squadron at Holton when war broke out. I remember that Sunday morning like it was yesterday. We'd been filling sand bags and all the boys had blisters or bleeding hands. We were filthy dirty and then we had to go and swing the props on these Gloucester Gladiators. They were buggers to start, those Glads. The engines were too heavy for the airframes.

We went out to France pretty quickly after that, to Hyeres, just 20 miles from the Italian frontier. We were fairly close to Malta, down there, and the old "Hermes" used to come out to practise deck landings. We had twelve serviceable Swordfish in the squadron and a few fighters. We were bombing the cork forests in the area – cork was very valuable. The Italians didn't like it very much, after all they hadn't declared war on us then, but, as far as we were concerned, it was a job we had to do.

When the Germans attacked France on 10th May 1940, George and his squadron had to get out pretty quickly. The pilots and aircraft could fly out. For the ground crews there was little option but to walk. Despite being machine gunned and attacked by the planes of a now-hostile Italy, the men eventually reached Toulon:-

In the harbour there was a little British coaster, a coal burner. Twenty five of us went on board and we became stokers! Imagine it, the Mediterranean in June, boiling hot. And there we were, shovelling coal. We'd work for an hour and a half and then they'd throw a bucket of water over us. It was the only way to get cool. We all worked, down there in the engine room, Flight Sergeants, Artificers, the lot. It took us three days to reach Algiers.

All the old aircraft from 767 Squadron were there. Four Gloucester Glads, I remember – Faith, Hope and Charity were three of them. I can't remember the other one, or what happened to her. I must have swung the props on those planes a thousand times. My mate Charlie Wills and I used to look after about twenty planes while we were out there.

We were sent to El Kebir, we had to fly. So they put us into the rear seats and off we went. Of course all the aircraft over heated as we went up over the mountains and we had to come down in a cornfield to let the engines cool a bit. Suddenly, over the hill, came these big – and I mean big, six foot every one – black men, all wearing red fezzes. My mate Charlie, he would stutter when he got excited and now, when he saw the great big bayonets these blokes carried, he couldn't utter a word, let alone stutter! And then the leading man said "Good afternoon, gentlemen, may we be of assistance?" He was a French officer who'd been stationed in London for some years before war broke out.

The Fleet Air Arm soon decided that the planes of 767 Squadron were needed at sea and George was once again put into the back seat of a Swordfish:-

We were told to land on the "Ark Royal." My pilot was only a trainee and, over the speaking tube, he said "I've never landed on a carrier before." You can imagine how I felt at that moment.

Anyway, we circled this great big flat thing, HMS "Ark Royal." I'd seen her before, in Pompey but at that moment she seemed quite huge. We circled twice, then tried to land. And we missed by a mile. We tried twice. The third time my pilot just closed his eyes and hoped for the best. Luckily we caught the arrestor wire but, unfortunately, we swung round and hit the pom-pom gun. We took the

The "Ark Royal" at sea.

whole main plane off but we were safely down. No.818 Squadron had no
maintenance crews then so I was transferred to them on board the "Ark."

After that George returned to Britain for a short time. He was working on a flight of
Fairy Fulmars at Worthy Down, just north of Portsmouth, bleeding their fuel tanks
because they were full of iron filings. After working all night he fell asleep on the
grass outside the hangar. The next thing he knew was a terrific smack on the back of
his head. It was a brick. The Germans were bombing the aerodrome, three hangers
being destroyed in the attack. A few weeks later it was up to Scapa Flow, to another
squadron of Fulmars. Often the ground crews would take to the air in the back seat
of the planes:-

They had a rear cockpit, those Fulmars, complete with machine gun. It was
fine but then you'd hear the radio – "Bandits!" – and you knew there was trouble
around.

In September 1940 I rejoined the "Ark Royal." She was refitting in Liverpool
and was shored up in dry dock. At night, when you lay in your hammock, you
could feel the ship swinging and moving. Liverpool, then, was a ring of fire from
the bombing raids. I felt so sorry for the people in the town, they caught it really
badly. I'll tell you what though - more people got killed by ack-ack than by
bombs. In a raid, when the guns were firing, all these white hot shell fragments
would fall down alongside you. If one of them hit you it was all over.

Pretty soon we started on the Malta convoy runs. I remember, once,
something exploded on the ship. We didn't know what it was but there was this
loud bang and next minute all these RAF boys from the planes we were
transporting were there in the lifeboats, all sitting there with their little cases in
their laps. It was funny, very funny.

Once, off the coast of Africa, we took a French ship – the Germans were trying to get it back to their home base. The ship was full of eggs, thousands of the things. Well, we were on rations, weren't we? We hadn't seen eggs in months, all we had were these powdered things. Once we captured that ship the whole of Force H was egg bound for weeks.

I saw several Swordfish pilots burned when their planes crashed on the flight deck. If you were close to them you'd try to help, to get them out. There were safety crews around, in special gear, but you'd still try to help, if you could. One Swordfish crash, in particular, I remember. The batman, the guy who guided the planes in, he was lying there and his head was missing, cut right off when the plane crashed. It sickened me. I remember thinking "This bloody war!"

Another crash I can recall involved a friend of mine. Lofty Woods and I had changed the engine in the plane and so we spun a coin to see who would go up in the back seat to check it out. Lofty lost so he had to go. On landing the plane went over the side – Sub Lt Guy was the pilot, I think. Anyway, they ended up in the drink and had to swim for it, both of them. I was so glad I'd won the toss.

A crashed and burning "Swordfish" on the deck of the "Ark Royal."

As part of Force H we were involved with the sinking of the "Bismark," of course. The weather was nasty, really nasty. The destroyers couldn't get out, it was so bad. Our deck was going up about 80 feet each time we hit a wave. I've never been sea sick but, I can tell you, I nearly was then. We were trying to get the Swordfish off so we were at the stern, on the flight deck, and all we could see was the deck just going up and up. It was terrifying. When you armed torpedoes they had a red nose, to indicate they were live. You just wanted to get them onto the planes and off. Every time we hit a wave there was this shudder, it ran right through the ship. And there we were with these red nosed torpedoes – frightening!

Sub Lt Guy going over the side of the "Ark Royal" – he survived!

Twice we sent the Swordfish off and the weather got worse. I've never seen the Atlantic in such a state. Of course we didn't know if the torpedoes had hit or not, we were just carrying on with our jobs. We knew that the "Bismark" had sunk the "Hood," not officially but the rumour was around. The "Hood" boys, we knew them, we'd often go drinking with them when we were on leave or off duty, so we felt it when she went down. You would, wouldn't you, 1000 men going like that.

Later on the weather calmed down a bit. And then we saw that she'd gone down, the "Bismark." She was upside down in the water and I remember the rust streaks on her bottom. There were men in the water but they were probably already dead. We couldn't stop to pick anybody up but I do remember those shapes in the water.

George was lucky. He was posted just before the "Ark Royal" was torpedoed and sunk. He was in Glasgow, with 898 Squadron, when he heard that the "Ark" had gone down. At the same time he saw the "Queen Mary," complete with buckled bows. She had just rammed and sunk the cruiser "Curacoa" off the coast of Ireland. He actually took passage on the "Queen" a few weeks later, landing at Boston and, from there, joining the carrier "Victorious" which was then undergoing a refit:-

The Yanks had never seen a carrier like her before. All their carriers were flat bottomed. We went out on exercise and they had these fast attack boats going for us. The Yanks thought they were something special but the old "Victorious" could do 36 knots. We left everyone standing.

We went through the Panama Canal to the Pacific. That was some experience, I can tell you. We were taking huge chunks off the side of the canal, handfuls of stuff coming off and dropping into the water. The canal starts in a river and there were crocodiles there, real live crocodiles. After that it was off to Hawaii.

Heavy shells dropping into the water.

We had to go eight miles up river to get to Honolulu and all you could see was sunken ships all the way up. Their guns were sticking out of the water – it was a terrible sight. Some of those Yanks, mind you, they were dangerous. When we were flying, well, the roundels on our aircraft, they saw them and thought they were Japs. So they just opened fire. Why they didn't know we were coming I just don't know.

We went up and down the Australian coral reefs, patrolling. We were linked up with the American carrier "Saratoga." We were so fast that we were something of a greyhound, running between Australia, New Zealand and the Pacific islands. The "Saratoga" was lucky to make 8 knots!

I was out in the Pacific when the atomic bomb was dropped but I can't say I remember it particularly. What I do remember, is having to drop all the lease-

Swordfish aircraft from the "Ark Royal" disabled the "Bismark" and left her helpless in the water.

lend planes that the Yanks had given us into the Indian Ocean. Dozens of them, after peace came, we just dumped them into the sea.

It was hard work keeping the planes flying during the war years, lots of long hours. If there was a job to do you'd just get on with it, work until the job was done. You were tired and sweaty but you kept on going. I had to cut my eye lashes to see through them sometimes, they were all stuck up with sleep. Often we'd look at each other and we were black from all the cordite and smoke. We were oily and smelly but we'd just laugh. Well, we were only kids, weren't we?

George Akerman was demobbed from the Fleet Air Arm in the 1950s. He was offered a commission but knew that he would not really be able to afford it. And so he came out:-

I'd had enough, really. I had married by then and had two sons. I wanted to do something with farming, I wanted to enjoy the good Welsh air. And so I came to Aberystwyth.

S R (Jim) Arnold - Merchant Navy
(Convoys – Atlantic – Far East)

Just 16 years of age when he first went to sea in January 1936, Jim Arnold came from the county of Pembrokeshire. He lived in the small community of St David's, the smallest city in Britain, but was determined to expand his horizons. He certainly did not want to spend his life on the family farm:-

I joined the Blue Funnel Line. They were based in Liverpool and, at one time, had almost a hundred ships. They sailed mainly to the Far East and for the four years of my apprenticeship I got to know quite a lot about Japan and China. I can still remember coming through the Inland Sea in March 1936 and seeing all the cherry blossoms blooming. It was a marvellous sight.

My apprenticeship ended just as the war began in 1939. We knew that preparations were being laid for war – in those final months you couldn't pass a naval vessel without it calling you up to practise signalling. As Midshipmen – the Blue Funnel Line had special permission to call its apprentices Midshipmen – we were always being called to the bridge to take over and do the signalling. So by the time war actually broke out we could read most of the signals made by the lamp as fast as the navy could.

When war broke out Jim Arnold was steaming along the American coast in the Pacific. The first thing the Chinese crew did was to paint everything on the ship a dull grey – funnels, masts, everything. Nobody on board realised that grey would be the primary colour of all ships for the next six years:-

When we arrived in Hong Kong they put a 4.7 inch gun on the poop deck. We all had to undergo training in gunnery. There were no DEMS gunners then, like there were later, and my job was sight setter. I remember having to shout things like "Sights moving, sights set." We left Hong Kong and sailed for home. It was only when we reached Gibraltar that we got any ammunition for the gun. Up until then we'd had the gun but nothing to fire.

It was after the fall of France that things began to really "hot up." We sailed in convoys out of Liverpool, then from Halifax back to Britain. There were always frantic preparations going on. The Master would be ashore for a convoy conference and then come back on board with all the information. This was then passed on to us as deck officers.

The first thing you wanted to know was how many ships were in the convoy. It was quite usual to have, perhaps, forty ships. They were all divided laterally – is that the right expression? – not lengthways. If there were forty ships there'd be 10 columns of 4 ships, not 4 columns of 10 ships. It was a broad front. The first thing you had to find on the form was the number of your ship. If it was, say, 3/1 it meant you'd be the leader of the third column. Ship number 3/2 would come behind you – and so forth. The Commodore's ship would be in the middle column or, if there was an even number of columns, to the right of the middle column.

There's an old expression about the speed of a convoy being the speed of the slowest ship. That was absolute rubbish. If it was, say, a ten knot convoy then all ships had to maintain that speed, 10 knots. If they didn't then they fell back. If they broke down it was just too bad. You couldn't slow a forty ship convoy down to, say, just 1 knot. That would have been suicidal.

In the convoy instructions, on the North Atlantic Chart, there were always three positions – A, B and C. After taking the noon position each day – always done by sextant, none of the global positioning like you have these days – the Commodore would hoist a signal flag. He'd say "The rendezvous for the day after tomorrow is to be X degrees, X miles from A or B or whatever." So any ship that had fallen behind or had to stop for repairs, she could try to put on speed and head for that position in order to rejoin the convoy.

Jim went on to sail in troop convoys from the Clyde. The first one carried soldiers out to Singapore, just before the island fortress fell. Within two months of landing the young British soldiers that Jim and his colleagues had carried were in Japanese hands. Other convoys he was involved with included sailing down to West Africa to pick up African troops and take them to India. The speed of these troop convoys was usually quite fast, perhaps as much as 14 or 15 knots, and the duties of a watch keeping officer were considerable. One had to be constantly on the alert:-

You had to keep on your toes, particularly in the more dangerous areas. It was very hard for young officers but, then, it was a very serious business we were involved in. You had to keep your position in the convoy, you had to keep a look out for the enemy. A sense of humour was important, essential to keep the right mental balance, but it was serious work we were involved with. You couldn't relax, not even for a moment.

At Singapore, just before the surrender, we discharged our troops and cargo and then we loaded up with women and children who were being evacuated, and took them down to Australia. There was a bit of a panic in Singapore just then – deserters and the like trying to get on board. I can't say I blame them, now, knowing what was lying ahead for them. But back then we were told that we couldn't discuss such things when we reached Australia. It's strange, looking back, how we were discouraged, actively discouraged, from talking and keeping things like diaries. Yet when you read memories of the war from all the "big shots" that's exactly what they did, keep diaries.

One thing I remember, when we reached Fremantle, was this little lad on board. He screamed out "Look, mummy, white coolies!" We had to keep him quiet, knowing how touchy the Australian stevedores were. Trouble with them was the last thing we wanted.

The convoys all had naval escorts but usually they were well ahead of the merchant ships, looking for submarines. Sometimes they'd come close but usually they left running the convoy to the Commodore. Some of those escort vessels, well they were little more than glorified trawlers. We didn't have a lot of faith in them but, as the years went by, things did improve.

Danger was ever present for Merchant Navy sailors like Jim Arnold. Sometimes it came in the shape of submarines and bomb attack, sometimes it came from the sea itself:-

Liverpool soon came within the range of German bombers and after that we spent more time based up on the Clyde than on the Mersey. I don't suppose we spent a lot of time in port, we just brought the ship in and the stevedores would get working to unload her and get her back out to sea again as quickly as possible.

Once my ship was bombed and sunk when we were in Gladstone Dock in Liverpool. The bomb went clean through No 2 Hatch and the ship settled in 30 foot of water. The superstructure was out of the water, safe enough, but the rest of the ship was beneath the surface. That December, 1941, Liverpool was heavily bombed and I was actually pleased to be at sea and out of it all.

We were also bombed, once, by Focke-Wulf Kondors when we were off Cape Finisterre. We had an ack-ack cruiser alongside us and we were the Commodore's ship at the time. We all wished he'd move his flag elsewhere. What surprised me were the near misses. They'd send the ship on a ten to fifteen degree list before she'd flop back down onto an even keel. We were all rather pleased they were near misses, not anything closer.

One time we ran into a tremendous north-westerly gale. There was such a horrible sea that, eventually, the order came for the convoy to scatter. With all the deck cargo we had and with such a dangerous sea running we couldn't have headed for safety, even if we'd wanted. So we just had to run with the wind and waves behind us. I remember the ship sliding down the sides of the waves into these great green valleys. We'd be up on the bridge and we'd be thinking "Oh, my goodness, how are we going to get out of this one?" You'd have that feeling, you know, don't look back, there's somebody following us! Next thing we'd see this huge wave behind us and we'd say "Come on, girl, get your bum up." And she did and then we'd slide down into the next trough.

I'd only ever experienced the south-west monsoon before that, out in the Indian Ocean. I remember thinking "If I survive this I'll pee to windward." It was frightening. And I can still remember it quite clearly.

Jim was fortunate. During the course of the war he served on nine different ships. Eight of them were sunk – but only after he had left them:-

I was lucky, I suppose. You tried to put the danger out of your mind, tried not to think about it. We all had these little scatter bags, a bit like the things you carry on your backs these days, and in there you'd put a bit of this and a bit of that, just in case you were torpedoed and the order came to abandon ship. You'd put in all your certificates and a bottle of amber coloured liquid, in case it was needed in the lifeboats, and keep it close to hand. But even when there was torpedoing and depth charging going on I tried not to let it worry me too much. Every night when I wasn't on watch I'd still climb into my pyjamas and get into my bunk. In my mind's eye I'd see the green hills of Pembrokeshire as I drifted off to sleep.

One of the things we were wary of was meeting an enemy ship at sea. Whenever we came across another ship we'd always have a signal flag to hoist – say F3J or something like that – and that flag would last for a day or so before it was changed. When we hoisted that signal we'd look to see what the reply was. If she was a genuine ship the reply would be accurate. If she was German she wouldn't know the correct reply. Maybe she'd have the White Ensign flying but not the correct signal flag. This was a method the Germans often used.

They almost caught one of our company ships like that. The Master ordered his ship to stop when he saw another ship bearing down over the horizon but the Chief Officer realised it was a fraud, a trick. And there was a fight on the bridge! The Master was holding the telegraph one way, the Chief Officer pushing it the other. Eventually the disguised German ship fired a torpedo but the Blue Funnel ship managed to turn around and get away. The Chief Officer said simply "There's your friendly ship for you, Captain."

German ships operating under our colours, often converted merchantmen, were a constant danger. The Captain of that vessel in the story, in a book after the war, said that only one British ship ever managed to get away from him – "the Blue Funnel one." He didn't realise the shambles that had gone on to enable the ship to get away.

Life at sea was not without its compensations, however, and sometimes there was humour to be found in the most unlikely of situations:-

We were in Oregon, once, shortly after the war broke out. Two of us were going ashore, just to have a look at the town of Astoria and see what it was like. We had no idea that we were three or four miles from the town. So we had to walk. A car stopped and an elderly man and woman asked us if we would like a ride into town. We got talking and they showed us around, pointed out where the explorers Lewis and Clarke had come down through the hinterland, and eventually took us to their home. The old man said "Switch the light out, mother. Can you guys see this luminous alarm clock?" He must have thought we lived in the wilds of Siberia or somewhere like that.

Anyway, on the way back to the ship the old man suddenly said "This is the bad part of town. It's where all the loose women live – they follow the salmon fishermen down the coast. We have our own name for them out here but, of course, back in England you call them Protestants!" We didn't correct him.

In recent years the question I'm most often asked is "Where you on D Day?" And the answer is in the Indian Ocean, after clearing the Red Sea. We were carrying troops, one of the many important jobs the Merchant Navy did during those war years. D Day, 1944, seems a long time ago now.

I don't think the Merchant Navy ever got the recognition it deserved for its service during the Second World War. I think the Royal Navy was a bit jealous, as if the glamour was meant to be theirs and theirs alone. That was the feeling we all got at the time. Perhaps they resented the publicity we were getting, in particular for the heavy losses we had during the war years.

One of the Blue Funnel ships, called the "Chilean Reefer," was twenty or so miles behind her convoy. She couldn't keep up and was overtaken and fired on by a raider – it turned out to be the "Gneisenau." Old Tommy Bell, the skipper, had the audacity to fire back at this battle cruiser with his little 4.7 inch gun. There were prisoners on the "Gneisenau" and they counted the salvos. In all 87 salvos were fired before they blew the "Chilean Reefer" out of the water. Two boats got away, the 2nd Mate in charge of one, Tommy Bell the other. Eventually they were rescued by the navy – apart from the 2nd Mate who was taken on board the warship – and were well looked after but there was no mention of the incident in the press or anywhere. It would have made a great story, that tiny little merchantman standing up to a German battle cruiser.

I sailed with Tommy Bell just after the war and he had a letter from the Merchant Navy Masters Union that said something like "we were shocked to find that after this gallant action there was no mention or reward for gallantry." Tommy just said "They didn't want to recognise me then. Now four years on they can forget it." I suppose it rankled with us quite a bit.

The number of merchant seamen who lost their lives was huge. In proportion it was far heavier in the Merchant Navy than in any of the fighting forces. Most of the deaths occurred in the lifeboats, not in the actual sinking, and they did so at an alarming rate. The first twenty four hours were the worst, it was almost like a shock effect after the torpedoing.

Jim Arnold, who was always known by his proper name of Stanley during his working life – Jim was the name by which he was known in Pembrokeshire - continued in the Merchant Navy after the end of the war. He was not to know that the Suez Canal, through which he had sailed several times whilst taking troops from West Africa, would become something of a prison for him 23 years later when, as Master of a merchant ship, he was held up there during the Six Days War of 1967. It was only one incident in a professional life and career dedicated to the sea.

When Jim retired, however, it was to his "green Pembrokeshire hills" that he returned. He lives, now, in Milford Haven, a bare stone's throw from the sea that has been so important to him.

Gordon Baker - Merchant and Royal Navy

(Air attack, during the Spanish Civil War – Armed Merchant Cruiser)

The following story was written by Gordon Baker, a Swansea man who sadly died a few years ago. It was never intended for publication but was put down on paper for his family. It has been preserved and passed on by Sarah Llewellyn, Gordon's granddaughter, and is presented here in an abridged form.

Gordon Baker began his working life in a shop in Swansea but as all his spare time was spent staring at the ships in the nearby docks it was almost inevitable that he should go to sea when the opportunity arose. The "British Corporal" was an oil tanker, owned by the British Tanker Company of London. Like many merchant ships at this time she also carried a few passengers and in 1937 Gordon was about to be taken on as a cabin boy:-

One day my mother came down to the shop with a telegram for me to join the "British Corporal" at Falmouth. However, I was not too sure how the manager would take my leaving. He was quite all right about it, as it happened, and even offered me ten shillings extra a week if I stayed. I wasn't tempted by this, I was keen to go. I put my coat on while he got my pay and was pleased to find he had paid me a full week although it was only half way through, and so we said our goodbyes. I went home with Mam to buy a new coat to take with me, then home to pack and have some tea.

I had never been on a train before and travelled all through the night. When I finally arrived I caught a taxi to the docks. I wasn't in the taxi more than five minutes and there was the ship in all her glory. It was before seven in the morning when I found myself standing at the bottom of the gangway. A steward spotted me and showed me where to go and what to do.

Amongst other things it was my job to look after the passengers. There were always a few of them on board. I was all right until the ship was out in the open sea. It was then I began to feel ill but I still had to look after the passengers. I went to the steward and told him but he said to keep on my feet and do what I could. He helped me and luckily it only lasted for two days before I was myself again.

Eventually we arrived in the Persian Gulf and there the passengers left us. We filled up with oil and left for Rotterdam and Hamburg. We sailed into Hamburg the same day that Adolf Hitler was visiting the place but I didn't know much about him then. That was to change later on.

Shortly afterwards Gordon found himself once more in the Persian Gulf. His ship sailed up the Red Sea and into the Suez Canal, an amazing experience for the young cabin boy and ship's steward. More amazing experiences were set to occur as the "British Corporal" was about to become a victim of the Spanish Civil War. Britain was not involved in the conflict but attacks on merchant shipping within range of the Spanish coast, often by German planes from the Kondor Legion that was helping General Franco, did sometimes take place. The "British Corporal" was one such victim. First, however, there was the sight of the canal to enjoy:-

It takes twenty four hours to go through the Suez Canal. It runs through two anchorages where ships can pass and then proceed on their way. It's really funny to see ships sailing across the sand – because that's exactly what it looks like.

When we were clear of the canal we went on across the Mediterranean, heading for the Straits of Gibraltar. Then, suddenly, there were three aircraft bombing and firing machine guns at us. It was early morning and we'd just got dressed. One bomb, I don't know if it exploded but it made a very loud noise as it dropped into the water beside us. When we heard that we rushed to the gangway, our way out, but then came the sound of machine guns firing so we jumped back into our "glory hole" until it went quiet.

When we thought the planes had gone we climbed back up the companionway. The other young boy on board, we called him Gissey, I can't remember his real Christian name, he was in front. Suddenly he turned around and flew back into the "glory hole." We asked him if the planes had come back. "No," he said, "I just needed to go to the toilet." I can't say what the others called him for that!

After that we turned round and sailed for Algeria. We had to wait for two days for a destroyer to arrive and escort us to Gibraltar. Then we went up the coast, through the English Channel to Fleetwood. The bosses were waiting on the dockside to see what damage we had suffered. After unloading we headed for Falmouth to get repaired. They paid us off at Falmouth and I went home so that everyone there could see I was not injured in any way.

Gordon did not go back to sea but took a job in a flour mill for a few years. Then, at the beginning of the Second World War, he was called up for the Royal Navy. After a full medical, he journeyed to Skegness for basic training on 28th December 1939:-

It was snowing the day I left Swansea and when I arrived at Skegness a lorry was waiting to take all the new recruits out to the camp. It was a Butlin's Holiday Camp and not made for living in at that time of the year. We weren't dressed for that type of weather, either, especially out there on the East Coast. There were three of us to each chalet and when we woke up in the morning we had to get rid of the ice on our blankets. We had to take it in turns to wash at the outside tap. There was no hot water. We were there for two weeks, then they put us on a train bound for HMS "Drake" at Devonport.

On the way through London another lorry was waiting for us. They said we were going to the Savoy for dinner before going on to Devonport. And we did – but it was under the Savoy we went, like a basement. Still, at least I can say I've dined at the Savoy.

At Devonport we were sorted out with hammocks and uniforms and somehow I managed to end up looking something like a sailor. We learned to drill and how to use rifles. I suppose we did this for about two months before we had a spot of leave and then came back to the barracks ready for our postings. I was sent to Belfast to join the "Asturias," an armed merchant cruiser. She had already been converted for war duty, had new engines fitted and had her speed increased to 20 knots. She had eight six inch guns and some anti-aircraft guns as well.

We sailed for Iceland, made two trips up there, before we went out to Gibraltar. While we were moored there a fire was discovered in the front of the ship and the Gibraltar Fire Brigade had to be called to come and put it out. It gave us an extra day in port. After that we escorted a convoy making for Britain.

The "Asturias" was mainly involved in patrol duties in the South Atlantic, most of the time being spent at sea. The ports of South America were defiantly neutral and were not prepared to allow the British ship to dock:-

After about a month they allowed us to come ashore but only for twenty four hours at a time. We had three ports open to us – Buenos Aires, Montevideo and Rio de Janeiro. Buenos Aires was very pro-German and left us feeling we weren't welcome when we tied up alongside the dock. There were one or two German sailors in the town. They must have been on the "Graf Spee," we thought. Now the pocket battleship was just a rusting sheet of steel, scuttled outside the River

Plate. We also went into Rio and Montevideo – I'll always remember the statue of Christ at Rio. The fingers are six foot long and you can see the statue long before you can see the town.

Most of the time we spent at sea, up to seven weeks at a time. We rarely saw another ship because we were outside the shipping lanes but one occasion I do remember, it sticks in the memory. It was getting dark when we spotted this other vessel. She wasn't answering our signals and so we went to action stations. The other ship just ran. We watched as her funnel began to glow – goodness knows what they were burning down in her engine room to make her funnel glow like that. They must have been sweating pints down there. Anyway, we kept signalling and at last they answered. It turned out she was a Greek tramp steamer and she thought we were German. She slowed and we watched her funnel cool down. We watched her disappear into the gloom and then we returned to our patrol.

One day one of our engineers was taken ill and died. We had to bury him at sea. He was wrapped in a canvas sheet and laid out on the deck with the White Ensign over him. Four sailors stood, one on each corner, with their rifles reversed. All the crew stopped work and the engines stopped, too. The Captain read a passage from the Bible and the engineer was lowered gently down the side of the ship. It was all very sad.

After a while the "Asturias" was relieved by the "Caernarvon Castle" and sailed to Virginia in the USA for a refit. It meant a period of well-deserved leave for Gordon and his mates. The Americans were incredibly friendly, happy to offer hospitality to the visiting British sailors:-

One day two of us were taking a walk into town when a car drove past and hooted. We waved back and thought no more about it. The next day we were walking along when the same car stopped and the woman driver wanted to know where we had got to the day before as she had turned round to offer us a lift but couldn't find us. We'd gone into a drug store for a drink, that's why she missed us. But that's how everybody was out there, so friendly.

Sometimes they were too friendly! We were walking past a filling station one day when a lad shouted, offering us a lift. The two boys in the car put us by the windows, one each side. We thought that was a bit queer and we were glad to get out. We had made friends with the local fireman and when we told him about it he said the police had been looking for those two boys for some time. The police would not be likely to stop a car with two British sailors in it – that's why they had given us a lift and asked us to sit like that. The fireman rang the police and we heard that a day or two later the lads were arrested.

When the work on the "Asturias" was finished she was like a different ship. She had six guns instead of eight, but much more powerful, much more modern, and also a catapult and a special hold made to house two aircraft. There was also a crane to hoist the planes out of the sea. Within a few days of rejoining we were off to sea, leaving the USA behind. It was back to patrolling.

One day, off Montevideo, we received information that a ship called the "Mendoza" was about to sail. It was a French ship but she supposedly had a cargo meant for war – we had to stop her. When we spotted her the "Mendoza" refused to stop, even when our Captain put a shot from our anti-aircraft gun across her bows. A gunboat from Montevideo had come out and she was supposed to chase us out of Uruguayan territorial waters. But when we turned our six inch guns on her she scuttled back to harbour. We followed the "Mendoza" and again we fired across her bows, this time with one of our six inch guns. And this time she'd had enough – you could see the water boiling as she went full speed astern. The shot must have scared everyone on board because all the passengers were running around half dressed.

We sent a boarding party aboard and then away we went with our lads sailing the "Mendoza" ahead of us. A cruiser soon arrived and they took over. They sent our boarding party back and away we sailed on patrol again. When we docked at Rio de Janeiro a few weeks later the papers were full of stories about "British pirates." We just ignored it – well, we were only in port for twenty-four hours so it didn't really affect us that much.

One day, out at sea, the Petty Officer was looking for a new masthead man, looking for someone to take turns as a lookout. They chose a nice young bloke from Derby and when it came to my turn for lookout this new lad was detailed to come with me. I was following him up the rigging and we'd got about half way when we suddenly stopped. "I can't go up any more," he said. I looked at his face and he was as white as a sheet. He was stuck to the rigging. I had a real job to get him down safely, one arm around him, the other holding the rigging. Just to get him to let go was a job – I reckon it took the best part of quarter of an hour to get him back to the deck. Not everybody can make a good masthead lookout.

We had been a lucky ship but, unfortunately, our luck did not hold out. We were making for Freetown one night when a U Boat spotted us and hit us with a torpedo. It was around midnight and like many of the others I was fast asleep. I was blown out of my hammock by the explosion. I picked myself up and ran to my action station. The ship quickly lost power as she'd been hit in the engine room. Everything was dead but we stayed at our posts until an officer dismissed us. I spent the time just looking at the oil on the water. I kept thinking I would have to jump into that. Water, that was all right, but oil? It made my blood run cold. It was a relief to learn that the ship wasn't going to sink, as long as they could keep the water down with the pumps.

We managed, eventually, to run her aground and then wait for a cruiser and a tug that were coming to help. We had no hot meals for two or three days but we were allowed two bottles of beer a day from the ward room. When the cruiser arrived at last she came alongside and they passed across some urns of hot tea. It was such a relief and a real change from beer.

Gordon Baker left the "Asturias" shortly afterwards. He was posted to the Flower Class corvette HMS "Snowdrop," going from one of the biggest vessels in the fleet to one of the smallest:-

We went to a place called Tacoradi and tied up alongside what was, really, just a river bank. I was on duty, belt and gaiters and all the usual white tropical gear. Suddenly there was a shout – "Stop that lad." A young boy had slipped on board and was now trying to run off the ship so I dropped my rifle and jumped onto the river bank after him. The slope was all slippery and I ruined my white suit. But I caught him and marched him back to the ship. The police came and took the boy away. When I had changed and resumed my sentry duties it was, like, the whole town was there on the bank, after my blood. I held my rifle and bayonet in front of me and said "If anyone tries to attack me I'll use this!" They hung around for about an hour before leaving, saying they'd wait until I didn't have a rifle to protect myself with. I never saw any of them again.

After that the "Snowdrop" sailed north to Gibraltar and then to the Clyde, Dundee and, finally, to Newcastle where Gordon Baker left the ship for the last time.

Frank Batterham - Royal Navy
(Destroyers - Russian convoys – D Day landings)

Frank Batterham served as a stoker on board HMS "Swift," a destroyer built at Cowes and commissioned in 1943. Commanded by Lt Commander J R Gower, she was part of the 23rd Flotilla, all six ships of the unit having names that began either with the letter O or S. Frank was born in Newport and after leaving school worked in the construction industry. As soon as he was old enough, however, he enlisted in the navy. After basic training he was taken by ferry to the Isle of Wight and there, for the first time, he saw his new ship. As Frank recalls:-

She was brand new, just as I was a brand new stoker. You could smell her fresh paint and her brass-work was dull because it had never been polished. When we fired up the boilers all her paint nearly blistered. She could make 38 knots, an incredible turn of speed for a destroyer in those days.

Two of the ships in our Flotilla were manned by Norwegian crews. They had a couple of British sailors on board. I suppose that was done for communication purposes. The "Swift" was a nice new destroyer and soon after we were commissioned it became clear that we were bound for the Arctic. We sailed north to Scapa Flow and that was wonderful. But soon we were going even further north, with the convoys to Russia. In between convoys we were on escort duty for strikes against the "Tirpitz," that type of thing – but always in the Arctic.

We were a lucky ship. Once, on one of the convoys, we'd been at action stations for three days and nights. We turned our helm away, completed a manoeuvre, at the exact moment a U Boat fired its torpedoes at us. HMS "Mahratta" slipped into the space we had just left and she caught the torpedo intended for us. She went down and most of her crew were lost.

And then, one day, we left Scapa but instead of heading north we went south, into the Clyde and up to Greenock. We'd been there once before, for a boiler clean, but this time it was different. We lay there and at any time we would shove off, with no notice, and sail down the Clyde. I remember, once, we were all lined up on deck, ready to go ashore for the evening. The klaxon went and that was it, we were off. Our night out in Glasgow was finished before it even began. By the time we got back to the wharf everything was shut.

Our gunners used to have a lovely time knocking lumps off the island of Jura, down in the Firth. Everyone wondered why they had to blast away at an island.

No-one knew but the buzzes, the rumours, would fly around the ship and most of them turned out to be right. We were being toughened up, preparing for the D Day landings. Although quite why they thought we needed toughening up after eight months on the Russian convoys we never could work out.

Eventually, the training was over and "Swift" headed south, joining an armada of vessels on the southern coast of England. The D Day landings were about to take place:-

There were all sorts of ships gathering from all the ports and creeks where they'd been hidden around the coast. Amongst them were some empty old merchantmen and their propellers made one hell of a noise whenever they came out of the rough water. How the Germans never picked up the noise when we were cruising around I'll never know. By now our skipper had told us we were on the eve of D Day – and remember, the invasion had been delayed for twenty four hours because of the bad weather. And then, suddenly, at 22.00 hours on 5th June 1944, we were told we were heading for France. We were off.

The battered remains of the destroyer "Swift," off the Normandy beaches.

We were all closed up to action stations, just waiting. Then, just before dawn, it seemed as if the heavens had erupted. The flashes and the crash of guns, the sound of bombs exploding on the shore – it was immense, almost unbelievable in its scale. As far as the eye could see the water was black with ships. There were landing craft full of soldiers. We felt so sorry for those men, it was really rough out there and I think most of them must have been very sick. Then they hit the beach, or close to it, and the soldiers just poured out. It was a sight we will never see again, not that anyone will ever want to.

Our job was to make for the beach, just behind the minesweepers, at a point close to Caen. We had an army liaison officer on board with us and, as directed by him, we were supposed to lay down fire with our 4.7 inch guns. There was a sudden bang off our starboard side. Our sister ship, the Norwegian manned HMNS "Svenner," had been hit by one, or maybe two, torpedoes from a German

E Boat which had come out from Ouistreham. We weren't supposed to stop but we did. It was a case of all hands on deck to pull the survivors out of the water.

We lowered scrambling nets over the side and I went down to the bottom to grab whoever I could. I managed to pull a few out and helped them up the net to shipmates on the upper deck. I got hold of one poor bloke and I could see he'd had his legs blown off. He couldn't help himself. Then I found myself getting lower and lower in the water and I realised we were getting under way again. I couldn't hang on to the chap against the force of the water and I had to let go. He gave one yell and then he was gone.

During one break in the action it was our job to feed the forward half of the ship. We got hold of whatever food we could. A Petty Officer gave me a fanny full of pineapple rings and told me to "do" the bridge. Off I went, telling everyone to just take two rings. There was no time for spoons or forks, it was a case of dip your fingers in and take your share. I got to the skipper last. He stared at me – "How do I get them out?" he asked. I looked at him with a straight face – "Same way as everyone else, sir, dig your fingers in." He looked a bit amazed but he did it and got his two pineapple rings. I said "Everyone's got greasy fingers," and then moved away – fast!

The "Swift" might have been considered a lucky ship but her luck was about to run out. On D Day Plus 15 there was a sudden and terrible explosion. The ship had hit a mine:-

There was no panic. I remember the skipper shouting "Don't abandon ship, the water's cold." That seemed to calm everybody down. We had to leave her in the end, mind you, as the explosion had torn her in half.

I was about to go over the side when I remembered I had no life jacket. I'd given it to an injured yeoman of signals who'd been blown off the bridge. So I went back to the mess deck to grab whatever I thought would float and then took my chance and went over the side. Strangely, for some reason, even though I couldn't swim, I knew it wasn't my day to die. The current washed me back towards the "Swift's" screws but I managed to get away and reached a marine landing craft about 300 yards away. I was just about exhausted, finished, when this marine threw me a rope. I couldn't catch it to begin with but then he threw it again and I managed to grab it. I tell you, there was no way I was going to let go of that rope once I'd caught it.

They gave us, the survivors, tea and rum and whatever clothes the marines could find for us. Then they took us to a merchant ship manned by Indians. It had been set up to cater for survivors from any ships that were sunk. And there, on that ship, we had another rum ration. Nobody seemed to be keeping count so we went round several times. We ended up quite drunk, I suppose.

The memories don't go. Some years later I went over to Ouistreham on the Caen ferry. Even after all those years I could see it all, in detail, the last moments of the "Swift." As the ferry passed, instinctively, I knew the exact spot where she had gone down.

Within a few days of the "Swift" being sunk Frank was back in Newport, re-kitted and sent home on leave. Within minutes of getting to the house he was fast asleep. It was his twentieth birthday.

George Blake - Merchant Navy

(Training for the Merchant Navy – danger from mines)

The end of the war did not lessen the duties or the pressure on Britain's merchant marine sailors. The country still needed to be fed, goods still needed to be imported and British raw materials still had to be sold in order to bring in much needed revenue for a country that had been made virtually bankrupt by the conflict. In addition there were thousands of soldiers, British and American alike, who needed to be transported home for de-mobilisation. So the need for sailors continued, and people like George Blake could still expect to forge careers for themselves in the Merchant Navy:-

I only sailed out of Cardiff once, right at the very end of the war. I joined the ship at Trafford Warf in Manchester and we sailed down the Manchester Ship Canal – always an interesting experience. From there we came around the coast to Cardiff and tied up in Queen Alexandra Dock, underneath the coal hoists, getting ready to load with good Welsh coal. Our destination was Valetta Harbour in Malta.

The company I was working for was a Cardiff based firm, Frank S. Dawson of Creighton House in Mount Stuart Square. I was apprenticed to them – I'd signed indentures for four years as a deck apprentice. The company was a small one. As far as I know they only ever had two ships, tramp vessels that carried general cargoes around the world. During the time I was with them it was mostly coal, iron ore and esparto grass – we were bringing that in from North Africa. Our regular routes were out to Algiers to load iron ore. Or we'd go to Arzew or Beni Saf for the esparto grass. I think it was used in the steel industry and we'd load up with that and carry it up to Middlesbrough.

George had been training for a career in the Merchant Navy for a number of years. Like many young boys in the 1930s and 40s he had always been interested in the sea and his schooling was geared to provide him with many of the skills and experience he would need:-

I went to this special sort of school, one that catered for boys who intended to make the sea their career. There were several of them around in those days, places like the "Conway" and the "Worcester." Ours was named after Lady Furness, the wife of the MP Christopher Furness. He was a ship owner, the Furness Withy Line, and he sponsored or subsidised this school for boys. It was down in Kent. We were there for most of the war years – late on in the war it moved to Devon but during my time it was located in Kent.

We wore a sort of naval uniform and most of the boys were the sons of Royal Navy or Merchant Navy personnel. We learned things like using a sextant, navigation –basic navigation - small boat work, that type of thing. You also had to do your normal lessons, maths and all that. It didn't guarantee you a job when you left but you had a better chance of a berth than someone who came out of an ordinary type of school.

Facing torpedoes and bombs was one thing. Merchant Navy men did not exactly take it in their George Blake - Merchant Navy

stride but they accepted it as one of the many challenges that war brought.

However, even after the end of hostilities the danger of mines and uncharted wrecks in shallow water remained strong:-

The biggest problem we had was mines. Our ship still had the degaussing gear, for use against magnetic mines, but that was no use against acoustic mines because, obviously, they were set off by vibration. We'd use the degaussing gear because the theory was that it would neutralise the ship's magnetism and that made us feel safe about magnetic mines. But it didn't solve the problem of the acoustic ones.

Sea Training – boys of the Lady Furness House School prepare to be sailors.

When we were sailing through an area where mines had been laid we'd go to the naval people in Liverpool and they'd give us a route through the minefield. We'd have to plot the route on the chart. Unfortunately, in heavy weather some of the buoys that were used to mark the minefields in, say, the Channel would drift and sometimes it was difficult to pick them up in the right positions.

I did hear about one merchant ship that was sunk off Gibraltar in Algeciras Bay. That was a short while after the end of the war. They'd obviously laid mines in the bay during the war years and this one must have been left behind when they cleared them all after 1945. She was an iron ore ship, the one that struck the mine, and she went down pretty quickly.

I spent twelve years in the Merchant Navy and was then invalided out. I'd caught TB which, I believe, is called the Seaman's Disease. I caught it out in the Far East but that was well after the war had finished. Even in the 1950s, you see, sailors were still going down with diseases like that. Conditions hadn't changed much since the 1930s.

Leslie Alan Boucher – Norwegian Merchant Navy

(Atlantic, Australasia)
Contributed by Malcolm Mort of the Cardiff Merchant Navy Association

With the consent of my father I joined the Norwegian Merchant Navy in 1941, as an Engine Room boy at the age of sixteen, because my friends had told me that they had better ships and paid more money than the British Merchant Navy. On a wage of fifteen pounds a month I was very happy when I got accepted and sailed from Newport, Gwent on my first foreign-going deep sea voyage. The eight months passed quickly by as I became used to their ways of living. They are mainly fish eaters. Salted fish with onions and tomatoes was a poplar very filling meal. There was also a cheese which looked like a bar of soap. On one occasion I was told to clean and scrub the engineers mess room table, and couldn't get the soap to lather.

When I told the person in charge of me about the problem. He picked up the bar and laughed before telling me that, "Cheese was for eating. Not for cleaning tables with." Needless to say that it wasn't long before everybody was laughing about it. Such was closeness and comradeship of the ship's crew who took an interest in me and started to teach me the basis of the Norwegian language.

I was fortunate to dock and pay off at Newport docks, Gwent in time to spend Christmas at home with my parents in Stanway Road, Ely, Cardiff. After my leave finished I joined another Norwegian general cargo ship named the MV Triton bound for Savannah in the USA. We loaded coils of paper which we discharged in Australia. Then we went to Port Pierie and loaded zinc ingots. From there on to Tasmania to load tinned fruit. We then went back to Australia to load bails of wool before sailing towards South Africa to become part of a Royal Navy escorted convoy of about thirty ships back to the UK.

In our previous ports the engineers had done the necessary routine maintenance work to the main engine and auxiliary plant, to cut down the risks of our ship encountering any breakdown problems and having to drop out of the convoy. The reality of the situation was that the convoy was unable to stop without presenting itself as an easy target for enemy submarines, warships or aircrafts.

On our way to South Africa we came across a ship's lifeboat with the survivors of a Panamanian tanker which had been torpedoed by a Japanese submarine. They told us that the submarine crew had machine-gunned them while they were trying to get off of the burning tanker. Those who had survived had managed to hide under the lifeboat or floating debris, until the submarine left them all as dead. We rescued and cared for them until we landed them in South African before joining the convoy bound for Loch Ewe in the UK.

Jim Brain BEM – Merchant Navy

(Malta, reported lost at sea, West Indies)
Contributed by Norman Date, Hon. Secretary, Merchant Navy Association, Bristol

Born at Barry Dock, South Wales in 1919 Jim left school in 1936 and joined the Reardon Smith Line ship `Bradfine`, not a happy start to his sea career as he developed appendicitis. Following his recovery he tried to join the Royal Navy in 1940, fortunately for the war effort and as later events will show, his application was unsuccessful. Later in the war he joined as Cook the King Line ship `King Edwin` which had been converted to an ammunition carrier at Suez, and which then in 1943 sailed in convoy from Alexandria to the besieged George Cross island of Malta.

The ship was loaded with drums of aviation fuel and coal in her forward holds and ammunition in the aft holds. Jim helped to man the ship's Oerlikon gun during a thankfully safe passage, and the ship anchored in Grand Harbour, Valletta, Malta. At this stage of the war the island was under virtually constant air attack by the Luftwaffe, which was attempting to destroy the port's installations and airfields, which together with indiscriminate bombing of the island's population, was intended to destroy this threat to the supply lines of Rommel`s desert campaign.

On the 26th April 1943, the cargo was being unloaded and Jim was checking stores, when at about 8.00 pm a terrific explosion occurred on the fore part of the ship as a bomb struck her. Jim's friend, steward Jack Britain called "lets get out, this is no place for us!" which in the circumstances seems like the best course of action. After fetching his bag containing essential belongings, Jim went up on deck and saw that the fore part of the ship was blazing and that the crew was moving towards the ship's jollyboat, which was moored astern. Captain Lewis then shouted to Jim to give him a hand to attempt to douse the flames. This Jim and other members of the crew did, being joined later by Royal Navy and shore personnel

The fire-fighting efforts continued until about 12.00 midnight, when the senior Royal Navy Officer brought the men together and told them that the fire had now reached the cargo of coal, and that it would be a short time until it ignited the ammunition, with disastrous consequences for the lives of the men, and destruction of the surrounding port area. The remaining men were then told that the only course of action was to flood the affected holds, and that volunteers would be required to undertake this action.

Despite the appalling conditions and ever-present danger the affected holds were flooded, enabling the remaining fires to be extinguished and the ship was saved. She was later returned to service and survived the war, one of the very few ships of the King Line to do so. Jim spent three weeks in hospital recovering from burns he had sustained while fighting the fire before he was told that he would be flown to Gibraltar by United States aircraft on the first leg of his journey home.

Fate, however had one more card to play, for when the aircraft reached Gibraltar such a strong cross-wind was blowing that the pilot, who had already made two attempts to land, warned the passengers to 'brace themselves' as he made the third and final attempt. This was almost a disaster for as the aircraft touched down, the crosswind caused it to 'ground-loop' and hurtle down the runway on its back until coming to a halt. Many of the passengers were injured in the accident, though fortunately Jim escaped scot-free.

After spending almost four weeks in Gibraltar, Jim managed to get a job as a Cook on a Dutch merchant ship and eventually landed at Newcastle. When he boarded a train on the first leg of his journey home to Barry, Jim himself admits that he must have been an unkempt sight, for he had not shaved for three months and was dressed in an old duffel coat, dungarees and a battered uniform cap. The train compartment was packed with R.A.F men returning to St Athan, but there was one empty space next to a W.A.A.F which was vacant and Jim sat down. As the train started the R.A.F men produced a bottle of scotch and passed it around, ignoring Jim, who fell asleep and then awoke to find one of the passengers looking at him intently. "Are you Merchant Navy, and have you been in trouble?" he was asked. "Yes" replied Jim, and told the story of his exploits. This broke the ice and the scotch was passed around again, this time including Jim who made full use of the generosity offered.

Having changed trains at Crewe, Jim reached Cardiff a little 'the worse for wear' and he was seen to the waiting room by the W.A.A.F., who apologised for having ignored him when first they had boarded the train. Having now recovered Jim finally returned to Barry, where after an absence of over five months he was met by his mother who told him that she had received an official telegram informing her that his ship had been lost and that Jim was not listed among the survivors.

After spending two months at home Jim joined a tanker bound for the West Indies working again as a Cook, later being appointed as Chief Steward. It was whilst serving on the tanker and when berthed at Port Elizabeth, South Africa, that Jim was summoned to the Captain's cabin and invited to sit down and pour himself a drink. Having done as ordered he was then congratulated by the Captain on the award of the British Empire Medal for his actions in Malta. Following which he was treated to a celebration of the news in a local club and his shipmates made sure that the occasion was properly marked!

The award of the British Empire Medal was published in the London Gazette on the 5th November 1943 with the following citation: - *"The ship was discharging cargo when a violent explosion occurred and fire broke out in one of the holds. This was followed by a further explosion in another hold. The cargo included drums of aviation and motor spirit and the flames spread rapidly. Fire-fighting appliances were manned immediately and orders were given to flood the two holds. Strenuous efforts were made to fight the fire and to save the ship but these proved unavailing and assistance was obtained from naval and shore personnel. It was not until two days later that the fire was finally extinguished. Ship's Cook Brain showed outstanding courage and devotion to duty in the fire fighting operations*

Chris Burt – Merchant Navy

(Atlantic Convoys, Merchant Aircraft Carriers)

Born 'down Cardiff Docks', Chris left school at 14 years of age, and there was not much work in Wales. He went to Kingston-on Thames and had three or four jobs, and ended up working as a pot-boy in the Railway Hotel, Teddington when war broke out. He was on a reasonable wage of £1 a week plus his keep, but returned to be closer to his family in May 1940, signing on for the Merchant Navy aged 16 as a ship's boy. His first ship was the SS Trevorian, where he sailed out of Cardiff from 1940-41. In 1941 he signed on the Sevilla, an old whaler built in 1900 (Salvesons of Leith, which also leased South Georgia as a whaling station), and converted to carry cargo such as lube oil. He never knew where the ship was heading when they left Cardiff for Barry Roads, and she laid off Milford to join a convoy.

The Skipper and Sparks went ashore for instructions, convoy position, speed and destination. We were in an 8 knots convoy, but could do only 5 or 6 knots in bad weather, so we were on our own after a day or so. It seems the captain would not give his slower speed to the convoy organisers. I was then sunk on the Harborough, where I lost some good friends. That was my most memorable trip, but there were many more frightening voyages, in and out of convoys. A large number of merchant seamen went through terrible experiences, but these ordeals have never been published or recognised. The sub came alongside the Harborough, and some U boat commanders had been merchant navy men so sympathised with us. He was one of the good ones. He gave us time to get the boats out and get stores on them. He will have known that the boats were stiff and they probably had never been moved for years, they'd have been painted in place, and he let us get stores into them. However, the mate started machine gunning us, and the captain hit him to stop him.

The full account of the Harborough's sinking is given by Chris in Part Nine, previously written for the relatives of the survivors.

I then served on the Leucer, making my way back from New York as a second cook and baker, before serving on the Forts. We went over as passengers to pick up the newly-built ships in Vancouver, BC. We brought the Fort Connolly home, and then returned for the Fort Bellingham, on a passenger liner, in October 1943. She was lost the following January when she was torpedoed.

The Fort Bellingham was sunk by U 957, in the Iceland to Murmansk convoy JW56A, as a straggler, carrying general cargo and cordite. There were 36 deaths and 37 survivors. Chris reckoned there were 36 Fort-class ships lost in the war.

To pick up the Fort Connolly from Vancouver, I sailed as a passenger on the Tafelberg, sleeping in a lifeboat. As the Tafelberg, she had hit a mine in the Bristol Channel. She was the largest whaler in the world at that time. She had hit a mine in the Bristol Channel and was beached at Barry Island, and it was thought that she could be towed to Cardiff, but she was beached over a rock under the sand and broke in two. She was then repaired in Cardiff and renamed the Empire Heritage. She was then in convoy from Cardiff to Canada after her repairs. However, we turned back after a few days for morerepairs. I was glad, as I took another ship to Vancouver. She was a massive target for U boats and planes.

She had a few voyages but she was lost with over 100 men in 1944.

The Tafelberg, owned by Salvesen's of Edinburgh, was one of the largest ships sunk in WWII, being over 15,700 tons. She was originally damaged on 28th January, 1941, and returned to service in February 1943 when Chris sailed for a few days on her. She was carrying cargo and 16,000 tons of fuel oil on September 8th, 1944, when she was torpedoed by U 482. There were 52 survivors and 112 deaths.

I then served on MAC ships. Many sailors know nothing of them and confuse them with catapult Ships of Woolworth's Ships. Even seasoned merchant navy men know little or nothing about Merchant Aircraft Carriers. There were 115 crew. I was the chief cook on the Amastra from 1943-44 and the Adula in 1944. My last ship in the war was the Naviceller from '44 to '46.

MAC-ships were oil or grain bulk cargo carriers with superstructures removed and flight decks added. They were manned by Merchant Navy crews, with Fleet Air Arm personnel to maintain and fly the aircraft - mainly A/S Swordfish and Sea Hurricanes. They flew the Red Ensign and some aircraft carried "Merchant Navy" instead of "Royal Navy" on their fuselage. There were 6 Empire class Grain Carriers - 8,000 tons, 12 knots, 4 aircraft; 4 Empire Class Oil Tankers - 9,000 tons, 12 knots, 3 aircraft; and 9 Rapana Class Oil Tankers - 12,000 tons, 12 knots, 3 aircraft, converted 1942-44, Anglo-Saxon Petroleum Company tankers. "Gadila" and "Macoma" operated under the Dutch ensign. No hangar and lift, aircraft maintained and stored on deck, 9 ships - ACARUS, ADULA, ALEXIA, AMASTRA, ANCYLUS, GADILA, MACOMA, MIRALDA, RAPANA. The Anglos Saxon Petroleum Company later merged with Royal Dutch to become Shell Oil. Apart from their convoy escort duties, the MAC-ships in the Atlantic carried valuable supplies of grain and fuel to Britain.

Our three Swordfish could only make about 85-90 miles an hour, and we served with the convoys out of Halifax. Each plane had a gunner, navigator and pilot, and many were from New Zealand. The Swordfish had an arrester wire to stop them on landing. One commander on the Adula ordered them up for practice off Nova Scotia, and fogs come all the time there, very quickly. The first made it back, and the second only just found the deck. We heard the other one passing over us as he asked Sparks where we were. He'd taken off at 6, and by 10 we knew their fuel had run out. The bodies were picked up, frozen, by a naval ship and given to us for burial at sea. They always took off well before reaching port, and landed at an unknown airfield. They also joined us at sea, to prevent spies from knowing the convoy had aerial support. They carried depth charges. Until 1943, deck guns on U boats could only traverse horizontally with a little in the vertical plane, to fire at ships. Not until then did they get anti-aircraft guns, and then shooting Swordfish was like pigeon-shooting, they were so slow.

Chris's first two ships had ice boxes, not fridges, so as the ice ran out the diet turned to haricot beans and canned meat. 'Rice cakes' were substitute potatoes. Curry powder was used well before the war to disguise bad meat (- as it had been for years in the Indian Army). Little was stocked in Britain because of rationing, but larger stores were taken on in good ports, such as those in America or Canada.

Sweet for most dinners was rice, tapioca or semolina pudding, but Sunday and Thursday was 'Board of Trade Pudding', the men's favourite. (Board of Trade

Pudding' is noted on many ship's menus, but there is only one Google reference to it.) They really enjoyed eggs when available. Petty Officers received extra portions at all meals, e.g. extra fish or chicken. Stokehole hands had extra water and oatmeal.*

Chris sent the following letter to Ken Holmes, who has since passed away, regarding the role of cooks at sea: 'We were discussing ships' meals, so here are a few facts for your book on M.N. conditions. From 1940, I sailed with cooks, both good and bad, we still had moans about the food. Never had much moaning about BAD Masters, Officers, Engineers and dare I mention sailors, firemen. Until the 1940's British Cooks had few supplies to work with. We had to make pastry from fat dripping or suet. Maybe 2 or 3 eggs allowed to make cake for 45-50 men. Also making their own gravy browning, soup stock, bread, cake etc.

I was on a tanker for fourteen months, 1944 into 1946, with a real misery of a skipper. Our main run was from ABADAN to INDIAN PORTS. No good stores either end, had to make my own yeast for the bread. Even in good ports bread was never bought. Of course, frozen vegetables were not around then. From 1940 ships' stores and food improved and by the end of the war were quite good, excepting some companies. On a BTC tanker in 1950, the Chief Steward still weighed out the galley stores. He allowed one tin of condensed milk to make two sweets a day for a full crew. Sundays and Bank Hols, 1 tin of EVAP Milk extra! Meat and bacon also doled out. Here's luck with your writings. Don't be too hard on the old time cooks.'

Intriguingly, Chris knew Robert Tapscott, the survivor of the Anglo-Saxon. The other survivor, Widdicombe, was a Newport man, and Tapscott was brought up and lived in Cardiff, settling ther. Chris lived in Hunter Street, in the area known as 'Rat Island 'down Cardiff Docks (because of the nearby junk yard which attracted rats). Tapscott drank in the Frampton, a long-gone pub in South William Street, off James Street in Cardiff docklands. Nearly all the old pubs have gone, but Chris referred to them in his poem, affectionately dedicated to Mr W.R. Henke (the same name as the commander of the U boat which sank the Harborough). If one refused to go to sea or missed a ship, one spent 6 months in civilian prison, so the sighting of a pool officer was not a pleasant experience for some men. It meant they were off to sea.

In the poem, the 'snake pits' were the cellar bar of the 'Big Windsor' to distinguish it from the Windsor Hotel. The Big Windsor is now a curry house. The 'pilot' was the Ship and Pilot, now the Orange Tree, and most of the others have gone. The Packet is the Steam Packet, and its bar fixtures were taken from the demolished Barry Dock Hotel, with its famous 'chain locker' bar. (The author was in the Chain Locker one Boxing Day, many years ago, when a fight broke out over the last ear on a boiled pig's head on the bar). The 'Six Bits' was actually nick-named the 'Six Tits' called after its three buxom barmaids, one of whom was one-eyed. The Rothesay Castle, another lost pub, was known as 'The House of Blazes'. Cardiff Docks and Tiger Bay also had a tavern called 'The Bucket of Blood'.

A POOL OFICER REMEMBERED
(With great respect to Mr. W. R. Henke, MBE)

YES... We remember Bill Henke, when missing a crew,
He'd dive round the Pubs, to shanghai a few.
The Castle, the Packet, and ma Bryant's bar,
The Frampton, the White Hart, were not very far.
The Pier and the Windsor, not forgetting The Mount,
Too many pubs for Bill Henke to count.
The Avondale, the Hope, and the Snake Pits,
And the one on the corner, nicknamed The Six Bits,
The Empress, the Sealock, the Old Ship Hotel,
The George and the Pilot, the Bute Dock as well.
We'd dodge in the Torbay, but he's on our tail.
The ship's in the docks, and she's ready to sail.
The ships are not there now, Bill has retired.
They have sold all the ships, and we have been fired.
Now he is older, and mellowed, we hear,
But, we still have a lookout, when drinking our beer.

Chris wrote the poem in response to a request in 'Despatch Boat' asking about the Cardiff pool officer who crewed the ships. During the war Mr Henke would cycle round the docks area, day or night, to find crew members missing from their ships, or pick other men to replace them.

There could be a knock on your front door at 2 or 3am if you were needed. If you happened to be in a pub during the day, someone might look out and shout "Here comes Henke!" This 'battle-cry' could lead to a mass exodus and unfinished punts on the bar. But like the Mounties, he always caught his men.
Serving on the MV City of Edinburgh in 1982, Chris had to cater for 29 adults and 5 children, 'boat people' fleeing Mainland China for Hong Kong. They were picked up from a sinking boat. Chris Burt stayed at sea, as a catering officer, until 1985, and now lives in Barry Dock with his wife Ena. Altogether, he served articles on ships for a little over 40 years.

Chris's ships during WWII were the Trevorian (40-41), Sevilla (41), Harborough (lost at sea 42), Leucer (42), Fort Conolly (43), Fort Bellingham (43), Amastra (3 voyages, 43-44), Adula (44) and Naviciller (44-46).

* Mr Burt kindly loaned Terry Breverton his 1941 'The Nautical Cookery Book: for the use of Stewards and Cooks of Cargo Vessels.' There are hundreds of recipes, some obviously intended for passengers and officers in peacetime, e.g. 'caviar sandwiches', 'angels on horseback', 'scotch woodcock', 'steak, kidney, lark, mushroom and oyster pudding '(using 6 larks and a dozen oysters). 'Mock goose' was a leg or shoulder of mutton with sage and onion stuffing. 'Sea pie' is a meat and potato pie with no marine element whatsoever. Among the less palatable offerings are 'conger pie', 'brain cakes', 'fried sweetbreads', 'tripe and onions', 'boiled tongue', 'tripe fritters', 'haggis' (using sheep's paunch, heart, liver and lights), 'boiled pig's

head', 'boiled calf's head' ('*garnished with the brains and tongue cut into dice*'), 'pigs trotters', and ''boiled sheep's head.' Those with a nervous disposition should not read the recipe for this: '*Skin and split the head in half, take out the brains and wash them, tie in a cloth and cook in boiling salted water for ten minutes, saving these for the sauce. Take out the eyes and inside bones of the nostrils and soak in salted water for one hour. Put the head and tongue into a saucepan, cover with water, simmer for one hour, skim thoroughly. Peel the vegetables and add them with the herbs and rice to the head and cook for another hour; in the meantime make the brain sauce. To dish, remove the flesh from the head, lay in the centre of a hot dish, coat with the brain sauce and garnish with the vegetables placed round and the tongue cut into strips. Serve with snippets of toast.*'

Graham Chadwick - Royal Navy
(Special translation duties – the Far East – in the Pacific with the Americans)

Graham Chadwick, later Bishop of Kimberley in South Africa, originally came from Radnorshire in Mid Wales but moved to Swansea when he was just 11 years old. The sea, therefore, was an element he was used to, regularly watching the ships as they came up the Bristol Channel and into the port of Swansea itself. He had always intended to work in the church overseas and, after being called up for the navy, a surprising opportunity presented itself to further or, at least, aid his future vocation and interest. It was a chance he leapt at:-

I did my initial twelve week training at Torpoint, HMS "Raleigh," and then moved on to the gunnery school. One day I was summoned to the commander's office, along with a few other ratings. The Admiralty, we were told, was looking for volunteers to learn Japanese with a view to becoming interpreters, interrogators and de-coders. As I left the office I began to wonder whether this might be a better way of spending the war than standing on the bridge of a ship, especially considering my proposed future vocation.

So I went back and asked for more information. In due course I was summoned to the Admiralty for interview. Most of the others being interviewed were older than me and included people with university degrees. But I think what got me accepted was the answer I gave to a psychiatrist. He asked me if I thought I could cope with the complicated hieroglyphics of the Japanese language. My answer was simply that they were obviously decipherable so why not have a go!

The year's course in Japanese started in August at the School of Oriental and African Languages, part of London University. Teaching us were two Canadian Japanese sergeants and Mrs Clarke, a beautiful young Japanese woman who was married to an Englishman. Mr Pilcher, a diplomat who had spent years in Japan, would also come sometimes to tell us about Japanese customs. He would sit cross-legged on the table. The only thing I can remember now about his talks was his comment that Japanese homes were so perfect and tidy that you could not possibly fart in them - that and the island of Bali which he described as "an island of tits and temples!"

All the people on the course were from the lower ranks, apart from one RAF Flight Lieutenant who tried to throw his weight about and an RAF sergeant called Richard Mason who later wrote a book, "The Wind Cannot Read," about forces personnel trying to learn Japanese. The only difference was that he set the book in Bombay. It seems that what he described as happening beneath a mosquito net in India between the hero and the lady teacher did actually happen – but in the Strand Palace Hotel in London, not India. His Japanese improved greatly.

Graham was one of the students chosen to concentrate on the spoken rather than the written word. His ability in spoken Welsh certainly helped and at the end of the course he was asked to join the teaching staff. He declined the offer as he wanted to see something of the world and also to get on with the war.

After completing the course he was commissioned as a Sub- Lieutenant and underwent a fortnight's officer training in Portsmouth. One of the lectures he attended was given by the chaplain who told the story of Harold Beardmore, chaplain on a warship. Beardmore was trying to write a sermon in his cabin. Within earshot were two matelots involved in scraping the deck. One said "I'm going on f * * * leave." The other said "I'm going on f * * * leave too and I'm going to have a f * * * good time." So the conversation went on. Finally Harold could stand it no longer, went out on deck and said "You're going on f * * * leave and you're going to have a f * * * good time. I'm trying to write a f * * * sermon. Now f * * * off!" It certainly grabbed the attention:-

At the end of 1943 I was sent to Ceylon, flying out from Lyneham on New Years Eve in an RAF Liberator. We were stuck in Gibraltar for five days and took part in a memorable party in the RAF Officers Mess. Being an innocent 20 year-old I poured most of the gin I was being constantly supplied with, into a handy flower pot. From Gibraltar we went to Cairo West. We flew out within a day but I was still able to spend an afternoon visiting the Pyramids and the Sphinx. I was certainly seeing the world.

When we eventually arrived in Colombo we were told that the urgency behind our posting had gone. The impending invasion of the Andaman Islands had been called off as all the landing craft were needed for the "second front" in Europe. We spent a few weeks in Colombo, being introduced to the mysteries of decoding and deciphering, and then were sent to Chittagong in N E India. How long the journey took to Calcutta I can't remember but it was certainly slow, travelling by train and a boat down the Hooghly River.

After some time in northern India, listening in to Japanese broadcasts, Graham was sent back to Ceylon, incredibly clean after what seemed to him to be a quite filthy India. From there he went to sea to fight for the first time:-

My first experience of action was on board the battleship "King George V" in which we left Trincomalee to bombard Penang in the East Indies. Not long after that I was on my way to Australia in the cruiser "Newcastle," to join Force X in Brisbane. We disembarked at Melbourne and then took a long, long train journey to Brisbane.

Force X was a laugh. Churchill and Roosevelt had decided there had to be a Royal Navy presence in the Pacific. The Americans had asked for six landing craft but, not content with that, the British also provided a headquarters ship with a Rear Admiral to boot. The ship was an old merchant vessel, the "City of

Edinburgh," renamed HMS "Lothian." She'd been prepared in a hurry, without any refit for the tropics. The seamen's quarters were so cramped there were desertions when she docked at New York and even a mutiny when she reached Panama! At the subsequent Court Martial all the defendants – and their legal representatives – were either Welsh or Irish. The necessary refit was carried out in Brisbane before I joined her.

One day the General commanding the Australian forces came on board for lunch with Rear Admiral Talbot. They piped "All hands to the Starboard side." But the additional scuppers that had been added in the refit had been left open and water began pouring in. The ship developed a really nasty list. So there was another pipe – "Hands to jump up and down." Can you believe it? It's absolutely true.

We had to listen to Japanese broadcasts, a section of twelve matelots in the charge of Ian Watt and myself. They intercepted the Morse code messages while we dealt with the decoding.

Gordon and his decoders were later transferred to the aircraft carrier HMS "Indefatigable," part of Task Force 57 attached to the US Fifth Fleet. The ship took part in Operation Iceberg, bombing airstrips on three islands in an attempt to keep the Japanese away from Okinawa. It was unrewarding work as the Japanese soldiers could simply repair the damage overnight using crushed coral to fill in the bomb holes. The next day the bombing missions would begin again:-

The American landings on Okinawa brought a strong reaction from the Japs and the first of many kamikaze attacks were launched against the Task Force. The first came on Easter Day, 1st April 1945, when the "Indefatigable" was hit. The Japanese aircraft hit the flight deck, a total of fourteen men being killed. The first Seafire, however, was able to land on the carrier less than an hour after the kamikaze's bomb exploded.

At Leyte in the Philippines we were transferred to another carrier, the "Formidable," and we sailed on 1st May to resume attacks on the islands. We were hit by another kamikaze at about 1000 hours on 4th May. A slice of its 500 lb bomb went straight down below and came to rest in a fuel tank. It says a lot for the quality of British carriers – and the crew – that aircraft were landing again by 1700 hours. Five days later we suffered another hit but the damage was minimal. Next day we "spliced the main-brace" to celebrate victory in Europe.

We left Sydney at the end of June to work with the US Third Fleet, our aircraft launching attacks on Japanese airfields on their mainland. On 3rd August with the weather good, a strike against the area around Hiroshima was surprisingly called off. Rumours ranged from an imminent invasion to the possibility of an Armistice. The truth reached us on 7th August – an atomic bomb had been dropped on Hiroshima the day before.

On 9th August I was listening in to a Japanese broadcast when suddenly the station, 25 miles outside the town of Nagasaki, was cut off. The second atom bomb had gone down on Nagasaki, exploding just above its cathedral. Our last day of operations was 10th August, and a few days later we heard that the war had come to an end.

We sailed for Sydney; the "Indefatigable" went with the US Third Fleet to

Yokohama. On the way they encountered a severe typhoon and had to batten down the hatches. When it was over the US Admiral signalled "How did you get on in the typhoon?" Captain Graham of the "Indefatigable" replied "What typhoon?" A typical British response!

Graham Chadwick did not go home immediately at the end of hostilities, as he had expected. Instead he was sent to Morotai, an island north-east of the Celebes, where he was attached to an Australian army unit looking after Japanese prisoners of war. Soon he was interrogating suspected war criminals:-

Most of the men I had to deal with were docile and easy to deal with. One, however, was extremely truculent. His name headed two lists of people suspected of a particular murder.

One afternoon I ordered that he should not be given a bed to sleep on that night, but made to lie on the concrete floor. Next morning, to my surprise, he confessed everything and signed the statement I had prepared, admitting his guilt. This was, I learned, typical of the Japanese for whom losing face was extremely demeaning.

Eventually it was time to return to Sydney. By now it was Christmas Eve. My plane to Melbourne went via Darwin, and fortunately I met up with someone there who wanted to go to Melbourne, but was on a flight bound for Sydney. We did a swap. After a month's glorious holiday, enjoying the outdoor life in a southern summer, I finally sailed for home.

Stanley Chandler - Royal Navy
(*Commando training – landing craft – prisoner of war duties*)

Stories that his father told him about life at sea during the First World War intrigued Stanley Chandler from the very beginning. His father, a miner, had begun his service life by serving in the Royal Engineers during the war but transferred when they asked for volunteers to work on the boilers of the destroyers of the Dover Patrol:-

They were lovely stories, the tales my dad told, and they really kicked off my interest in the navy. I joined in March 1942, a volunteer, as soon as I was old enough. On my 18th birthday I was stood outside the recruiting office door. It was my life's ambition to go into the navy. My dad wouldn't let me join earlier, as a Boy Entrant, so I said "Wait till I'm 18, then I'll go." And that's what I did.

I went for my basic training at HMS "Raleigh," in the seamen's branch. I was a gunnery rating, small guns, anti-aircraft. We did our twelve weeks at "Raleigh" and then we were dispersed.

I was sent on a draft to HMS "Brontosaurus." I thought she'd be a new destroyer or something. I didn't know where I was going or what she was. But I ended up on the side of a loch in Scotland. I arrived on a Saturday and reported in. On the Sunday we all fell in and were marched off to the stores. There we were kitted out with khaki battledress and webbing and given .303 rifles. "Where's the ship?" we said. There was no ship.

We were split into sections of eight and before we knew it we were undergoing commando training. Months it went on, over assault courses and things. They took us out to sea on a trawler and we practised landing from that. I requested to go back to sea, to the navy proper – no, they said, you're wanted here. There were about 180 of us there to start with but over the months they kept reducing us, slowly but surely.

Finally we were all paraded in front of this RN Captain from London. You'd go in one by one, in one door, out of another on the other side of the room. As I went in I saw my mate going out the other door and it seemed to me that he was shaking his head, sort of saying "Don't have anything to do with it." The Captain said "What I'm going to ask you, I just want you to say yes or no. If you say yes you'll go to London and have a good time. After that you'll work with canoes, and then go off to Iceland to acclimatise. If you say no then it's back to the navy." I told him I wanted to go to sea and out through the door I went. My mate and I went to the Clyde and joined a flotilla of landing craft. The other boys went to London – talk about a sprat to catch a mackerel.

Two years later, on the front page of "The Daily Mirror," I saw a picture of some of the boys who'd volunteered. They'd been shot in Belsen. One of them used to sleep in the bunk above me. He came from Preston, I think, and I remember writing to his mother. I never really found out what they were up to, but I know it could so easily have been me that ended up getting shot in that concentration camp.

After a period of intensive training Stanley was sent out to Sicily with his flotilla of landing craft. There were 12 boats in the flotilla and they were transported on the decks of merchant ships. When they reached the Mediterranean they were dropped into the water ready for action:-

We were a tank landing craft and I was manning one of the guns. We were there transporting Patton's troops and the men of the 8th Army for the invasion of Sicily. We went up to Messina with them. There was a bit of opposition, you could say. The first night we were there we were bombed all night long. And they always seemed to come at break time! I swear they knew when we'd brewed up.

During the Sicily landings they dropped a stick of bombs right alongside us. I thought the bottom had been blown out of the ship. But she righted herself – a good old girl, British made. They hit the boat next to us and she caught fire. You could hear all the boys on board screaming and shouting but you couldn't do anything about it. She had a deck cargo of jerry cans full of petrol. They hit her at the bows and all these cans were exploding, being blown up into the air. Next day the harbour was just a mass of cans. The ship was still afloat so they got a line across to her and towed her out of the harbour. What happened to her after that I don't know.

Another time, at Syracuse in Italy, we were going alongside an ammunition ship. I was on the stern with a rope, ready to toss it across. Jerry came along and dropped a couple of bombs. Before I knew it I was in the water, under the ship. My shoulder hurt like hell but I managed to grab onto a ladder and the boys pulled me up. I was lucky, very lucky.

From Sicily we took British troops and their tanks across to the toe of Italy. Once they'd landed, got a foothold, so to speak, we were busy taking them supplies and reinforcements. Then we were at the Anzio landings. That was bad show. We nearly got kicked right back into the sea there. It was quite quiet and calm to start with, then all hell seemed to break loose.

We had planes strafing us almost all the time. I was on the single pom-pom gun and I suppose I shot at lots of German planes. I don't think I ever hit any of them. You'd sort of close your eyes and pull the trigger and hope that their shots missed you. Luckily they all did.

The landing I really remember was when we went ashore in southern France. We landed the Free French troops and all of them just leapt ashore, ran up the beach and then kissed the ground. It was a very touching moment. Mind you, those French officers were something else. We picked up a lot of French colonial troops in Taranto but there were always French officers. They used to go round with sticks, hitting the men. They had a forty gallon drum of red wine and they'd be dipping into it all the time, popping up on it, and then start hitting all these poor soldiers. Our Captain said "Put it over the side." He'd had enough of it. So that's what we did.

Once, in Taranto, we saw soldiers dragging this pig along, tied up to a rope. They were heading our way. "What's that?" the Captain said. "Pig, sir." The skipper looked at them. "Well get rid of it," he said. "This isn't Noah's bloody Ark. It's a ship!"

We were in Marseilles towards the end of the war and we were billeted ashore in what had been an infants' school. I remember all these tiny chairs we were sat on! Suddenly there was a hell of a flap on. The Yanks arrived, doubled the guard. They were charging about everywhere. They'd had these Germans locked up in a U Boat pen and it seemed that they'd all escaped. Next morning the Germans were all there outside our school – with their girlfriends. They'd had a night on the tiles. The Yanks rounded them all up but those Germans had no intention of fighting. They were only interested in having a bit of fun.

It was a hard life on the landing craft. We were paid "hard lying" money. You'd get it on very small ships where the life was hard and you had to rough it a bit. It was about four pence extra a day. We had no proper cook or medic. One of the boys would cook, you'd take it in turns. Or you'd go to one of the bigger ships if you needed medical attention.

Stanley missed the D Day landings as he and his flotilla were still employed in Italy and the Mediterranean. They were still there when the war in Europe ended. One of the things that most annoys him is the way the men of the landing craft have had so little recognition:-

The soldiers who went ashore on D Day did a wonderful job, nothing can ever take away from that. But you never hear about the landing craft boys, the boys who took them there to the invasion beaches. I say boys because we were all just boys. I was only just over 19 years of age, the others not much older. No, you never hear about the landing craft boys. There's a lot of skill trying to land soldiers with dry feet. They never liked it if they had to get wet.

When they came back to the UK there was no longer any need for landing craft and they were billeted in a camp at Lowestoft. It was a "cushy" number and Stanley and his mates were enjoying something of a rest. Then, however, they were posted back to Portsmouth:-

About a dozen of us were sent to a camp near Havant, out in the country. When we got there we reported to the Ship's Office. A couple of sailors came past, pushing a wheel barrow. They had tapes on the backs of their hats. Must be Dutch, we said to ourselves. And then we realised. They were Germans, it was a prisoner of war camp. We had to patrol the place with rifles. It was a bit "Harry Tate," really, just a pair of gates with a guy on guard, a bit of wire and us walking around. If they'd wanted to escape all those German sailors had to do was cross the soccer field and get over the wire. They didn't, they were quite happy in there.

We got on well with them. They were sailors, like us. We played football against them and they beat us – nothing changes. We taught them to play darts and I remember saying "Give them a few more weeks and they'll beat us at darts too."

I remember Christmas Eve, being on guard duty. There was snow on the ground and I was crunching along, huddled up inside my greatcoat. I was checking the outside of one of the huts and all of a sudden I heard this wonderful singing. It sounded just like a Welsh choir. They were singing "Silent Night" – in German, of course. Whenever I hear that carol now I can feel the snow again, under my boots, and I'm right back there outside that hut.

I said to my mate "A few weeks ago we'd have been shooting that lot. Now we're out here in the cold and they're in there in the warm. There's something wrong somewhere."

It was lovely, though, that singing. Whenever I hear carols now it all comes back and I'm right there, Christmas 1945, the snow under my boots.

Stanley Chandler was demobbed in May 1946. He was thinking about staying in, making a career of it. Then he met his wife and that was it – he took his demob and came out into 'civvy street'.

Arthur Coxon - Royal Navy
(Training during the war years – the Far East)

Arthur Coxon lives now in Sully but came originally from Norfolk. His father had been a member of the Territorial Army unit from the Sandringham estate of the Royal family and, as such, had taken part in the now-famous assault by the Sandringham men during the Gallipoli Campaign. On 12th August 1915 Captain Frank Beck, the agent for the Sandringham estate, and his Company went "over the top" and simply disappeared. For many years nobody had the slightest idea what had happened to them. The whole unit was not totally wiped out, however, and some managed to survive, Arthur's father being taken prisoner by the Turks. After an eight day trip by cart he arrived in Istanbul where he was given parole but kept prisoner until the end of hostilities.

The Nautical College at Pangbourne, Arthur Coxon's sea training school.

Arthur had rather different ambitions from his father. The army did not interest him – but the navy certainly did. He had seen a film about Dartmouth cadets and the idea of a career at sea appealed to him. His father was not happy, always having been an army man at heart, despite having taken up his old profession as a doctor once he was discharged. And his mother, a nurse, had similar preferences. But for Arthur there was only one way to go – the navy:-

At the beginning of the war entrance to the officer ranks of the Royal Navy was through Dartmouth College. It was virtually a naval public school with entrance by exam and interview. My time came in the summer of 1940 when I was 13 years old. France had just fallen and there were a lot of young men about who fancied themselves as Lord Nelson. So there was an enormous field of applicants. I did well in the exam but didn't get through the interview – three old Admirals sitting there and making decisions about you.

So I went to Pangbourne College instead. It was a college for boys who wanted a career in the Merchant Navy, one of several establishments that specialised in preparing cadets, places like the training ships "Conway" and "Worcester." As well as entry to the Merchant Navy these colleges also offered a Special Entry to the Royal Navy when cadets were 18 years of age. The RN only took a fixed number of candidates and cadets from all three colleges competed for a place.

I went to Pangbourne at the start of 1941 when I was 13 years old. The college was close to Reading and was run on strict naval lines. It had been founded by the Devitt and Moore shipping line, all the training being originally based on board ship. They had vessels like the "Macquarie" and "Illawarra," beautiful wooden sailing vessels. The cadets did all their training on these ships. By the time I took up my place, however, the training was all shore-based at Pangbourne.

The discipline was hard but I never thought it was unjust. I can't say the education was that good – bear in mind, some of the instructors during that war period had been dug out of retirement – but the place certainly taught me to behave and obey orders. Rex Willis, the old Welsh international, was Captain of the First XV while I was there and our History teacher was one of just seven men to have won the VC before breakfast on the first day of the Gallipoli landings. We were Cadets RNR while we were at the College and I went for one of the RN special entry places in 1944. In fact I took my exam on D Day. I passed and was gazetted as Cadet, Royal Navy, on 1st January 1945.

To start with we had a term at the Naval College – but bear in mind, Dartmouth had been bombed in 1942 and so the cadets had been moved and were quartered and trained at Eaton Hall outside Chester. They'd put up huts in the grounds, brick ones for the Dartmouth cadets, tin nissen ones for the Special Entrants. It was as cold as hell in the camp, all the reservoirs froze and the water got contaminated. We all started our naval careers with diarrhoea or dysentery! The Pangbourne boys – Frobisher Cadets as they were called - were old hands at the game. The other Special Entry boys had come to the college as civilians and found it a bit harder to adjust. The Special Entrants used to have breakfast before the Dartmouth boys and Arthur Coxon remembers marching past their huts and banging on the windows to annoy them as they went past:-

They didn't like that very much, didn't like being woken up like that, but it amused us. The powers that be soon realised what we were doing and put a stop to it. We were looked after by old Pensioners, just the way they'd always done down at Dartmouth. Our old Petty Officer, he didn't like us getting caught in bed and he used to come in shouting a warning to keep us out of trouble. We used to play some awful tricks on the PO's – once somebody put a dummy in the bed and we fell about laughing when he started shaking it, trying to wake it up.

Marmalade Annie was the PO Wren cook and she always presided over breakfast. At dinner we'd shout "More chips, Marmalade Annie." She'd come to the hatch and bellow at us "Ain't no more!" And then she'd slam the hatch shut.

There was a lot of rivalry between the three huts, particularly with the Dartmouth boys. One day one of our boys climbed up onto the roof and stuck an old rugby jersey down their chimney. The hut just filled up with smoke, much to our amusement.

There were some strange people there for training, I must say. One of them was a bloke we called The Blue Man. He never washed and all the dye from his trousers used to come out on his legs. Eventually we picked him up and dumped him into the static water tank! It was January and that water must have been freezing. In the end he apparently robbed the Post Office in Horsham and was, shall we say, ushered out of the service.

Our second term as cadets took place on board the training cruiser "Frobisher." She'd been re-commissioned in the early part of the war and served at the D Day landings. Then she was refitted at Rosyth and by the spring of 1945 was serving as a training ship again. I had one term on board her – I joined her just two days before VE Day. At that time they called us the BEF Squadron – Back Every Friday. Once the war in Europe ended we got to venture a bit further afield. We went up to Scapa Flow – we were given a guided tour of a captured U Boat. It was dark and smelly, like any submarine, I suppose.

After a brief embarkation leave Arthur was sent by troop ship, the old P & O vessel

"Mooltan," to Colombo in Ceylon, Sri Lanka as it is now. The Japanese War had ended just before he sailed but, nevertheless, he joined the battleship "Nelson" in the summer of 1945:-

The "Nelson" flew the flag of Rear Admiral Harold Walker. He had lost an arm during the First World War. Now Walkers are always known in the navy as "Hooky" but nobody had told me that our Admiral only had one arm and that sometimes he wore a false limb complete with hook and at other times he'd just leave it off. One night, going up to the bridge – all dark, blue lights giving the place an eerie feel and look – I came face to face with a one-armed Admiral. He had a bare chest and was waggling his stump about. I just shouted in fright – and then tried to muster my dignity and say "Good night, sir." Goodness knows how it came out! I still thing their Lordships at the Admiralty must have had a sense of humour to put old "Hooky" Walker in the "Nelson."

The "Nelson" was on her way home and so, when we reached Mombassa, I was transferred to another battleship, the "Howe." We sailed around places like the Seychelles and the Maldives, it was quite beautiful. We were the first capital ship into Singapore since the "Prince of Wales" went down. I suppose that must have been quite traumatic for some of the men on board. Then, believe it or not, the "Howe" went home and they transferred me to the cruiser "Norfolk."

I suppose I was out in the Far East for about eleven months in all. Although the war had ended there were still a lot of prisoners of war and internees around. There were little pockets of soldiers here and there – nobody really knew where they were. There was so little communication. And, of course, the native population was rebelling or revolting, against the Dutch in particular. The natives were always taking pot shots at the Dutch. We had to protect British interests, although to be fair there wasn't much aggro directed at us. Even so, and strange as it may seem, we actually re-armed some of the Japanese, to help keep the peace.

While we were waiting to join the "Norfolk" we had to go to this little port where she was due to dock. We had a day or so before she arrived and the other Midshipmen and I thought it advisable to get ourselves a hair cut. So, I suppose, about half a dozen of us walked into the local village where there was a barber. It was funny, coming out of the dockyard, suddenly there in front of us, was the barrel of a machine gun and, behind it, the faces of these Japanese soldiers. They all stood up, saluted and bowed as we went past!

Anyway, we went to the barbers shop. Now the barber was a villainous looking bloke – and just then there were lots of stories doing the rounds, stories of people having their throats cut in the barbers' shops. We'd all heard them, a quick slash, an open hatch and the body dumped! I was the last one to sit in the chair and the others said "We'll meet you down the road." Then they were gone, leaving me there. I'll tell you what, as the old cut throat razor came down on my scalp I had my revolver out of its holster and my finger was on the trigger! When he'd finished I had to get it back in the holster before the barber whipped the sheet off.

In those days Midshipmen could still be beaten by the Sub Lt of the Gun Room. Once I was given four cuts of the cane for having the audacity to run my boat without taking in the fender first. A ship was known by the quality of her boats so the feeling was, I'd been sloppy. I didn't object; all of us knew the other crews might form a bad opinion of our ship and we didn't want that. Your pride in your ship was enormous.

Accidents did happen, of course. Once, somebody put the barrel of one of the guns in X turret through the awning that they'd slung over the quarter deck, ready for a party or reception. I remember watching the gun as it started to rise, thinking to myself "That's going to cause a problem." It went right through the awning and they had to get dozens of Indians on board, all sewing like mad to repair the split.

I was transferred to the aircraft carrier "Colossus" for a while. We were flying Corsairs. They were American planes but the Yanks never operated them, so they were given to us on Lease Lend. We also had an old Walrus bi-plane, a lovely old plane but so slow that we had to ask the ship astern to slow down whenever she was coming in to land.

Arthur came back to Britain in the summer of 1946. In due course he rose to the rank of Lt Commander, serving on vessels like the Battle Class destroyer "St Kitts." He was also "loaned out" to the Kenyan Government for a while, to help start their navy. It was a varied and interesting career. He left the navy in 1977, his final posting being Naval Liaison Officer in Cardiff and East Wales. Yet his career at sea was far from over and he went on to serve in the Merchant Navy for a further eight years.

Emlyn Davies - Royal Navy
(Landing craft – D Day landings)

Emlyn Davies lives now at Llangefni on the island of Anglesey but he joined the Royal Navy when he was just 18 years of age and served for four years. His memories of the war are vivid but recollections of the D Day landings are what remain strongest, as he explains in a letter and written memoir:-

June 5th 1944. Location - the southernmost tip of the Isle of Wight. It was referred to – unofficially, of course – as "Piccadilly Circus" and with good reason. Thousands of ships rendezvoused there that night. Their destination was the coast of Normandy.

I was serving on a Tank Landing Craft at that time. Our crew were all in high spirits that night, all of us having toasted the health of King George in "Nelson's Blood," not once but twice, and after a while we headed off in the direction of the French coast. Some hours later, with the coast in view, the effect of the rum began to weaken and the mood began to change. Now we were all dead sober and fear, although it was not too apparent, replaced the cockiness of before.

Astern of us the cruiser "Belfast" opened up with a salvo that went right over our heads. She was joined by the other "big" ships. The din was absolutely ear splitting but the return fire from the Germans was comparatively weak.

Pretty soon we hit the beach and our cargo of tanks rumbled off the ramp. They were there to support the infantry but, as for us, we just kept our heads

Emlyn Davies on board his landing craft.

down. After all, our job was done. But, of course, you couldn't help taking a look to see what was going on, to find out what was happening.

It was a pretty impressive sight, Gold Beach. Wrecked craft littered the coast line, mostly the work of mines. Then, suddenly, a nearby lorry blew up. The driver rushed out, screaming and holding his bloodied face. There were signs everywhere, reading "Achtung Minen."

As the skirmishes receded we decided to go ashore but we took care to walk along the paths which had been cleared by the Royal Engineers. They were marked with white tape, I remember. We could see a few dead Germans, some with their arms and legs blown off. One, I noticed, had only half his face left. I went into a nearby bunker – now I think, how stupid, hadn't I heard of booby traps? – and picked up some photographs and an Iron Cross that I found. They're still in my possession.

After that I strolled across to examine a coastal gun. It was heavily damaged, I assume by the RAF. At that moment a shot rang out. It was a sniper, still at

Emlyn Davies with captured German momentos.

work. Taking "Tommy's" advice I quickly retreated out of rifle range and went back to the landing craft.

We waited for the in-coming tide and when enough water surrounded the craft we were able to pull ourselves off the beach and, thankfully, head back towards England.

The men in the British landing craft had done their work well. By nightfall on 6th June Allied troops were well established on the Normandy coast and the story of the greatest armada in the history of the world was already going into the history books. There was more work ahead, however, for the sturdy landing craft:-

D Day plus 4 again found us on Gold Beach and, once again, we were high and dry. We had carried a load of heavy armoured vehicles across the Channel and were waiting for the tide to turn when a loud bang rocked the ship. We had suffered a near-miss. The smell of explosive filled our sleeping quarters, voices seemed to be coming from a long way off and my eyes were blinded. I fell out of my hammock and, along with the rest of the crew, scrambled up on deck. By now most of us had donned our life jackets, which was pretty foolish as we were actually still on dry land.

The stern of the landing craft had been heavily holed but luck was with us as we suffered only one casualty. Mind you, I noticed later that the string of my hammock had been cut, just inches from where my head had been. The landing craft was leaking water and so we kept ourselves afloat, all the way back to England, by working the bilge pump to full capacity.

Once they arrived back in port the landing craft was sent to dry dock for repairs and Emlyn and his

Emlyn Davies with captured German momentos.

shipmates went home for a few days well-earned leave. They were soon back at work, however, this time operating between Southampton and Omaha Beach where the Americans had landed on D Day:-

On this particular day we had made a successful trip over, carrying some Yanks and their vehicles. Just as we were setting out on the return trip we were warned about an impending storm and so we anchored about a mile or so off the French coast. Well, it wasn't long before we were struck by the full force of the gale. Winds of over 70 mph hammered at us and our anchor just wouldn't hold.

Our skipper decided to hang on to a bigger and heavier ship nearby, by means of thick hawsers. But it was of no avail. The hawsers just snapped like tiny match sticks. The engine room was getting flooded and one of our two engines was already out of action. We were at the mercy of the storm.

We had virtually no control over the ship's movement and were forced, by the fury of the gale, towards the coast. And, of course, we were being buffeted against the other ships that were trying to ride out the gale. Unashamedly, we prayed. When daylight finally came it was a great relief. But the storm had thrown us well up the beach, almost onto the nearby coastal road. We didn't know it then but we would be stranded on Omaha Beach for almost two weeks.

After a few days our food ran out and, hungry and thirsty, we would beach-comb along the coast in search of things to eat. What we found were mostly tins and things that were provided by ship wrecks, from ships not as fortunate as us to have ridden out the gale. "Dhobi-ing" was not at all pleasurable. Washing our shorts and clothes in sea water, with salt water soap, was quite an experience.

It was really just a matter of waiting for a high enough tide and then, with the US Army pulling and pushing us seawards with their heavy machinery, we managed to find enough water to get off the beach.

Eventually, Emlyn and his landing craft changed their route across the English Channel. As the Allied armies began their push through France and up into Germany, more and more occupied territory came under British and American control. Soon their new route involved the much shorter journey between Dover and Calais. Within a few months they were sailing to Ostend in Belgium:-

It wasn't as exciting as the D Day landings but running between England and the continent, keeping the troops supplied, was an important job. And I suppose we kept Channel hopping until well after hostilities were over.

Some memories fade as you get older but others remain vivid. I can't forget the sight of the German dead and the floating body parts on Gold Beach. I can't forget seeing the long lines of weary-looking POWs or the smells and sounds of wartime France. I can't forget the comradeship. And above all I can't forget those who did not return.

Evan Desmond Davies - Merchant Navy

(Coastal waters – convoys around Africa and across the Atlantic)

Evan Desmond Davies was born in 1926 in the west Wales town and port of Aberystwyth. Giving the name Evan to a male child was something of a Davies family tradition, each generation as far back as the 1760s having a child with that name in its ranks:-

My family have always been sailors, seven generations of them, so I suppose you could say that the sea was in my blood. I suppose it was inevitable that, once I was old enough, I would go to sea. It was certainly something that I always wanted to do, a career I always wanted to follow.

My father and grandfather before me were also called Evan and I suppose it was equally as inevitable that the name should come to me. I've kept up the tradition and my eldest son was also christened Evan. It's funny because Evan was the name I was known by when I was at sea but, for some reason, everybody in Aberystwyth has always called me Des, my second name.

My father had been at sea for years, serving on board vessels like the liner "Lusitania" but local people were more used to seeing him, after he came ashore, on the "Belle Isle," one of the boats that used to offer pleasure trips in the bay in the days before the war. He owned the boat and when I was a child I used to help him down at the harbour. I suppose I've been going out in boats ever since I could walk. When the wind was blowing I'd go down to the harbour with my father to put extra moorings on the boat. We used to have some terrific gales in those days.

I nearly drowned down there one day. Dad had gone into the cabin for some reason and, I don't know why, but I stepped off the deck and fell into the water between the boat and the harbour wall. I shouted for help and, luckily, Dad heard. He managed to pull me out. It could have been very dangerous.

There were lots of pleasure boats working out of Aberystwyth in those days. It was the time of the Depression and so many sailors just couldn't find berths. So they came home to live. Captain Julian Jones, later Harbour Master here, was one of them. Many of these sailors bought boats for themselves. Aber was a flourishing resort then and so they used to offer trips around the bay, that type of thing.

When the Second World War broke out Des was still a pupil at Ardwyn Grammar School but it wasn't long before he began to grow restless:-

Everybody seemed to be going away to the war, into the army or the navy. My mother didn't want me to go, after all nobody wanted their sons to go to sea in those days. But I was adamant I wanted to go to sea. I suppose I thought it would be a great big adventure. One day a local sailor, Captain Thomas Brodigan, came home from a voyage and my father simply asked him if he had a berth for me. Captain Brodigan said yes. And that was it. I signed articles as an ordinary deck hand for six months and my career at sea had begun.

The ship was just a little coaster, a general cargo vessel called the "Lottie R" – the R standing for Rolfe. She was owned by Stone and Rolfe from Llanelli and, in those early war years, she was used as a supply ship for the Royal Navy. The skipper had got an emergency war ticket, as Captain of a transport ship and we usually sailed out of Swansea and Llanelli. We were transporting mostly military stuff around the coast of Britain and up to the Faeroes and Iceland. There wasn't much convoy work in those days, escorts were hard to come by, and so we generally sailed alone, unaccompanied. I suppose it was dangerous but at the time we didn't think too much about things like danger. The Battle of the Atlantic was being fought and ships were being sunk all over the place but, remember, I was fifteen years old and it was all still like an adventure.

We sailed up to Scotland to join one of the Russian convoys. That would have been in 1941. But we never got as far as Russia. We were hit by a hurricane and most of our ship's lifeboats were lost. The ship was in a hell of a state. Anyway, we had to make for Reykjavik in Iceland for repairs and to get new boats. And what do you think? The replacement boats had been made in Aberystwyth, of all places!

It was a hard life in the Merchant Navy and Des is clear that conditions on board ships like the "Lottie R" were far from ideal, even making allowances for the discomforts of war:-

There weren't many of what you might call "home comforts." To begin with my bed was a bag of straw, what we used to call "a donkey's breakfast." You could buy it from the other sailors for a shilling. Conditions were pretty primitive, all the crew – fourteen of us in those days – living together, crammed into the foc'sle.

I went on to serve in other ships, most of them bigger than the "Lottie R." I sailed down the west coast of Africa and across the Atlantic several times. Being in the Merchant Navy you would be paid off at the end of a voyage, go home for a rest and then sign on again, usually on a different ship. In my time I've served in lots of different companies, from the Blue Funnel and Blue Star Lines to the Royal Mail and the RFA.

The Blue Funnel Line was almost a Welsh company, it had so many Welsh sailors in those days. You have to remember that a great many of the skippers came from the Cardiganshire coast. I served on the "Stentor," a Blue Funnel ship, with one of them, Dai Rees from Cardigan town.

Des Davies served in the Merchant Navy throughout the war and, even now, remains resentful at the way in which the MN sailors have been regarded and treated. The brave men of Britain's merchant fleet have never, he believes, been given the recognition they really deserve. It remains something of a thorn in his side:-

All the credit, I feel, has gone to the Royal Navy. I would say that, between 1939 and 1945, the men of the Merchant Navy probably saw more action than the RN boys. Certainly, wherever they went we went as well – and probably with worse conditions, too. I suppose I'm bitter about it, bitter that the Merchant Navy never got the credit it deserved. I'm not suggesting that we should have had more credit than the Royal Navy, just the same.

It does annoy me. After all, Britain wouldn't have had any food during the war years if it hadn't been for the men of the Merchant Marine. That's something that people tend to forget. The Merchant Navy brought in the food so that people in this country could survive. And they did it in unarmed merchant vessels.

After the war Des came ashore for a while. He got married and started a family. He became a fisherman for a while, then turned to land-based work once more. However, the lure of the sea always remained strong. So, invariably, he kept going back to his lifelong love, the sea. For 27 years he had interlacing spells at sea and then ashore, some of his sea-going activities taking him into danger spots like the Korean War, the Falklands and the first Gulf War. He lives now in a chalet on a holiday park in his beloved Aberystwyth, within sight and smell of the sea that has been his life for so long.

Trevor Davies

(Merchantmen, Middle East and Atlantic)

Among the papers handed to Terry Breverton by Fred Hortop is this account of the Welshman Trevor Davies surviving his third sinking: Trevor Davies and his close friend Charlie joined the Empire Cromwell in Cardiff on 25th May 1942. She was carrying Army stores for the Middle East and they sailed around the Cape of Good Hope and arrived at Lourenco Marques, where they lay at anchor for twelve weeks, awaiting the arrival of a replacement ballast pump.

They sailed eventually, alone and travelled safely through the Mozambique Channel, the Red Sea and Suez to discharge their cargo at Beirut, and the return trip was equally uneventful as they made their way back through the Canal and round the Cape on a heading for Trinidad. Then on the night of 28th November 1942, the peace of the Caribbean was shattered by a horrendous explosion as a torpedo struck the engine room.

"What a shambles. With lifeboats smashed, the engine room flooded, and men lying everywhere, dead or wounded, she was going fast. The Chief Engineer's cabin was right above the torpedo strike but I looked in to see in if I could give a hand, but the man was finished. Already the main deck was under water and two of the rafts had got away safely. That left one, but it was tangled in the rigging. We could feel the ship going under our feet, so we just clung like limpets to the raft and prayed that the suction might drag her clear. It did, but almost immediately it jammed under the cross-trees, and by now we were under the water and drowning. Then for no clear reason the raft broke free and shot to the surface, with seven very frightened men hanging on for dear life, to anything they could grasp.

We looked around and counted the heads on the other two rafts, there were twenty-two survivors in all, and of course my first thought was for my good friend Charlie and I shouted to ask if he was among them. The answer came to me in the most terrible words that still haunt me to this day. 'He went back to look for you'.

Twenty-one men had gone down with the Empire Cromwell, but a lot of them were dead before she sank, my pal had been safe, away in one of the rafts, and the only reason that he was dead was that he must have really looked for me, gone below and been trapped." Trevor Davies' grief was overtaken by events, for at that moment the submarine surfaced in a great swirl of white foam and the figure of its Captain (Oberleutnant Georg Staats) appeared in the conning tower. The survivors crouched silently, tensely wondering which type of U Boat Captain he was. Would they be machine-gunned? No. A request was made for the Skipper or Chief Officer. Informed that all the officers had gone down with the ship, the U boat Commander said in good English that he was sorry, and offered, if there were any wounded or injured to treat them on board the submarine and then return them to the rafts. There were no takers and the U boat quietly submerged.

Trevor Davies had now survived his third sinking in the space of two years. It is scarcely surprising that despite his lack of years, his shipmates listened to him when he said no water ration for the first few days. On the fifth day they were sighted by an American aircraft which dropped a parcel only a few feet away from them. It contained fruit juice, cigarettes and a message saying 'This is from the US Army Air

Force. You will be picked up some time this evening. Good Luck – see you on the beach" … The Americans were as good as their promise, and that night the survivors of the Empire Cromwell were picked up by two MTB's and taken to Trinidad, where for two weeks they were handsomely looked after before being shipped back to the United Kingdom.

For further details on the Empire Cromwell, see Part Five.

Bernard Peter de Neumann - Merchant Navy
(Bravery in the North Sea – South Africa- imprisoned by the Free French)

The following story was told by Professor Bernard de Neumann and is an account of an action in the North Sea when his father, 2nd Officer Bernard Peter de Neumann, was awarded the George Medal. Bernard Peter de Neumann went on to become a Master Mariner and after a variety of sea-going commands became Commander of HM Revenue Cruiser "Vigilant." In 1953 he joined the Port of London Authority but died as a result of an accident in Tilbury Docks in September 1972:-

My father's father was lost at sea in 1920. My father was just three at the time and six years later his mother also died, after a long illness. After that he spent time in an orphanage and with foster parents until he was sent to the Training Ship "Exmouth" which was then moored in the River Thames. On board the "Exmouth" he learned to play the French horn and trumpet – he later went on to play a solo at a Remembrance Day Parade at the Merchant Navy Memorial on Tower Hill.

Having left school in 1934 my father went to sea and, as is the practise, studied for his Board of Trade examinations whilst there, at sea. He joined the Alexander Shipping Line, a Cardiff based company that lost all 13 ships with which they began the war during the years 1939 to 1945. That is an exceptional record, albeit not one the company would want to have. It was while he was on board one of these Alexander Line ships, the SS "Tewkesbury," that my father earned both the George Medal and the Lloyd's War Medal for Bravery at Sea.

On 1st March 1941 the "Tewkesbury" was attacked by a German aircraft while she was in convoy off Aberdeen. Admiralty records commented "On the 1st March 1941, the 'Tewkesbury' was bombed by a German aircraft. Her defence was so good that the enemy was last seen flying low, with smoke streaming from it. The air crew were picked up later and the ship is credited with the kill.'

However, after the attack a large bomb of about 250 kilos was found, unexploded, on the second engine room grating. The ship was rolling in a North-Easterly wind and 2nd Engineer Turner, who was on watch, immediately sat on the bomb in order to stop it rolling off the grating and exploding. He was quickly joined by my father.

The "Tewkesbury" was flying the flag of the convoy Commodore and leaving him on the bridge to attend to navigation the Master, Captain Pryse, came down to the engine room to take charge of the disposal squad. However, my father and the 2nd Engineer had, by now, developed an almost proprietary interest in the bomb. They managed to get a rope sling around the missile and guided it clear of obstructions, at one point having to stand on the cylinders to do so. The engines were kept turning in order to maintain power and keep the "Tewkesbury" under way.

Due to the darkness down in the engine room and the decidedly awkward position in which the bomb had lodged itself the operation took over an hour to reach its conclusion:-

The Master and the two officers managed to get a second sling around the bomb and they hauled it up on deck. From there it was dumped over the side. At that point the Master issued a can of beer to the members of the disposal squad, went back to the bridge and the "Tewkesbury" proceeded on her way.

Unfortunately for 2nd Officer de Neumann his adventures were far from over. The "Tewkesbury" was torpedoed by U 69 on her return voyage from South America and he was adrift in a lifeboat, together with other survivors, for five and a half days, drifting helplessly in the tropics:-

The lifeboat was eventually spotted by the US ship "Exhibitor" and the occupants were rescued. Later they were transferred to HMS "Cilicia" which was attempting to trap U Boats and German commerce raiders by acting as a Q Ship. The survivors, including my father, were landed at Freetown on 17th June 1941.

My father immediately volunteered as 2nd Officer on the captured Vichy French ship "Criton" and they sailed, in convoy, for the UK on 19th June. The "Criton" had been sabotaged in a variety of ways by her French crew, however, and could not keep up with the speed of the convoy. As a result she was ordered to turn back to Freetown. On 21st June she was spotted by two Vichy French ships off Conakry.

One of the French ships cut off her escape, the other fired a warning shot and ordered the "Criton" to heave to and not send any messages. Despite this, the "Criton" signalled her predicament and, after a series of shouted messages through megaphone, the warship opened fire and swept the "Criton's" decks with machine gun fire. Opening fire with her main armament, the warship's shells went straight through the hull of the "Criton" and the Captain ordered the crew to abandon ship.

My father spent the years 1941 to 1943 as a prisoner of the Vichy French in Conakry, Timbuktu and Kan Kan – after being found guilty of piracy! While a prisoner he learned to speak French like a native – of West Africa! After being released he returned to the UK where he was finally awarded the medals he had won in the North Sea back in 1941.

Obviously the King had been briefed about the reason for the investiture so long after the event. When my father attended Buckingham Palace for that investiture on 11th February 1943 King George V1 said "Ah, you're the man from Timbuktu!" The title stuck for the rest of my father's life.

Two days after the investiture Bernard Peter de Neumann married Dorothy Eve Kimber, daughter of Horace Kimber, Chief of the Investigation Branch, HM Customs and Excise.

Reg Dunkley - Merchant Navy
(Across the Atlantic – up the Amazon – USA)

The following account of a voyage across the Atlantic, around the African coast and even up the Amazon River, right at the end of the war, was written by Reg Dunkley from Barry. He was then 4th Engineer on the SS "Clumberhall" and the written account gives a good idea of what life was like on board a tramp steamer, plying for trade around the world, during those years. The account was sent in by Reg's daughter Rita Dunkley.

Reg worked for the Blue Star Line for most of the war years, his first voyage early in 1939 being as Assistant Engineer on the "Africa Star." He was lucky as later that same year, after he had left her, the ship was a victim of the commerce raider "Graf Spee." For his second voyage Reg was again Assistant Engineer, this time on board the "Pacific Star." They sailed out to the River Plate and did not return to the UK for almost eleven months.

The voyage described here took place at the end of the war and in the first few months of peace:-

We left Barry docks in the late summer of 1945 and sailed across the North Atlantic. We arrived in Montreal some sixteen days later, hungry for a decent loaf of bread. The reason for this was the flour on board for consumption by the crew had gone bad and the taste was diabolical. The Skipper blamed the Second Cook and Baker for this and when we were lying in Montreal he brought ships' bakers from the other ships on board in an attempt to show our Baker how to bake bread.

S.S. Cumberhall at Santos, January 1946. Reg Dunkley on right.

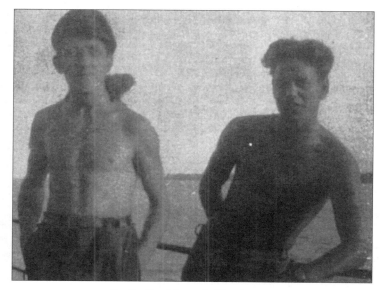

Reg Dunkley, left, on the River Amazon

All efforts to discredit our Baker failed, however, as the bread still tasted diabolical. Yet the Skipper did not give in and the flour store for the crew remained unchanged. When we sailed with a full cargo of grain a few days later the crew actually refused to eat the bread. As all the potatoes on board had already been eaten, for two weeks they ate almost nothing. Rice cakes became the alternative, to make up for the lack of bread and potatoes, but it wasn't really very effective.

The story is a good reminder of how bad food was not uncommon in Britain's merchant fleet. These days, with huge freezers and refrigerators, poor bread would not be an issue. Then it was a very serious affair. The story also puts the authority of the Captain into perspective. His word was law and if the crew chose not to eat the bread that had been provided for them then that was their problem. He had done all he could to help ease the situation:-

During our trip back across the western ocean our main feed pump failed and we had to put on line one that I had repaired earlier in Montreal. Our cargo of grain was sold six times by the Shipping Brokers or importers, each one making a profit on the sale, all without even seeing the cargo. And it was all done at such a high cost to the digestion of the crew.

Our 2nd Engineer, who'd had operations for ulcers some time previously, also became ill during the trip. He was laid up in his cabin. So the 3rd Engineer and I were put on six hour watches in the engine room to cover the 2nd Engineer's inability to carry out his duties. We finally reached our destination, Bone in Algeria, where we discharged our cargo. The sixth and final buyer of the cargo was, I suspect, the USA but that's something we will never really know.

While we were in Bone I went out on a motor lifeboat to inspect all the bombed wrecks in the harbour. Wrecks were a constant problem at that time. Even at Montreal there'd been over forty vessels sunk during the war. From Bone we sailed to Gibraltar where we bunkered. The 2nd Engineer was packed off to hospital in the Naval and Air Base and I found myself promoted to 3rd Engineer.

From there we went up to Oporto in Portugal. I remember the architecture in the city, really beautiful. We loaded brandy, port and almonds for Brazil before we dropped down to Casablanca in Morocco where we took on more coal for our bunkers. After that it was off across the Atlantic again, bound for Rio de Janeiro.

Rio was an interesting town. The crew, I seem to remember, were given Christmas dinner on Boxing Day by the Missions to Seamen. While I was there I was invited to smuggle opals and other precious stones across the Atlantic but I'll say no more about that apart from one simple statement – I declined. The last sight of Rio, as we sailed away, was of the illuminated figure of Christ on the Cross at the top of Sugar Loaf Mountain. It was an incredible sight.

A new 4th Engineer had joined us in Rio and after another bunkering call we headed off for Tutoya, a small island off the North East coast of Brazil. There were sand dunes and tiny huts with their roofs being made out of palm leaves. The only source of lighting came from paraffin lamps. The people all slept in hammocks, mainly to avoid the poisonous snakes, scorpions and tarantulas that littered the place.

We anchored out in the bay and you had to use a small rowing boat to go ashore or come back to the ship. There was only one hotel in the place and it had pigs and chickens running under the table and out of the door. That's where the Skipper had to conduct business. While we were there they held a dance in honour of the crew. It took place in the Town Hall, an old wooden hut, very rough, bare and sparse.

When we sailed from Tutoya we went down to Bellem at the mouth of the Amazon. It used to be known as Para. There was a carnival in progress when we arrived and that can only be described as a wonderful experience, quite fantastic. At Bellem the "Clumberhall" took on two pilots for a voyage up the Amazon, a 960 mile trip to Manaus. The pilots worked four hours on, four hours off until the ship reached its destination:-

The voyage up the Amazon was one of oppressive heat. There were mosquitoes and even piranha fish – we used to test them out with a stale loaf of bread. We had torrential rain with sheet lightning, and the visibility went down to nil in just seconds. Then you'd drop both anchors and lie there with the jungle on each side of you. At night all you could hear were monkeys screeching and paraqueets. There was floating debris everywhere, dead trees and alligators. We had to steam against an 8 knot current and it took us almost three weeks to travel those 960 miles.

After a while boredom set in, especially at night. We used to amuse ourselves by killing rats – we'd end up throwing them at each other. We had no cigarettes, only a few black cigarillos.

When we got to Manaus we found ourselves in the longest city on the Amazon. One good thing about the place, there was no racial discrimination.

White Portuguese and black seemed to exist on equal terms. As everything had to be brought up the river, the cost of living was very high. Beer was expensive and we bought many a glass with electric light bulbs! We loaded up with huge balls of rubber in their raw state, plus things like deer hides, mahogany planks and sandalwood oil. It was all expensive stuff and all bound for the USA.

It took only five or six days to travel back down the Amazon, thanks to the 8 knot current behind us. We stopped at one or two places on the way, to take on extra cargo – including 200 tons of Brazil nuts.

On our way up the river we'd bought three monkeys. Mine was a marmoset that I called Pancho. After leaving Brazil for Port of Spain in Trinidad two of the monkeys died and we gave them a burial at sea. I decided to leave Pancho in Port of Spain, otherwise he was certain to die of cold. There was real sorrow and anguish at the thought of losing a great friend.

After Trinidad the "Clumberhall" sailed north to New York, docking in Newark, New Jersey where she discharged part of her cargo. She also discharged hundreds of dead rats when the ship was fumigated. Mountains of the dead rodents soon lay on the quay wall:-

We went to look at the town while we were in New York, places like 42nd Street and Broadway. It was the sort of thing you did when you were in port. This time, there in a sideshow, was Jack Johnson, the great black American World Heavyweight Boxing Champion – well, the ex World Champion, anyway. Six weeks later he was killed in a car crash on his way up to Canada.

We sailed up to Boston where we discharged a part of our cargo and underwent another fumigation – more mountains of dead rats on the quayside.

Back in New York, in Hoboken, one of our Donkey Men, Paddy Driscoll, fell into the dock from the gangplank. He hit his head on a wooden pile and was killed. We buried him in New York. Paddy was a lovely old man. He must have been about 65 years old and had been a seaman all his life. There was a great deal of sorrow on board after Paddy's death.

But after New York it was time to head back over the Atlantic and make course for home. We were heavily loaded with timber on the trip, including a deck cargo about 10 feet high. On our trip across to Grangemouth in Scotland we had three major breakdowns. Firstly there was a problem with the main engine, then the LP bottom end boiler and, finally, the main condenser circulating pump. During the last problem our 2nd Engineer was badly scalded and was, really, a passenger for the rest of the trip.

We hit some very bad weather during the voyage. At one time we were blown back towards America – 87 miles in just one day. The ship was almost helpless, the deck cargo shifted and we developed a 12 degree list. It took us twenty-nine days to travel 2600 miles but you've got to remember that the ship wasn't steaming well due to dirty boilers. Eventually we arrived at Grangemouth, eight months and three weeks after leaving Barry. We steamed in through the Pentland Firth, between the Shetlands and the Scottish mainland. Luckily the weather was fine and soon we were tying up alongside the dock. They offered me the 2nd Engineer's position but I declined. I wanted to go home and see my family. My son was now 18 months old.

Reg Dunkley left Grangemouth on an early morning train that was full of soldiers, all heading for home and for demobilisation. He was armed with dozens of presents for his family and fabulous memories. It took him nearly 18 hours to reach Barry, standing most of the way. He arrived the following day – as he said, it was "lovely to be home."

He went on to become a town councillor and, in the year 1975 – 76 he was Mayor of Barry, a renowned and well respected member of the community. He died in 1990.

John Edwards - Royal Navy
(Cruiser HMS "Jamaica" – sinking of the "Scharnhorst" – Far East)

John Edwards' father was a miner, as was his father before him. His mother also came from mining stock, her father being killed in the pit at Abercynon when she was just three years old. When the war came, however, it was the Royal Navy that beckoned for John:-

After leaving school I trained as a teacher at the old Caerleon College but then, in June 1943, I was called up. Like everybody else I wanted to be a Spitfire pilot but at my medical they discovered I had a perforated ear drum. They offered me ground crew but I didn't fancy that – I didn't know one end of a spanner from the other. So I thought I'd try the navy. After all, you couldn't do much marching there. And I never regretted it. It was a marvellous experience. They wanted me, originally, to go into the Fleet Air Arm but there was the little problem of my perforated ear drum. So they said try coding and decoding and that's what I did.

My brother Ffrangcon had left school at sixteen to go down the pit but when war was declared he lied about his age, said he was eighteen, not sixteen, and found himself serving as an Able Seaman on board the cruiser "Jamaica." After I completed my basic training and my trade training as a coder I was ready for posting - where should they send me but to the "Jamaica." It did nothing for my mother's state of health, I can tell you.

I was waiting for the "Jamaica" on the supply ship in Scapa Flow and I suppose I'd been there about two or three days. Then, in she came and a drifter took me out to her. As I threw my bags on board there was a chap by the railings and he said "Are you Taff Edwards' brother?" And that was what I was known as for as long as I was on board, Taff Edwards' brother.

If someone had consulted the records they'd have realised that one brother was just six months older than the other. It was a biological impossibility. Of course my brother was drawing his rum ration, having lied about his age. Me, I was actually older than him but still too young to receive the rum. According to his "navy age" my brother was twenty and thus able to collect his ration. Anyway, I was a teetotaller – a non preaching teetotaller, I might add. So I was everybody's friend, they were all trying to get my rum ration off me.

We were operating in the Arctic, escorting the Russian convoys. The incredible bravery of those merchant sailors will always stay with me, sailing out there with no protection or any real armament. I must say that I found breathing a little difficult at first. I complained about it to the MO, told him I was having difficulty breathing. He said "My dear boy, this is probably the first time in your life that you'll have breathed pure fresh air."

One of the jobs given to the "Jamaica" was to help supply Spitzbergen. The place had been badly shelled by the "Schranhorst" and "Gneisenau," operating under the White Ensign, and the Admiralty did not want the Germans to realise the garrison was being supplied. As a Kondor used to regularly fly over on patrol at the same times every day the "Jamaica" had to be in after the first flight and out before the second. Everyone, from the Captain downwards, took a hand at unloading the supplies that were stacked up on every free inch of deck:-

Spitzbergen was the furthest north I've ever been and it was so cold. You had all these layers of clothes but it's amazing how quickly the layers came off. You really worked up a sweat unloading the supplies and, pretty soon, off would come the jackets and jumpers.

Once we went ashore at Polyano near Murmansk. The Russians were always suspicious of us. We were allowed to walk about a quarter of a mile but then we came up against soldiers with bayonets and they turned us back. And they were meant to be our allies. They were always quite formal and correct. When an oil tanker came alongside to refuel us I was amazed to see that she was crewed by women – well, I suppose all the men were needed for the front.

There are so many memories of those times. Like when we were ploughing through heavy seas in a snow storm and that song "White Christmas" was on the wireless. I can't say it went down very well. When we were rounding the North Cape the radio station we picked up most clearly was Radio India, a British station, broadcasting in English for the troops out there. Imagine that, us in the Arctic listening to an Indian radio station.

During the various convoys the "Jamaica" had several close encounters with German surface warships, including the "Prinz Eugen" but bad weather and bad visibility contributed to several near misses. On Boxing Day 1943, however, the "Jamaica" was one of several British ships to take part in the Battle of the North Cape:-

Destroyers had located the battle cruiser "Scharnhorst" quite early on but her radar was damaged and she was steaming straight for this huge screen of British ships and didn't know it. The battleship "Duke of York" was there along with us on the "Jamaica" and most of the ships of the 10th Cruiser Squadron.

My brother's battle station was on the 4 inch guns. I was at the back end of the quarter deck where I could hear messages being passed between our Captain and the C in C of the 10th Cruiser Squadron – and those to and from the C in C of the Home Fleet, too, come to that. I was able to move about – I suppose I was just a glorified messenger boy. My brother couldn't move as he was on the gun. I was concerned about him, just like he was concerned about me, and several times during the battle I'd divert away from my job to see if he was all right.

The "Scharnhorst" was just pounded to bits. She put up a hell of a fight but the result was a foregone conclusion. There was no need for radio silence and I heard the Admiral, the C in C of the Home Fleet, say "Jamaica is to go in and finish her off with torpedoes." Our Lt Cmdr was giving what he called "Boxing Day Bulletins," information for those people on the ship who couldn't see what was going on. He did a count down – 10,000 yards, 9,000 yards and so on. By now star shells were being used as it was quite dark. There was perpetual darkness that time of year up off the North Cape.

My lasting memory is of this huge vessel turning over in the water and going down. We'd dropped our torpedoes when we were probably just 1500 yards away, no more, and down she went. Emotions? I think I felt surprisingly little. I suppose I was exhilarated. After all, for a nineteen year old, used to the sheltered life of college, it was a great experience. I suppose there was a sense of just being there.

After she sank, the destroyers went in to try and rescue the "Scharnhorst's" crew. I did hear that the "Nord," a Norwegian vessel, went to pick some up but was told to get out of it because they were picking up the survivors on one side of the ship, then dropping them off the other! Whether that's true or not, I don't know.

We'd known the "Scharnhorst" was coming towards us, of course, knew that the battle was about due. We did think there was a possibility she might sink us but it was a fleeting thought. It's amazing how detached you can be at a time like that. And afterwards I, sort of, felt it had been worth coming, that I'd done something towards the war effort, however small.

When we got back to Scapa Flow the whole fleet cheered us in. Then Tommy Handley of ITMA fame came up and did a special show for us. To see all those characters you'd only heard on the radio – Mrs Mop, Colonel Chin Strap and all the rest – I'll never forget it.

I have this memory of a rehearsal we carried out a few days before the battle. The "Jamaica" played the part of the "Scharnhorst" and the other ships just lined up exactly as they did in the real battle. I spoke about it to my brother before he died and, like me, he remembered it. But I can't find any record of that rehearsal anywhere, it's as if it never took place.

After the battle the crew of the "Jamaica" were given a choice. The ship was to undergo a refit, ready for service out in the Far East. Crewmen could opt to stay with her or take a transfer. Both John and his brother decided to leave. Ffrangcon was posted to Portsmouth and spent the rest of the war there. John was sent to MNOAB, the Mobile Naval Operational Airbases, just north of New Guinea in the Admiralty Islands:-

I went to a place called Ponam. I was a full time coder and that was a bit difficult as we were in the American zone. I had to learn their ways of communication – Abel, Baker, Charlie, all those unusual words. They were just different. Ponam was where I encountered the cafeteria system for the first time, queuing up with a tray for your meal. It was also the first time I tried Coca-Cola. I'd never heard of it before but I must say I've liked it ever since. It was a great life, sitting there on seats made out of logs, in the open air, watching films like "The Road to Morocco." I must have seen that film twenty times. I think it followed me around the world!

One part of the island where John and his colleagues were not allowed access was the area where the locals buried their dead. The area was boarded up and decidedly off limits:-

One day I was standing, talking to the Padre. I was the editor of the camp paper and I'd just written a piece about the death of President Roosevelt. We were talking about that and about Truman, the new President. At that moment a native procession came along, the Headman in an incongruous top hat. I said "Padre, are they Christians?" He shook his head and said "Oh no, dear boy, Roman Catholics."

It was so very quiet out there and, as a non-swimmer, I thought it was about time I learned. They'd blasted out a pool for us and I spent quite a bit of time in there. Then I developed ear trouble and they told me that a piece of coral had penetrated my ear drum. So I was flown to Sydney, to hospital. They couldn't sort out the problem and decided that I had to go home, back to the UK. I was put onto the old Cunard ship "Mauritania" and given really great care. There was still something of the splendour of the old Cunarders about the ship, even though she'd been converted for trooping. I went home via the Cape and ended up in Liverpool. I was met at the docks and driven to hospital. It was really great care, the other side of war service, I suppose.

My chief memory of the "Mauritania" was on VJ Day plus one. We had just left Sydney and it came on dusk. Well, the ship stopped and put on all her lights. It was wonderful. I knew then that the war was finally over. I'd been walking down a street in Sydney when I heard the news that an atom bomb had been dropped on Japan. The sense of relief was enormous. I was quite religious then and I just offered up a prayer. Thank God, I said, because I thought it might be another ten years before we'd be able to get the Japs out of all those islands they'd occupied.

There are lots of good memories about my war service. Some of the best are about the entertainment we were offered. All the services had their special programmes. The Merchant Navy had Shipmates Ashore and the Royal Navy had what later became the Navy Lark. Much Binding in the Marsh started as a programme for the RAF.

Everybody knows what a great job Vera Lynn did but one entertainer who never received the credit she deserved was Ann Shelton. Gracie Fields was the greatest of them all. I saw her in Lancashire when I was training to be a coder and again in Sydney at the end of the war, at the cricket ground. There were thousands of people there and she was singing and doing cartwheels, all sorts of things. If ever there was a superstar in those years it has to be Gracie Fields.

After his journey home on the "Mauritania," John Edwards spent a few weeks in hospital at Bristol where they soon performed an operation on his nose. It sorted out his ear trouble in just ten days. He was demobbed early, on medical grounds, before Christmas 1945. Within a few weeks he was teaching in the city. He later went on to become a Head Teacher and then an Inspector of schools in North Wales.

Captain William Harrison

(Memories of Rene Harrison of her grandfather returning home to Swansea during an air raid)

My mother's memories of the war are of years of constant worry interspersed with periods of fear. She worried about her father, a Captain in the Merchant Navy, who was part of the Atlantic convoys. She knew that if his ship were to be struck by a German U-boat he would, as tradition demanded, go down with his ship. Her brother had also been called up to the army and was receiving training before being sent abroad. She was also writing to her best friend's brother who had just survived Dunkirk and was now in the Middle East. It was to be a fruitful correspondence as he became her husband at the end of the war and hence my father.

She lived in Port Tennant, a working class district near the docks in Swansea, South Wales. In addition to members of her close family she had an innumerable number of cousins, most of whom were also serving in the forces. She worked in a coal distributing office in the centre of Swansea and would come home every day to find that her mother was filled with worry about the latest rumour she had heard whilst shopping that morning. These varied from: the water had been poisoned by Fifth Columnists, the Germans had landed on the beach and Churchill had left the country on the Queen Mary bound for America. Whilst Churchill was regarded a good wartime leader he was generally not trusted. In South Wales he was remembered for ordering troops to fire on unarmed miners in Tonypandy and Llanelli, who were striking for better pay and conditions. In addition, the traditional Tory supporters; the shopkeepers and farmers seemed to be making a good profit from the war particularly through the 'black market'. Many people also felt that when Swansea suffered bombing raids the Fire Service attended businesses in the centre of town before areas of terraced housing such as Port Tennant.

As Port Tennant was near the docks, it was in the frontline when Swansea was bombed. The Harrison family was friendly with a grocer and his family who lived across the road. Since the shop had a cellar my mother and grandmother would shelter in the cellar together with other neighbours. As she sat there hearing the sounds of explosions outside my mother pondered something her mother had told her earlier in the day. The grocer's family was called Smith but the family came originally from Germany and were called Schmidt. Anti-German feeling during WW1 had caused the family had changed their name to Smith. My mother kept asking herself the same question time and time again. Why are one group of Germans trying to kill me and another group of Germans trying to save my life? She never found an answer to that question.

During one of Swansea's bombing raids her father's ship had docked at Barry, a port about 30 miles away, having just survived another trip to and from Russia. My grandfather had been away from home for several months and was looking forward to a few days leave with his family. He caught the train to Swansea only for it to stop 6 miles outside the town, because an air raid prevented it going any further.

Not someone to be deterred by the trivialities in life, he decided to walk the 6 miles home. As he arrived outside his house he saw, to his horror, that a bomb had fallen in the small back garden and all the windows, doors and anything breakable in the house had been destroyed. Running through the house he called out his wife's name but there was no sign of life. He stood outside the house looking up and down the street trying to ignore a terrible thought that kept flashing through his mind.

Had he survived the Atlantic convoys only for his wife and children to be killed in an air raid? The noise of the 'All-Clear' came sounding over the town, and from across the road he heard a voice calling "Dad". From out of the Grocer's cellar came his wife and daughter to run into his outstretched arms. Strangely enough it was a while before anyone commented that the house no longer had windows and doors.

The above story was posted on the BBC WWII People's War website, and elicited the following response from Germany, on 16th August 2004: "*I have read your article and found it very interesting. The thought that fire engines would go first to save businesses instead of family houses is strange to me. However I suppose businesses are there to serve the people, if there are any that have survived. I am from Germany and lived there during the war. We were bombed out 7 times in all and had to move from one place to an other, going from Berlin via East Prussia, my Grandmother's home (Russia now) to Silesia, my grandfather's home (Poland now) to Bavaria, where we stayed until the war ended and the Americans arrived. I have learned from a Russian Prisoner of War in East Prussia that there is no enemy amongst the people. The enemy are the politicians who will find reasons for war and then lie to the people until they feel that a war is necessary. Politics, Greed, Jealousy and Religion etc. make war, and soldiers have to have a reason to be able to fight. Maybe that would answer your question in your article, as to why the Schmidts across the road offered you shelter. They were ordinary people like you and me, and would not see an enemy just because the spoke a different language. Best wishes from Angela Valentine.*"

Ron Harry - Royal Navy
(*Destroyers – Arctic – South Africa – Mediterranean*)

When war was declared in 1939 Ron Harry and his friends from Cardiff enlisted in the local brigade of the LDV, the Local Defence Force Volunteers, soon to be renamed the Home Guard. They were too young to join the armed forces at that moment but they knew that, before too long, their turn would come:-

As young lads we had visions of another First World War, soldiers being up to their neck in mud and rat infested trenches. We talked it over, my friends and I, and decided that the navy would be a lot cleaner than serving in the trenches when the time came.

The recruiting centre for Cardiff was based in an old school on the Kingsway and that was where we went to volunteer. We went twice and on both occasions there was no navy man there. So we asked the RAF chap where the navy was. It was a big mistake. He was very persuasive, that RAF man, and when we came out we'd signed on for aircrew. And as we came out of the office the first thing we saw was a wrecked aeroplane sitting on a truck. We thought it might be best to try the navy again and so we went back later and there was someone there. We promptly signed up for the navy. We'd signed for both services.

Having enlisted for both the RAF and the Royal Navy, it was simply a question of

Destroyers at sea.

which service would call them up first. They had signed on in the navy as wireless mechanics, a brand new branch of the service. Ron's two friends were called up very quickly but he heard nothing. So he went back to the recruiting office:-

The man in the office said that as wireless mechanics were part of a new branch they were only taking a limited number of men, a few here, a few there. He said it would be quite a while before the next intake. I didn't want to wait and asked if there was anything else on offer. He said "Wireless telegraphist?" I said "Put me down for that."

It was an interesting trade. You had to transmit and decode messages. It involved a 14 week course to equip us with the necessary skills. I started off being able to do about 4 words a minute and worked up to around 24. I went in at the age of 19 years, in September 1941.

I started off at HMS "Ganges" where we went to kit out and have medicals. The floors in the huts were made of wood and every day we had to scrub them and then polish them afterwards. Trying to polish damp wood was virtually impossible. It wasn't about polishing floors, it was all about discipline, really.

My first posting was to the Isle of Man, to a holiday camp that the navy had taken over. We went there while we were waiting for a camp at Ayr in Scotland to be prepared for us. We were training and if you did well you had your choice of postings. I chose Plymouth. The CO was called Commander Harry and everyone asked if we were related. I said no but they didn't believe me. They moved me on pretty quickly from Plymouth because, I'm sure, they still believed I was related to the CO.

Ron was sent to a new Hunt Class destroyer, HMS "Catterick." They sailed out into the Irish Sea for trials before the Skipper was happy with the ship and signed to take her over. After that it was up to Scapa Flow, the base of the Home Fleet. That was at the beginning of 1942:-

Soon after that I went through the worst five days of my naval life. A report came in that the "Scharnhorst" and "Gneisenau" had been sighted in a Norwegian fiord and somebody came up with the smart idea of putting together a group of old merchant ships and destroyers as a decoy. When they came after the decoy we were supposed to pounce.

The weather was horrendous. The wind was howling, the waves were enormous and the rain was driving down. I have never been so seasick. I refused to get up for my first 4 hour watch because I was so ill. "Go away," I said, "I don't care if they shoot me." And I didn't, either. They could have shot me, if they'd wanted. I mean, I was deserting my post! But the boy who came to shake me awake – I was supposed to relieve him – he just went back and did my watch for me. He later became my best friend but I don't think he ever did a better deed for me.

I realised I couldn't go on like this and so, for my next watch, I turned out but sat there with a bucket between my legs. Do you know, I can still hear the screech of the wind, the howling it made through the halyards and the stays. It was awful.

As for the decoy plan, a German spotter plane sighted us and they soon realised what was up. The German battle cruisers went for a real convoy instead and we turned round and headed back to Scapa Flow. It was all a total waste of time.

After that little pantomime we sailed south to pick up a convoy at Liverpool. We were heading for the Far East and, in those days, the Mediterranean was closed to us as the Germans were more or less in control of North Africa, Crete

Refuelling at sea.

Table Bay at Cape Town, a happy base for many sailors.

and places like that. So we had to go down one side of Africa and then up the other. Our first port of call was the Azores. They belonged to neutral Portugal and, interestingly, a German U Boat had been there, in port refuelling, only the day before. I'd never been abroad before and so I climbed up the mast to see what the place was like. I was so disappointed. It was just a range of dirty, flat buildings. The only things that impressed me were the palm trees.

A few years later we were in the Med. and under attack from the air. In his excitement, our bridge pom-pom gunner shot our aerial off. Somebody remembered my escapade up the mast and I was sent to repair it. As I went past the pom-pom I said "Mind what you're doing with that gun." I don't suppose he heard me, what with all the noise, but I felt very unprotected, very vulnerable up there, especially around the nether regions. I mean, the gun was only six feet beneath me.

From the Azores HMS "Catterick" went south, sailing quickly in order to catch up with the convoy. And there was to be an unexpected surprise in store:-

We came upon a U Boat trailing the convoy. It might even have been the one that was in port the day before us but we saw her on the surface and when she realised we were there she crash dived. We plastered her with depth charges and soon we saw pools of oil coming to the surface. The Asdic people actually heard her breaking up. We were all so excited, it was our first kill. At the time we thought it was marvellous but I've often thought about that kill in the days since then. There would have been husbands and fathers on that submarine – and us supposedly Christian nations.

When we got to Sierra Leone we had shore leave. It was my first experience of so-called white supremacy over the black races. And I can't say I liked it very much. There were natives there who would carry you over the stream for three pence. They got wet, you stayed dry. My next shore leave was on the Gold Coast. I had one day ashore and flagged down a taxi. It was the most hair-raising drive of my life. Chickens and people were just diving out of the way. The driver had one speed – fast!

The first time I ever drank iced lager was in Simonstown, just around the coast from Cape Town. There was a pub there, the first one we went into, and it was run by a man from Cardiff. Amazing – you go half way round the world and meet a man from your home town. Durban was a really modern place, much more up to date than Cape Town which was just a maze of twisting streets. Durban was set out American style, dead straight streets with blocks, like in the States. We went into a cinema there. It had a sliding roof and you could look up and see the stars.

We were supposed to be heading for the Far East but as our tanks weren't big enough, on the way to Ceylon we had to refuel at sea from this cruiser. We shot a line across and all the ratings who were off watch were sent to the upper deck. We pulled the fuel line across and ran it to our tanks. One of the ratings on the cruiser managed to put his foot into a loop of the rope. Of course, the ships were heaving, pulling apart and moving all the time, and his foot was torn off. I thought I saw a boot flying through the air but it wasn't, it was a foot. We heard the screams and there were people running all over their deck. I never got to hear if the man survived.

As soon as Ron Harry and the "Catterick" reached Ceylon a decision was taken to send them back to Cape Town. The 11th South African Escort Flotilla, based at the Cape, had been formed, the intention being to pick up convoys off the island of St Helena and take them up to Mombassa. That would free up the escorts from the UK to head back to their home waters:-

As junior ship in the flotilla we always got picked to carry out any little extra duty. One day we were off duty and they sent out the Shore Patrol to call us all back on board. A U Boat had been sighted off the Cape and we had to go out and deal with the problem. Several of the crew were still "under the influence" but back we went.

Our lookout reported the U Boat on the surface, such and such a degree. The Skipper turned us around, firing all these star shells – it was really quite impressive. He was going to ram the submarine. And then, at the last second, he realised it wasn't a U Boat, it was a rock. I think the lookout was still drunk! However, our evasive action took us right over the top of the U Boat. We dropped our depth charges and sank it. We were all sworn to secrecy as the Skipper said a dim view would be taken of a destroyer charging a rock. When we got back to Cape Town we had quite a few pints off the locals – they all said we were heroes. They didn't know the truth.

From time to time we'd get bunker cleaning leave, four days off while they were cleaning us out. You could go as a guest to what we called the "up homers," people who lived out in the country who used to invite British servicemen for short breaks. The first place I went was a vineyard. The most special one, however, was about twenty miles inland from Durban. The bloke was an overseer on a sugar plantation and he took us to show us how the process worked. The cane was squashed until every last ounce of fluid was out and stored in big vats. We climbed up a staircase and looked down at the vats through a window. It was a horrible looking mixture. They made Golden Syrup and also white sugar.

At the end of the process they gave all the natives – and they'd come from all over the area – a party to celebrate. There must have been a fifty foot trench filled with burning coals and they had oxen turning on spits all the way down, whole oxen, not just bits of them. The natives were plied with what they called "native beer." The overseer told us not to touch it on any account. He reckoned you'd go blind after a few glasses of the stuff. There was a lot of dancing to an old wind-up gramophone and once they'd eaten the oxen the natives ran up and down and across the hot coals. They showed us their feet afterwards. They were dirty but there wasn't a trace of burning.

After the Battle of El Alamein the Suez Canal was reopened to Allied shipping and

German prisoners on board a British ship.

the "Catterick" soon found herself stationed in the Mediterranean, escorting convoys from Gibraltar to Malta. There was still a lot of activity in the area and most of the convoys were still being bombed on a regular basis. The "Catterick" sank her third U Boat at this time, picking up an echo on the Asdic and depth charging the submarine while the convoy sailed on unmolested:-

We were working with an American destroyer and afterwards we found out that she had claimed the kill. It annoyed us at the time. Mind you, they were very generous, those Yanks. All our food was dehydrated but they had canteen service and they were always inviting us on board. They must have had coffee machines every 20 yards along the deck and they had a cinema rigged up at the stern.

Out on the convoys we saw some terrible sights. The Liberty Ships, for example, they were just prefabricated, welded together, and couldn't take a hit of any sort. They did a job and without them I don't suppose we'd have won the war. But they were floating death traps, really. They'd been invented by a guy called Henry Kaiser and we called them "Kaiser's Coffins." I've seen merchant ships, carrying fuel or ammunition, go up in balls of flame. As junior ship we

Hunting for U Boats.

were always sent back after an action, to pick up survivors. There were never very many.

One day we were sent, along with the cruiser "Orion," to investigate a report that Germans had been seen on a Greek island. We launched a couple of motorboats full of marines and they went to explore the island. I was on the bridge, operating a ship to shore radio. The message came – "All we can see is one cat and two goats." And then came a burst of firing. The next thing we heard the Germans had surrendered.

The German in charge was a typical Nazi. He had a monocle in his eye and was screaming his head off at his soldiers. They were mostly old men and were obviously happy to be prisoners. We put the men into the engineers mess while the officer took one of our officer's cabins.

We took part in the Salerno landings and it was all a pretty "touch and go" affair. The Yanks had a really bad time of it, all these Tiger tanks being dug in, waiting for them. And they were nearly driven back off the beaches there. We were in quite close to the shore, firing our four inch guns. The battleships were further out to sea, firing over our heads. The noise was terrific. I remember seeing these American Lightnings, planes with a double fuselage. They came in over us in a V formation and dropped their bombs on the Germans. Because of the noise of all the gunfire the Lightnings seemed to be making no noise at all.

We were attacked by a glider bomb once, a radio-controlled weapon. The skill of our Skipper, Arnold Tyson, saved us. He ordered full speed ahead and the glider bomb dropped into the sea astern of us. We'd never seen a weapon like that before and our bridge anti-aircraft gunner never fired. Someone asked him why. He said "Because I thought it was a fucking great shite-hawk" – navy parlance for a seagull.

Ron Harry might have thought the world of Arnold Tyson but, soon, he was posted away from the "Catterick" and replaced by another commander. And this one, as everyone soon realised, was not quite of the same calibre as Tyson:-

I can't remember his name. He was the son of some Admiral and nobody trusted him. We'd get into our hammocks fully clothed at night, that's how much faith we had in his ability as a Skipper.

One day, as we were about to leave port, he decided to show off to the Yanks and take us around the bay in a fast circle. Unfortunately there were overhanging cranes and we ripped off all our aerials. He also damn-near hit the dockside. He didn't hang around but shot off out to sea which was just as well as all the Yanks were killing themselves laughing. That was another occasion when I got sent up the mast for repairs. The sea was very choppy and it was quite hairy up there. I had to hold on to the stays and then feel for the loose wire with my foot. Eventually I managed to gather it in but it was quite frightening up there in the open sea.

We were supposed to be escorting Canadian troops on a landing in northern Italy where some heavy guns had been seen. Our Skipper managed to ram the oiler when we were refuelling in Corsica and that bent the forecastle a bit. When we landed the Canadians it turned out the "guns" were just tree trunks painted to look like cannons. The whole affair was a farce from beginning to end.

We were the first British ship into Naples. That old saying, 'See Naples and die?' It was more a case of 'Smell Naples and die!' We went to an opera while we were there. The size of those Italian singers – the heroine would die and you'd see the stage going up and down where she'd fallen.

Ron had been away from home for nearly four years and was now due for relief. He was put ashore in Malta, then taken to Naples to await transport back to the UK. He sailed for home on an old P & O liner and landed in Greenock. The navy gave him a posting close to home after that, in Cardiff, and after four years away he found himself living at home for the next six months:-

We didn't do much when I was in Cardiff, it was a bit of a rest camp, really. Now and then we'd go out into the Channel, usually when some of the ships needed their direction finding gear re-calibrated. The Marconi man would be up on the ship's bridge and I'd be in the launch, "Beth." I was paid sea-going money for that. It really tickled me.

The war ended while I was in Cardiff but they sent me down to Plymouth to join a tank landing craft for a while. We were going across to Norway to pick up all the abandoned German equipment, Stavanger fiord mostly.

On our last trip we struck a rock when the navigator went the wrong side of a buoy. It tore our bottom out and for the first time in the war I was able to transmit. Usually we used signal lamps and received radio messages but didn't send any. Now I was able to transmit an SOS, the only one I've ever sent. Two tugs came and tied up one each side of us. They pumped us out and took us back to harbour in the fiord.

We were in dock for repair and only one generator was working. We kept that for the midday meal. Normally we'd just make do, cooking slices of Spam over a candle. We couldn't use our toilet so we had to use the one on shore. It was a bit like the Alamo, a circle of tree trunks above a drain. Then you were sluiced down with cold water. I can still hear the screams, all that cold water against your backside!

Ron was demobbed soon after he came back from his "shipwreck" in Norway. His ship was destined for San Diego in the USA and one of the ratings who had been there said it was an awful place. So, despite being asked to stay on, he took his demob and, complete with striped demob suit, returned to Cardiff.

Arthur Hellyar – RN Dems Gunner

(Atlantic convoys)

A Barry boy, the 18 year-old Arthur joined the Royal Navy, and was sent to HMS Glendower in Pwllheli in 1942 for DEMS training. His father had been a shipwright on the docks, and Arthur was desperate to join the navy as all his friends had also gone to sea. He then went to Cardiff to serve on 'Defensively Equipped Merchant Ships' as a gunner. He remembered from Barry, Ernie (Chippy) Haysham, torpedoed seven times, and 'Dicko Males' who was a friend lost at sea.

At HMS Glendower, after 6 weeks of basic 'seamanship', 37 of us were told we were 'volunteering' for D.E.M.S. Training), and proceeded with a further 6 weeks training in gunnery, everything from 6" guns, heavy and light machine guns, rocket launchers, bomb projectors and of course all relevant ammunition for the same. At the end of training, I was sent to Cardiff and joined an old coal-burner, the S.S. Barrington Court, with the captain being Hughie Felix from Quarrella Street in Barry.

We loaded with coal, bound for South America, and after several incidents we finally got there. Lucky, I suppose, as several ships wers sunk. We called at several ports on the way, Recife, Bahia and Victoria. At Bahia, we arrived at the same time as two lifeboats of survivors, who told us that they ahd been well treated by the U-boat captain, he ensured that they had enough supplies to reach dry land, but took their captain as proof of sinking. Of course, there were stories of lifeboats being machine gunned. One U-boat skipper and all his officers were, after the war, sentenced to death.

The Barrington Court was a pre-war tramp, and as such had seen much better days. She had no refrigeration, inly an ice-box and when this melted, all the meat went into a brine tub. It was like eating old boots, and sweat-soaked at that. We were starving. Even the rats were hungry. To tell how rusty she was, we were on passage from Brazil to Freetwon on our own, when the chains and pulley operating the steering gear ripped out of the deck. The only way we could steer was by clamping the rudder and altering position when required.

To top it all, on watch in the pitch dark, a light was signalling. We were informed from the bridge 'Do not touch gun'. One chap was all for loading it. I had to stop him, we were ordered to heave to. Then the moon came up, and as it does, it lit up everything. On one side of us was a cruiser (British, thank goodness), and on the other side two destroyers, all with guns trained on us. I asked the chap if he'd like to try loading the gun now, and he sheepishly declined. It appeared our Aldis lamp was out of action, hence the heave to. And so we arrived in Freetown, to find several ships damaged. One had a hole in her you could drive a bus through, I don't know how she managed to get there.

On our way home, a German plane was tailing the convoy, going back and fore across our stern. Our shells were exploding well below him. I altered the setting on one shell from 1000 yards to 1750 yards. We fired the shell right on his nose, he veered off heading for home. Then a message came from the bridge – 'Who altered the shell setting?' Anticipating a 'Well done', I answered 'I did, sir.' From the bridge came the reply, 'OK Taff, I've said it was me as he wants you court-martialled for leaving a hole in his umbrella.' (The anti-aircraft flak range was set deliberately for all guns to discourage a plane from getting too close and firing torpedoes or dropping bombs. The First Mate, who was also the chief gunnery officer, took the blame to prevent Arthur getting into trouble for disobeying orders.)

After a couple more incidents, we docked in Middlesbrough, where I left the Barrington Court and joined the Empire Prince and first met Popeye, the ship's dog, more of whom later. We sailed from Middlesbrough for Newport, where we loaded all the ammunition for the battleships King George V and the Howe. Our fore peak was loaded with gas bombs and we were given double gas clothing and gas masks, plus extra ammo lockers and guns. We then sailed for Algiers and all was peaceful until about 4-5 days out. The Bay of Biscay was like glass, really unusual, and with perfect vision for waves of enemy bombers, 16 at a time – 4-engined Kondors. The attack lasted well into the night. We hit a Kondor attacking us and it veered away and aimed at the nearest ship, the Fort Ash*, which had a bomb land either side of her, and also the ship astern of us was badly damaged. The Commodore then ordered us out of the convoy. Our skipper said that if they hit us, we would take half the convoy with us. I asked what of the two ships that had been ordered out of the convoy with us, and he said they were loaded with dynamite. That really made my day. Of course Jerry saw three ships being taken out of the convoy, realised what was happening and in he came. Then to our aid came the light cruiser, HMS Dido. She certainly saved out bacon.

Well, after having a few more incidents, inclding having a U-boat under us, necessitating us dropping out of the convoy once again, we arrived in Algiers via Gibraltar. We went ashore for a glass of wine (no beer) and at 2 o'clock the Italian dive bombers came in. Of course, they had been told the convoy was in port, with battleships. It was the biggest barrage I've ever seen. The King George V opened up, and all the barrage balloons were shot down, such was the intensity of the firing. She had 16" guns, with absolutely huge charges. The whole port was lit up with fires and flares and the like, and we were moored next to the ammo dump. Next moring, there were hundreds of pieces of shell shrapnelt stuck into out deck. I was on sabotage watch after that – there were looters in port. There was a fright in one of the ammunition sheds as smoke was coming out, but we sorted it. I saw the smoking ruins of a ship. Just before we got into port, a ship had gone up with all hands – they were loading landmines on it, and it had been full of army and DEMS men. Anyway, after a couple more alarms, we eventually got home. Mum said 'You're not looking so well this trip, Arthur.'

Next trip, same ship, we went in ballast to New York, where the incident ith Popeye and the fumigators took place. We loaded general cargo and set off for

Suez. I stayed with the Empire Prince for a further 18 months, seeing further action in her off Crete and then, to Africa and India.

It was night, when passing Crete, the alarm bells sounded, and there was a message from the bridge to expect torpedo bombers. Suddenly, with no sound of overhead planes, the sky over the convoy was full of parachute flares – of course outlining the convoy for attack. I was manning mid-ships Oerlikon; my mate tapped me on the shoulder and pointed. One bomber, flying parallel to us, started to turn. The fact that we could see him told us he was in range. I fired a full pan of 60 rounds at him. Our Petty Officer, a London chap named Beveridge, who was manning a rocket gun aft, aimed where I was firing and let go with 40 rockets, in batches of 20 at a time. My mate said that every round of ours was hitting. A couple of minutes later we saw fire and exploding ammunition as the plane hit the sea. At least we got one, before he got us.

We eventually arrived in Port Said and as was Norman were interrogated by the DEMS personnel, who informed us at once: "Please don't claim that plane as at least 6 Yanks have already claimed it." Our Petty Officer protested, saying that the only ones to fire at it were Taff (me) and himself. The officer said that he quite believed us, and said "Well done", but I don't think it went on record. Still, I did get a pat on the back. We then went through the Suez Canal and Red Sea to various ports on the east coast of Africa: Zanzibar, Dar es Salaam, Beira, then up to Mombasa and across the Indian Ocean to Ceylon and Colombo. We were sailing alone, when out on the horizon came a task force – two cruisers, one aircraft carrier and four destroyers. British, thank goodness, although it made the adrenaline flow in all of us.

In Colombo, to pick up the convoy – 3 merchant ships and one small escore vessel, naval authorities told us to be extra vigilant as several ships had disappeared on the same trip, without trace. Only recently they'd found out from a survivor (a champion swimmer by the way) that the Japs were capturing vessels and taking no prisoners. On this occasion they had lashed all of them to a sub and submerged. The survivor had managed to free himself, swam to some wreckage and was later picked up.** Hence our information. I can assure you, never was a more intense look-out kept.

We docked in Calcutta, not far from where our lads were fighting on the Burmese border and winning, thank goodness. We then went to Durban. All lights on, no blackout and shops full. It was another world. Then to Capteown and on our own to Buenos Aires. Then finally home in convoy to the UK. We had travelled, in mileage, twice around the world.

I finally came home and was sent to HMS Safeguard in Southampton – some rest, I'd rather have been at sea. From Safeguard I was sent to Liverpool, stationed in an old workhouse. I got there late and they put me in an attic, sleeping in my uniform – there was no mattress. I woke in the morning covered in snow – no glass in the window, just chicken wire to keep the   p i g e o n s out.

I then joined the British Justice, the worst looking ship I ever saw. She was full of rust, on her last legs and loaded with High Octane, bound for Russia. I'm firmly convinced that the powers-that-be thought she was expendable. Anyway, we sailed a few miles and she broke down so it was back in for emergency repairs, then off again, only for more serious faults to develop. Back in and they unloaded her, then they sent us back to the workhouse.

I was then sent to join the Manchester Shipper, a lovely, almost new passenger cargo vessel. After the last ship it was Paradise. I had two trips in her to Canada.

Then the war with Germany ended. One day we were tying up in Halifax when all the ships' sirens started going off. I was going up to the deck to take watch. The war was over. I couldn't believe it. There was an empty feeling – no more star shells, no more bombing attacks, no more watches for torpedoes. It was strange and I was sent to join HMS Vanguard in Portsmouth, an absolutely massive ship. You could walk upright through her hawse pipe and the shackles were immense. We were supposed to be sent to fight a Jap battleship as ours was the only capital ship big enough to take it on, but the Yanks sunk her with torpedoes. Then there was the atom bomb so I was sent to a holding camp to wait for demob.

You have no idea how dirty the ships were. In New York they used to fumigate the ships while we went ashore, and you could shovel the cockroaches up, there were so many. People have no idea. And the food was generally pretty poor. And the 'donkey's breakfast' attracted insects. On another boat, we were carrying copra, and 'copra bugs' came through any empty rivet holes and infested our beds, and were all over the ship. On my first boat I was seasick in the North Atlantic – she was small the the waves were huge, but you soon got your 'sea legs' Another time, we were sailing into Liverpool, so the convoy was in single file as it was a fairly narrow and shallow approach. A mate shouted to me "Taff, look at that!" and we reported seeing a conning tower to the bridge. We were told again that it was all right, it was one of ours, and then a Yank ship blew up. The escorts flew to the scene dropping depth charges – the U boat couldn't have stood a chance – there was not enough water to dive properly. He must have had a death wish, operating there. I rang the bridge and told them that the sub had just turned traitor and sunk a Yank.

They started putting stern guns on later in the war. Hitler had ordered captured DEMS gunners to be shot out of hand. Under International Law a ship with a forward gun was classed as a warship, but a stern gun was OK. When Hitler said that, it was decided that we might as well have a forward gun.

When a ship sank, they stopped the crew's pay at that moment! Not many people outside the sea realise that. But we DEMS gunners would have been paid normally. I don't know where they get such heroes from. They are the real heroes of the war, the firemen and trimmers below decks. They often only knew of an attack when they heard us firing, or if they heard an explosion when another ship in the convoy went down. And if we were hit, their chances were not good. Every one of them was a hero.

On one trip we went to Freetown and then broke with the convoy to go to Brazil on our own, carrying coal. We brought back the most dangerous cargo, even worse than coal, iron ore. If torpedoed, you had no chance of getting off. It was a dead weight in the bottom of the ship, and the water rushed in on top, so you were down in seconds. Firemen and trimmers had no chance, just possibly the deck crew.

DEMS gunners are never mentioned in RN records. At holding camp in Southampton we were next to some former DEMS gunners who were 'bomb-happy' – I found out they had no cigarettes so the boys organised a whip-round of ticklers (rolling tobacco) and matches and fag-paper and we threw it over the hedge to them.

I went to the Battle of the Atlantic 50th Anniversary celebrations in 1993, at Liverpool. Our little DEMS contingent of marchers got a great cheer. A German sub came to Liverpool Docks. I was asked if I would meet a couple of WWII U-boat crew. One shook my hand and broke down in tears, apologising for the war and that he was glad the war was over. His nerves had gone. The stress they were under must have been terrifying. Mind you, my own son joined the nuclear sub Trafalgar.

We were never really accepted by the Navy, as part of them, but the merchant boys accepted us as their own. There is a DEMS Memorial in an arboretum – there are 2000 trees there, one for every merchant ship lost.

On the Empire Prince, we shipped from North Wales and we had a fantastic dog on board. He rounded up the blokes when they were drunk in the bars, and I wrote this about him:

"POPEYE"
THE SAILORS' DOG

On June 13 after a trip to South America aboard the "Barrington Court" I joined the "Empire Prince". On joining the ship and after stowing my kit, our PO suggested that I take a turn round the decks to familiarise myself with the armament etc. I finally made my way up to the Monkey Island where I was pounced on by the biggest Alsatian I had ever seen. He knocked me flat on my back and proceeded to lick me to death, the so and so. That was my first meeting with "Popeye", the ship's dog. If ever I had seen a reincarnated sailor, it was him.

We sailed and found ourselves in convoy, loaded with ammo for the "King George V" and the "Howe" and bound for Algiers. Crossing the Bay of Biscay was, to say the least, lively. We were shot at, bombed and everything else. Popeye, to put it bluntly, must have been bomb-happy, as when we arrived at Algiers and the gangway went down Popeye was the first ashore, which was unusual as he had never left the ship before. He was promptly followed by a few members of the crew, swearing they would not come back until Popeye was found. The Skipper put up a reward for his return, but he didn't have to pay out because Popeye came back of his own accord three days later. No-one had any idea of where he had been, but I would like to bet that there would be a lot of half-breed Alsatians running around that port in a few months time. Popeye spent most of his time rounding up any lads from the ship that he found the worse for wear, and always saw them back to the ship safely, but he wouldn't have any truck with anyone from another ship. When he left the ship the crew thought that something nasty was due to happen to the ship, sailors being a superstitious lot.

From Algiers we sailed for a place called SAFI about twelve hours due south from Casablanca, where we loaded with phosphates for Leith in the UK. Our next trip was to

New York and during the trip we found that we were over-run with cockroaches, which resulted in our having to be fumigated on our arrival in New York. As a consequence of this we were billeted in a first-class hotel ashore, with room service laid on. My mate Dave Gowens and I had no trouble settling in. It was then that our thoughts turned to Popeye, where had he ended up? When we questioned the rest of the crew it appeared that no-one had any idea of where he was. We ordered a taxi and asked him to get us to the docks as quickly as possible. When we arrived we made to go aboard. But were confronted by a couple of guards built like the proverbial brick ----house. We explained that we had come for our dog Popeye, after which they contacted their boss who informed us that all was OK. Popeye had been put in the kennels for the night. As we were leaving, we heard one of the guards remark "Crazy Limeys risking their lives for a damned dog!" I was quick to reply that any of our crew would do that just for that dog, he was almost human, in fact he had a lot more sense than a lot of humans I knew. On those occasions when the Alarm Bells rang and he saw us running to our guns, he would make straight for the galley, where he would settle himself safely under the table. He had all his marbles, did Popeye.

When we were on Sabotage Watch, he would always be there with us, and if we had to go off anywhere for some reason he would take our place on the gangway head until our return. Then he would retire to a corner, as if to say "It's your turn now." He never barked, he just gave a low growl to let one know he had noticed something or someone. This brings me to another occasion, when we were in Durban. On watch me and Popeye often took a turn arou8nd the deck. We covered aft, midships, looking over the side etc. We then approached the fore-peak, Popeye walked half-way up the steps, then suddenly froze. So help me, every hair on his back stood straight up, he shook with fright and whimpered, running back aft and not acting at all like a hero. I put one up the spout of the rifle, and forced myself to go and have a look at what had scared Popeye so much.

Finding nothing, I went and found Popeye. I knew where to look. Yes, you've guessed it, under the galley table. After a while, I managed to coax him up forward again, but no way would he go to the fore-peak. I wondered what he had seen or sensed. I mentioned it to the lads, but they didn't have any answer. A couple of nights later, Popeye and I were on watch again. I was enjoying a smoke, sitting down on the forward hatch, when Popeye started to growl, and I glanced in the direction he was looking, and there was someone standing all in white, peeping around the corner of the cabins. I said, "OK, Pop", and put one up the spout. I jumped up, Popeye was growling like a caged tiger. "Halt or I fire!" I shouted and the figure screamed "Don't shoot Taff, it's only me!" It was one of the boys dressed in cleaning rags, but back came Popeye with the arse of his pants in his mouth.

Some time later the crew bought two monkeys. Did I say monkeys? They were more like demons from Hell, they would sit on the fiddley, waiting for the stokers to come off watch, then come screaming down the ladders at them, and when the lads turned away, they would piddle all over them. They tormented Popeye no end, he was scared to death of them. One of them would chase him around the deck, while the other would lie in wait to ambush him. As Popeye ran past he would jump on his back and ride him like a jockey, with all hands trying to catch Popeye and knock the monkey off his back.

After about 18 months to 2 years I was finally sent to HMS Safeguard at Southampton and reluctantly had to say my goodbyes to Popeye and the Skipper, a North Walian and a fine Skipper in every sense of the word. I asked him what would eventually happen to Popeye and he said "When this lot's over, I'm retiring and taking him to my farm." If there *is a special Valhalla for DEMS Gunners and Merchant Seamen, I hope to see Popeye straining at the leash at the Pearly Gates looking for his old shipmates from the "Empire Prince."*

*This attack on the convoy was also remembered by Nwport's George Williams (in 'Death and Donkeys' Breakfasts'), who was a 17 year-old on the Fort Ash. *'What should have been a 5 day trip (from Milford) to Gibraltar, due to enemy action, took 5 weeks... Sunday 15 August was a beautiful day. The sun was shining and the sea so calm it was like a shhet of glass. We were in the Bay of Biscay, somewhere off Bordeaux, when, at 07.55, the ship's alarm bell rang. An aircraft had been sighted on the port bow. Within seconds, the plane dropped three recognition flares. It was a Liberator bomber on patrol. The All Clear was sounded at 08.00 hours. Just 5 minutes later, more alarm bells rang. A Focke-Wulf had been spotted on the starboard side of the convoy.*

The convoy consisted of 81 ships, including 3 troopships, 8 tankers and various merchantmen of different nationalities. The escort vessels were 1 AA cruiser, 8 destroyers, 4 frigates, 2 deep-sea rescue tugs and a submarine sailing on the surface at the rear of the convoy. When the Focke-Wulf spotted the convoy, it immediately dropped its bomb load, in order to gain height. Despite intense anti-aircraft fire from all escorts and merchantmen, it managed to cross the convoy three times, presumably taking photographs, while also relaying our position to base, which we assumed to be Bordeaux.

Thanks mainly to the skill of the Convoy Commodore, who turned the convoy around when the Focke-Wulf left us, it was 17.00 hours before the bombers found us. They came through the glaring sun in waves of 15. The convoy was continually bombed until 22.25, when the first ship, one of the Harrison Line, was hit. Many ships had near misses. The Fort Ash had one stick of bombs – which we clearly saw leaving the aircraft – drop so close that I was knocked down and drenched by the water thrown up by the explosions. The carpenter, who came from St Mellons, picked me up. "You all right, Ginger?" he asked. "Yes thanks, Chips", I replied. Then the Chief Steward gave me a couple of whiskies. Yes, I was OK.

The deep-sea tugs took off what survivors there were from the Harrison boat. It was still daylight. Later, one of our escorts sank the vessel with gunfire to stop her falling into enemy hands. I don't know how many died in that ship, but all ensigns were at half-mast that day. Our DEMS gunner received congatulations from the Commodore for his work with the multiple rockets. Although we had not shot down any enemy planes, the intense fire from all vessels kept them at 1000 feet, thereby making it difficult for them to hit their targets. We had only lost one ship.'

**Eddie Hughes' reminiscences also recalled Arthur Hellyar's fear of being captured by the Japanese. Time and time again, Allied merchant seamen, adrift in lifeboats, were machine gunned by Japanese crewmen of the submarines that sank their ships. In the instance recorded by Arthur Hellyar, captured seamen were brought aboard the submarine, tied together and there on the deck many of them were beheaded by Japanese officers of the sub, before the others were cruelly thrown into the sea...still tied together with the headless corpses and dragged behind the submarine as it submerged. Further research has shown that this was the Dutch steamer Tsijalak, carrying 11 Dutch and 3 British officers, 10 gunners, 51 Hong Kong Chinese ratings, 22 Lascar seamen being repatriated to India, and 5 passengers including an

American Red Cross nurse travelling to join her British husband in Calcutta. On March 26, 1944, about 500 miles from Ceylon, the Tsijalak was torpedoed by the I-8 under Lt—Commander Ariizumi. Three Chinese died in the explosion, and the survivors were ordered on board the submarine. The survivors were tied up and then filmed being beheaded, one by one as the others looked on. The nurse was eventually shot, and 98 were murdered. The 5 survivors included James Blears, the 2nd radio officer who was a pre-war Olympic swimmer, and who is the person referred to by Arthur Hellyar above. (The English Blears was famous in the USA after the war as the wrestler 'Lord James 'Tally-Ho' Blears', appeared in films and retired to live in Hawaii). Blears was roped to apprentice Peter Bronger, and he hurled themselves into the shark-infested waters, but the injured Bronger ded soon afterwards. Two other Dutch officers threw themselves overboard. A Lascar sailor named Dhange was one of the last 20 left alive. The Japanese, tired of their fun, roped them together and the submarine dived. Dhange was the last man on the rope and managed to free himself. The 5 survivors scrambled onto a lifeboat and were picked up two days later, after being fired on by an Amercian merchantman which thought that their boat was a conning tower. More details of the above atrocity and 15 others are given by Bernard Edwards in 'Blood and Bushido: Japanese Atrocities at Sea 1941-1945'.

For the above crime, lieutenants Mononkato and Hattori were sentenced to 7 and 5 years respectively by a War Crimes Court. The I-8, with the same officers also had sunk the Jean Nicolet. The Japanese picked up 96 survivors on its deck, and then dived, leaving 23 survivors. The Langkoes was sunk by I-158. One lifeboat was machine-gunned and another rammed by the sub, leaving only 13 alive out of 94 survivors. The Samamoga had its lifeboat and raft machine gunned, leaving 1 survivor. When the Behar was sunk in 1944, 72 of her 108 survivors were murdered. One of the most horrific examples of Japanese cruelty was the POW ship Lisbon Maru, when 846 POW's died, many machine-gunned by Japanese ships while they were swimming for their lives. It is difficult for any modern generation to understand the atrocities and sustained torture carried out by the Japanese upon captured enemies, whether on land or sea. Bernard Edwards had this letter published in the International Heald Tribune, January 11, 1992.

Wartime Atrocities - More than 50 years after the attack on Pearl Harbor, it is high time the Japanese apologized for the atrocities they committed against Allied merchant seamen in World War II.

The Dutch merchantman Tjisalak was sunk in the Indian Ocean in March 1944, by the Imperial Navy submarine I-8, captained by Lieutenant Commander Tatsunoseke Ariizumi. All but three of the Tjisalak's crew survived the torpedoing and were taken aboard the submarine, where most of them were beaten unconscious before being dumped into the shark-infested sea. Five lived to tell the tale. In a final obscene gesture, 20 men who were still alive were roped together in a line and towed behind the submarine when it submerged. In researching my book "Blood and Bushido," I unearthed 15 such incidents, in which more than 800 noncombatant Allied seamen died at the hands of the Japanese in the most horrendous circumstances. The book is based on survivors' reports on file at the Public Record Office, London, and at the National Archives, Washington. I also was able to interview two of the survivors and the relatives of some of those who died. Lieutenant

Commander Ariizumi committed hara-kiri at the end of the war. Otherwise, the Japanese have remained silent on the matter.

Ray Hicks - Merchant Navy
(Convoys – Atlantic run – the "Queen Elizabeth")

Dr Ray Hicks, now of Gosforth, has led a life which is an example to us all, and gave the following interview to Terry Breverton on a visit to Dr Hick's sister in Barry.

I was born in 1925 in the industrial town of Ebbw Vale in one of the mining valleys of South Wales. As a result of the closure of its steelworks, about 50% of its male population experienced long periods of unemployment between 1929 and 1936. Since all my male relations were coal miners or steelworkers, it was generally assumed that I would follow in one of these industries. However, the result of growing up in such an environment had a profound effect on me. I developed a deep fear of becoming unemployed and became determined to avoid it at all costs.

The word 'education' was often used by my mother. She believed that if I had a good education I would not have to work in a coal mine or a steelworks. Her cherished ambition was to see me getting a clean job behind the counter in the Co-op. This objective was one that I had no intention of pursuing. The whole idea horrified me.

Although I won a scholarship to a grammar school, I prematurely dropped out with no qualifications. I then worked for seven years as a steelworker, a merchant seaman (1942-46), a builder's labourer, and as a trainee on an opencast coal site.

Ebbw Vale steelworks closed in 1929, for seven years, so my first eleven years were spent in poor circumstances. I was the first from our family to get a Grammar School scholarship, but dropped out and went to work in the re-opened steelworks. I those times young men from the area were trying to get out of the area to better themselves in the USA and elsewhere. I wanted to go to sea to get a knowledge of the world outside the steelworks.

At 16 I went down to Newport to try and get into the Merchant navy, but was refused as I was 'too young.' There were no vacancies for boys down there, so I stayed in the steelworks for another year and in 1942 went to Newport again and said I was 18. I got a job on a ship as a coal trimmer and was sent to Gravesend for training. I had to get my cards from Richard, Thomas and Baldwin's works at Ebbw, but as they showed I was not 18, I was too young to serve as a coal trimmer. I then travelled to Liverpool, the centre of the Merchant Navy's Western Approaches.

My uncle, a policeman on the dock, got me a job on a Dutch ship. Most of the Dutch fleet had been at sea when war broke out, and most joined up with the British merchant marine. Holland had been over-run in 1940, and they did not know what had happened to their families until the end of the war.

I wanted to serve in the war. I had been a dedicated boy scout, and then an ARP messenger boy and Home Guard. I knew that it was dangerous, but it was an adventure where you were not bossed around like in the Home Guard. We all knew that there had been sinkings. The whole crew was Dutch, with one Bristolian. All spoke Dutch naturally but were also fluent in English. There was a crew of about 40, including boys on the freighter. I also met some hard cases at sea during the war, as some young offenders were sent to sea instead of Borstal.

I was interviewed for the job by the Dutch First Officer.

He asked me if I was Indian because of the Valleys lilt in my voice! I was as 'green' as could be. I had no gear ready to go to sea, as I had gone to Liverpool

A painting by Ray Hicks, dating from 1944.

'on spec.' There was no training, I was just given four rules to remember:

1. Never undress out at sea, i.e. in the Atlantic – in an emergency you had to get out on deck immediately;

2. Always wear a lifebelt – if you were swept over the side, at least you stood some chance of surviving;

3. Keep your I.D. papers nearby; and

4. Ensure the cabin door is tied back so that it cannot close – explosions would deform the door frames so that they could not be opened.

During the four years I was at sea I served in two Dutch merchant ships and in six British ones. In those years we generally sailed in convoy as it was much safer – but not always.

There is little merit in talking about each voyage in detail since some were totally without incident. But the return convoy of my first voyage is worth mentioning. That was Convoy HX 229 and it was one of the most famous convoy battles of the war. Two convoys left New York in March 1943 and Donitz assembled forty two U Boats to attack them. I was a crew member of the "Ganymedes," a 2682 ton freighter registered in Holland.

On that first voyage on the Ganymedes we went to North America – you were never told where you were going until you were at sea. We sailed up to Loch Ewe to join a convoy, and at sea were informed that our first destination would be New York. There was terrible weather heading for the States. The USA came into the war at the end of 1941, and by 1942 was really involved, with U-boats

NAME *Raymond Hicks.*
DATE *April - Sept -1945*

*American GIs crowd the aft deck of the "Queen Elizabeth" – somewhere in the crowd is
Ray Hicks!*

causing havoc off its Eastern Seaboard.

There was brilliant camaraderie at sea. There had to be – you all had to rely
on each other. The officers 'belonged' to the shipping line, and often stayed with
the same ship, but the crew belonged to a shipping pool, which at the start of the
war was Liverpool for me. I was later in the Newport pool. I was universally
known as 'Taffy' wherever I sailed because of my strong accent. On this first
voyage I served on the Ganymedes in convoy HX229, and was involved in the
biggest convoy battle of the war, with 27 ships being sunk.
The Germans claimed to have sunk thirty-two merchant ships from the convoy,
plus one of the escorting destroyers. In fact only twenty-two merchantmen went to
the bottom. It was undoubtedly a one-sided affair, however, only one U Boat, the U
384, being sunk by the escorts. Old and out of date warships and the complete lack
of air cover were the main reasons for the disaster

Convoys sailed in a grid formation, around 8 deep, never using radio, just
semaphore and Morse code to keep in touch. We only used radio to receive,
never to send. When the war started, U-boats operated independently, attacking

ships by operating out of the Baltic. However, in 1942, Admiral Donitz started the wolf pack attacks. Germany now had 300-400 U-boats are they were all over the North Atlantic.

One U-boat found the position of a convoy, and signalled to HQ. Doenitz then directed all other U-boats in the area to assemble around the convoy. They were refuelled by what we called milch cows, much bigger subs which just carried oil. For convoy HX229, they had accumulated 42 U-boats off Halifax, Nova Scotia, to attack my convoy. You often did not know if another ship had been hit. We were out of sight of much of the convoy. Often, the only way you knew was when you saw fire at night. They operated as surface vessels, only attacking at night.

I served on the "Ganymedes" from December 1942 until July 1943. We survived the destruction of Convoy HX 229 and brought in our cargo of sugar. My second voyage was more or less a duplication of the first and again we encountered U Boat trouble in the North Atlantic. My "Ganymedes" records indicate that we were in the North Atlantic at the end of December 1942 and in New York and Trinidad in January 1943. That clearly puts us in the battle zone when a wolf pack attacked Convoy ONS 154 and fourteen merchant ships went down. I have no way of knowing whether or not we were part of Convoy ONS 154 although it seems quite likely and I do remember being under attack from U Boats on that trip.

Ray Hicks' comments are interesting. They show that knowledge of things like convoy numbers, destinations and ships sunk were often not shared with crewmen on a regular and routine basis. The Masters and ships officers would know what was happening, the names and numbers of ships involved in convoys, but unless they chose to share them most crew members were kept in the dark:-

With HX227, part of the convoy was diverted to the Greenland ice field to escape the carnage. One ship, a tanker called Suen or Sewin I think, struck an iceberg, but we know nothing about it. Some men survived. From New York, we went down to the West Indies, not in a convoy, and after a few days started getting disaster signals from a torpedoes ship. We were ordered to ignore them, and I was devastated. The problem was, of course, that the U-boat would wait for rescue ships to appear, and out cargoes were too precious to risk losing.

Cargoes were far more important than men, and we all realised that. Without the Merchant Navy, Britain would have quickly run out of the resources needed to fight Hitler. It seems that the Merchant Marine has never been fully valued for its service in the war, compared to, say, Battle of Britain pilots. It was also highly unlikely that any of the crew would be alive by the time we reached a sinking ship. Donitz lost two sons, both U-boat commanders, and later gave orders to shoot all survivors. Incidentally, if you were torpedoed, your pay stopped the minute you 'left the ship.'

You also did not expect to be picked up. There were lots of Merchant Navy prisoners-of-war from the first part of the war, before the shoot-to-kill policy, but again theirs is an unknown story. After I left the "Ganymedes" I served on a number of different ships. I worked as a steward on ships like the "Queen Adelaide" out of Hull and on the "Wild Rose," sailing out of Newport in October 1944, being discharged at Cardiff the following March.

My only really terrifying experience was on a small freighter, the Wild Rose, which I joined at Barry Dock in 1944. It was travelling back and fore to Normandy, and at night in the Bristol Channel there was a hurricane. I was in my bunk, and there was a huge bang, Water came into the cabin and I slipped on my lifejacket and rushed onto deck. Or cargo of coal, trimmed in Barry, had shifted and the ship was listing about 30 degrees. Somehow we got her into Swansea. It was a terrible experience because it was the type of crisis in which you were helpless – you could do nothing but hope.

The boys loved New York. We were not paid much, so we used to go to the Blood Donation Clinic and a pint of blood was worth $5. We youngsters used to spend the money on chocolate, but some of the old tars used to spend it on other things… There were $4 to the £1 then. If the ship was being repaired at New York we worked at fast food restaurants as dishwashers for a dollar an hour. I spent most of the war in the North Atlantic, and then on the troopship Queen Elizabeth.

I joined the "Queen Elizabeth" in April 1945 and made five voyages on her across the Atlantic. The "Queen Elizabeth" had been converted as a troop carrier in the early days of the war and when I joined her we were taking US servicemen back home. I've still got a photograph of the "Queen," her decks filled with thousands of American soldiers. I'm in there somewhere but I couldn't tell you where. That was her taking 15,000 Yanks into New York, the first load of repatriated GI's – that was before the war had ended. I remember James Stewart the actor visited, and Marlene Dietrich was on the quayside welcoming the troops. I always worked in catering, usually as a Mess Room Steward, as I was untrained, but on the Queen Elizabeth was given the grand title of Plate Pantry Steward – which just meant that I had thousands of dishes to wash.

I had always served on freighters until the Queen Elizabeth, and it was painted light grey, just like the freighters. It was not a 'real ship' though, not like a freighter where you can feel the sea, and hear the ship creaking in storms. 'Real seamen' don't like ships like the QE and Capetown Castle – they are like hotels, boring, and you don't serve on them by choice. I served on the QE for 6 months, but in 1945 I was with a gang of 'Valleys Boys' in the galley of the Capetown Castle, sailing around the Far East, to India, Singapore, Ceylon etc.

We were mainly bringing POW's home, and always used Japanese POW's to unload the ship where we could. That was a real morale booster for the former allied POW's. I accidentally met my school friend John Evans who had been a POW – he had been in the RAF. The NAAFI had taken over the famous Raffles Hotel in Singapore, and there I also met my next-door-but-one neighbour Tommy Cramp.

I also served on the Bolton Hall, a West Hartlepool ship carrying ore, and the Queen Adelaide which took timber from West Africa. My last voyage was on a Barry freighter sailing to Port Churchill in Hudson Bay to get grain, in 1946. The Resettlement Bureau gave me £5 to spend on a correspondence course so that I could matriculate.

By the end of this time, the wise words of my mother had finally penetrated my thick skull. I realised I would have to get an education if I wanted to be more than a manual labourer. As a result of taking a correspondence course and studying in my spare time, I finally achieved a school-leaving certificate by matriculating as an external student from London University. Additional part-time study at a technical school enabled me to win a scholarship to Cardiff University, where I graduated with a first class honours degree in civil engineering. A year later, I was awarded a M.Sc. as a result of research in applied mathematics. This was followed by winning a Royal Commission Research Award in the same subject which enabled me to get a Ph.D.

Subsequently I spent 27 years working in British industry. This included nuclear power, steelmaking, coal mining, building construction and general engineering. Since my life has been long, eventful and rewarding, it encourages me to hope that my experiences may help young people pursuing a career in 21st-century Britain, particularly those who may feel that they come from a deprived background.

Ken Higgins - Royal Navy
(Submarines – Western Approaches)

Ken Higgins came from the town of Brecon, more than a few miles from the sea. Brecon was an army town, being the long-time base of the South Wales Borderers of Rorkes Drift fame. It would be logical to expect a young man who was eager to serve his country to stick with what he knew. Yet it was the navy that appealed to Ken once the time came to join the forces:-

Right from the start I knew I wasn't going to join the army. Brecon was always full of soldiers and I'd seen and heard enough of the Regimental Sergeant Majors on

the barracks square. Mind you I was in the Home Guard from about the age of sixteen but that was different, it wasn't real soldiering.

In 1942 I went down to Cardiff for my medical. I had to go the night before because you just couldn't get from Brecon to Cardiff by nine-o-clock in the morning. I was the only one who passed for the navy that morning. You had to put your preference on the form – the navy was my first choice, RAF second. We did various tests as well as the medical. The maths test, I remember, a quick speed test as they used to call it.

Anyway, I came down the stairs and there, at the bottom, was this Marine RSM. He said "Come here, son." I

Ken Higgins in February 1944.

Ken Higgins during training – he is second from the right in the back row.

thought to myself I'm not his son but I'll humour him, see what he wants. So I went over. He told me I was the only one to pass for the navy that day. "Join the Marines, son," he said, "and you'll be a sergeant in no time." I told him exactly what he could do with his Marines. Only the proper navy would do for me.

It was ten months before I was actually called up. You used to have your medical at seventeen and then have to wait until you came of an age. I was doing my apprenticeship and they couldn't take me until I'd finished that. But I was called up the day I finished, the very day. That was in April 1943 and I was just eighteen.

Like most "hostilities only" ratings Ken went south to do his basic training, at HMS "Raleigh" in Torpoint. After that he was sent to Wilcove for training as a torpedo man. He was expecting a posting to a destroyer or some sleek cruiser. But then came something of a nasty shock:-

I was drafted into submarines. I was so annoyed, really upset. I was due to go on leave that weekend and on the day that I heard where I was bound, a Thursday it was, I went into the office. I was always in and out of the office as I was the PO's runner. The place was full of Wrens and this afternoon they all stared at me and said "What's up Taff? You're not smiling like you usually do." I told them the reason and then I said "I'm home this weekend and you won't be seeing me again. I'll find a cave up in the Brecon Beacons and stay there until the war's over." They were horrified. "You can't do that," they said. "You'll get into serious trouble." Of course I came back on the Monday and they were all so relieved to see me.

There was a way out, of course, several ways out in fact. You could fail "the tank." They had this deep tank and they sent you down to the bottom and you had to escape using the Davis Escape Gear. Fail that and you were out. Or you could fail the exam, the test they put you through. I had to learn every inch of the submarine, working off these drawings they gave me. But I didn't fail. I don't know what it was, you just wanted to do the best you possibly could. So I passed and went into submarines and I can honestly say that I've never regretted one minute of it.

I was sent to Blythe on the North Sea coast to do my submarine training. They used to take us out on a small sub called the "Tribune." The first time we went on board we were all sat in the fore-ends, just waiting to dive. We'd been going for some time and blokes were moving around, carrying out various jobs. As trainees we were just sat there. In the end someone said "When are we going to dive?" One of the crew turned around and said "You've been under for the last ten minutes." They hadn't sounded the buzzer and there was no difference in movement.

After completing his training Ken Higgins was posted to the "Unrivalled." The submarine was patrolling in the Western Approaches, hunting for enemy ships. There was not much likelihood of spotting German surface craft at that late stage of the war but the possibility of spotting a U Boat was always there:-

I only did two patrols on the "Unrivalled" and we never fired a torpedo in anger, at least not during my time on board. We certainly never saw any enemy ships. We spent a lot of time helping to train anti-submarine craft, corvettes and the like. And we worked with Coastal Command aircraft several times.

In August 1944 I was taken ill with acute appendicitis and rushed off to hospital. The operation was no problem but, of course, you couldn't go to sea for three months after an operation like that. By the time I was fit for sea duty again the war was almost over. They sent me to the "Saga" and that's where I met my friend John "Topsy" Turner, another Welshman. He was already serving on her. Later on I left the "Saga" to join the "Tantalus."

Aircraft were always a problem when you served in submarines. If you saw one you'd dive. It didn't matter if they were British or German, you didn't hang around to find out. To them we were just a shape in the water, how did they know if we were a British sub or a U Boat? They dived, you dived, it was as simple as that.

HMS *"Tantalus," returning from patrol.*

116

To young sailors like Ken the toileting arrangements on submarines left rather a lot to be desired. It wasn't a major problem but hygiene was sometimes the last thing people were concerned with:-

You didn't get to wash in clean water very often when you were on patrol. Fresh water was always in short supply. You'd fill a bowl and everybody used that water to wash in – great if you were first in the queue, not so hot if you were last. Then it was a case of washing in other men's water.

And toileting was interesting, too. If you went to the toilet you had to blow it out, over the side. You had to ask permission to do that. You'd phone the control room and ask "Permission to fire a shit shot?" There was a reason for it, of course. Urine could make bubbles as it went into the sea, waste matter could be spotted by any enemy ship that was prowling around. So it made sense.

I hadn't wanted to go to submarines to start with but I can honestly say that I loved every minute of it – once I got there. The camaraderie was superb in submarines and once you were in, nobody wanted to get out. I can't think of anyone who asked for a transfer out – not that they'd necessarily have given you one.

So although I was dead set against it to start with, once I got to Blythe and started my training I became fascinated by the job and by the people who worked on the submarines.

Ken came out of the navy in October 1946. He had qualified as a carpenter before the war and, after his demob, he returned to the building trade. He later ran a department in the Welsh Office.

Ken Hopkins - Royal Navy
(Submarines - Western Approaches - the Far East)

Born in Pontycymmer in the Garw Valley, Ken Hopkins came from a family of native Welsh speakers. His father was a minister in the church and soon the family moved, first to Cardiff and then, later, to Newport. When war broke out he was 14 years old and studying for his Higher School Certificate:-

Originally I wanted to join the RAF. Like all the other youngsters I wanted to be a Spitfire pilot but when I went for my medical they said that as I wore glasses there was no chance of that. So I chose the navy instead. I had no experience of the sea and there were no family connections or interest. My only involvement with the sea was the odd trip on the Campbell pleasure boats that sailed out of Cardiff and Penarth.

I signed on the dotted line and then they delayed my mobilization so that I could sit my Higher Cert. It was September 1943 before I joined up. They sent me to HMS "Royal Arthur," a holiday camp at Skegness that the navy had taken over as a training base. I did a month of basic training and then went on to a six month course for Radio Operators. The thing I remember most about that period was having to do guard duty in the winter months. The eastern winds came straight in from Siberia, howling over that flat East Anglia landscape. But I passed and was classified as a Telegraphist.

I volunteered for submarines in March 1944. I'm not sure why. I suppose it was something different and you also got a shilling a day extra. Every time you dived you got that extra payment. Later on, when we were going out to the Far East our Captain made sure he dived every single day. I did my submarine training at Blythe, after having done "the tank" and the Davis Escape stuff. I can't honestly say I found it a problem. I spent two or three months on the "Una," a U Class submarine, quite small, just 50 crew I suppose. We were finishing off our training really.

My first real posting was to the "Talent," a new super T Class submarine. We had to stand by her as she was still being completed at Barrow-in-Furness. It was a lovely time, living in "digs" up there. The two blokes in there with me were Lofty, a big lad, nearly six foot eight, and Bash from Lancashire. Bash was a really heavy drinker. Every weekend I used to jump on a train and come home. Lofty and Bash used to come with me and my mother would put them up. We'd go to the dances and they'd be off chasing the girls. I had my girlfriend, in college training to be a teacher, so I can't say I joined them in that. But they had a whale of a time.

We weren't really supposed to leave Barrow and one Friday I went to the toilet on Crewe station. Who should be there, in the next stall, but our Captain. "What are you doing here, Hopkins?" he said. "Going home to see my girlfriend, sir," I said. "Appear before me on Monday." I got 7 days No 7 Punishment for that but we still went off the next weekend. I think the Skipper turned a blind eye to it, unless he had no choice.

Our Skipper, Commander Flavell, was a lovely bloke who came, I think, from Devon. He heard we were bound for the Far East and he called us all together. "Look, boys," he said, "I've got two daughters and I want to be able to come home and see them. Agreed?" We agreed. This was a man who had been there before and had already sunk two Japanese warships. He didn't want to take any chances and neither did we.

The "Talent" sailed for the Clyde where she tied up alongside the Depot Ship and was soon involved in diving tests in the deep lochs. More practice saw the submarine patrolling out into the Western Approaches. They even pretended to fire torpedoes at Ailsa Craig, the huge rock that sits in the Firth of Clyde. Then, in the summer of 1945, the submarine received orders to proceed to Hong Kong:-

We sailed via Malta and Port Said, going through the Suez Canal. That was strange, sailing along with nothing but the desert on either side. It took us two months to reach Hong Kong and by then the Japanese had surrendered. When we reached Hong Kong we found that the Japs had blown up the power station so, for a while, we provided the power for the city - us and the "Tally Ho," 24 hours on, 24 hours off.

We also used to go out on pirate patrol, looking for these Chinese pirates that were supposed to be around. We never saw any and I suppose it was just showing the flag, really. But we'd stop off every so often and go ashore to play football on those lovely sandy beaches. That was good fun.

There wasn't a lot of damage in Hong Kong and the people were quite friendly. They preferred us to the Japanese, I suppose. The crew used to love going ashore. I looked after the money for them. I had Margaret, my girlfriend, at home and I wasn't interested in the things they were looking for. So I sat at the door with their wallets.

I was always troubled by sea sickness, the whole time I was in the navy. I never cured it but I got used to it. Of course it was only when we were on the surface, there was no motion when you were submerged. Sometimes I'd be in the Radio Room, being quietly sick, and the cook would be waving bacon or sausages in my face.

We were in Hong Kong until from the end of 1945 until March '46. The Captain said we were off on a "Round the World Victory Tour" but then my father wrote and said he'd got me the chance of a place at Oxford. I actually tried the exam sitting in the Captain's cabin underneath the Sydney Harbour Bridge. The Captain was there to supervise me. The next thing I knew there was another letter from my father – I'd been offered a place. And because of that I was given an early demob. The "Talent" was due to go to the east coast of the USA, I came back home and was demobbed in late September 1946.

I enjoyed my time in the navy, living with people like Lofty and Bash. It was a good experience, one that broadened my experience of humanity. And just coming across things like the rum ration, that was different. We never had alcohol in our house and I was faced with a dilemma – what should I do with it? One of the crew, an old sailor who'd been in submarines for years, he said "Want me to do your dhobying?* You give me your tot, I'll do your washing." That's what we did. It was strong stuff that rum and by the afternoon the old guy was well away. He was a lovely old bloke, helpful and nice.

I think I wrote to Margaret almost every day when I was away. Well, there wasn't much else to do in the Radio Room. You'd sit there, just waiting for something to happen, and writing letters was a great way of passing the time. There wasn't that much to do on a submarine, not when you were off duty. The food was all right, at least there was plenty of it. Not that I ate that much with my sea sickness. When you were patrolling it was just a case of working and getting your head down. When you docked, that was different.

I remember being given a fortnight's leave when we were in Sydney. They sent us up into the mountains, to a holiday resort. The people were very friendly and we had a great time, dances and socials, that type of thing. It was all paid for by the Australian Government.

We never fired a torpedo during my whole time on the "Talent" and the closest I came to the enemy was in 1943 when they brought in a captured German General on a destroyer. He looked shattered. But the navy was still a great experience – mind you, I was lucky. There were plenty of others who weren't.

After his demob Ken Hopkins spent four years up at Oxford. He became a teacher and finished his career as Director of Education for Mid Glamorgan.

* Dhobying is a naval term for washing clothes.

Eddie Hughes Merchant Navy Radio Officer
Atlantic Convoys

Eddie Hughes qualified as a radio officer aged 19, and joined Liverpool's Merchant Navy pool. He entered service with the Blue Funnel Line as a 2nd radio officer/purser.

My first ship was the Theseus, from Liverpool to London, where I joined the S/S Teucer, an 8000-tonner scheduled to sail through the Med-Red Sea-Penang-Singapore-Hong-Kong-Shanghai to Kobe, Japan. My first trip on her was around 6-8 months. I then served on a tramp the S/S Malampus (5962grt) for 16-18 months – it was one of 6 Dutch-flagged ships under the Blue Funnel Line. We were sailing around the Cape to Colombo and Penang, via the Malaya Straits, loaded with rubber, and we were very wary by this time of Jap subs in the Indian Ocean. One Blue Funnel ship had been captured carrying all the codes and plans for our base in Singapore – they knew all the defences and could break transmissions, so it was no wonder they took it so easily.

I was on the Malampus when the Japanese invaded Java. We were about 200 miles south of there on passage from Fremantle, carrying spares for the oil fields. They turned us around to head for New York. On the Malampus, in the Pacific Ocean, we were stopped by a British armed merchant cruiser, they were looking for a German raider.* We were on our way back from New York to the Dutch East Indies. There was a famine in India and we went to Australia to get wheat, but the Indians would not eat it.

When I was discharged from the Malampus, I served on the M/V Dolius, in convoy ONS5. The engine kept breaking down, and we stopped to repair her, but caught up with the convoy. We were stationed 01, in the front of the port wing of the convoy, which was attacked by over 40 U boats. About 13 of 36 vessels were sunk. We were expecting a torpedo from port, but one hit us from starboard, amidships at 11am, which must have passed through the convoy. It exploded in the DEMS gunners' cabin. There wwere sheet metal and sandbags protecting the radio cabin, as it was the first thing that any attacker tried to take out by shellfire or machine guns. When the torpedo hit, it jammed the door shut, and I was going to have to use an escape hatch, but as the ship listed, the door opened again. I got out but had to rush back and get the code books and throw them in a weighted bag over the side.

The convoy had gone on and left us, but a rescue ship came for us and picked us out of the lifeboats. One of the DEMS gunners had both legs broken and died in the boat so we buried him at sea. We were transferred from the rescue ship to the corvette Sunflower. The senior ship in the convoy was the frigate Snowflake and there were 4 corvettes. The action lasted 7 days. We were battened down below the bridge on the Sunflower so could hear everything that was going on. We could hear a shout that 3 torpedoes were coming in, followed by the order 'Hard Aport!', and we heard them go alongside the corvette.

Later, I was standing on the port wing of the bridge and we heard a ship on our port side, and then saw it was a U boat tracking the remains of the convoy. Again the skipper shouted 'Hard Aport' and went flat out towards it. Corvettes were slow and she had only reached about 10 knots going flat out, but the hit forced our bows up and then down, and we dropped the depth charges, which exploded almost immediately. The Sunflower was granted 1 known kill and 1 possible kill on that escort duty patrol. We were landed in New York and waited 4-5 months for transport to Liverpool.

The MV Dolius (5507grt) was built in Greenock in 1924, and sunk by U 638 on May 5th, 1943, when part of the famous convoy ONS5, mentioned in Part Fifteen as the 'turning-point' of the Atlantic War. At last, despite heavy losses, U boats were also lost. At 14.00 hours on 5 May 1943, the Dolius (Master Gilbert Robert Cheetham) in convoy ONS-5 was torpedoed and sunk by U-638 northeast of Belle Isle, on passage from Avonmouth to New York. Three crew members and one gunner were lost. The master, 57 crew members and eight gunners were picked up by the HMS Sunflower (K 41) and landed at St.Johns. The U-boat had been sunk by the corvette after the attack. The Dolius was the only ship sunk by U 638. It was sunk the same day, north-east of Newfoundland, in position 54.12N, 44.05W, by depth charges from the British corvette HMS Sunflower. 44 dead (all hands lost). The Sunflower was a new Flower class corvette, which in 1941 and 1942 had picked up survivors from the torpedoed Hawkinge, Shahristan and Richmond Castle. On October 17th 1943, the Sunflower also depth-charged and sank the U 631, and 12 days later the U 282.

I then served on the Fort McLeod, a MOWT seconded to the Blue Funnel Line, operating in the Far East. I'd sorted out a 'panic bag' in case I was sunk again. We sailed independently from Colombo to Fremantle to get wheat. We were again worried about enemy ships and subs in the Indian Ocean. A torpedo hit our rudder at 10 at night, and blew our propeller off. We were immobile so manned the lifeboats. I was standing on the end of the deck, holding the portable w/t transmitter – it was my job to put it into the lifeboat, but the rope had gone to lower it. I didn't know what to do. So the mate shouted to me to 'Send the damned thing down, Sparks!' Thankfully it missed the boat, as the ship moved. It would have gone right through her. The sub circled the Fort McLeod as she hadn't sunk and shelled her, but she still didn't sink. They had to use torpedoes again. We didn't hang around and had rowed away as fast as possible. We didn't know if it was a Jap or German sub, and the Japanese were known to machine-gun lifeboats. We all got away and spent about 8-10 days in a lifeboat in the Indian Ocean.

The S/S Fort McLeod (7127grt) was a new ship, delivered June 1942. Sunk 3rd March 1944 by Japanese submarine I-162 with gunfire and torpedo in the Indian Ocean 02.01N 77.06E - south-west of the Maldive Islands whilst sailing independently on a voyage from Colombo to Durban, Majunga, Tamatave and Aden to the UK, with a cargo of 2000 tons of copper and 1000 tons of military stores. The I-162** was commanded by Doi. 34 crew and 3 gunners landed 60 miles south of Lumbo, Portuguese East Africa and were returned to Colombo on March 8th.

A letter to The Times, 16th April 2000 reads:

Any photos of this ship?

The British merchantman SS "Fort McLeod" (7,127 tons; Capt. Alderton) managed for the Ministry of War Transport by Alfred Holt & Co/ Glen Line of Liverpool/London, cleared Colombo harbour on the morning of March 2, 1944, routed on a voyage to Durban/Lourenco Marques.

Late in the evening of March 3, she was torpedoed by a Japanese submarine (and later sank), but happily with all the crew surviving and being returned to Colombo on the March 8.

Does any photograph of the vessel (she'd been "tramping" around the Indian Ocean area for many months), taken at the time, exist, I wonder? I realise that unofficial photographic recording of shipping movements, in the conditions prevailing, would have been much frowned upon - to say the least but, one never knows!

R. Travers-Bouguse
Hampshire, UK

It's funny the things you remember. The Blue Funnel Line had Chinese crews, and they would not allow any of them ashore in New York. Because of their Immigration Laws, there was a $5000 indemnity on each Chinese crew member, which we would have to pay if any of them got ashore and disappeared into Chinatown. So we had to patrol the deck every night. In Brooklyn we tied up and the harbour was full of ice, it was so cold. I was on freezing on watch and had just popped down to get a hot coffee. A Chinese lad had tried to get off the boat and let go of a rope, falling between the harbour wall and the ship. We had a landline and phoned the authorities and soon there was the siren of a police car followed by an ambulance. A doctor stepped out, in immaculate whites, and wearing sunglasses. This was around 11 at night. He shouted 'Where's the Goddamn Chink?' And we shouted back 'He's still in the water!' We managed to get him out of the sea and he was rigid with cold. The Yank MD said he was all right and we took him back on board, covered him with a blanket on a bunk, and next morning he was serving us breakfast.

On another voyage the Chinese were tormenting a monkey on deck, and I told them to leave it alone. I took it back to my cabin, and he used to sit on the end of my bed, eating cockroaches.

On one convoy we were being bombed south of Malta and the Yank ship astern of us was firing its machine guns, and caused more damage to us than the Germans. 'Friendly Fire', they call it these days, but it's not what we called it.

We had a whale of a time in Australia around 1942 and 1943. We were in Melbourne for 5-6 months and they didn't know what to do with us. We were moored in Perth and Fremantle, a huge American aircraft base was nearby. I took some of the Dutch midshipmen ashore for a few beers. The bars were only open 6am-6pm, but there were clubs open in the evening also. We came out about 8 or 9 and went to a café to get some coffee, and I told the Dutch to go and get a spare table while I bought the coffees. I was swung around by my right shoulder and a Yank punched me on the nose. Some Yanks had gone for the table at the same time as the Dutch boys and a huge fight broke out. I grabbed a table and smashed it over the Yank's head, then we heard the whistles of shore patrol and spilled out into the street. My nose was bleeding all over my whites, so I headed home to the ship – I walked all the way from Fremantle to Perth. If you were ever in any trouble, the first rule was always to get back to your ship. Happy days! In 1944 I was discharged, after the second torpedoing, as being medically unfit for duty and they gave me a full pension for a year, but that soon ended.

Eddie worked for many years as a buyer with Dan Evans Department Store in Barry, and now lives in Bridgend with his wife Edna.

* This incident may be that when Captain Manwaring on HMS Cornwall was on the point of opening fire, as a British merchant ship would not stop. She then transmitted an RRRR message, and the attack was called off. Soon after, the Cornwall found and destroyed the German raider, the Pinguin, as noted in Part Fifteen of this book, and in the footnote in the entry on Theodore Pryse.

** The I-162 which torpedoed Eddie Hughes was one of Japan's most successful subs. She was completed in 1930, as the I-62 at Mitsubishi Shipbuilding's Kobe Yard, and her first war patrol for the Imperial Japanese Navy was in 1941. Later that year she was involved in the invasion of Malaya. In the South China Sea, the I-62 formed a patrol line with the I-57, -58, -64 and the I-66 off Trengganu, Malaya. After a second patrol she took part in the Invasion of the Celebes, Netherlands East Indies.

On 31 January 1942, she torpedoed and damaged the 9,463-ton British tanker Longwood 20 miles W of Colombo, Ceylon. On 3 February 1942, in the Indian Ocean, she torpedoed, shelled and damaged the 7,402-ton British tanker Spondilus. In March 1942 she left Penang for her 3rd patrol, and on 4 March 1942, S of Tjilatjap, she shelled and sank the 865-ton Dutch merchant Merkus en route from Tjilatjap, Java to Bombay, India. The same day, the I-62 torpedoed and damaged the 8,012-ton British tanker San Cirilo. On 10 March 1942, she shelled and sank the 235-ton British sailing ship Lakshmi Govinda. On 21 March 1942, the I-62 torpedoed and damaged an unidentified cargo and passenger steamer, but it escaped. In May 1942, she was renumbered as the I-162, and took part in the Battle of Midway at the end of May. On 6 August 1942, she left Sasebo on her sixth war patrol via Camranh and Penang for the Indian Ocean. Her assigned area was located between Madras, India and Trincomalee, Ceylon.

On 3 October 1942, the I-162 torpedoed and sank the 2,332-ton Soviet freighter Mikojan. On 7 October 1942, she torpedoed and sank the 5,597-ton British merchant Manon. On 13 October 1942, the I-162 torpedoed and damaged the 4,161-ton British merchant Martaban. The torpedo hit caused a large fire. In December she left port for a new raid into Indian Ocean, but had to return to Penang because of mechanical trouble. On 20 January 1943, the I-162 and I-165 left Surabaya for a diversionary raid. The I-162 also reconnoitred Cocos Island. On 14 February 1943, off the Lesser Sundas, the I-162 was attacked by the USS Thresher (SS-200) E of Thwartway Island. The Thresher launched two Mark 14 steam torpedoes, but one was faulty and the other missed and exploded harmlessly. The I-162 fired her deck guns at the Thresher, turned north and broke contact, returning to Sasebo for repairs and overhaul. On 12 May 1943, LtCdr Doi Mareshige assumed command. 26 September 1943 saw I-162 leaving Penang on her seventh patrol to raid enemy communications in the Indian Ocean.

On her 8th patrol, in the Indian Ocean, S of Ceylon, the I-162 torpedoed, shelled and sank the 7,127-ton British merchant Fort McLeod SW of the Maldive

Islands. The Fort McLeod was sailing alone from Durban, South Africa via Majunga, Tamatave and Aden to Great Britain with a cargo of 2,000 tons of copper and 1,000-tons of military supplies. On 18 March 1944, S of Ceylon, she torpedoed the 5,199-ton Dutch merchant Ittersum. LtCdr Doi claimed a sinking, but the Ittersum survived his attack. On 1 April 1945, the I-162 was configured to carry five "kaiten" human-torpedoes. The I-156, -157, -158, -159 and the I-165 were used in a kaiten-ferrying role in home and Korean waters. Later in 1945 she was surrendered and sunk by gunfire by USS Nereus.

John Humphries - Royal Navy
(Lease Lend destroyers – landing craft in the Mediterranean – the Maldives)

John Humphries was born in Bridgend and was already working in the construction industry when war broke out in 1939. His work involved travelling around the country and he was actually in the Midlands town of Derby when Prime Minister Chamberlain made his auspicious announcement. Twelve months later he decided that it was time to join up:-

I don't know why I chose the Royal Navy – your memory gets a little cloudy at my age. I think I was talked into it by a friend, all that free rum and tobacco, I suppose. Anyway, I went in to see the Recruiting Officer and I didn't have a clue about the various departments I could join, I just signed up. In the end I became a torpedo man and I can't honestly say I loved it or that I hated it. I suppose it was a bit of both. I didn't like the bureaucracy of the navy, they did everything by numbers and you always felt you were being punished for something. But I enjoyed the rest of my time, took it in my stride, I suppose.

It was July 1940 when I enlisted. To start with I was sent to HMS "Collingwood," outside Portsmouth, for my basic training and we all lived there in these great long rows of sheds. As soon as we finished training they sent me to America on the "Empress of Britain." She was a big liner, three funnels, very luxurious. We landed in Nova Scotia and then made our way down to New York. We had a great time there for a few weeks. The Americans loved us. Well, they'd all heard about the bombing of London and places and treated us like heroes. All of them were trying to trace their ancestry and find some British heritage.

We picked up these four funnelled destroyers, all part of the Lease Lend programme that Churchill had worked out with the Americans. "Four Funnelled Bastards" we called them. They were old and out of date and pretty early on we realised that they threw you around like a piece of cake – and we had to face the Atlantic on these things! I was on the "Broadway" and our Skipper, an RNVR man, gathered us all together on the upper deck. "Our torpedoes aren't working," he said, "they're all rusted up. But don't worry, chaps, we'll ram the first U Boat we see." A couple of the old navy sweats looked at each other and said "Fuck you, Jack, I'm overboard!"

Those old four stackers were all wet ships. They leaked like sieves. I was a seaman on the upper deck when we came back across the Atlantic, standing lookout and watches, but I never saw a thing, no submarines, nothing. When we got back we took the ships up to Scapa Flow for repairs and for conversion. It was awful up there at Scapa, the only living things you saw were sheep. We lived on board, there was no point in going ashore - all that was there were mountains. There was a canteen that sold this special Scottish beer in tins but that was all. The weather was cold and the place was bleak.

John was not at Scapa Flow for too long as he was soon drafted back to Portsmouth Barracks. It was an easy posting after the rigours of the North Atlantic and the Lease Lend destroyers:-

You were what they termed "a scientific loafer." You'd just pick up a crate or a box of something and carry it around until it was time to have lunch. Then you'd do the same again in the afternoon. They had some funny terms in the navy. It went on for months before they sent me off to Hayling Island for more training. Eventually they sent me back to the States again. I was in a shore establishment there, HMS "Asprey," until they decided to send us by rail down through Georgia and along the Mississippi to New Orleans. They were building these new Landing Ship Tanks and we were supposed to pick up one of them. The train journey down south was special. It was tiring – I mean, we didn't have bunks, we just slept in our seats – but it was a wonderful way to see the country and to find out all about the place and the people. It was a great experience.

The ship wasn't finished when we got there, they were still welding and plating, so we hung around until they were ready. Those LSTs were wonderful ships. You just fed military hardware onto them and they had a lift to take it to the upper deck. Once that was filled you'd start on the lower deck. They were designed to take tanks and troops right up onto the shore.

At last our ship was ready, LST 165 she was, and we sailed for Algiers. But when we reached Bermuda she broke down. Everybody was happy to spend a bit of time in Bermuda. Our Engineer, an old Merchant Navy man, reckoned he'd fixed the engine to break down so that he could enjoy the island. There were lots of Wrens stationed there, Wren writers and the like, so it's quite possible he did.

We were moored in Hamilton and I can still remember the red roofs of the houses and the wonderful turquoise sea. All the other LSTs had gone on and we had all these lovely WRNS to ourselves. They used to come on board for parties, it was a great time. We had to send to New York for a part for the engine and we were there for several weeks in the end. Mind you, our Engineer, the man who fixed it all up, got himself injured and he was flown back to the UK. So the pleasures he so eagerly sought he never got!

John Humphries and his landing craft did eventually make it to Algiers. There they worked with the famous Desert Rats, preparing and then taking troops and tanks to Sicily. From Sicily they more or less followed the Desert Rats, running up to Naples and then to Anzio:-

The LSTs were immobilised at Anzio. There was a sand bar and we just couldn't get across it. And of course the Germans were bombing the hell out of us. We had to get the tanks onto improvised barges and they carried them into shore. It was quite hairy, all these Me 109s attacking and firing at us all the time.

There was always a lot of enemy activity when we were unloading tanks, aircraft attacks and things like that. At Anzio we were fired on regularly by

Anzio Archie, this big gun the Germans had. He kept firing at us, time after time, but luckily he never managed to hit us. The bay at Anzio was about the size of Porthcawl, not very big at all. And the beach was tiny. We never got to the beach, just lay off unloading our tanks onto these barges.

While we were carrying troops to Anzio we saw the "Penelope" torpedoed. I was on the upper deck, on lookout at the time, and suddenly there was this great big flash. I think it was a one-man sub that did it. Whatever it was we were detailed to pick up survivors. They were up to their necks in oil and we just couldn't pick them all up. We were a very high-sided ship and we couldn't get at them. We lowered scrambling nets over the side but they couldn't climb them, they were so weak and covered in oil. They were screaming at us, calling us all sorts of names. It was understandable. It was a dreadful experience.

Shortly after that I was sent back to the UK, to Portsmouth again. It wasn't long after the D Day landings and we were taking tanks across the Channel and putting them into the Caen area. I suppose I was lucky, there as elsewhere. We were in the heat of the battle but I always came out unscathed.

Conditions on our landing craft were pretty good. Ours was American built, of course, so you had beds rather than hammocks. Lots of the lads preferred hammocks to beds – and they were quite cosy once you'd learned how to use the things. Not me, I preferred the conditions on our Yank ship, much better all round.

Even now I can still see the faces of the men I served with. There was such a great camaraderie back then. After we were demobbed I kept in touch with one lad, in particular. You'd meet others occasionally. One day I was working and a chap pulled up alongside me in a bakers van. "Are you Taffy?" he said. He'd been with me on the old LST. It was a great life, everybody laughing, drinking the navy rum, going ashore. But on a ship you never knew when somebody was going to put a torpedo in your guts. That thought was always there.

I was a loader for one of our guns on the LST. I never fired one in anger. I think the "real Navy" frowned on us as hostilities only ratings. I remember once my mate being asked what he did in Civvy Street. Teacher, he said. And the other guy, a regular, just turned away and looked ashore.

I got married in 1944, when I was in Barracks in Portsmouth. I'd known Mona before the war but I had to get permission and then came back to Bridgend – her home – for the ceremony. Mona stayed in Bridgend where she was teaching and I went back to Barracks, after a brief honeymoon in Bournemouth. Soon after that I was sent on draft to Ceylon. The Suez Canal was open by then and our troop ship sailed right through it. That was a strange experience, nothing but desert all around you. When we reached Ceylon we went into barracks in Trincomalee, more sheds designed to take in-coming personnel.

They put us on a trawler and sent us off to the Maldives. Our job was simple enough, working out the height of the waves. We had some sort of apparatus and we used to send all the graphs and measurements through to Ceylon. They were making all sorts of preparations for the invasion of Japan. As far as we were concerned it was great. You'd work for five minutes in the morning, five minutes in the afternoon, and the rest of the day was yours to do with as you liked. There was nothing much to do, mind you, just lie back and sunbathe. I was a deep golden brown inside a couple of weeks. All this white sand and blue sea, it was quite enchanting. I was there for about six months and I'd have been quite happy to stay there for another six.

I came back to the UK just before the war in Europe ended. After that it was just a case of waiting for your demob number to come up. I can't say I ever thought of staying in even though I had enjoyed all the fun and the companionship. You had the chance to stay in, if you wanted but I came out, got my demob suit and hat, and went back into the construction industry.

John came back to Bridgend to work and stayed with his firm for 40 years. He rose steadily through the ranks and in the end he became a Director of the company.

Beryl James (nee Jones) - Wrens
(Home service – Portsmouth – Poole – Swanage - Scotland)

Beryl James joined the Wrens in 1943, aged just eighteen. She had been studying at University and, immediately before joining up, revisited her family in West Wales. She arrived in Aberystwyth on a warm day in April and was amazed to see how little the place had changed. It was the start of the summer season, the band was playing on the prom and people were sitting around in deck chairs – it was as if the war had never happened. A few days later she reported to the Wren officer in charge of a huge barracks in Mill Hill:-

The White Ensign flew over a part of the parade ground which was called the Quarter Deck and we had to learn to salute it every time we walked past. Lining up for the first time in columns of three we stood on the parade ground, waiting for further directions. I was dressed in a rather glamorous maize-coloured woollen overcoat which had a front edging of fur. Unfortunately it formed something of a muff and I was immediately nicknamed "the kangaroo."

Sixteen of us were allocated to a cabin. The mattresses were hard and reveille was at 6 am. We each had tasks to carry out. Mine consisted of scrubbing the sick bay floor, burning lousy hair and used sanitary towels and generally being a dogsbody! Unlike the other women's services, Wrens were allowed a three week period to decide whether they wanted to remain in the service before actually signing on the dotted line and I was sorely tempted to ring my father and tell him that I wanted to come out. I resisted the temptation.

It was three weeks of learning the ways of the navy, three weeks of spit and polish, learning to tie knots (though I've never yet worked out why), learning to live cheek by jowl with complete strangers – a lot easier for those of us who had suffered the rigours of boarding school.

At one stage Beryl Jones, as she then was, was sent for interview to an address in Acton. The officers in charge were interested in the fact that she had a smattering of Russian, learned while in College. She was also asked if she minded spending her war in just one place and quizzed about her ability with crossword puzzles. Looking back now, she is sure that she was being sounded out about coding duties at Bletchley Park. She quickly denied any prowess with crossword puzzles and asserted that she didn't mind being posted anywhere, as long as it was close to the sea:-

The fact that I had attended physics lectures at University convinced the navy that I should train to be a radio mechanic, even though physics remained a complete mystery to me. I had really been interested only in art at College but as that was considered not quite respectable I had to attend lectures in physics as well. Now I joined a class of thirty-six other girls in the Technical College in Manresa Road, Chelsea. There was a lot of studying and a weekly test was held in order to weed people out. Only eighteen girls passed out at the end of the course and how I managed to find myself one of them I shall never know.

We were all told about flying bombs, doodlebugs. We learned to count up to eighteen after their engines cut out, then listen to the thump of the explosion. Then we knew we were safe until the next one came along. At the end of one day's lessons I was strolling across a small garden in South Kensington when a large man in overalls leapt on top of me and pressed my face into a flowerbed. I was very alarmed but then I heard the explosion. The ground shook. He had seen the doodlebug diving and was coming to my rescue.

By the summer of 1944 all of us on the course had got as far as building our own primitive receivers and early one morning one of the girls heard, on her receiver, a faint voice proclaiming that the Allies had landed on the Normandy beaches. We all downed tools and made for the nearest pub, the "Six Bells" in the King's Road. There was an enormous celebration, complete strangers embracing one another. We had all waited for this moment for so long.

After a while we were sent down to a Signals School in Hampshire and that was where I qualified as a Radio Mechanic. I must confess to feeling a complete fraud, having bluffed my way through the tests. But I passed and after being summoned to the Drafting Officer I was told that I would be stationed in Portsmouth docks. I was sent to Port Radar, situated in a row of ancient houses in the docks. When I looked out of the window I could see Nelson's "Victory."

In those days no Wren was allowed on board a ship unaccompanied and as I was expected to repair transmitters and receivers, they assigned me an "oppo" called Slinger Woods. He had a pretty low opinion of Wrens and called us "Gold braid chasers!" But somehow I won him over and we became good friends. When the call for assistance came he and I would wait at the King's Steps for the "cabbage boat" to deliver us to whichever ship was having problems. Sometimes it was pitch dark and it was difficult to see the ship looming up in front of us. I used to clutch my toolbox and say fervent prayers. Slinger was always cheerfully confident in my ability – which only made things worse.

Half of the time the problem was not faulty equipment but "finger trouble," with the Sparks having pushed the wrong switch. Somehow I managed to get away with it and wasn't found out! Before going ashore Slinger was always inclined to steer me in the direction of the Ward Room to meet young officers. It was a bit of a decoy as he then made his way below deck to wangle an illicit supply of tobacco, soap and brown sugar. I was quite happy with the arrangement and met some very charming young men. As they were always on the verge of sailing they were invariably "ships that passed in the night."

After three months in Portsmouth Beryl was posted to Swanage. She was mystified about the posting because, as far as she knew, there were no ships in Swanage. After a crowded train journey she and a colleague called June arrived on Swanage station in the pouring rain to be met by a young Sub-Lieutenant who, surprisingly, told her to call him Ronnie:-

It was even more surprising when he told us he was our commanding officer. Ronnie took us to a Guest House and told us to take the next day off to acclimatise ourselves and get used to the town. At breakfast the next day we saw a handful of Wrens who were also staying there. They were dressed in polo-neck sweaters and bell bottoms. June and I were hugging ourselves – we had escaped the rigid naval discipline of naval life in Portsmouth.

The previous spring, in preparation for D Day, a series of Radio Direction Finding stations had been set up along the south coast. They were going to be in direct contact with the beach-heads in France. It was all top secret and the first radio operators and mechanics weren't aware of the final details of the operation until D Day minus one. These RDF stations were heavily guarded and even the first Wrens who served there had to learn how to shoot. Our underground station, the Combined Operations Unit as it was known, was at the top of Dulston Hill and could only be approached on foot. The whole area was a minefield. It was in direct contact with the US troops on Omaha Beach and by the time June and I joined the unit it was the contact point for back-up troops, supplies and ammunition.

The operating room was manned twenty-four hours a day by American and British radio operators. My job was maintaining the transmitters and the masts above. It was the first time I'd worked alongside Americans. When I came off night duty I would walk down to the US base and breakfast on waffles, syrup, doughnuts and coffee. There was sometimes quite a lot of rivalry between American and British sailors and then the Wrens would try to cool things down. Dare I say that the presence of females diffused many a confrontation?

On Christmas morning 1944 I was guest of honour at a feast cooked by four American sailors in a farmhouse a few miles away. I was told that they had acquired a turkey – I might add that in wartime turkey, when you could get it, always tasted vaguely of fish as they were fed fishmeal as part of their diet. I was only mildly disturbed to see a row of very wet socks, hung over the ancient Aga stove, dripping into a large pan of gravy. We had the most enormous, unforgettable meal and then, later, went to a children's party in the local Church Hall. Santa Claus spoke with a strange Trans-Atlantic accent as he handed out presents to the children. Everyone had lots to eat.

Sometimes I had to test the quality of our transmissions and then I would chat to the US troops in Normandy. A group of them became very curious about my appearance so I told them I was tall, blonde and had green eyes. Being a disembodied voice you can re-invent yourself without fear of being caught out!

Beryl went home on leave for the New Year and early in 1945 was posted to Parkstone in Dorset where, for a few weeks, she worked on Motor Torpedo Boats in Poole Harbour. Once again discipline was relaxed and easy but then, suddenly, she and June were recalled to Portsmouth. It was back to rules and regulations, morning Divisions, roll calls and a smart appearance at all times:-

We were working on ships at Portsmouth but there wasn't the same urgency now as there had been earlier in the war. One of the ships we worked on was the battleship HMS "Nelson." She had just returned from the USA and we were asked to listen to some of the gramophone records the crew had brought back. They gave us a tin of peaches and we opened it immediately. What bliss! I hadn't tasted anything so delicious for a very long time. We were working on the "Nelson" for some weeks but I must say I preferred smaller ships. They always seemed to have more personality. It's hard to explain but the moment you board a ship it's possible to sense whether she is a happy one or not.

One day there was quite a stir when the Free French ship "Croix de Lorraine" entered the Solent. A Wren radio mechanic was required to work on board and I volunteered, with some trepidation, as my French had never really progressed beyond Fifth Form level. As I was the only woman on board they assigned me a Chief Petty Officer to act as my chaperone. The matelots made a big fuss of me and were very gallant. The Chief and I were able to keep up a tolerable conversation as he was from Brittany and Breton and Welsh do have some similarities. I ate in their mess and found the food very unusual, "foreign" you could say. It was cooked in olive oil and there was always heaps of red cabbage at every meal. It certainly didn't resemble the French cuisine I relished later in life.

April came and the few sparse trees in the dockyard burst into blossom. I was working on the cruiser "Jamaica" and on my way back to my quarters in early May when the sound of ship's hooters and church bells suddenly broke out. Such a cacophony of noise could only mean one thing – the war in Europe was over! The streets were full of happy faces with total strangers hugging and kissing each other. All the traffic came to a halt and I went off to a party on a double-decker bus.

Some hours later, when I got back to my quarters, there was an ashen-faced Third Officer, tears rolling down her face and a telegram clutched in her hand. She had just been informed that her husband had been killed when a Japanese kamikaze plane had hit his carrier. It was a sobering thought. The war was still being fought out in the Pacific.

That wasn't the only shock for Beryl. That same day she found herself posted to a Fleet Air Arm station called Evanton on the east coast of Scotland. While the rest of the country indulged in a giant party she was fighting her way to Euston station ready to catch the overnight train to the north:-

Transport met me at Inverness station and I was taken out to Evanton. I felt such an alien. I'd never been to an airfield before and the sight of the planes, the runway and the whole hustle and bustle of the place completely bewildered me. The CO was equally as disturbed – he hadn't been expecting me! After a few phone calls it became clear that the wrong Jones had been drafted. Another telephone call was made and I found myself with instructions to report to RNAS Drem near Edinburgh. The WAAFs on the station – the Fleet Air Arm shared the aerodrome with the RAF – thought naval discipline archaic. They were probably right. We even had to form a Liberty Boat (a small squad) before we were allowed to "go ashore." A bit later I was posted to Arbroath, to the shore-based HMS "Condor."

I felt quite settled in my new surroundings. When we were not repairing receivers in the workshop we had to take turns in the Control Tower whenever there was night flying. One evening the operator in the runway van couldn't contact the Tower. All he could receive was the voice of Jack Benny cracking jokes on the air! He'd forgotten to put the right crystals in the radio set. By now it was the summer of 1945 and the war in the Far East was still raging. At HMS "Condor" naval pilots were still in training.

My family came up to visit me one weekend and I came down with German measles. The local doctor said it was OK to keep enjoying the weekend but to steer clear of pregnant women. By the time my family went home and I reported to the Sick Bay it transpired that I had contracted Weill's Disease. I was taken to Kelly Castle, once owned by Ramsey McDonald, and put into isolation. There were only one other rating and myself there, housed in turret bedrooms at different ends of the castle. It was a lovely rest. One evening I was leaning out of my turret window when I heard a terrific commotion. The rating, my fellow inmate, was down below, in the courtyard. He was waving his arms and shouting "The war is over!" We commandeered a jeep and drove down to Arbroath where we joined ecstatic crowds. I think I kissed everyone in sight but I still looked out for pregnant women –just in case.

After a period of leave at home in Llandysul over Christmas and New Year, Beryl was amazed to find herself promoted to Petty Officer and posted to Scotland once again, this time to Abbotsinch outside Glasgow:-

Having sewn the gold anchor buttons on my jacket and donned my new tri-corn hat, I reported to my base. I was shown to my own cabin – no longer did I have to share my sleeping quarters. My duties were fairly routine but one I can still remember. I was to be in charge of organising a welcome ashore party to the off-duty crew of two American ships. I was a bit apprehensive, after all it wasn't an enviable task, overseeing the well-being of a group of Wrens entertaining American sailors. After a few hours I found myself helping several of the girls to their cabins. Several of the Americans were close to passing out, too. It seemed that two of my male helpers had spiked the beer with torpedo alcohol. Next day my group of Wrens were due to be entertained on board the USS "O'Hara" but the plan was scuppered as so many of them were suffering momentous hangovers.

When Beryl's demob papers arrived in the summer of 1946 she had mixed feelings. After all it was rather like leaving a large family:-

I was certainly not the same person who had been such a carefree student in Aberystwyth before the war. Walking out of the camp gates for the last time made me feel quite sad. I did the usual round of farewells and travelled south to Wales and home. Soon I would be twenty-one years of age and I had no idea what I would do with my new freedom.

Brian Jenkins - Merchant Navy
(Russian convoys – the Far East)

Born in Haverfordwest in West Wales, Brian Jenkins had always wanted to go to sea. He came from a farming family but the lure of life afloat was strong. It was not something he could ever account for but there is nowhere in Pembrokeshire that is much more than a stone's throw from the sea and so, perhaps, the sea was in his blood. In 1940, when he was just twelve years old, he joined the Sea Cadets:-

I was with the cadets for almost four years and by the time I came to join the Merchant Navy I could read Morse better than the officers who were supposed

Brian Jenkins taking a sight, using a sextant on board the "British Chancellor."

to be instructing us. I also went to the Outdoor Pursuit Centre at Aberdovey for a month before I joined. In 1944 I was apprenticed to the Cory Line. I must have written to about ten different shipping lines asking about apprenticeships. The Cory Line replied first. My father paid £10 for my first year's indenture and my salary was exactly that figure, £10 a year. It rose to £12 in my second year. There was no training, no pre-sea training, you just went straight onto the ship and you learned "on the job," as it were. My fellow apprentice was, like me, straight from school.

Looking back, now, I would say that, as apprentices, we were little more than unpaid deck hands. It was a bit like slave labour, really. My first ship was the "Fort Massac," one of the vessels the Cory's had built in Canada. She was a bit like a Liberty Ship. The government gave orders to build around 60 ships of that type, heavily armed merchantmen of about 7000 tons. We had a four inch gun on the forecastle and a Bofors gun each side of the bridge and another close to the 4th hold. There was another 4.7 inch astern. All the guns were manned by DEMS gunners.

I was sixteen years old when I joined the "Fort Massac" and I felt as if the world belonged to me. Then we came alongside this rusty, dirty ship and my mate said "Is this her? Is there some mistake?" and I looked and I remember saying "No mistake. Look, there's her name plate. This is her."

In February 1945 we were loading TNT at Middlesbrough when they offered us all three days training on guns. They were offering you fifteen shillings for the three day course and chaps were volunteering left, right and centre. I suppose the training was there in case the DEMS gunners got killed.

Brian's first trip took him from Middlesbrough on the Russian convoy route. The outward journey was uneventful enough but on the return trip they ran into a hurricane and the convoy was forced to scatter:-

It was bitterly cold and the weather was atrocious. We were up on the bridge, on watch, and the 3rd Mate said to me "Are you scared, Lofty?" Well, it was my first trip and I assumed such weather was normal. So I just said "No, sir." The Mate shook his head and said "Well I am. This is the worst I've ever seen."

In the end we had to put into the Faeroe Islands for shelter and to regroup. We were there about three or four days in all. Our next trip was to Murmansk, Convoy JW 65. There were 26 ships in that convoy and I can still remember the ship alongside us being torpedoed. We just kept going – there was nothing else you could do.

I was on the bridge, not long later, and I saw a shape sticking up in the water. It was like a long tube. The Skipper passed me his glasses – along with the comment that if I lost them over the side I'd be well advised to jump in after them – and asked me what I could see. "A spar buoy, sir," I said. The Skipper pointed out that the shape was almost as big as the frigate alongside it and I realised it was a U Boat. "Ah," said the Skipper – and that was all he said. The U Boat had been depth charged to the surface and her bow was sticking up in the air. Again, we just kept going, ploughing on at 9 or 10 knots.

It was so cold. The cold on those Russian convoys, that's what I really remember. There was ice everywhere. We couldn't have used our guns, even if we'd wanted to, because they were all iced up. We were told that we couldn't take photographs and that's a shame because it looked spectacular. I've seen so many photos since that I wish I'd just ignored the order and taken some.

They used to say that you'd have three minutes if you ever went into the sea but, really, they reckoned your heart stopped the moment you hit the water. The shock was just so great. They gave us lifejackets but we were carrying TNT and I remember thinking "We need parachutes, not lifejackets."

Once we reached Russia we could take a few trips ashore before we started back to the UK. I don't know why we went, mind you. Officially the Russian girls weren't allowed to talk to us and they were all a pretty dour lot. We'd go to the Russian Officers Club and they'd tell us "There's plenty of food in Russia." But, outside, people were starving, kids were even picking up potato peelings to eat. I remember, once, seeing a guard kick one of these kids in the stomach as he was trying to pick up some peelings. We snowballed him and he went away.

One girl, Natasha, we did manage to speak to her. If anyone saw us talking, she said, she would receive a visit. "Why do you speak to these foreigners?" she would be asked, "when there are lots of good Russian men. Do it again and you'll be in Siberia."

I thought the Russians were a shower. Stalin had had his purges and all that was left were "yes men." The Russian navy was meant to come out and escort us in but they always stayed put. We had no escort at all on the last stages of the voyage, not until we reached the White Sea but, because it was so cold, the U Boats couldn't get through and we didn't lose any ships.

During the Arctic Convoys Brian Jenkins and his colleagues endured attack by U Boat and by torpedo aircraft. Working four hours on, eight hours off for days on end, they endured some of the worst conditions imaginable. And they faced it all with incredible fortitude and courage:-

When we first joined the "Fort Massac" and learned where we were heading the other apprentice asked "What's our chances of getting back?" One of the old hands, an officer who'd made many trips, said "Don't worry about it. It's only the others who get killed."

On my first leave back in Haverfordwest I walked past the old Grammar School where I'd studied and one of the teachers called me in. I had tea in the Staff Room and they asked me about where I'd been. Russia, I said. "How old are you now, Jenkins?" one of the teachers asked. "Sixteen," I said. He shook his head. "Sixteen," he said. And that was all.

Brian was in Loch Ewe when the war in Europe ended and the next thing he knew he was heading to the other side of the world. He sailed first to New York and then New Brunswick, where the ship was loaded, before crossing the Atlantic again and passing through the Mediterranean on her way to the Far East:-

We were off Bombay when it all ended. I never enjoyed either VE Day or VJ Day as I was working both times. We had all been looking forward to the invasion of Japan, a bit like mice looking out for the cat. The first thing they did was to take off all our DEMS gunners – all but two of them, anyway – as soon as we docked in Bombay. After that we went up through the Persian Gulf, through the Med. and back home. The trip took about nine months, I think.

After the war ended Brian served as 3rd Mate on a British Tanker Company ship. The Skipper made Captain Bligh look, in his words, "like a member of the Salvation Army" and all the officers decided to come ashore. Brian did one trip as a deck hand and then returned to Pembrokeshire where, in later life, he owned and ran his own boat business.

Emil John – Merchant Navy
(Atlantic Convoys)

Emil John of Barry was a friend of Robert Hortop (see chapter 12) and recounted his experiences to 'The Barry & District News', beginning with the sinking of the Athelknight on May 26, 1942 (see Chapter 5 and Chapter 8).

There were 26 of us in the lifeboat with just 40 gallons of water. One Barry man died of his injuries and we had to put him over the side. There were 23 crew in the other lifeboat, and they were picked up safely but we must have covered 1500 miles before we were sighted off St Bartholomew in the West Indies. We were looked after by nuns at a hospital before making our way via St Kitts and Antigua where we joined a Cuban boat which took us to Porto Rica. Then an

American transport took us to Florida and we went by train to new York where I joined a tanker to come home.

Emil was serving on the Baron Dechmont when she was hit by three torpedoes off the coast of Brazil on January 3, 1943. Eight men died, all of whom were sitting on the No. 1 hatch, drinking coffee, when a torpedo exploded underneath them. One was Robert Hortop, one of the seven Barry brothers who served in the war.

The rest of us managed to launch a lifeboat and row for the shore where we were taken to a maternity hospital before getting to New York via Miami. Our skipper was captured by the U 507 and was killed when she was sunk 10 days later. I was on the Largs bay, a troop ship, when we hit a mine off Naples. About 100 US soldiers were killed but we managed to sail the ship to New York for repairs. There was an Irish bar tender in the pub next to our hotel in New York who got fed up of seeing me there! Next I joined a ship named British Character which was crossing the Bristol Channel to Avonmouth when she collided with another vessel moored without lights. I said to myself 'That's it I've had enough!' and took a medical discharge from the navy. Emile returned to the sea in 1947, however and then worked at Rhoose Cement Works and Barry Docks.

Barbara Jones - Wrens
(Home service – Pwllheli - Plymouth)

Barbara Jones was still living at home in Cardiff when the war broke out. She was working in a sweet shop, serving the customers, but on Sunday 3rd September her house was full of neighbours, all of whom had come to listen to Neville Chamberlain's broadcast as so many people did not have a wireless. When the Prime Minister announced that Britain was at war with Germany several of the women were crying and all the men looked very serious. But for youngsters like Barbara it was hard to see what all the concern was about:-

I don't suppose I quite realised the enormity of what was going on. It seemed to be more exciting than anything else. I suppose I expected the Germans to land by parachute any minute and come marching down our street but I can't say I was particularly frightened. There was an air of excitement about the place, more than anything else. We knew about war, of course, but only vaguely. All we'd seen of it was on the newsreels at the "twopenny rush," stories about the war in Spain. Reality came with the air raids – we weren't that frightened but it was something different again.

Right from the beginning I'd wanted to join up. I know it's awful but I didn't want the war to end until I was old enough to join up. There were propaganda posters everywhere and everyone just wanted to do something. I joined the Girls Training Corps where we did things like aircraft recognition and Morse Code and I really enjoyed that. But it wasn't like the real thing.

I joined the Wrens because I could join them when I was seventeen and a quarter – or, at least, I could go for an interview when I was seventeen and a quarter. For the ATS and the WAAF you had to be seventeen and a half before

Wren Barbara Jones, 23rd January 1945.

they'd even give you an interview. So off I went to the recruiting office and signed on the line. A bit later they called me for a medical at St John's School in the Friary in Cardiff and that was fine. Then, when I was old enough, off I went to Mill Hill in London, to become a Wren.

The training involved a bit of everything. Everybody had to take their turn in the Mess, to lay up and clear up. We scrubbed toilets and staircases – everybody had to do it, no matter what your job was going to be. At that time the only categories open were cooks, general stewards and officers' stewards. I thought I'd choose the best of them and become an officers' steward. Later on I put in for Fleet Mail but that was at the end of the war and before I could be drafted I changed my mind and took my demob.

I still remember getting my uniform. You went into what they called the "slops," the stores, and the Wrens behind the counter would look you up and down and then slap a jacket on the counter, then a skirt, two of each and a bit of everything. I saw these huge black bloomers, what they called "blackouts," with long legs and elastic. They were hideous. We said "We don't have to wear these, do we?" And they said "No, don't worry about them." You just kept them and pulled them out for kit inspection.

We were on parade one day and the woman inspecting us came and caught hold of the back of my greatcoat. She pulled it and said "I think this lady could do with four sizes smaller!" A friend of mine took it in at the back for me. I rarely wore the greatcoat, mind you. The Burberry was much more comfortable.

When we were training there must have been 40 girls in the one room, sleeping in double bunks. One night there was a doodlebug raid and the girl in the bunk above mine was really scared. She'd never been in a raid before, she came from the wilds of Yorkshire. The bunk was shaking and I could hear this muffled crying. I said "Do you want to come in with me?" Back home I'd always slept with one of my sisters so it was nothing to me. In she came. In the morning there was a Petty Officer shaking the foot of my bunk. "What's this?" she demanded. "Don't you know it's an offence to have two in a bed?" At the time I'd never thought of it. Every other bunk was alternating heads and feet so you couldn't breathe germs over each other, I supposed, and we'd had lectures on hygiene and head lice and things. So I thought that was what she was on about. It wasn't until after the war that I realised what she was concerned about. That's how green I was.

In those war time years Wrens were not sea-going. The slogan was "Join the Wrens, free a man for the fleet" and Barbara Jones' first job was in the Ward Room of HMS "Glendower," which was based in the Butlin's Holiday Camp in Pwllheli:-

It was just serving and waiting, really, but you had every other afternoon off and every fourth day you were off from mid-day. The hours were lovely. And the people, the girls I worked with and the officers, they were all very nice. What the life taught me was to understand other people. I don't think I'd ever heard of a Scouse person or a Geordie until I joined up and then, suddenly, there were all these different voices and accents all around. I'd be asked what part of Scotland I came from or whereabouts in Ireland, north or south.

I was at "Glendower" for about eighteen months. She was a training ship, what we called a stone frigate. So, of course, there were dances in the evenings and we had a ship's cinema and a drama group. In the evenings you could go into Pwllheli to see a film but you rarely saw the end because you'd have to catch the train back to camp. And, of course, the films usually broke down so that just made it worse. After the cinema you'd all rush back over to the railway station. The Wrens had to go in certain carriages, the sailors in others. The guard would come along and lock the doors of the Wrens carriages.

On our afternoons off some of my friends and I would go up to Llanystwmdwy and just throw stones in the river. It was peaceful and very nice there. Sometimes we'd see this rather short old man with lots of thin but grey hair. He used to wear a black trilby with a wide brim and a cloak that had seen better days. He'd often stop and chat, asking us where we were from and whatnot. He's chat for a few minutes and then go off, walking along the river bank. Or he'd sit on a stone. We had no idea who he was, he was just our "little old gentleman." And then we heard that David Lloyd George had died and all the papers had his photograph. It was our little old gentleman.

On the day of his funeral a notice was sent around. Anyone who wanted to go to the funeral could go and so those of us who were used to seeing him decided to attend. It was such a lovely sight and there was wonderful singing. It was a simple funeral. The coffin came up on a farm cart pulled by an old dray horse. It had trails of leaves all over the cart and coffin. And afterwards we looked at the coffin in the grave. Again, there were leaves, lines of leaves, reaching down into the bottom. I remember all the colours. On the other side of the river there were two fields and the people were a mass of colour, all singing the hymns. It was absolutely gorgeous.

After eighteen months at Pwllheli Barbara Jones was given a draft for Plymouth. That's where she was stationed when the war ended:-

They organised a big Victory Parade. I suppose they had them all over the country but with Plymouth being so special for the navy ours was a huge occasion. The navy, of course, had pride of place. In the parade the Marine Band came first, then the sailors and then the Wrens. For some reason we had the US band behind us and they were very jazzy. So with the Marines in front, the Americans behind – well, we weren't the best marchers to begin with but being stuck between those two bands we didn't know which foot to put forward. It must have been the worst marching ever seen.

We all had a demob number and every so often a list would go up and you'd have to check it to see if you were on it. My friend and I – we'd been together since we'd joined up – were going to stay in. We'd just applied for Fleet Mail and then she got homesick. So we both decided to come out when our numbers came up. I often wish I'd stayed in but there we are.

After her demob Barbara Jones returned home to Cardiff. She has lived there ever since.

Griffith John Jones - RAF, Coastal Command
(Pembroke Dock – above the Atlantic - Ireland)

Griffith John Jones, Griff as he was invariably known, joined the RAF on 14th June 1940. Despite an initial desire to become a pilot, he was trained as a wireless operator and special equipment operator. Posted first to Pwllheli for gunnery training, he soon found himself at the air base in Pembroke Dock, PD as it was always known in Coastal Command. The base at PD was, for many years, the largest flying boat base in the world, squadrons of Sunderlands flying out of the place for patrols over the Western Approaches throughout the war years:-

I was given the rank of Sergeant and posted to PD to wait for Operational Training. I didn't fly when I was there because I wasn't operational at that time but they did use me in Signals, to give me something to do, I suppose. The work was mostly at night. One night, in particular, I remember. I came off duty at about midnight and went out of the station gates, uphill to the old school where we were being billeted. Almost as soon as I got into bed there was this whistling noise. I was out and under the bed before the crash came. A stick of bombs had destroyed a lot of houses just down the road.

I also remember the bombing of the oil tanks at Pembroke Dock. Five of the firemen were killed fighting that blaze. Pembroke Dock suffered badly from bombing during the war, not just the tanks but also the houses of the town. They took a real pasting.

One day, being off duty, I was up on the Barrack Hill above the town. I was just sitting there, enjoying the sunshine, when a Walrus flying boat came in to land on the waterway in front of me. I was watching it and, I suppose, it must have hit a log or something because the next minute it leapt into the air and turned about three somersaults. And believe it or not, the crew all walked away unhurt.

The Sunderlands were at PD then. They always gave you a feeling of safety, those Sunderlands. You could see them whenever you walked through the town, moored out on the Haven or pulled up at the air base. As I was with Signals, rather than flying just then, I suppose I had a reasonably easy life. I remember going to Tenby one day and missing the bus back. I had to walk all the way back, about ten or twelve miles. I walked along the railway line and got back early in the morning.

After eighteen months Griff was promoted to Flight Sergeant. By now he was with 206 Squadron, flying Hudsons out of Aldergrove near Belfast:-

Serious bomb damage at Pembroke Dock, one of many British towns that suffered badly during the war.

Our crew consisted of two pilots, navigators, gunners and us, the special equipment operators. We used to vary our duties. Sometimes I'd be on the wireless, sometimes on the guns. You tended to stay with the same crew and that was good because you needed to develop team work. Some trips were as long as 15 hours, out over the Atlantic. That's an incredibly long time to be on patrol. In all, by the end of the war, I had 1021 hours operational flying time. When you add in non-operational flying, my total flying time was 1475 hours.

In all that time, six years, we had seven U Boat sightings. That was quite a lot. You have to remember that some crews never had any, not one during the whole war. We made five attacks, three of them in 1943. And, of course, we sank two subs. The first one was off the coast of Portugal, the second one out in the Atlantic. That time the U Boat fired back at us. Later, when we got back to base, they found shrapnel in the front of the wing. We didn't know we'd got the U Boat until the kill was confirmed after the war – U 338. You didn't feel particularly scared, you were too busy to feel either fear or excitement. Afterwards, when you got back, you felt that you'd done something. That's when the relief set in.

It might seem strange but I was also on the first 1000 bomber raid on Bremen. They pulled in Coastal Command aircraft in order to make up the numbers – Bomber Command couldn't raise enough planes and so they used six of ours. Two of those aircraft were shot down during the raid. I met Joe Speed, one of the survivors from the Coastal Command planes, a few years later. I think he was one of the few to get out.

Our navigator was a New Zealander and one day, out over the mid Atlantic, we flew into very low and very thick cloud cover. If the clouds were too low you had to turn back but it was always a judgement call and this particular day we were low over the waves when, suddenly, the navigator shouted. "Pull her up, Nobby, pull her up!" The pilot pulled back on the stick and our nose slowly rose up into the air. In a trough of the waves below us was a ship. The navigator reckoned we'd have hit her mast if we hadn't got up quickly.

I'd played a lot of sport while at school, even representing Welsh Schoolboys at cricket. And sport in the RAF was excellent. I played rugby and cricket for most of the stations where I was posted and sometimes, if an operation clashed with a game, they'd even bring our flight forward so that I could still play. I can still remember scoring 98 and 92 in one match and getting myself caught out on the boundary in both innings.

Posted to No 53 Squadron Griff flew Flying Fortresses and Liberators in the final stages of the war. Few people realise that the RAF actually flew "Forts" on an operational basis, thinking them the preserve of the US bombing squadrons, but, with their long range potential, they were also ideal aircraft for Coastal Command. In due course, after a period when he was working as an instructor in Scotland, Griff was posted to Nassau in the Bahamas:-

Up until then my only experience of real heat was on a day trip to Barry Island so, now, to find myself in the Bahamas, well it was a great experience. We were converting to Liberators, before starting another tour, and so we just flew and flew. And then, where do you think they sent us? Reykjavik in Iceland. We were all thinking, because we were in the Bahamas, that we'd be sent somewhere hot, somewhere warm. And we pulled Reykjavik. It was mid winter and we were frozen – well, we'd just come from the Bahamas, what else could you expect. We adapted, in time, but it certainly did take time.

Having been promoted to Warrant Officer Griff applied for his commission whilst in the Bahamas. He was appointed Flying Officer before he left the islands:-

We were all waiting for D Day, counting down the hours and days. We had a French Canadian in our crew and he was a professional ice skater before the war. His name was Cecil Le Blanc. Anyway, he went home after his tour of duty and we would write. He'd ask how things were and was there any news about the landings. I'd write back and say there were no indications. I wrote that, as usual, on one day and the very next day the landings took place. I had to write and tell him that my previous letter was wrong.

VE Day was celebrated while we were on our way back from Iceland. We were posted to St David's, back in Pembrokeshire, and so that was where we celebrated the occasion. The Squadron was then transferred to Transport Command. We'd never used oxygen when we were hunting U Boats with Coastal Command but we certainly did in Transport.

Griffith John Jones spent six years in the RAF, most of that time being based with Coastal Command, hunting U Boats out over the Atlantic. It was an unromantic war but one that was very necessary to the ultimate success of the Allied forces.

J S Jones – Merchant Navy
(Atlantic convoys – the Far East)

John Jones was born at Ty Gorsaf, the Brecon Station House, in 1920 his father being the youngest station master ever appointed by the Brecon and Merthyr Railway. Until his father's promotion to the Headquarters of the Great Western Railway in Oswestry in 1934, the majority of John's childhood was therefore spent in the immense Station House just north of the Brecon Beacons. Despite being land-locked for most of his childhood, however, John had always had dreams of a life spent on the oceans of the world:-

I had always wanted to go to sea. I had an Uncle who was an engineer with the Bank Line from Glasgow and he would come home every two years or so and

John Jones (left) and ship mates at Alexandria, October 1942.

enthral my brother, sister and me with tales of life afloat. I read everything I could lay my hands on about the sea and ships and wanted to join as soon as I was sixteen. My father was clear, however, that I had to matriculate first. Then the war came.

My sister was at Oxford and I can honestly say that the war released me from following the same path. The outbreak of war was, literally, an escape route to adventure for me. I had a friend, Geoff, who had gone to sea as a cadet but he'd broken his indentures and got himself blacklisted, as they called it then. Anyway he came along, I packed a bag and together we headed off to the Shipping Office in Cardiff. It was a bare, dismal place, full of seamen waiting for ships.

From time to time the clerk behind the grille would call out something like "Two AB's and a greaser" or "Six firemen and a bosun" and there would be a rush for the counter, Discharge Books in hand. The lucky ones would be let through to the back room to see the appropriate agent and Chief Officer or Chief Engineer of the various ships and to be told where their vessels were berthed. In effect, it was a Labour Exchange for unemployed seamen.

I hadn't got a Discharge Book at that stage and Geoff, because he had been "black listed," could have had a bit of a problem. But, nevertheless, they sent us to a ship called the "David Livingstone." Unfortunately, they couldn't take the two of us and we wanted to stay together. So we "worked by" on the ship - working on her while she was sitting there in dock - for a couple of days and that helped me find my way around the complicated workings of a cargo ship.

We dossed down in Cory's Mission to Seamen in Bute Street. It cost one shilling a night, bed and breakfast. We slept in these topless cubicles and the food was typical ship's fare – salt fish, curry and rice, burgoo and so on. Tiger Bay, then, was the old Tiger Bay of legend, a separate community of tiny terraced houses and mysterious little ethnic eating places. There were battered pubs and a hundred different nationalities around the area.

Eventually I had a chance of a ship and Geoff suggested that I sign

Going aloft to relieve the lookout, John Jones during the war years.

on, get some experience and also a Discharge Book. He was confident that he would get a berth soon enough. So that's what I did. I joined the "New Westminster City," one of the Reardon Smith cargo fleet. She was a coal burner, 2882 tons, and was the smallest deep-sea vessel I ever sailed in. I joined her while she was lying at Port Talbot.

John's friend soon obtained a berth on a coaster sailing to Portugal and, having made arrangements to keep in touch, the two friends went their separate ways. During the next few years John Jones sailed on eight different ships, two oil tankers amongst them. He was serving at the very end of an era, the last days of the coal burners. Four of the ships he sailed in were fuelled by coal and conditions were not easy:-

The food was terrible, just curry and rice. There were no vegetables or fruit unless you were lucky enough to be out east. The first few ships I sailed in didn't even have fridges. There were ice boxes but once the ice had melted you'd had it. The only items the company provided me with were a battered zinc bucket and my "donkey's breakfast," a palliasse filled with straw. And they logged sixpence from my pay for the privilege.

For my first voyage we left Cardiff and sailed along the coast to Milford Haven where we joined a small convoy. They didn't tell us our destination – they didn't during the war years - but we knew we were bound either for Canada or the USA. We ended up in La Fontaine, a suburb of Montreal, and took two weeks to load our cargo. At Halifax we joined Convoy HX 49 for the return trip, about 25 to 30 ships with just two escorts. And on the way back to Britain we were attacked by Gunter Prien in the U47. Of course I didn't know it at the time but from what I've read since, books and various sources, it was obviously Prien. The ship next in line to us was hit and sunk but he missed us, thank goodness. She was an oil tanker called the "San Fernando" and went up in seconds, a great explosion and clouds of black smoke. In two days they sank four ships from the convoy.

I mostly sailed out of Liverpool and the sailors, the various crews, were amazing. We had all sorts, men of seventy and boys of fifteen, and they were all quite articulate. Most of those sailors were true philosophers, they could discuss anything. They all read a lot, of course. Well, there wasn't much else to do. We had these book boxes delivered to the ship – I don't know who chose them but they did a brilliant job. And the crew would all discuss the books so intelligently. I was a Grammar School boy but I was put in my place quite quickly.

Some of the crew were real old "salts," men who'd been at sea for years. The Liverpool firemen I remember in particular. Theirs was a terrible job, down there in the engine rooms, shovelling coal. Most of them came off the Scotty Road and they were real hard men. They were, I suppose, the descendents of the old windjammer men.

John was lucky, he was never torpedoed. By the law of averages he probably should have been as he sailed across the Atlantic so many times. He also sailed into the Indian and Pacific Oceans and even ventured into the Mediterranean, carrying aviation spirit for the El Alamein campaign:-

I went all over the place, out to Australia and into the Caribbean. The early trips out east always took us around the Cape but later, once the campaigns in the Mediterranean were over and the Suez Canal was opened up, we were able to shorten the route. The voyages were always long, mind you – well, the ships did 8 knots at best so a voyage was always going to take a long time. I did one of 12 months and one of 14 months and, of course, you rarely or never got mail. My parents could have been dead for all I knew. Lots of the boys came back from a voyage to find their homes had been bombed. Liverpool took a bad hammering and that's where so many of them came from. I was lucky because my family was living in the country but the city boys didn't have that luxury. They'd get the bad news, just turn round and go straight back out to sea.

We always had plenty of work to do and even in the coldest weather we sometimes worked on stages slung over the ship's side, chipping rust, red-leading and painting. It was a dangerous time but, you know, I never once saw any sign of panic. During that very first attack by Prien, the behaviour of the Somali boys on board was incredible. They used to get down and pray five times a day, they really put us to shame. But during that first attack our escorts dropped depth charges and there were bangs and crashes going off all over the place. The Somali lads just calmly rolled up their prayer mats and started getting ready to climb into the boats. No panic, no fear, they were amazing.

One air attack in particular I remember very well. We were in the Bay of

Biscay and we were the Commodore's ship at the time. These bombs came down and straddled us. The skin of the ship was so thin that when the bombs dropped the blast blew out all the lights. And yet the boys in the engine room just carried on working, no fuss. They were all remarkable men, those merchant seamen.

After a while I volunteered as a DEMS gunner. They put a stern gun on the ships, 4 inch or 4.7 inch usually, plus some small arms and, as the war progressed, all sorts of other junk – rockets, Bofors guns and so on. Anyway, I trained as a gunner. It was done under the auspices of the Royal Navy, down on the "Eaglet," an old gunnery training ship. It was a very intensive course, run on strict naval lines. They had these big surface guns mounted in a huge shed alongside the ship and the old gunnery instructors ran us through the drills over and over again until we could work every position on the gun. To my surprise I passed out "Highly Commended" and was able to command sixpence a day as a Seaman/Gunner.

I was gunner on a twin barrel cannon, a long distance anti-aircraft weapon. They were very powerful shells, armour-piercing, and you had to have a harness to keep you safe. I must have fired hundreds of shells at enemy aircraft. Mind you, they weren't stupid, they kept pretty high up, out of range. What you did was to put up a box barrage and hope to keep them away.

In July 1943 I signed on the "Themistocles," a big Shaw, Savill Line ship of 13,000 tons. My Oerlikon gun was in a pit by the bridge and this day we'd fired so many rounds that I was standing on the cartridge cases. We had to get the deck boy – only a youngster of 14 years – to get rid of them. He was kneeling down, shovelling them into a sack. When he looked up all Hell was going on. The ship alongside us was hit and went down in four minutes. There were no survivors. On the other side of us the next ship had her steering gear damaged and she was going round and round in circles. Up above there were puffs of smoke everywhere. The young lad would look up every so often and just say "'kin Hell!" It was a good Liverpool expression that seemed to sum up what was happening.

U Boats, Stuka dive bombers, high level bombers, John Jones saw them all during his time in the Merchant Navy. One of the most interesting events of his career was when he became a DBS (Distressed British Seaman) in New York. He had signed on with the "Empire Widgeon," an American-built cargo vessel handed over to Britain under the Lease-Lend arrangements:-

It was a very civilised life on board the "Empire Widgeon." The crew all lived amidships in cabins and we even had showers and a proper mess room. We left Newport in November and sailed out to India and East Africa, carrying manganese ore. We were out in the Indian Ocean for a long time, then crossed the Atlantic and arrived off the Statue of Liberty on 8th April 1942. Of course, by now, America had come into the war and it transpired that the US Government wanted their ship back. The ship and her cargo were taken over by the Yanks and the crew, from Captain to cabin boy, had to quit the ship.

They put us into the Hotel Imperial on 33rd Street. It had lots of potted palms everywhere, very 20s or 30s. We all expected Groucho Marx or Mary Pickford to suddenly appear from behind them. We were paid off in US dollars and became Distressed British Seamen awaiting passage home. We still had to report to the Shipping Office every day and if there was a vacancy – say a man had been injured or taken ill – you had to take the berth. That would have meant another voyage, maybe for two years, out of New York.

I had an aunt in Long Island so after one night in the Imperial I went up there to stay with her and commuted back into New York every day. Meanwhile the boys in the city were spending their money – Dempsey's Bar, with the great fighter himself present, was one of their most popular haunts. I wanted to send some money home so I went to Barclay's Bank and a Welshman who was working there cabled it home for me. Mind you, I did spend money as well. I bought a suit for 27 dollars, about £4 in those days. It was, according to the American fashion of the day, a "zoot suit," as worn by the up and coming teenage idol Frank Sinatra. It was a grey herring bone with a long jacket and sloping shoulders. I thought I was a real "Jack the lad" but my aunt said I looked like a bookies' clerk. My mates said I looked like a different sort of clerk altogether!

Eventually they decided to ship us home. They put us on a train at Grand Central Station, full of people injured or sick after their ships had been sunk by U Boats. The whole of the American coast was lit up, no Black Out, and ships were just silhouetted against the lights. Dozens of them were sunk by the Germans and the boys we saw on that New York train were the survivors. It was a Pullman train with bunks that you pulled out at night. Two nights we were on it, going up through New Hampshire and into Canada. We pulled into Halifax, right into the docks, and boarded the "Orcades." As we boarded I was given a card marked "Deck F, Room 446, Berth Mat." And it meant what it said. I was sleeping on a mat on the floor, a thin mattress on the deck of a six berth cabin. The injured boys were in the bunks.

The Captain came on the Tannoy and welcomed us on board. "This ship," he said, "was built to carry 1000 passengers in peace time. Now we have 4000 on board. You can expect a little discomfort." There were troops on board as well, mostly Canadians and they spent the passage playing poker – until mal de mer set in. Us Merchant Navy men were excused fatigues and spent most of the trip walking up and down the promenade deck keeping a professional eye on the number and availability of lifeboats. The convoy was attacked but what I remember most is seeing one of the ship's stoke-hold gang, clad only in singlet and dungarees, jump from the foc'sle head into the grey ocean. His mind had cracked after who knows what experiences. Nothing could be done. The convoy had to plough on and in any case he'd probably been sucked in by the churning propellers and mangled.

I was never really interested in promotion. I could have gone to Nautical College in Liverpool. You could take your ticket from the foc'sle in those days, although I never heard of anyone actually doing it. But my eyesight was considered too bad, even though I never wore glasses at sea and kept lookout throughout the war. So I couldn't follow the course. I did make one trip as a bosun, after the original bosun had jumped ship. Some of the apprentices on board stirred up trouble, said that he'd never brought a ship home. And several of the boys left the ship because of that. There was always a great deal of superstition at sea.

The "Samtrusty" football team, John Jones is third from the left in the back row.

I made one trip up to Russia, almost at the end of the war. Murmansk was the worst place you can ever imagine. The place and the people had been the victims of total war. They'd had a terrible time of it and our ship was unloaded by women. There were no men anywhere around – I suppose they were all away fighting. I almost missed my ship in Archangel. I was walking down alongside the river when, suddenly, I saw her disappearing down the river ahead of me. Imagine the panic! But she was just moving berth.

When the war ended John was on a ship in the Pacific, carrying grain. His ship, the SS "Samtrusty," was actually one of the first Allied ships to sail into Singapore after the end of hostilities:-

The place was in a terrible state and was still under martial law. We were told not to drink the liquor because, they said, the Japs had poisoned it. Whether they had or not I really don't know. The only money around was Japanese and we took cigarettes to use as currency. They would always buy you a meal.

We had about a hundred Japanese prisoners working on the ship every day, just the "other ranks" as under the Geneva Convention the officers did not have to work. We had to use the derricks to unload as the Americans had bombed the docks and destroyed all the cranes. Several of the Japanese prisoners were injured working down in the hold. We had an electric winch and it was very jumpy. One day it crushed a prisoner's foot. He was so impassive, he just controlled his pain.

Another time we were unloading crates that had been bound with thin strips of metal. The tacks came loose and the wire sprang up and cut this Japanese soldier's throat. Quick as a flash, he just whipped off his cap and kepi and wrapped them right around his own throat.

We were away for about a year after the war finished. And I signed on for another voyage after that, carrying copper from Mozambique. Then it was off to the west coast of Africa where we loaded palm kernels for soap making. By then I'd had enough and so when we got back I sold all my gear and headed home. Everyone said "You'll be back" but I never did. My father was worried about me and thought I'd be spending my life at sea as an AB. All my friends were going off to University and he thought I was going to the dogs!

John Jones' father promptly investigated the possibilities of teacher training for his son, something John had long wanted to do. For a while he worked as an uncertificated teacher but he was soon called up to college and, after completing his training, found himself a post in one of the new secondary modern schools in Oswestry. The first thing he was given was a cane.

William Oswald Jones - Royal Navy
(Atlantic – Pacific - Indian Ocean – around the world)

Bill Jones with his wife Sal and daughter Freda, 1940-41.

Bill Jones was born in 1913 and worked as a coal miner in the Ebbw Vale area for many years. When Pinchie Colliery closed he was employed for a time in the steelworks at Ebbw Vale before being called up for service in the navy in 1941. He lived in Llanelly Hill, close to Brynmawr, and had been married in 1938. His first daughter, Freda, was born in 1940.

Sadly, Bill died in 1989 but his story is told here from a variety of different sources. To begin with there are notes made by his late wife Sarah - always called Sal by Bill and the family. Then there are the memories of his youngest daughter Mrs Gwyllis Hartshorn. Finally, there are letters, comments and a diary kept by Bill himself:-

Mrs Sarah (Sal) Jones

When Hitler declared war we had absolutely nothing so that it really hit us hard. Suddenly everyone, men, women and children, had to have identity cards. There was a rush from having no work to having plenty of it – a rush against time to prepare for war. We had no planes or bombs so there was real

147

chaos for a while. The country was frantically building aircraft, preparing ships, making ammunition and calling up men and women to serve their country.

Then came real hardship – rationing of food, clothes and fuel. I received just £2.25 a week to keep my daughter and myself. My husband had been called up to serve in the Royal Navy and things were tight. I had to use some of my clothes to make clothes for my daughter. I would make rag mats from sacks and old clothes or coats. I would stay up all night to make enough of them – I would be able to get ten shillings for a full sized mat. Our rations were in ounces, usually about two ounces of butter, one rasher of bacon each, two ounces of tea, hardly any fruit at all. There was very little in the way of vegetables. I was usually able to get about three eggs a week from a neighbour and half a pint of milk each day.

Bill went into the navy on 7th December 1941 and was sent to HMS "Raleigh" at Plymouth to undergo training. The Nissen Hut next to his was destroyed during an air raid and all the men in there were killed. He helped to "pick up the pieces," using a hat box for some of the more unsavoury tasks.

With his training complete Bill Jones had a brief period of leave and then travelled to Greenock in Scotland to join his ship. However, he was late returning from leave and arrived at the port only to find himself in trouble with the authorities. Overstaying leave was a punishable offence and Bill was duly put in "the slammer" for a brief period. However, as he wrote in his diary, it was a risk worth taking in order to see his family for a few more hours:-

Bill Jones

I go out from here at 2.15. I hope it will be the last time I'm in here but I've no regrets. I'd risk it again to try and be with Sal and Freda for a few hours. They are worth any punishment, the best wife and baby any man could wish for. May God see fit to send me back to them safely in the near future. I know they will never be happy without me. I'm very proud to know that but I, too, love them and I thank God for binding my life with them. We will always be happy together – apart we shall be unhappy.

I think I will bring these notes to an end. I'm glad I got them out all right. So I close this diary with one wish in my heart - that I'll soon be back with my wife and baby. May God bless and keep them safe until I return to them.

Released from Detention, Bill Jones found that his original ship had sailed, something of a fortunate accident for him as the ship was later sunk out in the Atlantic. Instead, he joined the crew of HMS "Engadine," an aircraft transport ship. Built at Dumbarton as the merchant vessel "Clan Bucanan," she was launched in May 1941 and subsequently commissioned into the Royal Navy. The "Engadine" had no flight deck and was a transport ship rather than an aircraft carrier in the traditional sense:-

Mrs Hartshorn

My father joined the "Engadine" for her three week sea trials and didn't get home for the next three and a half years. At least my mother managed to travel to Greenock by train in order to see him off.

Out in the Atlantic they hit such bad weather that it was impossible for the men on duty on the guns to get back below decks. All the men were certain that Dad had been washed overboard in the gale but he managed to strap himself into the gun pit and survived. Three days he was out there, without food or water.

The "Engadine" was due to enter Pearl Harbour on the very day that the place was bombed but she was delayed by bad weather and actually arrived on the day after the bombing – another lucky delay for Dad. A bit later, out in the Pacific, they were loading a carrier with aircraft. The alarm went and they were told to "get out of it." Just an hour later the ship they had been loading was sunk.

The pangs and pain of separation for sensitive and caring men like Bill are clear to see. And yet they carried on doing their duty, knowing that the quickest and safest way to get home was to see the job done as efficiently as possible. They hid their feelings from their mates and only in letters home, particularly at times like Christmas, did they let down their guard:-

Bill Jones (letter to his wife)

My Darling Wife and Daughter

It will be impossible for this to be a Merry Xmas for you. You will be in my thoughts more than ever on the 25th. Distance cannot lessen my love for you, dearest. Let us both pray that the last lines of that verse "Women" will come true in the very near future. May God bless you both.

From your Bill.

Bill Jones (letter to his mother)

Dear Mum

I trust you are in perfect health and all goes well. I dare say, as always, there is plenty going on around there to keep you occupied. I'm sure Freda is enough to keep you busy anyway. Does she still talk of me? I hope that it won't be many more months before I'll be able to trot her around a bit. I'm in the best of health, Mum, never felt better. If I were only home! It seems the doll I sent for Freda caused some excitement. I'm so glad it got home OK. I trust she is making use of it. Well, cheerio, Mum. May we meet again soon.

Your ever loving son.

The crest of HMS "Engadine," aircraft transport ship.

During his three and a half years in the navy Bill travelled right around the world. Other ranks and naval ratings were forbidden to keep diaries but, despite this, Bill – and many others like him – managed to keep a record (including photographs) of the many places they visited:-

Bill Jones

We travelled approximately 140,000 miles, the cruise lasting from December 1941 until July 1944. I crossed the Equator twelve times and the International Date Line five times. During the cruise I passed through both the Suez and Panama Canals and sailed in the North and South Atlantic, the North and South Pacific, the Indian Ocean, the Coral Sea, the Caribbean, the Mediterranean and the Red Sea.

I went to some amazing places – imagine a bloke from Lanelly Hill standing on top of the Empire State building. Because of the places we went all of the crew were awarded medals that many sailors didn't usually get, things like the Burma Star (with the Pacific Bar) and the Africa Star.

The food on board the "Engadine" wasn't too bad. For breakfast on Sunday we had bacon and eggs, then for lunch there were soup, pork chops, string beans, roast potatoes and prunes and custard for desert. We'd have buns and bread and butter for tea, then preserved meat and beetroot for supper. The meals on other days weren't too bad either – roast lamb, beef, meat pudding, that sort of thing. There was always supper as well as tea.

As well as visiting strange and exotic places – places that no Welsh miner would ever have dreamed of seeing – Bill met dozens of interesting people during his travels:-

Mrs Gwyllis Hartshorn

Dad made some lovely friends in the USA. The best were Cyril and Marge Thomas from San Diego. They used to send food parcels and letters to Mam, something that we really appreciated in those days of rationing. After the war they used to visit us quite regularly for many years. Other friends he made, also from San Diego, were the Greens. In South Africa he met the Weir family. They were lovely people. They wanted Mam and Dad to go out there and live with them after the war.

Mam and Dad hated being apart, they never wanted to be away from each other. So Mam wrote to the government and told them that he was a miner. There was a great shortage of miners and they needed every ounce of coal they could get for the war effort. It was agreed that he could be discharged but, of course, he was sailing around the world. So his Discharge Papers followed him around the globe.

A letter, dated 2nd June 1944, from the Admiralty to the MP G Daggar, Esq, who had become involved in the application, gave the official news that Bill could be discharged from the navy:-

I write on behalf of the First Lord in reply to your letter of May 20th about Able Seaman W O Jones who has applied to be allowed to return to coal mining. Normally a man who has volunteered for colliery employment is not drafted abroad until a decision on his application has been given, but in view of the numerous applications received, manning requirements may make it impossible to follow that course in every instance.

You will, however, be pleased to learn that arrangements are being made for the release of Jones for colliery employment as soon as he returns to the United Kingdom in a few weeks time. You will appreciate that his Commanding Officer is in a better position to know what is the first available opportunity for Jones' return.

Bill Jones was formally discharged on 4th April 1944 and returned home to Llanelly Hill where he resumed his former employment. Because of his service in the Royal

Bill Jones and friends on top of the Empire State Building in New York.

Navy he was, from that point onwards, known as Bill Jones Sailor in the area. Blessed with a beautiful singing voice, Bill almost took to the professional stage after he took a relative to an audition and was heard singing himself. Transport was not easy in 1949, however, and Bill was late for his own audition. By the time he arrived the star of the show, Kenneth Griffiths, had gone and Bill's chance went with him.

Bill Jones died on 7th October 1989. He and his beloved Sal had said that they never wanted to be parted again, after his three years in the navy, and exactly one month later, on 7th November, Sal suffered a stroke and died.

Peter Leech – Royal Navy
(submarines – Rosyth, Scotland)

Peter Leech was born in Ipswich but by 1939 his family had moved to Newport in South Wales. He did not want to wait to be called up as he had already decided on his career and in 1941, as soon as he was old enough, he joined the Royal Navy as a Boy Entrant:-

The sea, that was what I wanted, I wanted a career at sea. So as soon as I was able I joined the navy. I went into the submarine arm straight away, as soon as I'd done my training. It's difficult to say why I chose submarines – lots of the men in the submarine arm during the war didn't have a choice where they went. I volunteered for the submarine service.

I suppose there was the fact that you got extra pay for being in submarines. That had to play a part. But mostly, to be in boats – and submarines were always called boats – meant that you were a little bit special. Submariners were always regarded as individualists, a bit unusual, a bit different. I don't think that the surface seamen, the ordinary sailors, liked us very much. And they were probably right. We really did think of ourselves as being a bit special.

I spent most of the war up in Rosyth in Scotland. Remember, I was a Boy Entrant, not a Hostilities Only rating. So the training took some time and I was up in Scotland, doing my training, until the summer of 1945. When I did finally qualify the war in Europe was over, that had ended a month or so before. The war against the Japanese, of course, was still going on and, I suppose, that was where we were intended to go. As I say, I went into submarines once I completed my training.

Peter Leech was posted to HMS "Sentinal" and found that, no matter how the members of the submarine service viewed themselves, no matter how elite they thought they were, conditions on board the submarines were not always first class:-

Well, it wasn't easy, far from it, but you coped. You had to, there was no choice. We were quite young, most of us, and so we were quite happy roughing it. You didn't wash very often because fresh water was not always readily available. One bowl of water between everybody, that's how it was most of the time. You always tried to be first in the line but it didn't really matter.

The war out in the east finished before we could get involved so, really, my only experience of the Second World War was training and listening to the stories of all the men who were involved.

The thing I remember most is the "Perishers." That was the commanding officers' qualifying course. It was something all the skippers had to do if they wanted to command one of our submarines. It was pretty brutal stuff, that training. The navy didn't want anyone but the very best so the would-be COs had to succeed on the course or perish in the attempt – hence the name.

Of course, what that meant was that they were on your back all the time. Nobody wanted to fail and they weren't going to let up for a second. When our boat was involved with the "Perishers" we were on the go, morning to night. We'd be diving, then surfacing and then before we knew what was happening they had us diving once again. It was really hard work.

You had to sign on for submarines every three years and I suppose that was a good idea. It gave you the chance to consider your situation. If you wanted a change you could come out after your three years were up.

As a Boy Entrant and a regular serviceman Peter Leech did not come out of the navy when peace was declared in 1945. He remained in the service, operating mostly in submarines, until December 1956 when he finally retired and came ashore.

James Edward Luen – Merchant Navy
(South Atlantic – death in the North Atlantic)

The following story was told by Mrs Jenny Reynolds, the niece of James (Jim) Luen who died in November 1939 while serving on board the "Harlingen." In the years before the Second World War the Luen's were a well known family in Barry, Jim's mother Rebecca having literally established the Cold Knap area of the town. Almost single handed she established and ran the Cold Knap Hotel and funded the building of many of the properties in the area. Many of the boys in the family became sailors, as Mrs Reynolds recalls:-

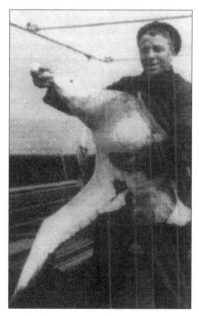

Jim Luen holding the albatross that fell onto the deck of his ship.

My Uncle Jim was one of eight children born to Rebecca and Albert Luen. Two of the children, Brinley and Jim himself, went to sea and both became sea captains. The family had a long-seated connection with the sea, originating from St Malo in France. For years the family ran ships in and out of St Malo, sailing across to Jersey and places like that. They moved to the Penarth and Barry area around the end of the nineteenth century, when the ports of South Wales were busy and work was plentiful.

Uncle Jim was a lovely man, a really nice guy. I was only a child, of course, so I only remember him as an Uncle who came home from sea every so often but everyone said that he was a wonderful person. I remember him bringing me presents home and that was nice because he had two daughters of his own. He didn't have to think of me but he always did.

There is a lovely story about Jim when he was a young boy, attending school in Barry. It seems that he got into a row with the teacher and it resulted in the man shouting at him. Jim apparently jumped to his feet and leapt through the open window. Nobody saw him again for two years. Imagine that, two whole years! Then, one day, his mother at the Cold Knap Hotel received a telephone call – well, having a hotel she was one of the few people in town to possess a phone. The call was from Jim. He had been at sea for the two years he'd been missing and his ship had just docked in Cardiff. Could she bring him some clothes and shoes, he wanted to know. Rebecca set off and brought him back home. Of course he went back to sea soon afterwards but at least now they knew where he was.

Jim Luen did return to sea and slowly but surely worked his way up the ranks. When war broke out in 1939 he was serving as Chief Officer on the Scandinavian cargo ship "Harlingen." The ship was in the Magellan Straits off the coast of South America and there a most unusual occurrence took place:-

One day an albatross just fell onto the deck of the ship. The birds follow the ships, looking for food, and an albatross can travel thousands of miles, just gliding along. This one had obviously become exhausted and just dropped down onto the deck. Uncle Jim picked it up and even had his photograph taken with the bird in his arms. It was enormous, having a wing span of 18 feet. They let the bird recover and, in the end, it simply flew off and was lost to view. That was probably a good thing as sailors are terribly superstitious and none of them would have wanted a dead albatross on their hands.

I don't know if it did Uncle Jim much good as he was drowned soon after that. On 25th November 1939 the "Harlingen" was off the eastern coast of Canada, off Nova Scotia, when they received a radio message. The ship was told to clear the area immediately as there were U Boats in the vicinity. The only trouble was the propeller was fouled, tangled with weeds, and she couldn't move. The weather was terrible. There were reports of icebergs in the area and a full gale was blowing. Huge waves were smashing into the ship, crashing over the side, and the wind was howling through the rigging.

The Captain asked for a volunteer to go over the side and clear the propeller. Uncle Jim volunteered. They tied ropes around his waist and he took a knife and over he went. It must have been terrible with the waves hammering into him. And the cold would have been awful. But he did it, he untangled the propeller and, cheering and shouting, the crew hauled him back onto the deck.

Uncle Jim was on the deck, standing there as the crew untied him. At that very moment a huge wave hit the "Harlingen" and poor Uncle Jim was washed overboard. He was never seen again. Of course they searched for him but they never found him and with the U Boat warning they couldn't afford to hang around for long. So they had to abandon the search. It was terrible, to die like that after such a brave deed, so tragic.

They made Jim a posthumous Captain in recognition of his bravery but the news of his death probably helped kill his mother. Jim had always been her favourite son and his death came hard on the heels of the army requisitioning the Cold Knap Hotel. His death, and losing the hotel, albeit temporarily, just devastated her. She was a broken woman and she fell one day and broke her hip. She never recovered and died soon afterwards.

I remember the day we received the news of Uncle Jim's death. It was the first time I knew that grown-ups cried. There was crying all over the place that day, it was awful. I was only eight at the time so I didn't really understand, I just saw all these adults weeping and wailing all over the place.

For Jim Luen's widow another problem soon surfaced. Although he had been made a Captain posthumously, his substantive rank at the time of his death was Chief Officer:-

When Uncle Jim's pension arrived his widow soon discovered that she was being paid only as the widow of a Chief Officer. A Captain's pension would have been worth so much more. So up to the Houses of Parliament she went and she began lobbying the members. She even petitioned Winston Churchill himself – this was in the days before he became Prime Minister. I think he was First Lord of the Admiralty at the time. Anyway she made such a nuisance of herself that they granted her a full pension. It was the least he deserved.

Uncle Jim was the second of the brothers to be made Captain as Uncle Brinley was already serving at that rank. The other brothers didn't go to sea. Clive was, we think, something to do with MI 5, Dudley was an electrician and Sid a schoolmaster. He was a bit of a character, was Uncle Sid. As well as teaching he used to write a column in the Barry and District News. He'd been a Colonel in the Black Watch during the First World War and I remember once seeing him come down the road in his kilt and full military regalia. He was a really handsome man in that outfit.

I often think about Uncle Jim, his bravery and courage. I think that to die in the way that he did was so wasteful. It was cruel, I think, more than anything else. I mean, he'd carried out his duty, saved the ship, and then, to die in that way, well it didn't make any sense.

Jim Luen's heroic action in going over the side of the ship to clear her propellers probably saved the lives of every man on board the "Harlingen." To die in the way he did symbolises the cruelty and utter futility of war. Merchant seamen faced the prospect of sudden death like that every day of their working lives but for the families and friends back home it was a hard cross to bear.

Thomas Marshall – Merchant Navy
(torpedoed in the South Atlantic)

Thomas Marshall has now, sadly, died and the following account of his wartime adventures has been told by his son Douglas. Born in June 1894, Thomas Marshall served in the Merchant Navy for many years, making several voyages as a Bosun. He finally decided to leave the sea in 1938. When war broke out the following year his immediate reaction was to try to join the army. He was too old, however, and wanting to "do his bit" he decided to go back to sea. He signed on as an AB and made two voyages during the war years:-

Dad ran away to sea when he was just 14 years old and, I suppose, spent most of his life in the Merchant Navy – apart from the First World War when he was in the army. He was a Sergeant in Haig's HQ platoon. Strangely, both Haig and my father had been born in Kirkaldy and they also had the same birthday, 18th June. He even called me Douglas Haig Marshall, after the Field Marshall. After the war Dad spent twelve to eighteen months with the Black and Tans in Ireland but he soon gave that up and went back to sea. He met my mother in Tiger Bay when he docked in Cardiff and they were married soon afterwards.

Dad and Mam moved up to Jarrow for a brief period and they were there during the time of the General Strike and then the Jarrow March. Dad was involved with that and was one of the men who marched all the way to London. He soon went back to sea – I can remember being taken out to his ship in a rowing boat, in order to see him before he sailed off on one of his voyages.

Rescue at sea, Thomas Marshall and the survivors of the "Baron Ogilvy."

Our family moved back to Cardiff, to the Ely area of the city, because that was where my mother's family came from. Dad was at sea but he left the ship in Cardiff and came ashore for good – at least that was the intention, until the war broke out. After the army turned him down he tried the ARP, the Home Guard and the fire service but they were all too tame for him. He wanted more adventure so going back to sea was more or less inevitable.

My father's first ship during the war was the "Empire Trader." It was a fairly uneventful voyage and he survived that one quite well. Then, on 15th July 1942, he signed on the "Baron Ogilvy" at Cardiff.

Thomas and his ship were heading for the South Atlantic. And there, on 29th September 1942, the "Baron Ogilvy" was torpedoed and sunk by a U Boat:-

The U Boat surfaced after the ship was hit and the crew were taking to the lifeboat. Dad never spoke much about the sinking, never said how he was feeling or what it was like. He was a quiet sort of man, even though he loved the adventurous life style. He never bragged about his adventures or the things he'd done. And I suppose he really wanted to forget about the torpedoing.

Anyway the U Boat came to the surface once the "Baron Ogilvy" had gone down. It pulled alongside the lifeboat and the Germans began questioning the crew. They wanted the Captain and so, rather than hand him over, the crew simply hid him in the bottom of the lifeboat. The Germans gave up the search and disappeared over the horizon, leaving the boat and the survivors adrift in the ocean. There were about thirty of them, all crammed into the one tiny lifeboat.

They were adrift for seven days and, once again, Dad never said much about the experience. He did say they were very short of food and water, wondering what was going to happen. But apart from that he never said too much about the experience. The longer they were adrift, of course, the worse conditions would have been. Eventually, however, they were picked up by a Portuguese cargo ship called the "Mousinho." Somebody on the ship stood there at the railings and took photographs as they were being rescued. And later he gave them to my father – I've still got them.

Once the survivors were on board the "Mousinho" they got lines or ropes onto the lifeboat and winched it up on deck – again, it was all captured on film by that anonymous camera man. The "Mousinho" was bound for Cape Town and so that's where the survivors were taken. They landed and had to wait for a ship back to Britain. It took several months but, at last, they managed to get back to this country.

Back in Cardiff we received a letter to say that my father's ship had been sunk. It didn't say if he was dead or alive, just that the ship had been sunk. It was a month before we knew he was safe. I remember writing in my diary at the time – "26th October. My father is safe and has landed in Cape Town."

When Thomas Marshall came home either he or his wife Lillian decided that enough was enough. He was discharged from the Merchant Navy on 27th March 1943. After that he worked in Cardiff and Barry Docks as a rigger, unloading the full cargo ships as they came into port. After the war he found a job in the Ely paper mills, his urge for adventure finally satisfied. Thomas Marshall died in the 1960s.

John McKeown – Merchant and Royal Navy
(convoys - North Atlantic – accident at sea - aircraft carrier)

Although he lives now in Prestatyn, John McKeown was born in the Liverpool area, just four hundred yards from the Gladstone Docks in Bootle. Indeed, the docks were his playground as a child, as they were for most young boys in the area, and so it was inevitable that the lure of the sea should be strong:-

It had always been my ambition to get away to sea. Playing in the docks as a child we used to see all the sailors and we would often make friends with them. Lascars, in particular, the poorest of the Indian sailors, were always very friendly. They were good people, those Indians, really nice.

I remember getting my first ship. "So you want to go to sea, son?" asked the clerk. I said "Yes please." And that was it, I was off. I was only fifteen years old but I'd got my first ship. She was the SS "Oropesa" and was bound for South America. It was September 1939.

I had signed on as Engineers' Boy. On board ship I was known as "Little Eng." – Eng. being short for Engineer - and my opposite number was called "Big Eng." because he had such a big nose. We sailed from Liverpool that September in my first convoy. For three days we had an escort but then the destroyers left us to go back and escort out the next convoy. We knew what to expect. That night I slept fully booted and spurred on the top of my bunk, lifebelt ready to hand. We were attacked and I grew up, quickly.

The ship just in front of us was torpedoed and went down fast. We couldn't stop to pick up survivors; that would have been asking for it. So we just ploughed on, hoping that the next torpedo wouldn't be in our belly. The convoy just scattered to the four winds. Well, there was no escort and we had to try to survive as best we could.

The very next day John was detailed to "Dump the gash," rubbish from the mess room. He picked up the sacks and went aft to throw the rubbish over the stern of the ship, as was the practise. And there he saw an incredible sight:-

Right aft I was astonished to see a periscope sticking up out of the water. It was quite close up to us and, later, I couldn't help wondering if any of the "gash" had got stuck in the periscope. I rather hope it did. I knew what I had to do. I phoned the bridge and told them what I had seen. We picked up speed but kept on course. If we had turned to port or starboard we'd have presented ourselves as an easy target.

We saw and heard several explosions over the horizon and I think we lost five ships from our convoy. But it was early days – things were only to get worse.

Our first landfall was Bermuda and then we sailed on to Havana and Panama. From there we headed south, down the coast of South America. After a few weeks we turned around and headed north towards Halifax in Canada. After all the heat of South America it was so cold in Canada. If your nose was dripping it would turn into icicles, it was that cold. We were in Halifax for about three days. The crew had sent off their mail and said goodbye to their girlfriends. We hauled in the gangways and set off, thinking that we would be home in about two weeks.

We located and joined our convoy and took up our allotted position. The weather was absolutely freezing and soon the convoy ran into patches or banks of fog. It got gradually worse and worse until, off the Grand Banks of Newfoundland – the graveyard of the "Titanic" – we hit thick pea-soup fog. All the ships were blowing their fog horns at intervals but we could only hear those nearest to us as the "pea-souper" dampened down the others. It was very lonely and eerie out there.

And then, suddenly, it happened. There was a terrific collision between us and the "Manchester Regiment". Our bows struck her amidships and her engine rooms were severely damaged. She was abandoned very quickly, even though she was still on a pretty even keel and there seemed to be plenty of time for the crew to get into the lifeboats. When you lower lifeboats the seamen have to work together on the falls, the ropes that hold the boats. If one releases faster than the other then the boat will dip and the people in it will end up in the water.

That's exactly what happened to two of the boats from the "Manchester Regiment." They went down like express trains, tipped out all the men and turned over. They all had lifebelts on but they were no use against the cold. The men struggled for a while but then they just seemed to give up. We tried to rescue them but they just floated past us. Hypothermia was the killer.

We launched our emergency boat, in the charge of the bosun. He was a big, strong, bullish sort of man and he got the boat heading towards one of the upturned lifeboats. There was a black man standing on it, legs apart to keep his balance. It was a choppy sea but the bosun managed to get alongside. He shouted to the man to jump but the chap just couldn't move or speak. He was paralysed. Time was valuable so in one breathless movement the boatswain leapt across onto the upturned boat, hit and grabbed hold of the man, slung him over his shoulder and jumped back into our boat. It must have taken about ten seconds at the most.

The "Oropesa" turned back to Halifax for repairs. Next day the rescued man went looking for our bosun to thank him for knocking him out and saving his life. We spent some time in Halifax, undergoing repair, and then headed back to Liverpool. I signed off and went home. I heard later that the old "Oropesa" was torpedoed on her next trip. I hoped the bosun was safe – no doubt he was.

John spent only two days at home before looking for his next ship. This was the SS "Nova Scotia" and it was not long before a convoy was formed. They sailed from Liverpool and two days out from land came across wreckage from the convoy that had left a few days before:-

That previous convoy was the ill-fated "Children's Convoy." They had put hundreds of children onto a passenger ship and evacuated them to Canada, away from all the bombing. The ship was torpedoed with very heavy loss of life. One boat, I think, was picked up a week later. How they managed to survive with hardly any food and water I'll never know. And the weather, it was a nightmare for them – and their parents.

I left the "Nova Scotia," signed off six weeks later because of the bed bugs. It was so bad I had to sleep with the sheet wound me like a mummy. Not just me, we were all like it. I suppose you could say there were eight mummies in the one cabin! Those bugs got their comeuppance a little later when the ship was torpedoed off Durban in South Africa.

The "Nova Scotia" was carrying a thousand Italian prisoner-of-war when she was torpedoed. There weren't enough lifeboats and there was a dreadful loss of life, Italians and British sailors alike. One of those who died was the boatswain who, apparently, went floating past on the ship's ladder, waving and shouting "Cheerio lads." He didn't survive.

John Mckeown joined the Royal Navy soon after leaving the "Nova Scotia," signing T124X Articles. By this arrangement Merchant Navy men took over the catering sections of RN ships. In John's case it meant that he was still on Merchant Navy pay, a princely sum of £28 per month. He was still only a young lad and was picking up more than many of the old navy hands with whom he was now working:-

I was posted to HMS "Smiter," what we called a "Woolworth's carrier." She had been built very quickly, for war service, in the USA. I remember going down the Mersey one day when one of our sailors fell overboard. As it happened he hit the gun platform and although he was a strong swimmer the fall probably killed him outright. They piped "Man Overboard" and launched the emergency sea boat but it was no use. The boat was being hoisted back on board when "Man Overboard" was piped again. This was unprecedented, very unlikely to happen, but there it was, the second call within the hour.

What had happened was our chief cook had imbibed a little too much rum and some "homemade" brew he had concocted. He was sitting on the stern rail, directly above the propellers, shouting out "I'll save you." And then he jumped. He hit the water and swam out of the ship's wash. He would have drowned but the ship's boat was ready to go and was just in time to save him. He was a lucky man – and he could also have been charged with breaking ship!

Jim McKeown served in the Royal Navy for the next four or five years. His service included time on the aircraft carrier "Empress" and on several of the Cross-Channel ships that had been requisitioned by the Admiralty for use in the Normandy landings. He left these ships just before the invasion took place.

After the war John returned to the Merchant Navy, joining the Cunard Line and serving on board both the "Queen Mary" and "Queen Elizabeth." In total, he spent 50 years at sea.

Aneurin Moller – Royal Navy

(Sinking the "Scharnhorst – the Russian convoys – action in the Channel)

The following story was contributed by Marita Ward, sister of Aneurin Moller. It was quoted in a book published in 1995 and gives a good description of the sinking of the "Scharnhorst" and of the work undertaken by the Royal Navy in escorting the Russian convoys. Aneurin Moller was of Norwegian heritage and came from New Quay in Ceridigion. He joined the Royal Navy in 1943 at the age of eighteen and was later to write the following account of his experiences:-

After finishing my training at the Signal Training establishment in Devonport I was drafted to HMS "Onslow," Flotilla leader of the 17th Defence Force. I was chuffed with this posting as, had I been given a choice, a destroyer would have been the one. I also knew of the "Onslow" as she had distinguished herself the previous year on New Year's Eve in the Battle of the Barents Sea. She and three other "O" class destroyers thwarted the attempts of the pocket battleship "Lutzow" and the heavy cruiser "Admiral Hipper" to destroy Convoy JW 51B. The "Onslow" was hit by three 8 inch shells from the "Hipper" and the Captain, Robert St Vincent Sherbrooke, was severely wounded.

I travelled from Devonport to join "Onslow" in Scapa Flow at the end of 1943 only to discover that she had sailed earlier that morning. But I took passage on another destroyer and caught up with the "Onslow" in the Faeroes where she was topping up with fuel.

The Captain of HMS "Onslow" at this time was J A McCoy, DSO, and within twenty four hours of joining the ship Aneurin found himself at sea. The "Onslow" was due to rendezvous with Convoy JW 55B off the coast of Iceland, 19 freighters and a heavy escort that consisted of nine destroyers, two corvettes and a minesweeper. Captain McCoy had overall command, as Captain D:-

We proceeded steadily on a North-Eastern course in slowly worsening wind and sea conditions. By Christmas Eve a full gale was blowing with thick snow showers and mountainous seas. Our convoy and Convoy RA 55A, the homeward bound convoy, were being covered by Admiral Sir Bruce Fraser in the

HMS "Onslow."

battleship "Duke of York." There were threats from submarines and when a reconnaissance aircraft spotted JW 55B seven U Boats were deployed to intercept. Only one of them made contact and all her torpedoes missed, luckily. The battlecruiser "Scharnhorst," together with escorting destroyers, had left Altenfiord on Christmas Day, her intention being to intercept the two convoys. British intelligence reported her departure and with Admiral Fraser in the "Duke of York" still 400 miles astern of Convoy JW 55B, it was crucial that the merchant ships slowed down. Captain D in the "Onslow" was ordered to reverse course for a number of hours in order to let the battleship and her escorts to catch up:-

In the weather and sea conditions the manoeuvre was impossible so we did the next best thing, which was to edge north at reduced speed, as close to the Arctic ice barrier as safety allowed. The homeward convoy was now past Bear Island and four of their destroyer escort arrived to reinforce JW 55B. The "Scharnhorst" was approaching rapidly and all the destroyers were ordered to join the "Onslow" and Captain D on the threatened side. We were prepared to defend the convoy as best we could but is seemed a pretty hopeless task against such a powerful unit.

Luckily the cruiser "Belfast", which had been partolling with the "Norfolk" to the south of Bear Island, picked up the "Scharnhorst" on her radar. The British radar was much superior to the Germans and now the "Scharnhorst" was lit up by star shells.

The German battle cruiser turned away from the two British cruisers but by now Admiral Fraser and the "Duke of York" arrived to add their weight to the battle. The "Scharnhorst" was battered by the big guns of the battleship and sunk. Convoy JW 55B arrived safely in the Kola Inlet on 29th December.

Aneurin Moller remained on the "Onslow" for the rest of the war. In 1944 he was involved in more Russian convoys:-

By this time our convoy escorts had been increased and strengthened by the addition of a cruiser and two "Woolworth carriers." At long last we had air cover for the full voyage. During my second convoy in 1944, in just three days, twelve enemy aircraft were shot down.

There was a bit of an interlude at the end of April when the "Onslow" was back in Scapa Flow. King George V1 visited the fleet and came on board to observe submarine attack exercises. After this peaceful event we sailed for Portsmouth in mid-April, in readiness for D Day. We carried out numerous patrols in the English Channel, or E Boat Alley as it became known because of the lightning strikes by German E Boats from the French ports. Two of these fast craft were sunk by the "Onslow."

On 6th June 1944, D Day, we sailed from Plymouth early in the morning, escorting and covering an assortment of ships of that great armada heading for the Normandy beaches. We lent our little ounce of 4.7s to the mass bombardment of enemy installations ashore.

On 8th and 9th June the "Onslow" joined with seven other destroyers in an engagement with the German 8th Flotilla out of Brest. In a night of fierce running action two German destroyers were sunk and others damaged. On 18th June we were patrolling north east of Barfleur, along with the "Offa," when we came under attack from seven JU 88s. They dropped nine torpedoes at us as we sped and zig-zagged along. One torpedo hit us on the starboard side but didn't explode. It split a seam in the Asdic compartment which then flooded. I was about fifteen feet aft of the point where the torpedo struck and had it gone off – goodbye Aneurin.

In the autumn of 1944 the "Onslow" returned to Arctic waters once more, this time under the command of Captain H W S Browning, brother in law to the novelist Daphne Du Maurier:-

We helped to fight off several packs of U Boats west of Bear Island and in January 1945 formed part of a successful cruiser and destroyer force attacking enemy shipping off Egersund. Several ships, including tankers and minesweepers, were sunk.

Convoy escort duty continued in appalling weather that February. Convoy RA 64, with 34 ships, sailed on 17th February and distributed among the convoy were the rescued population of the Norwegian island of Soray, some 500 in all. A U Boat pack had gathered. One U Boat was sunk clearing the boom at Kola but one sloop had her stern blown off and had to be towed back. Shortly after an American freighter was torpedoed but the crew and 41 Norwegians were rescued. Then the corvette "Bluebell" was hit in the magazine and blown to smithereens. Miraculously there was one survivor.

Storms of force 11 to 12 broke up the convoy, with waves forty to fifty feet high. Then JU 88s attacked a straggling merchantman carrying 70 Norwegians, mainly women and children. Amazingly, 58 of them were rescued. Eventually, the battered convoy reached Loch Ewe on 28th February.

After the end of the war the "Onslow" was part of the escort that returned King Haakon, his court and government to Oslo. It was appropriate that Aneurin Moller should have been on board for this event as his grandfather was Henry Christian Moller, a sailor who had left Norway to come to Wales to work on the sailing ships of the Ceridigion coast.

James Morton – Royal Navy
(*Russian convoys – Combined Services*)

James Morton's brother had joined the navy as a regular in 1937, being drafted to the cruiser "Glasgow" as soon as she was commissioned. When the time came for James to join up in 1942 he immediately dismissed the idea of the army. He came from Penally in Pembrokeshire and an army base lay just a few hundred yards below his house. He often saw the soldiers parading and marching and the idea did not appeal to him very much. With his brother already in the navy, that was the direction he decided to take and immediately applied to be posted to the same ship:-

The uniform of the navy appealed to me. It was very smart. These days it's not the navy I knew but then we had so many customs, so many traditions. We were like a great big family, really. I think my war service was probably the happiest time of my life. There were friends all around, regular meals and things like medical aid. Of course you could get killed but you always thought it was going to happen to

The cruiser "Glasgow."

somebody else, never you.

I was sent to Malvern to train and nearby was a big girls' college with a lake, ideal for boating drill, and a swimming pool. We took all our swimming tests there in that pool. On off-duty nights we'd go and pick fruit on the nearby farms. There were all sorts of fruit, apples, raspberries, all sorts. Being there, in the barracks, it was the first time I'd ever heard men crying. They were homesick, being away from home – a lot of big men, big posing men. We soon found out that they were mummy's boys, really.

While I was at Malvern I saw a notice asking for men to train for RDF – radar. I didn't want to be a stoker so I applied, was accepted and went into radar. They sent me to HMS "Valkyrie," a shore based unit at Douglas on the Isle of Man. I spent three months stuck on the end of a jetty in the harbour. It was all brand new to me but I found the work and the training very interesting.

After that I was drafted to Portsmouth, to the "Victory." They knew I'd applied for the "Glasgow" and she was on her way back from repair in the States. She'd been at Crete and had taken two torpedoes in her starboard side but she still made 17 knots on the way to Alexandria. I sat in Portsmouth and waited for her.

When James finally got to the "Glasgow" at Christmas 1942 he found that his brother was not on board. During the time "Glasgow" had been undergoing repairs at Alexandria he had been sent to a destroyer. The destroyer had, subsequently, been torpedoed and sunk. His brother was reported as missing:-

The Padre later told me that he had been picked up and was a prisoner in North Africa. It was good to know he was alive, I mean everybody was afraid of the telegram boy arriving at the door in those days. But, of course, it meant that I never did get to serve with my brother.

We were based up at Scapa Flow. One trip we were supposed to make was escorting the "Queen Mary" across the Atlantic. Winston Churchill was on board, going to the Quebec Conference. We were making 35 knots – everything was rattling – and the "Queen Mary" just left us in her wake. There was no way we could keep up so I never did get to see Canada.

We had new radar fitted in the States, transmitter receivers being set up on the masts. They had a range of about 30 miles and were just aerials really. Then we had surface radar which controlled the 6 inch weapons and high angle radar for controlling the anti-aircraft guns.

Coming back across the Atlantic we called into the Azores. Lots of the boys ended up in the brothels and that was fine, they were clean. Those boys who picked up girls in the streets almost invariably ended up with a dose! On a run ashore we'd all come up the gangway and there, at the top, were officers, Marines and Doctors. Everyone would be examined – cells, cells, sick bay! The boys all put away a lot of drink. They lived for today.

It was a good life. We were poor, mind. Pay was just ten bob a week. I sent three shillings home to my mother and that left me with seven shillings for the week. You rolled your own cigarettes. You could buy a pound of tobacco for half a crown and pipe smokers would make their own blocks of tobacco. They'd tie canvas around the tobacco leaves, bind it really tightly and let it soak in a bit of rum. Then, when they took the canvas off there was a solid block of tobacco. They would cut off slices and smoke them at their leisure.

Soon, the "Glasgow" was sent back to Scapa Flow and, from there, up to Iceland. It was not an easy time as the Icelanders would not speak to the sailors, feeling that the British were little more than invaders of their country:-

Our relaxation and leisure facilities in Iceland consisted of one jetty, a tin shed and several bottles of Canadian beer. There was nothing else to do. Then we'd steam out, pick up a convoy and head off to Russia. In the summer you could sail further north because there wasn't so much threat of ice. In the winter, of course, we had to sail much closer to the enemy coast and that was much more dangerous. We did the Denmark Straits patrol, the White Water Run as they called it.

One day the radar picked up an echo, 32 miles away. We closed fast and fired a star shell. It was a German freighter called the "Regensburg," trying to slip back home from Japan. And she almost made it – a few days more and she'd have been there. We assembled a boarding party, armed with cutlasses, and then there were two loud bangs from the "Regensburg.". The German skipper had scuttled her, blown out her bottom. There were only eight survivors. We threw scrambling nets over the side but the sea was wild and most of them never made it. They didn't call it White Water for nothing.

When the "Regensburg" went down there were so many bodies in the water, including women. We couldn't hang around to pick them up as there was always the possibility of German U Boats. I never understood why the German Captain did it. He'd been caught so why didn't he just come into Iceland with us? If he'd wanted to scuttle his ship he could have done it then, in shallow water. It would have saved a lot of lives. I can only think he was a fanatical Nazi.

It was very cold out there. We'd wear long johns, sea boot socks, uniform boiler suits (our working rig), duffle coats and gloves. The girls of the Notre Dame School adopted the ship and they knitted us long johns and balaclavas. They were very itchy but we still wore them – anything to try to keep warm. In my radar cabin there was ice inside the room. We never undressed while at sea, we slept in our clothes and the only wash we took was a quick swill or rinse every now and then.

It was about two weeks, a fortnight at sea, to get to Russia and we lived on sandwiches or, if we were lucky, a drop of soup every now and then. You never slung a hammock, just slept wherever you could, on the deck usually. Hard line, the navy men called it. John Brown's, the ship building yard back in Glasgow, had fitted trunking from the engine room in order to blow hot air into the ship. It didn't help much, just caused a lot of condensation.

You didn't like to think about being torpedoed or bombed. You'd be dead inside two minutes if you ever went into those seas. Even the spray froze as soon as it hit the deck. We seemed to spend hours chipping ice off cables and bare surfaces. Many of the old trawlers used to capsize because of the ice on deck. You had to keep the top deck clear or else you'd become too top heavy and then over you'd go. We much preferred the idea of the one big bang. At least that way it would have been quick.

The ice would just lie on the top of the sea, almost like sand on the surface. It looked quite horrible. The further north you went the colder it became and then you encountered icebergs and pack ice as well.

I don't remember ever being attacked by aeroplanes. There were lots of submarine attacks, of course, and we usually had to pick up survivors. The worst part of that was the oil. Men in the sea, after the ship had gone down, would swallow it. Just breathing in the fumes was enough. To get the oil off the survivors was difficult. It was like tar or engine oil. They had to be stripped right down and, of course, if it was on their lungs there was no chance.

When we got to Murmansk we were never allowed ashore. We'd just anchor and wait for the lighters to come alongside. We used to have these horrible herrings in tomato sauce and nobody ever ate them. "Herrings-in" we called them. When the lighters came alongside we'd throw these cans down. The seabed there must be littered with those tins and cans.

We always had a couple of trawlers following us, picking up whatever survivors they could find. Once, in Murmansk, the trawlers were tied up alongside us and I shouted down "Any Taffs down there?" And there was one, a bloke from Llanelli. So I went down and he gave me what they called "neaters," neat rum. It hit me like a sledge hammer. On the bigger ships you always had measures, two of water, one of rum. On small ships it was "neaters." I still like rum, it's probably my favourite drink.

Scapa Flow, despite the privations that made the naval base famous, was almost a holiday camp for the sailors after Iceland and the Russian convoys. Ratings were allowed ashore between 4.30 and 6.30 at night and there were just two canteens to choose from. One was dry, the other wet:-

We'd go to the dry one first to have a meal. Then it was down to the wet one to drink as much as you could before it was time to head back to the ship. We used to go ashore in these old Clyde puffers that they kept for the purpose. Coming back on board one night the Master at Arms was pushed into the sea. An accident? Who knows, it was certainly very crowded on those liberty boats. When the Yanks arrived at Scapa we'd put cold tea into a bottle and tell them it was rum. "Keep it out of sight," we'd say. All their ships were dry and, of course, by the time they found out the truth it was too late.

The King came for a visit one day and we only had time to paint half the ship, the half he was going to see, between the gang plank and the ward room. It must have looked very odd.

James has never been able to understand why the Germans did not make more use of their surface fleet during the war. Their ships were excellently made and the crews invariably well trained. The enemy destroyers were as large and heavily armed as many of the British cruisers and yet they always seemed more interested in getting back into port than taking on ships like the "Glasgow":-

I never understood their reluctance. Those destroyers, attacking from two sides, would have cut us to pieces. They never did. I'd have thought they'd have had some pride and come out to fight but, in the end, they stayed in port and got bombed to bits.

The Focke-Wulf Kondors were the worst, not because of the damage they did but because of what it meant when you spotted them. You could see them in the air but they always stayed well out of the way so you couldn't reach them with your guns. Once you saw them you knew they'd be calling in the U Boats. It was only a matter of time before the attacks began.

We fired our 6 inch gun at a Kondor once. He was so far away he thought he was safe but we worked out roughly how far away he was, set the time fuse and fired. We didn't hit him but we certainly frightened the bugger!

I always felt sorry for the Merchant Navy men. Once they were sunk their pay was stopped. They were off the books. One bloke I later worked with had been torpedoed in the Indian Ocean and spent three weeks in an open boat. He got nothing, no pay at all during those three weeks because the ship had been sunk. It was scandalous.

In 1942 James and the "Glasgow" were involved in one of the most bizarre episodes of the entire war when Admiral of the Fleet Sir Dudley Pound was buried at sea:-

He hadn't been well but his death was a bit of a shock for everyone. His funeral took place at Westminster Abbey and the casket containing his ashes was taken to Portsmouth where it was lodged on the "Victory" overnight. We were called in to Portsmouth and on 27th October we took his ashes out to sea. When we were thirty miles off the coast we put them over the side. The burial service was over by 1.15 pm. His wife had died only a few weeks before and her ashes went into the sea at the same time. The old guy had made a bit of a mess over the PQ 17 convoy and I suppose it could be argued that the chaos around that disaster hurried him on the way to the grave.

It wasn't all bad conditions up there in Scotland. The Minches was a lovely stretch of water between the outer islands and the mainland and we went through there one beautiful moonlit night. The land was so dark and yet it was

The ashes of Sir Dudley Pound are brought on board the "Glasgow," Portsmouth 1942.

so clear. Standing on deck, looking over the side, I was mesmerised by the flow of water. I almost had to be pulled away.

James eventually found himself drafted to a corvette but when she suffered damage and put in for repair he was sent back to base. After a few weeks he had had enough

James Morton and shipmates on board the "Cygnet," 1946.

and volunteered for Combined Operations. His blue uniform was taken away and he was issued with khaki. After the D Day landings his unit went up the coast from Normandy:-

I was still working with radar but this time, of course, I was ashore. Our unit was working between the army and the coast. We ended up at Knohle sur Mer, covering convoys coming in through the Scheldt to Antwerp.

Then they sent me to another corvette, HMS "Cygnet" and that's where I was when the war ended. We were training ratings how to use radar and I was there on board as an instructor. It was interesting enough but, of course, by then I was waiting for my demob to come through. I did think about staying in. They were almost begging us to stay because, after all, we were fully trained. But I'd missed out on so much, education and things, so when the time came I decided to come out and see what life was like on the "outside."

James was demobbed in 1946 and joined the police force. He was posted to Pembroke Dock and Milford Haven but, after the excitement of war at sea, found the work petty and boring – he had to have so many cases a year and even on days off he had to inform his bosses where he was going. He still regards his time in the navy as the best period in his life.

Ray Newberry – Merchant Navy
(nautical training – convoy to the Far East)

Ray Newberry left home in 1942 to take up a place at HMS "Worcester," a nautical training school based on an old wooden-wall battleship on the River Thames. Sea training for boys on board wooden ships had been a fairly common occurrence during the nineteenth century, many of the vessels being Reformatory or Industrial School Ships. By the beginning of the Second World War, however, most of these had disappeared and only "officer" training ships like the "Worcester" on the Thames and the "Conway" in the Menai Straits were left:-

When the time came for me to take up my place on the "Worcester" it was, obviously, war time and by then the old wooden ship had been requisitioned as a mother craft for the Thames Patrol of the Royal Navy. As a result of that, the "Worcester" boys were kicked off the ship and we lived ashore at Foot's Cray Place in Foot's Cray in Kent. We still did the same training but we did a lot of it on shore.

Despite losing the main ship the school still managed to keep the old tea clipper "Cutty Sark" which had been part of the establishment for several years and was moored alongside the old "Worcester." That was in the days before she was taken to Greenwich as a museum piece. We used to go down to the "Cutty Sark" for our seamanship training.

The "Worcester" had been going for many years and most of the officers in the Merchant Navy came either from her or the "Conway" – or the shore establishment at Pangbourne. We used to have annual rowing matches against the "Conway," all the cadets pulling at these heavy whalers to see who would

The MV "Empire Confidence," complete with "A" frame across the bows.

come out on top. There was an annual exam for boys who wanted to go into the Royal Navy and some even went into the army. But most of us were bound for the Merchant Marine.

By 1944 Ray Newberry's period of training on the "Worcester" was almost over. It was time to look for a job at sea:-

I left school in 1944, having signed indentures as a Cadet, the lowest form of human life on a ship! I signed with a shipping company called the Royal Mail Lines and in peace time their principal place of business was London. Their main trade routes were to South America, the West Indies and the far coast – that's the west coast – of North America. My indentures stipulated that the company would teach me to become a Navigating Officer and, in return, I had to undertake to look after their property and to obey their commands. It was war time, of course, and what generally happened was that we went wherever the army went. Or wherever the government wanted to send us – which was usually with the army.

My first ship was an interesting one. She was the ex "Dusseldorf" of Bremen and had been seized in the South Atlantic by a British warship, then brought back to the UK. Here she was re-named "Poland" for a while, then after a few months she was re-named again, this time as "Empire Confidence." It was a pattern they followed. You'll often hear seamen say things like "I was in a Park boat" or something like that. "Empire" ships, generally speaking, were vessels built for private shipping companies but managed by the Ministry of War Transport. I think all the ships captured by the British were called "Empire" something or other. I'm not certain that's true but it was what was put to me when I was a Cadet all those years ago.

Ray joined the "Empire Confidence" in Middlesbrough. As he says, as a young 17 year old who had spent his life so far in the south, he barely knew where Middlesbrough was – even though he used to be quite good at Geography in school! Soon after he joined the ship she sailed in convoy down the east coast and up the Solent. There they picked up another convoy and went around the coast to the Welsh port of Milford Haven:-

We went through the Dover Straits to reach the Solent and attacks in that area were from E Boats rather than submarines. Those E Boats were fast and heavily armed and they could run rings around any merchant ship. Luckily we managed to steer clear of them on that trip.

Milford Haven was a forming up place for convoys going out east. Most of the North Atlantic convoys seemed to go up to the Liverpool area and then they'd head out north of Ireland. We weren't crossing the western ocean, we were heading for Gibraltar and then, via the Mediterranean, out to the Far East.

We were moored there in Milford Haven for a short time, waiting for the convoy to form. I never thought about going ashore. When you're 17 and waiting to go to sea there's no point in going ashore. It's the ship that you love, as it were. You're desperate to become a sea farer and you're anxious to get experience, so that you can talk to people without them detecting that you don't have a damned clue about what you're doing, or about ships and the sea.

As I say, Cadets were regarded as the lowest form of human life in the Merchant Navy. My starting wage was £3. 10. 0 a month. In fact it wasn't too bad a salary, when you think about it. The company fed me and they housed me. They heated and lighted my cabin, too. I was 17 and was leaving wartime Britain with its rationing and here was this ship with all the goodies in creation. At that age you eat like a horse and when you're suddenly projected into the salt-fresh air, well, you eat like two horses! So, in hindsight, I suppose my salary wasn't that bad.

As a Cadet you're in the business of learning the trade of sailor, in my case Navigating Officer. I was there to learn how to be a ship's officer and to be taken through my first certificate of competency, the Second Mate's Certificate. Normally you had to do four years at sea before you could sit for this certificate but because it was war time and there was a shortage of young officers – so many had been killed – they reduced that to three years. And because I had been on the "Worcester," a recognised training ship, I had another year's remission. As a result I only had to do two years before I could sit the exam and try to get a decent salary.

Ray's first convoy was a large one, about 80 merchant ships although, as he says, the figure was never clear:-

As a Cadet nobody tells you anything. In those days I wasn't even aware that convoys had numbers. As far as I was concerned the convoy was just what I could see when I stood on the bridge. Mind you, there did seem to be ships everywhere. When the convoys formed they were organised in line abreast, perhaps nine or ten of them, and then there'd be a column behind each leading ship. You kept a fair distance away from the stern of the ship in front because that gave you a little time if something happened to her. The escorts were always knocking around. You didn't see much of them, not in the centre of the convoy, they were always on the periphery, working on the assumption that things didn't happen in the middle.

The U Boat threat was still quite considerable in 1944. And, of course, there was the weather. The weather doesn't care if you're British, German, Italian, Japanese, American, whatever. So we had the enemy and the weather to consider.

That first time out of Milford it was so bad the convoy broke up and we sailed on to Gibraltar on our own. I suppose it was dangerous but what was the option? Hang around or go on alone? There was no choice, really. Once the convoy had split we could go at our own speed and we had quite a lot in hand. I suppose, in those days, the average speed of a merchant ship was about 8 or 9 knots. Well we could turn in 13 or 14 without any problem. We were in Gibraltar well before the rest of them showed up.

Ray had his first run ashore as a sailor at Gibraltar but the next day the convoy reformed and they sailed on across the Mediterranean. By now the Suez Canal was open and from that point onwards ships sailed independently. The Red Sea was out of range for enemy aircraft, and even the U Boats which operated off the Cape would have had difficulty reaching the merchant ships there:-

As a Cadet I was involved in watch keeping, but I must say that I was just a boy standing in the corner. I wasn't qualified then to do anything else. There were two of us Cadets and one used to keep the 12 till 4 watch, the other did from 4 till 8 – it gave the Skipper an extra pair of eyes on the bridge. When we were in the North Atlantic the threat was a bit more imminent. Then we would do four hours on, four hours off. In places like the Red Sea it was much less arduous.

I suppose it was dangerous - that first convoy three ships were sunk -but you didn't think about it too much. The way I felt was, I was going to sea as a professional sea farer and I was keen to learn my business. The fact that somebody might be throwing bullets and bombs at me was purely incidental to the business of learning my trade. And, of course, when you're 17 things don't look half as dangerous as they do when you get older. You tend not to recognise danger when you're that age. I just thought, well if we get hit the lifeboats are there, we'll sail one of those into port.

The chaps in the engine room would ring the bridge sometimes and say "Was that a bomb or a torpedo?" We hadn't heard anything. They'd felt the shock wave as it impressed upon the hull and heard it down there, below the water line. Up top we'd never heard or felt a thing. It happened like that several times.

The threat of aerial attack was always strong, particularly around the coast of Britain. When you first left port you'd be firing the guns all the time and Action Stations was always being sounded, but as you got further away the chance of seeing anything got less. Out there the threat was from submarines.

Like most merchant ships we used to have guns mounted on board, but we weren't gunners in the sense that the Royal Navy boys were. We were just happy to have a go and try to shoot down an enemy plane or two. Anyway, one day an excited gunner was following an aircraft that flew past. Unfortunately, the mast was between the gunner and the enemy aircraft. Now, when you're trying to bring down an enemy plane you don't think about anything that might be in your way. And that time the mast got in the way. He literally severed the top of the mainmast and we had to have a collar, about two feet deep, put round it. When they did that they took the precaution of putting rails around the Orlikon pits. The rails prevented the guns from firing and hitting the funnel or the masts or even the chaps standing on the bridge. It was so easy to fire close to people if you were concentrating on enemy planes.

Mines were a problem, you didn't know they were there. Like lots of merchant ships, we had a device for dealing with them, an A-frame over the bows which you could lower into the water. It had something like a bucket on it and this started a hammering that would set off acoustic mines. We also had paravanes that you could stream over the bow and they were meant to keep us safe from moored mines, the paravanes would just sweep the mines away. And then there was a degaussing system which, broadly speaking, was a powerful electric coil running around the ship. It created a current to counteract magnetic mines.

The "Empire Confidence" football team with Ray Newbury on the right of the front row.

When the "Empire Confidence" reached India, the crew got together a football team and played several matches against other ships in the port:-

We were quite good, even if I say so myself. One of our players, an assistant steward, he'd had trials for Grimsby Town and one of the engineers had had trials for Sunderland. And there was a Scottish engineer who'd had trials for one of the Scottish league teams. So we were a pretty good side, those three boys and the rest of us "also rans." We were supposed to be going to Australia but we had some engine trouble. As the ship had been taken over from the Germans there were no plans or drawing for the machinery. So we headed back to India and spent the time playing football instead.

It's incredible how quickly we, the other Cadet and I, became useful. As I say, to start with we were just another pair of eyes on the bridge but soon we mastered the art of signalling. It was nearly all signalling with an Aldis Lamp which we used to have up on the monkey island, the uppermost deck of the ship. I was in Antwerp when the war in Europe ended, just back from the Far East.

The town had been pretty badly knocked about, I must say, I don't think there was one warehouse with a roof on it. On VJ Night I was in Liverpool. We'd been somewhere else in between but we were back in Liverpool by then.

With the war over and having obtained his Second Mate's Certificate Ray became Fourth Officer on a ship called the "Almonzora." Although the war had ended there were still troops to be brought home:-

Although my indentures were completed I wanted to stay with the Royal Mail Line and I was lucky because they sent me to the "Almonzora." She was old, built about the time of the First World War, and she'd undoubtedly have gone for scrap if it hadn't been for the Second World War.

Of course I wanted promotion but I must say a lot of the fun stopped as soon as I got that glittering gold band on my sleeve. The first thing you do when you get promotion is buy yourself a lot of clothes to save having to do so much washing. You get enough clothes to last you from port to port.

I don't say I was much better off, mind you. When you were attached to a ship at sea you were paid war risk money. During my first year it was about £5 a month. After the first year, when they regarded me as being of some value to the country, it shot up to £10. That was great money, far more than my salary. Of course it all stopped when the war ended.

Ray Newberry continued with his career at sea after the war. He rose to command his own ship and later went on to work for the Board of Trade. He lives now in the Vale of Glamorgan.

Doug Owen – Royal Navy DEMS gunner

(Indian Ocean, convoys)

Doug's family moved from Ystrad, Rhondda to Cadoxton, Barry, when he was 6 months old, and he grew up longing to go to sea, against the wishes of his parents.

I was trained at HMS Glendower at Pwllheli to be a DEMS gunner. Usually you had a 4.7" stern gun, and 12-pounders were added later to the bows. The merchant navy before the war was treated dreadfully, and things didn't improve. If they were torpedoed, their pay stopped immediately, but we were still paid.

I was sent out with a naval draft to Bombay. My first boat was an old Indian ship in 1942, the Jalarami. There were cockroaches and rats everywhere. There were 6 sheep tethered on deck for fresh meat. When one was needed it was killed and skinned in front of the other sheep, on the deck. I sailed on the Santa Clare (US) to Karachi and the Aurelia to Bombay, and the troopship Ormond to Cape Town. There was also a Dutch oil tanker, and I spent 9 months on the Persian Gulf to Durban run. There was also the Ocean Verity, a Blue Funnel ship. We went from Dar-es-Salaam to the Red Sea, up the Suez Canal through the Med and home to Middlesbrough in late July 1944. It was a lucky trip with no attacks on our convoy. I had a month's leave owing to me, and joined the Greenwich in a big convoy getting war supplies from New York. We also went to India, Suez, Cape Town and Buenos Aires and picked up grain and hide on the River Plate.

When the Greenwich reached the UK we were told to wait for a convoy at Gibraltar, so I missed VE-Day in Liverpool. We did some training of merchant crew members to fire the guns – it was an insurance policy if we were hit. On some ships we had 4 naval gunners and 4 army gunners from the Maritime Regiment.

After leave, I had a spell in gunnery at Southampton, and volunteered to go out to the Japanese war with the troopship Orion from Liverpool. We were carrying Australian and New Zealand army and navy personnel. It was terribly overcrowded and the food really poor. About 300 New Zealanders walked off the ship in Liverpool, disgusted at the conditions, and they had been POW's! On 7 August 1945 the troopship HMAT "Orion" set out for the southwest Pacific, but had not even reached the Panama Canal when news was received that the war came to an end. The Orion duly changed course and headed directly for Wellington, New Zealand and Australia. I spent 5 months then on the staff of the Naval Detention Centre until I was demobbed, and joined the Orion to get home. The Daily Express had a picture of the Orion with the headline 'Hell Ship' because of its overcrowding and food. In Fremantle there was nearly a mutiny on board, and the officers were going to put people ashore.

After demob, Doug worked at Rank's Mill, Barry Dock for two years, and then on a milk-round for 8 years in the town. He saved enough to take a year off and study in Cardiff for his w/t exams for 18 months. He then served 6 months with an experienced radio officer to fully qualify and joined the Lord Byron for 10 months, sailing to China. He then joined the Cardiff South American Saints Line on the St Helena, before serving on Blue Star Line container ships. In 1970 he joined ACT-1 and he served 9 years on container ships including the Bar and Swiftpool. For two years he then served on the California Star, and he used his time at see making model ships on a 1/16th inch to 1 foot scale. He made the Saxilby, which went down in 1933 losing 7 Barry men and a Barry boy aboard, and the ACT-1 and ACT-2, on which he had served for 7 years. He was also on the Melbourne Star, Brazil Star and Sydney Star. His models are in the Brisbane Maritime Museum and other museums, and there are models of the Baron Dechmont and Jedmoor (see Chapter 4) in the Mayor's Parlour in Barry. Because he had 8-12 and 4-8 watches, Doug could spend up to 5 hours a day making his models, which each required about 20-30 coats of paint 'to finish them off'. When he started each took 240 hours, but he got the time down to 120 hours by the time he finished making them a few years ago. Doug retired from the International Marine Radio Company after heart trouble which has necessitated two bypass operation, and reminiscences that the other services had dances and concerts and entertainments, but the poor old merchant navy got nothing at all. Doug served 28 years at sea and lives with his wife Irita in Barry.

Bill Peel – Royal Navy

(Battle of Cape Matapan – Crete – submarines – the Far East)

Bill Peel joined the Royal Navy on 1st January 1936 as a Boy Entrant and trained as an engineering apprentice at HMS "Fisgard." His first ship was the giant battleship "Warspite" although when he joined her, in May 1940, she was already in the Mediterranean as part of Admiral Cunningham's fleet, and Bill had to take passage to Alexandria on the cruiser "Carlysle." When he arrived in the Egyptian port the "Warspite" was waiting for him:-

She was a lovely ship, the "Warspite." She'd been built in the early days of the First World War and had fought at the Battle of Jutland. As a Junior ERA I was on her for two and a half years, getting my various tickets. It took one year to gain my auxiliary machinery ticket, one year for my boiler room ticket and six months for my engine room ticket.

Action in the Mediterranean

I suppose the biggest action I was involved with on the "Warspite" was the Battle of Cape Matapan, the first time the British and Italian fleets had gone head to head. Now normally it took us about four hours to raise steam. That night we did it in one! Admiral Cunningham received a message from the code breakers at Bletchley saying that the Italian fleet was either at sea or was preparing to sail. That was exactly what he'd been waiting for.

Alexandria was a real hot-bed of spies in those days, and Cunningham knew that if he left by day the news would be relayed to the Italians before we'd gone twenty miles. If the Italians realised what was coming their way, they'd have headed straight back to port and the chance would be gone. So he waited for night, then we got up steam and left. We left in such a hurry that we ran right over a sandbank and sucked up mud into our starboard wing condenser. It put the whole engine out of action. I was one of the team detailed to clear and clean it. Hours and hours it took us, taking off these big doors, hosing it through and then pumping it all out. At the end I was exhausted.

I'd just gone to clean up when they sounded Action Stations. So it was off to my post in the Number 3 Boiler Room – I never did have time to wash and clean up. At about 8.30 that night, a couple of hours later, the guns opened up. We sank three Italian cruisers that night and the racket was tremendous but being down in the boiler rooms I didn't get to see anything. And I was so exhausted from spending all those hours on the condenser. That, really, is my memory of one of the most important naval battles we ever fought in the Mediterranean.

The "Warspite" was also involved in the various actions around Crete between May and June 1941, covering the British withdrawal. During the latter stages of the battle she was hit by a bomb and seriously damaged:-

I was preparing to take my engine room ticket at the time so I had the control in the engine room. At about 2.00 pm there was this terrific explosion. It was like an earthquake and it really shook the whole ship. All the gauges went down to zero. The Chief of the Watch relieved me immediately and sent me over to the boiler room to see what had happened – the phones had all gone dead and we couldn't raise them at all. A pretty big bomb had hit us, destroying the starboard 6 inch magazine. There were bodies everywhere, it was horrible.

When I reached the boiler room I found that they had lost air pressure but otherwise they were OK. The Commander was there, directing operations, fire fighting and that type of thing. Of course, we had to prepare all those bodies for burial at sea and that was not a nice thing to have to do. We stayed on station for some time after the bomb hit but then it was back to Alex and, eventually, over to the USA for refit and repair.

I left the "Warspite" in November 1942, at Mombassa. I joined the "Royal Sovereign," another battleship, and sailed with her to Philadelphia, again for a refit. And from there I transferred into the submarine service.

Like many submariners, Bill Peel is reticent about why he went into submarines. It's not something that can be easily explained, not to the public at large and sometimes not even to the submariners themselves:-

I don't really know why I transferred into submarines. After all I had enjoyed my time on the "Warspite." Being in submarines was different and I suppose I just fancied trying it. Now, all these years later, I can honestly say that I wouldn't have changed any of it. It was a wonderful experience. The relationships between all the crew members on the boats were great. You could go ashore with your officers, no trouble. Back on board there was respect for their role and their skill, for the job they had to do – in the same way they respected us for our skill and abilities. And that was how it should be.

I "stood by" while my submarine, the "Statesman," was being built at Cammel Lairds. That was in September 1943 and I was the Chief ERA. Then we were sent out to the Far East and based ourselves in Trincomalee in Ceylon, Sri Lanka as it is now. We sank dozens of ships during our time out east and we were also depth charged lots of times. Once you fired a torpedo you knew what was coming. I have to be honest, it was terrifying. I didn't like it one little bit, none of us did. But you tried not to show it. You just looked at each other and tried to keep calm. Nobody broke, that was the important thing.

Except when once, our engineer, an old bloke called Bert, he totally lost it. He went round the bend. He was running round the boat shouting "I can't stand it!" The Skipper ordered him to be restrained and he was confined to the ward room for the rest of the patrol.

I was awarded the DSM and, do you know, I'm really not sure why. On the citation it just says "For devotion to duty." The one thing I can remember was our starboard hydroplane seizing up and our Skipper, Lt Bulkeley, asked me "Can you fix it?" I just said "Yes." Then I spent two or three hours under the covering, working there, knocking out the pin and replacing it. We were in the Malacca Straits at the time, it must have been 1944, and there was always the danger of Japanese ships appearing over the horizon. I suppose that could have been the reason for the award.

The "Statesman" is credited with firing the very last British torpedo of the war. Bill Peel remembers the incident, and the build up to it, very well indeed. There were two fleets out in the Far East during the war years, the Pacific and Far East Fleets. Each of them was under the command of an Admiral:-

The Admiral of the Pacific Fleet and our Admiral, John Power, were supposed to have had a bet as to who would get into Singapore first once the war against Japan ended. That was the story. It's probably not true but we'll never really know. As it happened the Japanese war ended quite swiftly and, so the story goes, our Admiral leapt into the cruiser "Cleopatra," escorted by four destroyers, and took off for Singapore in order to win the bet.

Anyway, on 15th August 1945, we were on patrol in the Malacca Straits and the signal came through for us to cease hostilities but to remain aware of potential problems. We had to be on the lookout for any Japanese treachery. We surfaced and ambled along, feeling pretty good about things. Then, on 18th August, we spotted a shape in the water ahead of us. We closed, carefully, and it turned out to be a burned-out Jap cargo ship. She's been attacked from the air, probably by rockets, and had been abandoned by her crew.

Our Skipper reckoned she was smack bang in the path of Admiral Power and his armada. They were coming along behind us at 25 knots or more and we couldn't take the risk of leaving the hulk there. She had to go.

We came alongside and fixed demolition charges but they failed to go off. We tried again – still no result. So finally we stood off to 800 yards and put a torpedo into her side. It just blew her to bits. The Admiralty later acknowledged that to be the last British torpedo fired in anger during the Second World War.

Life on board the "Statesman" was busy during the war years. Conditions were never easy in the cramped confines of a submarine and sometimes the atmosphere was more than a little stressful:-

You did your patrols, came back to port and refuelled and rearmed as quickly as possible. Then, usually, you went straight back out. It could be a little stressful and that affected men in different ways. One day our coxswain got drunk on rum. I imagine he'd saved up his ration. Anyway, he got drunk, stripped off and dived into the sea. He just missed the liberty boat that was going past at the time.

He was hauled back on board and taken before the Duty Officer. He was told to go and get his head down, to sleep it off. Did he? No way, he went straight back on the rum. Eventually he crashed out – in the bed belonging to the Captain, Submarines. That was it, the Marines were out, he was arrested, charged and in due course reduced to his substantive rank, which was AB. We all signed a petition saying we thought the punishment too severe. After all, he was a married man! But it was no good, reduced he was.

Submarines weren't very good on the surface but once they'd dived you wouldn't have known you were at sea. They were always better below the water, particularly in rough weather.

Toileting was an interesting exercise. You had to ask permission to blow the waste matter over the side. A mate of mine once phoned the control room – "Permission to fire a shit shot?" he said. That was the standard request. The trouble was the Officer of the Watch answered and he was a bit of a stickler. "Don't you realise this is the Officer of the Watch?" he shouted. "Sorry," said the rating. "Permission to fire a shit shot, sir?"

As a regular Bill Peel remained in the navy after hostilities ceased. He remained in submarines, renewing his engagement every three years, as was the common practice. He did not retire until August 1965 and lives now in Cardiff, the Welsh capital city.

Bill Phillips – Merchant Navy
(Shipwrecked in the North Sea - Convoy PQ 17)

Although he lived for most of his childhood in Haverfordwest, Bill Phillips was actually born in Belfast. His father was discharged from the navy after the First World War and began working for the Harland and Wolf shipyards in the northern Irish city. This was at a time when the Irish troubles were escalating. As a Protestant who had married an Irish catholic, as well as taking a job that an Irishman might otherwise have occupied, Bill's father was given a warning. He had just 48 hours to get out of the city. The family returned to Haverfordwest:-

I went to school at the old Grammar School in Dew Street and Reggie Lang, the Head, implied that I wasn't going to go a lot further than 5B. I was good at Latin, History and English but not much use at anything else. And so I joined the Merchant Navy. My father's family had been sea farers and we talked about it. I signed indentures and joined a tramp steamer company from Cardiff, Cory's. I spent my 16th birthday at sea in 1937.

When war broke out in 1939 I was serving on one of the Cory ships – they only ever had three – called the "Coryton." The Captain was a Cardigan man, from New Quay and like 90% of all Cardies he was called Evans. We had been down to Buenos Aires in South America but coming back across the Atlantic I was taken ill with food poisoning. I was too ill to work and so they landed me in Freetown, West Africa. I think I was in the hospital at Freetown for about three months.

Eventually they sent me home as a DBS, a Distressed British Seaman. None of the shipping lines wanted to take me but, in the end, one of the New Zealand companies fitted me on board and I was landed at Gravesend on the Thames. I

Bill Phillips on board ship during the war years.

had gone from 11 stone to about eight and was lucky not to have died.

Bill Phillips rejoined the "Coryton" in London and despite his physical condition set off almost immediately on another voyage. This time the tramp steamer was bound for Canada and the weather in the North Atlantic was bad:-

The weather was awful, all the way across. But we made it and loaded steel, a deck cargo of timber and a couple of holds of grain. Before too long we started back. We crossed the Atlantic in convoy but that only took us across the ocean. Our orders were to proceed to the Firth of Forth and there pick up another convoy for our destination, which was Hull. I was on watch as we came down the coast towards the Farne Islands and the weather was a bit foggy.

I was about to come off watch – it was 7.45 – when I saw a thin black buoy ahead of us. I reported it and went to call the new watch. Suddenly there was a hell of a bang and the whole ship shook. We took soundings and it was clear the ship was making water. We had no idea what we'd hit, maybe it was a mine. But because she was taking water the "old man" decided to beach her.

There was a long strip of land south of Holy Island and the Skipper ran her up onto the beach. We dropped the two bow anchors and put out two kedge anchors off the stern. We took those out in the lifeboats. The "old man" said that once we found out the damage we would be able to get her off. The Holy Island lifeboat arrived and took the Skipper ashore, for a conference I suppose, to debate what to do. When he came back it was with the news that the lifeboat men were saying that if the crew didn't get off now they probably wouldn't be able to later as the weather was deteriorating, beginning to blow up a SE gale. The Skipper said "Take what gear you can, boys, you won't have another chance." And so we went ashore. I remember taking a 25 lb bag of sugar with me. I'd bought it for my mother in Canada and it was all I saved from the ship.

We put up at a Guest House on Holy Island. I still remember the name of the family who owned the place – Moody. They were very kind to us. The next day the Boatswain and I went to have a look at the ship. Both masts had gone. There was a torch light on deck but we couldn't see any movement. That was about

Trying to salvage the "Coryton."

8.00 am and three hours later they found the "old man's" body on the beach. He'd stayed on board until he'd cleared up all the paperwork, he wouldn't leave. He was that type of man. I don't know if he'd been washed overboard or been drowned while trying to get ashore.

Later that day I watched the "Coryton's" funnel fall over the side. The people of Northumberland did quite well out of the shipwreck. A friend of mine later visited that part of the world – he said they had the finest crop of grain he'd ever seen. All the timber went as well. And we never did find out what it was that we had collided with.

By 1940 Bill was serving on the Royal Fleet Auxiliary tanker "Aldersdale." For twelve months or so they were operating in Arctic waters, mainly carrying out oiling at sea. It was hard work for the crew, trailing copper hoses astern and working in the most arduous of weather conditions. To begin with the "Aldersdale" was based in Scapa Flow but soon they moved to Iceland:-

It was difficult work, particularly in the winter months. Often we would lose the escorts in the fog or heavy seas. And there were always ice growlers around, mini icebergs that lay mostly beneath the surface of the water.

This one day we were doubled up on watch, two officers at a time on the bridge. The man with me on watch was Charlie Cairns, an oldish chap who'd been called back for service because of the war. I heard this noise, rather like a motor-ship. We had no radar in those days and I remember saying to Charlie "There's a ship out there." Something passed by, only a couple of hundred yards away. All we saw was a slight disturbance in the fog. And after, only after the other ship had gone, did we realise it had been a German destroyer.

The very next day a growler hit our bow and pulled out both anchors. They ran out almost to the end of the cables. Fortunately they were shackled but it still took us half a day to get them back in and there was a lot of damage on deck, valves and rails bent, that type of thing. They called us back to the Clyde

The "Coryton" before the disaster that saw her wrecked and abandoned.

after that and we joined Convoy PQ 17.

By the May of 1942 Bill and the "Aldersdale" had already completed a couple of Russian convoys. However, nothing could possibly have prepared them for the horror and the carnage of what was to come:-

As soon as we cleared Iceland the German reconnaissance planes picked us up. The Icelanders didn't want us there and I still reckon that someone tipped off the Germans. The policeman in Hval Fiord was undoubtedly a Nazi. He didn't like us at all. He insulted our Maltese greasers, called them black men. We got our own back by letting down the tyres on his bike – it gave us a great deal of pleasure.

Nearly 40 ships left Iceland in PQ 17 and we didn't put out one drop of oil because we were attacked almost from day two, high level bombing to start with, then dive bombers. It was summer time and there was bright sunlight for 24 hours a day. The "Alderesdale" was attacked several times. We had a 4 inch gun on the foredeck but that was no use as we couldn't elevate it high enough. We had two oerlikon guns on the bridge wings and a Hodgkiss machine gun. The Mate wanted to rest it on my shoulder so he could fire. I told him "No bloody way!" The gun was useless anyway.

The escort force left us after the second day. Dudley Pound, Admiral of the Fleet, believed the "Tirpitz" was coming out and so he withdrew all the escorts. All that was left were a few trawlers. Before the escorts withdrew they had launched the Walrus flying boat from HMS "Norfolk" and, of course, by the time it came back from its reconnaissance mission the "Norfolk" and all the warships had gone. So the plane had to land on the sea. The Commodore managed to get the plane and crew picked up and taken on board his ship. I later saw the pilot, Sub Lt Wignall, in Archangel and he was furious. "We got left behind," he said. "The bastards left us!" The Admiralty decided that the Walrus should be given to the Russians and there was a ceremony where Wignall officially handed it over.

Once the escorts had left the convoy to its fate the Commodore had little option but to order the ships to scatter. The thinking behind the decision was that there was no way the cumbersome merchant ships could have defended themselves when grouped together. Independent sailing seemed to be the only way to avoid utter disaster. It was a tactic, however, with which Bill Phillips disagreed at the time and one he still discounts now, many years later:-

I still think we'd have been better off staying together. We still had two flack ships, ex fruit carriers, and a rescue ship. And there were the "Northern Gem" and another trawler – they could at least have done some damage. Imagine it, 40 ships scattering in bright sunlight. They picked us off one by one. Less than a dozen made it into port.

It was mostly bombers that did the damage. We were just sitting targets. They were flying so close to us, between the ships, that you could actually see the pilots and the gunners in the cockpits. They picked out the tankers first. The very first one they hit was a Russian ship, crewed by women. She was carrying linseed oil and it was under pressure. A huge column of linseed oil shot up into the air when she was hit. The crew still managed to get off, they didn't lose anybody.

We were hit by a bomb that bounced on the deck. It didn't go off but it knocked some of the lids off. We were carrying aviation fuel and fuel oil for the naval ships, diesel and black oil. We were a motor ship and the vibration of the bomb hitting knocked out the engines. The "old man," the Skipper, was Hurricane Hobson and he said we'd better 'Abandon Ship'.

Charlie Cairns was busy getting rid of the charts and I was dumping the weighted code books. When we reached the deck our lifeboats had gone. The Skipper, the First Officer, Charlie, an engineer and me, that's all that was left on board. We found a bottle of rum in the "old man's" cabin and went aft to the jolly boats. We launched these and got in. We had what we were stood up in, nothing else – oh yes, and my sextant. I would never part with that.

The jolly boats had no engines, just oars, so there we were, rowing for northern Russia. We must have been in the boats for five or six hours. It was a day of bright sunshine. The water was freezing but not the day. We had these big sheepskin coats, Admiralty issue with waterproof lining, and they kept us pretty warm. But the prospects didn't look too good for a while.

And then a small minesweeper, the "Britmart," came along and picked us up. Our ship was listing badly by this time but she was still afloat. The Captain of the "Britmart" decided to sink her and fired incendiaries into the pump house door. We stopped him doing that as he was likely to blow us all to blazes and so he put some 4 inch shells into her hull instead. Four hours later she sank slowly by the stern. It was American Independence Day, 4th July 1942.

After the loss of the "Aldersdale" Bill Phillips was taken to Russia and, eventually, ended up in Archangel. In all he was there for two and a half months:-

When we landed we had no clothes or baggage. The Russians were terrified of typhus and they took us into a big room, a bit like a schoolroom, and told us to take off all our clothes so that they could be disinfected. The official behind the table was a woman and she stood there while we stripped off. We didn't have a stitch on. They wrote down our names phonetically and sent us to be showered.

It was a big room and there were roses on the ceiling and a boy controlled the water. Russian nurses in oilskins came in with brushes and attacked us, scrubbed us down. Then they issued us with white pyjamas that were tied at the wrists and ankles – we looked like Cossacks! And that's what we wore until we went home.

The ordinary Russian people were very friendly but the military and the police were suspicious of us, suspicious of everyone. They were utterly ruthless. They caught one Russian sailor coming off a ship with two tins of coffee on him. They just took him round the back of the shed – bang, bang, that was the end of him.

They put us into a big military hospital. Some of the officers went to hotels but I was placed in charge of 60 Chinese crewmen. They'd refused to go back to China by sea, they'd only do the trip overland, and so I was left in charge of them while the authorities worked out what to do.

During the time Bill was in Archangel the town suffered badly from German bombing. Virtually every other night the planes came droning across and the scream of high level bombs became a common occurrence for the townspeople and the British sailors alike:-

Our Chief Wireless Officer was a man called Harries. He came from the Welsh valleys and was built like the side of a house. During one bombing raid people were trapped in the wooden houses of the town. The flames were leaping from one house to the next and we were trying to help by fighting the fires and by getting the furniture out of the houses before they were destroyed.

With the Russian fire fighters we decided to create a fire break by knocking down one of the wooden houses between these great big flats. We found this huge telegraph pole and Harries took one end, I took the other, the Russians in between. We aimed at the house and charged – bang! We hit the doors and Harries disappeared. It was a cess pit and he'd fallen right in. He was up to his waist in it. We pulled him out and took him to the river, on to one of the rafts that were moored there. And then we dropped him in. He was freezing. Then we took him back to the hospital for a bath. He stank to high heaven.

Bill's ship had been sunk in July and it was October before transport could be found to bring him and the rest of the crew back to Britain. He continued to serve in the Merchant Navy, rising to the rank of Chief Officer before becoming an acting Master in British research vessels. When he retired he returned to Haverfordwest and in due course became a County Councillor and was, for a time, Chair of Governors at Pembrokeshire College.

Herbert (Bert) Powell – Dock Worker
(*Barry Docks*)

Bert Powell on his wedding day.

Bert Powell has now died and the following story has been told by Terry Powell, his son. Bert Powell was a Barry boy, all of his family coming from the town. He started work with C H Bailey's, the ship repair firm on the docks in Barry, on 6th November 1922:-

When he first left school my father worked on board a sailing pilot cutter in the Bristol Channel. She was called the "Britannia." In those days the Channel pilots worked single handed and only had one young boy to help them. When they heard that a ship was beating in from the Atlantic they'd go down the Channel, often as far down as Lundy Island, and there was always a great deal of competition to get the ship. It was all private enterprise in those days. If they were lucky and got to the ship before the other pilots then they'd go up her side and leave the young boy to get the cutter back to port. He'd have to sail it back single handed. That was the job my father was doing when he was just 14 years old.

My father wanted to become a pilot but his eyesight wasn't good enough. He wore glasses all his life. One of his brothers was a Channel pilot and Dad would have loved to follow in his footsteps. But it wasn't to be and in 1922 he began work at C H Bailey's. He did his time with them as an electrician and was foreman with the company for 40 years.

When war broke out the docks at Barry became busier than ever. Ship repairing was one of the main jobs, working on vessels that had been damaged out at sea. The men in the docks must have worked on hundreds of them during the war years. They also fitted degaussing gear onto the ships, putting metal wires over the bows of the ships in order to counteract magnetic mines. There used to be an electrical current running through the wires, that's how the system worked.

It was a reserved occupation, being a docker. Well, they needed all the supplies they could get and they weren't about to lose any skilled workers off the docks. It was a hard time for the men. They'd have to start work at about 7.00 am and wouldn't finish until 5.00 at least. The docks were full of men, working for firms like Bailey's, Hodges and the Barry Graving Dock.

My father was an electrician but a lot of the repair work involved riveting. They had charcoal burners with foot pumps to get them really hot. Then they'd heat the rivets. They'd be sat there in a metal tray and when they were hot enough they young boys would catch them in a pair of pincers and throw them up to the man on the scaffolding alongside the ship. He'd catch them, place them in the hole and the guy on the other side would hammer them in. To begin with it was all done by hand but, eventually, they brought in steam hammers to do the hard riveting work.

All the workmen were very conscientious, Dad always said. They knew that they were working for the war effort so there was no skiving or slacking off. Everyone had a job to do and they did it to the best of their ability.

During the war there were a lot of women employed on the docks, doing the sort of work that before the war was only ever done by men. You wouldn't have dreamed women would end up doing it. Really heavy work it was, too, things like plating, boiler making – well, there weren't enough men to do all the work in those days as so many of them were in the forces.

Barry docks were not just involved with ship repair. The docks had begun life in the nineteenth century as an outlet for Welsh coal and this was a task that continued during the war:-

Ships were always sat there under the tippers, waiting for coal. The whole of the docks area was covered in a film of coal dust. There were also whale oil ships that used the place, they used to unload at the old Cory's Dock. There was a terrible stink from that whale oil, it used to cover the whole town.

After the Dunkirk evacuation there were a lot of ships in Barry docks, ships that had been brought back to the UK. They were moored there while the government thought what to do with them. My father used to come home with all sorts of things. Once he brought home two brand new ladies' bicycles. They were French-made, obviously off a French ship.

Another time he brought a brand-new electric cooker. Electric cookers were very rare in those days. He wired it up and it sat in the kitchen alongside the old gas one. The trouble was all the dials were in French! It used to drive my mum mad. "What does this stand for?" she'd demand. She got used to it in the end.

He also used to get petrol, goodness knows how. He had this old three-wheeler car and, of course, you weren't supposed to be able to get petrol in those days. But Dad managed it somehow. He even had a French radio and ran loudspeakers to all the bedrooms in the house. And an alarm was fixed up to it. It was quite posh in those days – one of the earliest ever radio alarms, I suppose.

One of the other things I remember Dad doing was to convert ARP helmets into bed warmers. Can you believe it? He'd put in a bulb and a lead and they were very effective. Whether or not they were safe was another matter.

Bert Powell was appointed as an Air Raid Warden for C H Bailey's Dry Dock and although he worked a regular day shift he was often back on the docks in the night, performing his duties as an ARP warden:-

There were so many men working on the docks and the hardware and things were so important that they had to have a warden. My father was the foreman electrician, the ideal man for the job really. They gave him the old helmet and uniform and a big torch and he'd go off patrolling the docks and the workshops and things. I only know of one bomb dropping on the docks during the war but there could have been more. The one I know about fell on the Barry Graving Dock although whether or not my father was involved I couldn't say.

He had a watch post on the top of the firm's offices and they used to have a rota for duty. He was always there, watching for fires or making sure that lights weren't being shown. The boilermakers and the shipwrights would sometimes have to work during the night, especially if there was a rush job on, and they couldn't afford to show lights in case the German bombers saw them.

We had an air raid shelter in our garden, an Anderson Shelter*, and my father managed to rig up an electric light and heater for it. He made it quite comfortable and warm in there, very unusual for those shelters. Normally they were cold and ended up full of water or, at least, quite damp.

As kids we used to go out on the morning after a raid and collect shrapnel. I know it sounds strange now but it was a real craze then, seeing who could get the biggest bit of shrapnel. I can remember collecting all this stuff and taking it home. And my father was furious – remember, he was the ARP warden on the docks – because it was dangerous.

One day I brought an incendiary bomb home. It hadn't exploded and I thought it was a great find. He went berserk. He knew how dangerous those things were. As a child you just collected them, like everybody else.

Bert Powell worked for C H Bailey's on Barry Docks for 42 years in all, finally retiring in 1946.

* The Anderson Shelter was named after the Home Secretary John Anderson and was a corrugated iron air-raid shelter.

Terry Powell – Dock Worker
(Barry Docks)

Like his father before him, once he left school Terry Powell went to work for the firm of C H Bailey in Barry docks. It was right at the end of the war when the place was still full of ships and repair work as well as cargo handling were an important part of the daily routine:-

It was hard, dirty work. There was coal everywhere and even though I was starting an apprenticeship as an electrician there was no escaping the dirt and noise. We used to spend a lot of time putting in temporary lighting for workers in the various trades. The docks were still going full blast in those days and there were even ships tied up or moored in the centre of the basin, waiting for repair. You rarely saw an empty berth in those days – as soon as one ship left another came in to replace it. The dry docks were always busy, too.

My family had always been involved with the docks. My father worked for Bailey's and his father had been a coal trimmer there. My mother's brother was a fitter turner with Hodges and my Uncle Percy was a launch driver for Barry Graving Dock. Dad's brother Leonard was a dock policeman. One way or another almost all the family was employed there. Well, the docks did use to be

Terry Powell working in Barry Docks (on the ladder).

the main employer in the town for many, many years.

Before the D Day landings they had lots of small craft in the docks, frigates and landing craft, ships like that. Then they were moved down to the south coast ready for the invasion. Later on, of course, there were many small ships laid up in the docks, waiting for breaking or disposal.

I remember six landing craft being moored for years alongside the mole in No 1 Dock. A friend of mine had the job of starting their engines once every week, to make sure they didn't seize up I suppose. In the end those landing craft were sold off and used as ferry boats around the Greek Islands. I can't imagine they'd have been very comfortable but there we are. There were also frigates and corvettes laid up in the docks, all with netting and things over them.

The docks were really busy during the war. I can remember, long before I went to work there, seeing American troops landing in the docks and then marching up into town. Black American soldiers I can remember. They marched into King's Square (in the centre of Barry, adjacent to the old Town Hall) and then out to their camp.

Terry's brother-in-law began his working life on the docks in Barry but in 1943, when he reached the age of 18 years, he was called up. However, he did not go into the forces. Rather, he was told that he would be serving his country by going down the mines as a Bevin Boy. With the need for coal miners becoming increasingly important, from 1943 onwards every tenth conscript was sent to the mines rather than into the army, navy or air force:-

My brother-in-law was called Lionel Wiggin was very popular with his fellow-apprentices. And when his call-up came they were shocked to discover he wouldn't be going to the air force or whatever, he was going down the mines. So the apprentices decided to go on strike as a protest. There were a lot of boys working in the docks then and so a strike like that was quite significant. But nothing came of it. Lionel still had to go down the mines. It was a waste of time but at least they tried.

I enjoyed working on the docks. Of course, as a young apprentice, you'd get all the usual tricks played on you – go and fetch me a bucket of holes, that type of thing. There were so many apprentices there in those days and we'd all gang together. It was good fun. The pay was terrible, mind you, less than a pound a week after stoppages. You'd make up your money by working overtime in the evenings and at weekends. When the docks were busy you could get almost all the hours you wanted.

There was a main canteen on the corner of No 1 Dock, run by Solly Andrews. He was a famous name in the Cardiff area and used to run buses and all sorts of things. It was a rough, tough place, that canteen, with sawdust on the floor. You used to get a mug of tea and a piece of toast in there. There was another canteen for railway workers at the other end of the yards. During my apprenticeship they sent me, for a while, to the docks in Cardiff. That was after the war and they had a big mothball fleet there. I used to go in on the train every day. I was amazed – in their canteen they even sold beer!

Mostly we just made cups of tea for ourselves in the workshops. We'd boil up a can on a gas ring. But if you wanted then the canteens were always there. You'd bring in your food each day but sometimes, if you fancied something extra, you'd pop into the canteen.

Terry Powell has now retired from work and, sadly, the great docks at Barry have been run down over the years. Terry still lives in the town.

Theodore Pryse – Merchant Navy
(North Sea – the South Atlantic)

The following story was recounted by Bernard de Neumann whose father served with Captain Pryse on board the "Tewkesbury" when the ship was attacked in the North Sea. Pryse came from an old Cardiff family and had been at sea since the age of seventeen. He completed his apprenticeship with Common Brothers and attended the Reardon Smith Nautical College in Cardiff before joining the Blue Star Line and then Houlder Brothers:-

Captain Pryse joined Capper Alexander, a Cardiff shipping line, and served as Mate aboard the "Queensbury," "Tewkwsbury" and "Bibury" before the war. His first appointment as Master was on the "Aylesbury" but the ship was torpedoed and sunk during his first voyage as Captain on 9th July 1940. The crew were rescued by the "Harvester" and "Havelock" and subsequently landed at Liverpool.

On 1st September 1940 Pryse was appointed as Master of the "Tewkesbury." On 1st March the following year, while in convoy heading down the east coast of England, the ship was attacked by a German bomber which she subsequently managed to shoot down. After the attack an unexploded bomb was found rolling on the engine room grating. Two officers, Bernard Peter de Neumann, my father, and Gerald Turner were awarded the George Medal for disposing of the bomb and Captain Pryse was awarded an OBE for his part in the incident, although none of them knew anything about the awards at that stage. (For a full account of the incident see Bernard de Neumann's story in this book.)

Following the incident the "Tewkesbury" continued with her voyage. She picked up a general cargo at Monte Video and was bound for the Cape Verde Islands when disaster struck. Captain Pryse was later to write –

"On 21st May - - - there was a violent explosion on the starboard side in way of the bridge about halfway between the bow and the stern. I was on the midships deck at the time with the Chief Engineer. A terrific column of water was thrown and the Chief and I were knocked down by the force of the water and washed along the deck. There was a strong smell of cordite; the ship gave an upwards lurch and listed to starboard about 10 degrees."

The "Tewkesbury" was duly abandoned and the crew were about 500 yards from the ship when the submarine fired a star shell. Then she began to shell the ship. About 25 rounds were fired and according to Captain Pryse they appeared to hit every time. Captain Pryse commented –

"My ship was still afloat and at 2238 (local time) the submarine fired a second torpedo which struck the ship in the stokehold. There was a terrific explosion and flash and my ship sank bows first about 7 minutes later. We did not see the submarine at all, not even when she was firing."

The Radio Operator* had managed to get away an SOS signal, and after several days afloat the Captain's lifeboat was picked up by an American steamer, the "Exhibitor," and taken to Freetown. The other boat under the command of the Chief Officer was adrift for 11 days before it, too, was picked up and the crew rescued. Captain Pryse commented that the crew had fared quite well in the lifeboat –

"We had about 200 lbs of biscuits and 12 gallons of water. As well as this we had about 24 lbs of tinned meat and sardines. I had also seen to it that we had a supply of cigarettes and tobacco kept in the boats. I think that it would be a good idea if all lifeboats carried a supply of fruit juice and less biscuits."

The "Tewkesbury" had been sunk by the U 69, under the command of Kapitan Lt Jost Metzler. On the same day he also sank the American ship "Robin Moor," an action that led to protests from President Roosevelt and went some way towards bringing the USA into the war:-

After he returned to Britain, Captain Pryse was given command of the "Newbury." He was gazetted with his OBE on 7th October 1941 but, unfortunately, he had already sailed on his new ship. On 15th September 1941 the "Newbury" was spotted by Otto Ites in the U 94 and torpedoed. She was lost with all hands. Strangely, a Radio Officer friend received the last distress message from the "Newbury," the last that was ever heard of her. Captain Pryse never knew that he had been awarded an OBE for his part in the "Tewkesbury" incident of 1st March 1941.

Later, his four-year old daughter Rosemary, with a heavily bandaged burnt right hand from an accident at home, received his award from King George V1 at Buckingham Palace. The King asked her "What have you been doing little girl?" Rosemary was not too impressed by the King, and was disappointed that the two Princesses were not present.

The story of Captain Theodore Pryse is one of quiet courage and dedication to duty. Undoubtedly he did not consider any of his actions, the disposal of the bomb and the abandoning of the "Tewkesbury" after she had been torpedoed as anything more than what was expected of him. The tragedy of Captain Pryse is that he died not knowing how that he had been honoured.

* Radio operators were real heroes, sending out distress messages while the ship was sinking, and usually being the last off ships, if they survived. One of the first actions of an attacking U-boat or ship was to try to smash down the masts and radio equipment of a merchant, so it could not radio for help, and thereby give away the position of the attacker. For example, Radio Officer John Thomas was directly responsible for the sinking of Germany's most successful raider, the Pinguin. His bravery allowed HMS Cornwall to finally find and destroy the Pinguin on the following day. The Pinguin had sunk or captured 32 Allied ships in 320 days at sea, on a remarkable voyage from the Atlantic and through the Indian and Southern Oceans. Bernard Edwards is and has been the foremost historian and researcher of maritime actions in World War II, and the following is taken from his excellent book 'Beward Raiders! German Surface raiders in the Second World War':

At dawn on the 7th he (Kapitan-zur-seer Kruder) closed the range and opened fire with a full salvo from his port guns. On this rare occasion, perhaps because they were too eager, the Pinguin's gunners were less than accurate. The shells that were meant to carry away the British Emperor's aerials missed their target and fell over her. The surprise was lost and the tanker's radio burst into life, sending over and over again the terse message, 'QQQQ de (from) BRITISH EMPEROR 0830N 5625E.'

The Pinguin's guns opened up again, this time deliberately bracketing the fleeing tanker, for Kruder desperately wanted this ship intact. The raider's signal lamp urgently flashed the order to stop and surrender, but the British Emperor, black smoke pouring from her tall funnel, continued to run for her life, with 32 year-old Radio Officer john Thomas at his key pounding out the QQQQ message.

Despite her advanced age – she was built in 1916 – the British Emperor had a good turn of speed, and, reluctantly, Kruder ordered that she must be stopped by force. He ordered his gunners to shoot to sink and the next salvo burst on board the tanker, setting her on fire and smashing her steering gear. She began to circle out of control and some of her crew could be seen jumping overboard. She finally drifted to a halt and her radio fell silent.

It did not end there, for while the Pinguin's boats were alongside the British Emperor taking off her crew, her radio was heard transmitting again. Radio Officer Thomas was back at the key and broadcasting his ship's plight to the world. Kruder could not open fire again while his boats were alongside the tanker and it took some time to clear them. Then the Pinguin's guns opened up again, pounding their target mercilessly. Only when the British Emperor's bridge was destroyed and her accommodation on fire did Thomas cease transmitting.

The burning tanker was now sending up a huge pall of smoke, which must have been visible for many miles over the horizon, and the raider's wireless office was reporting other ships relaying Thomas's QQQQ signal... (Captain Manwaring was on the cruiser HMS Cornwall, 500 miles away, searching desperately for the Pinguin) *...As he* *sipped a cup of hot, strong tea, Manwaring was handed a signal form with the British Emperor's QQQQ message. Minutes later, orders were received from the C-in-C East Indies Station to steam northwards to intercept the German raider...*

Glyn Rogers – Merchant Navy
(last letter)

The following letter is the last communication sent by Glyn Rogers of Wrexham. It was submitted by Sue Woodfine who comments that "My uncle, Glyn Rogers died at sea, aged 20, on 20th November 1940 whilst serving as Second Radio Officer on the SS 'Bradfine.'" The letter was written in August, just three months before he died and was sent to his sister Nell. It begins with Glyn Rogers on his ship in Canada and is filled with hopes and ideas for the future, all the more poignant for knowing that the plans were never to come true:-

Dear Nell

I hope you received my last letter OK. I'm sending you this one when we get back to England (It may be Ireland that we are going to but I hope not, and the chances are against it). This letter, when finished, will be a diary of daily events of interest – at least I hope you find them interesting. It's easier than writing the letter all at once.

I see from my diary that my last letter to you was dated 10th July so I'll start from there. But wait – we spent such a hectic time in Three Rivers that I didn't find time to write the damn thing up. The only entries for a fortnight are 10 dollars drawn, 15 dollars drawn and 5 dollars drawn. Perhaps that tells you something anyway. We spent many of our evenings in a small nightclub called "The Green Pansy" whose orchestra is occasionally on the air from the local radio station. This place is smaller than Wrexham, yet what a difference.

A night club (open till 4.00 am every night except Saturday when it closes at 1.00 am), a club with an orchestra, taverns open until 1.00 am every night and none of the "Time gentlemen, please" stuff. It's generally about 2.00 am before you are finally requested to remove yourself. And a radio station. Don't you wish Wrexham was something like that? There's something radically wrong with our country.

We spent a couple of days in Sunderland before we came away and after 10.00 pm each night there was nothing to do but walk the streets, not even a café open. I'd like to go to Canada to live after the war. One of the crew, namely the 5th Officer, found a girl to his liking over here and deserted the ship for a week. He came back on the Saturday before we left but scrammed again on the Sunday. The Captain had the police after him but they didn't get him so we had to leave without him. You're bound to find a job in Canada but when Hitler's finished with poor little England the chances are there will be more unemployed than employed there.

This letter is beginning to ramble but here begins the diary of events.

July

Tuesday 23rd. Left Three Rivers at 1400 hours with slight regrets for having to leave the "Green Pansy," the taverns, Yvette the publican's daughter and many other charming things and people. The "old man" (your hardened and experienced seafarer will know that this refers to the beloved Captain) had brought a curious little dog aboard. He looks like a cross between a bull dog and a terrier but I understand that he is a thoroughbred.

Wednesday 24th. Fog nearly all day, ship's whistle going every few minutes. That whistle is a super-test for the nerves. When you're in the wireless cabin you are almost on top the "goddamn" thing – "goddamn" being Canadian for "dashed." The river pilot left us in the evening.

Thursday 25th. About 4.00 pm we passed between Cape Breton Isle and Nova Scotia. The channel narrows down to about a mile and you get a very pretty panorama each side. Late evening a "pea souper" descended on us, so thick that we had to anchor. Give me a break for a minute, will you? I must roll myself a cigarette. Yes, I'm getting expert now. Incidentally, I hear that cigarettes in England have gone up again. Woe are we! End of day.

Glyn Roger's use of the term "England" when referring to the British Isles owes more to the attitudes of the times than any preconceived notions on his part. There is no disrespect intended to Wales and the Welsh people, it was simply how people thought in those days. The concept of Welsh nationalism was then very limited:-

Saturday 27th. We reached Halifax, Nova Scotia and anchored in an inland harbour in which there were about 20 ships waiting for convoy. We had some good swimming here off the ship's side and obtained a slight colour. On Wednesday 31st the ships moved out, one after the other, to form up a little way out to sea. In the afternoon we were off, with a fortnight's run ahead of us.

I decided not to write a day to day précis coming across because it would, no doubt, bore you as much as the trip bored me. A few days out a small convoy joined us from Bermuda. It was escorted by the "Montclair," one of the "Mont" ships, now an armed merchant cruiser. On 8th August a moderate gale rose, whipping up a nice swell which gave the ship a helluva roll. The decks were awash half of the time.

On the evening of the thirteenth we had a little thrill. The escorting naval sloop signalled that there was a submarine around. All the ship's aft guns were manned and the sloop dropped a few depth charges. However, we carried on unmolested. At the time of writing (1400hrs, 14th August) we are north of Scotland and in a few hours will be passing through the Pentland Firth. Our destination is somewhere on the east coast, most likely the NE again.

14th August. Passed through Pentland Firth, a narrow channel between the north point of Scotland and the Orkneys, wherein is situated Scapa Flow. The Orkneys look very grim and forbidding – high cliffs rising sheer from the water and twenty days out of a hundred there are gales. We had one when we passed through the Firth. You could hardly stand up against it. Someone suggested, rather weakly perhaps, that the Scots wore kilts because their legs got so brawny striving against the wind all the while and they wanted to show them off.

Friday 15th August. We arrived at the little Scottish port of Methil. A great many ships were waiting in harbour for a convoy. It's grand to be back again in the old homeland. Two and a half months is not a short time. It seems ages since

I staggered around the docks of Middlesboro' with a case getting heavier every minute, and with a feeling of dejection and homesickness almost to be wondered at now. However, the initiation into the sailor's life was soon over.

Incidentally, it is a most mysterious fact that throughout the trip I was never anywhere near being seasick and we had many a stormy day when the ship was rolling so much the side rails, called the gunwhales or, more correctly, the gun'ls, were under water. On the Channel crossing I used to feel seasick at the slightest movement of the ship.

As I sign off for the 16th it is a moonlight night, or morning rather, and I've just received a message that there are planes over the south coast. So far there are none up this way. We are now near the mouth of the Tyne, having moved off in a southbound convoy this morning.

Saturday 17th August. Arrived, at last, at a port a few miles up the Humber. It seems that we'll be away again in about ten days.

Sunday 18th August. We have received the very unwelcome news that there must always be sufficient numbers of the crew to man our defensive gun while in port. It works out that I have to be on watch once every four days. However, my mate, the chief operator, is going to take one week and I the other. That means I will be able to get home for a week. I will go to London first as I have several things to buy and also I want to get rid of the cash accumulated in the last couple of months. But I'll be up in North Wales for two or three days. I'll write you from London when I'll be going up there.

You may find there's a penny postage to pay on this letter as I've only got a 2d stamp and the PO here is closed. There may be a slot-machine, however. Well, here's wishing you all the best.

Glyn

The letter is a fitting testimony to a brave man, to all the brave men of the Merchant Marine, who so willingly went to do their duty, knowing that death lurked in the wave troughs waiting for them to sail by.

David Simpson

(Atlantic Convoys)

Although a Liverpudlian, David sailed with many North Wales sailors out of Liverpool, and has lived in Barry since 1966. He is presently using Fred Hortop's research as a basis for a study of Barry merchant seamen lost in WWII. He served full-time in the Merchant Navy from 1940-46, and after the war worked for Butlins in the summer and went to sea in the winter, until Butlins needed him full-time in 1963.

I was at Birkenhead, in boarding school when war broke out, and wanted to go in the RAF but my maths then wasn't good enough. A friend's father was a chief engineer with Coast Lines and I managed to become a cadet and served on small coasters. However, the pay was only 12 shillings and sixpence a week, so I became an Ordinary Seaman. On Liverpool ships there was always a bunch of Scousers, and a mix from other parts of the country. I remember one ship there were 6 form, I think, Porthmadog, and they all spoke Welsh all the time, not in front of you, though.

It was fairly iniquitous, the 'us and them' approach at sea. Deck and engine-room were very different. Lots of Barry men were 'down below' as firemen and trimmers, I couldn't stand the heat and noise, and lots of the men lost were firemen, not deck personnel. With my first ticket, the Master pulled me to one side and told me I'd have to make changes to my life. He'd seen me talking to the 3rd engineer, and I was 3rd mate. I said I knew him from shore, but he told me that 'oil and water don't mix.' He said it was very important to keep a water-tight compartment between deck and engine crew members. It's unjust – you see these men with chestfuls of medals, but the poor firemen, those most at risk, below the waterline, got nothing. During the war, tt was a mark of pride for us on shore leave, jut to wear our silver M.N. badge, no medals.

In convoys, you had no idea what was going on – I was in one of the biggest convoy battles - SC118 - of the war, but was unaware of it at the time. I remember a US troopship going down with hundreds dying but little was heard of it, and also I always thought that the Commodore's ship was a Blue Funnel line, but that seems not to be the case.

I would be on the wheel or on look-out on the bridge as lookout and usually warmly dressed. I was aware that I was lucky. A mate had told me to get any girlfriend to cut off the feet of any old silk stockings – they kept your feet warm. On either side of me, clipped to the rigging were great life rafts. You didn't have to lower them – you just knocked a clip off and they fell into the sea. The men down below were in singlets and dungarees. If they managed to get out and up the ladders to the deck, it was freezing and they'd come from a hundred degrees of heat, wearing next to nothing. I'd have preferred to be ashore rather than in that job. In the Anglo-Saxon, two young sailors survived – few firemen made it to a boat, let alone survived. I started writing this stuff on Barry because no-one seems to care any more. You compare it to Liverpool, where it is still part of their heritage.

It was hard work. At sea there was no slack on the boats – if anyone was ill you had to cover and work longer than your normal 10 hours a day. And on the average tramp, the food was absolutely terrible. You don't feel fear when you're 17 and growing up in the war – you feel invincible at that age. The main thing I remember is the food was awful. The captain and chief steward bought the food, and lots of it was inedible – I suppose some might have been on the fiddle. The best meal of the day was curry and rice for breakfast – it was curry added to the remains of what the saloon had had the night before.

I was at the doctor's recently, and I told him that I was a doctor as well. He asked how, and I told him that 2nd mate was usually the ship's doctor with the key to the medicine chest. You were so busy at sea that the 2nd mate was the only one who had the time between navigational duties and watch-keeping. I still have 'The Shipmaster's Medical Companion'. In a case of suspected appendicitis it tells you that the appendix is sited 'in the south-west corner of the abdomen'. You couldn't make it up, could you?

Typically in the Merchant Navy you came home and had to be given your 2 days leave a month. As an average trip was 3 months, that meant 6 days shore leave. You'd then go to the pool officer and ask what was available. I suppose some of the pre-war men tried to stay on the same ship, as they were used to it, and most of us didn't want a little tramp steamer with lousy food. I served mostly on tramps as Ordinary Seaman and then AB.

David still lives in Barry with his wife Tina, who he met when they were both appearing in pantomime in Blackpool in 1963. After the war, David's maths had improved, and he attained his 2nd Mate's Ticket in 1949. David's ambition was to be a comedian, and he was given a 6-week trial in a theatre, but his 'American' style was too early for British audiences. Butlin's, with many different revues and shows, suited him better. He assisted his father to arrange the Royal Variety Performances, which included the Beatles, Flanders and Swan, Joe Loss, Charlie Drake, Steptoe and Son, Dickie Henderson and Marlene Dietrich in 1963. He was offered the position in 1967 by Bernard Delfont upon his father's death, but he much preferred Butlin's! The line-up for 1964 included Tommy Cooper (twice), the Shadows, Cliff Richard, Cilla Black, Millicent Martin, Kathy Kirby, Brenda Lee, the Tiller Girls, the Bachelors, Morecambe and Wise, Gracie Fields, Ralph Reader's Gang Show, Jimmy Tarbuck, Bob Newhart and Lena Horne. David sold cars at Motors in Barry and also was entertainments manager at Butlins in Barry. After retiring from Butlins, he worked at Geest's at Barry Docks as a relieving officer, and Tina opened the Take 5 Tea Shop in Barry's High Street.

* The most important convoy battles were during 1942-1943. After May 1943 the wolfpack threat had gone, and after that most U-boats faced the convoys on their own and had to deal with the escorts by themselves. Each battle could be last a week, have about 60-80 ships and a few thousand men fighting over shipping and goods worth several hundred million pounds. The convoy battle referred to by David Simpson was, the slow Halifax/UK Convoy SC118, escorted by the British B2 group. >From 4th-7th February, 1943 it was attacked in mid-Atlantic by a pack of 20 U-boats. 13 of the 63 merchantmen were sunk. However, on the 4th U-187 was detected by HF/DF, hunted down and sunk by the destroyers Beverley and Vimy. Three days later, the Free French corvette Lobelia sank U-609 and a RAF B-17 Flying Fortress sank U-624. 1 in 26 mariners serving aboard US merchant ships in World WW II died in the line of duty, suffering a greater percentage of war-related deaths than all other U.S. services. Casualties were kept secret during the War to keep information about their success from the enemy, and to attract and keep mariners at sea. The same occurred in the UK, which is why these seamen are neither recognised nor remembered properly. The losses for Barry alone equated to at least 1 in 20 of all able-bodied men in the town.

Ray Steggles - Royal Navy
(Norway campaign – corvettes – submarines in the Mediterranean)

Although he was born at Ferndale in the Rhondda, Ray Steggles came to Cardiff at an early age when his father, who worked initially on the Taff Vale Railway, transferred with the Great Western Railway to Severn Tunnel Junction. His father's original idea was to move with the Great Western down to Cornwall or Devon but his mother didn't like the idea. She was a bit homesick and as she was from Cardiff that was where the family came to live:-

I joined the navy on 24th January 1938, as soon as I left school. I was just fifteen years old and was in Boys' Service until I reached the age of eighteen. Some boy entrants went to the "Ganges" at Harwich but I was sent to train at HMS "St Vincent" in Portsmouth. I was there for 18 months and finished my training just as war was declared. I trained as a wireless operator, a Telegraphist as the navy called us. "Sparkers" we called ourselves.

I was on the old battleship "Iron Duke," Jellicoe's flagship at Jutland, at the time. She was being used as a training ship, giving young boys like me practical training afloat, and sailed from Portsmouth to Falmouth where we were due to pick her up. Quite why they wouldn't let us sail on her I don't know. They sent us down by train – how stupid can you get. I was only on board a few days, 17th till 23rd August, and then we were recalled because of the war. Otherwise we'd have been away, at sea somewhere.

I kept a diary during the war years, lots of blokes did. You weren't supposed to, of course, it was all strictly illegal. I don't know what they would have done if they had ever found it, confiscated it, I suppose. It didn't matter, I wanted some sort of record of the places I went and the people I met. So I kept my diary, wrote it up all through the war. I still have it.

We went into barracks at Portsmouth for a short time after we came off the "Iron Duke" and then I was drafted into the cruiser "Effingham." She was the first cruiser lost in the war. She ploughed into some rocks during the Norway campaign and we always said she was sunk by "soft pencil." We were landing troops in one of the fiords of Norway and we didn't have many good maps of the region. What our navigator was using was an old school Atlas, we reckoned. And he ran off the course with a soft pencil rather than a hard one. The line covered up the rocks and we drove right onto them.

I was in the Recreation Space at the time, waiting to go on watch. I felt a shudder and the ship slowed. Next thing we knew there were destroyers alongside to take us off. And the "Effingham" slowly sank. I was then on the destroyer "Echo" until they transferred a group of us to the "Coventry." We went into Harstad, spent the night in a furniture storeroom, and from there they put us on a Polish transport, ready to go back home. Then some bloke on the sloop "Fleetwood" went sick and I was detailed to take his place. When the campaign was over we towed the destroyer "Eskimo" all the way back to Scapa Flow – stern first as her bows had been blown off.

Ray was back in barracks at Portsmouth when the news of the Dunkirk evacuation came through. After the French surrender the docks were full of French ships and he was one of several sailors detailed to take over the destroyer "Leopard." There were several Free French sailors on board but most of the crew were British:-

The trouble was we couldn't get her working properly. Every time we went out to sea she'd come back with a list. We just couldn't work out what the problem was. I wasn't on her for long as I was soon sent out to Ireland, to Belfast, to help pick up a new Flower Class corvette. She was named the "Gentian." We were based in Liverpool and from September 1940 until January 1941 I was involved in convoy duties across the Atlantic.

The "Gentian" rolled like hell, same as all the Flower Class Corvettes. Well, she was only a glorified trawler, after all. They had no draft, those corvettes, and in bad weather they were very, very wet. The water seemed to come in everywhere.

Conditions were pretty basic on those convoys, particularly in a bad sea. Just trying to get a meal was a problem - it was a stupid design because the messes were for'ard and the galley was aft. Imagine trying to carry pots and pans all the way along the deck in bad weather! Most times we'd make a big urn of stew. Everything you'd care to name went in. We'd just tie it to the ladder and you'd scoop out a mug full whenever you wanted something to eat.

There were usually two or three corvettes in each convoy, maybe a destroyer or cruiser as well. Several ships were sunk in our convoys. I really can't remember how many but certainly a few. The first thing you knew about it was an explosion, and then we'd shoot in and drop our depth charges. I don't think we ever sank anything.

There was great camaraderie on those corvettes, we were all in it together, that was the feeling. I had a bunk in with the stokers and that was lucky. Stokers didn't have to sling a hammock like the rest of the lads. Very comfortable it was, unless the weather was bad. We didn't think much about the danger although we all knew it was there.

Ray left the "Gentian" in January 1941 when he volunteered and was accepted for duty in the submarine service:-

I was fed up with all the rolling on the surface! I reckoned that at least down below it would be stable. And you did get an extra shilling a day for being in submarines. The first thing they did was to send me on a course to HMS "Dolphin" at Gosport. That took a couple of weeks and we had to do things like go through the escape tank. You'd go down on ladders alongside the deep tank and then float up to the surface using the breathing gear. You wore a sort of rubber apron that was supposed to keep you balanced. It was a little claustrophobic down there in the tank but I didn't find it any real problem. Several men failed it, mind you. They couldn't handle the pressure.

It was a long course, mine lasting from 17th February till 1st May 1941. We did one trip out in a submarine but most of the course was classroom-based. And after it was over they sent us up to the "Cyclops" in Rothesay on the Clyde. She was the depot ship but I didn't wait long on her. I got there on 2nd May and on 13th I was drafted to a training sub, the H 32, First World War variety. We did day trips down the Clyde and I was on her till September.

I was sent out to Malta on P 36, a modern U Class sub. Churchill had said that all our submarines had to have names, rather than numbers, but early on in the war some of them didn't and some of them got sunk before they could be named. It was very cramped on board. We lived in the fore ends, alongside the spare torpedoes. After you fired the first four torpedoes and they reloaded the tubes you tended to have a bit more space.

I was what they called 'spare crew'. It meant that, once I got to Malta, I relieved people who were on the sick or on leave, so I served in lots of different boats. I was there from December '41 to sometime in 1943. It was during the siege of the island – they even awarded me the Malta Medal. I remember seeing "Faith," "Hope" and "Charity," the three biplanes that defended the island, flying many times. They looked like real string bags but they certainly did a good job.

We made our patrols out from Malta and there were so many different targets in those days. You tended to spend 10 days at sea, then four in harbour. If you fired all your torpedoes inside the 10 days you'd just come back in, reload and go off again. You had to be out for ten days. One of the Skippers I served with, on the "Unicorn," was Anthony Daniel. I spent six months on the boat with him and we sank several enemy ships, Italian mostly.

When I was on the "Ultimatum" we sank an Italian submarine. She was on the surface, we were submerged. That was probably the worst time because we knew what they would be feeling and doing.

I was on the "Ultimatum" when we heard that the depot ship "Medway" had been sunk. Rommel was too close to Egypt, they decided, and she had to be moved to Haifa. But she was torpedoed on her way there. I think she'd have been better off stopping in Egypt.

Normally we fired our torpedoes when we were submerged – and usually at night. We had a gun, a little 3 inch thing, and we'd use that if we were after small ships. Once we bombarded the Italian mainland with that gun, us and several other submarines at different points along the coast. They told us the targets and we went out and tried to hit them. Whether we did or not is a different matter.

When a torpedo hit its target you'd hear the sound of the explosion, even though you were down below. You'd feel the shock waves. It was worse than the shock from depth charges but then, of course, you knew that it wasn't you who was getting it.

We did all sorts of unusual and dangerous things out there. I wrote in my diary about several of them –

"Friday 9th January 1942, arrived off Cannes. Surfaced at 1850, a few yards from the shore, and landed agents in two separate Folbots.* Set course for Malta."

That was a typical sort of exercise. We carried secret agents several times and what happened then was you stowed collapsible boats in the racks where you normally kept the spare torpedoes. It meant more cramped conditions for us!

Other diary entries read like this –

"10th September 1942, sank one 8000 ton supply vessel. Three torpedoes fired, three hits. She sank in two minutes. No counter attack due to heavy rain and bad visibility. Escorted by eight destroyers and aircraft. Only one boatload of survivors seen."

"19th August 1942, P 44 arrived off patrol. She had fired one torpedo at point blank range whilst on the surface. Target was an ammunition ship which blew up with such force that a destroyer alongside taking off ammunition was never seen again. P 44 was so near that the blast almost blew her conning tower away. Her main ballast tanks were also damaged. She is now in the dockyard."

We were depth charged lots of times. On one occasion they dropped 123 depth charges on us, over a period of 24 hours. Then they gave up and went home. Of course we were frightened, especially when the shock made the corking come down off the ceilings. We generally held it together but it would be wrong to say that we weren't afraid. And it wasn't just torpedoes. Once we were machine gunned by two ME 109s as we came in through the boom at Malta. That was on 27th February 1942.

Malta was constantly bombed during the months that the "siege" was taking place. To begin with the Italians attacked from fairly high altitude but soon the German Luftwaffe joined in the assault and then the attacks were lower and much more accurate:-

They bombed the P 36 when she was alongside at Valetta. She took a direct hit and went down. There were crewmen on board at the time but luckily nobody was killed. Coming back into base after a patrol you always flew the "Jolly Roger" if you'd sunk any ships. The flags had all sorts of emblems, crossed guns for a gun action, ships to represent the enemy ships you'd sunk and so on.

It wasn't all work, mind you. I remember, once, having five days leave in Jerusalem as a guest of the Palestinian Police. We went to Bethlehem and Nazareth and even went down to the Red Sea. In Jerusalem itself this Inspector took us to places that the guide books didn't even know about. It was a great experience.

Back in Malta the people were lovely. The famous "Gut" was a great place. There were so many little booths and places to eat and drink all day long. There were always Maltese men on the doors – "Come inside Jack," they'd be shouting, "all your ship's company inside here!"

I remember Lt Commander Wanklyn VC, the great submarine ace. Once when the place was bombed he got us all together because he wanted help in finding some Penny Black stamps. They were in one of the bombed out buildings but we never

managed to find any for him. He was a really nice bloke. You spoke to him just like you spoke to another rating.

I came back to Devonport in September 1943. That was on board the "Unison" because it was the end of the commission. And that's when I got married. I came home in September, was engaged in October and married in November. I stayed in submarines, serving on a whole variety of them like the "Upshot," "Vulpine," "Surf" and "Unbending." I stayed on boats until the end of the war.

After the war Ray remained in the navy, serving in submarines until 1948. At that point he decided it was time for something different. He changed his branch and became a Leading Patrolman, in effect a naval policeman. He left the navy in 1958 and lives now in Cardiff.

* A folbot is a type of collapsible canoe or kayak, made in the USA since 1933.

John Stephens – Royal Navy
(Far East)

John Stephens came from Abersychan in South Wales and was just seventeen and a half when he volunteered for the navy. At the time he was working as a brick layer, building warehouses in Newport docks. A Greek cargo ship came up the river and moored alongside them. His mate decided that a life at sea was just what they both needed:-

We went looking for the boatswain. And when we found him he was the biggest man I've ever seen. He was a Greek and he had this huge, bushy beard. "Do you want any lads?" we asked. Of course the answer was yes. My mate signed on, then and there, and went the same day. I came home and told my parents what I was going to do. "Oh no, you won't," my dad said. "If you want to go to sea you can join the navy." And that's what I did. Looking back on it now I must have been nuts!

I went down to Plymouth on the train and still remember crossing over the river into Cornwall. I spent 10 weeks in training at HMS "Raleigh." The third day I was there I got into trouble when I thought the CPO had cracked a joke. I laughed and that was the start of naval discipline for me – gas mask and full uniform, around the parade ground I went.

In those days rugby was my passion. I'd captained Pontypool and Monmouthshire Schoolboys and was even reserve for the Welsh Schoolboys. Wherever I went in the navy they had a rugby side and there were always plenty of Welsh blokes playing in them. Several years later, out in South Africa, we played the South African Air Force. They were undefeated but we beat them by 9 points.

John Stephens and shipmates at Pietermaritzberg. John is sitting, right, without a shirt.

Anyway, after basic training I was sent off to Gunnery School, just outside Plymouth. Then I was sent on draft to join the "Zulu," a Tribal Class destroyer. At the time she was based in Alexandria and so four of us were put on a Dutch merchant ship for passage out to the Mediterranean. The MV "Rembrandt" had a Dutch crew and none of them could speak English. We just lay in our hammocks, ate the food and played cards. It was a great life until, one day, we heard three blasts on the whistle. It was the signal for a submarine attack.

There was absolute panic with people running everywhere. In fact what had happened was that one of the DEMS gunners had borrowed a duffle coat off us, and when the watch changed he threw it to the other men so that he could use it. The coat got tangled in the wires that were used to give the warning signal and off it went.

Eventually we arrived in Durban. Nobody said anything to us or told us what to do and so we sat tight. The rumour was the ship was heading back to Britain and we thought that if nobody said anything we'd take a trip back home. But at the last minute we were transferred to another ship. At Durban there was a woman dressed all in white and she used to stand at the end of the jetty and sing "Land of Hope and Glory" whenever a ship sailed out. It made all the hairs stand up on the back of your neck.

John joined the "Zulu" in June 1942. He sailed on one convoy to Malta but nearly all the merchant ships were sunk. At that stage in the campaign the Germans had almost total control of the area and the only way to get through to Malta was by using fast minelayers:-

I stayed on the "Zulu" until 14th September 1942 and in that time we were involved in several interesting exploits. Finally we put to sea with Marine Commandoes in an attempt to disrupt things at Tobruk but everything went badly wrong. As dawn began to break we were picked out by searchlights. The first to go was the AA cruiser "Coventry." Then our sister ship the "Sikh" was hit. We tried to take her in tow, but a million to one shell from the shore batteries broke the line and we were ordered to clear out by Captain D.

Aircraft were attacking us all the way. I don't know what I felt at the time. We were so busy that there wasn't really time to be afraid or to think very much. I was on anti-aircraft, close range weapons, and I was firing Oerlikons at the Junkers 88s or Stukas as they came in to attack. They were good guns for anything close up but not much use for anything a bit further away.

Then, suddenly, whoosh, we were hit. The immediate sensation I had was that something had gone. I didn't know what but that's how it felt. And in fact the whole stern had been blown away. By now we were about 100 miles short of Alex and when the order to Abandon Ship was given I just jumped into the water. The next second the "Zulu" had gone.

It wasn't cold in the water. At that time of year the Mediterranean was at its warmest. There weren't many life rafts around because she had gone so quickly, but at Action Stations you always wore your life jacket. We had a crew of about 250 and all we lost were 22. I think that's the number. We weren't in the water all that long before one of the MTBs picked us up and took us into Alex (Alexandria). We were sent to the hospital ship "Maine" to be checked over and at that stage everyone thought it was all over, that the Germans would be there soon.

They put about 300 of us on a train, into carriages with the shutters down. They gave us a rifle each and five rounds of ammunition. We thought we were going out into the desert to fight. The next morning when they opened the shutters all we could see, a long way off, was a boy on a donkey and, of course, somebody had to take a pot shot at him. He missed, thankfully. Trigger happy matelots!

With no ships left in the flotilla John and his colleagues were unsure of their future. Indeed, the navy did not seem sure what to do with them either. In the end they were put on board another liner and taken down to Durban in South Africa. From there they sailors went hundreds of miles inland, to Pietermaritzburg, the capital of Natal:-

They really didn't know what to do with us and so we were stuck there for about two months doing absolutely nothing. We got together a good rugby team and spent as much time as we could travelling around playing other service teams – and, of course, the South African Air Force.

On Trafalgar Day several of us were detailed to march through Johannesburg, along with the Marine Band from HMS "Revenge." We had a great few days, dances and parties being laid on for us, and we ended up at the High Commissioners Garden Party. We were supposed to be a burial party because everyone thought he was going to die. But he didn't and so we had to clear out back to Pietermaritzburg.

Eventually, however, I was drafted and joined the cruiser "Frobisher." She had just refitted at Durban and was off to join the Eastern Fleet. We called in at Bombay and there we had curry for lunch. Nobody had ever heard of it before, let alone tasted it. The cooks of the day, two ratings from our mess, collected the trays of curry and we ate it. Then one of the cooks went back to the galley to find the milk for the rice – we thought it was rice pudding. It was something we had a good laugh about afterwards.

One night they were going to have a dance on the quarter deck and a few ratings were sent to scrub the steps. We were on the top gun decks where they stored the fruit and veg. A bloke called Mason was strumming on a guitar and somebody threw a potato at him. The next minute the whole deck was full of fruit and vegetables that had been thrown everywhere. They read the Minor Mutiny Act but I don't think anybody got charged.

One day we came across a French destroyer, her engines stopped and put out of action by rough seas. She had also lost a few men over the side. We lowered our boats to take them food and water – you could hardly row for all the sharks and barracuda in the water. One of the sharks was hauled up after being caught on a boat hook. Big Joe, a Marine Lieutenant, drew his revolver and shot it. The shark fell back into the water – what a sight, all the others ripping it apart.

We took the French destroyer in tow, our Captain screaming for us to keep a look out for Japanese submarines, and we towed her all the way to Madagascar. It was a trip of 1200 miles and was officially recorded as the longest tow undertaken in the whole war.

HMS "Frobisher" – did she fire the first shells on D Day?

We got on well with the French crew, very well, until we went ashore in Madagascar. I don't know what the drink was, but spill it and you'd burn a hole in the table. It looked like lemonade but it certainly didn't taste like it. Fighting broke out all over the place. Men were escaping from the cells, breaking away from the Marines in order to get back and continue with the fight. They were being chased from one deck to another, and lots of them ended up jumping over the side. The ship's boats were launched in order to get them back on board.

Everybody loved South Africa and when we towed that French ship into harbour we somehow managed to hit the dock. You've never heard a cheer like it when the Skipper announced that we'd have to proceed to Cape Town for repair.

When the "Frobisher" arrived in South Africa the crew were given leave. John and some friends went to De Hook in the Transvaal, a train journey of three or four days. They were dropped, not at a station, but on the trackside and billeted miles from anywhere:-

We were being looked after by people who ran a Portland Cement factory and we had a great time. They had tennis courts and that was where I hit a golf ball for the first time in my life, in a field close to the plant. At night we'd lie in bed and hear baboons calling in the darkness.

After a while the "Frobisher" was repaired and we rejoined the ship. >From South Africa we went back to the UK and there we prepared and took part in the D Day landings. We've always believed that the "Frobisher" actually fired the opening shot. Another ship has also claimed that honour but the "Frobisher" crew has always believed that they were the first to open the account. We were at Sword Beach and I can still remember the sight – destroyers in front, then cruisers like us and, finally, battleships like the "Warspite" out to sea. We took a lot of the minor casualties off the beach but really we were there to support the landings by putting as many shells as we could into the German positions.

I had a brother in the Merchant Navy and he was involved in the landings, too. Years later when we met again he said "I knew you were there. I had the earphones on and all I could hear was the pilot of our spotter plane shouting 'Oh, good shooting, Frobisher.'" What it was that we'd hit a line of tanks inland – and that's how my brother knew I was involved with the landings.

On 8th August 1944 the "Frobisher" took a torpedo when she was lying off Sword Beach. We were stationary at the time and had just caught a pair of frogmen trying to attach limpet mines onto the hull. Suddenly there was this great thump and you knew something had happened. The torpedo hit us in the forecastle and the hole was so big you could have driven a bus through it. It didn't matter because she had such a terrific chain locker and the water tight doors kept her afloat.

It meant a return to base and another period of leave for John. After that he requested a shore posting for six months, something you were entitled to do – and state your place of preference. He asked for Cape Town – he ended up in Birkenhead on a brand new destroyer. This was the "Hogue," a Battle Class Destroyer destined for the war in the Pacific:-

She was a wonderful ship, being twice the tonnage of other destroyers and having automatic magazines and turrets. The Skipper got rid of the old Oerlikon guns and replaced them with twin and single barrel Bofors. The kamikaze planes had just begun to function and the Skipper said we had to hit them while they were up in the air, not let them come down. We frowned at that and said that if the kamikazes came down we'd be jumping over the side – our PO, a Scotsman, said we'd have to follow him as he'd be in first.

And so we went out to the Pacific, calling at Malta and sailing through the Suez Canal. The war against Japan had just ended and I remember seeing Yokohama and Tokyo. In many respects they were just like Plymouth and Devonport. But the destruction, I've never seen anything like it. The places were just razed to the ground, a few columns left standing but that was all. The Yanks were in command out there and they let the Japs know it. If a Japanese man or woman was walking up the pavement towards you they'd leap out of the way onto the road because the Americans would just give them a belt if they were in the way.

In Yokohama there was an old destroyer that the Japs had captured at Hong Kong. It was really old and below decks you had to bend over double to walk through some of the compartments. We were told it had to be brought back to Hong Kong, so we took it in tow. Well, this terrific storm blew up but we carried on towing. We were being tossed about like corks and we didn't see the rest of the escort for three days. Pride demanded that the old destroyer was brought back to Hong Kong – bloody silly, really, but there you are, that was the navy.

The only currency worth anything just then was cigarettes. I remember paying 10 Players for a watch and shortly afterwards the thing stopped. When I took the back off there was nothing there – how it had kept going for even a minute I'll never know. Lots of the boys got conned – the Japanese would take the cigarettes and then ride off without passing over the goods. After a while we set up hosepipes on the deck and we used to turn these onto them. At Shanghai you couldn't get up river for all the sampans trying to barter and sell stuff to us. We even bought a dog off them but he never grew, and we ended up burying him in Sydney harbour.

With the war now over we were involved in a round-the-world cruise, and after visiting places like Singapore and Hong Kong and several islands in the South Seas we ended up in Darwin. From there we slipped down the coast of Australia, along the Great Barrier Reef to Sydney. Four Battle Class destroyers were there, along with the "Duke of York." We had a fabulous time.

By now, however, John's demob was due and he left the "Hogue" for a shore base, the "Golden Hind," to await transport back to Britain. He was eventually given a passage on the cruiser "Berwick" and landed in Plymouth where he was demobbed. His round-the-world cruise had taken him to places like Hong Kong, Singapore, Perth and Formosa (Taiwan). He arrived home on 11th February 1946, just in time for the heaviest snowfall in years. He was also in time to watch the Kiwi touring party play Monmouthshire at Pontypool Park. Monmouthshire won in front of a crowd of about 30,000. He resumed his career in the building trade and now lives in Cwmbran.

Gerard (Jerry) Turner – Merchant Navy
(torpedoed in the South Atlantic)

The following information was supplied by Bernard de Neumann, whose father served with Jerry Turner and won the George Medal for the same act of bravery in 1941. Born in the NE of England, at Sunderland, Jerry Turner moved with his parents at about the age of three to live in Aberaman. The family later moved to Abercwmboi and, after his schooling was completed, Jerry joined the Merchant Navy prior to the outbreak of war. Jerry was serving as Second Engineer on the SS "Tewkesbury" when she was attacked by a German bomber in the North Sea on 1st March 1941.

When an unexploded bomb was found on the ship after the plane had been shot down, Jerry held it steady, sitting astride the 250-pound missile, while Second Officer Bernard de Neumann attached a sling. Working in total darkness and with assistance from the Captain, Theobald Pryse, the bomb was eventually hauled on deck and dumped into the sea. In recognition of their courage Jerry and Bernard de Neumann were awarded the George Medal, Captain Pryse an OBE. For a full account of the incident see Bernard de Neumann's story in this book. After the incident the "Tewkesbury" proceeded on her voyage but on 21st May, en route for the Cape Verde Islands, she was torpedoed by the U 69. They were about 900 miles from land in the South Atlantic and after the first torpedo struck the ship's two lifeboats were quickly launched. Captain Pryse took command of one, the First Officer the other. The German commander allowed the crew of 42 to pull well away before he sank the "Tewkesbury" by shell and a further torpedo. Twenty one sailors were in each boat and while the Captain and his boat were soon picked up, the other boat, containing Jerry Turner, was adrift for 12 days. The "Aberdare Leader" for 16th August 1941 ran an account of the experience –"Readers will already have heard on the radio the thrilling story - - - All the crew of 42 officers and men got away in two lifeboats and were twelve days on the broad waters, twice being attacked by sharks and circled by whales before being picked up by an American steamer "Antillus" and landed in Cape Town."The first shark attack came as the crew were taking to the boats and the creature was driven off by an axe blow. About the second attack Jerry said – "On the sixth day we were again attacked by a shark which struck at the stern of our boat. The Chief Mate waited for the shark with an axe and buried the axe head in its snout. We did not see it again."A bigger fright for the crew came when a whale circled the lifeboat, sometimes only a few feet away, before it dived and disappeared. The whale could easily have upset the boat and tipped all of the crew into the shark-infested water.

After eleven and a half days in the open lifeboat the survivors of the "Tewkesbury" were picked up by the "Antillus" and taken to South Africa. From there they were returned to Britain as soon as transport was available. When the news reached Abercwmboi about the award of the George Medal to Jerry for his part in the incident in the North Sea, a reporter from the "Aberdare Leader" went to Jerry's house for the story:-"Calling for an interview, I took it for granted that the honour had come to Abercwmboi as a result of Second Engineer Turner's adventure of last May after his ship had been torpedoed in the South Atlantic. He and 41 other officers and men spent twelve days at sea in an open boat. 'No,' said his brother Morris, 'that was nothing, to be torpedoed happens to hundreds of seamen, that was just ordinary, he didn't do anything out of the ordinary then.'"

There is no doubt that Jerry Turner's act of bravery in securing the bomb on board the "Tewkwsbury" was something that was very out of the ordinary. Yet Jerry, like many brave men, rarely spoke of the incident - or of the award of the George Medal.

John (Topsy) Turner – Merchant and Royal Navy
(tugs in the Bristol Channel - submarines)

John Turner – Topsy as he and all men with the surname Turner were known in the navy – was born in Cardiff. His family were mainly seafarers, his father having spent all his life at sea. Cardiff, in those days, was still one of the most important ports in Britain and it was logical and natural for families who lived close to the docks to turn to the sea as a way of earning a living:-

My father's brother, my uncle, had been lost at sea and my Dad spent all his working life afloat so it was a way of life I was used to. All of us, my family, my friends and me, we were all "docks boys," always down there alongside the ships, playing on the jetties or just watching the ships coming and going. Almost as soon as I left school I went to work on the ships.

I became a deck hand on the tugs that operated out of Cardiff – the Bristol Channel Towage and Salvage Company, that was the firm. They had their base in Cardiff, down in the docks area. During the war we used to go out and tow ships into Cardiff and Barry. You see, if there had been mines dropped in the Channel – and there often were – they'd put an embargo on merchant ships turning their propellers and then, of course, they needed us to tow them in. It didn't seem to matter about us but they wouldn't be allowed in under their own power.

Quite a few ships went down in the Bristol Channel, usually after hitting a mine. The most famous one, the one I remember, was the "Tafelberg," a big Norwegian vessel. She was blown in half by a mine but the two halves were towed into port and they just welded her back together. There was quite a shortage of ships in those days and they couldn't afford to waste anything that could sail, even if it was in two halves. They re-christened her – I suppose they thought it was unlucky to keep the same name – and called her the "Empire Heritage." It didn't do any good. I think she only made two trips before she was sunk (see the entry on Chris Burt above).

Working on the Channel tugs we were classified as Merchant Navy and therefore in a reserved occupation. So I didn't have to go to the forces when the time came. But I fancied a change and I decided to join the Royal Navy. There was no way I was going into the army but I did quite fancy the navy.

It was 1943 when Topsy Turner joined the navy and he went to HMS "Raleigh" at Torpoint to carry out his training. He volunteered for submarines right from the beginning of his service and only served in the submarine arm:-

I can't really say why the idea of submarines appealed to me. I think that most submarine men were individuals and if you had that bit of independence about you then you were quite suited for the boats. It was like a big family where you all worked together. With most Skippers you could get away with murder, as long as you did your job properly. You couldn't have done that on surface ships.

Mind you, I could have joined Combined Operations once I'd finished training. That was one of my options. But I didn't fancy that, it all seemed a bit dodgy. Overall, I thought submarines were a much better bet. And I was right. I loved my time in the navy and I loved serving in submarines.

My first boat was the "Oberon," then I went to the "Taku" and then the "Saga." I spent all my war years in the Western Approaches, based in places like Dunoon and Rothesay on the Clyde. I was also at Blythe on the east coast, just down from Newcastle, for a while.

Conditions on the submarines weren't great but you were young and somehow it didn't seem to matter too much. If you could get one, you had a hammock – very comfortable. If not you slept on the deck and that wasn't nearly as good. Or you could "hot bunk" with one or two other crew members. All that meant was you would share a bunk. You'd come off watch, shake your mate and he'd go off for his duty. You'd climb into the bunk he'd just left.

And toileting, that was fun. You had to ask for permission to use the "pig's ear." It was a sort of funnel that would take the urine down over the side of the boat.

It was a bit cramped on board, obviously. There were communal lockers and you put most of your gear in there, stuff you probably wouldn't be needing at sea. You kept out your hammock and things like your oil skins and anything you might need to get at quickly.

Overall, though, it was a really great atmosphere in the submarine service. You seemed to know everybody and you all got on well. The one thing you didn't want was to be sent back to general service. That would have been the ultimate disgrace, the worst punishment ever.

I enjoyed being that little bit different. Of course, everybody knew you were in submarines. They could smell the shale oil*. It was supposed to be used for the torpedoes but, in reality, you cleaned everything with it. Everything! And the smell used to linger something terrible.

Topsy Turner left the navy after the war, taking his demob in 1946. He returned to live in his home town of Cardiff.

* Torpedoes were powered by an engine using a mixture of compressed air and shale oil. The torpedo could weigh around 5000 pounds, 250 pounds of air and 30 pounds of shale oil, and have a range of up to 5000 yards at up to 45 knots. In practice, around 1200 yards was the 'ideal' firing range.

Arthur Walker – Merchant Navy
(South Atlantic)

The following story was sent in by Mr A T Bradshaw of Penarth. It concerns his wife's father, Arthur Walker, who has now died but whom, when war broke out, was just 20 years old and serving a 4th Engineer on the SS "Ashlee." Arthur was a Penarth man who had lived close to the sea all his life. Penarth had been one of the major coal exporting ports of South Wales, the docks only recently having closed and turned into apartments and a marina. In 1939 the "Ashlee" was trading out of Liverpool, running down to the east coast of Africa:-

The "Ashlee" was sent to Cape Town at the end of September 1939 where she was loaded with a cargo of sugar. She set out to return to Liverpool but just a week out of port, in the early morning of 7th October, she was caught by the German commerce raider "Admiral Graf Spee." The pocket battleship ordered the "Ashlee" to stop engines and a boarding party was sent across. The Captain and crew were told to get their belongings together and to row across to the "Newton Beach," another British ship that had also been captured and was lying there.

The "Newton Beach" had left Cape Town just a few days before the "Ashlee", so the crew knew her quite well. Anyway they left their ship and rowed across. When they'd climbed on board the "Newton Beach" the German boarding party set charges and blew up the "Ashlee." Later in the day the two captured crews were told to come aboard the "Graf Spee." They were put into a darkened mess room, given medical aid and food and then left to sleep.

Shortly afterwards the crews heard the sound of loud explosions. This was the "Newton Beach" being sunk. The "Graf Spee" then sped off at full speed. Some days later the battleship met up with its supply vessel, the "Altmark," and the captured crews were transferred, along with the crew and cargo of the SS "Huntsman" which had also been captured and sunk.

Arthur Walker was always quite reluctant to talk about his time on board the "Altmark." Certainly the prisoners did not feel as well cared for in the holds of the supply ship as they had been on board the "Graf Spee." Captain Langsdorf of the

"Graf Spee" was a humane man and treated his prisoners with dignity and respect, something that was not always replicated by other German captains:-

Arthur did say that it was quite boring, being stuck there in the hold of the "Altmark." He was never very talkative about the experience and we had to get bits and pieces out of him whenever we could. He'd let out little snippets every now and again. There wasn't much to do down there, he said, out of the fresh air, locked away for days on end. He said they played cards and the younger prisoners even played football with a ball they'd made out of bits and pieces.

Arthur spent his 21st birthday in the hold of the "Altmark." That was 1st November 1939 – imagine that, celebrating your 21st as a prisoner. I can't imagine there was much of a celebration! Just six days later his first daughter, Jean, was being born in Cardiff. Of course he didn't know that at the time.

The rest of the story is quite well known. The "Graf Spee" was hunted down and ran for the safety of neutral Montevideo. Believing he was totally outnumbered and out-gunned Langsdorf ordered the ship to scuttle herself in the shallow waters outside the port. Langsdorf shot himself a few days later. That was a shame because he was an honourable man. He didn't want to kill civilians and it was civilians who crewed the merchant ships. The crews of all the ships he captured and sank – I think there were about nine of them in all - were lucky that the man had a heart.

Early in 1940 the "Altmark" was making her way back to Germany when she was cornered in a Norwegian fiord and boarded by sailors from the "Cossack." Arthur was down below decks, in the hold with the other prisoners, and like all of them didn't know a lot about it until the action was over and they'd been rescued. They obviously heard the noise but they had little or no idea about what was going on. The rescue was one of the most famous actions of the war.

After the rescue Arthur Walker and the other prisoners were taken back to Britain. He returned to sea and spent the rest of the war in the Merchant Navy. He was not sunk again and, after the end of hostilities, came back to Penarth to live.

Doug Watkins – Royal Navy
(Fast attack craft – east coast)

Doug Watkins joined the Royal Navy in 1943. He had registered at the age of seventeen, as required, and then sat back to await the call up after his next birthday. He chose the navy because his uncle was already serving at sea and several of his friends, local boys from the Kenfig Hill area, had also chosen the navy:-

I did my basic training at Portsmouth and was then sent up to Scotland, HMS "Scotia" in Ayrshire, to train as a telegraphist. A lot of the training involved visual signalling, semaphore, because I was destined for small attack craft and that was what they used on those boats.

Six months the training lasted and up there with us we had these Cadets who'd done two or three years training of sorts. So they were well in advance of the rest of us. We were just HO's, hostilities only ratings. At the end there were exams, quite strict exams, and if you did well you were eligible for advanced promotion, Accelerated Advancement as it was called. It was a real fiddle because our Chief could recommend whoever he liked. He picked out two or three of these Cadets, no-one else. I was the only one who had sufficient marks to deserve it but I wasn't one of his favourites so I wasn't on the list. In the end he kept quiet because of this and didn't tell the other Chief so, in the end, none of us got it.

After training I was sent to do sea training. That was on board HMS "Attack," an RML, Rescue Motor Launch, and then it was time for the real war. I was drafted and went to Lowestoft, the Coastal Force base. There were 22,000 men there and the place even operated its own command structure. I always say that I joined a wooden boat sailing the North Sea, just like the Vikings of old.

We were operating short Motor Torpedo Boats, just 72 feet long. They were built on the Isle of Wight but powered by American Packard engines, 1500 horse power, very powerful. We had a crew of 17 and those boats were, for their size, the most heavily armed ships in the Royal Navy. Guns, torpedoes, depth charges, we had everything. There were bigger models, some of them having crews of up to 30, ours were the smaller variety.

Every night, almost, we were over to the enemy coast, raiding and attacking. Everybody thinks Coastal Force meant our coast – it didn't. It was their coast we were operating on. We sailed over to the Hook of Holland, to places like Texel. Sometimes we patrolled, other times we took part in planned attacks on German convoys that were bringing in iron ore from Norway.

We'd be disappointed if we didn't encounter the Germans every night we were out. After a while we recognised the different enemy boats and we even knew the names of their commanders. It was no place for shrinking violets. Once this new Flotilla came in, and there weren't enough flak jackets to go round. So we loaned them ours as they were just about to go over "the other side" on an operation. Later we heard the news that she was gone, last seen on fire in the middle of a German convoy.

I don't think you felt fear, not real fear. You'd be frightened for the first few minutes of an action, perhaps, but then you were usually too busy. You used to think that if you could see it, then it had missed you. Of course there was sadness when somebody you knew was killed but you had incredible pride in the uniform. And it was all a bit of an adventure in those days.

Doug and his companions slept ashore but, if they were not out raiding, they had to leave a record of where they were going. If needed, they had to be back at the base within twenty minutes. The MTBs always had two men on board and the engines were always ready. It meant that the boats could leave for sea almost as soon as the crews returned:-

This particular night I was at the cinema with a group of mates. Suddenly it flashed onto the screen – "Fourth MTB Flotilla report to base immediately." About twelve of us squeezed out, everyone cheering and shouting "Sit down, sit down!" The cinema was full of Yanks and other troops.

When we got back to base we were off immediately, over to the Dutch coast where this convoy was gathering. There must have been five merchantmen and 16 escorts, everything from destroyers and 'flak ships' to E Boats. Those flak ships were barges, steel barges from the Danube. The Germans built platforms on them and mounted anti-aircraft guns – those guns were mainly intended for use against aircraft but they also turned them on ships as well.

We had a young boy with us that night. His name was Mortimer Henderson and he came from Kilmarnock in Scotland. He was a new lad. Anyway I was in the wheelhouse and we'd been under gun attack. I glanced down the hatch and saw three men down below. Two of them were holding up the third. His head was hanging down and it wasn't until they laid him on the couch that I could see it was Mortimer. A phosphorous-coated shell had gone clean through him. I stayed with him all night and, in the end, he died in my arms. I've tried to get in touch with his family many times since then but I've never been able to find them.

Another time I was on deck, behind the bridge, because the other "sparker" didn't like being on deck. "You go up," he'd say. There was a canopy behind the bridge, just canvas and paint but it gave the appearance of solidity. We saw search lights reflecting on the clouds and thought that Lowestoft was getting it. But no, it was the Dutch coast. What looked like cigarette ash was falling on us, falling down almost gently through the air.

That night we attacked a German minelayer. We were the last boat - our Skipper was away on a course and a junior Skipper took over. It meant that they put us at the back of the line of eight boats, normally we were second. It meant that we hadn't got rid of our torpedoes and so we took on the minelayer.

I still remember the gun on the German's stern firing at us. The first shell went into our stern, into the engine room. The second one hit the mast and exploded. The Coxswain was at the wheel and he fell to the left with the force of the explosion. The Skipper shouted for someone to take the wheel, then he turned to me and told me to help the Coxswain. He was a big man, the Coxswain, but I helped him to his feet and got him into the cabin.

As I was doing that the gunner off our forward gun also fell into the cabin. He had a hole in his neck you could put your finger in. Blood was spraying everywhere. The gunner said "Got you, too, did they?" I stayed there and looked after the pair of them as best as I could. The Coxswain died just as we came into harbour the next morning. The shell had exploded and caught him. His blood just soaked into his kapok suit and he bled to death. His whole back had been shredded.

A lot of the Coxswains, in particular, were Barnardo boys for some reason. I don't know if the navy picked them especially but it certainly seemed like it. Our Coxswain who died, he had no family and I always wondered if he came from Dr Barnardo's.

With MTB 455 seriously damaged Doug and his crew were sent down to the Isle of Wight to pick up a new boat. MTB 470 was fast new vessel and Doug and his Flotilla now found themselves moved from Lowestoft:-

We sailed through the Straits of Dover at about 11.00 am. Suddenly we saw white puffs of smoke coming from the enemy coast – shells from German coastal guns. We didn't hang about there for long.

When we reached the Solent the place was full of ships, in particular landing craft full of Yanks, all waiting for the D Day landings. We weaved in and out and gave them a bit of a show – well, we were spectacular looking boats when we got speed up. We were in arrow-head formation and there was an 8 foot high plume of white water behind us. Suddenly a light from the shore started flashing – Stop! We stopped. "You haven't saluted the Commodore's flag," said the message. It was on a tiny Martello tower and we had to turn around, go back out and come in again. That's the navy for you.

They sent us down to the easternmost point of the Normandy coast with orders to watch out for any German ships trying to get up the Channel. Then we'd send a message and other MTBs would intercept. We had to be 20 miles off the French coast during daylight hours and after D Day I suppose we all got a bit careless.

MTB 469, seriously damaged off Normandy in 1944.

On 21st August MTB 469 was hit by shells from a shore battery. She lay there with her engines stopped, a sitting target. The frigate "Thornborough" went in, making lots of smoke, threw across a line and got the MTB lashed to her side. Then she brought her out to sea and safety. Our MTB470 took over the tow, but the weather was bad and our engines over-heated and so we had to pass over the tow to another ship. It was awful, we were low on fuel and rolling with our deck almost under water.

I was on watch and went up on deck to give the boys a hand. And in the water I saw debris and wreckage - and heads. Men were in the sea, waving their arms. We picked up 17 Canadians that day, the other boat, the 469, found 14 of them. When we got back we found out that they had been on the HMS "Alberni," on their way to Normandy, when they'd been torpedoed by a U Boat. It was only 75 feet deep there and everyone assumed that the U Boats would be operating in deeper water. The crew was mustering for their rum ration and she went down in under a minute. Sixty men went with her.

The MTBs weren't particularly comfortable vessels. They gave us crash helmets to help protect our heads because, at speed, they bounced about all over the place. There were bunks that you could lower but somebody would always have to sleep on top of the ammunition. It didn't bother us at the time, we never thought about the potential danger. We had one chap in the crew who would dismantle bullets with a stone on the quay side, in order to get the brass!

We always wore big kapok suits when we were at sea. They were like big padded oilskins and made you look like the Michelin Man. To see us walking about in those suits you'd think we were all twenty-stone giants.

It wasn't just patrols against enemy shipping that the MTBs did. One of the boats slipped out of harbour one night and, in the company of a Norwegian boat, went across the North Sea and up this fiord. Then some of the crew went ashore with axes. The Norwegian King had expressed a wish to have a Christmas tree from his home country and so the boys cut down half a dozen of them for him. I believe that started the Trafalgar Square tradition – MTB 666 in 1943. That boat was later captured by the Germans. Three days later, they had her up on a cradle, examining her to see what they could find out about her design, when she suddenly exploded. Nobody ever knew why.

Doug Watkins and his MTB returned to Lowestoft shortly after the bridgehead was established in Normandy and remained there until the end of the war. Then he was posted to Largs in Scotland, to a Motor Launch that was working in conjunction with an Underwater Research Establishment:-

They were all Cambridge undergraduates and none of them would speak to us. They were carrying out experiments with X Craft and things like that. George Blake, the Communist spy, was one of them and we later reckoned that everything they discovered was in Moscow within hours. We sat at a buoy out in the Clyde most of the time. But then they transferred the base to the south coast and we had to tow a motor fishing vessel attached to the squadron. A storm came up and we were driven into Cairnryan, the loch leading to Stranraer. They had two huge jetties there – it was where the "Queen Mary" and "Queen Elizabeth" used to unload the American troops after they'd brought them across the Atlantic.

Doug Watkins was demobbed in 1946, glad to be out after an exciting and adventurous war service. As he said, he was probably too independent-minded to stay in the navy for long once, war had ended. He came back to Wales and, as a carpenter, worked all over the country on various building sites.

R J K Watkins – Merchant Navy
(convoys – North and South Atlantic)

Keith Watkins was born in 1925 and joined the Merchant Navy in the early years of the Second World War. He has now died and the following account is an abridged version of the story he wrote for his family. Born in Varteg, Keith was 14 years old when the war began. In 1940 he found a job packing bananas for Elders and Fyffe in Cardiff Docks' Bute Street but this job finished when bananas became rare because of the war. After a few other jobs he decided to join the Merchant Navy:-

I joined the Merchant Navy at Newport. No guns, no uniform, no drills – I

Lowering the boats to pick up survivors,

was just sixteen and able to join the Armed Forces but I was away on my first voyage for six and a half months. The SS "Veerhaven" was my first ship, a Dutch vessel that couldn't return home after the Germans invaded.

I was met at the gangway by a junior officer who showed me to the deck crew quarters, down the companionway to the mess deck where about fourteen men were sat having a mid-day meal. It was worse than Varteg Colliery with dust everywhere. They had all washed their hands but from the wrists up they were black with the dust. In the centre of the table was a big dish of pig's trotters with several plates of bread, a gallon kettle of tea at one end and one of coffee at the other. I told them I was a new boy, but only a few spoke to me for just five were British and the rest were Dutch.

It was an impossible task to get the place clean while we were still loading coal. I scrubbed the wooden table and benches and it looked like I was winning until the deck crew came in for breakfast (which I would get from the cook in the galley) and brushed off most of the coal dust that clung to them. This went on for a week until our holds were full and the crew hosed down the whole ship.

We sailed the next day and as soon as we passed through the lock gates I began to feel queasy and a bit sea-sick. We steamed to Barry Roads where we anchored amongst other ships, waiting to form a convoy. Our ship was forty-eight years old, a typical tramp steamer of about ten thousand tons, top speed 12 knots – a bit better than the convoy speed of ten knots.

While waiting for the other ships I made a big effort to clean the quarters, using lots of hot water. As the crew were due for a meal I grabbed some old signal flags from a locker and spread them around to keep the floor clean until it dried. When the crew came in, a Dutch sailor grabbed one of the flags from the floor and started ranting at me in Dutch. An English AB from London came in and calmed him down enough to find out the problem. I had put the Dutch national flag down on the floor to be walked on. I apologised, explaining that I had no idea what the Dutch flag looked like, but I felt sure that some of them never forgot my insult.

In the Bay of Biscay the conditions were terrible, the ship pitching and rolling all over the place. I felt absolutely terrible with headaches, dizziness, an unsteady walk etc., sea sickness. I felt rotten but I just had to carry on. One day I saw a man I hadn't met before. He looked about seventy and seemed very ill. He was a 40 year-old Dutchman who had been with the ship for 10 years and was in the final stages of syphilis. He could have been put ashore in Britain, but because he knew no-one there the Captain kept him on board so that he could die amongst friends. Two days later, off the Canary Islands, he died and was buried at sea.

The convoy was near Freetown when the U Boats struck. Five ships were lost during the first night attack, four the following day, one of them a tanker in the line next to the "Veerhaven." The sailors suspended a large cargo net over the ship's side in an attempt to rescue the survivors:-

We could see many men in the water which was covered in thick oil. We watched the men trying to swim, gasping for breath as the oil entered their lungs. We stood there, helpless, and I noticed several of our crew, hardened sailors, with tears running down their cheeks. Two men managed to reach our net but were too exhausted to climb up. Four of our sailors went down and with two either side of the survivors helped them on board. One was fairly well but the other was in a bad way, having swallowed and inhaled a lot of oil. He died in the night, the other we took to Freetown.

The "Veerhaven" sailed on to Uruguay and up the River Plate. In due course she moved on to Buenos Aires and then Rosario. Keith was made welcome by many of the families he met, and when the time came to sail once more he knew that there was no way he could put up with the surly, miserable Dutch crew:-

I walked off the ship and caught the train to Buenos Aires, where I went to find the family who had been so kind to me. I stayed with them for some time. Then they had a letter from an elder brother who had been away in the army. There would be no room for me. So I went to the British Consul and despite saying that I should go to jail as a deserter, when he realised I was only seventeen and not eligible for military service, he sent me to the Hostel for British Seamen. I stayed there, along with four other British sailors who had been left behind in the port because of illness, until on 27th June 1942 I joined the SS "Nagara," a Royal Mail Ship homeward bound from Australia.

We sailed for Freetown on our own and there we waited at anchor for a convoy to form. Eventually there were 39 ships gathered together and we sailed for home. A week later we had lost twelve of them. When we got past Gibraltar we did have a little air cover, but we still lost five more ships before we docked in Avonmouth on 8th September.

I sailed on several other ships after that, but on 27th April 1943 I joined the oil tanker "El Aleto." Nobody knew our destination, apart from the Captain, but we soon arrived in Scapa Flow. A convoy of thirty ships assembled. When we left, it was with an escort of two destroyers and two corvettes. They kept steaming around and around the convoy, reminding me of sheep dogs rounding up the sheep. We still hadn't been told where we were going but from the course we were following it was obviously Canada or the USA. But why, I wondered, were we taking oil to the USA? A few days later all was revealed.

From the hold we dragged on deck long lengths of 10-inch reinforced hosepipe and used it to refuel our escorts. It happened several times on that voyage. They'd come alongside, the sea usually rough, and a line would be fired from our ship onto the destroyer's deck. They pulled in the line and the hose, attached to the line. We would start pumping and all the while the two ships were about 50 feet apart, pitching and tossing about. Sometimes we were 30 feet above them, sometimes 30 feet below. The whole operation would take about three hours and, as we were very vulnerable to U Boat attack, I was always glad when it was over.

On 11th September Keith joined the SS "Empire Don" at Newport. She carried guns, ammunition, ambulances and medical supplies. On deck there was also a railway engine and tender. They were heading out to the Mediterranean to supply the Eighth Army:-

It was very rough in the Bay of Biscay. Suddenly the Bosun was shouting "All hands on deck!" Grabbing oilskins and life jackets we dived out on deck expecting a submarine attack or dive bombers. But it wasn't either. The railway engine was breaking free from its fastenings, and was moving up and down the deck with every pitch of the ship. As it weighed more than sixty tons it could have unbalanced the ship with the possibility that we might capsize. After many hours pulling on blocks and tackle and putting chocks under the wheels, we managed to secure the monster. A man was put on guard to make sure it didn't move again and we were all called to the First Mate's cabin and given a generous tot of rum, plus the thanks of the Captain, for our efforts.

The next day was much calmer and the bombers arrived. We were attacked almost every day but our army gunners were great. The fire power they put up with the Bofors guns was amazing and we beat off the planes every day. We managed to shoot one of them down and every ship in the convoy promptly claimed it. But I'm sure it was our army gunners that were successful.

Five ships were sunk from that convoy. There were so many men in the water but we weren't allowed to stop or slow down to pick them up. All we could do was say a silent prayer that they would be rescued and wonder when it would be our turn. When we reached the Mediterranean they fitted us with a huge metal net, stretching almost the full length of the ship. Apparently it was to catch any torpedoes fired at us. We only had it on one side and we crept along as close to the shore as possible on our undefended side, hoping it would be too shallow for the U Boats to attack from that side.

On the fourth day, without warning, there was a huge explosion followed by lots of smaller ones. The ship next in line to us had been torpedoed. She must have been carrying ammunition because she was still exploding as she sank. It was all over in minutes and I doubt if anyone survived.

At daylight we saw that a torpedo had been caught securely in our net. The escort ordered us to raise the forward derrick, bringing the torpedo to just below the surface. We cut our speed and the destroyer moved in, ahead and a little to our right. All the crew went to the stern and the destroyer opened fire. After four shots the torpedo exploded. The shock wave lifted the ship and even threw us off course.

With their cargo unloaded, Keith and the "Empire Don" returned to Britain. He joined the SS "Empire Welfare" at Sunderland at the end of 1943. She was a "Liberty Ship," one of hundreds built for Britain in the USA:-

Unlike traditional British ships, which were riveted, those "Liberty Ships" were welded. It caused me some apprehension because stories were already circulating that in bad weather these welded ships sometimes broke in two. When we left port we found her motion very strange. Most ships are different in their reaction to heavy seas. Some roll from side to side, others pitch and roll. This one had a peculiar action, a half roll, then a sort of corkscrew motion into a deep pitch. It was most uncomfortable especially as we had been ashore for so many weeks.

It was very cold out in the Atlantic, especially at night when we had to keep a lookout in the crow's nest, forty feet up the mast. We had to try and wrap up warm in whatever clothes we had or could borrow. The crow's nest was about 4 foot long by 2 foot 6 inches wide, just enough to move a few steps so you could see all the horizon. It was during one of my spells in this little box that I realised it was 8th February – my birthday had been two days before.

We ran into a terrible storm. The rain and hail lashed down and the sea became very rough. Usually a storm like this one lasts only a few hours. This one went on and on and seemed to get worse all the time. It was extremely difficult to walk along the deck. We fixed lifelines and greatly reduced speed. One moment we were at the bottom of a great trough and the next we were on the crest of huge waves with propellers thrashing wildly at the air. Then with a sickening lurch we would drop into the next trough. I was on lookout during the hours of darkness and I could only guess at the size of the waves. But at dawn it was terrifying. At the crest of the wave, being more than 40 feet up the mast, looking down into a trough about 30 feet deep, it was a sight never to be forgotten. The storm lasted for more than three days and nights.

Keith Watkins went on to visit places like New York and Durban in South Africa. He also sailed to India, anchoring for a long time in Bombay:-

We played quite a lot of football in Bombay. In the cool of the evenings we would play against any ship that could manage to raise a team. We weren't very good but our goalkeeper was six foot tall with hands like shovels. He had once played in goal for West Ham. When we couldn't find a ship to play against we'd play one of the local Indian sides. They played in bare feet and were much too fast for us. But at least we enjoyed the exercise.

One of the places we sailed to on that trip was the remote island of Tristan da Cunha. We dropped anchor about half a mile from shore. High cliffs faced us with a small beach in the centre. Through binoculars we could see lots of activity on the beach and soon a rowing boat was launched. It was rowed by six oarsmen, all big and powerful looking men. I learned later that they were all of Portuguese descent, from ships that had been wrecked on the island hundreds of years before. We had passengers on board, the relief party for the weather and radio station that were maintained by the British government. Ships only called every two years and this remote island was to be their home for that length of time – and there were three small children in the party.

I had a chat with the island's Council Leader, the man responsible for governing the community. He brought out some goods to barter – sheepskin rugs, hats and gloves. I bought a pair of well-polished and mounted cow horns. In return I gave him a pound of apples that I'd "acquired" from the stores that were being taken ashore. The horns are still in my family, fifty years later.

When we reached Buenos Aires I tried to find the Argentinean family who had been so kind to me years before, but I was unable to find them. I had some pain in my stomach and took myself to the hospital run by Dr Zimmerman, a German working in the British Hospital. He said I had appendicitis but that it wasn't serious and would be all right until I reached home. I explained about the conditions on board ship and he agreed to admit me. I was operated on the next day.

My mate Taffy Howells from Pengam had been admitted to the hospital, also with appendicitis, the previous day. When I came to I found myself in the next bed and between us sat a Staff Nurse. She was speaking Welsh to us, having heard that we were both from Wales. We had to explain that not all Welshmen spoke Welsh. She spoke perfect Welsh, English and Spanish. Her grandparents had emigrated to Patagonia many years before and she was overjoyed at the thought of speaking Welsh to real Welshmen. We knew the odd word and the National Anthem but it wasn't enough and she was very disappointed.

A week later the Captain came to see us. He told us that the ship was about to sail and as we were not well enough to work we would have to be paid off and left behind. I was discharged from hospital on 22nd April 1945 and went to stay in a hostel run by the British Missions to Seamen.

With the war in Europe now over, Keith Watkin was given passage home on the "Empire Driver." When they sailed down the River Plate the masts of the German battleship "Graf Spee," sunk in 1939, were still clearly visible in the shallow water. They docked in Newport on 12th July after a year and a half at sea. VJ Day was soon celebrated and the Second World War was finally over.

Homer Wenderling – Merchant Navy
(Atlantic Convoys, Middle East, Palestine)

Homer and other Barry seamen started the King's Square Action Group, lobbying the council for many years for a memorial to merchant seamen in Barry. When the white Portland Stone memorial was eventually unveiled outside the Vale of Glamorgan Council offices, about half a mile down the main shopping street, Holton Road, Homer made one of the opening speeches, upon May 8th, 1996. Homer was insistent that the Atlantic should be called the Western Ocean on the memorial, and corresponded with its sculptor Philip Chatsfield and elsewhere to this effect. As he said, 'you returned home on the Western Ocean Roll.' He knew Ernie (Chippy) Haysham, who was torpedoed seven times, and reminisced about conditions at sea.

No-one really realises how bad conditions were in the merchant navy, not just during the war, but before it. You had to buy your 'donkey's breakfast', a sack of straw, down Barry Docks, and that was your bed. It cost two shillings to half a crown and you had a bunk with metal laths across. If you were overweight, you felt every one of those iron bars. You bought your donkey's breakfast from 'Dirty Annie's' down Dock View Road, and Dai Woodham's father used to bring it down to the ship with a horst and cart. (Dai Woodham was responsible for collecting hundreds of stram trains down Barry Docks after the war, in what was known as the 'engine graveyard', most of which wer bought by societies and saved for restoration). My first ship in the war was the Selvistan, a Newcastle ship, and the worst was the Homeside – it was a terrible ship.
A 'Donkey's Breakfast' was the sailor's name for the straw-stuffed bag of hessian which up to the Second World War was the only sleeping paillasse used by merchant seamen. It is even referred to in an early sea-ballad of 1400; "A sak of strawe were there right good." As the seaman headed toward his ship on sailing day, with a seabag over one shoulder, he would call on a dockside chandler, buy his donkey's breakfast, and hitch it up over his other shoulder. If it was pouring with rain, he'd sleep that night on its sodden straw, and before the voyage was over the straw would have wormed itself into great knotted lumps and become the home of vicious bedbugs. It was the seaman's duty to provide his own bed, and it was dumped after every voyage and a new one bought from a chandler. At least by the time Homer was buying his beds, they were delivered 'dry' and by horse and cart. Many used to get washed up at Bendricks Rock to the east of Barry, and sailors hurled their beds over the side as they approached Cardiff or Barry on their homeward journies.
At school I used to earn some money handing rivets to the boilermakers down Barry Docks, and aged 17 joined the shipping pool to go to sea. The usual

trip was around 3 months which meant you had 6 days leave when you returned home, after which you had to report to the shipping pool again. You couldn't refuse a ship. A one-armed man named deacon ran the shipping pool for the Shipping Federation in Barry, and you had to have a really good reason to refuse a ship in wartime. I remember a bunch of us Barry boys walking up the gangway of a tanker called the Schuykill to see the CO. We were led by two local Maltese boys, Ronny Montero and his brother. Someone called down 'Are you all Maltese down there?' and we all turned on our heels and walked back to the Fed. Deacon's assistant tried to get us to go back, but we refused. He told us that if he couldn't get another crew by 5, we'd have to go, and fortunately he found a crew before he reported us to Deacon. Deacon would have sent us into the army.

I sailed on the Filleigh, a Tatem ship, which was torpedoed later in the war. They said of Tatem's, 'T on the funnel and nothing in the galley' – that was their reputation for looking after you. The food was lousy. The milk came in a big tin and went off within 3 weeks. There was no refrigeration, just an ice box, so we had to make do with salt beef or salt pork when the ice melted. In our plate of porridge for breakfast, we had to take out the weevils and place them around the plate. All you needed was the slightest damp in the oats, and the weevils came. Probably the oats stayed dry for a week at the most when you sailed.

This opinion of Tatem's as a company is backed up in Vernon Upton's "Upon Their Lawful Occasions": *'The Tatem Line possessed a fleet of fine, well-found ships, manned by good men, but spoiled by the rule of niggardly and oppressive tyrants, devoid of any human attributes. I did not serve in another of the ships of the Tatem fleet.'*

On the Homeside we went to load iron ore in Pepel, up river in West Africa, then waited for a convoy. The ship was full of bugs and cockroaches. We had a boat drill every Saturday morning and always had a life-jacket on or near you as a pillow. We shook our beds over the side – the water was black with bugs. After we docked we used to lift up the beds, pour paraffin in the joints and set fire, listening to the bedbugs and other insects crack. I never brought clothes home – they were dumped. My wife used to burn what I wore home.

The Homeside was a 4617grt freighter carrying 7,100 tons of iron ore from Pepel, the she radioed that she was leaking and the crew taking to the boats (January 28, 1941). There were no survivors and the Arbitrator decided that she was a marine loss rather than a war loss. Homer's friend Jummy Cambell, her 3rd officer, was lost. (See the account in Chapter IV)

I served some time on the Isaac, taking coal to Iceland for the mine sweepers and rescue ships - we had to bunker it at sea, so we never went ashore at reykjavik. The Icelanders didn't like us because we took over the country, us and the Americans, to stop the Germans taking it and disrupring our supply routes even more effectively.

On the convoys, only the captain knew where we were going, but you had a good guess after a few days out. The captains met ashore before we set off. If under attack, the flag system told us to disperse. The big ships used to sail to Oban or Liverpool and little coasters used to take cargo down the East Coast. It was really dangerous for the coasters. Just as dangerous was off the East Coast of the USA. It was all lit up like Piccadilly Circus. U boats could see a ship coming out from miles away, silhouetted against the glare. It was like shooting rabbits in a bucket until the Yanks realised what was happening and imposed a black-out.

I sailed on a captured German ship, the Rolfborg towards the end of the war. We were chartered to take coal from Methel in Scotland to Hamburg, but in Germany there were still snipers in the hills overlooking the river. There were huge U-boat pens there. On one trip down the river it was really foggy, so the pilot said we should anchor until morning. I was on the 8-12 watch, on the focs'l, ringing the bell to warn other shipping. The Empire Swordsman came right into us and caught the no. 4 hatch, so we went to panic stations. The port lifeboat was launched, with me and a shipmate named Willo' on one fall, and the mate and chief officer on the other fall. We swung the boat out, someone called out 'Hang on a minute!' and all the crew were throwing their clothes and possessions into the boat. We lowered the boat into the water, then the mate kicked the Jacob's ladder over the side and we got in and started to row away. The mate then told the captain it was imperative that he went back to the Rolfborg. The captain said no, the ship was sinking, but then relented; telling him to be quick or we would leave him there. The mate lowered a cat and 5 kittens into our ship's boat, and came back into our boat with a new pair of shoes and two bottles of rum. We watched the ship go down. Then the mate got up, and shouted at the crew 'If you think more of your clothes than your lives, swim for them!' and threw all their clothes, suitcases, everything into the river. The men just looked stunned but none dared argue as he was right. He gave a bottle of rum to me and Willo', but we passed some on to the men. There were three Barry men in the boat, me, Willo' House and Gerry Carroll, and we rowed her to go on board the Empire Swordsman.

I served on 'Yankee Jeeps' with Ivor John of Barry, the Cyrus Sears and Bailey Foster spring to mind. My biggest ship was the Port Melbourne, which went to Buenos Aires for meat. We had orders to divert to South Africa as the Graf Spee was about. Generally you were on your own, not in convoy on a big ship as she was that much faster. In convoys were pulled the log in – you steered by log at night to keep in convoy to the right speed. It was a filthy ship. I heard they raised the Plimsoll Line up a foot so we could carry more cargo. That was on the Filleigh. There was also a fire in her bunker, and the deck crew had to lend a hand, shovelling coal away, helping the firemen/trimmers. After the war ended I was the Ocean Vigour, supposed to go to New York with general cargo, after unloading at Malta and Naples, but there was a change of orders and we carried on around North Africa, ending up at Port Fuad, off Port Said. We didn't know what was happening as hundreds of bunks were installed in no. 1 and no.2 hatches, and they were covered with tarpaulins so air could get in, but no rain. All the firemen and sailors were living aft. This happened about three months before the end of the war, but I spent two years in the Middle East. There were terrible problems – we had these Jewish refugees to Palestine, and the scenes in Haifa were unbelievable. They hated our soldiers. (The Ocean Vigour was damaged by a Haganah bomb later). It took two galleys to feed them. We saw one little ship of refugees come in, and it was crowded to the rigging. They said she carried twice as many passengers as the Queen Mary could hold. There was a holding camp for the refugees at Famagusta on Cyprus.

However, I managed to play a lot of football out there, playing for an army team, O/C Troops, up and down the Suez Canal. We were usually anchored off Port Fuad meeting refugees to go to Haifa. I was picked twice to represent the army in representative sides, but the blokes I was playing with said I'd just been posted, not letting on that I was an AB. In the Metlock we carried troops home from Salonika. On the Metlock the troops were't allowed ashore at any port, so if we met any Welsh soldiers, we used to lend them our 'civvies' so they could come ashore with us.

When I came home it was Easter 1947 and I couldn't find my wife. When I did it was in two foot of snow – so deep you couldn't open doors. It's a pity they never widened the lock gates at Barry – it could take up to 53' of water. It would have opened the town up to more trade and opportunity. I carried on playing football for Sea View in Barry and managed them. There weren't many jobs about.

Homer took a painting job in the Distillers plant in Barry, then shovelled coal in the boiler room there, before moving to work rigging in Barry Dock. He then worked in maintenance of the coal tips and cranes for the Docks Board, and finally in maintaining the main lock gates and pier head. Homer still lives with his wife Bet in Barry.

W (Bill) Whomes – Royal Navy
(Royal Naval Patrol Service – trawlers in the North Sea)

Bill Whomes went to HMS "Raleigh" at Torpoint in September 1943 for his basic training. He had been keen to join the navy and volunteered at the age of seventeen and a half:-

My first draft was to HMS "Kestrel" at Worthy Down near Winchester. It was a Fleet Air Arm flying field and was where, as still a very young lad, I experienced all the highs and lows of wartime service. I wasn't there very long before they transferred me to the Royal Naval Patrol Service at Lowestoft. Again, I was only there for a short time before they sent me north, to Scapa Flow, to join HMS "Whitehorn." There was another Seaman with me – we weren't called ABs in the RNPS, just Seamen – and his name was Richard Nielson.

The journey north to Scapa Flow was by train and it took a very long time. In wartime train travel always seemed to take a lot longer. We ended up staying the night in Thurso and the following morning we were taken out from Scrabster Harbour to the Flow. We were landed on the old liner "Dunluce Castle" which was used as an accommodation ship and there we were told that the "Whitehorn" wasn't at Scapa Flow at all. She was in Aberdeen.

We spent that night on the "Exmouth," a replica of an old three-decker sailing ship. She had been a training ship for boys, moored on the Thames for years. She was built of iron and to all intents and purposes looked like an old wooden wall. But she wasn't. I think she was actually built as recently as 1905.

The Training Ship "Exmouth," a steel built replica of an old wooden wall battleship.

They'd moved her up north for war service.

Next morning it was back to the mainland and then we had to face another train journey, this time to Aberdeen. In due course we presented ourselves at the Dock Gates and were directed to the "Whitehorn" which turned out to be a Tree Class trawler. She was numbered T127, had a displacement of just 530 tons and had been built by Smith's Dock in 1939.

We went to sea the following morning and I was pleased and very relieved at how easily I fell into place as a member of the For'ard Party. All the time I spent aboard the "Whitehorn" – about 14 months in all – I can honestly say that she was a very happy ship. We all seemed to get on with each other and in such a small ship that was something that was quite important.

That first trip we sailed for Lerwick, along with two sister ships. One was called the "Wisteria," the other I can't remember. We were escorting the ferry ships that carried RAF personnel for the Sunderland flying boat base in the Shetlands.

Sailing in those waters was to prove far from easy for many of the trawlers' crews, as Bill was to discover during this first trip. On their return from Lerwick the first sight to meet his eyes was the row of ambulances on the quayside:-

It seems that they were there for bad cases of sea sickness. And there were plenty of them. During the return trip we ran into a South Westerly gale and my sea sickness was in second place to my awe at the waves we encountered. My mate, Richard Nielson, lived up to his namesake* and was violently ill throughout.

After a few weeks we left Aberdeen and went up to Scapa Flow. There we spent several months patrolling the Pentland Firth, mainly on anti-submarine work. We ran four hour watches on the "Whitehorn." That meant one hour on the wheel, one hour top bridge lookout, one hour spare hand – taking messages, making Ki (cocoa) for the rest of the watch – and one hour on the aft Oerlikon gun platform as lookout. It was there, on that gun platform, that I discovered just how cold you could really feel.

I still remember the day that I was lookout on the gun platform when I became aware of a swishing and thrashing noise coming up astern. Suddenly, out of the mist, loomed a huge grey shape. At the same time, on the starboard quarter, I made out the shape of a destroyer overtaking us at quite a speed. The grey shape passed us at a distance that was a little too close for comfort. I remember staring up at it. She was challenged by our "Bunts" and replied that she was the "Renown." What a cheeky challenge. There she was, one of the biggest ships in the fleet at 30,000 tons or more, and we weighed in at a mere 570 tons!

I'm convinced, to this day, that she did not know we were there, not until we challenged her. Come to that, we didn't know she was coming, either. And that was despite both ships having radar.

When the war in Europe ended in May 1945, Bill and his trawler were sent down to Plymouth. They left Scapa Flow for the last time as escort for an old RFA tanker that was being sent to Rosyth. Although the war was officially over it soon became apparent that the need for an escort was still very necessary:-

As we left Scapa Flow we saw this long line of submarines being escorted in – U Boats. They had surrendered and were being gathered together in places like Scapa Flow. Later, as we approached the Firth of Forth, we noticed that there was a great deal of activity going on. There were ships all over the place. Obviously something was up. We were told that the "Avondale Park," a Dominion steamer, had just been sunk by a U Boat. After torpedoing her it seems that the U Boat surfaced and surrendered.

When we reached Plymouth our first task was to head out into the Irish Sea, and turn back some trawlers that had been sent to fish in mined waters. The threat of mines was still very real in those first few months of peace, there were still minefields about as well as loose mines which had broken away.

We found one of the trawlers but she turned out to be faster than us. We were delighted to be able to fire a shot across her bows. Even then they were reluctant to turn back. They must have had a death wish.

In late 1945 "Whitehorn" sailed, in company with T231 "Bonito" and T368 "Grilse," for Holland. We were towing these barges which were to be filled with concrete. Then they were supposed to be sunk in order to plug or fill gaps in the Dutch dykes. There had been a lot of damage to those dykes in the last few months of the war. It was an adventurous trip. The "Grilse" had her tow parted by an American freighter which was off course through the Goodwins. Then we came across another American ship. This one had actually foundered on the Goodwins. She was carrying a cargo of military vehicles and as we went past we could see them being taken off by landing craft.

I was at the wheel, during my one hour period, when we saw a mine floating on the surface. We only just missed it. The mine was spotted from the bridge when "Bunts" was checking his signalling lamp. But for that happy accident we would surely have hit it. We took evasive action, I swung the wheel hard over, and then we waited to see if the barge we were towing would also miss the mine. Luckily it did.

Mines seem to have been something of an occupational hazard for Bill Whomes.

He was soon drafted to an American-built minesweeper, BYMS 2070, and spent several months sweeping the Channel area as far as the Dunkirk Roads. They went on to clear the areas around Boulogne and Dieppe. For the minesweepers and the men who crewed them the war clearly did not end in 1945.

* Nielson is often pronounced as Nelson.

Ernie Yeats – RN DEMS Gunner
(Atlantic convoys, Pacific)

Originally from Aberkenfig, Ernie Yeats now lives in Barry with his partner Joyce.

I was in the Home Guard and used to get so wet in exercises I thought I might as well go to sea, anyway. I travelled to HMS Glendower at Pwllheli on St Patrick's Day, 1942, then trained at the gunnery school at HMS Wellesley and then was on the Chrysanthemum on the Thames. We took a ship to Iceland and we made roads there out of lava. We had picks and shovels and the Yanks had excavators. The Icelanders didn't like us being there. (The Icelanders were not overly sympathetic to the Allied cause). It was a strange country – no trees, just shrubs. The cows were full of TB so we were told only to use the NAAFI, which was OK.

In Iceland I went about 20 miles up the coast to a Russian ship, with an Oerlikon gun for them to take on board. They had an armed guard at the top of the gangway to stop us going on board. Only the P.O. went on board, but I did notice that there were quite a few female members of the crew, something the British MN did not have.

I then joined the PLM-14, a collier out of Leith, which was standing off the port for the Russian convoys. She had a French 4-pounder and Lewis Guns and Marlins. She was then refitted with 2 Oerlikons, a 12-pounder and they left the Marlins on her. It was mid-winter and it was absolutely freezing. Every seaman will tell you that the winter of 42-43 was terrible – not just the temperature but the storms at sea. On PLM-14 there was a cabin boy, only 14-15 years old, who had already been torpedoed twice. In one storm he tried to take the skipper's food across the gangway over the holds – the deck was awash. The skipper told him never again to worry about his food, never to risk himself again.

The PLM-14 was originally a French ship, of 3754grt, capable of 9 knots, and sailed in convoy OS 51 in July 1943. Before we left to join the convoy, we loaded with coal at Barry Docks, and we also lost the radio operator, when he fell in the docks. We made every attempt to save him but it was too dark and the water was black. The PLM-14 then carried coke and coal from Milford to Gibraltar, and the convoy was attacked by U 135, which itself was sunk. In 1931 on a voyage carrying coal and coke from Cardiff to Salamis, she had collided with and sunk a Greek freighter.

Our convoy was about 18 ships including troop carriers, and there was a huge storm in the Bay of Biscay which dispersed the ships, it was so severe. A liner broke its shaft, and there were 40 foot waves, huge rollers. It was 2 days and nights before we could turn the ship around, and there was 6 foot of water in the bunkers. The ladders were wrapped around the guns, and the lifeboats wrecked. On the way back I saw a flash off the port bow and told the skipper and we altered course. A destroyer later told us that one of our ships had gone down. We were the commodore ship – although she was old she had a new engine and could make 9 knots. We had taken coal to Fremantle and then returned to the Clyde. We had to stay very close to the bank as the Queen Mary was making her way out. I stayed in the PLM 14 until around August 1943, when we unloaded coal at Devonport. I think she was called PLM after Paris-Le Havre-Marseilles. There was a new engine in her so she could take 9 knots so could be a commodore ship in a convoy. She was built around World War I and was a bit of a rust-bucket. We collided with another PLM boat in the Firth of Forth. We developed a 30 degree list, before we unloaded coal in Devonport. The ship inspector hit the bulkhead with a hammer, and broke through – she was falling apart. We took her to dry dock in Birkenhead for repairs, where she was for 4 months, and then taken to Cardiff for more repairs, before going to Barry to join a big convoy to the South Atlantic.

I then was sent to Plymouth, carrying out drill on the Hoe, before joining the Polperro, a 1937 motorship. She was a little 600-ton coaster, and we carried China Clay, scrap iron and grain and the like, up and down the South Coast, up to Murrayport and to Barry once. It was very hairy business. We were on shore rations out of the ice box. Once, in a storm at Milford there was a huge storm and we sheltered there, but there was no food. We lived on ships' biscuits, and they couldn't get a boat out to us. There were rats all over the ship. And cockroaches – 'steamflies' we called them. (They are called steamflies or steambugs because, as well as kitchens, they are found in laundries. In Sweden, they are called 'bread-eaters'). Once I was on watch at night and saw two phosphorous streaks heading towards us in the pitch dark. I had no time to call the skipper, but thank heaven they were dolphins. Another time the Polperro was sailing to Murrayport and I was on watch and it was pitch black again. I called the skipper and he said, "What do you want, Guns?" I asked the skipper if he could hear something, and he said no. I asked him again, and said it was the sound of pebbles on a beach rolling with the waves. He sprang into action – we must have been 50 yards off the shore. I'm not surprised that she was sunk after I left her – it was so dangerous. The skipper was from Swansea.

On the night of January 5th, 1944, a flotilla of German E-boats torpedoed the Polperro's coastal convoy WP457 and sank 5 ships including the trawler escort. All 8 seamen and 3 gunners were lost on the Polperro, off the Longships, carrying coal from Manchester to Penryn.

I then served on the Maja, a tanker for 12 months, on convoys to New York, and Perth Amboy and Port Elizabeth in New Jersey etc. We were always a tail-end ship on convoys as halfway across an engine valve became faulty so we could only operate on one screw. I saw a burnt hulk in Port Amboy, a Liberty ship. Around Scotland, there were old Liberty ships everywhere, split in half and derelict and damaged.

I was on gun watch once in the Atlantic on the Maja and an escort ship came racing up to tell us to turn off a light in our stern. I couldn't find anything, I looked over the side, looked everywhere. She came up, all agitated again, to warn us, and there was no light in any port-holes, but I chanced to look up. The Chinese crew had caugh a fish about a foot long, and had tied to to some rigging to dry. It was glowing with phosphorescence.

The Maja was attacked at dusk in the Med on one occasion by planes. Once we were anchored off the Isle of Wight, loaded with high octane and with 2 big Yank landing craft next to us. In a storm, they both broke loose and crashed into our bow. We dragged our anchor. We were lucky they didn't break through our degaussing gear, otherwise, BOOM! The worse thing to carry was car petrol because of the gas it gave off – the ship stank, and you daren't smoke anywhere. On one ship I was unloading shells – it was incredibly hot and dusty. When the Maja went down, three months after I left her, 8 gunners and 3 crew were killed. I know where the torpedo went in – into the gunners' quarters where 8 would have been sleeping or resting. It was next to the engine-room. The two gunners on watch survived.

The motor tanker Maja, 8181grt, was carrying 10680 tons of gasoil and motor spirit when torpedoed by U 1055 on January 15th, 1945, south of the Isle of Man. The master, 37 crew and 2 gunners were rescued by a Dutch freighter and landed at Holyhead. She was en route from Swansea to Belfast to Reykjavik.

I was taken off the Maja in mid-September and taken to HMS Boldon outside Totten, Southampton, for drills etc, till after Christmas 1944. It was a sort of rest camp. They then asked for volunteers for foreign service. No-one moved a muscle. The call then was 'First two ranks step forward!" and I was on my way to Australia on the SS Empress of Scotland (formerly the Empress of Japan). I was in a big camp, HMS Golden Hind on a racecourse for a month, and then was sent fleet training on HMS Coventry, a submarine depot ship. HMS Coventry had landing craft, and scramble nets on the side. It also had a leak in one of its tanks of petrol, so we had to go down two at a time for 10 minutes at a time to sort it and got petrol rash on our feet, until the MO made them give us sea boots.

We left Sydney for Leyte and on arrival there were put on a ship called the Empire Spearhead. On the side of the ship the word Altmark was written in big white letters. They were not far off the truth. After working on the ship unloading six-inch shells we started to get 'prickly heat', so some of the lads went swimming, with a patrol boat keeping watch. About an hour after they came back on deck we saw a ten-foot long hammerhead shark swimming around the ship. I went under a salt water shower with salt water soap for about thirty minutes and it got rid of the prickly heat.

Before I left for Leyte, I had to go to Sydney and was sent to an office to be presented with my first good conduct stripe by Commander Keyes. He was the same officer who was in charge of us on the Howe in Plymouth. After I left the Empire Spearhead, I joined the Fort MV Langley, a Blue Ensign ship. Fort Langley was a brand-new Vancouver ship and we sailed through the Admiralty Isles. We carried aircraft parts and were near the Equator. Some of the gunners did not realise how dangerous that area was. One got pneumonia and another went mad and had to be taken off and put in sick bay on an aircraft carrier. We went through the islands to Leyte in the Philippines. The skipper told us to keep a good watch out for Jap subs, for it they didn't get us, the cannibals would.

Ashore, there was ENSA, and I was surprised to see how people lived – in straw huts like pigsties, but the girls dressed beautifully. Of course, the Yanks had the money and had their pick – they didn't want to know us. They then put us on the Empire Stanley, a depot ships, 4 bunks high below decks. All the hatches were welded down so you just sweated on your mattress – it was bad. We were off the Admiralty Isles when the Japanese surrendered. When the Japs gave in we headed for Brisbane, and dumped all the aircraft parts over the side. The sergeant in charge gunners on that ship was Bill Cowan from Murches Gardens in Cardiff. I was then sent to Liverpool, not in the old camp but in a new one, full of Allied POW's. Some were thin as laths. I then went to signal camp in Plymouth.

Ernie's discharge book has the following entries: HMS Glendower 17-3-1942; HMS Wellesley 6-6-42 Liverpool; HMS President II 4-7-42 London; SS Leinster 1-9-42 to Iceland; SS PLM14; MV Polperro; HMS Devonport; MV Maja; HMS Drake; MV Empress of Scotland (Japan); HMS Golden Hind (Australia); HMS Maidstone (to Latie Fell); Empire Spearhead; MV Fort Langley; HMS Walamallou; HMS Queen; HMS Boldon 11-5-1946. After the war, Ernie worked for Catons Dry Cleaners in Cardiff for 9 years, then for Super Oil Seals in Western Avenue, Cardiff until retiring.

PART FOUR

Brief Letters

The following brief letters, stories and pieces of information were sent by people from across the country. They were either not long enough to include in the main text or, because of a range of issues, were not able to be enlarged upon. They are offered here in the hope that they may add something to the text or might be used for further research by others:-

1. Letter from Mike Cole –

My grandfather Alfred Ford served throughout the war on a destroyer, HMS "St Mary." He was mainly serving in the Russian convoys. Sadly, he died in 1984 and his widow, my grandmother, passed away in 2000. My mother is a sprightly 65 year-old and can remember him coming home on leave, bringing navy rations, etc., with him.

Her uncle, my grandfather's brother is the only surviving sibling out of a family of twelve. Three of the brothers were, I believe, in the navy. They were –

Alf, who served in the "St Mary." I have his official war record and discharge papers which show how he was wounded during an exchange and was mentioned in despatches. He mainly served in the North Atlantic and especially the Russian convoys. There was a ship's writer on board and some of his writings were used for the film "In Which We Serve" with Noel Coward. He was a fantastic character. After the war he brought home the ship's cat "Olaf," a fierce old moggie they acquired in Iceland.

Harry served on the "Ark Royal." On one occasion the "St Mary" and the "Ark Royal" were in the same convoy and the brothers were allowed onto the bridges of their ships to signal to each other.

Glyn – I'm not sure which ships Glyn served on. I think he was out in the Pacific, at least for a time.

2. Letter from Victoria Davis

My late Dad, a Spaniard called Manuel Ray, served during the war as a Fireman on the Neil and West trawler "Kyata." Unfortunately, the ship was lost at sea with no details as to how and where.

My father was a lovely man and his name is now on a plaque at Tower Hill in London. My late Mum, my sister and myself attended the Memorial Service in London, a very sad occasion which the Queen attended. Whenever I hear the hymn "Eternal Father Strong to Save" I remember that day.

My late husband, Bob Davis, was also a victim of the war at sea. His ship was torpedoed and he spent six days in an open lifeboat. It was November in the Atlantic and as a result of that experience he lost the tips of his fingers with frostbite.

3. Letter from Trevor James Evans

I am an ex Royal Marine, Portsmouth Division. I joined at the age of 17 years along with many others of the same age. After basic training at Eastney Barracks we were sent to Lymstone, Devon, for the commando training course.

From there we went to the south coast to train under naval officers as crews of assault landing craft. We were eventually formed into one of the first Royal Marine Flotillas, No 538. I believe there were only two or three Marines Flotillas formed and all were involved in the D Day landings.

4. Letter from Mrs Evans (nee Harvard)

I had two uncles at sea, one was a Merchant Navy Captain by the name of Cecil Metcalfe – an uncle of Jean Metcalfe of BBC fame – and the other was Arthur Hopkin, his nephew, from Barry.

They both served on convoys in the North Sea and were transferred onto the same ship in mid-ocean when one of their ships was torpedoed. Both came back without further mishaps. Unfortunately, Cecil died of a heart attack on board his ship in London Dock at the very end of the war. He is buried in Battersea Park Cemetery near Wandsworth Common where he was living.

Arthur was the son of Arthur Hopkin Senior, grandson of Evan Hopkin of St Athan in the Vale of Glamorgan. Young Arthur was a well-known Barry boxer although he never let that fact be known while he was at sea. Both my grandmothers, Lydia Hopkin and Minnie Harvard, worked in the SRD at Barry Dock. Lydia was the Red Cross Nurse and Minnie packed Red Cross parcels for the troops. They lived together throughout the war years, in a flat opposite King's Square in Barry.

5. Letter from Mrs Margaret Jones

I was only eight when the war broke out but my late father was in the navy and told us many tales about his service during the First World War. My brother Iorwerth was in the Merchant Navy during World War Two, fetching German prisoners of war from France to Southampton.

My brother told us one story about a POW asking him for a drink of water. When he was given it he insisted that Iorwerth take a lovely ring with a red stone in exchange. My husband, whom I lost in 1981, aged just 48, was also in the Merchant Navy. When he was 16 years old he was sailing across the Atlantic to the USA. I still have the Xmas Card he sent home to his parents.

6. Letter from Doug Lloyd

I served on the destroyers "Tenacious" and "Onslaught" during the war. When I was on "Tenacious" we escorted tank landing ships to Anzio, ready for the push on Rome. We were actually in harbour at Naples when Mount Vesuvius erupted in May 1944 – quite a sight.

We did many operations in the Adriatic and were based for a time at Taranto and Brindisi. We sank the U 453 in the Ionian Sea, just off Mount Etna. That was on

21st May 1944 and we managed to pick up 49 survivors from the U Boat. Fifty years later, on 21st May 1994, we had a reunion in Blackpool. Twenty five of the survivors, together with their wives, came over for the week and I have also been to their reunion in Koblenz on the Rhine.

7. Letter from Les Owen

Perhaps you would be interested in learning about Radio Officer Jonathan Islwyn Davies who I had the honour and pleasure of serving with when I was also a Radio Officer during the war.

Dai Davies came from Lampeter and was the son of a minister of the church. I think I am right in saying that his sister married the Archbishop of Wales. Anyway, Dai was Chief Radio Operator on the SS "Peterton" when she was torpedoed off West Africa in 1942. She was sailing independently at the time.

They managed to launch two lifeboats and one was picked up within a day or so. The other one, however, was adrift for 49 days and this was the boat where Dai Davies was located. The occupants suffered terribly and if they had not been rescued when they were it is certain that many would have shortly died. As it was there was only one death in the boat and that was the young apprentice.

Sadly, Dai died in 1964, never really having recovered from that ordeal in the lifeboat. I served with him between 1944 and 1945 in the tanker "Voco."

8. Letter from Russell Owen

As far as possible I have tried to verify what I have written. Some of the memories, but by no means all, are shared by other members of my family.

Alan Cooper was my cousin and he served on minesweepers in the Mediterranean. He lived with my grandmother in Llandudno. On one occasion, when he was home on leave, I remember him telling my Dad that when his ship was berthed in a Yugoslavian port he met a group of Marshal Tito's partisans. Some of them were women and I recall him saying "They were a tough looking bunch, Uncle Dick. You wouldn't want to cross swords with them – certainly not the women, anyway."

At Alan's wedding at Holy Trinity Church, Llandudno, in 1945 I remember being concerned that he only had one wavy ring on each arm. I said "You're a Lieutenant, you should have two." He laughed and said "I couldn't be bothered to sew the other ones on."

Alan's younger brother also served in the Royal and Merchant Navies. He was a stoker on the carrier "Illustrious," joining her after VE Day but before VJ Day. After he left the Royal Navy he worked on the "Queen Mary" for many years, also as a stoker.

9. Letter from June Perrot-Firth

My father William George Perrot was born in Llanelli in 1918 and so was one of the first to be called up to serve in the Royal Navy in 1939. He was aged just 21.

He spent most of the war years in the Mediterranean, having trained at Chatham Barracks. He was involved in Operation Pluto, laying oil pipelines, and was paid "danger money" because of the nature of the work. He served on three different ships, the first and second being torpedoed and sunk. During this time he was courting my mother – they married in 1943 – and throughout the war he sent her love letters written on the back of photographs of himself and his shipmates.

My father had a very basic working-class education and so did not learn to read and write until he joined the navy. This enabled him to study for naval exams and he was promoted from Ordinary to Able Seaman.

10. Letter from Mrs D Roberts (nee Phillips)

You may be interested to know that my first husband, Raymond Phillips, army no. 3964379, was a gunner on board merchant ships during the Second World War. One of the ships he was on was the SS "Staffordshire." She was torpedoed and he was picked up and interned by the Vichy French in Martinique. They were eventually released by the Canadian Red Cross.

The gunners were mostly men from the Royal Artillery and they were known as the "Maritimes." Sometimes I think that these men weren't properly recognised for

Barry Docks Office Clock – the glass blown out by the explosion which hit the SS Highwood in July 1941

The SS Highwood badly damaged when hit by a sea-mine from an aircraft. The first mate, on watch at the time, was killed.

the part they played during the war. The Maritimes were disbanded, I think, in 1944.

11. Letter from Mr George Wainwright

I am a Somerset man but my parents were Welsh by birth and were both Welsh speakers. I served with many Welsh sailors both during and after the war. I served on the "Fort Vercheres," joining her at Hull in 1944 just after she had returned from Russia. Her Captain was T Dene, the First Mate was Mr Legge and the Chief Engineer was Mr Rowe – all men from the Cardiff area.

On my next voyage all the catering staff were Welshmen from the Cardiff/Penarth area. After I paid off from the "Fort Vercheres" I joined the MV "Harlesden" and we were away for nine months, bringing iron ore from Australia into Swansea. The crew then paid off, with the exception of myself and another boy seaman. The new crew were all from Wales, mainly from Cardiff and Newport but some from places as far away as Carmarthen and Lampeter.

I sailed on several voyages with Peter Davies from Swansea. His brother Basil was an AB on tankers and his ship was torpedoed. He was the mainstay in his lifeboat, keeping up everybody's spirits. They were eventually picked up and landed in the Bahamas. Basil then joined a ship bound for the UK but she was sunk in the North Atlantic and went down with all hands. Basil showed outstanding leadership in the lifeboat and has never been recognised for it.

When I was on the "Harlesden" the Second Officer was Robert Morris from Porthmadog. I was his "bridge boy" and kept the 12 to 4 watch with him. When we were in convoy we sent and received signals by flag hoists, and instructions from the Commodore were answered by each ship copying his hoist. Mr Morris would pick up the instruction hoist through his binoculars, chalk the relevant flag letters or numbers on the sleeve of my oilskin and then I had to make the hoist. He used to love to be first with all the hoists and took a special delight in beating any American ship in the convoy. He used to insist that the flag locker was kept in immaculate condition, all flags and pennants neatly folded and connecting clips hanging over the locker edges.

12. A Memoir by Gwilym Evans of St Athan of his father's story of working on Barry Docks.

THE DAY THE MINES CAME DOWN

Selwyn Evans came to the best part of his A.R.P. (Air Raid Patrol) circuit, walking down the hill to the little café in a shed outside the Barry "Graving Dock". It was 12 midnight and the men on nightshift were streaming out of the gates towards the café.

"Tea, John", said Selwyn, and when served, headed for an empty seat. "Thompson Street not bombed yet, Sel?" asked Vernon, a fitter's mate.

"No, all quiet", said Selwyn. The air raid siren sounded and all eyes instinctively looked at the ceiling. "Another false alarm", said Vernon.

Meanwhile, a lonely German bomber looking for Bristol had got lost, and decided to turn round and return to base. Relocating the River Severn, the pilot followed it to the Bristol Channel, and realised that he didn't have enough fuel to get home with its mines aboard. He decided to ditch them. He put the plane into a dive to lose height, and was about to release them when he saw what looked like a dock entrance. He levelled off, thinking, "Well, I may as well cause a bit of chaos."

In the café, the sound of aero engines, and the scream of the mines falling left a stunned silence, followed by a frantic diving under the tables. A deathly hush followed, broken by a voice saying "They missed!" and ended by a huge explosion that shattered the café windows, and sent thousands of shards of glass hurtling through the room.

Selwyn braced himself. "There'll be deaths and horrendous injuries here", he thought. He climbed up into the ankle-deep glass and looked around. Men were dusting themselves down, checking for non-existent injuries.

"Anyone hurt?" shouted Selwyn. "I've got a piece of glass in my bum!" said Vernon. "You always were a pain in the bum" answered Selwyn.

They all headed off to the gates of the docks, the Dock Office clock staring facelessly down at them. "You can't come in here, we've been hit, you must all go home!" shouted the security man at the gates. "I've got to come in, I'm ARP" said Selwyn.

"Sorry, orders are orders", answered the security man.

"You'll let me in at 7 in the morning, when I start my dayshift", fumed Selwyn, a fitter by trade, and stormed off to his depot to write up his report. With luck he'd get two hors sleep that night before he started work next morning.

The mines had fallen on the quay between ships in two dry-docks, and blown both ships off their blocks. These ships had shielded adjacent building, and all the housing on the exposed streets overlooking the docks, saving many lives and complete devastation in the area. For all the size of the explosions, there were only minor injuries to dock personnel.

There was a fatality, though. On one of the ships, a crewman decided to go to the toilet. He should have gone ashore to the dockside toilets, as the ship was in dry dock, but it was cold and drizzling, so he decided to use the crew's toilet instead.

Unknown to him, the storm drains had been removed for replacement of their leather seals. These 'drains' were in fact pivotal valves, which allowed toilet water out, but flapped closed if a wave hit the hull of the ship. When the mines exploded, the blast flew up the open toilet waste pipe, lifting the crewman off the seat, and killing him instantly as he hit the deck-head (ceiling).

(This may have been in 1940, when a lone plane bombed the docks. An unarmed fighter plane from St Athan, just being taken out for a spin after a service, harried the bomber as it flew back towards Germany.)

13. Memories of Leslie Thomas, the Newport Author

It has proved impossible to contact Leslie Thomas, but the following is extracted from a newspaper article he wrote about his stoker father Jim, lost on the Empire Whale. The source is unknown, as the following has been taken from an old photocopy of a newspaper article, where Thomas pays tribute to the fact that Newport lost more men from the merchant navy in the war, than from the other three services combined. (There is more information on the sinking of the Anglo Saxon later in this book.):

'When my younger brother Roy and I asked him where he had voyaged, he often admitted he was not sure. "East," he would say, pointing out of our front window. "Somewhere. I go below and then the ship sails and sometimes I never come up till she comes back home again."

One of my schoolmates was a boy called Eric Hansen. "The milkman gave my father a lift down to the docks," he once recalled. "We never saw my dad again." Oscar Hansen had joined a crew, mostly of local men, aboard a freighter called the Anglo Saxon at Newport in August 1940. Sixteen days out, off the Azores, she was pounced on by a German warship and blown out of the sea by its big guns.

There is a caustic note of regret in the log entry of Helmuth von Ruchteschell, captain of the attacking Widder: "I ordered a torpedo to be fired but I did this without enthsuasm as I had only seven torpedoes left."

My schoolmate's father was not among the survivors but seven of the Anglo Saxon's crew managed to launch the little jolly boat – the shallow 18-footer that was normally used for shore leave. Five of them eventually died. Two of these, parched and starving, jumped into the sea in a suicide pact after bequeathing their shirts and vests to the others. They kept their trousers on "for fear of mermaids", they joked.

The jolly boat had no oars and no sail. It drifted 2,275 miles across the Atlantic in 70 days, an open boat voyage comparable only to that of Captain Bligh after the mutiny on the Bounty (47 days) – and he had supplies, oars and men to man them. Two men from the Anglo Saxon, Robert Tapscott, 19, and Roy Widdicombe, 24, were all but dead when their frail craft was eventually washed up in the Bahamas. Their last drink had been alcohol from the compass. "After that, we couldn't even see which way we were drifting", said Tapscott. Recovering in hospital, they were visited by the Duke of Windsor, then Governor of the Bahamas, and they and their boat were paraded in neutral America as propaganda for the British war effort. In New York, Widdicombe boarded another British ship to return home. It was torpedoed and he drowned.

Today, their jolly boat can be seen in the Imperial War Museum in London. It was found in a storeroom at a museum in New England and brought back by a benefactor and a group of Newport men. It is a poignant sight, and the most poignant thing about it are the notches that Widdicombe and Tapscott cut into its wood to mark the desperate days they were drifting. There are only 24 grooves. "We got confused after that," Tapscott said. He went to the Nuremburg War Trials in 1945 and gave evidence against Helmuth von Ruchteschell, who went to prison for ten years on other matters. His widow told me that he rarely spoke about the ordeal…

Because the had no uniforms – only a small button-hole badge which was introduced later – they (merchant seamen) were often accused in the street of being war service dodgers or conscientious objectors. A woman once gave my brother Harold a white feather – the sign of cowardice. He had been bombed at sea and returned in such a state that he decided life would be safer in the Royal Air Force. He went off without telling anyone and sent his civilian clothes home in a parcel. My mother thought he must be dead. When he turned up in his RAF uniform it was with the news that, because of his sea-going experience, he had been posted to an air-sea rescue launch used to pick up ditched airmen. "The Jerries machine-gunned us", he related dolefully. "I think they're after me,"

Lindon, my eldest brother, was a uniformed officer. His ship was torpedoed and he ended up drifting in a lifeboat off Labrador. "What was it like, Lin?" I remember asking. He said "Freezing." When he came home he went to see his great friend Guy, a handsome and humorous young officer who played the ukulele and taught me to draw sailing ships. All the way back to the bus, lin wept. Guy had gone doen with his ship.

My father would sail off with a convoy – or without it if the ship was too slow – and then come home without saying much. He was glad to be in full employment. When I was a child, he used to take me aboard ships to show the captains how thin I was, going for the sympathy vote so that they would give him a job. He was an everyday, ordinary hero. He had seen men die in boiling oil and in the bitter Arctic but he rarely mentioned it. He often came home drunk and one night my mother threw the chamber pot down at him. Another time he arrived at midnight and, because we had not drawn the black-out curtains, my mother, for a moment, lit a candle. A pompous air raid warden, years younger than my old man, accused us of helping Hitler. There were a few Welsh words said about that.

One of the bonuses of my father risking his life at sea was that we had an abundance of free knitwear. He would bring home scarves, pullovers, and balaclava helmets, in navy, air force blue and khaki, knitted by busy, patriotic ladied. "There's a glut of this stuff", he said, handing it around. In winter, we went to school in the colour of a different service every day. When our Sunday School teacher asked our mother to help with the Christmas crib, she obliged by knitting small garments for the depleted figures in the Bethlehem stable – unravelling some of the wool from our free balaclavas and scarves. The Virgin Mary was in RAF blue, Joseph in navy and the baby Jesus in his khaki swaddling coat.

Throughout the six years of the hostilities, 30,421 merchant seamen died, their passing almost unacknowledged because of war secrecy. On the very first day of war, September 3, 1939, the passenger ship Athenia was torpedoed off Scotland with the loss of 118. The Jervis bay, a converted cargo ship armed with a couple of ineffectual guns, fought off an enemy pocket-battleship so that the rest of the convoy could escape. One of the men who survived told me that, clinging to a raft in the icy sea, he and his shipmates had tried to keep one man warm by rubbing his skin. "We rubbed it all off", he said.

And so on, though every day of the war. And yet their recognition was scant and has remained so. Every time they sailed, they were in the front line. There were no medals for the Arctic voyages to Archangel to get supplies to Russia, although one convoy – PQ17 – through an Admiralty blunder, was left at the mercy of the Germans. Out of the 33 merchant ships in that convoy, only 11 reached Russia.

Once we received a letter from my eldest brother, posted in besieged Malta, where the supply ships were incessantly bombed. Attached was a patriotic label thanking the Royal Navy and RAF for getting the mail through: no mention of the Merchant Navy in which many Maltese served...

One morning I heard my mother and dad singing in the back kitchen, some old semtimental song from the days when they were young, in love and went by motorbike to dances where they danced the tango. He was going to sea that day. He had some bread and cheese (all he ever seemed to eat). When he returned, they would start a new life. He kissed our mum, and then Roy and me, slightly beery kisses, picked up his sea-bag and, with his cornerwise grin, went off down the stree to the docks. We never saw him again.

In February that year, 1943, 108 ships were lost in the Atlantic. In the first three weeks of March, another 107. Then suddenly came the miracle of breaking the Enigma Code, improved sea and air operations, and the packs of hunting U-boats were defeated. Another month and Britain would have been unable to sustain the losses and the war might well have been lost. But only 11 ships were sunk in the last week in March – my father's was one of them, on March 29. He was 54. ("The same age as Hitler", he would say.) ... The insurance man came around and paid out £110. We had never seen so much money. My mother bought a new three-piece suite, a sort of memorial to Jim Thomas.

Six months later my mother was dead, and Roy and I were sent to Barnado's.'

As a footnote to this sad story, Jim Thomas was killed on the Empire Whale. She was built in 1919, of 6159grt, carrying 7870 tons of iron ore in convoy SL126. 425 miles NW of Cape Finisterre, she was torpedoed by U-662 on March 29th, 1943. 47 died and 10 survivors were picked up.

PART FIVE

The Contribution to the Merchant Navy of one Welsh Port

Before we move on from the 80th anniversary of Armistice Day, may I put in a word for the officers and men of the Merchant Fleet, who, throughout the press and television coverage, never got so much as a mention? Without their devotion to duty and their heroism, we could not have survived two world wars, let alone have won them. For month after month, year after year, these men faced death in its most horrible form, hunted continually by packs of U-boats and, when torpedoed, either drowning miserably in icy waters on the Atlantic or Murmansk convoys or being roasted alive in a sea of blazing oil. Should they be rescued, their pay was stopped until they had found a new ship. To the best of my belief, they did not even get a pension, nor were they even awarded a campaign medal. The way these men have been treated is an absolute disgrace. Now, when everybody else is being remembered, they are again forgotten. Our debt to them is immeasurable.

(Letter from Colonel Maurice Willoughby, Daily Telegraph, November 18th, 1998. Merchant seamen could actually claim a medal by applying to the Registry of Shipping and Seamen, whereas the British Armed Forces were sent theirs by post.)

John Harrop has been researching the contribution of the Newport area's merchant seamen in World War II. No less than 654 were lost at sea. On certain ships, there was a high density of Newport men. On the Castlemoor 10 died. All we know is the men's names. The 6,574 ton ship was en route from Halifax, Nova Scotia, for the Tees, and last seen on February 25th, 1940, 800 miles west of Ushant. On the Anglo Saxon there were also ten Newport deaths, recounted later in the chapter, and in Part Six.

It has been calculated that there were about 185,000 merchant seamen including Asians on British ships, with 144,000 being at sea at any one time. 31,000 were killed (plus 900 fishermen). This is an incredible percentage of deaths, and the example of just one Welsh port can show the terrible tragedies that World War Two gave to the people of Wales. 265 merchant seamen from Barry died in the First World War, but in World War Two the toll was even higher (at least 360). Indeed, Bernard Edwards stated that around 1941, '*the port of Barry had gained an unsavoury reputation among seamen, for the records showed that one in three ships that sailed from the docks fell victim to the enemy.*' (- 'Attack & Sink', Bernard Edwards).

In World War II, 5,150 Allied merchant ships were sunk, of which 2,898 (56%) were sunk by U boats. U boats were also responsible for the sinking of 148 Allied warships, including 3 aircraft carriers and 2 battleships. Of the 1131 U boats commissioned, 785 (69%) were lost. Of the 831 U boats which sailed on operational patrols, 754 (91%) were lost. Of 39,000 U boat mariners, 27,491 died (70%) and c.5000 became POW's, giving an 83% chance of death or capture. Admiral Doenitz was sentenced to 10 years in gaol by the Nuremburg War Crimes Tribunal.

We should put into perspective the merchant losses at sea:

MERCHANT SEAMEN	DEATHS
British	22490
Indian lascars on British ships	6093
Chinese on British ships	2023
USA	5662
Norway	4795
Greece	(est) 2000
Holland	1914
Denmark	1886
Canada	1437
Belgium	893
South Africa	182
Australia	109
New Zealand	72
TOTAL	**49556**

Merchant seamen from neutral countries	(est) 6500

Royal Navy (DEMS) Gunners	2713
Royal Artillery Maritime Regiment	1222
US Navy Armed Guard	(to end 1944 only) 1640
Gunners on Merchant Ships TOTAL	5575

The then national newspaper 'Reynold's News' in 1943, ran a headline 'Port That Craves Adventure', and stated 'Barry Dock, Wales' famous coal seaport, has lost more merchant seamen in the war than any other seaport of comparable size in Britain. When the war record of the Merchant Navy comes to be written, the seamen of Barry will feature prominently in it. There are few streets in the town and dock area which have not lost men at sea as a result of enemy action. Scores of Barry seamen have figured in dramatic front page stories of the seas since the war began. Several have spent 30, 40 and more days in open boats after the sinking of their vessels by enemy planes or submarines; a number, since rescued by the Eighth Army, have experienced the hardships of Italian prison camps; many have dodged Jap planes and submarines after the fall of Hong Kong, Singapore, etc. Many died in eastern waters not to mention Jap hands. Today it is safe to say that there are Barry seamen in every United Nations' convoy sailing the seas of the world. Heavy losses of life and incredible hardships suffered by Barry men have not dismayed the youth of the port. They are still entering the MN as soon as they are old enough and can be absorbed by the service.' (-reported in 'The Barry and District News' July 2, 1943). The Barry DEMS gunners lost are not included in the 360 merchant seamen lost in the war, but if we use the total British casualties of 22490, then 1 in 62 deaths were of Barry men, at a time when Barry had 1 in 1250 of the UK population. Again, if we reckon that a fifth of the then population of Barry was capable of serving in the war, omitting restricted occupations, females, the elderly, young and infirm, then 1 in 20 Barry men died in the merchant navy (plus of course there were other deaths in the army, DEMS, navy and air force). When this author was growing up in Barry, it was commonly said that every street in the town lost someone at sea.

The late Fred Hortop took fifty years researching his fellow seamen from Barry who died in World War II, coming to the conclusion that Barry, for a town of its size, had proportionately more deaths at sea than any other port in Britain. Hortop also researched the First World War, and his efforts and those of his colleagues were responsible for the Merchant Navy memorial outside the Vale of Glamorgan Council offices in Barry. These were the men, in unglamorous jobs, without whom Britain would have succumbed. They were donkeymen, firemen and trimmers, greasers, stokers, boatswains, stewards, galley boys, cooks, bakers, carpenters, daymen, engineers, officers, apprentices, mess room boys, steward's boys, ordinary seamen, engineering officers, able-bodied seamen (AB's), chief officers, electricians and captains. There are hundreds and hundreds of untold stories, from just this one port in Wales. For instance, four Barry men survived the Italian submarine Malespina sinking the Guelma of Swansea in 1941. They were rescued and lived in cramped conditions on the submarine Thunderbolt.

Hortop notes, in his Barry Merchant Navy Roll of Honour the poignant circumstances of youngsters who died. Galley boy George Bryant was just 15, when he was lost on the SS "Empire Kingsley" in 1942. The list of under-18's from Barry who died in the Merchant Navy in WWII is as follows:

NAME	TRADE	SHIP	LOST	AGE
William Bennett	apprentice	Victoria City	1940	17
George Bryant	galley boy	Empire Kingsley	1942	15
Rowland Davies	assistant steward	Jedmoor	1941	17
Gordon Illtyd Down	galley boy	MV King Malcolm	1941	15
William George	ordinary seaman	Nicoya	1942	16
Frederick Goodfellow	mess room boy	SS Shakspeare	1941	17
John Goule	ord seaman	Magdalena	1940	16
Barrie Higgins	mess room boy	Stornest	1942	16
William Hopkins	asst steward	Petrel	1941	17
Raymond Hurn	cabin boy	Fort Longueuil	1943	16
Frederick John	cabin boy	Tunisia	1941	15
Terence Lewis	deck boy	Rose Schiaffino	1941	15
William Locke	snr. ord. seaman	Ashbury	1945	17
Clifford Maidment	deck boy	Petrel	1941	15

Of course this was nothing new. In the First World War, the Bubbins brothers of Barry Dock were just 15 and 16 when sunk by German submarines and killed. On the Barry War Memorial, 385 merchant seamen were listed, more than 1% of the

John Quinn	cabin boy	Tunisia	1941	16
Charles Stiff	mess room boy	Rose Schiaffino	1941	16
Frederick Tagoe	cabin boy	Marslew	1941	17
John White	galley boy	Jedmoor	1941	16
James Whittaker	cabin boy	Dalblair	1940	16
John Xenophon	ship's boy	Fort Longueiul	1943	15

population of Barry at the time. Some are not included in Hortop's list. Fred Hortop recorded the following 360 merchant seamen losses of Barry men in World War II.

Age was no barrier to service at sea in either war – among others in the Barry World War II Roll of Honour are Magnus Anderson (63), Gustave Arthur Blamander (aged 64), William Burke (63), Percival Harry Bloodworth (aged 63), John Daly (62), Klaas de Wit (60), Carl Hogstrom (64), Frederick Jansson (62), Peter Johansen (65), J.H. Johlgreen (64) and Charles Linton KC (60). Some mariners died shortly after the war from their injuries.

Age < 19	20-29	30-39	40-49	50-59	60+	unknown
Dead 31	114	73	84	44	10	4

Also some mothers in Barry lost more than one son at sea. James and Catherine Ashford lost their sons, the ship's cook Clarence Ashford (aged 21) dying in 1941 on the Cardiff ship "Kervegan", and their other son AB Septimus Ashford (aged 25) dying on the "Baron Newlands" in 1942. The sons of John and Elizabeth Bradford also died, steward William Bradford on the "Fiscus" in 1940, and donkeyman John Bradford on the "Empire Wagtail" in 1942. Louie and Adeline Goule of Barry Dock lost ordinary seaman John, aged 16, in 1940 when the SS "Magdalena" was sunk. They lost his brother, cook Louis Goule, on the "Hamla" two years later. The brothers fireman Ernest Holmes and cook Trevor Holmes perished together on the "Tunisia" in 1941. Ordinary Seaman John Hopkins of Cadoxton, Barry also died on the "Tunisia", and his brother assistant steward William Hopkins died the following month in the "Petrel". Two brothers from Barry Island perished on the 4th of May and the 5th of May in 1943. Third Engineering Officer John McGillivray died on the "Harperley", and junior engineering officer Donald McGillivray was lost on the "Dolius" the following day. The Cadoxton, Barry brothers Christian and William Poulsen were both firemen, and Christian died in May 1942 on the Athelknight, while William died in October of that year on the "Stornest". The brothers Frederick (30) and Thomas Cunningham (22) died on the same ship, the "Embassage", in 1941.

Ernest and Elsie Stiff of Cadoxton lost three sons at sea. In 1941 they lost 16 year-old Charles, a mess room boy on the "Rose Schiaffino". In March 1942 they lost his 21 year-old brother Joseph, a cook on the "Baron Newlands". In October 1942 they lost their third son, the 19 year-old William, on the "Magdalena".

Many cousins died, the Colemans, the Davies's, the Browns, the Hobbs, the Howells, etc., etc. Fathers and sons died, for example Frederick John aged 15, noted above as dying on the "Tunisia" in 1941. His father, fireman and trimmer Frederick

Benjamin John, tragically died on the "Stornest" in the following year, leaving a grieving widow in Cadoxton, Barry. John Xenophon died aged 56 on the "Swiftpool" in 1943, and his son John on the "Fort Longueuil" in 1943, aged just 15. From Fred and George Hortop's accounts we see that they lost their elder brother Robert on the "Baron Dechmont" in 1943, and another brother Dan never truly recovered from his wounds.

We also must not forget Gordon Bastian of Barry, who won the Albert Medal (translated to the George Cross in 1973). Born in Barry in 1902, he joined the Merchant Navy in 1927 as an engineer, and in 1942 had been appointed an MBE for his services in the battle of the Atlantic. He was watch-keeping in the engine-room of the "Empire Bowman" on March 30, 1943 (his 41st birthday) when she was torpedoed. Bastian shut down the engine, and was leaving the engine room when he remembered that two firemen had been on watch in the stokehold, below.

Water was rising fast in the engine-room, but he left the ladder to safety on the upper deck and forced and groped his way, waist deep in swirling waters in the smoky pitch black engine-room, to the water-tight door to the stokehold. He managed to wrench it open, and the inrush of water swept the firemen into the engine-room. Another few minutes and they would have drowned. They were both in a bad way.

Bastian dragged one up the ladder to the deck and then returned for the more seriously injured fireman, whom he saved. Bastian's lungs were irreparably damaged by cordite smoke, and he had to be invalided out of the navy. His portrait hangs in the Imperial War Museum, and Bastian Close in Barry is named after him. Perhaps another new road in Barry should be named after Ernie Haysham (sunk seven times) or after the 7 Hortop brothers who fought for their country.

Several ships' masters from Barry died in merchant navy service. Charles Milne (47) of Barry was commanding the Bramden when it hit a mine off Dunkirk on September 16th, 1939, and is buried at Calais Southern Cemetery. Captain Neil Macdougall (52) of Barry Island was lost with all crew in February 1941, en route to Buenos Aires, sunk by the U 52. Captain Henry Isaac (48) was lost with 50 hands (15 survivors) hands on the Cornish City, July 29th 1943 (see below). Captain Alexander McLean (56) died on July 27th 1941, when the SS Kellwyn was torpedoed by U 203, west of Cape Finisterre. Captain Charles Linton KC (60) was lost with all crew when the Radhurst was torpedoed by U 525 in February 1943 en route for New York. Captain William Care (45) was lost when the Tregenna was torpedoed by U 65 off the Hebrides on September 17th, 1940. Captain Henry Edwards died on October 21st, 1941, when the Treverbyn was sunk with all hands in the Atlantic by U 82.

The origins of this book lay in the need to record memories of the survivors of the war at sea, and the men and women who backed up this effort to save Britain. However, the authors realised that this would be a disservice to those who died, especially in the 'forgotten service', the Merchant Navy. The great losses in Barry were sometimes made even worse at home, when several men were serving on the same ship. Ships sailing out of Swansea, Cardiff, Newport or Barry were particularly likely to get friends and relatives from Barry signing up to sail together. Thus, in the first three ships listed below, 49 Barry men lost their lives out of crew deaths of 118.

(We also must remember that more Barry men perished in the Royal Navy, but naval deaths, service and heroism have been far better documented). To read the following is to understand how local people who knew each other, died together. The firemen in particular were vulnerable, stoking in the engine rooms of ships. In all 360 Barry men were killed on 174 different merchant ships.

We can see by the following losses, that Welsh seamen were unsafe all over the globe, and were subject to constant danger from planes, submarines, MTB's, capital ships, mines and unlit shipping lanes, collisions and terrible conditions at sea. There were 22,000 British merchant seamen lost, but 27,491 Ubootfahrers also met their ends in their 'iron coffins'. The particular circumstances of the sinking of the "Anglo Saxon", "Stornest" and "Athelknight" are recounted in the following chapters 6-8.

Let it never be forgotten that the British merchant sailor is always in the front line in wartime, and that the front line of war at sea was always active – never still. Day in and out, he faced the menace of bombs, torpedoes, shells and incendiaries, of machine guns and mines; he was beset from above the water, on the water, and beneath the water. And still there remained the old hazards of the sea: hurricanes, fogs, rocks and storms. The winter of 1941-42 was especially severe; in the North Atlantic there was a "flaming gale" for months, with often a 75 mile-per-hour wind and nothing much less than 35 miles-per-hour, and waves anything up to 65 feet high. Cold and frostbite, starvation, madness or death from exposure, and an end with the sharks were often the lot of the shipwrecked sailor. The odds against the merchant seamen were tremendous. They were unequalled in the history of the sea. But no ship left port undermanned, and few ships, ready for sea, were ever seriously delayed for lack of a full crew. (extract from Britain's Merchant Navy, edited by Sir Archibald Hurd).

LIST OF MERCHANT SHIPS WITH MULTIPLE DEATHS OF BARRY MEN:

TUNISIA (registered Swansea) – 4,337 tons, 10.5 knots, built 1927 (18 deaths)
This steamship was captained by W.A. Shute O.B.E., and was bombed and sunk by German aircraft 350 miles west of Achill Head, County Mayo, on August 4th, 1941. The crew took to the boats but only Captain Shute and four others survived*. 38 men died, half of them from Barry. They were: Thomas Atwell (aged 21) sailor, Albert Baade (46) fireman and trimmer, John Dooley (21) fireman and trimmer, James Forsyth (18) galley boy, James Garland (32) AB, Hector Garn (21) fireman and trimmer, Patrick Hamilton (30) AB, Ernest Holmes (27) fireman and trimmer, his brother Trevor Holmes (29) cook, John Hopkins (21) ordinary seaman, J.H. Johlgreen (64) donkeyman, Frederick John (15) cabin boy, Manuel Martinez (37) steward, Ralph Painting (33) fireman and trimmer, W.J. Pook (18) ordinary seaman, John Quinn (16) cabin boy, Frank Slade (40) fireman and trimmer, Joseph Taylor (37) fireman and trimmer. Captain Shute died on the Hamla a year later (see below).
* The four men who escaped in the boat with Captain Shute included J.L. Benson

of Barry, who was later lost on the 'Pacific' (see below). Shute's interview is noted later, mainly because it appears that many more men should have been saved, and the note in his report about Ernie Haysham of Barry: *"This is E. Haysham's fourth experience, having been once mined, twice torpedoed in other vessels and now bombed in this vessel."* Ernie survived the war and lived in Barry until the 1990's, having been sunk no fewer than **seven** times, perhaps a record for the war at sea, but nowhere recorded.)

ROSE SCHIAFFINO (Cardiff) – 3,349 tons, built 1920 (18 deaths)

This Ministry of War transport sailed from Wabana on October 6th, 1941, carrying iron ore to Cardiff. She left St John's, Newfoundland on October 31st to join her convoy. Nothing more was heard of her the ship or its crew of 37 and 4 gunners. It seems that she was sunk by U 106. (U 106 was sunk in 1943 off Cape Ortegal, by British and Australian bombs). No less than 18 of the 41-man crew of the Rose Schiaffino were from Barry: Ahmed Mohamed 55 fireman, Thomas Baston 48 AB, Daniel Cadogan 41 AB, Klaas de Wit 60 steward, Karl Eriksen 58 boatswain, John Foley 56 AB, William James 28 cook, Jheai Ahmed 53 fireman and trimmer, Terence Lewis 15 deck boy, Mohamet Nagi 47 greaser, Joseph Norton 58 AB, Jose Ocampos 48 AB, Jose Pires 44 cook, Maelgwyn Richardson 20 ord. seaman, Arthur Robertson 29 fourth eng. officer, Salem Mocabil 40 fireman and trimmer, Charles Stiff 16 mess room boy and Emanuel Teuma 42 carpenter. Charles Stiff's two brothers were lost on the Baron Newlands and the Magdalena.

STORNEST (Newcastle-on-Tyne) – 4,265 tons, built 1921 (13 deaths)

The Stornest was torpedoed by U 706 en route from Swansea to Boston at 2.33am on October 13th, 1941. (U 706 was sunk by American bombs, off Cape Ortegal in 1943). Carrying coal and listing heavily in a heavy gale, the Stornest lost her boats and called for assistance. The neutral Irish steamship Irish Oak stood by on the 14th until the Stornest sank, but was unable to save any men because of heavy seas. All 29 crew and 10 gunners perished, including 12 men from Barry: Anton Andersen 55 donkeyman, James Edwards 27 fireman and trimmer, AB Edward Fellows 22, Sydney Flynn 50 donkeyman, Clifford Gurd 18 asst. cook, Barrie Higgins 16 mess room boy, Frederick Benjamin John 41 fireman and trimmer, Thomas Lamb 42 fireman and trimmer, William Poulsen 24 fireman and trimmer, Idris Pritchard 19 cook, William Robinson 27 fireman and trimmer, William Weeks 23 sailor, Charles Williams 28 fireman and trimmer. Poulsen's brother Christian had been lost 5 months before on the Athelknight. Chapter 7 recounts the sinking of the Stornest in more detail. The Irish Oak (master, E. Jones) was sunk in broad daylight on May 15, 1943 by U 607, although showing her neutral colours.

KING MALCOLM (London) – 5,120 tones, built 1925 (9 deaths)

This cargo ship under Captain James Wilson sailed from Haifa, via Table Bay and Sydney, carrying potash to Belfast and Garston. She left Sydney on October 17th, 1941, and on October 21st was reported at 47* 40'N., 51* 15'W., but was never heard from again. It was a straggler, not being able to keep up with its convoy. U 106 claimed the kill, and that the ship sank in just three minutes on October 28th. However, U 374 claimed the kill on October 31st, and was the only U boat off

Newfoundland at this time. Its report stated that the king Malcolm sank in just 30 seconds before it could make a distress call. (U 374 was sunk in the Western Mediterranean off Catania in 1942, by torpedoes from the British submarine 'Unbeaten'. U 106 was sunk by depth charges from Sunderland aircraft in 1943).

34 crew and 4 gunners were lost from the King Malcolm, of whom 9 were from Barry: George Ashton 24 fourth eng. Officer, George Cliff 38 greaser, Patrick Cullen 38 greaser, Gordon Illtyd Down 15 galley boy, Matis Jacobson 47 carpenter, Albert Manning 40 cook, Ernest Pettersen 22 greaser, Juan Rufo 54 greaser, AB Jan Snyder 53. The King Malcolm had sailed around Africa and up the Suez canal into the eastern Med, returning the same way, but was diverted to Sydney in Canada because of 'Operation Torch' when off the north-west coast of Africa. She made her way across the Atlantic to join convoy SC 50 back to Liverpool. Depending upon which U boat torpedoed it, she sank either 11 or 14 days after leaving Sydney, but was only 450 miles from Sydney. She was an oil-burner and if she had broken down, perhaps she was attempting to repair a piston. Or perhaps she was returning to port for repairs. She was out of any radio contact in all this time. It is a mystery to this day.

BRITISH DOMINION (London) – 6.938 tons, 10 knots, built 1928 (8 deaths)

Captain J.D. Miller was in command of this tanker, and in Atlantic convoy TM-1. Mid-way between the Canary Islands and Madeira, she was torpedoed by U 522 on January 10th, 1943. (The U 522 was itself sunk a month later in the mid-Atlantic off Madeira, by depth charges from the British coastguard cutter Totland, with all 51 crew dying.) Captain Miller and 14 crew survived, but 38 men were killed, 8 from Barry: John Aistrope 32 boatswain, AB Daniel Barry 29, Michael Carabott 44 greaser, Charles Chislett 37 greaser, William McAlinden 35 greaser, Samuel Taylor 29 greaser, David Tobin 38 greaser, Alfred Tolan 36 fireman and greaser.

BRITISH MONARCH (London) – 5,661 tons, 12 knots, built 1923 (7 deaths)

She was torpedoed by U 48 and sunk on June 19th 1940, 200 miles N.N.W. of Corunna, Spain. (U – 48 was stricken at Neustadt in 1943, and scuttled in 1945, see the addendum on the Magdalena). Captain F.J. Scott and 39 men were killed, 7 from Barry: Christmas Aspinall 18 asst. cook, AB Gerald Azzopardi 35, Thomas Bennett 38 chief officer, George Huebner 26 cook, AB Claude Melvin 23, AB Michael Reynolds 46, Saleh Ali 40 donkeyman.

SHAKESPEAR (London) – 5,029 tons, 10 knots, built 1926 (6 deaths)

This is a wonderful story of bravery at sea. The Shakespear, with a crew of 40 and 2 gunners, fought the Italian submarine Commandante Cappelini (later renamed UIT 24) off Senegal, West Africa. The action lasted two hours, on January 5th, 1941, as skilful manoeuvring allowed the steamship to use its single small aft-mounted gun. The Shakespear refused to surrender until its gun had been knocked out, and both gunners and 18 crew were dead. The survivors, including the captain, took to the boats and the submarine sank the Shakespear by gunfire. Lt. Cdr. Salvatore Todaro of the Commandante Capellini took the ship's boats in tow to near land, and helped the survivors with rations and medical aid, although he himself had lost 2 crew members and several were injured. (The Commandante Cappelini was taken over by the Germans in 1943, then taken over by the Japanese and scuttled by the US in 1946). 6 of the Shakespear's 20 dead were from Barry: Gustav Blamander 64 carpenter (buried at St Vincent Cemetery, Cape Verde Islands), William Burke 63 fireman and trimmer, Thomas Cridland 41 chief steward, Frederick Goodfellow 17 mess room boy, AB Frederick Jansson 62, Frederick Lorenson 25 boatswain.

PETREL (London) – 1,354 tons, 12 knots, built 1920 (6 deaths)

The route of the HG series of convoys from Gibraltar to Liverpool took them within range of Luftwaffe FW 200 ('Condor') aircraft. These acted both in a reconnaissance role, able to guide U-boats operating out of the French Atlantic ports onto the convoys, and as effective bombers against shipping. Despite the difficulties most convoys completed successfully, but of the 570 merchant ships which took part in the 28 separate convoys in 1941 on this homebound route 25 were lost, together with a further 5 stragglers. Experience in the other direction (designated OG) could be a little different because Germany was denied the intelligence information on sailings available from agents in Spain for the homebound stretch - 1004 ships took part in 30 OG convoys in 1941, with 21 lost in convoy, though a further 34 losses were classified as stragglers. 1941 was by far the most dangerous year for convoys on this route in either direction.

Convoy HG 73 saw the heaviest losses of all. A total of 25 merchant ships formed the convoy from Gibraltar on 17 September, together with an unusually strong escort including a destroyer and Fighter Catapult ship, although as usual most escorts were Flower class corvettes. Hastily brought together for the task, the escorts' lack of training as a team was subsequently blamed by C-in-C Western Approaches, Admiral Noble, for their lack of success. In retrospect, though, the convoy was unlucky to have been subject to concerted attack from three of the most able U-boat commanders of the war.

The convoy seems to have been spotted by a FW 200 off Cape St Vincent and shadowed by U-371 and a group of three Italian submarines for several days, whilst a U-boat pack was assembled. On 24 September a FW 200 again established contact and guided U-124 and U-203 to the location. U-201 and U-205 joined later, although U-205 was attacked on 27 September and damaged, and was unable to press home any effective attack. The other U-boats withdrew after expending all their torpedoes. The following merchant ships were lost from the convoy:

date	time	ship	gross tonnage	built	nationality	cargo	lives lost sunk by
25 Sep	0744	Empire Stream	2 911	1941	British	3 500 tons potash	8 U-124
26 Sep	0031	Avoceta	3 442	1923	British	88 passengers 469 tons general	123 U-203
26 Sep	0031	Cortes	1 374	1919	British	general cargo	31 U-124
26 Sep	0031	Varangberg	2 842	1915	Norwegian	4 100 tons	21 U-203

						iron ore	
26 Sep	0223	Lapwing	1 348	1920	British	750 tons	24 U-203
						pyrites & cork	
26 Sep	0223	Petrel	1 354	1920	British	405 tons general	22 U-124
26 Sep	2303	Margareta	3 103	1904	British	400 tons general	0 U-201
26 Sep	2335	Cervantes	1 810	1919	British	500 tons potash	8 U-201
						400 tons cork	
27 Sep	0211	Siremalm	2 468	1906	Norwegian	iron ore	27 U-201

The Petrel was torpedoed and sunk in the North Atlantic by U 124. Two other ships in the convoy were sunk by U 124. Captain Klemp of the Petrel survived, but 22 men died from that ship, 6 from Barry: William Fowler 23 greaser, William Hopkins 17 asst steward, Clifford Maidment 15 deck boy, William Nelson 41 fireman and trimmer, Harold Weeden* 21 fireman and trimmer, Walter Whitchurch 25 fireman and trimmer.

U 124 was depth charged by the corvette HMS Stonecrop off Oporto in 1943, and all its crew were drowned. Her commander was Germany's most celebrated U boat commander, Kapitanleutnant Jochen Mohr. In her short life, she was the third most successful of all the hundreds of Axis and Allied submarines, sinking 49 ships totalling 226,949 tons. A Barry man, Fred Hortop (see earlier) was a depth charge operator on the Stonecrop (see Dartford entry later).

*An account of fireman Weeden's death and the rescue of some crew of the Petrel is given below. This was given to Terry Breverton by Fred Hortop before his death, and the source is now unknown. However, there is also a log of the lifeboat's journey extant, written by Chief Officer Woodhouse of the Lapwing. Woodhouse and Klemp received the Lloyds War Medal:

"PETREL was torpedoed at 1.20 am on September 25th 1941, almost at the same time that the steamer CORTES... was sunk. Captain Klemp, master of PETREL was in his cabin when the ship was struck. He immediately went on deck to find that the torpedo had hit the ship right aft. The sea was by then covering the deck as far forward as the bunker hatch, although it was only about 20 seconds after the explosions. All lights had gone out and the engines had stopped.

The boat began to sink very quickly. Realising that there was no time to get the boats away, Captain Klemp gave orders for the rafts to be released and for everyone to jump clear. When this was done and the master could see quite a number of his men in the water, he himself jumped and swam to one of the rafts which was already supporting the 2nd and 3rd officers of the PETREL, 'Sparks', 3 AB's and a passenger, Mr. Roy Warne of Messrs Gonzalez Byas & Co of Portugal. On looking back, Captain Klemp saw the PETREL almost vertical in the water with only the foredeck above the surface. She remained in that position for some minutes and then disappeared.

About twenty minutes later the LAPWING came into sight and by her slow speed Captain Klemp guessed she was coming to the rescue. A few minutes later they were haled by the Chief Officer of the Lapwing Mr. J. R. Woodhouse, who was in charge of the lifeboat. The Captain told him to pick up those men who had nothing to hang onto first, and then come back for those on the raft. This took some little time and the sea was rough and getting worse. At about 5am the boat returned but was so crowded, having picked up about 17 of the PETREL's crew and a number of those from the CORTES, that those on the raft decided to remain there until the other survivors had been put on board the LAPWING. This being done the LAPWING was torpedoed amidships. She sank in about one and a half minutes. As far as could be seen no other boat was lowered from the LAPWING.

After the LAPWING had disappeared the boat tried to get back to the spot to pick up survivors who might be in the water. But the sea was very rough and the lifeboat's crew exhausted after their five hours rowing and those from the raft were numbed with the cold. Consequently only five men were picked up, three of whom were from the CORTES. All the next day the boat rode to a sea anchor. Then at 8am on the 27th they set sail and headed for the Portuguese coast. This course was maintained for nearly four days, when headwinds were encountered, so it was decided to make for Ireland.

There were now 22 men in the lifeboat. In addition to those already mentioned from the raft, there were the 1st and 3rd officers and seven men from the LAPWING, one more from the PETREL, terribly injured, and three men from the CORTES – an Arab and two Philippinos. The injured man, Fireman Weeden, died on the morning of Sept. 30th. He had been suffering terrible pain from his injuries, both feet were crushed and the right leg had a compound fracture, the bone protruding right through the flesh.

They had three beakers of water – one half empty and somewhat brackish, one of about 22 gallons fresh filled at Gibraltar, and a naval beaker which had been salvaged from a jolly boat which was probably from a corvette and had been left adrift after rescue work owing to heavy seas…

… There were some ships biscuits, 12 tins of Nestles milk and 24 of Ideal milk, two tins of corned beef and a case, somewhat damaged, taken from the jolly boat. Captain Klemp calculated that it would take 15 to 21 days to make land – and so the course was set.

One ships biscuit per day and three ounces of water, with the occasional addition of a little Ideal milk spread on the biscuit, like jam, and every three days a tin of bully beef; such clothing as the men had constantly soaked by the seas which broke over the lifeboat; feet continually soaked, for the boat, which had been damaged, was leaking, and had to be baled out every six hours or so – how can the life of the ship's crew be pictured! Small wonder that the badly injured man died after two days and was buried at sea, and that the Arab and one of the Philippinos died before the voyage ended. And yet the others struggled on until, on the fifteenth day, land was sighted – as fine a bit of navigation as we could wish for wrote Mr. Wearne, the passenger. Mr Wearne wrote a long and vivid account of this voyage, here is his account of the last two days of this epic voyage.

"In the afternoon of the 13th day we were all scanning the horizon for the sight of a ship or plane, or even land, when a large cormorant flew by. I remarked to the helmsman that land could not be too far away, even if only bare rocks, as seldom, if ever, I believe do these birds fly far from their homes. That night we were hove to, owing to rough seas, and about 1am we had a very heavy rainstorm. We cut a hole in the canvas covering us and caught the rain water, passing round the tins we filled so that all of us had as much water as they could drink, which was a great relief after so many days of thirst, but at the same time, we had all become soaked and it did not seem possible to get warm, in marked contrast to when we were soaked with sea water which, although cold, did not seem to chill us as much as the rainwater did.

The next morning, October 10th a lighthouse was sighted and the excitement was great. The cover was rolled back; we all had to see it. One man, a born pessimist, said that he thought it was Ushant (This is Ouessant, the northwestern point of France, in Finistere). I asked the captain and he replied that he was certain that it was not Ushant. He knew its light well and, in any case, belligerent countries were not showing lights, and therefore it must be a neutral country, most likely Eire.

We immediately sent up flares but received no answer or signal. A big sea was running and the wind freshening, so we shortened sail as we were nearing the lighthouse too fast to be safe, and therefore ran on slowly until dawn. What a glorious sight it was to see land. But the wind was rising and the waves becoming mountainous. It was decided to run to the starboard of the lighthouse and try to get under the lee of the land and to find a landing place. The captain went up into the bows in order to direct the helmsman, as rocks were plentiful. In the meantime I had got the time and handed water round to all, since it did not seem to matter how much we had.

There seemed nowhere at all where we could land, and the sea was running unpleasantly high, and frequently breaking over the boat.

Suddenly the captain saw a fisherman's boat drawn up on the sand, and he said that if that fisherman could get up there so could we. There were rocks to the right and to the left and also in front of us...

The captain remained in the bow, shouting instructions to the helmsman. If we struck it would mean another swim for us all, and possibly severe injuries on the rocks. We could see someone running down the beach towards us. Swiftly we moved on. We had put tins of Ideal milk in our pockets because we had a long walk ahead of us to the nearest town. Suddenly there was a crunching sound and we were running up on the beach. Willing hands were there to help us. Some, in their excitement, jumped too soon and fell headlong into the sea, thence to scramble onto the beach. I climbed over the bow and slid gently on to the sand. Little, until then, had I realised how weak I was. My knees gave way and I fell flat on my face. Soon afterwards a fisherman's wife brought down a jug of scalding hot tea and milk. This revived the men more than anything.

Shortly afterwards an ambulance arrived. There were three stretcher cases. Others were taken in private cars. The captain, Mr. Woodhouse and myself said we would walk towards where the cars were going and they could come back and pick us up. However, we did not quite realise how far it was , and, when we started we found that Mr. Woodhouse could not walk, so he had to carry him, the fisherman showing us the way. After about two miles we saw some cottages. We went into one where the owner had a roaring peat fire and made some tea. She also started to dry some of our clothes until the cars returned. We were then motored into Clifden, the nearest town, about six miles away, where we were put into the Railway Hotel. The manager and manageress, who represented the Shipwrecked Mariners' Society, were also kindness itself and did everything possible for us that wa in their power. Those who had been conveyed in the ambulance were taken to hospital and put to bed.

I shared a room with the captain. We awoke often during the night and talked and drank all the water we could lay our hands on, for we had an insatiable thirst. But it was marvellous to be able to stretch out at full length on a soft bed… The next morning we received a message that the Philippino was dying. We hurried out of bed and into our clothes and went to the hospital but were too late as the poor fellow had passed away. He was buried the following afternoon. All the village turned out and the villagers did him the homage of carrying the coffin on their shoulders the whole way to the cemetery. Klemp laid two wreaths on the grave from the officers and crew of PETREL and LAPWING.

On Monday we left for Galway having to leave behind six men in hospital. On Tuesday morning we left by train for Dublin. When we reached Dublin the British authorities would not allow us to travel the next day, our feet were so swollen and painful. Klemp and I went to buy some things, then returned to Jury's Hotel to rest our feet. We then caught the bus to Kingstown to board the boat early next morning. The organisation and kindness of the General Steam Navigation Company was amazing – everything had been arranged for us. When we arrived at Holyhead we were taken off the boat first, then straight through Customs etc., so that we should not have to stand too long. Carriages were reserved for us on the train, but only four of us went through to London, where we were met by our various relations and friends and so home… Captain Klemp and Mr. Woodhouse later both received Lloyds War Medal.

BARON DECHMONT (Ardrossan) - 3675 tons, 11 knots, built 1929 (6 deaths)

Barry men were unlucky on this ship – of the 7 dead, 6 were from Barry, probably caught below decks. Not sailing in convoy, it was torpedoed by U 507 off the north coast of Brazil in 1943. Captain D. MacCallum was taken prisoner and the 35 surviving crew landed ashore the next day. U 507 was sunk by American bombs off Natal in 1943. The Barry dead were: Michael Buckley 26 donkeyman, Bertie Burge 22 fireman and trimmer, Percival Burnett 25 greaser, Robert Hortop 35 carpenter (brother of Fred, whose story is given later), Frederick Lean 59 fireman and trimmer, Norman Reeves 21 fireman and trimmer. The captain, Donald MacCallum, was lost with the masters of the James and the Yorkwood, and an apprentice from the Oak Bank, when POW's on the U 507.

BARON NEWLANDS (Ardrossan) – 3,386 tons, 10 knots built 1928 (6 deaths)

In 1942, she was torpedoed and sunk off Liberia by U 68. The U 68 was sunk off Madeira in 1944 by bombs from aircraft of the US escort carrier Guadalcanal. 18 men on the Baron Newlands died, 6 from Barry: AB Septimus Ashford 25, Alfred Barnes 42 fireman and trimmer, AB Jeremiah OConnell 33, Joseph Stiff 21 cook, AB Jaan Wahter 56, Frank Warner 33 steward. Joseph Stiff's two brothers also appear on this list of Barry deaths.

JEDMOOR (London) – 4,392 tons, 9.5 knots, built 1928 (5 deaths)

The Jedmoor was sailing from Santos and Sydney to the Tyne, and had reached a position 300 miles west of the Orkney islands. On September 16th, 1941, she was torpedoed and sunk by U 98, losing 26 crew and 5 gunners. (The U 98 itself lost all hands when bombed by British planes west of Gibraltar in 1942). The Jedmoor lost the following men from Barry: Rowland Davies 17 asst steward, AB Lawrence Gayton 23, Carl Hogstrom 64 carpenter, Eric Stocker 23 junior eng. officer, John White 16 galley boy. There were only 5 survivors, including Barry's Dan Hortop (see earlier), who had suffered injuries when the SS Maclaren had hit a mine on 3rd December 1941. (However, of the 5 killed in Fred Hortop's account, it seems that Eric Stocker was from Machen. 64 year-old Carl Richard Hogstrom is noted as being Swedish in the return of deaths to the Ministry of Shipping, although he may have been resident in Barry. Lawrence Gayton is not listed, but may have died of injuries later.)

The vessel was the second ship in the third column of the SC-42 convoy (see the entry on the Empire Crossbill). On the morning of the 9th the convoy was steaming parallel to the coast of Greenland on port at a distance off 15 miles. At that moment the Jedmoor's engine slowed and then stopped. Chief Engineer Robert Adamson reported to the bridge that the fuel lines were blocked and it would take some time to clear them. In the meantime the ship was drifting and two black balls were hoisted at the masthead, indicating the ship was "not under command". Fifteen minutes later, the last ship of the column, the ore carrier Hampton Lodge, steamed by. Some time later two stragglers, Southgate and Makefjell, also passed while they tried to catch up with the convoy.

U-85, which had sighted the convoy's smoke was closing in on the convoy.

As standard procedure for the first boat of a wolfpack that sighted the convoy Greger did not engage but reported the convoy to BdU. Although U-85 slowed down to keep the convoy at a distance the U-boat slowly closed in on what appeared to be a lone ship. When U-85 was about 10 miles from the vessel it became clear she was alone and stopped. Since the ship was at a safe distance from the convoy Greger decided to attack her. The Jedmoor had been lying stopped for two hours and the convoy was barely visible on the horizon to the northeast. The lookouts were doubled up and all guns manned. Suddenly the lookout on the port wing shouted a warning as the two tracks of torpedoes were streaking across her bow from port to starboard. Even though the ship was stopped the torpedoes missed the ship by 50 yards or more. Then a periscope was seen and distress rockets were fired to inform the convoy of the attack. That the Jedmoor escaped destruction was due to a combination of circumstances.

When, at 09:59 (13:59 CET), Greger fired his first torpedo, it proved to be a tube-runner, sinking deep and passing below the merchantman's keel. When the U-boat's ballast tanks were filled too slow to compensate for the loss of weight, the U-boat porpoised, disrupting Greger's aim when he fired the three other torpedo tubes, all of which consequently missed. It was the tracks of two of these latter torpedoes Jedmoor sighted. Greger now turned U-85's stern to the steamer and fired a final shot - which also went wide. With all tubes empty, Greger then dived deep to reload. At 11:50, having reloaded his tubes, U-85 went to periscope depth to find that the destroyer Skeena and the corvette Orillia had abandoned the convoy and were standing guard over the Jedmoor. For the next forty minutes the warships circled the merchant dropping depth charges and U-85 was forced to retire.

Subsequently Jedmoor's defects were repaired and she managed to rejoin the convoy.

In the night of 16 September the convoy was now only little over 24 hours from British coastal waters. U-98 (which was part of Gruppe Bosmüller - 9 U-boats) had penetrated SC-42's ring of escorts and then lay submerged between columns 3 and 4 on a parallel course, and keeping pace with the merchants on either side of her. Gysae decided to attack the ships on his port side. These were, in the lead Jedmoor, followed by the Campus, the Maplewood, the Nicolas Piancos and the Hampton Lodge. From 2,000 metres the four bow torpedoes were fired in quick succession, one at each of the first four ships. One muffled thud was heard, and that was all.

The only one of U-98's torpedoes to hit struck Jedmoor in her No 1 cargo hold. The pyramid of iron ore in the Jedmoor's forward hold, stowing only 12 cubic feet to the ton, occupied less than a third of the space, leaving two thirds to be filled by the sea pouring in through the hole in her side. She began to go down by the head. As her stern rose in the air, her propeller still running, there was a loud rumble as thousands of tons of iron ore in the holds shifted and ran towards the bows. One by one, the steel watertight bulkheads of the holds collapsed under the weight, and the Jedmoor stood on her head as the whole of her cargo ended up in the forward part of the ship and the ship quickly sank. Eyewitnesses to the sinking gave the time she took to sink as anything from nine seconds to two minutes.

Although she sank very fast two distress rockets were fired. These were seen by the corvette HMS Narcissus, which immediately increased speed to 14 knots to hunt for the U-boat. Douglas, Skate and Alberni also joined in for the hunt, firing starshells and snowflake rockets. A number of depth charges were dropped but U-98 had already left the scene. Narcissus then searched for the Jedmoor, which was believed to be still afloat. Throughout the remaining hours of darkness, Narcissus and Alberni searched in vain for the Jedmoor. After sunrise the two corvettes came upon a large patch of oil, in the middle of which floated some debris from Jedmoor. The convoy had travelled at 7.5 knots, and it was the biggest sea battle in the war at that time. Five days after the battle, the Jedmoor was sunk (q.v.) by U 98 when approaching Scotland. Carrying a valuable cargo of managenese ore used to manufacture steel, she sank like a stone. She had loaded at Santos, Brazil and covered 8000 miles.

FORT LONGUEUIL (London) – 7,128 tons, 11 knots, built 1942
(5 deaths)

On 16 Jul, 1943, the Fort Longueuil left Barry Docks with a cargo of government stores, including ammunitions, and arrived safely at Alexandria on 8 August. After the cargo was discharged, she sailed through the Suez Canal two days later, and docked at Aden on 8 September to bunker. The next day, the ship left for Australia after loading phosphate. She was due to arrive at Fremantle, Australia and then to sail to Port Kembla and Newcastle, New South Wales, but was reported missing on 15 October. By 3 November, it was known that the ship had been lost at the estimated position of 10°S/68°E.

On 19 Sep, 1943, the unescorted Fort Longueuil (Captain George Edwards) was torpedoed and sunk by U-532 southwest of Chagos Archipelago. The complement consisted of 49 crew members from Britain, India and Canada and ten British gunners (the ship was armed with one 4in and five 20mm guns). Only two Indian crewmen, Thakar Miah and Mohamed Aftab, managed to survive on a raft and became Japanese prisoners on 1 Feb, 1944, when the raft drifted ashore on Sumatra after 134 days at sea. The following men from Barry died: Raymond Hurn 16 cabin boy, Arthur Lacey 26 cook, AB Sydney Livermore 20, AB Alexander Mitchell 24, and John Xenophon 15 ship's boy. The U 532 remarkably ended the war by surrendering at Liverpool in 1945. It had sunk 8 ships of 46,000 tons and damaged two others.

RUNA (Glasgow) – 1,575 tons, built 1930 (5 deaths)

Travelling with a cargo of coal from Barry to Lisbon, she was torpedoed on September 21st, 1941, 700 miles west of Cape Finisterre. 12 crew and 2 gunners were lost, including five Barry men: stewards' boy Ivor Brown (19), cook James Carthy (23), AB William Nott (32), fireman and trimmer Thomas Taylor (37) and galley boy John White (16). The Runa was sunk by U 201, which was itself depth charged off Newfoundland in 1943 by the destroyer Fame, all 49 crew being drowned.

EMPIRE HAWKSBILL (London) – 5724 tons, built 1920 (5 deaths)

She was sunk by the U 564 in July 1942, about 200 miles north of the Azores, on her way from Barry Docks to Table Bay. (The U 564 itself was sunk by British bombs off Cape Ortegal in 1943). All 37 crew and 9 gunners were lost, including the following men from Barry: Harry Batchelor 26 second officer, AB William Brown 43, Jose Duran 45 donkeyman, William Evans 27 carpenter, AB Karl Hofgaard 54.

BARON CARNEGIE (Ardrossan) – 3178 tons, 11 knots, built 1925 (5 deaths)

On June 11, 1941, she was sailing in convoy west of St David's Head, Pembroke when attacked by German aircraft. Captain G.S. Cumming survived but bombs killed 25 crewmen. The Baron Carnegie was taken in tow, but sank before reaching port. Men from Barry who died were: Arthur Begley 35 fireman and trimmer, Thomas Gervaise 24 ordinary seaman, Marcus Nicholls 24 sailor, Horace Partridge 22 ordinary seaman, Edward Wallace 22 ship's boy.

PEARLMOOR (London) – 4,581 tons, built 1923 (5 deaths)

She was travelling from Pepel to Immingham when torpedoed and sunk 80 miles west of Donegal Bay on July 19th, 1940. At 18.28 hours on 19 Jul, 1940, the Pearlmoor (Master James Rodgers), a straggler from convoy SL-38, was hit by one torpedo from U-62, broke in two and sank 62 miles west of Malin Head. 13 crew members were lost. The master and 25 crew members landed at Gola Island, Co. Donegal. Lost from Barry were Mohamed Masul 48 fireman, Mohamed Rajah 45 greaser, Abel Mosham (age unknown) fireman, George Newton 50 3rd engineering officer, Salih Tabit 22 fireman. This was U 62's only merchant sinking and the unlucky Pearlmoor was the only ship in the convoy of 30 to be sunk. U 68 was scuttled at Wilhelmshaven in 1945. Captain James Rodgers was lost on the Eastmoor (see below), but the following is his account of the sinking:

"We were bound from Freetown to Immingham carrying a cargo of 7,860 tons of iron ore. Our hull was black, superstructure buff, and the funnel was grey with a black top. We were armed with a four inch gun and two Ross Rifles. Wireless was on board; we were not flying the flags of the ensign at the time of the attack. The crew numbered 39 including myself, and 13 members are missing and one injured. The vessel was degaussed, but it was not on at the time of the attack.

We left Freetown at noon on the 3rd July, I carried out the instructions given to me by the Admiralty Authorities, and we zigzagged continually, using No. 8 zigzag. We proceeded without incident until the 7th of July when the Engineer reported to me that he had trouble with the boiler tubes. I signalled this information to the convoy, and as we were able to continue on only two boilers, making 7 _ knots, we had to drop astern and so became detached. The repairs actually took about 24 hours, and it was not possible to catch up again so I opened the sealed instructions and proceeded accordingly.

When we approached the Irish coast, at about 3.50pm on the 19th July a Sunderland Flying Boat was sighted, nd we watched it pass over and go right astern.

We were in position 5523N 0918W and travelling at 9 knots; there was a gentle breeze and a choppy sea but visibility was good. I left the bridge and went downstairs to have a wash. I had just taken off my coat when suddenly, and without warning, there was a dull explosion right in the engine room, about 210 feet from the bow on the starboard side. A big column of water was thrown up on the starboard side which wrecked the starboard lifeboat. There was no jolt, but the vessel immediately listed slightly; corrected herself, and then went down within 1_ minutes, by the head.

As soon as I realised what had happened I gave orders to abandon ship. I instructed the Radio Officer to try and get a message away then rushed down the ladder, picked up the bag with the confidential papers in and threw it over the side. Meanwhile we had been able to successfully launch the port lifeboat containing seven men; the remaining crew, as far as I know, went into the water. I had managed to get on my lifejacket and the next minute I was in the air and the ship had gone. All the men in the water were picked up b the boat. I was picked up by a boy of about 16, he was on a raft which had overturned so the oars were underneath. He had no knife to cut the oars away, but we had some calcium flares tied to the raft and we used these to burn the oars free. We managed to pick up the boat and were taken on board. I took command as soon as possible, and we proceeded to search the wreckage for any possible survivors, but none were found.

We then set sail for land. The sea was very choppy and the men soon became exhausted from rowing, soon we saw a lot of broken water and rocks, and approached very cautiously until daylight when I saw a rowing boat. I hailed the boat and asked where I could find a safe landing. The boatman told me to follow him and he led me to Gola Island in West Donegal. There we were transferred to a motor boat and went to Bunbeg. After I had made myself known to the guards at the barracks we were treated very kindly and eventually worked our way to Belfast where I closed the accounts of the ship.

HAMLA (London) – 4,416 tons, 10.5 knots, built 1929 (4 deaths)

Captain William Shute OBE had escaped the sinking of the Tunisia in the previous year (see above), and the Hamla sailed from Rio de Janeiro for Freetown on August 11, 1942, with 38 crew and 4 gunners. At 23.37 hours on 23 Aug, 1942, the unescorted Hamla was hit by two torpedoes from U-506 southeast of Fernando Noronha, Brazil. U boat commander Erich Würdemann observed two hits under the bridge and the aft mast. After the explosions, the vessel was disappeared. All hands were lost, including 4 from Barry: James Britt 19 fireman and trimmer, Louis Goule 24 cook, William Hobbs 22 sailor, William Jemmett 58 steward. The U 506 was sunk west of Vigo in the North Atlantic by American bombs in 1943.

ANGLO SAXON (London) – 5596 tones, built 1929 (4 deaths)

She was sunk by the German raider Widder, en route from Newport to Bahia Blanca. Two survivors landed on Eleuthera Island. Barry losses were fireman and trimmer Verdun Green (24), donkeyman Alfred Nicholls (37), greaser Charles Williams (29) and fireman and trimmer David Williams (20). Chapter 6 recounts the loss of the Anglo Saxon in more detail, including the death of the young Newport cook Leslie Morgan, who went mad from thirst on the ship's boat.

ATHELKNIGHT (Liverpool) – 8,940 tons, built 1930 (4 deaths)

This tanker was torpedoed on May 26, 1942, by the U 172, sinking the next day. According to records 5 gunners were lost, and in actuality all five deaths were of Barry men, 4 of whom were in the port bridge lifeboat.* See the chapter on Captain Hugh Roberts, OBE for more details of the loss of this ship, including the captain's report. The Barry men killed after the Athelknight had sunk were: AB Sydney Gaisford or Gainsford (34); AB Martin McGrath (37), Fireman John Moore (18) and Fireman Christian Poulsen (24), whose brother William was lost on the Stornest five months later. Ten Newport men also died, Walter Allnatt, William Prowse, Charles Wallace, Lars Rasmussen, Charles Stuart, Phillip Takle, Trevor Keyse (whose brother Donald died on the Koranton), Albert Ely, Leslie Morgan and George Bedford. For the story of those who survived, see the entry on Emil John, above.

*These four men from Barry, with an AA gunner named Oliver, managed to get into a lifeboat. Oliver received two shrapnel wounds in his forearm, and Gaisford (spelt as Gainsford by Captain Roberts) and McGrath died in the boat of shrapnel wounds. The fireman Poulsen (the correct spelling, but spelt Paulson by Roberts) had a shattered left shoulder and jaw. Ordinary Seaman Moore had a deep wound in his abdomen. Both were given morphine and their wounds dressed, when taken on Roberts' lifeboat, but both died the day after the attack.

For more information on this sinking, U boat 172 and its 'first-class ace' Captain Emmermann, see Chapter 8 on Hugh Roberts. Could Emmermann have been convicted of war crimes, instead of dying in comfortable prosperity in 1990? The port bridge boat had only 5 men in it. Two dead, two dying and one badly wounded in an arm - they would not have been able to launch the lifeboat, let alone get into it. They were obviously shelled when in the lifeboat.

WHITFORD POINT (London) – 5,026 tons, built 1928 (4 deaths)

She was voyaging from Baltimore and Halifax, carrying steel to London in convoy

HX 79 with a cargo of 7,840 tons of steel. On October 19th, 1940, 400 miles west of the Hebrides, she was torpedoed and sunk, according to Lloyds Shipping Register. However, for the 20th October, she was claimed by U-47. This U boat had become famous when, on October 14, 1939, under the command of Günther Prien, she managed to enter the base of the British home fleet at Scapa Flow through a hole in the defence line, and sank HMS Royal Oak.

U-47 carried out ten combat patrols and spent a total of 238 days at sea. She sank 30 enemy merchant ships (164,953 tons), the Royal Oak (29,150 tons) and damaged eight more. She went missing 7 March, 1941 in North Atlantic near the Rockall Banks. There is no certain confirmation of

how U-47 was lost. For years was it believed that the British destroyer HMS Wolverine sank U-47 on 8 March, 1941 after depth charges attacks, but the Wolverine actually attacked Eckermann's U-A. Possible reasons for the loss of U-47 include mines, by its own torpedoes or by an attack by British corvettes HMS Camellia and HMS Arbutus. The Barry men on the Whitford Point killed by U-47 were fireman and trimmer Ali Kassim (45), chief steward John Conibear (45), cook Thomas Hilberg (44) and the ship's captain, John Young (51).

EMPIRE STANLEY (Greenock) – 6,921 tons, built 1941 (4 deaths)
At 15.50 hours on 17 Aug, 1943, the unescorted Empire Stanley (Master Arthur John Pilditch MBE) was torpedoed and sunk by U-197, south-southeast of Cap Sainte Marie, Madagascar. The master, 17 crew members, six gunners and the passenger were lost. On 20 August, 19 crew members and one gunner were picked up by the British motor merchant Socotra and landed at Bombay ten days later. Eight crew members and one gunner were picked up by the British corvette HMS Thyme, and landed at Durban on 29 August. U boat 197 was sunk 20 Aug, 1943 south of Madagascar, by depth charges from 2 British Catalina aircraft. 67 dead (all hands lost). The Barry dead were: dayman John Arnold (26), AB William England (22), sailor John McCarthy (22), and AB Cyril Thomas(36)

VICTORIA CITY (Bideford) – 4,739 tons, built 1929 (4 deaths)
She sailed from New York to London with a cargo of steel, leaving Halifax, Nova Scotia on November 21st, 1940. She was sighted north of Ireland on December 2nd, and wreckage found on December 8th off Portstewart. From the records of U 140, we learn that at 21.42 hours on 3 Dec, 1940, the Victoria City (Master Alfred Longstaff), a straggler from convoy HX-90, was hit underneath the bridge by one G7a torpedo from U-140 and sank by the bow within 15 seconds west of the North Channel. The master and 42 crew members were lost. The U 104 sank 3 merchantmen and was scuttled at Wilhelmshaven in 1945. The dead from Barry were: Apprentice William Bennett (17), boatswain Thomas Pender (24), and firemen and trimmers Falsh Mohamed (43) and Ali Omar (27).

OCEAN CRUSADER (London) – 7178 tons, 11 knots, built 1942 (4 deaths)
This was a 'Lend Lease' ship built in Portland, Maine, and on her maiden voyage. She was west of Newfoundland, on a voyage from Portland to the U.K. via Panama

and New York with 8891 tons of general cargo. In heavy weather on 25th November 1942, she became a straggler of convoy HX 216 comprising 42 ships. The following day she sent out a submarine distress signal and was sunk by U-262 commanded by Heinz Franke. The Welsh Master, Captain Ellis Wynne Parry and the crew of 44 were lost. The Barry men killed* were: firemen Wilfred Hobbs (33), Charles Moseley (28), William Vaughan (29) and George Weaver (31). Other Welsh seamen were lost, e.g. John O'Brien of Cardiff. U 262 sank 4 ships in 10 patrols, and was bombed at Gotenhaven in 1944, and stricken at Kiel in 1945.

* They had survived the sinking of the Harborough two months previously, and an account of its sinking was written by a fellow survivor as a memorial to them. See Chapter Nine following.

KERVEGAN (Cardiff) – 2,018 tons, built 1922 (4 deaths)

This little ship was carrying pulpwood for Loch Ewe and London, from Halifax Nova Scotia, when she reported that she was in distress and in danger of sinking. Wreckage was later washed up in Nova Scotia. Barry men on board were: Clarence Ashford 21 cook, Sedonis Jacobs 27 third eng officer, AB William Jones 45, AB Cyril 'Dicko' Males (unknown age). The ship's master was Tom Tippett of Cardiff (51) and steward Sidney Pain (25) was also from the capital.

EMBASSAGE (Newcastle-on-Tyne) – 4954 tons, 10 knots, built 1935 (3 deaths)

Travelling from Leith to Pepel, she was torpedoed by U 557 100 miles off Achill Head, County Mayo, on August 27, 1941. Captain W.E. Kiddie and 38 men died. The only survivors were the boatswain and two other men who clung to an upturned boat for three and a half days before being rescued. The Barry dead were: Frederick Cunningham 30 steward, his brother Francis Cunningham 22 baker, Charles Roberts 29 donkeyman. U 557 sank near Salamis in the Mediterranean, losing all her crew, after a collision with the Italian submarine Orione.

EMPIRE CROSSBILL (London) – 5,463 tons, 10.5 knots, built 1942 (3 deaths)

She was travelling in convoy SC-42 from Philadelphia via Sydney British Columbia to Hull when torpedoed by U 82 on September 11, 1941. Captain E.R. Townend and all 37 crew, 10 gunners and 1 passenger were lost. The Barry dead were: Winsor Banks 31 cook, Edmund Gough 20 asst. steward, Sigvard Gronhaug 45 greaser. U 82 was sunk in 1942 off the Azores, by depth charges from the British sloop Rochester and the corvette Tamarisk.

There were 67 ships in Convoy SC-42. The convoy passed Cape Farewell, Greenland on Sept. 7. Being aware the convoy was being shadowed the Admiralty ordered it even further north, closer to the east coast of Greenland. It seemed like it had managed to shake off its followers, but on Sept 9 a ship that had lagged behind reported having sighted a periscope and the wake of a torpedo, so the convoy changed course from N to NE. At about 21:30 that same evening U-432 (Schultze) unleashed several torpedoes, 2 British ships went down, then several more U-boats joined the attack. Another 2 ships were torpedoed, one of which sank. In the early morning hours the attacks continued, a Dutch and a Danish ship went down, then the Norwegian D/S Stargard was hit by U-432; D/S Regin rescued 9 of her survivors. The convoy continued while 14 U-boats followed. Another British ship went down. By this time the escort had been reduced because one of the corvettes had taken a torpedoed tanker in tow for Iceland. 2 Canadian corvettes, en route to reinforce the escort, sank U-501 with all men, and this took place so far away from the convoy that they couldn't assist when the battle started in earnest. The Norwegian book "Nortraships flåte" adds that by Sept. 11, 16 ships had been sunk, 1 was damaged, and the Norwegian Bestum was missing, but it later turned out she had become a straggler and had reached Iceland safely.

The captain of D/S Vestland reported that when the British Gypsum Queen was torpedoed on Sept. 11 he didn't have the heart to ignore the men in the sea crying for help, and against orders he stopped and rescued 26, but 10 died. 2 independent attacks took place on the 16th and 19th (1 ship damaged, another sunk) but at this time the main force of the U-boat group was concentrating on a new eastbound convoy, SC 44. U-boat information is slightly different to the above, but of the 67 ships in the 7-column convoy, 16 were sunk, including Dutch, Norwegian and Greek vessels. Another 19 ships were sunk later in the war. The SC series of convoys started in August 1940, for vessels which could not keep up with the minimum 9 knots speed of the HX series of convoys from Halifax, Nova Scotia.

GRELHEAD (London) – 4,274 tons, built 1915 (3 deaths)
Voyaging from Baltimore to Swansea, she was torpedoed by U 562 at midnight, December 1st, 1941, 2 miles off Punta Negri, Morocco. 35 of her crew of 37, and all 6 gunners were lost. She was carrying iron ore from Spanish Morocco. The 2 survivors were taken to Tangiers. The Barry dead were: firemen and trimmers Rufus Tyne (45), John McAuley (52) and David Jackson (44). The U 562 sank 6 ships. It was sunk 19 Feb, 1943 in the Mediterranean north-east of Bengazi, by depth charges from the British destroyer HMS Isis, the British escort destroyer HMS Hursley and a British Wellington aircraft. All 49 crew were lost.

MAGDALENA (West Hartlepool) – 3118 tones, built 1923 (3 deaths)
En route from St John's, Newfoundland to Liverpool, she was torpedoed by U 48, about 600 miles west of the Hebrides. All 30 of its crew and its gunner were lost. The Barry dead were: Ivor Davies 21 boatswain, John Goule 16 ord. seaman, William Stiff 19 sailor. The U 48 was stricken in Neustadt in 1943 and scuttled there in 1945. William Stiff lost his brothers on the Baron Newlands and the Rose Schiaffino.

Note on the U 48
The U 48 was the most successful U boat in the war, and was responsible for Barry men dying on at least three ships (Tregarthen, Magdalena and British Monarch). Launched in 1939, she sank 10 British, 1 French and a Greek ship from September of that year until the New Year. In 1940, she sank 30 merchantmen, of which 20 were British, 3 were Norwegian, 3 Dutch, 2 Greek, 1 Swedish and 1 Finnish. In 1941 she sank 10 British, a Greek and a Dutch ship. In addition she sank a naval sloop and damaged other vessels. In her time at sea, she sank 54 merchant ships

totalling 322,292 tons.

PACIFIC (Hull) – 2,816 tons, built 1923 (3 deaths)

She left Sunderland in convoy in bad weather, carrying a cargo of coal to London, but the convoy became scattered overnight in bad weather. Next day, the 9th February, 1943, the Pacific and two other ships had been lost. All 38 of its crew perished, including from Barry AB John Benson 39, William Betts 37 cook, Geoffrey Lake 23 cabin boy. Poor Benson had survived the sinking of the Tunisia (see above), when 18 Barry men died.

CREEMUIR (Newcastle-on-Tyne) – 3997 tons, built 1924 (3 deaths)

She was bombed and sunk by German aircraft on November 11th, 1940, between Stonehaven and Aberdeen. 26 crew and 1 gunner were lost, including carpenter Alfred Clanford (58), donkeyman William Nelson (28) and AB Walter Frampton (20). The German planes were probably also responsible for sinking the Ravnanger off Teesmouth, and the Trebartha near Aberdeen on the same raid.

FISCUS (Cardiff) – 4,815 tons, 10 knots, built 1928 (3 deaths)

Sailing in convoy, she was torpedoed and sunk by U 99, about 120 miles west of the Hebrides, on October 18th, 1940. Its convoy, SC 7 arrived at Liverpool just three days later. Captain E. Williams and 37 crew perished, there being just one survivor. The Barry casualties were: William Bradford 39 steward, Clifford Hopkins 24 cook and Gethyn Richards 20 cabin boy. 2 days after the Fiscus, the Whitford Point was sunk (see above). In just 3 days in October 1940, in the Battle of the Atlantic, 34 ships were sunk and 2 damaged. Carrying scrap iron, the Fiscus sank within a minute of being torpedoed.

There was another tragedy regarding the Fiscus. For two Cardiff brothers, Kenneth James Lewis and Raymond Leslie Lewis, it was their first ship, Within a few weeks both would be dead after the ship was torpedoed and sunk by U-99 while sailing to the Clyde from Sydney, Cape Breton in Convoy SC-7. They should never have been onboard as Kenneth Lewis was only 14 years old. His brother Raymond was 15. The two boys are believed to have forged a letter from their father stating he had given permission for them to join the ship. Kenneth and Raymond Lewis are commemorated on the Tower Hill Memorial in London on Panel 49 and are two of the youngest serving Merchant Seamen killed in WWII.

Survivor Report – Fiscus (from Kew Public Records Office)

Deposition of Ordinary Seaman Edward Sidney King - Sworn at Cardiff, Nov. 19-1940

"This vessel had reached a point about 350 miles West of Eire. Position in Convoy, third ship in column three from port. Other columns having from three to six ships in each. Deponent was lying dozing in his bunk when a violent explosion occurred and ship took a heavy list to starboard. One packing case was lying alongside No. 2 hatch. It was not lashed to the deck. Deponent got on to the packing case, when the sea washed him into No. 2 hold, the hatches of which had been blown off by the explosion. Evidently, the torpedo had struck No. 2 hold, starboard side, blowing off beams and hatch covers. The hold was full of water. Deponent sank and rose to the surface when he grabbed the rope lashing

around the packing case. The case floated away, the fore deck of the ship being by this time under water. The packing case swept clear of the ship and when deponent looked around the ship had disappeared, and the sea was a mass of wreckage. In deponent's opinion vessel sank within a minute of the explosion. After about two hours on the packing case deponent sighted three Indian firemen clinging to the ice box about 20 yards away. He called to them and helped them on to the packing case. They died from exposure the next morning. Deponent did not see any other members of the crew. He remained on the packing case until picked up on 21/10/40 by a lifeboat full of survivors from Norwegian ship Thalia.(This is incorrect. The Thalia was Greek and was sunk about 90 minutes after the Fiscus, sailing in the same convoy.) The lifeboat was sighted by a flying boat on 24/10/40 and the occupants picked up on the same day by HMS Clematis. The boats of the Fiscus were swung out ready for launching. One raft was in the starboard fore rigging and two others aft in main rigging, one on each side. Master had given strict orders on 17/10/40 that every man was to wear his life-saving waistcoat continuously and deponent knows that all deck personnel wore them accordingly."

JOSEPH SWAN (London) – 1571 tons, 9.5 knots, built 1938
(3 deaths)
This collier was torpedoed and sunk by a German motor torpedo boat (MTB) off Lowestoft, with Captain Pirie of Newport and 16 men dying, including AB Albert Bauman 40, Noel Brown 30 fireman and AB John Johanssen 47 of Barry

SWIFTPOOL (West Hartlepool) – 5,205 tons, 11 knots, built 1929
(3 deaths)
She was carrying a cargo of ore when torpedoed in the North Atlantic by U 372. Between 01.50 and 01.59 hours on 5 Aug, 1941, U-372 fired four single torpedoes at ships in the convoy SL-81 west of Ireland. First the stern torpedo struck the Belgravian, which burned out and sank the next day. Neumann reported that the second torpedo missed the intended target but exploded on a ship beyond, the third torpedo was a dud and the fourth hit an ammunition freighter, which exploded and sank by the bow in 50 seconds. The ship missed was the British steam merchant Volturno, but a hit on another ship is not confirmed. The ship sunk was the Swiftpool. The master, 36 crew members and five gunners from the Swiftpool (Master Harry Raymond Clark) were lost. Two crew members were picked up by HMS Bluebell and landed at Greenock. The Barry men lost were: Magnus Anderson 63 carpenter, Demetrius Xenophon 56 donkeyman and Alfred Cusworth 25 fourth eng officer. U 372 was sunk 4 Aug, 1942 in the Mediterranean south-west of Haifa, by depth charges from the British destroyers HMS Sikh and HMS Zulu and the escort destroyers HMS Croome and HMS Tetcott and by depth charges from a British Wellington aircraft.

MARSLEW (London) – 4,542 tons, 11 knots, built 1926 (3 deaths)
Carrying 6000 tons of general cargo, she was torpedoed 300 miles north of Rockall on February 23rd, 1941. Of the 36 crew, the Welsh Captain H.R. Watkins and 12 crew were lost when the ship broke in two. The Barry men were: second engineering officer David Jones (age unknown), fireman and trimmer Sali

Mohamed (48) and cabin boy Frederick Tagoe (17). U 69 (or U 95) fired one G7e torpedo and hit the Marslew amidships after Convoy OB-288 had dispersed. The survivors were picked up by the Empire Cheetah. 10 ships in the convoy were sunk.

CAPE CORSO (Glasgow) – 3807 tons, 10.5 knots, built 1929 (3 deaths)

Cape Corso (Master W.C. Montgomery) arrived in Reykjavik as part of Convoy PQ 14, but did not sail with it to Murmansk. She joined the next convoy, PQ15 and on May 2nd, 1942 was attacked by German torpedo-bombers and sunk. She went down almost immediately, as she had been carrying fuel and ammunition. There were only 6 survivors, of whom 3 were injured, of the 56 man crew. Firemen and trimmers William Brown (50), John Davis (28) and Jose Gomez died. A Cardiff greaser, Tom Toby, also died. The summer route to Russia was to meet in Iceland and take the long loop on the other side of Iceland, with Greenland to the west, sailing as far from the European mainland ports and planes as possible. The winter route went up through the Norwegian Sea and the Barents Sea – considerably shorter but far more dangerous.

EMPIRE HOUSMAN (Sunderland) – 7359 tons, built 1943 (2 deaths after war)

She was en route from the UK to New York and was torpedoed by U 545 on December 30, 1939. It was also possibly hit by U 744 later that night. The convoy ON-217 left it behind as a straggler, and she was torpedoed again by U 744 on January 3, 1940, and finally sank on January 5, after superhuman efforts by its crew. One man died and 44 men were rescued and taken to Reykjavik. Two Barry men, hurt during the hostilities, died shortly after the war. The chief steward John Britton died aged 51 in Barry in 1951. A donkeyman Charles Svendsen died in Barry aged 48 in 1952. U 545 was bombed and sunk west of the Hebrides in 1944. U 744 was torpedoed and badly damaged by the destroyer Icarus in 1944. The Icarus and other naval ships tried to tow it, but had to depth charge it after taking off survivors.

PIKEPOOL (West Hartlepool) – 3,683 tones, 10 knots, built 1909 (2 deaths)

This old ship had the misfortune to strike a mine 20 miles E.S.E. of the Smalls Light on November 22, 1940. Captain Atkinson and some survivors were picked up after being adrift for 48 hours on water-logged life rafts. 6 officers and 11 men were killed, including the Barry men: Paul Boucheron 22 mess room boy, Reginald Crook 35 boatswain.

EMPIRE LAKE (West Hartlepool) – 2582 tons, built 1941 (2 deaths)

She was off the east coast of Madagascar, en route from Durban to Aden when sunk by U 181 on July 15, 1943. She sank in one minute with the loss of 25 of her crew and 6 gunners, including from Barry Chief Officer Hiram Brock (aged 45) and Chief Engineering Officer Ronald Marr (28) from Penarth. The U 181 was taken over by Japan in 1945 and became I 501, before being scuttled after surrendering at Singapore.

BALTISTAN (London) – 6,803 tons, 13 knots, built 1937 (2 deaths)

This ship was torpedoed and sunk 400 miles west of Ireland, with Captain Hadley, 46 crew and 4 passengers all dying. The submarine was Italy's Bianchi. The Barry men killed were 3rd engineering officer Leslie Wharrad (32) and Chief Officer Edgar Pritchard (37). It was a Ffyffes ship sailing out of Liverpool on February 23rd 1941 in Convoy 209. Four days out the convoy scattered as the Baltistan was hit and sunk with all hands. Other ships sunk by aircraft and torpedoes in this convoy on 26th February, 1941 were the Solferino, Mahanada, Llanwern, Kasongo, Swinburne, Teneriffa and Leeds City. The Leeds City had picked up the sirvivors of the St Elwyn the previous year – see part 11 of this book, the account by Philip Thomas of the sinking of the St Elwyn. The submarine "Severn", on patrol for U-boats attacking HG convoys west of Gibraltar, torpedoed and sank Italian submarine Bianchi on the 7th August, 1941.

LISSA (London) – 1,551 tons, built 1927 (2 deaths)

This was lost without trace travelling from Barry Docks via Milford Haven to join a convoy for Lisbon with a cargo of coal. She left Milford on September 11th, and her last report was September 21st. All 21 crew and 5 gunners were lost, including AB John Battin (33) and fireman and trimmer Patrick Welsh (48). At 23.20 and 23.21 hours on 21 Sep, 1941, U-201 fired torpedoes at the convoy OG-74 north-northeast of the Azores and reported two ships sunk. The ships hit were Lissa and Rhineland. The U 201 itself was destroyed by depth charges from the destroyer Fame, in February 1943 off Newfoundland. The U 201 was also responsible for the destruction of the Runa (see above).

LADY GLANELY (Cardiff) – 5,497 tons, built 1938 (2 deaths)

Travelling from Vancouver to London, she was torpedoed and sunk by U 101, 400 miles west of Ireland, on December 2, 1940. All her 33 crew perished, upon the 20th ship to be sunk by U 101. The Barry men were junior engineering officer James Evans (37) and chief officer Arthur Hewitson (58).

HARMALA (London) – 5,730 tons, built 1935 (2 deaths)

Sailing from Rio de Janeiro and New York to London, she was torpedoed and sunk by U 614 on February 7, 1943. 40 of the 64 crew died, including from Barry, fireman Arthur Farley (31) and AB Steffan Lonnberg (43). The unfortunate Harmala was the only ship sunk by U 614. On 29 July, 1943, north-west of Cape Finisterre, U 614 was sunk by depth charges from a British Wellington aircraft, with all hands lost.

REEDPOOL (Stockton-on-Tees) – 4,838 tons, 11 knots, built 1924 (2 deaths)

She was about 100 miles north of Georgetown, in then British Guiana, when torpedoed and sunk by U515 on September 20, 1942. 2 officers and 4 men were killed, and 7 officers and men wounded. Captain Downs was taken prisoner. From Barry, the dead were AB Phillip Dunn (22, buried at Buenos Aires) and fireman and trimmer Thomas Pardoe (32). U 515 was sunk north of Madeira, by bombs from the US escort carrier Guadalcanal, and depth charges from the destroyer escorts Pope,

Pillsbury, Chatelain and Flaherty. The U 515's commander, Werner Henke, also sank the Harborough and 24 other ships, and his patrols and sinking are recorded in Part Sixteen. Peter Ratnek was a Barry man lost when the U 515 sank the California Star and 46 crew were killed.

ALMEDA STAR (London) – 14,935 tons, 16 knots, built 1926
(2 deaths)

She was a liner with the Blue Star Line, torpedoed and sunk 350 miles west of the Isle of Lewis, on January 17, 1941. All 360 persons on board, 194 passengers, 27 gunners and 137 crew were killed. The Barry crewmen killed were 2nd engineering officer Edwin Griggs (38) and chief electrician Thomas Lewis (28). From the Blue Star Line website we read: *'The Almeda Star, a 16-knot vessel of about 15,000 tons, built in 1926, was normally used for the passenger and refrigerated cargo service between the United Kingdom and South America. During 1939 and 1940 she continued on that service, sailing independently. At 9.0 p.m. on December 22nd, 1940, while lying in the Mersey, she was damaged by a bomb during one of the air raids on Liverpool. The damage cannot have been very serious for on January 15th, 1941, she sailed from Liverpool, commanded by Captain H. G. Howard, Commodore of the Blue Star Line, with a crew of 166 officers and men and 194 passengers. The year 1941 opened with tempestuous weather in the North Atlantic, gale succeeding gale with dismal regularity. It spelt tribulation for all ships at sea. The Almeda Star was unescorted. Suddenly, from out of the blue on January 17th, came her signal of distress. She had been torpedoed. Her position was 58'17'N. 13'40'W., which put her about 35 miles north of Rockall, that lonely hummock of rock some 35 miles to the west of the Outer Hebrides. No further message came through. Destroyers and other vessels were at once ordered to search the area; but without result. Not even a waterlogged boat was found, no wreckage, no trace of anything. Nothing recognisable as belonging to the Almeda Star was washed ashore. Except that she sent off that one signal of distress giving her position and saying she had been torpedoed, nothing is known of what happened, even from German sources. We do not even know if the ship was abandoned, and if the survivors tried to get away in the boats. All that we are aware is that she appears in the official list as having been torpedoed by a submarine in the position given. The weather at the time being very bad with a heavy sea, it is probable that the stricken ship was overwhelmed and sank in a depth of more than 200 fathoms carrying those 360 souls with her.'*

U 96 was the responsible U boat, and not sunk until March 1945, by US bombs at Wilhelmshaven. She had made 11 patrols, sunk 27 ships totalling 181,000 tons, and damaged 5 others. There is a connection between U 96 and the famous film 'Das Boot': Lothar-Günther Buchheim joined U-96 for one patrol as a war correspondent. This resulted in the internationally best-selling novel of submarine warfare Das Boot (The Boat), and other books. Buchheim was ordered aboard as an official artist to send back renderings of the German Navy in action for propaganda purposes. A camera was to aid his work and over 5,000 photos survived the war. Buchheim witnessed the meeting between U-96 and U-572 during a heavy storm. This probably occurred in November 1941. At this time U-572 was commanded by Kptlt. Heinz Hirsacker (who was condemned to death by military tribunal in 1943 charged with "Cowardice in the face of the enemy" - the only U-boat commander to have that fate, being executed on April 24th, 1943. U-572 was lost later in 1943.

ASHBURY (Glasgow) – 3,901 tons, built 9125 (2 deaths)

All hands were lost when she was wrecked on January 8th, 1945, and the entrance to the Kyle of Tongue. It was the worst incident at sea not caused by the enemy. The Barry men were second officer Ivor Morgan (buried at Thurso) and senior ordinary seaman William Locke. 'WW2 People's War' archive has the following contribution from Alasdair Sutherland which he *has kindly allowed us to reproduce: 'On the 8th of January 1945, the British tramp steamer SS Ashbury foundered and sank at the mouth of Talmine Bay, with the loss of the crew of 42 men. It was the worst loss of a merchant ship during World War Two, in an incident not caused by enemy action. The Ashbury a three-island cargo ship of 3901 tons built at West Hartlepool in 1924, had returned from the Mediterranean in late 1944,with a load of iron ore. The cargo was discharged at Workington in Cumbria; the Ashbury was then told to go to the Tyne for repairs on a faulty engine condenser. Captain David Morris set sail from Workington in ballast on the 31st of December 1944 for Lochewe, where the weather deteriorated badly and the ship lost an anchor. The Ashbury then sailed from Lochewe as part of a convoy on the 6th of January 1945, straight into a force nine gale.*

The Ashbury soon fell behind the convoy, becoming unmanageable to the crew in the heavy seas. A tug was sent to her assistance as the Ashbury drifted alongside the Norwegian ship 'Bestik', off Strathy Point. The Canadian frigate "Ste Theresa" tried in vain between 2am and 4am to pass a line to the Ashbury, but had to move away as there was a danger of running aground on some rocks. A retired merchant seaman, on coastguard duty in Melness reported a light in the Kyle of Tongue around 3:30am; this light is believed to have been from a liferaft. News soon spread of a possible shipwreck and local people began to scour the beaches for survivors.

No survivors were found, as people discovered that a ship had run aground on Dubh-Seir Mhor (The Black Rocks) of Talmine, at the mouth of the Kyle of Tongue. Twenty-seven bodies were washed ashore and taken to the mortuary in Thurso; where fourteen were buried in war graves in Thurso cemetery, eleven bodies were claimed by the next of kin, the remaining fifteen had no grave, but the sea. Two crew members from the Ashbury are buried in war graves in Tongue cemetery; one is the ship's third engineer J T Eddicott, who had replaced the regular engineer at Lochewe when he was taken to hospital with appendicitis. The other grave in Tongue cemetery is that of an unknown sailor whose body was found on Island Rhoan several weeks later.

A formal investigation into the sinking of the Ashbury concluded that the loss of the ship was due to it hitting the Talmine rocks under stress in heavy weather. The ship was unable to maintain safe course in her light condition with only one anchor and short cable; the report also stressed that had it not been for the war conditions the Ashbury would not have been deemed fit to sail from Lochewe.'

BARRWHIN (Glasgow) – 4,998 tons, 10 knots, built 1929 (2 deaths)

She was carrying 8,200 tons of grain and military stores from Halifax, Nova Scotia to London. At 21.18 hours on 29 Oct, 1942, the Barrwhin (Master Thomas Sydney Dixon) in convoy HX-212 was hit by one torpedo from U-436 and sank quickly south of Iceland. Barrwhin had rescued 60 survivors from the Kosmos II, which had been sunk by U-624 (Capt. Soden-Fraunhofen) at 03.05 hours the same day. 12 crew members of the Barrwhin and 12 survivors of the Kosmos II were lost. The master, 41 crew members and 48 survivors were picked up after about eight hours from rafts by the HMCS Kenogami and landed at Londonderry. >From Barry, chief steward Martin Pereira (47) and boatswain Peter Antman died. (Hortop names Pereira as Preiera). The Barrwhin had been adopted by Radnor Girls School in Wales. Two casks of oranges from the crew to the girls, meant as a 'thank you' gesture, were lost in the sinking. 38 merchant seamen from Barry died in October 1942, in 15 separate sinkings. Vernon Upton GM had served on the Barrwhin for 9 months on Arctic and Atlantic convoys, and then took his full leave entitlement on September 8th, 1942. The Barrwhin was lost on her next voyage. Captain Upton's account of the loss of the Start Point is Part Ten of this book.

The U 436 sank 6 ships for a total of 36,208 tons and damaged another two. It was sunk 26 May, 1943 in the North Atlantic west of Cape Ortegal, Spain, by depth charges from the British frigate HMS Test and the British corvette HMS Hyderabad. All 47 crew died. From the website Uboatnet we get the following description of the ill-fated convoy of 45 ships HX-212, and the battle that ensued from 26-29 October, 1942. The convoy was first sighted by U 432 on 26th October. *"The escorts were The American escort group A3 (Cdr. Lewis) consisting of the destroyer Badger, the cutter Campbell, the British corvette Dianthus and the Canadian corvettes Rosthern, Trillium, Alberni, Summerside and Ville de Quebec.*

The wolfpack code-named Puma consisted of 13 boats: U-224 (Oblt. Kosbadt), U-301 (Kptlt. Körner), U-383 (Kptlt. Kremser), U-436 (Kptlt. Seibicke), U-441 (Kptlt. Hartmann), U-443 (Oblt. von Puttkammer), U-563 (Kptlt. von Hartman), U-602 (Kptlt. Schüler), U-606 (Oblt. Döhler), U-621 (Kptlt. Schünemann), U-624 (Kptlt. Graf von Soden-Fraunhofen), U-753 (Korvkpt. von Mannstein), U-757 (Oblt. Deetz). After the fruitless pursuit of convoy ON-139, the patrol line Puma is reinforced and searches further. On the 26th U-436 runs into HX-212.

In the night this boat attacks and scores hits with all her five torpedoes. One ship is sunk and two are damaged. U-606 damages a large ship and finishes off one ship damaged by U-436. Then this large ship is again torpedoed by U-606 and U-624 also before it sinks. U-621 and U-563 have no success. During the next day the U-boats are kept at bay by Liberators coming from Iceland. Only in the night does U-224 manage to sink a straggler and U-624 sinks one ship from the convoy. On the 29th the air escort drives off all boats trying to close in and the operation is broken off. 6 ships were sunk - a total of 51.918 tons from convoy HX-212."

From ex-Able Seaman C G Humphreys, DEMS Gunlayer CJX336950

In 1942 at the age of 18 I had to register for war service and I chose to go in the Navy. Waiting for call-up I went back to work to continue with my apprenticeship in the printing trade. Soon after I became 19 the call came and I had to report to a training camp in Pwllheli, North Wales, where the new intake had square-bashing, a bit of seamanship and training for being a member of a gun crew. It appeared that we were to be in the DEMS (Defensively Equipped Merchant Ships) designated to be gunners on merchant ships.

After six weeks followed by some leave I was drafted to Cardiff to be put on a ship. We were billeted in an infants' school and while waiting to be drafted we did duty fire watching at Cardiff docks.

Eventually I was told to pack my kit and report to SS *Barrwhin*, a coal-fired merchant ship of pre-1914-18 vintage it seemed to me. In our quarters there were eight of us. Five other naval ratings and two army fellows from an artillery unit I got to know, all under the charge of a Leading Seaman. Mounted aft there was a 4-inch gun for shooting at U-boats. On the bridge was a Lewis machine gun and on one side of the ship was a piece of armament for fending off attacking aircraft. A rocket was fired up trailing a cable with a parachute on the end. Fortunately we never had to use it.

Eventually we set off up the coast and joined a convoy collected off the Scottish coast to sail across the Atlantic. As the ship was empty, apart from some ballast, it was a rough journey that my stomach didn't like and I ate ships' biscuits mainly during the two weeks that it took to get to our destination, which was Halifax, Nova Scotia. We used to go on watch, two at a time, for four hours throughout the voyage. It was now about October/November time and bitterly cold in the North Atlantic.

In Halifax the ship was loaded with vehicles in the bottom of the holds, tanks I think they were, all cocooned with some sort of sealant as grain was then poured on top of them. Finally loaded we set sail and formed up with the rest of the convoy for the voyage back home. My stomach didn't appreciate going to sea again and it was back to ships' biscuits. The convoy consisted of all manner of ships; I particularly remember we had a Norwegian whaler as it had a distinctive shape. There was also an escort of Navy vessels.

We had been sailing for about a week, chugging along at about 7 knots, when one night things started to happen. Ships were being torpedoed. Tankers carrying fuel sending flames up into the sky. The Navy ships chased around dropping depth charges but whether they sunk any U-boats I don't know. There were 30 or 40 ships in the convoy and quite a few were sunk that first night. So we plodded on during the day, apprehensive as to what the night would bring. Then we knew. More sinkings, including the Norwegian whaler. We managed to pick up some survivors from one of the ships.

The next night the convoy was in disarray and the ships were ordered to scatter and the following morning we were on our own. I heard afterwards that a U-boat had been sighted not far from our ship during the day. That night the inevitable happened and the ship was torpedoed on the port side and started to go down. Fortunately, my boat station was on the starboard side with the lifeboat operational. The merchant seamen started to lower the boat. It was a metal one fortunately, as it crashed against the ship's side on its way down. I had managed to get into the boat and as other men crowded in I found myself lying on my back in the bottom. Eventually we got ourselves sorted out and I was able to get onto an oar with some other fellow helping to keep the boat head-on to the waves. Others were not so lucky, having to make do with life-rafts, after perhaps being in the water. One thing I did find though, my stomach like the motion of the boat more than on the ship and I felt fine in that respect.

It was a moonlight night and there we were in the middle of the Atlantic, just keeping the boat head-on to the waves with the oars with the life-rafts around. So what did we thank about at that time? I can't really remember how I felt. Being only 19 I just left it to the experienced merchant seamen.

As it was wintertime the nights were long. I am not sure how long we were in that situation but it was still dark when out of the night two grey shapes appeared. They were Canadian Corvettes on their way across the Atlantic to Ireland and completely unaware of *our plight but an eagle-eyed lookout had spotted us.*

Rope ladders were let down and we were soon aboard and in two or three days we landed in Londonderry. We were kitted out and sent on our way to our respective bases, mine being Chatham. After booking in I was given travelling warrants and food coupons and I was on my way home for two weeks survivors' leave.

BULLMOUTH (London) – 7519 tons, 10.5 knots, built 1927
(2 deaths)

On October 30th, 1942, this tanker was sunk by U 659, about 100 miles N.W. of Madeira. Of her crew of 54, 47 died, including carpenter John Howells (35) and chief engineering officer Arthur Hutton. It appears that the Bullmouth was first damaged by U 409, became detached from convoy SL-125, and was then sunk by U 659. U 409 was sunk by depth charges from HMS Inconstant in 1943. Also in that year U 659 sank after a collision with U 439 in the mid-Atlantic. Other known Welshmen on the Bullmouth included 3rd radio officer George Chiles, of Rhiwbina, Cardiff, and steward Brinley Lewis of New Tredegar. The chief officer and 5 crew landed in Bugio Island near Madeira.

CANFORD CHINE (Swansea) – 3,364 tons, built 1917 (2 deaths)

With a crew of 33 and 2 gunners she sailed from the Clyde on February 6th, 1941 for Buenos Aires. She was renamed, from SS "Bryntawe", in 1936. At 14.35 hours on 10 Feb, 1941, the Canford Chine (Master Neil MacDonald), a straggler from convoy OG-52 since 8 February, was torpedoed and sunk by U-52 south-southwest of Rockall. The master and 34 crew members were lost. U 52 was stricken at Danzig in 1943, transferred to Kiel, and scuttled there in 1945. Barry crewmen lost were ship's master Neil MacDonald (52) and steward Wyndham Wiggin (40). (Hortop names MacDonald as McDougall). Another Canford Chine was sunk in the First World War.

CORNISH CITY (Bideford) – 4,952 tons, 12.5 knots, built 1936
(2 deaths)

This was the flagship of what came to be known as the 'Jervis Bay convoy'. On November 5th, 1940, she was wearing the flag of the commodore of the convoy, Rear-Admiral Maltby, when the ships were attacked by the German pocket battleship Admiral Scheer. It was shelled but survived to trade for another two years. She was voyaging in 1943 from Lourenco Marques to Durban then Aden and Suez with a cargo of coal. After leaving Durban, at 06.00 hours on 29 Jul, 1943, the Cornish City (Master Henry Thomas Isaac) in convoy DN-53 was torpedoed and sunk by U-177 southeast of Madagascar. The master, 31 crew members and five gunners were lost. Five crew members and one gunner were picked up by the Australian destroyer HMAS Nizam and landed at Port Louis, Mauritius. U 177 sank 14 ships and damaged one, sinking almost 90,000 tons of shipping. She was sunk by depth charges from US Liberator aircraft in the South Atlantic in 1944, with 50 dead and 15 survivors. The Barry men killed on the Cornish City were AB Gerald Buttigieg (35) and the ship's captain Henry Isaac (48).

THE CONTRIBUTION TO THE MERCHANT NAVY OF ONE WELSH PORT

DARTFORD (London) – 4,093 tons, 10.5 knots, built 1930 (2 deaths)

She was in convoy ONS-100 in the North Atlantic when torpedoed and sunk by U 124, on June 12th, 1942. (The French ship Mimose was also sunk by the U 124). 25 crew were killed on board and another 2 died after being picked up. The Barry dead were firemen and trimmers Joseph Bonnie (46) and James Williams (55). The U 124 sank 46 merchantmen for 219,000 tons, 2 warships of 5,775 tonnes, an aircraft and damaged another 4 ships. These were occasioned on 11 patrols, latterly under the command of the U boat ace Jochen Mohr. The phenomenally successful U 124 was sunk on 2nd April, 1943 west of Oporto, by depth charges from the British corvette HMS Stonecrop and the British sloop HMS Black Swan. All the crew of 53 died. (The emblem of U-124, the Edelweiss, was inspired by the loss of U-64 in April, 1940 as the boats were largely manned by the same crew, including the commander, and saved from the Norwegian waters by members of the German mountain troops using that same emblem.) The U 124 also sank the Petrel (see above).

EASTMOOR (London) – 5,812 tons, built 1922 (2 deaths)

At 04.53 hours on 1 Apr, 1942, the unescorted Eastmoor (Master James Basil Rodgers) was torpedoed and sunk by U-71 about 600 miles east of Hampton Roads. The master, 12 crew members and three gunners were lost. 29 crew members and seven gunners were picked up by the British merchant Calgary and landed at Capetown. She was carrying 7500 tons of general cargo from Savannah to Britain. The Barry men who died were carpenter Frank Bettley-Cooke (51) and fireman and trimmer Augustus Vanburgh (26). Captain Rodgers had earlier survived the sinking of the Pearlmoor (see above).

EMPIRE CROMWELL (Sunderland) – 5,970 tons, built 1941 (2 deaths)

At 02.17 hours on 28 Nov, 1942, the unescorted Empire Cromwell (Master Philip Dent) was torpedoed and sunk by U-508 about 160 miles southeast of Galeota Point, Trinidad. She was carrying 1000 tons of chrome ore. The master, 20 crew members and three gunners were lost. 19 crew members and six gunners were picked up five days later (other sources say two days) by British MTB's and landed at Port of Spain, Trinidad. The Barry men who died were AB Peter Johansen (65) and chef officer John Ritchie (30). U 508 sank 14 ships totalling 74, 000 tons. The U boat was sunk 12 Nov, 1943 in the Bay of Biscay north of Cape Ortegal, Spain, by depth charges from a US Liberator aircraft, with 57 dead (all hands lost). The story of survivor Trevor Davies and his third sinking is told earlier in this book.

FORT ATHABASCA (London) – 7,132 tons, built 1943 (2 deaths)

She was bombed and sunk at Bari, Italy on December 2nd, 1943. 36 crew and 3 gunners died, including from Barry steward Robert Peart (27) and 2nd officer William Watson (25).

Note on the Bari Disaster – 'A Second Pearl Harbour'

Courtesy of the Naval Historical Society of Australia Inc., the following is an abridged account of the unknown disaster at Bari. Bari is located on the toe end of Italy, on the Adriatic with a population of about 200,000. It had become the main supply base for Montgomery's Eighth Army, plus the new HQ for the US 15th Air Force. On the 2nd December 1943, the port was crowded with 30 Allied ships. One of these, the Liberty ship John Harvey, carried a secret load of 100 tons of mustard gas bombs, a precaution in case Hitler decided to invoke the use of chemical warfare.

The Allies gave little thought to a German air raid on the bustling port of Bari. The harbour was crammed with shipping, stuffed with supplies, including aviation fuel for the US bombers crowding the Foggia air base 75 miles away. At sunset, on the evening of the 2nd December in 1943, with the urgent need to hasten the unloading of ships filling the port, the harbour was brilliantly lit so that cargo might be unloaded though the night.

However, there had been a German reconnaissance flight during that afternoon. Unmolested by any AA fire, the pilot made a second pass of the port, and turned North for home, to report that the proposed target was crowded with unloading ships, perhaps 30 plus. Field Marshal Wolfram von Richthofen, in command of Luftflotte 2, had suggested to his boss, Field Marshal Kesselring, that an attack on Bari could slow down the advancing 8th Army, and retard attacks from the newly arrived US 15th Air Force.

He thought he might manage to gather 150 JU 88's for the attack, but in the event, 105 was all he could muster. His aircraft were ordered to fly east to the Adriatic, then turn and approach Bari to the west. The Allies no doubt would anticipate any German air raids to come in from the North. The aircraft would drop Duppel, thin strips of tin foil to confuse the defensive Radar. Parachute flares would be dropped to light up the targets in the harbour at about 7.30pm. Then the JU 88s would attack at a low altitude, hoping to avoid Allied Radar installations.

The Captain of John Harvey was not officially informed that his ship would carry a load of lethal mustard gas bombs. These were 4 feet long, 8 inches in diameter, and each held 60-70 pounds of the chemical. Mustard gas forms blisters, and irritates the respiratory system, leaving the skin burnt, with raw ulcers. Her cargo including 2,000 M47A1 gas bombs filled with mustard gas, which remained a secret, and meant she was not given any priority to unload, so she had to wait her turn.

Arriving on schedule at Bari, Flight Lieutenant Gustav Teuber, leading in the first wave of bombers scanned the scene below, brilliantly lit, cranes busily lifting cargo from ship's holds, the east jetty crowded with ships. The attack was a complete surprise. Liberty Ship Joseph Wheeler exploded from a direct hit, John Motley was hit in No. 5 hold, John Bascom next to her, shattered by a rain of bombs, was abandoned. John Harvey was on fire, and suddenly blew up, disappearing in a massive fireball, casting pieces of ship and her deadly cargo of mustard gas all over the harbour. Mustard gas gives off a garlic odour, and now it combined with oil in the harbour, a deadly and volatile mixture. People were noticing a smell of garlic in the air, already doing its deadly work. Another Liberty ship, Samuel Tilden was sunk.

In all, 17 ships were lost, 5 American, 5 British, 2 Italian, 3 Norwegian, and 2

Polish. Aanother 7 were heavily damaged. This Bari raid was a disaster on two fronts. It was a Second Pearl Harbour, with 17 ships totalling 75,936 tons sunk, and another 7 ships with a tonnage of 27,289 tons heavily damaged by this sneak air attack by German aircraft, one of the Luftwaffe's success stories. The Bari raid produced the only poison gas incident associated with WW2, made worse by the perceived need for secrecy in wartime. There were over 1,000 military and merchant marine casualties, some 800 were admitted to local hospitals. 628 suffered from the mustard gas, of whom 69 died within two weeks. The port was closed for three weeks, as it had been rendered into rubble.

Although US records did mention mustard gas, Winston Churchill insisted all British Medical records were purged and mustard gas deaths were merely listed as the result of: "Burns due to enemy action." No doubt his insistence of secrecy could have caused more deaths, as victims, especially Italian civilians might have sought proper treatment for their injuries, had they known the real cause.

TREVERBYN (St Ives) – 5,281 tons, built 1920 (2 deaths)

She was carrying 7,800 tons of iron ore from Pepel to Cardiff, and left Freetown on October 15th, 1941. She straggled behind her convoy SL-89 and was never heard from again, except for a German broadcast over a year later claimed she had been sunk by a U boat. All 38 crew and 10 gunners were lost. From U boat records we find that at 22.31 hours on 21 Oct, 1941, the Treverbyn was hit amidships by one torpedo from U-82 and sank in 3 minutes southwest of Cape Clear. The Barry men lost were Captain Henry Edwards OBE (47) and ordinary seaman Edward Lewis (32). Other Welsh seamen lost were mess-room boy Francis Harrison (15) of Cardiff, carpenter Harry Godfrey (28) of Newport, 3rd engineer officer Brinley Colwill (23) of Pembrey, fireman and trimmer William Pratt (24) of Newport, cook Frederick Vimpany (34) of Newport, ordinary seaman Frank Burke (23) of Newport, 2nd engineering officer Vincent Broughton (48) of Cardiff, and ordinary seaman Robert Brimble (15) of Newport. Fireman Herbert Jones (25), AB Andrew Morgan (23), fireman William Pearce (20) and 3rd officer Phillip Jones (26) were also lost, giving a total of 14 Welshmen dead including 5 from Newport. The U 82 sank 8 ships, but was sunk in 1942 off the Azores from depth charges from HMS Rochester and HMS Tamarisk, with no survivors.

HAIG ROSE (Liverpool) – 1,117 tons, built 1920 (2 deaths)

Captained by Owen Roberts, she left Barry Dock on November 5th, 1940, for Plymouth. She was never seen again and perhaps struck a mine. The Barry men who died were ordinary seamen Dashwood Caple (23) and Gordon Jenkins (24).

HARTINGTON (London) – 5,496 tons, built 1932 (2 deaths)

She was heading from Halifax, Nova Scotia to Belfast, and torpedoed on November 2nd, 1942, 450 miles east of Belle Isle Strait. 22 crew and 2 gunners were lost, including chief officer Owen Clements (37) and cook William Usher (31). The U 521 sank 4 ships. It was sunk 2 June, 1943 in the North Atlantic south-east of Baltimore, by depth charges from the US patrol craft USS PC-565. (51 dead and 1 survivor).

HOMESIDE (Newcastle on Tyne) – 4,600 tons, built 1924 (2 deaths)
This ship was lost in the North Atlantic on 28th January 1941, but information is scarce about the ship and the circumstances of its loss. She left Pepel for Middlesbrough, leaving Freetown on January 8th, 1941, with 35 crew and 2 gunners, and carrying 7100 tons of iron ore. A wireless report on 28th January stated that the ship was leaking and the crew were taking to the boats. The Barry dead were 3rd officer James Campbell (24) and cook Harry Smith (55).

GEORGE BALFOUR – 1,570 tons (2 deaths)
She left London October 12 1942 for Blyth, in ballast. In an E-Boat attack (E-Boat S-75) she broke in two and the bow sank. The after part was towed to Great Yarmouth and then to South Shields where a new forepart was welded on. She was in convoy FN 38, and the Lysland was also hit but was towed to Immingham and repaired. The Barry men who died were: Chief Engineering Officer James Gronhaug (56) and Captain Harry Mawson (47).

LIEUTENANT ROBERT MORAY (Belfast) – 3176 tons, 2 deaths
She was travelling from Southampton to Barry, in ballast, when bombed by German aircraft, February 10, 1942. Of the 26 crew and 8 gunners, 2 men were lost, both from Barry. They were firemen and trimmers Thomas Phillips (28) and James Yeoman (25). She was berthed at Penzance and then towed to Falmouth for repairs. Information about this ship is extremely scarce, even to the extent of its unusual naming.

BELLEROCK (Gibraltar) – 1199 tons, built 1909 (2 deaths)
She struck a mine off Porlock, Devon and sand with the loss of 17 lives, including from Barry, cook William Piper (24) and boatswain Charles Williams (26).

BIBURY (London) – 4616 tons, 11 knots, built 1929 (2 deaths)
West of Africa, she was sunk by U 46, on September 2nd, 1940 with 38 men dying. The Barry men were fireman and trimmer William Bennett (31) and Chief Officer John Trollope (42).

CLARISSA RADCLIFFE (London) – 5754 tons, 10 knots, built 1915 (2 deaths)
She left New York for Barrow carrying 41 crew, a sick seaman and 10 gunners. It appears that she was torpedoed by U 663 on March 9th 1943. There were no survivors, and the dead included firemen and trimmers Pedro Lopez (58) and Paul Phipps (age unknown).

EMPIRE STREAM (Greenock) – 2922 tons, built 1941
Voyaging from Gibraltar to Dundee, she was torpedoed and sunk by U 124, 800 miles west of Cape Finisterre, on September 25th, 1941. 4 crew, 2 gunners and 2 stowaways died, including boatswain John Gilmore (54) and donkeyman John Haughton (30).

CYPRIAN PRINCE (London) – 1,988 tons, built 1937 (1 death)

While there was only one death of a Barry man on this ship, recent events show the terrible moral decisions that had to be made by the captains of merchantmen in times of war. Divers have located the wreck of the destroyer HMS Exmouth, which was torpedoed and sunk with all hands, in waters off the coast of Wick in Caithness. HMS Exmouth was torpedoed by a U-boat in January 1940, while the Cyprian Prince from Aberdeen to the Scapa Flow naval base. The Cyprian Prince carried urgent cargo - searchlights, anti-aircraft guns, trucks and ammunition - and it was deemed imperative she make it to Orkney. Accordingly, when the destroyer was hit the Cyprian Prince did not stay to pick up survivors, lest she too be torpedoed; by the time the Wick lifeboat got to the scene, all 189 crew had been killed or drowned.

The captain of the Cyprian Prince was so affected by what he had been forced to do, he resigned his commission on reaching Orkney. His feeling of guilt was heightened when the Royal Navy claimed at an Admiralty Board of Inquiry that it would have been impossible for a U-boat to have sunk HMS Exmouth, and it must have been a mine she hit. It was not until recently that the captain was vindicated: German records showed that it had been U-boat 22 that sank HMS Exmouth. On the divers' first inspection of the wreck, they found ample confirmation.

The Cyprian Prince was later bombed and sunk by German planes on April 6th, 1941, in Piraeus Harbour during the invasion of Greece. In the same attack, the 7,529 ton Clan Fraser blew up (she was carrying ammunition), destroying other ships and damaging the port. Apart from the Cyprian Prince and Clan Fraser, other ships lost in the explosion and air attack were the 7,108 ton City of Roubaix (also carrying explosives), the 1,706 ton Patris, the armed boarding vessel Surf, the salvage ship Viking, and the Greek ships Elpis, Evoikos, Syyliani, Petalli, Kyrapanagia II and the Halcyon. 4 of the 36 men on the Cyprian Prince perished. The Barry man who died in this terrifying attack where 13 ships were destroyed were 2nd engineering officer Francis Garrett (29). The ship was beached near Salamis and was a wreck by 1945.

PART SIX:

The Loss of the Anglo Saxon

The Anglo Saxon left Newport on 8th August 1940 with a new, mainly Welsh crew, carrying coal to Bahia Blanca, Argentina. There were 41 officers and men, and one deck gun. She joined the outward-bound Liverpool convoy OB 195 at Milford Haven. On August 21, she met the armed merchant raider "Widder" 800 miles west of the Canaries. The "Widder" was one of 9 heavily armed German ships which were disguised as merchant vessels, known as Hilfskreuzer. They approached unsuspecting Allied ships, sank them by concealed torpedoes and cannon, and sunk over 900,000 tons of shipping. Commanded by Hellmuth von Ruckteschell, the Widder sank 10 ships totalling 58,645 tons between June 13 and September 8 in 1940. She usually tracked her victim by day, made a fast approach at night, and opened up fire when close in.

At 8.20pm on August 21, 1940, in darkness, the Widder opened fire on the Anglo Saxon, which had not seen her approaching. Her first 5.9 inch shells were fired from a mile away, and landed on the Anglo Saxon's poop and gun platform, exploding the Anglo Saxon's ammunition and killing the gun crew. Moving in closer, gunfire and flak smashed the bridge and wireless room and damaged the boats which the crew was trying to launch. There were many dead, and the captain gave the order to man what boats were available. The ship was ablaze, and finally sunk by a torpedo. The Widder fired tracer bullets into two life rafts and did not search for survivors before steaming off.

Only 7 of the 41 men managed to escape, in the portside jolly boat, which had not been seen by the Widder (it had attacked the starboard) and so was luckily undamaged. The survivors were the mate, Barry Denny (31 year old); the sailor Robert Tapscott (19); the sailor Roy Widdicombe (21); the assistant cook Leslie Morgan (20) who had been injured in the right foot; the gunner Francis Penny (44) who had been shot through the right forearm and leg; the 2nd radio operator Roy Pilcher (21) who had been hit by gunfire and also had a badly crushed right foot; and 3rd engineer Lionel Hawks (23). The boat was just 18 feet long, and its maximum beam was 6.5 feet. It was not meant as a lifeboat, but fortunately was supplied with a tin of ship's biscuits, 11 tins of condensed milk, 18 pounds of canned mutton but only 4 gallons of water. There were also 6 pairs of oars, a compass, a sea anchor, flares, matches, a boat cover, a medical kit and a sail. After spending the night anchored, to avoid attracting the Widder's attention, the next morning she set sail westwards.

On September 1st, Roy Pilcher died from a gangrenous foot, 10 days after the sinking. The survivors began to deteriorate physically and mentally. The mate Barry Denny noted in his log: 'Do not feel particularly hungry but suffer from parched throat owing to low water ration.' He later wrote that they were unable to chew on the ship's hard biscuits because of the tiny ration of water. His last entry in the log was September 2nd, suggesting improvements in the list of rations to be stored in lifeboats.

From September 4th, the log was written by another crew member, who stated that the gunner Francis Perry had 'slipped overboard'. On 5th September he notes tragically that Barry Denny and 3rd engineer Hawkes 'go over the side no water.' On September 9th, cook Leslie Morgan 'goes mad and dies.' The only two left alive were Roy Widdicombe and Robert Tapscott. On September 12th a cloudburst gave them some water for six days, and on September 20th another cloudburst gave water for four days. They had no biscuits or water at this time, and had spent 5 weeks in the open jolly boat.

They drifted westward, surviving marginally on seaweed, and once a flying fish landed in the boat. There was minimal water from the occasional shower. They broke their compass to drink its mixture of alcohol and water. Two ships passed and missed their signals, and Widdicombe broke his front teeth trying to eat his shoes. Tapscott spent his days lying in the bottom of the boat, and both were slipping into insanity. On the 68th day, Widdicombe spotted a seagull, which gave hope at last. Next day they sighted an island and guided the jolly boat to land.

On October 30th, 1940, after 70 days and 2500 miles, the sun-blackened men landed on Eleuthera in the Bahamas. Emaciated, dehydrated and exhausted, they were found lying on the beach by a farmer. The authorities were noted and they were placed in hospital in Nassau, where they were visited by the Duke and Duchess of Windsor, the Duke then being Governor of the Bahamas.

Widdicombe recovered more quickly, and in February 1941 sailed from New York on the "Siamese Prince". She was lost with all hands just one day out of Liverpool, torpedoed by the U 69, the first of the 16 ships she sank. Robert Tapscott's health was almost broken, but in the summer of 1941 he went to Canada and joined the Canadian Army. However, he rejoined the Merchant Navy in March 1943, arriving back in the UK in May 1943. He served at sea until his premature death aged 42 in 1963.

The captain of the Widder was sentenced to 10 years (commuted to 7) by a British War Crimes Court, and died in prison, aged 58, just before his release. A report of the rescue was delivered to the Colonial Secretary at Nassau, which included the log of the jolly boat of the Anglo Saxon. Spellings and sense begin to ramble in the log entry for September 4th, written by Hawkes, and the last entry is probably by Widdicombe on September 24th, 7 weeks before the survivors made land.

Sinking of SS Anglo Saxon by armed German raider on
August 21st, 1940 at Lat. 26. 10 N. Long. 34. 09.

Sir,

On Wednesday, October 10th, a ship's boat containing two men came ashore on the island of Eleuthera. The men were discovered lying on the beach in an advanced state of exhaustion by a farmer named Martin who was working in a field nearby and had seen the boat approaching. He obtained help and the men were removed to the Governor's Harbour and the resident Commissioner reported the circumstances to the Colonial Secretary at Nassau, who issued instructions for their removal to the hospital at Nassau by aeroplane. The Chief Medical Officer went with the plane from Nassau and they were brought back and placed in hospital the next day. Although in a very weakened and emaciated condition, every hope is entertained of their recovery.

2. The men, Wilbert Roy Widdicombe and Robert Tapscott, were able seamen on the SS Anglo Saxon, 5000 tons, of the Lowther Latta line, bound from Newport, Mon to Bahia Blanca with a cargo of coal. They are, apparently, the sole survivors of a crew numbering about 40.

3. They had with them in the boat three pocket books containing papers, the property of the junior wireless officer Pilcher. These were delivered to the Colonial Secretary who turned them over to me for examination. Among these papers I found a rough log kept by the Chief Officer B.C. Denny from the time the boat was launched up to a short time before his death. A few entries were made subsequently by Widdicombe, AB. As the events recorded therein tell the story of this frightful outrage by the German raider, I give it in full as follows:-

AUGUST 21ST, 1940. At 8:20pm in Lat. 26.10 N. Long. 34. 09 W. attacked by German raider assumed by crew to be SS Weser or Weber, Hamburg America Line. Vessel not lighted until she had steamed to within a mile of us. Pitch black night. First sent four shells 4 inch crashing into poop and gun platforms aft. Many of crew in fo'castle were killed. She then steamed to within 3 cables (about a third of a mile) and raked the decks with incendiary machine gun bullets coloured red, yellow, white and blue. Then a shell hit engine room starboard side and main boiler burst. The bridge and wireless room were raked with pom-pom shells and machine gun bullets. Some of the crew went to boats on boat deck but were mowed down by machine gun fire. The two big boats were badly damaged. Senior wireless operator reported wireless installations smashed, unable to send S.O.S. On reporting to Master, found him presumed shot down by machine gun bullets in his cabin, saloon amidships was wrecked, poop by this time blazing and the crew few in number were told to take to the boats. The port gig, under my orders, was lowered and contained seven of the crew comprising: Chief Officer B.C. Denny; 3rd Engineer H.L. Hawkes; 2nd W/T Officer R.H. Pilcher; AB Widdicombe, W.R.; AB Tapscott, R.G.: Gunlayer F. Penny; Assistant Cook L. Morgan – of whom the 2nd operator was badly injured in the left foot by gun fire, and the 2nd cook in right foot, while gunlayer was shot through right forearm and right leg.

When the gig pulled away from the vessel, the raider was lying off a half a mile to port and a few minutes later fired tracer bullets into two life rafts launched from the vessel. The vessel sunk stern first and shortly disappeared altogether. Raider headed off to the eastward. Assumed that Germans wanted no members of crew left alive, and were fortunate in this boat's crew escaping observation. We lay hoved to all night with sea anchors out and at dawn could see no trace of any description. Having no instruments for navigation except boat compass, we set sail dipping lug and course started west to make W.S.W. time, trusting to God's good grace to either finding a vessel en route or striking somewhere in the Caribbean Sea.

THURSDAY, AUGUST 22ND, 1940 Wind N.E. 3. Slight sea, slightly confused easterly swell. Course by compass W. All's well. Medical treatment given.

AUGUST 23RD, FRIDAY. Wind E.N.E. 3. Slight sea, slightly confused easterly swell, partly cloudy. Half a dipper of water per man 6am, also half a biscuit with a little condensed milk. Sighted a vessel showing no lights at 11pm. Showed sea flare. She cruised around but was of the opinion that she was a raider as she was heading N.N.E. We were about 100 miles from our original position. Kept quiet and let her go off.

AUGUST 24TH, SATURDAY 85' Crew's spirits cheerful. Wind N.W. _ Cloudy, steering S.W. time. Issued half a dipper to each man and half a biscuit, hoping for rain showers.

AUGUST 26TH, MONDAY 24' 12' 36'. Crew all well though 2nd cook and 2nd W/T wounded feet very painful and starting to swell. Rations half a dipper of water at 6am and again 6pm with one biscuit per man per day, with a little condensed milk, hoping for rain showers but none around yet. Wind N.N.W. 2 cloudy, slight sea. D/L sail set. Course W.S.W. true. Nothing sighted and becalmed all day long. 6pm opened 6 pound tin of boiled mutton; crew ate half which greatly improved their morale which is splendid. No sign of giving up hope. Sun set at 6:35 A.T.S. on leaving ship estimated distance covered 225 miles W.S.W. true.

AUGUST 26TH, MONDAY Bosun bird flew overhead. Sun rose at 6:52 am A.T.S. Becalmed, occasional fitful gusts. 6am issued meat rations out from day previous, wrapped in canvas, little taken, half a dipper of water per man, little drop of condensed milk, spirits of whole crew keen, no murmur from wounded men. Hoping to sight vessel soon, but praying for squalls and a decent wind. During a.m. medical treatment given by 3rd engineer and myself. W/T operator's left foot which is badly crushed bathed with salt water for an hour and last linen bandage applied, well covered up but swelling badly. 2nd cook's right foot swollen badly, ankle badly strained with bullet wound just above ankle, bathed with salt water and well bandaged. Gunlayer's right forearm washed first in fresh water, then iodine applied and bandaged. All day long blinding sun's rays and cloudless, becalmed. During afternoon first officer, 3rd engineer, gunlayer, AB's Widdicombe and Tapscott dipped their bodies in water over side, taking care to keep their faces out of the water, result greatly invigorating. Rations still half a dipper of water per man at 6am and 6pm, only eat half a biscuit per day, no need for more, and a little condensed milk. The boiled beef (he means mutton) kept in canvas is still good and the fat is appreciated. Although the W/T is weak, everyone else in good spirits and very cheerful. Keeping two watches, one myself other 3rd engineer, two AB's, four on and four off. Having no nautical instruments or books on board can only rely on the compass and stars at night. Trusting to make a landfall in vicinity of Leeward Island, with God's will and British determination. 10:30pm, wind freshening from eastward skimming along fine at about 5 knots.

AUGUST 27TH, TUESDAY Wind E.N.E. 3 to 4, partly cloudy, no rain yet. 6am ration given, half a dipper of water, no one felt hungry. Managed to give each man a cigarette made out of newspaper and half a can of tobacco, but only 8 matches left so this luxury will soon be stopped. On Port tack heading S.W. true making about four knots and throughout night, held a lottery in evening as to who gave nearest date of being sighted or making landfall. Sun set 6:42pm A.T.S.

AUGUST 28TH, WEDNESDAY 160' During afternoon, Chief Officer, 3rd Engineer, Widdicombe and Tapscott had a dip over side, felt greatly improved as body absorbed the water leaving salt on skin, saliva came to mouth which (was) previously parched. Moderate to fresh E.N.E. trade, heading S.W. true. Bosun bird and ordinary black seagull flying around.

AUGUST 29TH, THURSDAY On our eighth day in the boat, crew's spirits extremely cheerful. W/T operator weak owing to left leg going dead. Ration still half dipper of water per man 6am and pm. Noon half a biscuit with light condensed milk. Wind E.N.E. 4, moderate sea and swell. Gig running free on Port tack heading S.W. true. High hopes of picking up a ship or making landfall shortly, we are all putting our trust in God's hands, everyone is fit except a weakness in legs and of course great loss in weight. Do not feel particularly hungry but suffer from parched throat owing to low water ration, pity we have no lime juice or tins of fruit, which would ease matters considerably, but no one is complaining. All day long strong E.N.E. wind with strong swell, shipping a little water everywhere.

AUGUST 30TH, FRIDAY 50' Moderate N.E. trades and swell, course W.S.W. true, rationed half a dipper of water at 6am and again at 6pm. Now a quarter biscuit per man, hardly touched owing to slim measure of water, small issue of thin condensed milk, crew's spirits cheerful, but W/T op getting weaker, during evening becoming becalmed, W/T op delirious kept everyone awake at night with moans.

AUGUST 31ST, SATURDAY 30' Becalmed, partly cloudy, nothing sighted whatsoever, have had not one speck of rain yet but living in hopes. 6:15am water issue half a dipper also at 6:30pm. Opened our second tin boiled mutton (six pounds) have one left, also five tins condensed milk and three-quarters case hard biscuits, water breaker half full, nine days in boat.

SEPTEMBER 1ST, SUNDAY 30' During Saturday night crew felt very thirsty, boiled mutton could not be digested and some felt sick, doubled the water issue that night. 6:15 am half a dipper of water per man and same in pm. Wind S.S.W. 2 slight northerly swell, steering West true. W/T op failing slowly, hope to see something soon. 8am W/T operator R.N. Pilcher passed peaceably away. Committed his body to the deep with silent prayer.

SEPT. 2ND MONDAY 6:15am issued half a dipper of water per man and same in the evening with a little condensed milk diluted with it. Wind E. 2 slight sea, steering W. true. Crew now feeling rather low, unable to masticate hard biscuit owing to low ration of water.

  Suggestion for life boat stocks. At the very least two breakers of water for each
  boat, tins of fruit such as peaches, apricots, pears, fruit juices and lime juice,
  baked beans, etc. Our stores consisted of:
  One tank filled with dry biscuit

11 tins condensed milk
3 tins each 6 pounds of boiled mutton
One breaker of water, half filled
[Note by R.O., at this time the writing is visibly much weaker and subsequent entries in different hand]

SEPT 3RD, TUESDAY 120' One dipper of water per man at 7am and again in evening. Things going from bad to worse, 1st mate who wrote this diary up to this point going fast. Good breezes from E.S.E.

SEPT 4TH 100' Everybody much weaker. The mate is going fast now. 1:30pm Sunday, Penny very much weaker slipped overboard. From 10pm tonight 14 days out, tried to make the Leeward Island or Porto Rica, Hayti, but the German raider gave none the right to take a sextant, chronometer, extrer (sic) water, tin fruit or bottled fruit, no rum or brandy for wounded crew. Evidently intended to smash all life boat gear to kill all inquiry, but we got the small gig, seven of us by wind somewhere in vicinity of Leeward Islands.

SEPT. 5TH Chief mate and 3rd Engineer go over the side no water.

SEPT. 9TH 2nd cook goes mad dies. Two of us left.

SEPT. 12TH A cloud burst gives us water for 6 days.

SEPT. 20TH Rain again for four days. Getting very weak but trusting in God to pull us through.

R. Widdecombe
R. Tapscott

SEPT. 24TH All water and biscuits gone but still hoping to make land. R.W.

A truly graphic account of the events surrounding the sinking of the Anglo Saxon and the trials in its jolly boat is found on the website rbls-kirkwall.org.uk/memorials:
  "On a pitch-dark evening, Wednesday 21st August 1940, she was suddenly attacked with diabolic fury by a German raider in latitude 26∞ 10' N and longitude 34∞ 09' W. The nearest land to the eastward lay a 1000 miles or so to the Canaries or the Cape Verde Islands. Westwards the West Indian Islands were 2800 miles west-southwest.
  It was 8.20 p.m. when the first salvo from the unseen raider ploughed into the Anglo Saxon's poop, demolishing her gun and killing everyone in the starboard fo'c'stle. The first salvo was followed very quickly by three more and thereafter a hail of lead and steel from pom-pom and machine guns raked the doomed ship fore and aft. Shell fragments tore the ship all along her starboard side. Incendiary bullets criss-crossed into her in burning lines as the noise of destruction rose to a crescendo.

Machine gun bullets poured into the bridge structure and the Master, Captain Flynn, was riddled as he attempted to drop the ship's papers over the side. The wireless aerials and sets were smashed at the outset of the holocaust, so there was no chance of sending an S.O.S. Within 6 minutes the ship was a shambles, most of her crew killed, but her engines still turned pushing her ahead.

The Third Mate had been on watch and an Able Bodied Seaman named Roy Widdicombe, 21 years of age, had been at the wheel. A breastwork of concrete building blocks protected the wheelhouse and this gave the seaman some cover, but the officer was killed outright early in the massacre. Widdicombe left the shelter of the wheelhouse but dived back immediately when the hail of fire moved forward again. He was then joined by the Chief Officer, Mr. Denny, and by the Senior Wireless Operator. All three realised that their only hope of survival was to get off the ship as quickly as possible. They left their shelter and ran to the port side, but only the Chief Officer and Widdicombe reached it and they found that the lifeboats had been smashed by gunfire.

They did find, however, that the jolly boat by some miracle had escaped serious damage. They managed to lower it, not without injury to Widdicombe whose hand got jammed in a running block, and as the boat was passing the deck below two men jumped into it. The mate and Widdicombe then slid down the lifeline into the boat and they were immediately followed by the Second Wireless Operator, who just managed to slide down before the boat rope parted. As the jolly swept by the ship which was still going ahead, two more men dropped into it as it went round the stern, missing the propeller by inches.

The Raider was so intent on the kill, she hung on the "Anglo's" blazing trail and failed to observe the jolly boat which drifted by on the swell only 30 yards from her. Lights suddenly appeared bobbing up and down on the crests of the waves. The men in the jolly boat realised that the lights were on life rafts from their ship and they started to row towards them, when the Raider swung her guns on the rafts and streams of incendiary bullets soon obliterated them and also some men who had been seen clinging to them.

At 9 p.m. on the Mate's wrist watch an explosion rent the "Anglo Saxon" and she slid by the stern into the sea. The Raider, her work of destruction over, headed off into the east, evidently satisfied that she had sunk her prey and all her crew without trace. In the jolly boat, or gig, which is an 18 feet small boat used to ferry members of a ship's company from ship to shore or for painting the hull etc. were seven men: The Chief Officer (or First Mate), Mr. C.B. Denny, who was a Londoner, 34 years old; the Third Engineer, Leslie Hawkes, aged 22 from Sunderland who was making his first trip to sea; the Second Wireless Operator, R.H. Pilcher, also a Londoner who, according to his shipmates was a cut above the usual article; the Gunner, a Royal Marine named Richard Penny, a Devonshire man aged 42; The Second Cook, Leslie Morgan, aged 20 from Newport and 2 A.B.s Roy Widdicombe (21) and a fellow Welshman named Robert Tapscott who was 19. Tapscott had trained as an officer cadet but had broken off his training as the pay was so poor.

Mr. Denny immediately organised his crew and began keeping a log. He found that the jolly boat was not properly provisioned or equipped. The water breaker holding 6 gallons was only half-filled. Provisions consisted of one tin of ship's biscuits, eleven tins of condensed milk and 3 six-pound tins of boiled mutton.

To make matters worse, the Wireless Operator Mr. Pilcher, who had rowed in the darkness for some time, was found to have been shot in a foot which was reduced to a pulp of mangled flesh and bone. The Royal Marine, Richard Penny, had been shot through the right forearm and a piece of shell splinter had torn through his thigh. Tapscott had been wounded in the back when fragments of a shell, which had blasted him across the deck, were lodged there. Morgan the 2nd Cook had been wounded just above the right ankle and he also suffered from a badly contused hand. The medical kit in the boat consisted of a bottle of iodine, two rolls of bandages, a packet of medical lint and a small pair of scissors. They set a sea anchor and waited for morning.

In the morning the sun's rays lit up the surface and with one accord, all who were able stood up and scanned the sea. In all that turbulent plain they could see nothing – nothing but empty miles of water, nothing on the ocean's surface and nothing in the sky. They were completely alone. The Mate then announced that there was no use going east as wind and current were against them so they set course for the Leeward Islands 2,800 miles to the west-southwest. Their only instrument of navigation was the boat's compass. Making the wounded men as comfortable as possible and dividing the fit men into watches, they stepped the stubby mast, hoisted the lugsail and with a good breeze blowing from the east, made all of 4 knots.

The Mate had considered their chances of making land, the minimum food and water to sustain life and the amount of each, which they had in the boat. He set half a dipper of water for each man, a little of the condensed milk with it, and half a biscuit three times a day. On Sundays there was to be an issue of mutton so long as it lasted. The mate's calculations, however, were based on fair wind and good weather – neither of which they experienced to any great extent.

At 11 p.m. on 23rd August, two days after their hip had been sunk and about 100 miles from their original position, they sighted a steamer showing no lights and which was heading NNE. They lit a flare, which was seen for the ship turned and came back in a wide circle as if fearing a trap. As she swung round they saw that her build was German. The men in the jolly boat lowered sail, crouched down and waited. After some minutes of cruising very slowly and suspiciously, the stranger turned, gathered speed and resumed her course. The men in the jolly boat breathed again and all agreed that they were lucky not to have been detected. A British ship would have shown her searchlight, but a German could not risk such publicity.

On Sunday 25th August the wind dropped and the boat lost way. Pilcher and Morgan were suffering increasing pain from their wounds. Their lacerated feet had swollen during the night and were swelling more. It was necessary to loosen their bandages. When this was done an odour permeated the atmosphere – the horrible stench of gangrene. As the boat drifted or lay becalmed under the burning sun and with no rain having fallen since the men abandoned ship, their pores closed up, their skin became scorched and crisped and salivation ceased. The direct rays of the sun upon them caused great torture. Their mouths and throats became so parched that talking was painful. Physical function practically ceased – their bodies had little waste to eliminate. The able men baled seawater over the wounded and when they had them thoroughly doused, went over the side themselves, being careful at first to keep their faces out of the water.

By the 28th August, the stench of gangrene was terrible. The Gunner's torn hip was going the way of the wounded feet of Pilcher and Morgan. Yet Pilcher never complained. The only words, which passed his lips, were words of apology for the terrible reek, which his shipmates were being forced to endure. On the 30th August that brave man became delirious and the Mate decided that the foot would have to be amputated. The majority of the men agreed and the Mate took an axe, which was on the boat, and with the help of Widdicombe and Hawkes, who were to hold down Pilcher, prepared to operate. When, however, it came to the actual business of lopping off the foot with a rusty and blunted axe, even the resolute mate quailed. "I can't do it" he said, "He'll have to take his chance".

That night nausea and cramp seized the Mate, causing him to retch in agony. When the morning dawned the others saw to their consternation that he, the symbol of discipline and fountainhead of knowledge had suffered some sort of internal collapse. Pilcher too was very low, but he was lucid. When they took him his morning ration of water, he turned his head away and croaked a request that it be given to someone who needed it more than he did. At 8 a.m. Morgan, from his place next to Pilcher in the bow sheets, said suddenly "Sparks has gone". It was indeed so, Sparks had gone as silently and unobtrusively as he had done everything in life. Tapscott and Hawkes lifted the body over the gun'l and lowered it gently into the sea. Very little was said in the boat during the rest of that day.

By September 2nd, all hands were very low and were unable to masticate the biscuit owing to the low ration of water. No rain had fallen and no great progress had been made for over a week due to the lack of wind. On that day the Mate made his last entry in his log and it included a detailed list for bettering lifeboat equipment based upon his all too practical experience. He was very ill during the night and in the morning he could not get to his feet. A bed was made for him in the thwarts using boards and lifebelts. He was too ill now to command. Leslie Hawkes, the Third Engineer, took over. Morgan and Penny were weakening fast.

That day Widdicombe suggested that a whole dipperful of water be issued to each man, instead of the usual ration, and it was clear that a fight would follow if he did not have his way. His argument was that the water would not last much longer anyway, so why not let everyone have a decent drink. He got his way.

On 4th September Penny, the wounded Gunner quietly went over the side, but not for a swim. He did what he deemed best and it was impossible to bring the boat round in time to try and pick him up. Morgan was delirious and kept up an incessant noise of meaningless chatter and song. That day Mr. Hawkes, the young Third Engineer, made his last entry in the log and it was a record of the inhuman ferocity of the German Raider in his determination to kill all inquiry. The next morning they drank the last of the water. During that morning a heavy swell carried away the rudder, which had lacked a lower pintle when they left the ship. Tapscott and Widdicombe got out a steering oar and shipped it in place of the rudder.

With the sun mounting higher in the sky and adding further to the agony of all, the Mate suddenly raised himself on his elbow and mumbled from swollen lips "I'm going over – who's coming with me?" The Third Engineer, Hawkes, said that he would but Tapscott and Widdicombe refused. Morgan, in a lucid manner, begged them not to leave him, as he did not want to die. Their decisions made Mr. Denny and Mr. Hawkes lay down in the boat and they went to sleep. The dread of what they must witness overwhelmed the other three – IT WAS THE FORMAL END – THOSE IN COMMAND WERE LAYING DOWN THEIR ARMS.

Tapscott thought that perhaps they would change their minds, for he could not imagine anyone making such a dreadful decision and then calmly going to sleep. Tapscott and Widdicombe neither remonstrated nor tried to interfere. Not only were the officers senior to them and entitled to make decisions without question, but also they had decided the most private question in life. Interference would have been presumptuous and moreover Tapscott and Widdicombe were too dazed and miserable to formulate much more than their own desires to hold on to the end.

Approaching 10 p.m. on 4th September, Hawkes sat up and said "Ready". The Mate opened his eyes and then got up to his feet with surprising sureness, considering his condition. Hawkes then announced that he was first going to have something to eat and drink. He thereupon dipped a can into the sea and gulped the water greedily. He filled the can again and drank that off. He then softened a biscuit in seawater and ate it. The Mate drew off his signet ring and handed it to Widdicombe with a croaked request to give it to his (the Mate's) mother should Widdicombe get through. He also told them to keep going west – no more south. They shook hands all round and Mr. Denny took off his light uniform jacket. Mr. Hawkes did likewise. Then they stood up in the thwarts near the port gunwale, shook hands with one another and fell over the side.

Tapscott had turned his head away and Morgan, with surprising clarity and sense, said that they ought to pray. The three were at a loss for a minute and then decided on the Lord's Prayer. They stumbled through to the end of it. The passing of the Mate and the Third Engineer had a curious effect upon Widdicombe. It vitalised him into hope and action. He took to himself command, but Tapscott and Morgan were sunk in despair. Widdicombe on the contrary was full of energy. He trimmed sail, set the course and rallied the others to new energies. The three in the jolly boat had absolutely nothing to sustain life, but Widdicombe was sure that somehow, miraculously, they would come through. His enthusiasm died down however, as they drifted and sometimes sailed through days of absolute agony.

On 9th September Morgan raised himself and said in a voice firm and clear without the detached quality of insanity "I think I'll go down the street for a drink". He stumbled aft and stepped overboard. There were now only 2 survivors from the "Anglo Saxon". How these two lived through days of sheer horror and agony is one of the inexplicable things in life. More than once they were on the point of quitting. In fact they did go over the side together on one occasion to end their misery and together, not being able to agree, climbed painfully aboard again a little refreshed by their bathing activities. It rained and they became new men. The water they obtained and preserved from a cloudburst only lasted a certain number of days, then it was agony all over again. They drank the pure alcohol in which the boat compass card floated and got gloriously drunk. They slept for several hours and woke to find rain falling. On two separate occasions a flying fish landed in the jolly boat and on another occasion they picked up some seaweed through which they sailed. Raw fish and seaweed were devoured gratefully.

Seventy days after the "Anglo Saxon" had been sunk, the jolly boat grounded on the shore of Eleuthera Island in the Bahamas. It was on 31st October 1940 that Tapscott and Widdicombe were found lying on the beach, a short distance from one another, by a coloured farmer and his wife, Mr. & Mrs. Lewis Johnson. Mrs. Johnson had dreamed a strange and compelling dream during the previous night. In her sleep she had been urged to "go to the beach" where she would find "something". The beach to the local folk meant a lovely and lonely stretch of white sand, fronting the Atlantic at Alabaster Bay. To reach it the farmer had to slash a way through the bush with his machete. When they got to the shore they saw the jolly boat slewed sideways just as it was left by the receding tide. But directly in front of them lay a man – or what had been a man:

Claw like hands protruded from the remains of a uniform jacket, wasted knobbly legs from what had been a pair of shorts. Such parts of him as were not covered with rags or hair were burnt a deep mahogany. His head thrown back on the sand, was a bearded skull; the cheek bones pressing through the tight drawn blackened skin, the closed eyes sunk in deep sockets, long black locks hung down his forehead and cheeks and tangled in his black beard. The second survivor was as ragged, bearded and emasculated as his companion. His large nose was a ridge of cartilage and bone; his cheek bones as salient as the other's, the rest of his face caved in. Through the tatters of a pair of underwear shorts, his sunburnt, withered thighs were visible. His skull-like face was blurred with an unkempt, yellow beard. His head, twisted back convulsively, lay in a shock of bleached tow like hair, showing a corded and craggy neck, no thicker than a child's. With the fingers of his out flung pipe stem arms, he plucked feebly at the sand. Both men were obviously utterly spent.

After some days rest, with food and drink in Eleuthera, Tapsett and Widdicombe were flown to Nassau and taken to the Bahamas General Hospital. For eight days they were only allowed to see Doctors and Nurses. They were suffering from pellagra and their blood pressures were alarmingly low. On the ninth day, they were visited by the Governor of the Bahamas and his wife, the Duke and Duchess of Windsor. The Duke had given special instructions for Tapscott and Widdicombe to be flown to Nassau and he also made arrangements for the preservation of the jolly boat. Word had already been dispatched to the survivors' families in Britain.

Tapscott was in the worse condition. There were grave doubts about his ability to survive. The mental and nervous systems of both boys were badly deranged. They suffered from insomnia. Both were frequently hysterical, or sunk in deep apathy. Tapscott, who had held up so well in the boat, now had long spells of melancholia during which he wanted to die. However, under the skilful treatment of the Chief Medical Officer, Dr. J.M. Cruikshank, and his staff, the two young men improved. In February 1941 Widdicombe was well enough to start on a journey home and he proceeded to New York, to join a Furness Withy Liner named "Siamese Prince". Tapscott, although improving, was not well enough to accompany him..." The ship was sunk with all hands on that voyage.

The Imperial War Museum has purchased the jolly boat. There are only 24 grooves cut into its wood to mark the days it was drifting. Robert Tapscott said 'we got confused after that.'

Robert Tapscott returned to live in South Clive Street, Grangetown, Cardiff, after the war. His father and grandfather had been Cardiff pilots, and it had been natural that as a 15 year-old he had joined the merchant navy in Cardiff in 1936. After 15 days on his 2275 mile voyage in the 18-foot jolly boat, the water had run out. One injured man had died after 11 days, and the next quietly slipped over the side two days later. 33 days after the sinking, another survivor gave Widdicombe (from Newport) his signet ring to give to his mother, and stepped into the water with another survivor. They held each other as they sank beneath the waves. They had given their vests and shirts to the survivors, but kept their trousers on 'for fear of mermaids.' A day later, another Newport man, Morgan, told Tapscott he was 'going down the road for a drink' and stepped off the boat. Twice after this, Tapscott and Widdicombe almost committed suicide together. Once Widdicombe pulled himself back into the boat, and Tapscott said 'If you're not going, I'm not', but could hardly clamber back into the jolly boat. A vessel passed half a mile away but missed them. By the time they made landfall, each man had lost over six stone in weight. Both men were suffering from starvation, exposure, prolonged dehydration and damage to their nervous systems. The men had been in an open boat in the Atlantic for 70 days.   For two days it was thought that Tapscott would not make it. Roy Widdicombe's death must have also held horrors for Tapscott, and a verdict of suicide from a deliberate overdose was given when he died in 1963. However, his wife Norma disputed the verdict. It had been three years before he told her what had happened on the boat. She believes that his death was a tragic accident – 'He had taken (sodium amytol) tablets and a cigarette set fire to the carpet and he was overcome by fumes. What he experienced dring the war eventually led to his death.'

Robert Tapscott had seen his captain shot while dumping the ship's papers overboard. He had seen men dead and dying and the lifeboats shot to pieces. As tracer shells and flames lit the sky, he and six others had managed to elude the Widder in the darkness and escape. Five of his shipmates died in the next 70 days, and Widdicombe a few weeks later. His memories must have been horrendous.

And what of the captain of the Widder? He had taken or sunk 7 Allied ships when he spotted the Anglo Saxon. She was en route to way to Argentina with a cargo of Welsh coal, and a crew of 41and Captain Ruckteschell decided to employ the same style of sudden attack, without any warning that had recently brought success against the Beaulieu and Oostplein. The Widder retired to wait below the horizon until after dark. It was not pitch dark until 8 pm, and with moonrise due at 08:18, Widder's captain had only 18 minutes during which to surprise the enemy.

Having approached on a directly opposite course, the raider opened fire at 08:08 from 2.500 yards, immediately hitting the freighter's deck gun and setting its ready-use ammunition on fire. Von Ruckteschell had refined this method of attack, tracking his prey by day, a fast approach by night and then a sudden assault with main armament, accompanied by raking AA and machine-gun fire to prevent any resistance. Ruckteschell then fired a torpedo, causing a large explosion, which sank the ship. She was the 8th of 10 Allied victims on the Widder's 1940 cruise.

Lights were observed in two lifeboats, as Morse signals were briefly seen passing between them, but as no one appeared to be seeking assistance, and as it appeared as if the boats were attempting to evade capture, making any rescue impossible, Ruckteschell said that he decided not to wait to pick up the survivors. Besides, the explosion that sank the freighter would have been seen for a great distance, and, as he recorded in his war diary, the boats were "only 800 miles from the Canaries" and "the wind was favourable".

Anglo Saxon's Seaman Robert G Tapscott testified at von Ruckteschell's trial that the Widder had opened fire on the boats as they moved away from the sinking ship. Ruckteschell's defence countered that due to the noise of the guns firing over the men in the boats, it was difficult to communicate the "cease fire" command. Somehow, Ruckestell was acquitted on this charge.

Von Ruckteschell was the only one of the merchant raider commanders to be tried for war crimes, being convicted of failing to pick up the crews of Beaulieu and Anglo Saxon, and of continuing to fire on Davisian after her Captain had signalled that she was being abandoned. He was sentenced to 10 years in Hamburg-Fuhlbuettel prison, the sentence subsequently being reduced to seven years, due to the fact that the charges concerning Beaulieu could not be upheld. He died there on 24 June 1948, shortly after hearing that he was to be released due to his worsening heart condition.

PART SEVEN:

The Loss of the Stornest

The following is from an article in *Sea Breezes "The Magazine of Ships and the Sea"* (Vol.66 No.564 December 1992), whose editor has kindly given us permission to republish:

In Memory of Idris Thomas, Lost at Sea
Introduced by Sid Davies

Some five years ago my brother noticed that the war memorial at Penmaenmawr, North Wales, did not carry the name of Idris Thomas. It was known that Idris had been lost on his first trip to sea in 1942 and the omission probably lay in the fact that his family moved to Wallasey at about that time. Having from time to time been struck by the sadness of the loss of such a young life - he was 18 - I became interested in finding out about the loss of his ship, the Stornest. A small paragraph in Sea Breezes brought a lot of information and advice concerning further sources and I now have a thickish file of letters from some very interesting people.

Idris Thomas had completed a course at the Wireless College, Colwyn Bay, and was sent to join the Stornest at Swansea where she was loading coal for Boston, USA. With a crew of 29 and 10 gunners she sailed from Milford Haven and the graphic details of her subsequent fate are given in the following report from the Ministry of Defence, Naval Staff Duties Section (British Crown copyright 1992/MOD reproduced with the permission of the Controller of Her Britannic Majesty's Stationery Office):

"The Cliffside Shipping Co steamer Stornest 4,265 grt, sailed from Milford Haven with seven other ships on the afternoon of October 2, 1942, to rendezvous in the northern Irish Sea with convoy ONS 136, which was due to leave Liverpool on October 3. The Stornest, which was bound for Boston, Mass, with a cargo of coal, joined ONS 136 on October 4 and took up station in position 52, which was in the centre of the convoy immediately astern of the commodore's ship. The convoy then proceeded into the Atlantic through the North Channel.

Virtually continuously bad weather was encountered in the North Atlantic, gale-force winds making it impossible for the escorts to keep the convoy together throughout the whole of the crossing. Ships were repeatedly falling astern and on October 11 the Stornest was one of a number reported by the Senior Officer of the escort to be straggling.

Just under 36 hours later, at 2202 (all times quoted are in GMT) on October 12, the ship was sighted some 130 miles south-east of the convoy by U706, under the command of Kapitanleutnant Alexander von Zitzewitz. She was then, according to von Zitzewitz, steering 250 deg at an estimated eight knots.

U706 thereupon shaped course to haul ahead of the steamer to attain an attacking position, but the U-boat made slow progress owing to the visibility, which varied between three and four miles but dropped to one mile in the frequent rain showers. The U-boat's speed of advance was further affected when, at 2316, the port thrust-block began to run hot and she was forced to proceed on only one engine.

It was thus not until 0138 on October 13 that U706, having reached a suitable attacking position, ran in and fired a spread salvo of two electrically-driven torpedoes from the bow tubes at a range of 900m. Both torpedoes appeared to run normally but no explosion ensued. The U-boat's crew, convinced they were on target, suspected pistol failure.

U706 thus ran in again and at 0205 a second spread salvo was fired from the other two bow tubes at a range of 800m. This time the attack was successful, the left-hand torpedo striking the ship abreast the foremast after running for 34 seconds. There was a large explosion plume, the Stornest fired off three red rockets and von Zitzewitz could see the flashing of lights on the upper deck.

The Stornest reduced speed and commenced transmission of a distress signal, giving her position as 57deg 25'N, 27deg 42'W, which von Zitzewitz tried unsuccessfully to jam.

Despite being badly holed in No.1 hold the Stornest remained afloat on an even keel. Von Zitzewitz thus decided to finish her off with another torpedo, which was fired at 0234 from close range from the stern tube. Inexplicably the torpedo missed. U706 then having emptied all five torpedo tubes withdrew to reload one bow torpedo tube for another attempt.

Reloading was completed an hour or so later and U706 ran in again, firing at 0403 at a stopped and drifting target. Once more, however, there was no result, which caused von Zitzewitz to wonder if the ship was fitted with torpedo nets. If not, he considered the only explanation was deviation of the torpedo from its track owing to heavy seas, despite its having been given a depth-setting of as much as 4m.

Von Zitzewitz reckoned he still had time to reload another tube before daybreak but had to dive to carry out the operation because of an increasingly high sea.

U707 resurfaced at 0533. There was then no sign of the torpedoed vessel and, after a search had failed to find anything other than an apparently empty lifeboat drifting northwards from the steamer's last know position, von Zitzewitz called off the search at 0714 on the assumption that the ship had sunk. U706 then withdrew from the scene, setting course to regain her position in the patrol line.

In reality the Stornest had not gone down and was actually still afloat some 24 hours after the attack. By 0429 on October 14, however, her situation had clearly become critical for at that time she reported from position 54deg 34'N, 26deg 39'W, that she was listing heavily, water was gaining rapidly and she was unable to hold out much longer.

At 0444 the Irish Oak, independently bound for the United States from Ireland, responded to the Stornest's distress signals, informing the stricken ship that she was about 90 miles away in position 53deg 45'N 24deg 47'W, and, if any use, would come along. The Stornest requested her to do so and inquired if she had direction finding gear.

A few minutes later, at 0450, the Stornest reported to the Irish Oak that the ship was being abandoned but that the Irish ship should keep coming.

To a further inquiry from the Irish Oak the Stornest confirmed that she had rafts (she had earlier reported the loss of her lifeboats which, on being lowered, had probably either been swamped or drifted away from the ship in the heavy weather, which is a possible explanation for the empty boat seen by U706).

In addition to the Irish Oak, the rescue tug Adherent in company with the anti-submarine trawler Drangey, which had been dispatched on Admiralty orders on October 13, were proceeding to the Stornest's assistance. Two corvettes had also been ordered to detach from the following convoy, ONS 137, and search for survivors.

At 1357 on October 14 the Irish Oak signalled that owing to heavy seas and a westerly gale she had abandoned the rescue.

The tug and trawler arrived in the Stornest's last known position early on October 17 but their search was without result. The weather then turned foggy but they were nevertheless ordered on October 18 to continue searching.

On the afternoon of October 19, however, the Admiralty decided in the light of continuing bad weather to call of the search and the tug was ordered on the morning of October 29 to return to base. None of the Stornest's crew had been picked up."

Mr Davies continues...

"U706, which was on her first patrol when she sank the Stornest, was herself sunk by a US Liberator aircraft north-west of Cape Ortegal on her fifth trip in July, 1943. Survivors were picked up by HMS Waveney. The Irish Oak was torpedoed in May, 1943, but most of her crew survived. I do not suppose that the fate of Idris Thomas was very different from that of many others during the war at sea, but his death at such a young age and in such appalling conditions makes sad reading. As memories dim I hope that, as a nation, we do not forget the sacrifice of so many young lives."

PART EIGHT:

Captain Hugh Roberts O.B.E.

In Chapter Five, The Contribution of One Welsh Port to the Merchant Navy, we see that all the Athelknight's dead were all from Barry. We are fortunate to have the records of that ship's captain, the remarkable Hugh Roberts, who was also previously sunk on the Athellaird. The following is his story, by kind permission of his family, and with the permission of www.rhiw.com, a superb website devoted to the Llyn Peninsula.

Hugh Roberts (1895-1987) was from Edern, and like many young men from the Llyn, chose the sea as his career. But three things made him a special Welshman. First, he worked his way up from a mess-boy to Captain; secondly he was awarded the O.B.E. for his leadership and sheer courage during WWII; and third he kept a detailed account of his life at sea. His first trip at fifteen years of age was on a tramp steamer, and he served in WWII, commanding tankers, the most feared vessels by seafarers, as the loss of life on them was horrific. The following is his story, beginning with his service at the end of WWI. It puts into perspective the role of the merchant marine in peace and war, showing the movements of materials in and out of Cardiff, Newport and Swansea, and the practice of 'paying off' after each ship returned home:

"I joined Radcliffe's, S.S. Wimborne 3689 tons net, at Portland on the 17th of March 1918. This was my first three mate ship, and I signed on as Second mate, and having bunkered we sailed for Newport News. We met with strong wind and heavy sea off the island of Flores, in the Azores, and the Master Capt J. W. Jones O.B.E. of Cardigan was very annoyed at the course the vessel was making good. In this ship it was not the practice to tow the log, and the Second Mate was the only one who did navigation. Neither the Mate nor the Third Mate had sextants, and the Master never took sights. When I found we were only thirty miles North of Flores, instead of about 120 miles, I reported that the ship was steering badly, and he said that there must be something wrong. The next I saw of him was coming from the poop, and he then informed me that our rudder plate from the 12 foot mark to the bottom was missing. He then said that on their previous voyage, they had been ordered to dock at Boulogne, North France, but when they tried to enter the locks, they found that the ship was too wide to enter, they then had to back out and in doing so, their stern had struck the bank, and they had to pull her out clear of the piers, stern first, as she could not possibly turn inside as she was also too long.

We made Newport News and entered port, nothing being said to the Pilot about the rudder, until the vessel entered the dry dock, which had been arranged for her beforehand. Quite a few times between Cape Henry and the dry dock the Pilot had asked sarcastically, what was wrong with the steering, as he had always found this an excellent steering vessel, but he got no reply. When he found the reason for dry-docking, he declared that he would not have brought us into port without the help of two tow boats, iIf he had been aware of the fact that we had only barely five foot

290

depth of rudder. The propeller and rudder were removed, the vessel taken to her loading berth, and loaded with 1500 tons of steel billets and filled with oats, which brought her down to her full load line. She was then placed in dry dock and the propeller and rudder repaired, and put back. This cargo was discharged at Dunkirk. This ship was manned on deck by ten apprentices, 5 Malay seamen and a Portuguese Bosun. We again came into Portland Harbour after leaving Dunkirk, and when berthing, some of the Malay crew started to fight with the Apprentices. This was seen by the Harbour Master, who asked me to tie up as well as I could, and that he would be back soon. He came back with a squad of Naval Police who took all the Malay seamen ashore, to be dealt with for insubordination. Before sailing it was reported that the Chief Steward was missing, and I was told by the Master to check the stores in the Steward's storeroom. This did not take long to carry out as there were no stores left, although we should have had sufficient to get back to the USA. When searching the Steward's room, we discovered some letters that had been given him by army people in Dunkirk for posting on arrival U.K. This was a serious matter, and they were handed over to the Naval people. In the letter, was evidence of where the stores had gone in Dunkirk and notifying the people, to whom the letters were addressed, that the Steward promised to send them some stores also from Portland.

He was arrested in London and punished. Our next cargo, consisting of oats and with our double bottom tanks full of fuel oil, was landed at New York. The oil was discharged at Portsmouth and the oats at Dunkirk, and when we called at Portland on 1st August 1918 I was paid off. I then went to study for my Mate's Certificate at Liverpool and obtained it at the first attempt at the end of September 1918. As the 1914 – 18 war was soon over, I decided to have a holiday and my next employment was with Howard Houlder and Partners of London. I went across to La Pallace, France to join their SS Doonholm 2776 tons, signing on there on 24th January 1919. This vessel was supposed to proceed to Philadelphia but at the last moment we were ordered to Cardiff where we loaded a cargo of coal for Gibraltar, and then in ballast to Freetown, Sierra Leone, where we took on board the usual crowd of crew boys to do the cargo work. Having taken in 1000 tons Manganese ore at Secondu, we loaded at Lagos and four other coast ports before calling at Freetown to land the crew boys. On our passage to Liverpool, we called at Las Palmas taking 5000 crates tomatoes on our foredeck and 5000 crates bananas on our after deck.

We anchored in the Mersey for a week awaiting a discharging berth, and were then sent to Manchester, where on our arrival, all hands, except the Chief Officer and Chief Engineer were informed that their services were at an end. Our Master was a real old timer, one Smith, from the Tyne, whose nose shone like a lighthouse, but who always swore that he had been a teetotaller. He had known for some time that the vessel had been sold, and I was later informed that he had dismissed with our services without authority from the old owners. My date of discharge from this ship was 14th June 1919. My last couple of months on this ship had been spent in agony owing to an abscess on the jawbone, which kept me from joining a ship that was offered soon after arriving home.

I remained home until May 1920 when I was instructed to join the ex Hamburg American Liner, SS Bosnia at Leith, where she was being handed over by the

Germans as Reparations. We eventually took this vessel to the Tyne, where she had been built by Palmers in the 1890's as an emigrant carrier, and as she was not suitable for Houlders trade, she was eventually sold to Nemasis of Hong Kong as a pilgrim ship and was renamed the Frangiestan, under whose ownership she was lost by fire in the Red Sea in about 1923. I then joined the same company's SS Franktor 2297 tons net at Cardiff on June 25th 1920 as second mate and made two voyages in her with coal from the Bristol Channel and ore from Agulas homewards to Barrow and Cardiff. On the 12th November 1920 the vessel was renamed Jalavijaya and registered at Bombay. The Scindia Co of Bombay, a newly formed Indian company, having bought all Howard Houlders remaining ships, we were only too glad to serve the new owners, and so sailed from Newport loaded with Railway material for Bombay.

After discharging our outward cargo we entered the Indian coastal trade and remained on it until the end of March 1922. We then loaded for Hamburg and Dunkirk, and I was promoted mate, and the 3rd Mate a Cardiff man became 2nd Mate. We were the only ones left of the Officers and engineers who had come out with the ship. We were paid off at Barry Dock on the 10th May 1922. I now decided to sit for Master and went to Liverpool, and received my Master's Certificate at the end of July 1922. Having had a holiday, I was required to relieve one of the Chief Officers in a sister ship to my last one at Liverpool in early October 1922, and went with her to Manchester and Barry Dock, at which dock I was asked to proceed as passenger with this ship to Port Said to await the return of my previous ship on her next return voyage from India.

I rejoined the Jalavijaya at Port Said on the 11th December 1922 and arrived at Hull on the 3rd January 1923, where I was ordered to proceed to Tyne Dock to join the SS Jaladuta 2592 tons reg, as Chief Officer, loading coal for Port Said and then in ballast to Rangoon to re – enter the Indian coastal trade once more. We were transferred to the Calcutta – Karachi coastal trade after getting rid of our Rangoon cargo, and remained on that trade until the vessel was sold to Japanese buyers on the 5th December 1925. I was then appointed Master of the SS Jalatarang of 4200 tons deadweight, which vessel had been built by Thorneycroft, on the Isle of Wight three years earlier. This was an oil burning vessel, and we traded between the Burman Rice ports and South India or Ceylon. When leaving the port of Akyab, fully loaded with rice, early May 1926, we received warning of a cyclone to the south of our track, so having gone just out of sight of land I decided to stop and await development. That ship with her extra large hatchways and deeply loaded, would not have much chance if she met a cyclone. Next day we re-entered port just before the cyclone arrived, and managed to hold her with both anchors down and the engines working as necessary, until the worst was passed. That night the storm crossed the Aracan Coast 60 miles north of Akyab and nearly 1600 people lost their lives. I left the ship at Bombay at the end of August 1926 and came home as a passenger, having in my own heart said goodbye to the Indian Coastal Trade.

I remained home until the 28th April 1928, when I joined the tanker, Athelbeach 3472 tons net at Birkenhead, as Third Mate. I had not been Third Mate previously, and had never been near a tanker, but within an hour of joining her I was left in sole charge of pumping operations. She was discharging a molasses cargo into the owner's own storage depot and I managed to keep things going from midnight until 8 am without any complaint. We loaded next at Holland for New York this was all Best Molasses. In August of 1928 I became 2nd Mate, and again Mate in December. We sailed from Amsterdam for Baltimore on 1st January 1929 with a cargo of beet molasses, and off the Azores we ran into extremely heavy weather which continued for the remainder of the 26 day passage. She was an excellent sea boat, but even so the sea smashed in the wheelhouse windows. She had a large hatchway forward, and after the wheelhouse windows were smashed, it was seen that something had gone wrong with the hatches, but no one could get near until just before dark, fourteen hours after the sea had done its damage. We went to investigate, whilst the Master and 2nd Mate nursed her with the engines, and found the forward hatch sections had been driven over the second section and only tarpaulins covered the forward section, the only wedges left were those on the fore end. Had another sea dropped on that tarpaulin, nothing could have saved us.

Things were put right in quick time without any injuries. We arrived in Baltimore with swept bunkers, and only five tons small coal and dust left. This vessel used coal as fuel at that time, because until suitable storage was arranged, there was too much risk of the cargo of molasses being contaminated by fuel oil. This vessel owned by the United Molasses Co. of London was sold to Norwegian buyers at Hull early November 1929.

I came home and having married that same month I was promoted to Master of the new 14000 ton twin screw motor tanker, Athelprincess which I joined on 26th December 1929 at Greenock. This vessel was fitted with a Sperry Gyro Compass and Automatic Helmsman. We left the Clyde after trials, on the evening of the 31st December for Tjilatjap, on the south coast of Java, where we loaded a full cargo of cane molasses for London and Rotterdam. I remained as Master of this vessel, until mid October 1939. Our usual voyages used to be from home in ballast, through the Panama Canal to California, where we usually loaded crude oil for Japan and then on in ballast to the Philippines, Java or Calcutta to load molasses for either the UK or the USA. When bound to the latter country we usually went around South Africa. Occasionally, however, after discharging in Japan, we went back to the Hawaiian Islands where we always loaded molasses for the UK. On one voyage, we remained on the California/Japan oil trade for sixteen months.   During all the time I was on this vessel, the only delay we had due to machinery failures, was seventeen hours changing a piston, and another short delay due to a faulty lubricating cooler, we were free of any serious damage to the hull of the vessel throughout. On one particular voyage from Java to New York non stop around South Africa, when we were north of Bermuda an old AB from this village, asked me if I thought the engines would stop if required to do so, we were at that time 48 days out of Java, and both engines had been running continuously. When war was declared in 1939 we were just south of Madagascar, and called at Capetown and Dakar before coming to Liverpool, where I left, as I had Gall Bladder trouble.

THE LOSS OF THE ATHELLAIRD

In February 1940 I took over the Mv Athelmonarch for one trip to Cuba and back, and then transferred to the Mv Athellaird, making one trip to Cuba and Everglades in Florida, and returning to Liverpool, sailed again on the 29th June. We were in convoy until 7pm on the 2nd July, when it dispersed, and from then on until dark the ships were in all directions. At 10.20 pm I was on the bridge arranging the course to be steered during the night, when a torpedo struck the vessel abreast of the fore mast on the port side, her stern came out of the water, and she became difficult to manage, so it was decided to stop and leave her in two out of four lifeboats, and then if she were not attacked again, we would come back. There was no point in risking the lives of those in the Engine Room unless we could be certain of help, and escort vessels were very short at that time.

At 1040 we were clear of the ship in the two boats, and about 300 yards away from her. In our boat there was some difficulty about clearing the sea anchor rope, and I moved into the middle of the boat to help clear it with the aid of my torch. Then suddenly there came a whirring noise under the very middle of the boat, and my first thought was that the submarine was passing right underneath us, but I suddenly saw the phosphorescent track of the torpedo, which made us all rather scared. I do not believe that the submarine had fired a torpedo at that boat knowingly, but in the dark had seen a light and then fired. If fired at the ship it was wide of the mark.

We could still see the ship until 2 am at which time a terrific explosion occurred abreast of the engine room, and we lost sight of her soon afterwards. Our position at that time was about 600 miles W.S.W. of Land's End. When dawn came we could not see the other boat, but later he spotted us and came closer to discuss the position. These lifeboats were 25 feet six inches long, of 8 foot beam and 3 feet 4 inches depth, and were certified to carry 20 persons. We had heavyweights and the other boat had 23 not so heavy men on board. Our provisions consisted of 20lbs biscuits in ten airtight tanks, two by ten gallon kegs of water, one case condensed milk, and four 7lb tins of corned beef, boiled beef and mutton.

We both decided to keep together and to head to the North East as we had no desire to be set East or South East which would have landed us in occupied France. Our first issue of water and biscuits was made on Wednesday evening, and afterwards these were given out at 5 am and 10 am, 3 pm and 8 pm, if the weather permitted us to open the bread tanks and water barrels. We also had a few cigarettes and a good supply of hard tobacco and matches. These biscuits were the circular ones usually carried in lifeboats at that time, one biscuit with a teaspoon full of condensed milk was issued at 5 am and 3 pm, a small portion of corn beef replaced the milk issue at 10 am and 8 pm, and about an ounce of water was issued at the above times. In these boats we also had eighteen grey blankets, which were issued to those people who had only thin clothes, and even when soaked through with water, they kept wearers reasonably warm. We did not do any rowing in our boat but relied entirely on the lug-sail and jib. The Bosun, an old Finn, domiciled in Hull for many years, and myself took turn about on the tiller.

The greatest difficulty in these boats is to find space to lie down, so all had to rest as best they could sitting down. One man, a fireman and cleaner, was caught putting a dirty old sweat-rag down the bunghole of the water cask at night in order to quench his thirst, so the water casks were brought right aft. Our Radio Officer also began to act curiously and one night threw our only bucket over the side, but he soon settled down. I discovered that he was very shy, and found it difficult to do everything he had to do in front of all on board, but he was all right soon afterwards. He was not the robust type and he died about eighteen months after this experience. On Thursday night it came on to blow rather fresh and we had to lay to our sea anchor. At dawn next day, we could not see our other boat but at noon he was sighted coming up astern and we could see him until we got into a calm on the Sunday.

He then rowed across and I found that his stores were not eking out as well as ours, and as he was faster than we were, owing to our heavier load, we decided that he should carry on without bothering to wait for us. We lost sight of him on Sunday evening. Monday night was our worst night with strong wind and heavy rain, and at 2 am we had to lower the lug sail, leaving only the jib standing and with the sea anchor dragging behind to try and prevent the boat being thrown broadside on to the sea, just before daybreak however our sea anchor was cut, a clean break close to the canvas, and thereafter we had to use our heaviest oar to keep the boat stern on to the sea. I had to get more help to work this oar over the stern on to the sea as the Old Bosun and myself were very tired. At about 10 am we were able to hoist a double reefed lug sail, and were going through the water at the fastest rate so far, we were able to do this as the sea was truer in direction, but the weather was too bad to allow us to open the biscuit tank or water barrel.

We could steer with the rudder now and I was constantly scanning the horizon in case someone should come our way, and at about 1230 I thought I saw a pole jutting up above the waves, a little later I saw two poles, but I did not say anything in case I was mistaken, however, when I saw several more, I fully realised that we were heading for an outward bound convoy, and when I told my boat's crew it was difficult to make them sit down, as they could easily have caused the boat to capsize in that sea. We now shook out the reefs (sails) and cracked on in earnest, but, we were not spotted until we were less than a mile from the nearest escort vessel, which turned out to be the sloop H.M.S. Sandwich, Commander Yeatman R.N.

She stopped and allowed herself to drift down on to us, and when we got alongside, it was comical to watch the antics of my crew trying to climb on the boarding net. When my turn came, I realised that they had not the strength to climb up, and I myself was very unceremoniously grabbed by the seat of my pants and by the neck and landed on deck, where I slumped like a sack of potatoes. I could not stand up, and after a bath I was put in the Commander's bed where I slept for twenty four hours with the aid of a few sleeping tablets given me by the ship's doctor. Whilst we were in the boat I insisted on everyone wearing his socks and boots or shoes, and was therefore able to avoid having any of the men suffering from swollen feet, a complaint that troubled most boat crews.

When we were picked up we still had 13 gallons of water, 30lbs biscuits, 30 tins of milk and 3 tins of meat. Our Brandy bottle was intact and about 5lbs hard tobacco still remained. H.M.S. Sandwich was on escort with an out bound convoy when she picked us up, but by the next day she had left them to meet an inward convoy. She eventually landed us at Greenock on Sunday morning, the 14th July 1940. We had sailed our boat 350 miles and were about 60 miles south off Queenstown when picked up.

The other boat had been more fortunate having been picked up by the vessel on the Liverpool to Limerick run on Monday morning, off Fastnet Rock, South West corner of Ireland. Some of that boat's crew had badly swollen feet and legs. The Chief Officer was Capt Vincent, who has been for many years on the staff of the Board of Trade (Ministry of Transport) at Liverpool as an examiner.

Having travelled overnight we arrived at Liverpool at about 3 am on the 15th July, and had to proceed to the Admiralty on Wednesday 17th to give details of the occurrence. At that meeting I was informed that my message was the first received of an attack by submarine in the particular area at that time, but they knew that two ships had been sunk by the same submarine on the previous day, but these ships had been alone and not able to broadcast any warnings. Following this incident the Chief Officer and myself received Commendations from the Admiralty.

CAPTAIN'S REPORT OF SINKING OF ATHELLAIRD

On July 2nd (1940) at approximately 22.40 B.S.T. vessel z. z. No8 at time violent explosion occurred abreast of foremast, apparently a torpedo, vessel going down rapidly forward, engines were stopped, Radio officer ordered to broadcast S.O.S. requesting immediate assistance, which was answered by Valentia and Lands End, 5 verey lights (Red) and a distress rocket were fired to warn shipping of what had happened. Engines were put ahead and vessel headed to N. E. but as steering was difficult owing to trim, and also because I feared the carrying away of further bulkheads forward, (Apparently the vessel being extensively damaged from forepeak to No. 2/3 Bulkhead) I ordered engines stopped, and that the crew take to the starboard boats (lee side) and lay to for the night, so that a better estimate of the possibility of returning to port could be made in daylight. Both boats got into position about 200 yards to windward on the vessel's Port bow, and whilst lying in this position a torpedo passed right underneath my boat, we watched its track carefully but it must have passed astern of ship as no explosion was heard.

At about 1 a.m. a terrific explosion occurred abreast of the Athellaird's funnel on the port side, and it was noticed that the vessel was settling down rapidly after this. I last saw the vessel at about 2 a.m. and when dawn came there was no sign of her at all, neither could we see the Chief Officer's boat, as the sea and swell had increased considerably during the night. At about 7 a.m. we sighted the Chief Officer's boat a mile to N.W. of us, but did not speak to him until dusk on Wednesday evening when it was decided to head North Eastward as soon as weather permitted. The boats did not sail in company but sighted each other at intervals until Sunday noon when we closed on each other and discussed what would be our exact position. It was decided to keep on the N. Eastward. Rough weather alternating with calms and heavy rain made life miserable in the closely packed boat. On the night of Monday the 8th the wind backed to S.W. and S.S.W. and increased to a fresh gale at about 3 p.m. Tuesday, boat was hove to, stern on to the sea anchor with reefed jib up to keep boat from coming broadside, but seas were curling aboard over stern and a re-arrangement of the men in boat became necessary to lessen risk of swamping.

Although we had been compelled to heave to 3 times previously, it had been to lessen our drift more than anything else. This morning however, things appeared very serious and to make matters worse the sea anchor rope and tripping line both carried away at the same time, we then ran before the wind and sea until the wind decreased slightly around 9 a.m. when we once more tried to head E.N.E. by compass. We set a reef lug at 11 a.m. and at about 1 p.m. sighted a convoy ahead and by keeping on our course, we sailed right up alongside the H.M. Escort vessel (H.M.S. Sandwich) which so kindly took us aboard.

It should be mentioned that whilst turning vessel round to N.E. on Tuesday night, the 2nd I heard the 47 gun being fired and on asking the poop what they were firing at, was told that they had fired at a submarine on the surface at 1000 yards range. I was looking in the direction indicated at the time the gun was fired but could not see anything except the silhouette of the M.V. Lobos to the N.W. which I thought might been mistaken for the submarine and I ordered them to cease fire. The gunner fired in accordance with previous instructions i.e. not to await orders if he saw any enemy craft at close range.

I did not see any sign of submarine at all, either from the ship's deck or from the boats. During the early hours of Thursday, the 4th I saw three blue flashes, rather dim, but as these were not in accordance with the Mate's torch flashes I did not reply, and when questioning Mr Vincent on Sunday he stated that he had shown no blue flashes at all.

Soon after noon on Tuesday, the 9th inst., I sighted a vessel ahead which proved to be one of the leading ships of the West bound convoy, and we were picked up by the escort vessel H.M.S. Sandwich at about 1.30 p.m. We were given every attention possible on board this vessel, and no words of mine can adequately describe the kindness shown to all of us. We were landed at Greenock at 8 a.m. yesterday, Sunday 14th July, and arrived Liverpool at 0.40 a.m. to-day.

Report written by Capt Hugh Roberts, Master. Monday 15th of July 1940.

NORTH ATLANTIC CONVOYS

The end of October 1940 I was appointed Master of the MV Athelregent at Birkenhead, and sailed in ballast with a South bound convoy, and we were sent off on our way. When well Westward of Ireland, passing close to the Azores and then into the South Atlantic. Soon after crossing the Equator, one engine had to be stopped for 18 hours due to the main engine compressor jacket having burst. A new coil was available on board and the jacket was repaired and the engine restarted, and having put into Cape Town for routing instructions, we had to get a seaworthy certificate for these repairs. We were delayed there for a week as the Surveyor insisted on a new compressor jacket being made and fitted at that port. We then loaded a full cargo of molasses at Durban, leaving that port on Christmas Eve for Liverpool. We joined our convoy at Freetown, and just before arriving at that port we must have crossed the path of the Graf Spee as she was in that area at that particular time. The homeward convoy was a slow one, which came north to the

West of the Azores, and our only escort consisted of three small whalers. When about 500 miles westward of Ireland our Commodore informed us that we were to proceed as if we had no escort, and we proceeded as if we were alone until we arrived off North Ireland, when, as if by magic, the convoy reformed on its own, with only two ships having gone on ahead.

We discharged at Liverpool and again sailed in convoy for Halifax, on the 3rd February 1941. We had the Commodore and his staff on board, also a Naval Sub-Lieutenant as passenger. This convoy started off through the North Channel, then West until we reached 20 degrees West Longitude, then South until due West of Ireland where we turned Westward and proceeded independently. The night before we dispersed was very dark with patches of cloud, and about 11 pm two planes passed overhead and soon afterwards flares were seen to the South West at considerable distance away. Before leaving us the, Senior Officer of the escorting destroyers came close to enquire if we had any idea as to what those flares were, but we never found out, on that night they could easily have been 70 to 80 miles away. We had a fine passage across, and when we were approaching the Grand Bank, at 8 am, one fine day, the ss Trelawney sent out a message that she was being attacked by a strange Warship, the position was 240 miles astern of us, and it was the Scharnhorst and Gneisenau beginning their famous raid on Atlantic shipping. We passed through a considerable field ice after passing Cape Race, and arrived at Halifax to land Commodore Galer R.N.R. and his staff We then proceeded towards New York. When the Pilot boarded, he said he had instructions for me, these told me I was to enter New York if I needed fuel, but if not, I was to return to Halifax, which we did, and had a full gale and blizzards the whole way.

I had an idea when approaching Halifax the first time that we might be needed as we had heard a sister ship's S.O.S. message saying she had been badly damaged by heavy sea on her way from Bermuda to join a homeward bound convoy from the Canadian ports, and his later message was to say she was proceeding to Halifax. We arrived and found that my surmise was correct, we were to take over her cargo, we managed to take in about 10,000 tons of molasses the rest had been lost, or mixed with water. This we took to Philadelphia, and having discharged, had left the berth and cast off the tugs, when the electric steering gear went completely haywire. We piled up on a mud bank but soon got clear and the steering returned to normal once more. We then went to Baltimore for dry-docking, and although the steering gear was carefully examined nothing was found wrong. We loaded at Cuban ports with molasses and joined a convoy at Halifax for home.

When in convoy the steering gear again caused trouble and to avoid running into other ships, we dropped out at 10 pm one night and stopped to overhaul everything at 2 am. We got away again and I took the wheel to see if I could find out at what particular place the disturbance was, but off she went again, but this time I thought I had detected a flash somewhere about the steering standard and soon smelt burning. We found two small indicator wires wrapped together with insulation tape. The wires being bare were shorting at intervals and this proved to be the cause of all the trouble, they gave us all grey hairs. We arrived in the Clyde during an air raid and were ordered next day to proceed to Hull, as our discharging berth at Greenock had been fouled by unexploded bombs. We made one more trip to Cuba and back to Hull before I left this ship, it had become necessary for me to undergo an operation for the removal of the Gall Bladder.

THE LOSS OF THE ATHELKNIGHT

At the end of April 1942 I was appointed to the Athelknight, then in drydock at Barry, and we sailed eventually in convoy for Trinidad. This was a convoy of vessels bound to the Mediterranean, South Africa, South America and Westwards, and having left it somewhere westwards of Gibraltar we proceeded on our own, on a track contained in our sealed orders.

At about 1030 pm on May 26th 1942 we were hit by a torpedo on the starboard side amidships, the position was Latitude 28 N Long. 45 40 W, Mid Atlantic. At the time I was reading a book in my room, a thing I rarely did at sea in time of war. The engines were stopped and orders given to abandon ship. The boats were being lowered when the submarine began to shell the vessel, and no gun flashes could be detected. One of the first shells hit the ship's side above the 3rd Mate's boat, and the boat fell into the water with only five men in it. I had to haul my boat forward, as jagged plates where the torpedo had hit were damaging it. When I went over the side into the boat I found it full of water, it had been badly damaged and obviously would not keep afloat very long. Shells were constantly pounding the bridge. Sparks, or the Radio Officer had sent out the SOS message but he could not say if it had been successful, and anyhow, no one was likely to come near.

We managed to pull clear and contacted the 2nd Mate's boat and we all got into that one. Our boat went under in no time at all. Some time later the submarine approached us, spraying machine gun tracer bullets over us, but none hit the boat and he came alongside. He asked for me, and he told me to come on board. He asked where we were from and where bound, and the name of the ship. He apparently did not believe me when I said we were British, but kept repeating, "You are American". I insisted we were British, and apparently satisfied, he asked if we had provisions, I said yes, but could do with more, whereupon he gave some orders, and a bag containing half a dozen loaves of bread were passed into the boat. During the interview on the submarine's deck I was fully aware that a man stood behind me with a Tommy gun. When he ordered me back to the boat, he also remarked that he was sorry for us, and I replied that he could not possibly be sorrier for me than I was for myself and all ahead of us.

The nearest land was Barbuda in the West Indies, and this was nearly 1200 miles away. The Azores were also about the same distance away, but prevailing wind would favour the West Indies. During the night he kept shelling the ship and eventually one hit the oil fuel tanks, which burst into flames. The ship's poop was 140 feet long and the whole length was a blazing inferno in a couple of seconds, and remained so until the sunrise the next day. At that time we saw the submarine send another torpedo into the engine room and in a couple of seconds the stern went under, the bow at the same time standing like a massive pillar out of the sea which very slowly sank beneath the waves, leaving just three comparatively small blobs on the vast surface of the ocean, our boat, the Mate's boat and the submarine.

After being ordered back into the boat the previous night we came across the lifeboat that had been cast adrift in the first shelling, and found two of the men dead, two badly wounded and one with two wounds in his forearm. We got the wounded on board and could do nothing for the already dead except leave them in the nearly sinking boat. The two badly wounded men were given morphine from our small first aid box and their wounds dressed as well as possible. After the ship sank the enemy left us and steamed westwards. We contacted the Mate's boat and found it necessary to even up the number of men in the two boats. We were left with 25 men, including two badly wounded and the other boat had 26 men.

These boats had the following provisions :- two dozen tins of small biscuits about 2" square, specially made as lifeboat rations, 1 case, 48 tins condensed milk, about 24 by 14 ounce tins of Pemmican, some Horlicks tablets and bars of Rowntree's chocolate, and four ten gallon tanks of fresh water. On this occasion the ration of water was fixed at 2 fluid ounces early morning, one at mid – day, and another two at sunset, this procedure lasted until the 24th day when all the biscuits and pemmican were exhausted. We kept on sailing the whole distance and were fortunate enough to land on St Bartholomew, a Vichy French Island 60 miles from our intended destination on our 28th day in the boat, when we landed in a small cove. On our second day the two badly wounded men died of their wounds, the other wounded man had recovered, except for a slight swelling in the arm.

The boat was fitted with a canvas cover, which could be used as protection against wind and weather, sun and rain, but with the latter, it also helped to gather small quantities of rain water to quench the thirst. We tried fishing with a line but could catch nothing. One small fish about half pound weight was jabbed with a sheath knife and shared out and eaten raw. Flying fish were also found and eaten raw. Flying fish, especially the small ones which landed in the boat were very rarely reported, and quite a few must have been eaten by those that were lucky enough to have them land against him in the dark. The general topic used to be, the first meal they would have when they made the Islands, none expected to be picked up by passing ships, anyway we saw none during the whole 28 days, nor did we see any smoke. We could see our other boat during the first four days but after that we saw nothing more of them.

What bothered me most was the heat of the sun, and when we sighted the Islands at dawn on the 23rd June 1942 my strength was fast ebbing. I now realise, that following a major operation for the removal of the Gall Bladder I was not in a fit state to do such a journey as this. At times it became necessary to warn all the men against drinking sea water. Some pretended to wash their mouths out only, but this had to be prohibited. The youngest on board was only sixteen, and the eldest, an old Kinsale seaman was well over sixty five. When we touched the beach at Bartholomew, the Islanders did not come near until we were actually ashore. The boat's crew with the exception of myself and the Kinsale man managed to get over the side of the boat and crawl ashore.

We had to be carried and were laid down inside some boat shelters where we were given coffee. It was about noon when we landed and two hours later a Police Boat arrived and we had to re enter our lifeboat to be towed to the harbour about four miles away. We stayed there for two days, some, like myself in a hospital under the tender care of a very old Breton nursing sister, others in Hotels. A small Dutch West Indian schooner then took us all aboard for the sixty miles trip to St Kitts. On our arrival, the Port Medical Officer came on board and examined us all. Most of us were prevented from moving hand or foot, and the ambulance had a busy time bringing us up the hill into the hospital at Basseterre, under the care of Dr. Steddefer, the hospital Superintendent, who had fled from Hitler's Germany before the summer of 1939.

In this hospital, the man (Oliver) whom we thought had bullets in his arm was found to have two pieces of shrapnel which were removed. It was found that I had lost 54lbs weight on the 28 day boat trip, I was in bed for ten days and when I was allowed up, had to be assisted to my chair. We had to leave hospital to make room for another ship's crew who had been 13 days in their boats. The reminder of my time on the Island was spent at the Doctor's home. Seventy shipwrecked mariners eventually left the Island by a Cuban ship for San Juan, Puerto Rico, where an American Naval store ship took us to Newport News, then by rail to New York. We eventually left there by rail for Halifax where about 280 of us boarded the Trooper Strathmore, landing at Glasgow before the end of September. In New York I received a cable from the owners informing me that the Mate's boat had been picked up by a South African bound ship after 24 days adrift, at that time they were 350 miles behind us so they were extremely lucky, as I understand that most of their stores had been used up.

The Chief Officer was D.J. Davies of Glanfa, Dinas Cross Pembrokeshire. We both received the O.B.E. from His Majesty King George V1 at Buckingham Palace February 3rd 1943. I was told by the Naval People that we had used our provisions in a manner not recommended by their medical advisors, this was that we should have given at least 10 fluid ounces of water the first day and to have reduced this and the other rations as we went along. This would have been a task, which would indeed be most difficult to carry out.

CAPTAIN'S REPORT – SINKING OF ATHELKNIGHT

Lat 28 O N Long 45 .40 W. At 22.15 hours, on 26th May 1942 vessel was struck by torpedo on star side under bridge, (No 6 tank and pump room and possibly No 7 tank).

I then ordered the boats be lowered at approximately 22.40 hrs. My own boat No 1 on star side of bridge caught on a bulge on the ship's side just above the water and was later cleared, but as I feared it would be further damaged if left there ordered it to be hauled forward, clear of the jagged plating. The remainder of the boat's crew and myself slid down the painter with the boat. As the boat was being lowered the submarine started shelling from ahead and as I went over the ship's rail a shell passed through my accommodation and also through wheelhouse chartroom and wireless cabin. I found my boat to be full of water up to the thwarts but we managed to pull clear of the vessel, and when about 100 yds away, stopped and tried to bail, but the boat was water logged, apparently through damage received when it caught on the bulged plates when lowering.

Meanwhile the submarine kept on shelling the vessel as well as spraying the sea on both sides with a large calibre machine gun using tracer ammunition, some of which passed over us. Later this shelling ceased and we closed the 2nd Officer's boat and in doing so forgot the boat radio transmitter which was underwater in my boat. Some little time later the shelling ceased and the submarine was observed approaching on the surface. He hailed us and ordered us alongside. I was then ordered aboard by the Commander who asked if we were an American ship. When I said we were British (but) he still maintained we were American and that we were from Freetown. After satisfying him (that) we were British he said he was very sorry for us. He gave those in my boat about 12 loaves which in daylight we found to be full of green mould. Before he left I asked him if he would tell our other boats to get in touch with us so that we could place some more of our men in them.

He said he would, but apparently he did not do so. When he left us he circled out of our sight at a fast speed and later resumed the shelling of our ship, causing the starboard side bunkers to catch fire which later enveloped the whole after end. This fire continued all night, we lost count of all the number of shells fired, but the number was considerable. We remained stationary after the submarine left us and later saw lights flashing. We closed (approached) this and found it to be the port bridge boat with five men in it, of whom two Gainsford and Mcgrath were dead from shrapnel wounds. Two seriously wounded Paulson and Moore, and AA Gunner Oliver with shrapnel wounds in the right forearm. These three were transferred to our boat as their boat appeared to be badly damaged by shrapnel.

Paulson, a fireman, was found to have a badly shattered left shoulder and severe injuries to the left jaw. Moore O.S. had a shrapnel wound in the abdomen. These men were attended to by the Chief Steward Boniface who did all that was possible for them with the first aid kit in the boat. Their injuries were so severe that I doubt if any treatment could have saved them. Moore died during the forenoon of the 27th May and Paulson at about 8 pm. At dawn we thought we could see the other boat close astern of our vessel but we soon found this to be the submarine as he again resumed shelling the vessel. Later we saw a huge column of water on the starboard side abreast of the engine room and sound resembling a torpedo explosion. In about 3 minutes after this the vessel had gone under, stern foremost, the bow from the fore mast forward being completely out of the water for a few seconds before it finally disappeared. Soon afterwards we sighted out other boat, and when we came close we arranged to transfer some of our men into that boat leaving us with 23 men and the 2 badly injured. Previous to this transfer we had 39 in our boat. The Chief Officer informed me that he had had considerable trouble with his rudder during the night and that either the lower pintle or the gudgeon had carried away. I informed the Chief Officer that our best course would be S W x W True and that the distance to the Islands in the vicinity of Antigua was about 1150 miles. We had no navigation equipment other than the Boat Compass.

The first three days we were favoured by fair wind and had the other boat in sight astern, but after that time we did not sight them again, as the weather changed completely. The wind remained at about S. S. W. to West with squally rain for the next five days and I do not think we could have made any progress during this period. After this the wind backed to the East of South but at no time afterwards did it become much eastward of S E magnetic.

This boat made considerable water during the first few days but the pump was able to cope with it and towards the end of the passage it was only necessary to pump out twice a day. The lifelines or grab lines of two and a half inch rope fitted from gunwhale to gunwhale under the keel at Barry were taken off because they slowed up the speed of the boat and were collecting masses of Gulf Weed that had to be frequently cleared. Later on we found that weed collected on the righting bars fitted to the keel, although fortunately these bars had remained throughout on a closed position.

The biscuits were strictly rationed from the beginning. 1 biscuit and 2 spoonfuls of condensed milk at daybreak with 2 ozs water. 1 biscuit 1 spoonful of pemmican and 1 oz of water at noon, 1 biscuit 1 spoonful of pemmican at sunset with 2ozs of water. In between we were issued Horlicks Milk Tablets and chocolate.

During the period of squally weather some rainwater was caught with the aid of the rubber suits and from the sail, the latter being much coloured by the dye in the sail, but otherwise quite fresh. We could not save any of this as we had no empty tank to put it in and we did not like to mix it with any of our water. When we had an empty tank we could get no rain at all.

Around the 18th day I and some others experienced considerable difficulty in swallowing the biscuits and pemmican, but we could manage the Horlicks and chocolate quite well. A few however managed quite well by pounding the biscuits into a powder with the aid of a small canvas bag and the hammer and then mixing it with the pemmican.

The biscuits and pemmican were exhausted on the day before we landed at St Barts, we still had a few days supply of Horlicks and chocolate as well as 8 galls water, and about 20 tins of condensed milk. Oliver the AA Gunner, although he must have been in considerable pain with his wounds was never once heard to complain and by the time we landed these wounds were healed. In the hospital at St Kitts the X-ray showed that there was still something in the arm. An operation was performed and three small pieces of shrapnel were removed.

Soon after leaving the vessel the donkeyman J Smith seemed to have something like a whitlow on one finger. Everything that could be done under the circumstances was tried but the pan continued, and on arrival at St Kitts this finger was amputated as gangrene had set in.

It is very doubtful if many of us would have survived were it not for the protection afforded by the canvas hood during the day. The only drawback being that the hood did not afford the man who happened to be on the tiller any protection at all, as it only covered just over two thirds the length of the boat from forward. The sides of the hood were doubled in under the overhead part to make an awning only and this allowed free passage for whatever breeze might be around. After twenty eight days the sails showed very little signs of wear. The sea anchor was tried out during the period of squally weather mentioned earlier on and I again found that it would not hold the boat head to sea with 23 men on board. It always seems to drift at the same speed as the boat itself. It appears to me that a sea anchor out aft and with the jib sail set, is the best method to adopt in rough weather.

On 23rd June we sighted land and the boat was beached on the S E end of St

Barts at about noon. By this time I could not stand up and was therefore carried ashore where we rested under the boat shelter for a couple of hours. The inhabitants did what they could for us and one of them took the 2nd Officer and Chief Steward by boat to the harbour some five miles west of where we landed to report to the French authorities. Later in the day a motor launch arrived and took our boat in tow with all of the crew on board and finally brought into the harbour, where about half of us were accommodated in the hospital and the rest in the town.

We were placed on board a Dutch W I schooner on the evening of the 28th and landed at St Kitts on the morning of the 26th June. Thirteen of us including myself were placed in hospital and remained there until the 9th July and on that date we had to leave the hospital to make room for other survivors just landed. Everything that could possibly be done for us was attended to by the European inhabitants in St Kitts.

The submarine appeared to be similar to the 750 ton type with one gun forward of about 4" calibre, another abaft of the conning tower appeared to have similar bore but a much shorter barrel. There also appeared to be a machine gun of the Oerlikon type on the after end of the conning tower. The upper part of the hull was painted a very light grey forward and much darker colours at the after end. This was noticed at daylight next day. We had very bright moonlight on the night of the 26th May and on one occasion before daybreak the submarine passed us about 200 yds away, but nothing of the hull could be seen. The noise of the exhaust was clearly heard and the wash of the sea at bow and stern were clearly seen. The submarine went away on a Westerly course after the vessel sank.

The Commander appeared to be about 26 to 28 years old, about 5'10" in height and slim. He wore greenish khaki shirt, shorts with a cap of similar material. He appeared to be a German, but it is possible that the crew may have been Italian from what I saw of them. One of the crew armed with a Tommy-gun stood by me whilst I was on the deck of the submarine.

List of the 23 Survivors (All British Subjects) From the British M/V Athelknight, Official No 161143, of Liverpool, who embarked at St Kitts, British West Indian. On Cuban S/S Libertad, and transferred at San Juan P. R., on July 22nd. To a U.S. Naval Transport for conveyance to a port on the East of the U.S. In the Captains Lifeboat were

1.	H. Roberts	Master
2.	D. Crook	2nd Mate
3.	P. Watson	2nd Eng (Sen)
4.	G. Bates	2nd Eng (Jun)
5.	J. Walsh	4th Eng (Jun)
6.	E. B. Boniface	Chief Steward
7.	E. Mills	Radio Op (3rd)
8.	J. R. Nicholson	App
9.	K. Taylor	App
10.	G. Steenson	Bosun

11.	D. Buckley	A. B.
12.	R. Aspinal	A. B.
13.	A. Hughes	A. B.
14.	W. Dumphy	A. B.
15.	J. Smith	Donkey
16.	Corcoren	Fireman
17.	E. John	Fireman
18.	D. Sonior	Cabin Boy
19.	B. Millet	2nd Cook
20.	E. Taylor	Mess Stwd
21.	G. Hebenton	Naval Gun
22.	S. Oliver	Army
23.	H. Parry	Army

ADDENDUM ON THE U 172 AND A POSSIBLE WAR CRIME

S. Oliver of the Army, a gunner, was the only survivor in the port bridge boat. From Captain Roberts account of the Athelknight's sinking, the U 172 was firing as boats were being launched, and after a brief respite, continued firing. Because of the circumstances of the port bridge boat (see the chapter on The Contribution of One Welsh Port), it appears that the four Barry men who died, and Oliver, had escaped to a lifeboat which was then shelled. This possibly constitutes a war crime.

The U 172 from November 5 was under the command of Kptlt. Carl Emmermann (Knights Cross) until October 31, 1943. Until its destruction on December 13, 1943 it was under the command of Oblt. Hermann Hoffmann. Emmermann had sunk 26 ships for a tonnage of 152,738 Allied shipping lost. Ob 11 Aug, 1943, while rescuing men from the just-scuttled U-604 the U-172 was attacked by an aircraft and 1 man from its crew was killed. On 13 December, 1943 in the mid-Atlantic after a 27 hour fight west of the Canary Islands, the U 172 was sunk by depth charges and Fido homing torpedoes from Avenger and Wildcat aircraft (VC-19) of the American escort carrier USS Bogue, and by some 200 depth charges from the US destroyers USS George E. Badger, USS Clemson, USS Osmond Ingram and USS Du Pont. There were 13 dead and 46 survivors. Carl Emmermann (1915-1990) was a seekadett in 1934, rising by 6 promotions to a korvettenkapitan in 1944. He was decorated 7 times, including the Knights Cross with Oak Leaves and the Iron Cross, 1st Class. From 1941 to October 1943 he was at sea with the U 172 for 368 days on 5 patrols. In 1945, he made no patrols on the U 3037.

For some years after 1934 Emmermann was training officer on the Marineschule Mürwik, where future officers got their training. In 1939 he joined the U-boat force and in November 1940 became the I WO on U-A (built for Turkey) under the command of Hans Eckermann. On her first patrol U-A only damaged the British steamer Empire Attendant of 7,524 tons. In November 1941 Emmermann took over his own boat, U-172. He completed five patrols with this boat, in the

Caribbean, with the wolfpack Eisbär in South African waters, and in the North and South Atlantic. His greatest success was the sinking of the British liner-troopship Orcades of 23,456 tons. His fifth patrol with U-172 was dramatic, in that the boat brought back half the crew of U-604 which had been so heavily damaged during two air attacks that she had to be scuttled. After that patrol Emmermann became the commander of the 6th Flotilla in St. Nazaire, France in November of 1943.

In August 1944 Emmermann became the chief of the "Erprobungsgruppe Typ XXIII". There in late 1944 he wrote the battle instructions for the new Elektro Boat Type XXIII. In March 1945 he was commander of U-3037 for one month, and in the last month of the war he commanded the 31st Flotilla in Hamburg. Along with some other U-boat men he took part in infantry duty around Hamburg as Commander of "Marine-Batallion Emmermann". His first sinking in U 172 was the Athelknight, and records of the U 172's sinkings, and apparently of Emmermann's exaggerations, can be found on the internet in the report on the interrogation of survivors from U-172, sunk 13 December 1943. Emmermann's greatest success was the sinking of the troopship Orcades, 0f 23,456 tons. He died in 1990, an honoured and respected citizen aged 75 years old.

PART NINE

The Loss of the Harborough

By Chris Burt of Barry

Chris Burt was one of the survivors of the Harborough, and his life at sea is detailed in Part Three, 'The Sailors' Stories.'

I am writing an account of the SS Harborough's last voyage, for Billy Vaughan, nephew and namesake of William Vaughan, who with his mates Harry Hobbs, George Weaver, and Charles Mosely was lost at sea on the SS Crusader which was torpedoed by a German U Boat in the Atlantic Ocean.

I signed on the SS Harborough, in Cardiff, we sailed round to Barry Dock, where on January 17th 1942, we signed on more crew. We loaded arms, ammunition and other military equipment and sailed from Barry, destined for the Middle East. First port of call was Freetown, W. Africa to take on Bunkers, then to Durban S. Africa. From there we went through the Red Sea to the Suez Canal. We discharged cargo at R.A.O.C. depot, Abu sul tan, which is in the Bitter Lakes, near Ismailia.

We sailed light ship, back to Durban, loaded coal for the River Plate, Argentina, there we discharged cargo upstream, then loaded grain and hides in Buenos Aires. We sailed around the coast to Rio de Janeiro, Brazil. Topped up cargo with more hides and cotton bales, we left Rio, bound for the USA.

Our ship had been sailing without convoy for the last seven months or so, covering vast areas of oceans, and seemed to be doing OK, without escorts. Then, Sparks received a message from Royal Naval sources, ordering our ship to change course into the Caribbean and join a convoy leaving Trinidad bound for New York. In the crew's opinion a grave mistake as packs of U boats were known to be in that vicinity.

The SS Harborough was torpedoed September 14th, 1942. The watches had just changed at 0900 hours. She was hit on the port side amidships, in the Engine Room, the boiler burst and the boat deck and port Lifeboat were blown sky high.

It was very difficult to launch the starboard Lifeboat, as apart from the heavy list, the ship had sunk to the gunnels of the welldeck. When we did get free of the falls, the heavy swell was pushing our Lifeboat into the welldeck. Our keel was scraping on the bulwark and there was a danger of being dragged into the rigging.

The U boat surfaced a few hundred yards away and started shelling the ship. The Commander must have been one of the good Germans. He could see that we were trapped, as our boat was between his Sub and our own sinking ship. He stopped the gun crew firing and motioned us to continue striving to get clear. After what seemed to be an eternity we broke free (a few of us bruised) and drifted astern of the ship. The Sub continued with the shelling, it seemed to take hours for them to sink her, she went down stern first.

Others of the crew had managed to launch 3 rafts and the jolly boat. Because of the heavy swell we had drifted apart from each other, it was evening before we grouped and took the rafts in tow, only to discover that two men were missing, the

2nd Engineer who was from the Tyne and my cabin mate (Taff) G. Coxe from Nelson.

One of the rafts was leaking badly, we cut it loose on the second day, the lads crowded aboard the two remaining rafts and the Lifeboat, we took it in turns to change over between boats and rafts, the boat was fairly dry but it was wet on the rafts most of the time.

The Donkeyman who was from South Shields was on the middle platform of the Engine Room when the boiler exploded and he was scalded very badly. He was lying on a blanket at the bottom of the Lifeboat, we could not make out his features, his face seemed to be one big blister. The terrible thing was we could do little to alleviate his suffering as we had a limited first aid kit aboard, throughout the days and nights he was groaning with the pain. We tried to keep the sun off him during the day with the few garments we had. I like to think that his senses had gone beyond feeling too much pain. The last I saw of him, was when the Padre on Tobago Island took care of him.

For the first two days on the Lifeboat there was no sign of land, but two of our older sailors had worked out our position and we were on course for Trinidad. I think these two AB's saved our lives, Dick Sheehan from Waterford and Big Gus, from Ukraine.

From July to December 1942, the Caribbean was overrun by German Submarines. At that time there were very few Royal Navy ships in that area. Each night the U boats were surfacing and signalling to each other with Aldis lamps. On the third day we sighted Trinidad. But with the flow of the sea it was decided it would be easier to make for Tobago.

The sails were up throughout most of the journey and we took turns manning the oars, not making much headway as we had the two rafts in tow. As we came closer to the island our next problem was how to get through the reef. By now we could not see the land as the boat was so low in the water, and the seas and spray breaking over the reef obscured all else. The boat's keel was scraping the submerged reef and there was a danger of capsizing. Then suddenly appeared a couple of islanders in canoes. They guided us through the seemingly impassable reef to the sandy beach.

The people of Tobago Island were wonderful to us, they gave us water, fruit and food. We were there for two nights and then got a boat over to Port of Spain, Trinidad. There were hundreds of survivors there. So, how many ships had been sunk? During that period there were three or more merchant ships, being destroyed in a day, by the enemy.

We were in Trinidad for a few weeks, where we were fitted out with trousers, shirt and sandals, we slept under the grandstand of a football field as all proper accommodation was full up. I will skip the many happenings in between but we eventually got a passage to New York, on an American ship. I can't remember if the name was SS Washington or SS George Washington.

In merchant ships, crew's wages were stopped on the day that their ship was sunk which was hard on the men who had families to support. So we joined the New York shipping pool, hoping to get a ship homeward bound. We were put up in a hotel in West 49th Street named the Van Courtland. Some of us earned a few dollars working in a factory on West 26th Street, during the weekdays. The first evening we were fitted out with clothes, shoes, a suit and overcoat by the American Women's Empire Association. They took us to a large department store in the city.

The Barry men along with other survivors from the SS Harborough, were sent to join a new ship SS Ocean Crusader at Portland, Maine. The few of us left in New York, saw them off at N.Y. Central, annoyed that we were not joining the same ship as them. Weeks later three of us from the old crew joined SS Teucer, bound for Liverpool. I arrived in Cardiff on Christmas Eve 1942. Within a few days, I inquired at 'Harrisons' shipping office, James Street, about the men who had joined the SS Ocean Crusader, as there was no news of them, although they had left the States long before us, As it was wartime the manager could not give me much information but did admit that the ship was long overdue and presumed lost. This is a condensed version of the last voyage of these men. Having survived the sinking of the Harborough, it was tragic that they were killed so close to home."

A local man, Mr Fred Hortop, has devoted many years of painstaking and dedicated research, compiling a book on the Merchant navy in wartime and a Roll of Honour, for Barry merchant seamen. I have taken the liberty of copying the following facts: The U 262, which sank the Harborough, also sank the Ocean Crusader. She sailed from Portland, USA, November 13th 1942, to join a convoy at New York bound for Avonmouth UK. She strayed from convoy due to heavy weather, November 25th. Next day she sent out a 'Sub. distress' signal, position 50 30N, 45 30W. No further information was received. All hands, 45 men, lost, including W. Vaughan 29, H. Hobbs 33, G. Weaver 31, C. Mosley 29, R. Sheehan, J. O'Brian from Cardiff. K. Laking, R. Ward from Cleethorpes and others whose names I cannot recall.

The Harborough had lost 26 men and 3 gunners, when sunk 60 miles off Tobago by Commander W. Henke and U 515. The U 515 sank 26 merchantmen and two naval ships, for a total of 166,000 tons, before being sunk by American aircraft in 1944. Henke survived and was shot on June 15th, 1944 while attempting to escape from an American POW camp. In the Fort Hunt, Virginia interrogation centre, he walked towards the perimeter fence in daylight and was ordered to stop, and then shot. It is thought that the commander of the Guadalcanal, after Henke had been captured, had threatened him with war crimes during the interrogation process, so hence committed deliberate suicide.

During the Second World War, more than 31,000 British merchant seamen and 900 fishermen lost their lives – a higher percentage than any service losses. The seaport of Barry lost more M.N. seamen than any port of comparable size in the UK.

PART TEN

Vernon Upton, George Medal

From Cardiff, Vernon was awarded the George Medal for his bravery and leadership on the Start Point and its lifeboat in 1942. The Start Point was a 1919 steamer of 5293 tons. At 14.02 hours on 10 Nov, 1942, the Start Point (Master David George Evans), dispersed from convoy ON-141, and was hit amidships by one of two stern torpedoes from U-128, She sank by the bow southwest of the Cape Verde Islands after being hit near the bridge by a coup de grâce at 14.21 hours. Two crew members were lost.

The Germans questioned the survivors in the lifeboats and were told that the master had gone down with the ship. The chief officer George S. Johnson and chief engineer Jones were taken prisoner, landed at Lorient on 15 Jan, 1943 and taken to the POW camp Milag Nord. The master, 38 crew members and seven gunners were picked up after 12 days by the British merchant Eskdalegate and landed at Pernambuco.

The U 128 which sunk the Start Point, was commanded by Ullrich Hesse, and in its career sank 12 ships totalling 83,639 tons. She was sunk 17 May, 1943 in the South Atlantic south of Pernambuco, by gunfire from the US destroyers USS Moffett, USS Jouett and depth charges from two Mariner aircraft. There were 7 dead and 47 survivors.

The following is the report of Vernon Upton, the Start Point's 2nd engineering officer:

Tuesday 10th November 1942.
At 13.05 GMT 1130 A.M. S.A.T. in D.R.

Position 13-35 N. 27-27 W. course 127 degrees true, speed 9 knots. Vessel struck in port side after end number two hold by one torpedo. Force of explosion blew away fore part port side of bridge – port jolly boat and port number three derrick smashed. Port lifeboat smashed while being lowered under supervision of Chief Officer. Vessel listing to port and going down slowly by the head. I immediately superintended lowering of starboard lifeboat, which was got away from vessel in charge of 3rd Officer. (32 men were in this boat). Then proceeded to lower starboard bridge lifeboat, assisted by 3rd Engineer. 12 men, including the Chief Officer and 3rd Engineer got into this boat. Then disposed of all confidential papers and documents before leaving vessel at 13.25 G.M.T., 1150 A.M. S.A.T. Master appeared to be dazed and would not leave the vessel although the Chief Engineer and I made several attempts to get him over the side into the boat. When last seen he was pacing the lower bridge. The 1st Radio Officer remained on board to re-transmit the distress message and his conduct was highly commendable throughout. The Bosun, M.P. Casey, and an A.B., W.H. Gordon showed great coolness in getting rats away from vessel and their conduct in the lifeboats was very good.

At 1330 G.M.T., 1155 S.A.T., the vessel was struck by a second torpedo in number two hold and went down within two minutes. 1st Radio Officer managed to get away in one of the rafts, but master was not found although 3rd Officer made a thorough search of the wreckage.

A submarine then broke surface and approached the boat I was in, then in charge of the Chief Officer. This submarine proved to be Italian and appeared to have been on station for some considerable period of time, judging by the condition of her hull and paintwork. Shortly afterwards, a submarine flying German colours broke surface and approached. We brought our boats alongside the Italian submarine under orders from her commander and the Chief Engineer and Chief Officer were ordered to board her. The German submarine had by then drawn abeam of the Italian, and it was apparent from the condition of her hull and paintwork that she was newly on station. A member of the crew of the Italian submarine told us that they had sunk an oil tanker the previous day. The crew of the Italian submarine appeared to be in good health and spirits and not unfriendly to us. Relations between German and Italian crews appeared to be good. All members of both crews including the commanders were very young. Both submarines appeared to be of the 750-ton class. The Italian mounted a 3 or 4 inch gun on the after deck, and a light anti aircraft weapon, possibly 20-mm, on fore deck. The German mounted no heavy gun, but had two light weapons of the type previously mentioned, one forward and one aft.

We were ordered to cast off from the submarine and the Chief Officer and Chief Engineer retained on board. I then went alongside the rafts and transferred all stores and provisions to my boat while the 3rd Officer did the same to the stores in the damaged motor boat, which was still afloat, Both submarines were last seen heading east in company.

We then set course N.N.W. true, close hauled on the starboard tack, wind E.N.E. moderate, sea moderate: and steered this course for the night, burning red distress flares at intervals of one hour. At day-break I decided to strike west to take advantage of the prevailing winds, as it would have been difficult to make any headway to the eastward in the face of the fresh E'ly winds then prevailing. My object was to make the north coast of Brazil at the same time crossing the route for southbound ships.

One fireman, Norman Gillian, age 19, had been badly injured when the vessel was torpedoed and was in the 3rd Officer's boat. He had a severe wound in the right side over the pelvis, which was bleeding profusely. This wound was dressed by the Chief Steward and Cook under the supervision of the 3rd Officer and the bleeding was partially stemmed. He was made as comfortable as possible and was kept warm. The dressing was changed on several occasions and the wound was washed with warm sea water and painted with iodine. Although badly injured as he was he never made any complaint and was cheerful at all times.

Throughout the 12-day passage we kept the boats lashed together with my boat towing the 3rd Officer's, as mine was faster; and with fresh and strong east to N.E. winds, at times approaching gale force. We had great difficulty in keeping my small boat afloat in the high seas and at times had to lay to the sea anchor. The boat was almost swamped on several occasions and it is only due to the willingness of my crew and the co-operation I received from the inexperienced members from the engine room department, notably fireman G.A. Matthews, that we kept the boat afloat. Despite the fact that everyone was constantly soaked spirits were remarkably high and morale good; and an example to the crew of the larger boat who were not suffering such hardship.

The 3rd Officer reports on the poor conduct of the crew in general (on his boat), and the exceptionally good conduct of the 1st Radio Officer, T. Jenkins, 4th Engineer H. Marshall, AB S. Pascoe, AB J. Williams, Cook J. Daniel and Chief Steward L. Hendry. We have provisions in both boats to last approximately 30 days and collected considerable amounts of rain water during squalls. The men had to keep regular watches and had regular meal times. The 3rd Officer and I also saw that they washed or soused their bodies regularly and thus absorbed moisture through their pores. During calms regular rowing watches were kept, and extra food and water given out.

Antonio Mizzi, Greaser, caused trouble from the outset, and was gradually going insane during the passage. He died between 9 P.M. and midnight on Saturday 21st November. I examined him on the morning of the 22nd at 6 A.M. Rigor mortis had set in, his body was hunched up and his face a mottled purply colour. No response from pulse or heart. He was suffering from piles before death. I read a burial service over his body and buried him at 6-15 A.M.

At 4-0 P.M. on the 22nd, smoke was sighted bearing N.E. and course was altered towards it. We burnt smoke flares and sent out a distress message by W/T. At 5.30 P.M., the vessel altered course towards us and we were taken aboard at 6-0 P.M. All hands were treated with the utmost kindness by the Master, Officers and crew of this vessel.

During the passage I had been able to ascertain our daily latitude with some degree of accuracy, having saved my sextant, and this did much to keep up the morale among the boat's crews".

Copy of Vernon Upton's Log from 10-11-42 to 22-11-42

TUESDAY 10TH NOVEMBER 1942 Latitude 13-35 North, Longitude 27-27 West. At 1305 G.M.T. vessel struck by first torpedo. At 1330 G.M.T. second torpedo struck vessel, sinking her. Set course N.N.W. true, and burnt flares during the dark hours. Wind E.N.E. moderate, sea moderate.

WEDNESDAY 11TH NOVEMBER 1942 At daybreak set course W.N.W. true, Wind E.N.E. gentle, sea moderate. Latitude at noon 13-32 North. Gave all hands three-quarters of a dipper of water, and one biscuit each for breakfast. Towards afternoon, wind fresher, with heavy swell. Boats lashed together, and making good way through the water. My boat taking a lot of water aboard. Third mate's boat not such a good sailer as ours, but much drier. Had a picnic towards evening. Two biscuits, half inch cube of pemmican, one half of a dipper of water, one teaspoonful of condensed milk. Spent a miserable night. Both boats taken aback during a squall.

THURSDAY 12TH NOVEMBER 1942 Fine and clear. Wind Easterly, moderate, sea and swell moderate. Course S.S.W. true. Both boats making fair speed. Still towing third mate's boat. Latitude at noon 12-35 North. We have all got over our sea-sickness.

Morning meal consisted of two biscuits, cube of pemmican, half a dipper of water, with one teaspoon of milk, two chocolate tablets, two Horlicks tablets, which have been christened "Maltesers", and which are not popular, as they are conducive to thirst. Towards evening wind fresher with heavy rain squalls. Boat taking a lot of water. We are all soaked to the skin, and do not sleep very well.

FRIDAY 13TH NOVEMBER 1942 Fine and clear. Wind still E.N.E., moderate, sea rough. Boats making good way. Latitude at noon, 11-52 North. Paid visit to Third mate's boat and found spirits to be good. Injured man in good spirits, and feeling better. We are now getting things properly organised. Food lasting well. Morning meal consisted of one biscuit, teaspoon of milk, two chocolate tablets, two Maltesers, three-quarters of a dipper of water. Towards evening heavy rain squalls and fresh wind. Boats racing along but my boat making heavy weather of it. Towards midnight, wind veered to the southward, with very heavy rain squalls. Everyone in our boat thoroughly drenched.

SATURDAY 14TH NOVEMBER 1942 Calm, fine and clear. Smooth sea and heavy swell. Plenty of sharks and fish about. Boarded the third mate's boat to look at the injured man's wound. Heated some sea water over flares and washed off the old dressing, which had stuck in the wound. Had a large piece of flesh torn out of his back between floating ribs and pelvis. Abdominal wall had not been pierced, but was visible. The actual hole in his back was about four to five inches wide, and roughly round, and the wound was looking as healthy as could be expected, although it was beginning to smell, and probably was infected. Heated some more sea water to just under boiling point, and thoroughly cauterised the wound, and dressed it again. Increased the water ration, giving a mid-day meal. We have plenty of food. Towards evening had a very heavy rain squall, and collected a considerable amount of water. Wind freshened from the N.N.E. with very heavy swell. Both boats making good speed. Cast off tow for a short while, but had to resume towing the third mate's boat, when the main tack parted during a heavy squall. A thoroughly miserable night with everyone soaked to the skin.

SUNDAY 15TH NOVEMBER 1942 Cloudy and clear. Light N.N.E. wind, slight sea and moderate swell. Latitude at noon 10-57 North. Went aboard other boat to effect repairs to the damaged sail, which was soon mended. Got away again at 0800 with both boats making fair speed. Becalmed during afternoon and evening. Heavy rain squall at 2300. Rode to sea anchor for a while, but got away close hauled on the starboard tack later on. Wind W.N.W. strong, sea rough. Our boat diving about a lot.

MONDAY 16TH NOVEMBER 1942 Calm and light airs during day. Fine and clear. Latitude at noon 11 – 01 North. Rowed for a short while, and gave the hands extra water which was collected during the night. About a dipper each extra. Cut down on food at tea time, because the calms are putting us behind in our schedule. A bit of a grumble from the hands, but that cannot be helped, and they will have to make the best of things, in their own interests. Have now organised day and night watches. Working very well. Don't get much sleep myself though. When will this wind come? 870 miles to do. Will steer South true, and let the leeway and Equatorial Drift to take me to the Westward. Evening meal the same as usual:- two biscuits, cube of pemmican, teaspoon of milk, two Maltesers, three-quarters of a dipper of water. Calms and light airs during the night, with heavy E.N.E. swell. Third Mate's boat rowing with us in tow.

TUESDAY 17TH NOVEMBER 1942 Light E.N.E. wind alight, slight sea and heavy E.S.E. swell, fine and clear. Got away again, and took the other boat in tow. Morning meal as usual. Latitude at noon 10-42 North. 835 miles to do. Took stock of food in the boat. 1200 Biscuits, 44 tins of milk, 35 tins of pemmican, 1200 chocolate tablets, 3600 Maltesers, 20 gallons of water. Am working out for at least 20 more days, as we have to cross the Doldrums, and it will probably be about 30 or more if this weather holds. However it is obvious that wind is on the way following this swell. I now make a point of going aboard the other boat daily to try and keep up morale, which is not high. Take my sight from his boat, and have a sweep on the day's run. If over 30 miles give the hands a small bonus of water. One Maltese and one of the firemen becoming a bit of a nuisance. Always grumbling, Towards afternoon wind freshening and both boats making fair speed through the water. Towards evening still freshening, with rough seas and heavy swell. We are towing the big boat.

WEDNESDAY 18TH NOVEMBER 1942 Fresh N.E. Trade Winds, rough sea and heavy swell. Cloudy and clear. Boats still in tow. Have had several arguments re. going aboard the other boat in heavy weather. Have to swim across via the tow rope. Will not be able to go aboard if the present weather holds. Latitude at noon 9-49 North. Not too bad. Meals as usual and at same times. Breeze constantly freshening with high seas and heavy swell. Our boat making water through the seams. Still in tow during the night. We are making a habit of dousing our heads under the water to keep cool during the day. We are getting pretty thin.

THURSDAY 19TH NOVEMBER 1942 Strong wind to moderate gale, very high breaking sea and heavy swell, cloudy and squally. Latitude at noon 8-41 North. Tow rope parted twice today, and mast has started to crack. Have repaired same. Making a lot of water and jumping about a good deal. Still in company at noon when tow rope parted again. Gale continues during the day with similar conditions, and weather. Lost the other boat for a while when the tow parted again, but resumed towing when we made contact again. Tow parted twice again during the night, but was re-connected. We are getting good at this drill.

FRIDAY 20TH NOVEMBER 1942 Gale continues with precipitous sea, and heavy confused swell. Cloudy and squally. Tow parted again at noon. Latitude at noon 7-42 North. Greaser Mizzi, in the other boat has gone mad. Several men drinking sea water. Wind continuing to freshen with heavy rain squalls. Miserable wet night with all hands soaked to the skin. Compass light continually going out, and we have run out of matches. Trying to steer by the stars, but some of the hands are not too adept at doing this.

SATURDAY 21ST NOVEMBER 1942 Strong E.N.E. wind, rough sea and heavy swell, cloudy and clear. Boats still in tow, and making good way through the water. Towards noon very heavy rain squalls. We collected about 13 gallons of water. Filled all tanks. Very heavy swell and rough confused sea rising. Other boat now towing us as we can carry no sail. Making very bad weather of it. Have asked Third Mate if he will stand by to pick us all up if we sink, which appears to be a certainty. Towards evening the sea is abating and the wind has gone S.E., gentle. Cannot make southerly course close hauled, so will make W.S.W. Again towing other boat towards evening. Wind and sea dropping. Mizzi reported to have died around 2000.

SUNDAY 22ND NOVEMBER 1942 Light S.E. wind, slight sea, and heavy swell, cloudy and clear. Latitude at noon 6-58 North. Went aboard the other boat at 0600 to perform last rites for Mizzi. Rigor mortis had set in and his face was a mottled purple in colour. Read burial service and committed body to the sea. Commenced rowing. Meals as usual. At 1600 smoke sighted by the Third Engineer to the N.E., which proved to be a ship on an apparent southerly course. Commenced rowing to cross her bows and get between her and the setting sun. Two boats rowing independently and burning smoke flares alternately. Sending out wireless messages giving position of 6-50 North Latitude, 31-30 Longitude West. At 1730 vessel turned towards us. At 1800 boarded SS "Eskdalegate" in darkness. Found that my latitude was correct to the mile but longitude was 30 miles out to the westward."

Captain Vernon Upton received the George Medal, and his 2004 biography "Upon Their Lawful Occasions" is essential reading, detailing not only his fortunate escape from the fate of the Barrwhin (see above) but also recording all shipping losses during the war on a monthly basis. His treatment by the Government after the war, as was the case of virtually all merchant seamen, was scandalous. In all the other allied countries, they received pensions, honoured treatment and preference for their efforts and suffering. >From his book, an essential purchase for anyone interested in not only the war at sea, but life in the merchant navy, we learn the following\;

Vernon Upon was born in Kobe, Japan, and described his life at sea. He mentions the hatred of Tatem's crews for their owners. When the owner of the line, Lord Glanely, was killed in an air raid in 1942, a fellow officer mentionwed that his epitaph should have been 'Under one sod lies another.' He recounted that Tatem ships were known as 'T on the funnel but none on the table.' Similarly, the prominent S on Reardon Smith funnels signified the 'Starvation Smiths' line. H. Hogarth ships were known as 'Hungry Hughie Hogarths', and the two white and one red band on the Harrison Line funnels meant 'two of fat and one of lean.' He mentions the filthy work and terrible treatment of apprentices on Tatem ships, victims of 'callous policies of the wealthy owner of the ships under the Tatem house flag, and those of his equally callous direcxtors and subservient sycophants.'

On his 24th voyage, in 1937, Vernon was serving on the Appledore, which received a shot across the bows from a Spanish cruiser and was forced to stop. Fortunately, the battle cruiser HMS Hood intervened. On his 25th trip, as a midshipman to British Columbia, he describes the new first mate, a 'nepotistic bully', replacing useful seamen with his cronies from west Wales fishing villages, and being refused permission to see his mother after 20 months without leave.

His 30th voyage was in the Appledore in convoy HX9, where the Royston Grange and Usmouth were torpedoed. The Appledore, heavily loaded, became almost unmanageable in a Force 9 gale. The lifeboats were smashed, there was damage to cargo and the ship began listing heavily in the blizzard, with the steering gear disabled. The Appledore limped back to Britain, behind the convoy, but grounded on the Goodwin Sands before reaching Hull to unload and get repaired.

For his 31st trip, to New Orleans, Vernon had been trained on a merchant seaman gunnery course. He recalled with fondness a Malay bosun on the Appledore who could not pronounce the letter 'F'. He referred to Vernon and his friend Phil Harris as 'puckin prentices'. He was a fine seaman, so Vernon and Phil used to regularly ask him what the weather would be like, and get an answer along the lines of 'Soon come plenty pog. We carry puckin pog for two days. The puckin pog clear, get plenty puckin pine weather.' After a few days of this, the bosun responded 'You puckin prentices ask me abpout puckin pog just to pull my puckin leg.' This voyage was in convoy OB79 from Liverpool, which dispersed after 3 days out. During her corssing, 31 ships were torpedoed in the Atlantic, but this particular convoy lost no ships. He was then in convoy OB316 (lost 5 ships), convoy HX 49 (lost 4 ships) and HX74 on the Istok. The Istok was a ex-Yugoslav rustbucket, and its engines needed overhauling, but she still went to sea with a cargo of pig iron. Vernon said there was no time to check the rescue or safety equipment or boats before she went to sea. If she was sunk, she would have gone down so quickly that there would not have been time to launch the boats, anyway. Arriving in Swansea, there was almost a catastrophe. The engine telegraph cables had been cut through in Halifax, by saboteurs, and only prompt action by the ship's engineer prevented the Istok ramming the lock gates.

He left the Istok and singed on next day on a Tatem's ship, despite avowing never to serve those owners again. Vernon was on the Filleigh (torpedoed in 1945) as 3rd Mate in 1940 in convoy OB227 to St Lawrence, and then convoy HX91 and on coming home took 3 months unpaid leave in Cardiff to gain his certificate of competence as a 2nd Mate. In 1941, he was serving on the Appledore's sister ship, the Hadleigh, and was attacked in convoy in the North Sea by a Junkers, despite flying anti-aircraft kites and balloons. As the mast was falling, Vernon rushed to tackle the master out of its path, severely damaging his arms. The Somali was sunk, and the hadleigh joined OB304 to the USA. After two more convoys, Vernon left the Hadleigh, which was torpedoed later in the war. In Cardiff he sought advice on his injured arm. The fractures from almost six months previously had not been treated, so his lower arm and wrist were misshapen and he needed a major operation to reset them. He was unfit for service for three months, and then joined the Barrwhin in Newcastle as 3rd Mate, destined for the Arctic convoys. He remembered freezing on watch on the voyages to Murmansk, and the ingratitude of the Russians for their efforts.

In January 1942, Vernon qualified to fire Marlin machine guns in the DEMS Traiing Centre in Leith. In this year, on leave, Vernon married his sweetheart Betty Mitchell in Cardiff, and they had a one-day honeymoon in Weston-super-Mare. On his next trip on the Barrwhin, in convoy ON89, he fell ill and was diagnosed as having scurvy. Two members of the Barrwhin's crew committed suicide around this time, one after going mad and fracturing an American night watchman's head with a hammer. After several more voyages in his 9 consecutive months on the Barrwhin, Vernon took his full leave, despite the captain asking him to remain on board. On its next voyage, it was sunk off Iceland (see above). Vernon joined the Start Point as 2nd Mate in October 1942 and put to sea in convoy ON141. Its sinking is recorded above, and in his book is a graphic account of the event.

When rescued by the Eskdalegate, he recognised the voice of an old friend: 'Pull the puckin tarpaulin across the puckin derricks.' He sent a telegram to his wife that he was safe, but it went missing. She was refused his pay as the ship had been sunk, and believed that he was dead. Pay was stopped from the moment of sinking. Vernon sent another telegram, but Betty had had no news of his fate for 2 months. In January 1943, Vernon boarded the Pilar da Larrinaga in convoy SC119 in New York. Its steering failed and emergency steering had to be rigged up in mid-Atlantic. It was full of explosives, so Vernon, for the only time in the war, went to sleep in pyjamas, rather that 'fully booted and spurred'. If she was hit amidships, it would have been pointless to even try to escape death. He then used his leave to take his First Mate's certificate. Betty commented on meeting him at Cardiff General Station that he looked 'like a scarecrow', following his privations at sea. She had seen him from a distance and did not recognise him. Vernon passed his examination and joined the Liberty ship Ocean vagrant in Swansea in June 1943. When in convoy ON190 to New York, it was announced in the London Gazette that Vernon had received the George Medal.

He was then in convoy UGS13 to Algiers and Bone, and GUS56 from Alexandria to new York, where he heard the news that he had been awarded the Lloyds War Medal for Bravery at Sea. Taken ill with gall bladder and ulcer problems associated with his exposure in the lifeboat, Vernon was repatriated on the Queen Mary. She made up to 29 knots, outrunning any U-boat, and for a time he stood watch on her. He was certified unfit in Cardiff, but with no income found a job with poor conditions and poor pay as Assistant Port Health Officer in Cardiff. During this time he learnt that his good friend Frank Howe had lost his sixth ship. After six months, Vernon signed on as First Mate on the Empire Spey in Barry, aged only 23. It was the former Blairspey, with a new bow section. He sailed in convoy OS82 to Italy, but in convoy MKS63 he started vomiting blood. He was discharged as unfit for duty in October 1944, and set up a small manufacturer's agency in Cardiff. Without Vernon's wonderful book, we would have very little of this information. It was published in 2004, when Vernon was 83 years old, just a year before he died.

PART ELEVEN

A Remarkable Escape

The Story of Philip D. Thomas of Cardiff after the Sinking of the SS Elwyn

The Barry Shipping Company was formed in 1926 and renamed the South American Saint Line in 1936. One of its ships, the Bryntawe was sold in 1936, renamed the Canford Chine and torpedoed (see above). Another, the St Winifred, was bombed and damaged badly by Spanish nationalist aircraft in 1938. In World War Two, its following ships were sunk: St Merriel bombed by aircraft; Chaucer shelled by a surface raider, and the St Elwyn, Ripley, St Essyllt, St Glen, St Lindsay, St Margaret and St Usk torpedoed.

Philip Thomas was a 4th engineer on the SS St Elwyn, and this is his personal account, passed to Terry Breverton by Fred Hortop:

"When the torpedo struck it was more like a nudge, but in the explosion that followed everything in my cabin that could move, moved fast, including me. Fortunately, in those days it was the custom at sea for cabin doors to be hooked open permanently and a door curtain used instead, otherwise I would not be here today.

The s/s St Elwyn was a vessel of some 9,800 tons (other records state 4,940 tons), a standard five hold cargo vessel owned by 'The South American Saint Line of Cardiff'. A fairly modern vessel built in Sunderland by J L Thomson in 1938 on which I was serving as 4th Engineer. She was on an outward voyage to Santos in South America fully laden with coal.

The passage commenced in a coastal convoy from Hull to Methil, then a further coastal convoy North about to Oban in Western Scotland. It was at Oban that the Atlantic convoy was assembled, about 20 vessels with an escort of a couple of armed trawlers, which sailed on 26th November 1940. For those of you who do not understand the convoy system, it consists of three or four lines of vessels, with a convoy commander on the front lead vessel. Prior to sailing all Masters attend a briefing where they receive their sealed orders concerning courses and patterns (of) manoeuvre. All vessels keep station on attendant vessels by manoeuvring their engines, and altering course at the same moment of a signal from the convoy commander, to steam on a zigzag pattern.

The British Navy at that time was stretched to the limit and desperately short of escort vessels, so on 28th November the convoy scattered, and all vessels proceeded independently. We had sailed into a developing gale, so in worsening weather it was not long before St Elwyn was sailing on her own, but still maintaining a convoy zigzag tactic to confuse any submarines as to the true course. We all knew that the German submarines would be waiting some hours further on to pick off any vessels which got within their torpedo range.

We had some protection, a 4" breach loading gun and a Mills bomb thrower mounted aft, but these were early 1914-1918 vintage. We had a retired naval gunner to teach the crew how to use these, and during firing practice on the previous voyage, we were good if we got within 5 yards of the target barrel.

We were obviously sighted, and perhaps followed, for at 7.40pm that evening, 28th November, the first torpedo struck on the portside in the engine room below my cabin. The weather had deteriorated; it was very cold, with a high sea and strong wind and storm clouds scudding across the sky which occasionally exposed a partial moon. We were quite well North in position 55.30N, 19.30W about 500 miles west of Oban.

On leaving my cabin my first thoughts were for those on watch in the engine room, but on opening the door of the alleyway I could see how hopeless it was, all the access ladders and gratings had collapsed. All I could hear was the hiss of escaping steam, the rush of water pouring into the vessel and cried of help from those below who were about to die. At that point the lights went out as the water reached the generator, and it was time for me to go.

It took a shoulder charge to open the alleyway door to the deck, my allocated open wood lifeboat was the one on the portside, the motor boat, and I reached it at the double. In the semi-darkness, I saw to my horror it was hanging in two halves from the davits, as the torpedo had struck the engine room directly below it. I quickly ran around to the starboard boat, to find a few people desperately trying to get it launched.

It was a very labour and time consuming job to swing out a boat from its stowed position inboard using rope falls and radial davits. Therefore, during the war, it was the practice to sail with the lifeboats swung out ready for lowering, and held against shipside wood chocks by gripe wires.

Within seconds of me reaching the starboard boat, the second torpedo hit the vessel portside in No 4 hold; sending tarpaulins, hatches and coal upwards like a volcano. As the noise and debris died down it was then that I saw it, a mountain of water about 30-40ft high, poised and ready to descend. The vessel had either broken its back and was sinking like a stone, or was rolling over prior to sinking. In the semi-darkness the threat of that wall was terrifying, especially as it appeared to grow each split second.

When it struck it was like the hammers of hell, I was tossed around like a rag doll in a gale. Everything I hit was hard; stanchions, bulkheads, davits – a most painful experience. Suddenly, as quickly as it had started, it stopped. Everything went still and quiet, the first of three miracles had occurred, possibly air trapped in the vessel, just held it up from going to the bottom, which was a long way down.

I quickly chucked off the rope in which I was partially entangled, but where was the surface? Up, down, left or right, I'm afraid I just flailed out in desperation. All this had happened so quickly, I had no time to take a deep breath before being overcome by the seas, so by now I was gulping down large quantities of salt water. Then came the second miracle, suddenly I was taking in air instead of water, but had I surfaced or was I in an air pocket in a sunken vessel? If the latter, I was a dead man as soon as the air ran out. Literally just before my eyes was a wall and as soon as I touched it I knew what it was, it was the side of the lifeboat which I had last seen swinging in its davits as the water struck. The third miracle had occurred – the lifeboat had somehow launched itself into such a position that I had surfaced directly alongside it.

It is said that desperate men have phenomenal strength, and I then proved that to be true. As waterlogged as I was, I was into that boat before Jack could say Robinson, and was possibly the first one in. By now I could hear men call for help, one by one hands appeared on the gunwales as we called out where we were, and men were hauled into the boat. The most difficult was the 2nd Officer who had been on watch on the bridge, so had on a duffel coat, which had become waterlogged. He was about the last in, as it took the combined efforts of a number of us to haul him out of the water. Fortunately, the sea had become damped down by the fuel oil escaping from ruptured tanks, but a strong wind was blowing which whipped up the stinging spray. It was bitterly cold, and only a little light when the moon very occasionally came out from behind the storm clouds. As each man was hauled in, they fell on the thwarts or side benches retching to remove fuel oil and salt water they had swallowed.

After about 15 minutes or so we heard it, the steady beat of the submarine's engines as the hunter came in to examine his kill. At that period German submarines were cock-a-hoop, they considered the war was won, so prisoners were not taken, or men in need assisted, their main purpose was to ascertain what ship they had sunk. Knowing this, we all huddled down and kept the most seriously ill as quiet as possible. Fortunately, he didn't see us and he steamed through the area where men were fighting for their live, and in the darkness we didn't see him. The sound of his engines died away into the night, there were no more cries for help from survivors, only the wailing of the wind and the lap and bang of the seas on the lifeboat.

Some years after the war, a friend of mine was allowed to examine the German naval archives, and he was able to tell me not only the number of the submarine, U103* but that on one voyage she had sunk two other Cardiff ships.

s/s "Graigwen" – 9th October 1940
s/s "Daydawn" – 21st November 1940

The entanglement of life is very strange, soon after the war when I came ashore, I became a consultant to Claymore Shipping who owned the Daydawn (until they ceased business), and I was technical director of Graig Shipping PLC for 30 years who were the owners of the Graigwen. In fact, I built the replacement Graigwen for them in 1977.

The U103, a type 1XB submarine of 1051 tons was built in Bremen in July 1940 and captained by Lieutenant Victor Schutze. Whilst under his command, she sank 27 ships during the period July 1940 t- August 1941. What happened to her? After sinking 45 ships of 231,940 tons she was decommissioned in March 1944, was transferred to Hamburg then to Kiel where she served as a generator boat, and was scuttled at Kiel in May 1945. Kapitan Lieutenant Schutze had a distinguished record in submarine service, serving ashore after leaving U 103 and died at the age of 44 of natural causes in 1950**

By the time U 103 had vanished into the night, the fuel released from St Elwyn's tanks hd mainly dispersed, and we were being subjected to the full force of the sea and wind. Some action had to be taken, as the lifeboat was broached or broadside to the seas which were breaking over it, so it was necessary to get the sea anchor out to turn the boat's head into the waves.

I soon found that apart from the two young apprentices, all the others were too ill with swallowed fuel and sea water to care whether they lived or died.

Together we got the sea anchor from the forward locker, rigged it, attached the line to the stern of the boat and launched it. This was quite a task, we were soaked to the skin and constantly being drenched by the seas and bitterly cold, so tying knots with frozen fingers was most difficult. Unless you have experienced it, extreme cold is torture, you physically ache in all your bones, shake like Parkinson's disease and cry to get relief.

For any non-maritime sailors, a sea anchor is made of canvas, held open each end by cane supports in the shape of a stubby drogue. The larger end is attached to the boat's stern by a floatable rope about 30-40ft long, it floats on or just below the surface and acts as a sort of brake when the boat surges by the actions of the waves. This brings the boat stern round so the boat faces and rides over the seas.

In our case, the head began to come round so very slowly, and with waves constantly breaking over and into it, it was full of water almost to the thwarts or side benches. It was therefore decided to ship the oars and the rudder, so the action of both would turn the boat faster. Here there was a problem with everyone so ill, but with the desperate situation we were in, and with a few curses, men were induced into action. Bit by bit the head came round and began to meet the waves bow on and to ride with them, but with so much water in the boat, it rode them very sluggishly. It was obvious we had to get the water out, so the oars were un-shipped, and all hands commenced to bail out using bailers and buckets found aboard, caps, hands, and any bit of equipment which would do.

After some 40mins or so, the level of water was still the same, and although some waves still broke into the boat, our efforts should have shown some success. The horrible truth then dawned. We were trying to bail the Atlantic into the Atlantic. The boat was damaged and taking in water. We were 500 miles out into the Atlantic in bad, bitterly cold weather, in a damaged lifeboat that was floating only by virtue of its buoyancy tanks, and its wood construction, and with a very sick crew.

By now, everyone had been exposed to the elements for many hours and we were dispirited and tired, but the extent of the damage had to be ascertained. Firstly it was checked that the drain plug was fitted and screwed up tight, then the hull had to be examined by hand, as it was very dark and the boat had seawater both inside and outside. The bottom was examined by lifting the floorboards and the sides by leaning over the gunwale headfirst into the sea, and running one's hands along whilst someone held on to your legs. This, however, still left some of the hull that could not be reached, but an hour or so later the damage was found on the portside forward behind a buoyancy tank where the timbers were stove in. It was difficult to assess the full extent until daylight, but we did manage to stuff a blanket into the hole which reduced the inward flow to some extent. Baling was now more successful, and we managed to drop the level of water in the boat, but it required constant bailing night and day and we always had about 10" remaining to slosh around in.

Whilst all this was going on I was thankful for my training in the Boy Scouts, where I learnt that the main danger leading to death in cold adverse conditions was hypothermia, so everyone not capable of examining the hull was busy either rowing or bailing. Sleeping was out but at least the following morning everyone who had got into the boat was alive, if not in a very good condition.

What was left of the night passed as if in a nightmare and dawn that day came ever so slowly. It was a grey, heavy dawn completely overcast with heavy rain showers. The weather had deteriorated further with a fairly high sea which the boat rode sluggishly and (there was) a strong, very cold wind. I suppose we were just about at out lowest ebb, but as it became light enough to see, there we were, 17 black men sitting in a boat, covered by fuel oil, even our hair was standing up like black barley. Strangely enough, we saw the humour of it and our spirits rose as we were able to laugh, especially as one of us was a black man, the cook was from west Africa, and still had his tribal marks on his face.

After the first surge of laughter, the reality of the situation was apparent; none of us had a lifejacket on, or was dressed for the occasions. The torpedo had struck at 7.40pm, as all those in the boat, apart from the 2nd Officer, were getting changed to go on watch. I had on very little more than the others; singlet, underpants, trousers, socks and shoes. Although we did not enjoy our coating of fuel oil, there is no doubt it insulated us from the cold, wet conditions and contributed to the fact that so many of those aboard survived.

With daylight, it was time to assess the full situation, first was to check who was aboard, and what injuries had been sustained, which revealed the following:

Officers – Chief Officer, 2nd officer, 2nd Radio officer, 4th engineer (me) and two cadets – all British.

Crew – Carpenter, 1 DEMS (see Glossary) gunner – all British; Cook and 1 catering boy – African and British; 6 assorted sailors and fireman – Dutch or Arab.

Passenger – 1 young Jewish German refugee on his way to a new life in South America, having lost all his family in the Holocaust.

Seventeen survivors out of a crew of 41, and it left us thinking about our shipmates who had perished.

Most of the injuries, apart from the sickness due to swallowing fuel and sea water, consisted of bumps, bruises and cuts sustained during the water turmoil as the vessel sank. This I consider amazing. The Chief Officer reported broken ribs with difficulty breathing, and the 2nd Officer was also in a very bad way due to sickness, so I could see that neither of these would be a lot of use in navigating the boat home. Using the first aid kit aboard, everyone was patched up as much as possible. The Chief Officer was strapped with bandages and made as comfortable as possible using the soaking wet blankets, but the 2nd Officer could only be given an aspirin as little else could be done for him.

It was about the that I realised with horror, that at the tender age of 20 years and 10 days, I was the only officer in a fit state to do anything towards getting the damaged boat, floating on its buoyancy tanks and (with) mainly sick survivors, back to Scotland or Ireland, some 500 miles to the east, under bad weather conditions. (It was the end of November). I suppose it was then that I sank to the lowest point, which took a monumental effort of will to avoid just sitting down and giving up, and it was then that I became a man.

The extent of the damage had to be checked, and this could only be done by going over the side attached by a line. It proved to be such that the boat would not be likely to break up, and the blanket filling the hole was pushed in tighter and secured.

Whilst all this was going on, the apprentices were given the task of checking the stores and equipment that were aboard, which were hardly the stores for a cordon bleu menu. The cook and one apprentice then had the job of organising and distribution of meals, there had to be rationing, to allow that we possibly had a couple of weeks before we reached land, unless we were picked up beforehand.

The lifeboat unfortunately was not completely stored due to it being fair game to steal from lifeboats when a ship was in port, so they are destocked and the stores and equipment put into the wheelhouse for safety. Due to the bad weather St Elwyn's boats had not been fully restocked.

Breakfast the first day, and in fact all meals from then on, consisted of a ship's biscuit coated with condensed milk, a dipper of water (about a small coffee cup), a couple of glucose sweets and a cigarette as long as they lasted. The tinned sausages and tomatoes were tried and rejected as they were too salty. The brandy was given out in tots at sick parade every day until it was finished, and I can assure you, never had a sick parade been so popular.

For those of you who have never had a ship's biscuit, they are about 4" square and _" thick and are so hard it requires a saw or hammer chisel to cut them. Most licked off the condensed milk, then dipped the biscuit in the water to try and soften it, but many were thrown away. One or two tried dipping in the sea, but this had to be stopped very quickly.

The equipment was adequate for the position we were in, but fortunately this, together with food, has been vastly improved today.

When all this was complete and breakfast over, it was time to think about getting on our way home. The mast was stepped, stays secured, the book sail and guys fitted and secured and the sail hauled up by the halyards. All this was a problem as none of us had any experience under these conditions. It was a difficult job by any means due to the cold and the movement and lurching of the boat, stiffness of the elbow and knee joints and that everything had a coating of fuel oil to various degrees. But where were we, somewhere 500 miles out in the Atlantic without charts or radio, only a small compass to steer by and with both the navigation officers out of action. The sea anchor was taken aboard, a course set dead east, and I suppose we began to make three or four knots. We had no idea of our drift, but Scotland, Ireland, Wales and Cornwall were that way somewhere. We were on our way; the sail filled as fortunately the wind was in our favour.

Hypothermia was still a problem, so bailing and rowing was continued, exhaustion however was starting to take over. Men were therefore split into two watches, four hours on and four off, or near enough, as all watches were either damaged or had stopped – my watch had stopped at 10.40pm. Those off watch could huddle together under a wet blanket, but I doubt if many slept, I know I didn't.

Those on watch continued to bail and row and were each given a sector of the sea to look at as we breasted each wave in case any ships were sighted. I suspect some off watch also did this. The most difficult job was that of helmsman, taken on by the two cadets and myself. Due to the damage and the wind direction, the boat tended to crab to port, so the rudder had to be held hard over to counter this. Spells on the helm were restricted to about 40 mins, even then it took a lot of massage to bring the arm back into use again.

Things progressed in this dismal manner until about noon, then came the call everyone was waiting for, "SHIP AHOY!!" Sure enough, on the top of the next wave we all saw it, it was a merchant ship close to the horizon, outward bound fully loaded about 30 miles or so from us. Shouting and waving was no use, so we used two of our distress rockets and a flare. Either he didn't see us or our rockets, or was too nervous to come to our aid we will never know, as he continued, disappearing over the horizon and we lost sight.

I would like to think it was the first of those reasons; it is the lore of the sea that a seaman in distress gets first preference. During that part of the war however, it was the custom of submarines to follow lifeboats and to torpedo any vessel that stopped to pick them up.

We must have reached our very lowest point after that, even the laughter and banter ceased, but remembering my Scout camps, a sing-song was started including Ging Gang Goolie, Agi Agi Agi and the Grand Old Duke of York would have been proud of the number of times we "marched to the top of the hill and down again."

One thing it did do, was bring a spark of life to the navigating officers, who recovered enough to give us a course to steer, so that raised spirits.

During the afternoon the weather appeared to ease a little, and we all felt a bit warmer in the chill cold. It wasn't in fact getting warmer; our blood was beginning to gel with the onset of frostbite, which bedevilled us later.

Just about dusk we shipped the sail so we could lay to the sea anchor during the night. The mind works in funny ways under these circumstances, as we all felt the necessity of sailing the boat 40ft or so to starboard before we anchored, to get off the main route for safety during dark hours.

Another strange thing happened during the afternoon, the cook whose nationality was West African advised me that he had spoken to his sister who had told him not to worry (as) we would be saved and picked up in due course. He claimed he spoke ot her every day, and I listened with some scepticism, as I thought conditions were getting to him, but not so, as will be explained later.

The next crisis occurred after we had anchored and the evening meal was being served. It was reported that the 2nd radio officer was not reacting and appeared to be cold and lifeless. Now I'm an engineer not a doctor, but even I could see he was dead, he had no pulse and I tested for breath using the signal mirror. I tried to give him a sip of brandy to no effect. During the course of my examination I found a most horrendous wound at the base of his spine, and he had either died from loss of blood or shock.

I will always remember that young man Kenneth Peter Berry aged 30 of Southport. When I went around with the first aid kit and asked if he had any injuries he replied, "No, I'm fine, use what little you have for the injured." **A truly brave, unselfish man.**

The same daily routine continued for the next six days and in a strange way I began to enjoy it. Fear never entered into it, I suppose it became like the regimented life in a hospital or institution, repetition and routine can be enjoyed.

We did consider sailing at night to speed up the journey but decided against it until the weather improved, but that time didn't arrive. We felt there was a risk of broaching and turning over the boat in boisterous seas during darkness.

Two meals a day was the routine and became part of getting through the day. It may sound odd but thirst was a problem, due I suppose to the fuel and sea water we had swallowed. Health-wise, we were all obviously going downhill, and with a few it was very noticeable at sick call. People lost interest in the food so weight began to fall off, and the gaunt unshaven look began to appear.

I think it was about the second or third day our biggest problem began to show itself, salt water boils began to break out all over the body, and were painful to the touch, so sitting or holding anything became a problem. Increasingly, frostbite also added t our woes, our hands and forearms, feet and lower legs began to swell up and go a darker colour. All this we had to put up with, as our first aid box had nothing for it.

We did sight two more ships in the distance as we crested waves during our cruise and we used up our stock of rockets and flares to try and advise them of our presence, but in each case they continued over the horizon. After each one our sense of despair grew less as we felt it was going to be by our own efforts that we would make it back to safety, especially as our last flare died away.

A few items broke the monotony and even raised a laugh, none of us had any fear as we had gone beyond that.

1. One day a fairly large whale took a look at us but decided we were not edible, or of little interest, and continued on his way!

2. Another night we were sure we were not too far from a submarine charging his batteries whilst on the surface. He was gone at daylight, but it worried us in case he was shadowing us should a vessel stop to pick us up.

And so it went on, day and night, until just after midnight on the seventh night, the 4/5 December 1940. We were laying to sea anchor with watches running, when out of the darkness loomed the black hulk of a vessel, not more than 20 or 30ft away, and going in our direction. All hands were called so we could start shouting and the lifeboat compass was lit and waved s it was the only light we had left.

The good Lord was obviously looking after us, for on the vessel the Chief Engineer had decided to take a walk on deck after seeing the engine-room watches change at midnight. He thought he could hear voices calling in the wind and saw what he thought a cigarette glowing in the darkness. He ran to the bridge to inform the officer of the watch and fortunately the Captain was there, who stopped the engines, put a torch in a megaphone and flashed it in the direction the Chief Engineer thought we would be. He also called out his full crew to line the handrails, each one with a heaving line.

We in the boat spotted the torch flash and for the first time felt fear; rescue and safety were so near and was ours for the taking. The sea anchor was cast adrift, quite stupid if we had not been picked up, the oars shipped and leant to with a will. We covered the distance to the ship in record time, salt-water boils, frostbite and lethargy forgotten. How long did it take us I don't know, 20 or 30 mins as the ship had steamed past us before stopping and had drifted in the weather.

Suddenly there it was, the large steel side heaving up and down in the seaway, but to our horror and consternation we ended up stuck on the vessel's stem or prow. From what I was told later then came another miracle, the Captain thinking he was drifting away, rang down for the engines to start half ahead. On a premonition he stopped the order, otherwise our boat would have been cut in two.

It was then they found us, a line was quickly attached and the boat pulled to portside amidships where a rope ladder was waiting. With our problems of boils and frostbite it was not an easy climb, especially as the lifeboat was riding up and down and ranging on the shipside in the waves. It had to happen, as one of our apprentices Bob Davies of Cardiff was halfway up he lost his grip and fell into the sea between the lifeboat and the vessel. When the lifeboat ranged back against the vessel's hull, no-one would have given a jot for his chances, but on the next wave as it ranged away again, up he popped and we had him aboard in a flash – uninjured but mightily scared.

The vessel's bosun and an A.B. came down to the boat after that with a line, and everyone was hauled up like a sack of coal. Tragedy nearly struck again when the line attaching the boat to the vessel came adrift and we drifted away, but someone aboard threw out a heaving line, which landed across the boat. From then on it was only minutes before we were alongside again, with everyone aboard the lifeboat cast off and the vessel's engines going full ahead. What happened to the lifeboat, it was never reported washed ashore, so it either broke up in the bad weather or was run down by another vessel.

The association with Cardiff vessels continued, as our rescue vessel was the s/s "Leeds City" owned by the Reardon Smith Line of Cardiff, inward bound fully loaded with general cargo and grain.

When I stepped on deck a voice called "any engineers?" When I replied, I was taken to the Chief Engineer's cabin. He and the 2nd Engineer cut off all my clothes and hair, dumped them, then washed me down with paraffin to remove the fuel, then I was shaved, scrubbed in a hot bath and put to bed. When in bed I declined food but asked for a drink and was given a bottle of whisky to warm up my circulation. I remember putting it to my mouth, taking a swig, and woke up the next day 6th November 1940 as the vessel went through a submarine boom at the head of the River Clyde, known to sailors as the tail of the bank.

We had made it back, **"A Remarkable Escape"** was complete, about 250 miles in the lifeboat and the remainder in the Leeds City, which was to land us 40/50 miles from Oban where it had all started.

The master, Captain Ward, had broken radio silence as he came through the boom to report he had survivors aboard, so as the vessel anchored a hospital launch was waiting. We all said our goodbyes and thanks and were taken to Greenock Harbour where ambulances were waiting for us. When we arrived we must have looked a weird lot without any hair, with odd and poorly fitting clothes the Leeds City crew had provided, gaunt, and with skin still a strange brown colour from the fuel oil.

I was only one of only a few who could walk in, and I was first asked to go into a side room where I was interviewed by two men, who I later was told were from MI5 or MI6. There were concerned with anything strange that happened regarding the cook, so I told them that every afternoon he used to talk to his sister, who told him that we would be rescued. It then came out that a coloured lady had arrived at the hospital from Portsmouth two days before we landed and told them to prepare for her brother and 15 other survivors (- there were 16 survivors). They thought she was just a bit strange until the "Leeds City" broke radio silence, when she was promptly arrested. As far as I am aware, she was released with no further action when explanations were given, if not understood.

Now followed some weeks of painful treatment for the salt-water boils and frostbite. Treatment appeared to be in the experimental stage, as different means were tried and we would be asked to report on pain and progress. Today the treatment is to immerse the person in a bath, keeping them as flat as possible and slowly bring up the body temperature. This is more or less similar to how the engineers on the Leeds City treated me.

The modern treatment was developed as a result of German medical experiments at Dachau concentration camp during 1940-42 to establish a method of cold weather survival, when many prisoners suffered extreme torture and death under the direction of Dr. Rhum***. The principal evil doctors at Dachau were caught after the war, two were hung, two were given life sentences and Dr. Rhum was killed by his own SS troops, so justice was at least partially carried out. Some of the doctors however continued to work in the USA after the war (they were pardoned of war crimes, for this purpose), to develop the system for the Apollo space programme. It is now used extensively in the air-sea rescue service, so some good came out of evil.

Unfortunately, in our case gangrene set in with some who lost fingers and/or toes, but thankfully no arms or hands or feet or legs. As the shock began to come out, nightmares became common and we all lost weight. I dropped about six stones, but the good food and attention we received, especially when we arrived home, soon put it on again. The saddest case was Allan Brightwell, the 2nd officer who was very ill on arrival at hospital and was there for many moths before going home. He returned to sea about 18 months later, but on the first voyage back caught smallpox and died.

One by one we improved and were released from hospital. I was first to leave after just 18 days and made it home for Christmas. Perhaps this was because I was young and fit and played as lot of sport, but I also like to think it was the **"DRAM OF WHISKY"** I was given on the Leeds City, which the doctors condemned outright. Whisky has been my favourite tipple ever since.

In due course, after recovery we were informed that we were excused from further sea service and offered jobs in various defence or shipping businesses. Some went back to sea, including me, but those who had lost body parts were given disability pensions and worked ashore in various jobs.

The 24 men lost from the St Elwyn were amongst the 31,908 merchant shipping seamen manning 2,284 vessels and 251 trawlers lost during the war, mainly in the early years of the Battle of the Atlantic before Bletchley cracked the Enigma Code. I don't think people realise the depth of what they owe to those men of the merchant navy, when Britain came within a whisker of losing the "Battle of the Atlantic", which could have lost us the war through starvation and lack of supplies.

Very recently an old house magazine of the Reardon Smith Shipping Company dated December 1979 came to light. In it was a short article written by Mrs Ward, the wife of the Captain of the Leeds City****, detailing the story of our rescue, she also included a copy of the Christmas card we survivors drew up in hospital dated December 1940 addressed with thanks to our rescuers on s/s Leeds City from the 16 survivors of the s/s St Elwyn. This written verse typifies the feelings of the merchant seamen to one another.

> May good luck be your Captain
> And happiness your freight
> May laughter be your pilot
> And sunshine be your mate
> May every port you enter
> Bring every pleasure new
> And good health be your steward
> And good friends be your crew

Plagiarising the famous lines which Churchill used to describe the RAF in the "Battle of Britain" and applying them to the merchant navy in the "Battle of the Atlantic":

> Never in the field of human conflict
> Has so much been owed by so many
> To so many who gave their all
> In the hours of need

Philip D. Thomas, Cardiff
February 2002

From the website uboat.net, we learn that the St Elwyn was carrying a cargo of coal from Hull to Santos, Brazil, and sunk east of Bishop's Rock:

*'At 20.24 hours on 28 Nov, 1940, the St. Elwyn (Master Edward Thomas Alexander Daniells*****, DSC and bar), dispersed from convoy OB-249, was hit near the bridge by one torpedo from U-103 about 500 miles east of Bishop Rock. The U-boat had spotted the ship at 09.51 hours and had to overtake her again after a first submerged attack failed due to the zigzag course. The ship sank by the stern after being hit by a coup de grâce in the engine room at 20.27 hours. The master and 23 crew members were lost. 16 crew members were picked up by the British merchant Leeds City and landed at Gourock'.*

* Official records state the U 103 sank 45 ships, totalling 237,596 tons and damaged 3 others. Schutze was awarded a Knights Cross, as was his successor in 1941-42, Werner Winter. It was taken out of service in March 1944. In Jan 1945 U-103 went from Gotenhafen to Hamburg and in April 1945 from Hamburg to Kiel. It was sunk 15 April, 1945 at Kiel, by bombs.

** Conditions in U boats, breathing in carcinogenic fumes from explosives and fuel, meant early 'natural' deaths for many unterseebooten mariners.

*** This must be Dr Sigmund Rascher, not Rhum. He experimented with hundreds of prisoners in freezing water and decompression chambers, but crossed Heinrich Himmler and ended up himself a prisoner in Dachau, being shot by an SS guard. The prisoners Rasher killed in Dachau included Russian POW officers.

**** The Leeds City was torpedoed just a couple of months after rescuing the St Elwyn survivors, in convoy OB290, with another 8 ships – see the entry on the Baltistan above.

***** Apart from the fact that Captain Edward Thomas Alexander Daniells was a Cardiff man, it is difficult to find out more. His DSC and Bar were possibly awarded when he was in the Royal Navy in WWI, as it is a military award.

The following is a log of the U 103's activities, showing just how effective U boats could be:

Operations information for U-103 from ubootwaffe.net

21.09.1940 - 19.10.1940

First Sailing - active patrol

U-103 left Kiel under the command of Viktor Schütze on 21st Sep 1940 and arrived at Lorient on 19th Oct 1940 after four weeks. Viktor Schütze hit six ships on this patrol, four of these ships were in convoy: One was from convoy OB-227 and three were from convoy SC-6.

- On 6th Oct 1940 he sank the Norwegian 6,123 ton *Nina Borthen*.
- On 9th Oct 1940 he damaged the British 3,697 ton *Graigwen*, sailing with convoy SC-6.
- On 9th Oct 1940 he sank the Greek 3,816 ton *Delphin*, a member of convoy SC-6.
- On 9th Oct 1940 he sank the Greek 4,407 ton *Zannes Gounaris*, part of convoy SC-6.
- On 13th Oct 1940 he sank the Estonian 1,186 ton *Nora*.

On 15th Oct 1940 he sank the British 4,747 ton *Thistlegarth*, from convoy OB-227.

09.11.1940 - 12.12.1940

Second Sailing - active patrol

On the 9th Nov 1940, U-103 left Lorient under the command of Viktor Schütze and returned to Lorient on 12th Dec 1940 after more than four weeks on patrol. Viktor Schütze hit seven ships on this patrol, five of these ships were in convoy: two were from convoy OB-244, one was from convoy OB-248, one was from convoy OB-252 and one was from convoy SLS-56.

- On 21st Nov 1940 he sank the British 4,768 ton *Daydawn*, sailing with convoy OB-244.
- On 21st Nov 1940 he sank the Greek 6,085 ton *Victoria*, a member of convoy OB-244.
- On 27th Nov 1940 he sank the British 4,393 ton *Glenmoor*, part of convoy OB-248.
- On 28th Nov 1940 he sank the British 3,578 ton *Mount Athos*.
- On 28th Nov 1940 he sank the British 4,940 ton *St Elwyn*.
- On 8th Dec 1940 he sank the British 9,515 ton *Calabria*, from convoy SLS-56.

On 9th Dec 1940 he sank the British 5,186 ton *Empire Jaguar*, sailing with convoy OB-252.

21.01.1941 - 24.02.1941

Third Sailing - active patrol

U-103 departed under Viktor Schütze from Lorient on 21st Jan 1941 and arrived back at Lorient on 24th Feb 1941 after nearly five weeks on patrol.Viktor Schütze hit four ships on this patrol, three of these ships were in convoy: One was from convoy HX-106 and two were from convoy HX-107.

- On 13th Feb 1941 he damaged the British 10,516 ton *Arthur F Corwin*, a member of convoy HX-106.
- On 17th Feb 1941 he sank the British 10,455 ton *Edwy R Brown*, part of convoy HX-107.
- On 18th Feb 1941 he sank the British 5,459 ton *Seaforth*.

On 19th Feb 1941 he sank the Norwegian 7,034 ton *Benjamin Franklin*, from convoy HX-107.

01.04.1941 - 12.07.1941
Fourth Sailing - active patrol

U-103 left Lorient under the command of Viktor Schütze on 1st Apr 1941 and returned fourteen and a half weeks later to Lorient on 12th Jul 1941.Viktor Schütze hit thirteen ships on this patrol, four of these ships were in convoy: One was from convoy OB-310, two were from convoy OB-313 and one was from convoy OG-60.

- On 25th Apr 1941 he sank the Norwegian 2,267 ton *Polyana*, sailing with convoy OG-60.
- On 1st May 1941 he sank the British 1,494 ton *Samsô*.
- On 3rd May 1941 he sank the British 4,253 ton *Wray Castle*.
- On 6th May 1941 he sank the British 4,752 ton *Dunkwa*, a member of convoy OB-310.
- On 6th May 1941 he sank the British 5,529 ton *Surat*.
- On 9th May 1941 he sank the British 7,120 ton *City of Winchester*, part of convoy OB-313.
- On 11th May 1941 he sank the British 5,828 ton *City of Shanghai*, from convoy OB-313.
- On 20th May 1941 he sank the Egyptian 3,575 ton *Radames*.
- On 22nd May 1941 he sank the British 6,857 ton *British Grenadier*.
- On 24th May 1941 he sank the Greek 4,236 ton *Marionga*.
- On 25th May 1941 he sank the Dutch 7,789 ton *Wangi Wangi*.
- On 8th Jun 1941 he sank the British 4,853 ton *Elmdene*.
- On 29th Jun 1941 he sank the Italian 6,619 ton *Ernani*.

10.09.1941 - 09.11.1941
Fifth Sailing - active patrol

On the 10th Sep 1941, U-103 left Lorient under the command of Werner Winter and arrived back at Lorient eight and a half weeks later on 9th Nov 1941.

Werner Winter hit two ships on this patrol and both of them were in convoy, both of them were from convoy SL-87.

- On 22nd Sep 1941 he sank the British 5,003 ton *Edward Blyden*, sailing with convoy SL-87.
- On 22nd Sep 1941 he sank the British 5,591 ton *Niceto de Larrinaga*, a member of convoy SL-87.

03.01.1942 - 01.03.1942
Sixth Sailing - active patrol

U-103 departed under Werner Winter from Lorient on 3rd Jan 1942 and returned to Lorient on 1st Mar 1942 after just over eight weeks on patrol. Werner Winter hit four ships on this patrol.

- On 2nd Feb 1942 he sank the American 6,182 ton *WL Steed*.
- On 4th Feb 1942 he sank the Panamanian 3,627 ton *San Gil*.
- On 5th Feb 1942 he sank the American 8,327 ton *India Arrow*.
- On 5th Feb 1942 he sank the American 8,403 ton *China Arrow*.

15.04.1942 - 22.06.1942
Seventh Sailing - active patrol

U-103 left Lorient under the command of Werner Winter on 15th Apr 1942 and arrived back at Lorient on 22nd Jun 1942 after more than nine weeks on patrol. Werner Winter hit nine ships on this patrol.

- On 5th May 1942 he sank the British 5,966 ton *Stanbank*.
- On 17th May 1942 he sank the American 2,612 ton *Ruth Lykes*.
- On 19th May 1942 he sank the American 5,037 ton *Ogontz*.
- On 21st May 1942 he sank the American 3,372 ton *Clare*.
- On 21st May 1942 he sank the American 4,727 ton *Elizabeth*.
- On 23rd May 1942 he sank the American 6,625 ton *Samuel Q Brown*.
- On 24th May 1942 he sank the Dutch 1,828 ton *Hector*.
- On 26th May 1942 he sank the American 5,588 ton *Alcoa Carrier*.
- On 28th May 1942 he sank the American 6,414 ton *New Jersey*.

21.10.1942 - 29.12.1942
Eighth Sailing - active patrol

On the 21st Oct 1942, U-103 left Lorient under the command of Gustav-Adolf Janssen and returned nearly ten weeks later to Lorient on 29th Dec 1942. Gustav-Adolf Janssen hit three ships on this patrol, two of these ships were in convoy: One was from convoy ON-149 and one was from convoy SL-125.

- On 31st Oct 1942 he sank the British 6,405 ton *Tasmania*, part of convoy SL-125.
- On 6th Dec 1942 he sank the British 5,025 ton *Henry Stanley*, from convoy ON-149.
- On 13th Dec 1942 he damaged the British 13,945 ton *Hororata*.

07.02.1943 - 26.03.1943
Ninth Sailing - active patrol

U-103 departed under Gustav-Adolf Janssen from Lorient on 7th Feb 1943 and arrived back at Lorient more than six weeks later on 26th Mar 1943. On 24th Mar 1943 in square BF 48, U-103 came under attack from an aircraft of RAF 224 Squadron. U-103 was not damaged by the attack.

24.04.1943 - 26.05.1943
Tenth Sailing - active patrol

U-103 left Lorient under the command of Gustav-Adolf Janssen on 24th Apr 1943 and returned to Lorient on 26th May 1943 after four and a half weeks on patrol.

At 0015 HRS on 27th Apr 1943 in square BF 45, U-103 came under attack from an aircraft of RAF 172 Squadron.

At 1448 HRS on 22nd May 1943 in square BF 47, U-103 came under attack from an aircraft of RAF 10 OTU Squadron. The boat defended itself with flak without destroying the aircraft.

25.07.1943 - 26.07.1943
Eleventh Sailing
On the 25th Jul 1943, U-103 left Lorient under the command of Gustav-Adolf Janssen and arrived back at Lorient on 26th Jul 1943 after one day.

18.09.1943 - 01.01.1944
Twelfth Sailing - active patrol
U-103 departed under Gustav-Adolf Janssen from Lorient on 18th Sep 1943 and after fifteen weeks arrived at Bergen on 1st Jan 1944.

03.01.1944 - 07.01.1944
Thirteenth Sailing
U-103 left Bergen under the command of Gustav-Adolf Janssen on 3rd Jan 1944 and arrived at Kiel on 7th Jan 1944 after four days.

PART TWELVE

Captain W.A. Shute's account of the sinking of the Tunisia

This was the greatest loss of men from Barry on any ship, with half of the 38 missing coming from the town. Just as importantly, it highlights our lack of knowledge of the men who served at sea. The captain's report notes that for Barry's Ernie Haysham, it was his fourth sinking (once by mine, twice by torpedoes and once by bombing). Ernie was sunk on another three occasions, and this fact seems to be unknown. Try to find anything about this remarkable man, who lived happily in Barry for many years after the war, and it is as if he never existed. Another Barry man of the survivors, John Benson, died later on the Pacific. Captain Shute was later torpedoed and died on the Hamla.

CAPTAIN'S REPORT ON THE LOSS OF THE TUNISIA (4,337 grt)
Strick Line, Swansea

Straggler from Convoy SL 81
<u>Bombed and sunk by German Aircraft on 4th August, 310m WbyN Slyne Head</u>
Passage: Freetown to Workington with 4,000 tons manganese ore and 2,250 tons iron ore
Crew: 36 crew and five army gunners and two naval gunners
Casualties: 38 missing
Armament: 1 4", 1 Bofors, 2 Hotchkiss, 1 Savage Lewis, 2 PAC rockets, 1 Schermuly pistols and 2 kites
Confidential Books thrown overboard in weighted box, all confidential papers burnt

<u>Report of interview of Master, Captain W.A. Shute.</u>

We left Freetown on 14th July and joined up in convoy SL 81. We straggled from the convoy about 28th July owing to engine trouble, and by the time the engines had been repaired we found out that we were 2_ hours astern of the convoy, with no extra speed with which to catch up. I therefore steered for the rendezvous for the following day, and although I steered through this position I did not see the convoy. I made several runs across the assumed track of the convoy in order to try and pick it up, but without avail. On 1st August I received a W/T message from the Admiralty instructing me to report my position, speed and prospects. We later received routeing instructions from the Admiralty and these instructions were closely followed.

We had been zigzagging but had to stop on account of the bad weather. We had been flying a kite until 0930 on 4th August, when the wire parted. We had just repaired the wire when at 1135 a Focke Wulf Kondor appeared out of the clouds on our port beam with his engines turned off. We were in position 53 degrees 53' N 18 degrees 10' W the sea was rough with the wind NW force 6-7. The weather was fine, cloudy and visibility was good. A little before the aircraft was sighted a splash was seen in the water on our port beam. The look out on the port side of the bridge came over to the Officer of the Watch who was standing on the starboard side and reported seeing a splash, and at the same time the look our on the monkey island also reported seeing the same thing. We did not know that there were any aircraft in the vicinity. The plane approached with its engines shut off flying at a height of about 300-400 feet. The plane flew straight over the ship from the port beam to the starboard quarter, avoiding both masts and the bridge, and as he came out of the clouds, we fired out 2 PAC rockets, but these were fired too soon and did no damage. I had two more rockets, but was unable to get the cartridges out of the pistol to reload them, and the opportunity of firing other PAC rockets was lost.

The first time the plane flew over the ship it did not drop ay bombs, but we opened fire with our Bofors and machine guns as soon as he was within range. The aircraft circled round and attacked, dropping 4 bombs which fell about 20 feet away, along the port side, the bombs falling more or less abreast of each of the four main hatches. The plane then flew across the ship and machine gunned the Bofors gun crew, but caused no casualties. It then circled round again flying very low crossing the ship from the port beam to the starboard quarter and dropped 4 more bombs, one which fell in the No. 4 hold, 1 on the poop and 2 fell astern clear of the ship. The force of these bombs blew the 3rd Engineer and gunner overboard, but they were picked up later by a lifeboat. The 4 near misses burst the main steampipe, and the main injection valve and the steering gear and dynamo were put out of action.

When we were being machine gunned one of the shells cut the rope fall of the starboard lifeboat, with the result that the boat dropped and some of the crew were thrown into the sea. The boat on the after deck was also damaged by machine gun fire.

We eventually lowered 3 lifeboats and 2 jolly boats. The port jolly boat remained alongside so that I and the men with me could get away from the ship. We then abandoned ship and transferred men, stores and gear from the damaged lifeboats into other boats leaving us with 22 men in the lifeboat, 16 men in the port jolly boat, and 5 men in the starboard jolly boat. I was in the starboard jolly boat with 4 men. Later I managed to transfer the food from the damaged lifeboat into our jolly boat and the sound lifeboat.

I had always made it a practice of carrying additional water in all the boats, and we also had a bottle of liquid paraffin in each boat. We carried as well a bottle of whisky and a bottle of brandy in the boats, but these were lost overboard while the boats were being lowered. The whisky and brandy sank, but the bottle of liquid paraffin floated and we got it back into the boat.

During the time we were in the boat we tried to eat the biscuits and some of the tinned meat, but they were very dry and made us thirsty. We could only eat about _ of the biscuits each day and during the last three days in the boat, 3 of us did not eat anything at all. We were in this small boat for 8 days and were wet through all the time. We had several showers of rain, but could not collect any water, as we had nothing suitable to use for catching it in.

We threw everything that was of no use, overboard. The boat had no sail and for the first 5_ days we pulled at the oars as much as possible after which we rigged up a blanket as sail with an oar for a mast and sailed to Eastward.

At about 23.30 on 11th August we sighted land and continued to sail until 08.30 on 12th August when we landed on the beach at Ronston near Galway.

During the time we were in the boat we saw 6 planes, 5 we recognised as being Focke Wulf Condors, and 1 British plane. The German planes saw our boat on 3 consecutive days, and I think it strange that the British plane did not see our boat.

Before leaving the ship we sent out 3 Wireless messages giving the ship's position and I fully expected assistance to be sent either by plane or surface craft, but none came. The other two boats with 38 men in them are still missing although they must be within 200-300 miles from the West of Ireland, and I see no reason why they should not be picked up as their boats are well found in every way.

During the attack we fired between 100-150 rounds from our machine guns, and I saw the bullets hitting the enemy aircraft. Our firing definitely silenced two of the aircraft's guns.

One of my boats was fitted with a wireless, but I consider that these sets are too delicate for use in boats.

The four men in the boat with me were J.W. Stone 3rd Officer, and Able Seamen J. Gillies, J.L. Benson and E. Haysham. This is E. Haysham's fourth experience, having been once mined, twice torpedoed in other vessels and now bombed in this vessel.

NOTE: There was no sign of the other boats and 38 were reported as lost. J.L. Benson was lost in 1943 when all crew of the Pacific was lost (with another 2 men from Barry).

PART THIRTEEN

The story of the Hortop Brothers at War

Robert, Dan, Fred, Harry, John, Ivor and George

The Hortops arrived in Barry from Devon in 1883, and during the war years there were seven brothers and five sisters. All seven brothers saw active service, six at sea. John had been in the merchant navy, but joined the army and fought in Burma and Malaya. Fred, George, Ivor and Harry served in the Royal Navy, and Dan and Robert served in the merchant navy. Some of the following information came from Fred before he died in 2006, and some from George. George specifically requested not to be included in this book, wanting to give pride of place to his brothers, but the author has included him to complete the story. Like all the men and women interviewed for this book, George sees no 'glory' in what was achieved – the times were incredibly difficult for all who served, in whatever capacity – but unless we record what happened, it is forgotten. And without a knowledge of our history, we are condemned to repeat the mistakes of the past. It is the duty of present generations to not only remember, but also to record for future generations.

Robert Hortop
Merchant Navy - Atlantic convoys
Robert was the eldest brother and did not survive the war, being killed on the Baron Dechmont, as noted previously in this book. She was torpedoed off Brazil on January 3rd, 1943. Robert's captain Maccallum was taken prisoner by U 507 and died 10 days later when U 507 was sunk by US aircraft. He had also been in the crew of the Minnie de Larrinaga, which was sunk by German bombers September 7, 1940 in London Docks. It was then filled with Blitz rubble and used as a scuttle ship in Dover Harbour. Emil John said that when one of Robert's ships had been torpedoed, all the crew were allowed to get into lifeboats, and the German captain said, in perfect English, 'pick up your cat' from the water. Robert left a wife and two very young sons.

Dan Hortop – Merchant Navy
Merchant Navy – Atlantic convoys
Dan Hortop served in the Merchant Navy from 1931, until he was invalided out in 1941. During the war, he completed the Merchant Navy A/A Gunnery Course in the firing and maintenance of machine guns, at the DEMS Training Centre in Cardiff, October 28th, 1941
February 1940
Able Seaman Dan Hortop was serving on the Clunepark of Greenock (3,491 grt, built in 1928), and it was one of 19 ships in the unescorted Convoy SLS64 which left Freetown, January 30th 1940. On February 12th, the German warship Admiral Hipper began firing its 8" guns from 3000 yards. Despite a heroic defence, 8 merchantmen were sunk, the Shrewsbury, Warlaby, Westbury, Borgestad, Nailsea Lass, Perseus, Oswestry Grange and Derrynane. Indeed, the carnage was so great,

Painting by George Hortop of the Baron Dechmont leaving Barry Docks, 1942.

Dan Hortop, on the Clunepark,
February 1941

that the Admiral Hipper sank 6 ships in just one hour. Two ships were badly damaged, the Lornastar and Clunepark, as well as another ship the Ainderby, which was not officially in the convoy. It was the greatest loss of ships in a convoy to any warship, principally because the Royal Navy let it leave Freetown unescorted, although it was known that the Admiral Hipper was at large.

Dan Hortop remembered the events, as recounted in *"The Atlantic Star 1939-45"*: *'We left Freetown, West Africa, with a cargo of iron ore bound for Middlesbrough. We were one of nineteen ships in ConvoySLS64. We had no escort. On the morning g of 12 February we were attacked by the German heavy cruiser Hipper. She sank several of the convoy very quickly... There was a lot of confusion aboard Clunepark. The bosun came down to our quarters shouting, and we dashed up on deck just in time to see one ship going down and another being smashed by heavy gunfire.*

Someone, presumably the captain, had given the order to abandon ship as her lifeboats were in the water. Dan said *'Although we ourselves hadn't actually been hit, our skipper must have ordered "Abandon ship." How else was it that boats were actually in the water by the time our watch got on deck?'* The skipper had served in World War I, and Dan believes that he saw that there would be no chance to lower boats when the Clunepark was inevitably hit in the next few minutes. With its cargo of iron ore it would sink in under two minutes. Large smoke floats were ignited and dropped astern to disguise the boats' progress. Dan said that after the smoke was effective, *'We then stripped No. 3 hatch, because the hatch boards would come in handy when we*

The Clunepark at Madeira, February 1941

338

The German Cruiser Admiral Hipper, which attacked the Clunepark, February 1941

were hammered by the Hipper – we thought that it would be our turn at any moment – and we also had a couple of rafts we made on the previous voyage.' Because of confusion concerning the amount of damage, the Clunepark was only partially abandoned. Dan Hortop was now at the wheel and the ship got under way again, and Hortop recounted that *'what remained of the convoy was scattered, but eventually after sinking the seventh ship the Hipper made off.'* The Clunepark returned to look for her lifeboats but only found debris and wreckage from other ships. *'The next day we put into (Funchal) Madeira. A few of the other ships of out convoy had arrived and we were reunited with two of our crew who had been picked up by the Blairatholl. Unfortunately however, eight of our crew who had abandoned ship prematurely were lost.'* The Clunepark joined Convoy HG 54, a week later. The convoy left Gibraltar on February 20th, arriving at Liverpool on March 12th. Dan was paid off in Middlesbrough: *'When we were paid off, there was quite a row in the shipping office. One of the Clunepark's crew had lost a brother in one of the missing boats. We heard there was an enquiry but never heard the outcome.'* On Dan's return to Barry, his father John gave Dan a large G.W.R. hand whistle (see picture). He urged Dan never to be without it, for it could save his life in the future.

May 1941

Dan Hortop joined Captain Robert Collins' Jedmoor at Barry on May 15, 1941. She was a motor vessel, capable of 9.5 knots, and sailed with a cargo of coal for Santos in Brazil. Around this time one in three of ships leaving Barry were being lost to Axis forces, and Dan had already seen action. The 5,200 mile passage was to be made unescorted, "at highest possible speed". She crossed the Equator and a day later her engine stopped in a heavy swell. There was a blockage in the fuel pipe line, requiring difficult and dirty work to fix it. While she was disabled, a large warship was spotted, heading straight towards her. Captain Collins called Action Stations, and her guns were manned. There was a 4" ant-submarine gin and a HA/LA (high angle/low angle) 12 pounder aft, and two Hotchkiss and two Lewis machine-guns amidships. Dan Hortop though he was seeing the reincarnation of the Hipper incident. Captain Collins noted the warship's many 6"and 8" guns trained on his ship. The cruiser held off from firing and signalled as it passed the Jedmoor.

Thankfully, she was HMS Sheffield. Soon after, the fuel line problem was fixed, and the Jedmoor discharged her cargo in June. Having arrived at Santos, the crew were entertained by expatriates and even played a cricket match at the English Club there.

The Jedmoor left Santos in August, carrying 6000 tons of manganese ore. This was a 'deadweight cargo.' If torpedoed, she would sink like a stone. When in the open seas, she would steer stiffly, rolling badly even in moderate swells. Instead of being able to return direct, the Admiralty had ordered the Jedmoor to Trinidad to take on fuel oil, and then to Sydney, Nova Scotia, to join a convoy. On August 30th, convoy SC42 started to leave. It was a huge convoy of 64 ships, with a very weak escort of a destroyer, HMS Skeena, and three Canadian corvettes. After 4 days of terrible storms, the convoy hove to, for two days on September 5th, rather than risk severe damage. The convoy was taking the most northerly route of any convoy thus far. On the afternoon of September, 9th, the Jedmoor was spotted by U 85. The Jedmoor had stopped for repairs, and saw a torpedo pass its bows. In all 5 torpedoes were aimed and missed her. A corvette detached itself from the convoy and protected the merchantman while she regained her station. Unknown to the Jedmoor, that morning the straggler, Empire Springback had been sunk by U 81. The sighting of the Empire Springback, Jedmoor and corvette was sent to Germany. Admiral Donitz signalled to his available U boats '*This convoy must not get through – U boats pursue, attack and sink.*'

Between Greenland and Iceland, Dan Hortop was at the wheel when he saw the Muneric torpedoed and sunk of the Jedmoor's port side, on the night of September 9th..The Jedmoor's gunners started firing, but hit nothing. Ships were now being attacked by 13 U boats in the Markgraf group. Dan Hortop recounted (in 'The Atlantic Star, 1939-45'): '*just before midnight, another two were sunk. In the early hours of 10 September, three more ships were torpedoed, two almost simultaneously. Themn, except for the occasional depth charge exploding, things became quieter for a while. However, just after daybreak, the ship on our port beam was torpedoed, the explosion lifting the funnel a little way into the air. This was the 'Empire Hudson' which, apart from being a freighter, was known as a CAM ship. Like all CAMs she carried a Hurricane fighter perched on a ramp over the foredeck… to combat the German long-range Focke-Wulf Condors.*' A ship on Hortop's starboard was torpedoed and sunk, and after dusk another two ships were sunk, one of them a tanker which lit up the entire convoy before it went under.

Dan stated: '*It was my turn on the wheel – that night we were steering from the monkey island above the wheelhouse, from where the Second and Third Officers and the master had a good view of the situation. The Chief Officer was aft with the gun crew who had been firing a number of rounds ahead off the starboard bow… After midnight two more ships were torpedoed, and not long after that we left the convoy, steering south on a zigzag course, while to the north we could still see flashes lighting the sky from explosions spread over a large area. During these early hours of 11 September three more ships in the convoy were sunk. Late in the afternoon we rejoined the convoy and took up our old station at the head of the third column.*' On September 11, Canadian and naval reinforcements arrived to assist the embattled convoy and U 501 was sunk. Soon air cover from Iceland also was available, but 5 U boats managed to keep in contact with the convoy.

The Jedmoor was within 24 hours of Britain but again straggling from the convoy, and fog was starting to come down, but U-98 had penetrated the escorts and fired four torpedoes at the Jedmoor from 2000 yards. On her aft 4" gun platform, the DEMS gunlayer Andrews, bosun Charles McQueen and AB Dan Hortop were knocked off their feet, McQueen injuring his head on the bridge bulkhead

There was a pyramid of ore in the forward hold, and two-thirds of the cargo space was unoccupied, so the inrush of water meant that the Jedmoor started to go down by the head. As her stern rose out of the sea, thousands of tons of ore shifted towards the bows, accelerating her sinking. Andrews had managed to release the nearby life raft, and dived after it, and Dan Hortop followed. He fell through the fog into the icy waters and thought he was going to drown, but was pulled up to the surface by his lifejacket's buoyancy, his lungs bursting.

Luckily, in the pitch black, he bumped against the wooden life raft, and was followed onto it by Andrews. Dan helped senior apprentice Wardle and the radio officer to get onto the raft. Hortop remembered that *'by now the ship's stern was high in the air, and you could hear the ore cargo rattling down inside the holds.'* The Jedmoor went down, one eye-witness saying that the Jedmoor

SEPT. 26ᵗʰ 1944.

NAZIS' NEW U-BOAT TACTICS

Barry Seaman's Escape

A battle between a number of German U-boats and a large British convoy in spasmodic attacks which lasted for about a week, was described to a "Barry and District News" reporter on Wednesday by Mr. Dan Hortop, of Wyndham Street, Barry Dock, whose ship was torpedoed and sunk during the attacks.

Mr. Hortop said he was on the aft-gun platform at about 10.20 on a dark night when suddenly a mighty explosion shook the ship, which sank in 1½ minutes. So violent was the explosion that Mr. C. McQueen, the Australian bo'sun, who was standing directly in line of the torpedo when it exploded, was blown back to the rigging on the bridge.

Although his back was badly injured he had the presence of mind to cut two rafts free and jump on to one of them.

Meanwhile Mr. Hortop had run to the lifeboats but he was too late, so seeing a raft floating near by he jumped over the side and swam to it. He clambered on to it and blew a whistle to attract the attention of others in the water and was able to assist a naval rating and a senior apprentice on to the raft, which was equipped with water and biscuits.

He was only on the raft about 20 minutes when another ship in the convoy picked them up. He is now safely home and enjoying a welcome respite from the hazards of the sea.

Mr. Hortop was born at Barry and attended Holton Road School. He has been seafaring regularly since the outbreak of war and was once in a convoy which suffered a terrific shelling from a Nazi Hipper class cruiser. Mr. Hortop's ship escaped on that occasion.

Report of Dan Hortop's escape from the Jedmoor

had sunk in nine seconds, but Dan's second piece of luck was that someone had managed to fire two distress flares from the bridge. It was seen by HMS Narcissus, which sped to the spot and searched for survivors, being joined by three other

Dan Hortop with bosun Charlier McQueen of the Jedmoor after their sinking, Dan with fractured skull, spine and right arm.

escorts. They tried to depth charge U 98 but it had gone – there were no asdic contacts. The Narcissus' captain then ordered a search for the Jedmoor, and failed to find the small life raft. For half an hour Dan Hortop blew on the whistle his father had given him. They had been in the middle of the depth charges and starshells had not shown their boat to the searching corvettes.

This was Dan's third piece of luck. The ship astern of the Jedmoor, the Campus, had seen her go down, and its master was reluctant to risk his ship by searching for survivors. It was highly unlikely anyway, he reasoned, but his chief officer insisted. Eventually, the jolly boat was dropped for a cursory search and they heard the last of Dan's whistles – he was out of breath. Even more fortunately, the injured bosun McQueen was floating and freezing in the North Atlantic swell when the last ship in the convoy, the Norwegian ship Knoll, spotted him. It was the 7th ship in column 7, and the Jedmoor had regained its convoy station at the head of column 3. There were 12 columns with between 6 and 7 ships in each. Of the 64 ships, 16 were sunk and others damaged.

As related above, 31 men went down with the Jedmoor, including 5 from Barry. There were only 6 survivors. It was Dan's misfortune to already have been in the convoy which suffered the most at the hands of a German capital ship. On this later voyage, no less that 16 ships were sink in convoy SC42

December 1941

In October, Dan completed a DEMS course and joined the SS Maclaren. On 3rd December, the 2330 ton Maclaren , owned by Stuart Ship Management Co., was en route from Liverpool to Barry. She was 7 miles south of Dan's home town of Barry, near the Breaksea Lightship, when sunk by a mine at 51° 21′N 03° 17′W. Dan Hortop was badly injured. He was in the mess, and the shock threw Dan off his seat into the deck head when he fractured his skull, and he double fractured the base of his spine when he landed. He also fractured an arm and was invalided out of service. In the picture he is seen on the left with bosun Charlie McQueen, who survived the Jedmoor sinking with him. Dan is standing awkwardly because he was encased in plaster of Paris from his neck to his hip, protecting his fractured spine. His left arm was still in plaster and he had head injuries.

Dan's injuries were such that for months he had to wear a 'plaster of Paris' jacket to enclose his chest and back. He later wrote to the British Consulate in Santos, asking about the British Club, or Santos Atletico Clube and was told that there were very few British members left. After the war, Dan served as a leading dock gateman for 34 years at Barry Docks.

Fred Hortop – Royal Navy
(depth charge operator, Western Atlantic Approaches, destroyer Hesperus and corvette Stonecrop)

Fred Hortop at St. John's Newfoundland, while serving on the Hesperus

Fred was a carpenter when he joined up, aged 20 in 1939, and has unfortunately died since this interview. He lost one brother on the "Baron Dechmont" (see earlier in this book), and campaigned for a Merchant Navy Day, and successfully for a monument to the Merchant Navy in Barry. At his own expense, he compiled and published a Roll of Honour of Barry merchant seamen killed in both world wars, because of the town's disproportionate losses, and the death of one brother and the sinking of another in the Merchant Navy. His first ship was the destroyer HMS "Hesperus" which had been built for the Brazilian Navy, but war broke out and the British Government had commandeered it.

After serving briefly with the 9th Destroyer Flotilla of the Home Fleet, "Hesperus" was attached to Western Approaches Command for most of the war. On 25 October 1941, "Hesperus" and the destroyers HMS "Electra" and HMS "Express" escorted the battleship HMS "Prince of Wales" for the first part of her journey to the Far East. The destroyers refuelled from the "Prince of Wales" south of Ireland. "Hesperus" then departed for Gibraltar. "Hesperus" attacked and sank the enemy German submarine U-208 (all 45 crew were lost) while in company with the destroyer HMS "Harvester" in the Atlantic west of Gibraltar on 7 December 1941. Fred's destroyer was the first to fire 2-ton depth charges.

Fred served until 1946 and remembered the time on Boxing Day, 1942, when the Hesperus sank a U boat, and had to be repaired. The Hesperus was homeward bound with convoy HX219 from St John's, Newfoundland. *'We went into action stations around noon, and I was in the depth charge crew on the heaving quarter-deck. We forced the U boat to surface early in the evening.'* The U boat submerged, and the Vanessa and Hesperus spent about 90 minutes searching for it, and then spotted its periscope. The U 357 had been forced to surface after repeated depth-charging. The "Vanessa" just missed ramming it, glancing off the side of the U boat and forcing some submariners into the sea. The U boat sped away from the chasing Hesperus on the surface, zigzagging and too damaged to submerge.

Fred remembered the chase from the quarterdeck: *'The order was passed, so very*

The Hesperus entering Gladstone Docks, Liverpool with a damaged bow after ramming the U-boat.

rare in modern sea fights: "Stand by to ram!" The enemy disappeared under the flare of the fo'c's'le, we cut her neatly in half and she sank at once, leaving only a spreading pool of oil and a handful of survivors. We picked them out of the sea in the darkness. One of the German seamen died in the night and next morning we hove to for his burial service at sea before proceeding to rejoin the convoy. Speaking for myself, I recall the elation of victory very soon replaced by a feeling of remorse at the killing of our fellow seamen, which, in spite of a situation of kill or be killed, must, I feel sure, go through the minds of friend and foe at such times.' There were just 6 survivors. As an Able Seaman in the depth charge crew on the "Hesperus" and then the "Stonecrop", Fred was involved in the sinking of 3 U boats. He noted that the top speed of a surface U boat was 17 knots, the same as the corvette "Stonecrop".

Next, on 15th January 1942, the "Hesperus" rammed and sank U 93 off St Vincent. U 93 had sunk 8 ships, tonnage 43,000, on 7 patrols, and there were 6 deaths and 40 survivors. The "Vanessa", (adopted by Barry), and the "Hesperus" (adopted by Yeovil), were protecting convoy HX 219 when the "Vanessa" spotted a surface U boat Christmas Day, 1942. Both destroyers headed towards the bearing, and the "Vanessa" laid down depth charges for 90 minutes. The "Vanessa's" captain then saw the U boat's periscope as it tried to aim torpedoes at her. However, the Hesperus laid down a pattern of depth charges and the U boat submerged again. The U boat was forced to surface again, in darkness, and was spotted by the "Vanessa", which signalled that she was going to ram it. "Vanessa" engaged the U boat with gunfire while U 357 tried to fire its stern torpedoes at her. "Vanessa" collided with the U boat's starboard side, but U 357 headed off again at full speed. She now tried to dodge the "Hesperus", but misjudged her course and the

"Hesperus" sliced her in two. The "Hesperus" returned for repairs at Gladstone Dock, Liverpool with German prisoners on her deck.

The photograph of Hesperus entering Gladstone Docks shows the damage to her bow. There was also a rip along the destroyer's bottom stretching nearly a quarter of her length. As the "Hesperus" needed lengthy repairs to its bow, Fred joined the corvette "Stonecrop". Launched in 1941 in Middlesbrough, it was a Flower Class corvette of just 925 tons. The U 124, under the ace commander Jochen Mohr, was sunk 2 April, 1943 west of Oporto, in position 41.02N, 15.39W, by depth charges from the British corvette HMS "Stonecrop" and the British sloop HMS "Black Swan". There were 53 dead (all hands lost). The Stonecrop and Black Swan were escorting the 27-ship convoy OS-45, when the Black Swan located U 124 with radar. She then spotted U 124 diving, and set depth charges on a shallow setting.

Fred Hortop's corvette, HMS Stonecrop

She turned over the spot where U 124 was still diving and laid down another pattern, then lost contact. The Black Swan was in danger of colliding with the convoy, so returned to her station at the head of the convoy, seeing the Stonecrop approaching at full speed. The Stonecrop now dropped charges over the estimated position, and turned for another run when the asdic operator reported that he had lost contact. However, a huge oil slick had appeared on the surface, so Stonecrop returned to escort the fleet. George Hortop noted that human lungs were found in the sea where the U 124 was sunk, recovered in buckets and taken to Gibraltar for proof of the U boat's sinking. Germany mourned the loss of Jochen Mohr, a 'born convoy fighter'. A few weeks after the incident, the captains of the two navy ships were told that they had sunk U 124, but did not discover her commander's name until 17 years after the war. Jochen Mohr's U 124 had sunk 46 Allied merchant ships and two warships. There are accounts in the chapter on Barry's contribution to the Merchant Navy of her sinking of the Petrel, Dartford, Eastmoor and Empire

Stream, all of which occasioned multiple deaths of Barry men.

On 23rd April, 1943, the Hesperus sank U 191 with depth charges off Cape Farewell, Greenland, with all 55 hands lost. Later, on 30th August, 1943, the German submarine U 634 was sunk in the North Atlantic east of the Azores, in position 40.13N, 19.24W, by depth charges from the British sloop HMS "Stork" and the British corvette HMS "Stonecrop", on which Fred was serving.

Fred was motivated to help the Merchant Navy get the recognition it has never received. He campaigned fiercely for a Merchant Navy Day for September 3rd. He remembered the 'slaughter in the Atlantic' of 1942, when 646 British vessels and 8000 lives were lost. A copy of a 1999 letter from Glenda Jackson when she was Under Secretary of State for the Department of the Environment, mentions Fred and the fact that the government could not support this simple recognition of the men who in reality saved Britain in WWII. However, a Merchant Navy Day was established in 2000 to mark the anniversary of the founding of the International maritime Organisation. Cardiff was the first city in Britain to give the Freedom of the City to the Merchant Navy Association, and Fred was responsible for the Vale of Glamorgan also honouring the MNA on April 16th, 2005.

Through his membership of the International Military Music Society, Fred also instigated a march arrangement of the song "Shipmates o' Mine", made famous by the Australian singer Peter Dawson. This was adopted by the Merchant Navy Association of Wales as their march. Arranged by Alan Bourne, Bandmaster of the RAF St Athan Voluntary Band, it was first played at the annual MNA service and concert at Barry's Memorial Hall in 2002.

Harry Hortop – Petty Officer, Royal Navy
PO HMS Tyne, HMS Indomitable – Atlantic and Pacific

Harry served from 1943-45 on HMS Tyne, serving in the Atlantic, at the

Normandy Landings, Burma and Pacific Landings. Tyne was a 14,600 destroyer, built by Scotts in 1940 which served as a depot ship. He was temporarily blinded for several days when a torpedo hit the wireless room on one of his ships.

A note by George Hortop records Harry's war: *'Harry Hortop , shipwright petty officer who served on the destroyer depot ship HMS Tyne at Scapa Flow, also the aircraft carrier HMS Indomitable and was on board the carrier when she was attacked and hit by two Japanese suicide bombers which exploded on the carrier's deck; Harry did invaluable work repairing damage on cruisers, destroyers and carriers – also when on the Tyne Harry took part in the D-Day June 6th 1944 Normandy landings & Northern France. He also took part in the savage landings in the Pacific in Leyte,*

Harry Hortop

346

HMS Tyne

Philippines, Lozon, Mindoro (which was opposed by suicide planes alone), Iwo-Jima (whose formidable defences were found to be more than expected, with a terrible loss of life), Okinawa (another very hard-fought action), Brunei Bay, Labuan Islands.

Harry holds the Atlatic Star; the France and Germany Star (for D-Day); the Burma Star; the Pacific Star; and the War Medal. Harry met many Barry boys serving in the Pacific, two in particular, an old friend (-) Gibbon and Fred Cook RAF, now country councillor of Glamorgan.'

John Hortop – Army
Burma and Malaya
Formerly in the merchant navy from 1922, the second eldest brother John joined the army in 1928. He served in Burma and Malaya and spent five years fighting the Japanese. He was a staff sergeant in the Royal Corps of Signals.

Ivor Hortop

Ivor Hortop – Royal Navy Marine Commandos
HO Combined Operations Royal Navy, Landing Craft and Tank Landing Craft
The eldest of the Hortop boys was attached to the Royal Naval Marine Commando Groups and took part in the Lofoten Island raid in Norway. He was also in the D-Day Normandy landings, and on the landings on the islands of Spitzbergen north of Norway.

Dan and John Hortop, 1941

George Hortop – Leading Torpedo Operator, Royal Navy

HMS Hotspur and HMS Orion

Aged 17, George joined the Royal Navy in 1943. After training at HMS Raleigh, he went to torpedo training school at HMS Defiance. His brother Harry had recommended torpedo training as these sailors were in charge of all electrical maintenance on the ship, which would give him skills for 'Civvy Street' when the war ended. He trained with depth charges, but his main work was electrical maintenance and standing watch in the main control rooms. There was a control room with a plan of the ship on each deck. He became a Leading Torpedo Operator (LTO) and saw action throughout his years at sea. He felt lucky in the Royal Navy – *'on a big ship, you were young and you felt invincible, not like in the merchant navy. I went on one ship and couldn't believe it. There was a ship's rope dangling from a fanlight into the holds, perhaps 60 feet long. If the ladders had gone, it was your only way out. Climbing 60 feet in a sinking ship?'*

George first served on HMS Hotspur before joining the Orion. In World War II, the Leander class cruisers' armament was altered substantially. Their anti-aircraft weaponry was much improved, with sixteen 2-pounder guns and varying numbers of 40 mm Bofors and 20 mm Oerlikons being fitted. The Orion was very heavily damaged in the evacuation of Crete, before George Hortop joined her. A friend from Bendricks Road, Barry, Billy Parfitt, was killed on 'A' turret. He was told that the ship was showered with confetti after the explosion – it was the gunnery orders from 'A' turret.

In July 1943, the Orion bombarded Rosolini (inland of the south-eastern tip of Sicily) before it was occupied by British troops, before helping with the full-scale invasion of Italy.

In September 1943 the Orion was supporting the great assault at Salerno, where she was the flagship, and the following article from The Daily Telegraph of the time records its contribution:

H.M.S. ORION'S SHARE IN INVASION OF ITALY –
OFFICER DESCRIBES HOW GUNS HARRRIED GERMANS

"Magnificent! Give 'em some more!" The voice of the Forward Observation Officer, forgetting the stereotyped spotting rules in his enthusiasm, came over the wireless to the bridge of the cruiser Orion. The ship's company of the Orion were having the time of their

Photograph taken from HMS Hotspur, escorting an Atlantic convoy, 1942

lives. *They were in action at short range against a moving column of German tanks, and their 6 inch shells were knocking "seven bells" out of them. This was just one incident in the hectic career of HMS Orion, commanded by Capt. G.C.P. Menzies, while supporting the army throughout the Sicilian Campaign and on the beaches of Salerno.*

The Orion was the first British warship to pass through the Straits of Messina since before the war. Her exploits were described in London yesterday by her navigating officer, Lt. P.F. Manisty, son of Paymr. Rear-Adml. Sir Eldon Manisty, "father" of the convoy system.

The Orion considers herself the "ace" bombarding ship of the Mediterranean Fleet. She bombarded: Pantelleria (and also the smaller island of Lampedusa, the taking of which the Telegraph reporter on board the Orion described in detail)); Enemy positions on the east coast of Sicily and on the toe of Italy; German troops in the first days of the Salerno landings; Tanks on the move.

The first indication that the invasion was contemplated was the arrival on board of a mass of charts and orders. The ship sailed that night and made "rendezvous" south of Sicily, with troop and supply convoys coming from both west and east. At dawn the troops landed on the Sicilian beaches, and it was soon obvious that the landing was successful. On board every warship was a military Bombardment Liaison Officer, who worked in the closest co-operation with the Forward Observation Officer ashore. These BLO's and FOO's know each other personally and are trained together as a team, a factor which contributed greatly to the effectiveness of our naval bombardments.

Lt. Manisty paid high tribute to the "Intelligence" which was made available and to the planning of both the Sicilian and the Italian landings. "We had charts, maps, descriptions and photographs of the whole coast," he said, "many of them the result of peace-time holiday snapshots. There was nothing that we did not know about it. It was amazing how

George Hortop on HMS Orion,
in pale boiler-suit

the hundreds of ships and landing craft all arrived at the right place at the right time. The planning must have been terrific." Day after day the Orion worked off the Sicilian coast on the right flank of the army, frequently bombarding the enemy's rear. "Request fire on – (a map reference)" would come the voice of the FOO, and in a matter of seconds that point would be bombarded. On one occasion members of the crew of the Orion were taken by the Army to the front line. "It was a terrifying drive at high speed over bad roads and temporarily repaired bridges. What impressed me most was the traffic organisation. There were thousands of newly erected signposts and direction boards. The whole country seemed to be a mass of moving vehicles, but there was no confusion."*

A few days later the army began to push northwards again. And the Orion led the 16in gun battleships Orion and Rodney into the Straits of Messina for the bombardment of the toe of Italy. Before the fall of Messina, the Orion went through the Straits to bombard the enemy's rear. The first sign of the impending invasion of the Italian mainland was the provision of Italian charts. The Orion joined up before dawn with the rest of the great convoy for the initial assault on Salerno. The day seemed extraordinarily peaceful, and at 7pm came the news of the Italian armistice. It was received with mixed feelings on board, where it was at first thought that the operation on which they had embarked might not be necessary.

An air attack shortly afterwards, however, showed that resistance was still to be expected. That night the Orion lay off Capri, which, to save shells, was not bombarded. Before dawn the minesweepers and little ships led in the first flight of the assault. These were followed by the larger ships and cruisers. During this first stage of the operation the Navy's guns were the only artillery available to the Army as it stormed the strong enemy positions. "The scene off the Salerno beaches was astonishing," said Lt. Manisty. "The sea seemed to be so full of ships of all sorts and sizes that confusion and collisions seemed inevitable. Yet there were neither, even when we had to dodge bombs during air attacks which were fairly frequent. Everyone knew exactly where to go and what to do. There was no confusion even when we found ourselves bombarding enemy positions ashore and defending ourselves from air attacks at the same time."

The FOO's ashore were encountering great difficulties and there were several casualties among them… our ships were using special bombarding shells with great effect. Sometimes they were firing at short range at targets which could be seen directly from the ships. The guns' crews worked incessantly. In the turrets they kept a careful record of the number of shells fired by each gun, as it was necessary to make corrections for wear of the guns so as

HMS *Orion*

to preserve the accuracy of the bombardments. *The targets were as varied as the methods of bombardment – building housing enemy headquarters and nests of resistance, enemy guns, and enemy troops, tanks and vehicles on the move. The latter were the most satisfactory targets from the point of view of the sailors. They enjoyed it most when the ship went right in as close as the depth of water would allow and engaged enemy troops which could be clearly seen from the ships.*

By day the Orion worked close off the beaches, and her main preoccupation was supporting the Army with her 6-inch guns. By night they hauled off to seaward and provided cover and anti-aircraft defence. After several days of this the Orion's shell rooms were almost empty. She pumped her last shells over a high hill and into the approached to Naples, and steamed off at high speed to replenish her ammunition.

In January, 1944, George was at the Anzio landings, and George noted that the Orion fired 2650 6" shells in 11 days of bombardments. The Orion was now the flagship of Rear-Admiral J.M. Mansfield, and on one occasion her Forward Observation Officer (FOO) was so excited by the accuracy of her shelling that he reported *"Fire effective... Effect beautiful... Wizard! ... All rounds on the target..."* One day the Orion took over a target from the destroyer Loyal because it was out of Loyal's range. The Loyal withdrew, signalling to the Orion, *'Thou shalt not pinch thy neighbour's FOO.'* The Orion immediately signalled back *'Many are called, but FOO's are chosen.'*

The Orion was in action from January 23rd to February 18th at Anzio. She was, along with the cruiser HMS Spartan, responsible for naval gunfire support on the beaches where British troops were landed. The Spartan was sunk by a glider bomb during an attack by 18 German planes on January 29th. The beaches where US troops landed were supported by the cruisers USS Brooklyn and HMS Penelope. After only 22 hours, the Allies had landed 36,034 men, 3069 vehicles and 90% of the U.S. VI Corps' assault equipment. Losses were only 13 killed, 44 missing and 97 wounded.

HMS Orion was later in action for five days from D-Day June 6, 1944.

A note from Lieutenant-Commander S.E. Glover, OBE, MBE, DSC states *'I was the gunnery officer of the cruiser HMS Orion of Force K which supported the landing at Gold Beach and opened fire on my appointed target, a gun battery, at 5.21 am on the morning of D Day. Being positioned on the east flank directly opposite Arromanches, I was able to observe between shoots the landing and the bulldozers at work to clear a way for vehicles and also to view the early stages of the build up of the harbour. I was then moved to the west flank next to Omaha and was able to see what happened to the US forces on landing. To visualise what is happening during the course of the action, when one's concentration is thoroughly absorbed is most difficult.*

We had on board with us the war correspondent named Harrison of the "News of the World", who seemed to be enjoying himself with what he saw during our five days at the beachhead, during which time we had worn out our 6-inch guns or 152-mm and it was necessary to withdraw and have new gun liners fitted and then to proceed back to the Med to prepare for the South of France landing, which my ship led in at St Tropez.' The Orion was congratulated for its engaging of Panzer tanks and troop concentrations at a range of up to 24,000 yards.

On 14th August, 1944, the cruisers Orion and Royalist led the fleet of almost 300 ships in the landings in the south of France. HMS Orion had been heavily involved in the battle of Cape Matapan, the British troop evacuations of Greece and Crete, and as a bombardment cruiser on the Sicily, Salerno, Anzio, Normandy and South of France landings from 1943-44, and the relief expedition into Greece, 1945. HMS Orion was awarded 17 battle honours in World War II.

George was demobbed in 1946 and worked at Collis's then in the electrical and electronics workshops in BP, Barry. For many years he and his brother Fred worked to have a monument to merchant seamen raised in Barry.

PART FOURTEEN

Welsh Ships Lost (and damaged) in World War II

(2)(3) = second or third ship of that name

Around 100 Cardiff ships were damaged and destroyed in the war. Famous Cardiff shipping lines included the (South American) Saint Line, formed by the amalgamation of the Barry Shipping Co and the St Quentin Shipping Co to become the B&S Shipping Co and then the Saint Line, with most of its ships named after saints. 12 ships were lost, and it seems that those ships prefixed with Saint were registered at Newport, rather than Cardiff.

The R.B. Chellew Steam Navigation Company lost 5 ships in the war, and was taken over by Cory Bros in 1952. Claymore Shipping lost both its ships, the Daydawn and Dayrose in the war, and closed in 1963. John Cory and Sons lost all its 3 ships in the war, the *Ruperra, Coryton* and *Ramillies*. J.T. Duncan's 3 ships survived the war. The Emlyn Line had stopped raiding in the 1930's, because its owner's criticisms of General Franco had killed off its Spanish trade. Constant (South Wales) operated from Cardiff and had only three ships left by 1945. Evans and Reid were known as the E.R. Management Co. Ltd and lost at least 4 ships. Graig Shipping (Idwal Williams) lost the *Graigwen, Graig* and *Newton Lass* in World War II, leaving only the *Graiglas*. The Hain Steamship Company lost 16 of its 34 ships in World War I. and it was bought by P&O but its operations remained at Cardiff and it lost 28 of its 40 ships in the war. Most of its ships were prefixed with Tre-.

Although many Reardon Smith Line ships were registered at Bideford, they are included in the following list as they were operating from Cardiff and owned by a Cardiff shipping line. Lovering & Sons had three small ships which survived the war. Many of Morel's ships were named after villages in the coalfields, and it lost four ships. Neale and West lost the two Cardiff trawlers with Japanese names, *Oyama* and *Naniwa*. W.H. Seager & Co lost 7 of its 8 ships, with only the Campus surviving.

The Tatem Steam Navigation Company lost 8 of its 16 ships in World War I. W.J. Tatem was knighted in 1916 and made Baron Glanely of St Fagans in 1918 for war services. He died in a bombing raid on Weston-super-Mare in 1942, a fate met with joy by some of his crews, as Tatems was notorious for bullying, poor conditions and poor food. Tatems lost several ships in the war. Evan Thomas, Radcliffe & Co lost 20 of 28 ships in World War I, and 11 of 16 in the Second World War.

CARDIFF SHIPS

(This list is probably incomplete as regards casualties and ships – further information would be welcomed. Ships with incomplete information are not registered in bold type.)

Allende-(Morel)-17.3.42- torpedoed & sunk by U 68, 20 miles S of Cape Palmas, Liberia outward voyage Calcutta - Freetown - UK (7700 tons of general cargo)- 6 dead – mainly Cardiff crew interned by Vichy French on Ivory Coast.

Amicus(3)-(Seagar)-19.12.40- torpedoed & sunk by Italian Sub Bagnolini 240 miles W of Blacksod Bay, Co.Mayo - all 36 crew lost.

Ampleforth-(Charles Cravos)- torpedoed & sunk by U101 west of Hebrides, a straggler from convoy OA199, carrying ballast from Hull to Jacksonville, Florida – 29 survivors - 9 dead.

[**Aurillac**- this has been recorded elsewhere as a 'Cardiff' ship, and was a Ministry of War transport sunk by the Italian sub Tazzoli on 15-4-1941 in the Atlantic 37.09N 18.42W -1 dead].

Barrdale-(Reardon Smith)-17.5.42 – torpedoed and sunk E. of Martinique by U156 - carrying government cargo and goods from New York to Table Bay and Abadan- 1 dead and 52 survivors.

Beatus(2)-(Seager)-18.10.40- torpedoed & sunk by U123 N. Atlantic 100 miles S of Barra Head, carrying lumber, steel and aircraft. Convoy SC7 Sydney NS to Tyne - master and all 36 hands saved.

Beignon(2)-(Morel)-1.7.40- torpedoed and sunk by U 30, 300 miles SW of Lands End in convoy SL38, carrying wheat Fremantle-Freetown-London. She had previously picked up 84 survivors from the Avelona Star.

Bradford City(3)-(Reardon Smith)-1.11.41- torpedoed and sunk by U 68, 300 miles off Walvis Bay, SW Africa, carrying sugar and rum. All 44 crew survived.

Bradfyne-(Reardon Smith)-22.11.40- torpedoed and sunk by U 100, in convoy SC11 from Sydney NS to Belfast, S of Rockall - 39 dead, 4 survivors

Bradglen-(Reardon Smith)-19.9.41- hit mine and sunk in Thames Estuary - 9 dead.

Chaucer-(South American Saints)—29.7.41-Shelled and sunk by the 'merchant raider', auxiliary cruiser Orion in N. Atlantic. She was the 15th and last ship sunk by the raider, and her crew taken off before she was finally sunk.

Clarissa Radcliffe(4)-(Evan Thomas Radcliffe)-10.3.43- torpedoed and sunk by U 663 with loss of all 55 hands 42N by 62W, west of Boston, a straggler from SC122 Pepel-New York-Barrow.

Chulmleigh-(Tatems)-6.11.42- bombed by Ju88, then ran onto rocks in a blizzard and beached at Spitzbergen – 13 survivors of 58 crew – most died from starvation and exposure, some buried in Tromso. Welsh captain, D. Williams.

Cornish City(3)-(Reardon Smith)-29.7.43 - torpedoed and sunk by U177 SE of Madagascar – convoy DN53 Lourenco Marques-Durban-Aden-Suez. 37 dead, 6 survivors, carrying coal.

Coryton-(John Cory)-16.2.41- bombed and sunk by German aircraft just off Bamburgh Castle en route from New Brunswick to Hull with grain.

Dallas City-(Reardon Smith)-4.7.40- bombed and sunk SE of Portland Bill.

Daydawn-(Claymore)-21.11.40- torpedoed & sunk by U103 off NW Ireland in convoy OB244 – outward voyage Barry - Santiago (coal) - 2 lost.

Dayrose-(Claymore)-14.1.42- torpedoed & sunk by U 552 S of Cape Race Newfoundland, outward voyage St.Johns, NF - Halifax, NS – 4 survivors, 38 lost.

East Wales(2)-(Gibbs)-16.12.42- torpedoed & sunk by U159 off Brazil outward voyage New York - Trinidad - Durban & Alexandria (coal & stores) - 17 lost, 28 survivors.

[**Empire Heritage** - this was the former whaler Tafelberg, mentioned previously as mined, beached and broken in two at Barry 28.1.41 and repaired at Cardiff. It was renamed as a MOWT in February 1943 but not a Cardiff ship. Torpedoed by U482 8.9.44 - 112 dead].

Empire Sky-(Claymore)-14.11.42- torpedoed and sunk by U 625 S of Spitzbergen. Hull-Reykjavik-Archangel – all 41 hands lost.

Ethel Radcliffe-(Evan Thomas Radcliffe)-17.4.41- torpedoed by E Boat off East Anglia – beached, and then -14.5.41-bombed after beaching on Yarmouth Sands - total loss.

Everleigh-(Tatems)-6.2.45- torpedoed and sunk in English Channel off Durston Head by U 1017 en route from London to Barry Roads and New York carrying ballast – 50 survivors 7 lost.

Filleigh-(Tatems)-18.10.45- torpedoed and sunk North Sea by U 245 in convoy TAM142 from London to Antwerp carrying military cargo – 49 survived, 5 lost.

Fiscus(2)-(Seager)-18.10.40- torpedoed & sunk by U100, carrying 5 tons of iron ore - 120 miles W of Barra Is. Convoy SC7 - master & 37 crew lost.

Fort Lamy-(John Cory)-8.3.43- torpedoed and sunk by U 527, a straggler from SC121 from New York to Liverpool. She was a former French ship seized at Falmouth to act as a MOWT. She sank off Cape Farewell, with 5 survivors and 46 dead.

Fresno City-(Reardon Smith)-5.11.40- shelled and sunk by Admiral Scheer in convoy HX84 - 1 dead.

Fresno City(2)- 12.4.43 - torpedoed and sunk in mid-Atlantic, a straggler from HX 232 Bombay-Cristobal-New York-Liverpool. Damaged by U 563 and finished off by U 706.

Goodleigh-(Tatems)-2.12.40- torpedoed and sunk by U 52 in convoy HX90 – 1 lost.

Graig – see Newton Lass

Graigwen-(Idwal Williams)-9.10.40- torpedoed and damaged by U 103: 10.10.40 torpedoed & sunk by U123 in convoy SC6 en route from Montreal and Sydney to Barry with maize – 24 survivors, 7 dead.

Grelhead-(Cardigan Shipping) - 2.12.41- torpedoed and sunk 2 miles N of Punta Negri Morocco by U562, carrying iron ore – 35 crew and 6 gunners lost.

Grelrosa-(Cardigan Shipping)-28.1.41- bombed and sunk off NW Ireland – 5 lost.

Hadleigh-(Tatems)-16.3.43- torpedoed and sunk by U77 NW of Oran, Algeria in convoy ET14 en route to Gibraltar, 50 survivors, 2 dead.

Helmspey-(ER Management)-11.2.43- torpedoed & sunk by U 516 off Port Elizabeth - 4 lost, 46 survivors.

Henri Mori-(H. Gonville)-27.4.41- a Breton cargo ship belonging to the Union Industrielle & Maritime Line which was seized in Swansea in July 1940. She was torpedoed and sunk by U 110, 330 miles WNW of the Blaskets Islands, en route from Pepel-Freetown-Barrow. 28 dead, 4 survivors.

Houston City-(Reardon Smith)-21.10.40-mined & sunk near East Oaze buoy, Thames Estuary.

Iddesleigh-(Tatem)-17.8.44- hit by 'one-man torpedo', and sunk off Sword Beach, Normandy outward voyage Hull & Southend - Normandy (stores). She was also previously torpedoed and damaged on 10.8.40. (These manned torpedoes were simple weapons which consisted of a carrier-body which looked like a large torpedo, in which the operator in the bow section sat in a Perspex-covered cockpit, which reached up to 18 inches above the waterline. Thus they were not submarines, and the cockpits were extremely simple with only start, stop, fire and a lever to turn left or right. The operators had usually only about 50:50 change of surviving in these boats and they were manned by volunteers for Opferkämpfer or sacrifice missions - but in reality these were little different from suicide missions

Jeanne M-(Mooringwell)-2.12.40- torpedoed & sunk by U 37 off Port Roca, Portugal in convoy OG46 from Cardiff to Lisbon carrying coal-19 survivors, 7 dead.

Jersey –(Morel?)-23.4.42- mined & sunk off Suez?

Jersey City(2)-(Reardon Smith)-31.7.40- torpedoed & sunk by U 99, NW of Tory Island, in convoy OB191. 3 dead, 43 survivors. Bob Edwards of Newport survived the sinking, and his story is told in 'Death and Donkeys' Breakfasts.'

Justitia-(Chellew)-22.11.40- torpedoed & sunk off NW Ireland by U100 - convoy SC11 - 13 lost, 26 survivors.

Kervegan-(Evans Thomas Radcliffe)-9.2.41- left Halifax carrying wood pulp the previous day - reported in distress & capsizing - Cardiff master and all 25 crew lost. Wreckage found by 'Cape Agulhas' off Nova Scotia, 12.2.41.

King City-(Reardon Smith)-24.8.40- suffering mechanical failure before being shelled & sunk by merchant raider Atlantis N of Rodriguez Is.- 6 crew killed.

Lady Glanely-(Tatem)-2.12.40- torpedoed & sunk by U101 in convoy HX90 – 400 miles off Bloody Foreland, Ireland - outward voyage Vancouver & Bermuda - London (lumber & spelter) – 30 dead.

Llanarth-(Evan Thomas Radcliffe)-27.6.40- torpedoed & sunk by U 30 200 miles off Ushant.

Llanashe-(Evan Thomas Radcliffe)-17.2.43- torpedoed and sunk by U 182 off Cape Colony – 33 dead, 9 survivors.

Llancarfan(2)- (Evan Thomas Radcliffe)-30.5.43-bombed & sunk 2 miles south of St.Vincent., carrying tinplate and aluminium.

Llandilo-(Evan Thomas Radcliffe)-2.11.42- torpedoed and sunk south off St. Helena by U 172, carrying US military stores, en route Durban-Bombay. 24 dead, 20 survivors.

Llanfair-(Evan Thomas Radcliffe)-11.8.40- torpedoed & sunk by U 38, a straggler from SL 41, west of Ireland en route Freetown-Avonmouth. 3 dead, 30 survivors.

Llanishen(2)-(Evan Thomas Radcliffe)--23.8.40-bombed & sunk SE of Wick.

Llanover-(Evan Thomas Radcliffe)-12.5.42- torpedoed and badly damaged by U 124, in convoy ONS92, SE of Cape Farewell, then scuttled by HMCS Arvida.

Llanwern-(Evan Thomas Radcliffe)-26.2.41- bombed by Focke-Wulf Kondor 240 miles off SW coast of Ireland. Frank Plaister of Newport remembered 'It sank in minutes. My friend Ginger Perkins, from Pill, ent down with her. I was terrified, but you don't have time to think. The next thing I remember was coming around in the sickbay of HMS Weston. I never expected to survive and thought I was in heaven. Only 11 of the crew of 60 survived.' (From 'Death and Donkeys' Breakfasts.')

Lorient-(Evans Thomas Radcliffe)-5.5.43- former French ship, torpedoed & sunk by U125 south of Cape Farewell, a straggler from convoy ON55 from London to New York - all 40 dead.

Maclaren-(Guardian Line of Cardiff/Stuart Management Co.?)-3.12.41-sunk by a mine en route from Liverpool to Barry - 2 dead.

Mervyn-(Mervyn Steam Shipping Co-Martyn, Martyn & Co)-1.11.39 sank after collision with SS Langleeford in the Barry Roads. The Mervyn was a regular visitor to Barry Docks, and was known to the coal tippers there as "The Rattle Basket", because of the noise generated by the sound of the cargo when being loaded. She was struck amidships, causing considerable damage, developed a heavy list, and started to sink. The crew scrambled into the lifeboats and cast off before she finally went down. 4 dead.

Moidart-(a Cardiff ship?)-27-7-40 sunk by mine off Harwich en route London to Newcastle 9 dead.

Nailsea Court-(E.R. Management)-10.3.43- torpedoed & sunk by U 229, in convoy SC121 New York to London, S of Iceland - 45 lost, 4 survivors.

Nailsea Lass-(E.R. Management)--24.2.41- torpedoed & sunk by U 48, a straggler from SLS64, 60 miles W of Fastnet - 5 lost.

Nailsea Manor-(E.R. Management)-10.10.41- torpedoed & sunk by U 126, a straggler from OS7 Newport-Belfast-Freetown-Suez, near Cape Verde Is - all saved.

Nailsea Meadow-(E.R. Management)-11.5.43- torpedoed & sunk by U 196 off Cape Colony - 2 lost, 45 survivors

Newton Lass, Graig -(Graig Shipping is said to have lost both these ships along with the Graigwen noted above, but more information is needed)

Newton Pine-(Idwal Williams)- 15.10.42- torpedoed and sunk by U410 in Atlantic- UK to New York carrying ballast, a straggler from ONS136 – all 47 dead.

New Westminster City(2)-(Reardon Smith)-3.4.42- bombed & sunk Murmansk.

Nordeflinge-(Constants)-30-5-44 (night attack) - in convoy KMS51 from Algiers to Italy, attacked by over 30 bombers and sunk with 12 dead.

Ocean Vanguard-(Seager)-13.9.42- torpedoed & sunk by U515 70 miles E of Trinidad - 10 crew & 1 gunner lost.

Orminster-(Saint Line)-25.8.44- torpedoed & sunk by submarine U480 NW of Cap d'Antifer, a straggler from FTM74, PJune Beach, Normandy-Portsmouth – 4 crew lost, 59 survivors.

Pengreep/Empire Fal-(Chellew)-2.7.45- In June 1941 she was seized by Vichy French at Casablanca & renamed "St.Jacqueline" - regained in 1943 and renamed Pengreep and then Empire Fal. Scuttled in Atlantic 2.7.45 with gas ammunition cargo.

Penolver-(Chellew)-19.10.43-Mined & sunk near St. Johns, Newfoundland - 27 lost- no survivors.

Penrose-(Chellew)-3.9.42- torpedoed & sunk by U 107, 3 miles from Cape Sines, Portugal - 2 lost.

Pensilva-(Chellew)-19.11.39- torpedoed & sunk off Cape Ortegal by U 49.

Pontypridd(2)-(Morel)-11.6.42- torpedoed and damaged by U 569, & then sunk E of Newfoundland by U 94 outward voyage Immingham - Father Point - Sydney (ballast) - straggler from convoy ONS100 – 2 dead.

Porthmeor-(Care Lines)-20.8.41- 8 dead. Incomplete information.

Prince Rupert City-(Reardon Smith)-2.6.41- bombed & sunk NE of Cape Wrath.

Quebec City-(Reardon Smith)-19.9.42- torpedoed & sunk in convoy SD415 by U 156 N of Ascension Island.

Queen City-(Reardon Smith)-21.12.42- torpedoed by Italian submarine Enrico Tazzoli & then sunk by gunfire E of Para, Brazil, en route Table Bay to Trinidad and UK.

Radchurch-(E.R. Management Co)-9.8.42- torpedoed & sunk by U176 carrying iron ore from Wabana to Sydney to Barry, SE of Cape Farewell – sank in 10 seconds - 2 dead.

Ramillies-(John Cory)-8.5.41- torpedoed & sunk by U97, in dispersed convoy OB317, en route Oban to Baltimore, off Cape Farewell- 29 dead, 12 survivors.

Ripley-(Saints Line)-12.12.42- torpedoed & sunk by submarine U161, SW of St Paul's Rocks, carrying palm oil - all 41 crew saved.

Rose Schiaffino-3.11.41- This was a former Tatems ship sold to France, but seized by the RN off Gibraltar, and its homeport was thereafter Cardiff - torpedoed & sunk by U374, 225 miles E of St Johns carrying iron ore – all 40 crew and Master Thomas Evans died.

[Rossmoor?-Cardiff?-25.3.41-bombed and sunk by aircraft- 6 dead]

Ruckinge-(Halford Constants)-19.12.41- torpedoed by U108 west of Lisbon in convoy HG76, later shelled and sunk by HMS Samphire-41 survivors, 3 dead.

Ruperra-(John Cory)-19.10.40- torpedoed & sunk by U97, in convoy HX79, from NY to Leith, 90 miles SW of Rockall- 31 dead, 7 survivors.

Sacramento Valley-(Reardon Smith)-6.6.41- torpedoed & sunk by U 106 W of Cape Verde Islands, in convoy OB324 from Cardiff to Pernambuco. 3 dead, 46 survivors.

St.Elwyn-(Saint Line)-28.11.40- torpedoed & sunk by submarine U 103 E of Bishops Rock - 29 crew lost.

St.Essylt-(Saint Line)-4.7.43- torpedoed & sunk by submarine U375 W of Algiers-1 dead.

St.Glen-(Saint Line)-6.9.40- bombed & sunk by aircraft off E coast of Scotland- 3 dead.

St.Helena-(Saint Line)-12.4.41- torpedoed & sunk by submarine U124 SW of Freetown - 38 crew all saved.

St.Lindsay-(Saint Line)-14.6.41- torpedoed and sunk by U 751 SW of Iceland, from dispersed convoy OG64 – sank vertically in 80 seconds with all 43 hands.

St.Margaret-(Saint Line)-27.2.43- torpedoed & sunk by U66 SE of Bermuda – dispersed convoy ON165 – carrying general cargo and coal - 3 crew lost & Master taken prisoner.

St.Merriel-(Saint Line)-2.1.43- bombed & sunk by aircraft in Bone Harbour- 3 dead.

St.Usk-(Saint Line)-20.9.43- torpedoed & sunk by U161 SE of Bahia, Brazil. Master taken prisoner on U 161 and died when it was sunk a week later.

Salvus(2)-(Seager)-4.4.41- bombed & sunk in North Sea off Cromer- 4 dead

Santa Clara Valley-(Reardon Smith)-23.4.41- bombed & sunk Nauplia Bay. She had carried munitions, horses and mules for Greek and British troops, and was evacuating British soldiers. She was attacked by 41 bombers in a small convoy, 25 miles from Piraeus, hit and set on fire, carrying 200 tons of explosives. With 2 other ships she managed to reach the bay and start unloading, but was constantly attack by Stukas for 18 hours. There was only one death, with the crew rowing to shore despite being machine-gunned by planes. The ship was raised in 1952 for scrap.

Shakespear-(Saint Line)-5.1.41- torpedoed & sunk by Italian submarine 'Commandante Cappelini' after several hours of fighting (see Part Five), off Senegal. 20 dead.

[Statira-(Cardiff?)-3.8.40- bombed and sunk in The Minches, carrying aircraft]

Stokesley(2)-(J.T.Duncan)-24.4.40- mined & sunk near Nore Light, Thames Estuary- 12 dead.

Tacoma City(2)-(Reardon Smith)-13.3.41- mined & sunk Formby Channel , Mersey.

Thomas Walton-(Coronation Shipping-Frank S. Dawson)-3.12.39- torpedoed & sunk by U 38 S of Svolvaer, en route from Port Talbot to Narvik. 13 dead. The U 38 then fired a torpedo (which was fortunately defective) at the ship rescuing the 31 survivors, the German merchantman Sebu.

Vancouver City-(Reardon Smith)-14.9.39- torpedoed & sunk by U 28 off Cork, en route Suva, Fiji to Liverpool carrying sugar. 3 dead, 30 survivors. Raymond Keyse of Newport had a lucky escape when he fell out of the lifeboat, and returned to Newport to sign on at the Shipping Federation in Dock Street. His brothers Trevor joined the Anglo-Saxon and Donald joined the Koranton, and both died on these ships (their sinkings are dealt with in this book). His 3 remaining brothers all served their country - Bernard was on the aircraft carrier Illustrious, Augustus on the cruiser Newcastle and Clifford in the Royal Engineers. There is a parallel with the Hortop brothers of Barry, with 6 brothers at sea and one in the land forces (see Chapter 13)

Vera Radcliffe-(Evans Thomas Radcliffe)-30.3.44- used as a blockship in Normandy landings.

Vernon City-(Reardon Smith)-28.6.43- torpedoed & sunk by U 172, in dispersed convoy OS49 in S. Atlantic, outward voyage Oban to Montevideo.

Victoria City-(Reardon Smith)-2.12.40- torpedoed & sunk by U 140 NW of Ireland – en route Halifax NS to London carrying steel - all 43 crew lost.

Vulcain-(Tatems)-24.5.41- former French ship torpedoed & sunk by U38 in dispersed convoy OB318, 160 miles NW of Freetown en route from Newport and Barry – Captain Jack Lewis – carrying coal -34 survivors and 7 lost.

West Wales(2)-(Gibbs)-29.1.41- torpedoed & sunk by U94 off NW Ireland – outward voyage New York & Halifax, NS - Newport (steel) - 16 lost - Convoy SC19.

Wilamette Valley-(Reardon Smith)-26.9.40- she was requisitioned by the Royal Navy in 1939 and converted to a decoy ship, the special service vessel HMS Edgehill (X39), and was torpedoed & sunk by U 51 in the S.W. Approaches. Cornelius Blake of Newport served on her, and believes that she was discovered to be a 'Q ship' by the deliberate ramming of a Spanish tug in Gibraltar, which exposed the guns behind her shutters – his story is recounted in 'Death and Donkeys' Breakasts'.

Winkleigh-(Tatem)-8.9.39- torpedoed & sunk by U48 500 miles W of Brest outward voyage Vancouver – Panama - Manchester (lumber & grain).

LLANELLY (sic)

Afon Towy-6-8-41- 9 dead when she grounded on Haisbro' Sands and broke her back.

Sarastone- this Llanelli collier, when a straggler from OG47 damaged an Italian submarine around 25.12.40 carrying coal to Lisbon, and Captain Herbert did not press home the attack as he was under orders not to risk his cargo. She was bombed and sunk by a FW Condor 29.10.41, with the 70 year-old ship's engineer dying. Another crew member died of his injuries 3 years later and has been awarded war grave status, being buried in Bronllys.

SWANSEA

Canford Chine-(Chine Shipping)-10.2.41 – torpedoed and sunk by U 52, SSW of Rockall carrying coal from Cardiff to Buenos Aires, a straggler from OG52 for two days. All 35 crew lost.

Dione II–(Ambrose, Davies & Matthews)-3.2.41, a straggler from SC20 from Sydney NS to Cardiff, carrying iron ore, bombed and damaged by Condor aircraft. 4.2.41- shelled and sunk NW of Co. Galway by U 93. 5 survivors 28 dead.

Fort Medine-(Reardon Smith managed)- 20.2.41- a French ship seized at Falmouth, 2.7.40, and managed as a Ministry of War Transport, mined off Mumbles Light, 1 dead (its French master).

Katvaldis-(Stockwood, Rees)-25.8.42- torpedoed and sunk SE of Cape Farewell by U 605. A former Latvian ship, requisitioned as a MOWT. 40 survivors, 3 dead.

Kellwyn-(Stockwood, Rees)-27.7.41- torpedoed and sunk by U 79 outward voyage Oban to Lisbon carrying coke, 350 miles WNW of Cape Finisterre – 14 dead, 9 survivors.

Medjerda-(F.C. Strick)-18.3.44- torpedoed and sunk by U 105, a straggler from SL68, north of Cape Verde Islands. Inward voyage Pepel-Freetown-Middlesbrough carrying iron ore. Sank in 30 seconds. All 54 drew dead.

Shelbrit I –(British Tanker Company)-19.9.40- this coastal tanker, on a voyage from Grangemouth to Inverness in ballast, blew up, caught fire and sank on September 19th, 1940, in the Moray Firth. All her crew of 20 and the gunner were lost. The most likely cause is a mine. We can see the effects of a 'local' ship's loss upon its home port, on the Tower Hill Memorial Panel 96, where 18 of the 21 deaths were of Swansea men:

AIRD, Chief Officer, GEORGE FREDERICK, M.V. Shelbrit I (Swansea). Merchant Navy. 19th September 1940. Age 40. Son of Albert and Phyllis Aird; husband of Hilda L. Aird, of Gravesend, Kent.

BOLTON, Second Engineer Officer, STANLEY, M.V. Shelbrit I. (Swansea). Merchant Navy. 19th September 1940. Age 38. Husband of Florence B. Bolton, of Gosforth, Newcastle-on-Tyne.

BREJDER, Greaser, ARTHUR ARVID, M.V. Shelbrit I. (Swansea). Merchant Navy. 19th September 1940. Age 62.

CAPPER, Pumpman, SAMUEL, M.V. Shelbrit I. (Swansea). Merchant Navy. 19th September 1940. Age 57.

GILL, Able Seaman, JOHN THOMAS, M.V. Shelbrit I. (Swansea). Merchant Navy. 19th September 1940. Age 29.

GRAHAM, Greaser, EDWARD, M.V. Shelbrit I. (Swansea). Merchant Navy. 19th September 1940. Age 28.

HUNTLEY, Greaser, WILLIAM HENRY, M.V. Shelbrit I. (Swansea). Merchant Navy. 19th September 1940. Age 30. Husband of I. Huntley, of Sunderland, Co. Durham.

JOHNSON, Steward's Boy, DENIS, M.V. Shelbrit I. (Swansea). Merchant Navy. 19th September 1941. Age 16.

JOHNSON, Greaser, HENRY GILL, S.S. Shelbrit I. (Swansea). Merchant Navy. 19th September 1940. Age 27.

KAVANAGH, Able Seaman, EDWARD, M.V. Shelbrit I. (Swansea). Merchant Navy. 19th September 1940. Age 58. Husband of Annee Kavanagh, of Arklow, Co. Wicklow, Irish Republic.

MANT, Able Seaman, FREDERICK GARNETT, M.V. Shelbrit I. (Swansea). Merchant Navy. 19th September 1940. Age 45. Husband of Helen Mant, of North Kessock, Ross and Cromarty.

MARTIN, Master, WILLIAM, M.V. Shelbrit I. (Swansea). Merchant Navy. 19th September 1940. Age 65.

MINISTER, Able Seaman, ROBERT STANLEY, S.S. Shelbrit (Swansea). Merchant Navy. 19th September 1940. Age 42. Son of Robert and Henrietta Minister; husband of G. E. Minister, of King's Lynn, Norfolk.

McVICKER, Third Engineer Officer, EDWARD, M.V. Shelbrit I. (Swansea). Merchant Navy. 19th September 1940. Age 38. Son of Matthew and Margaret McVicker.

OLIVER, Chief Engineer Officer, THOMAS VARDY, M.V. Shelbrit I. (Swansea). Merchant Navy. 19th Sep-tember 1940. Age 36. Son of Thomas Vardy Oliver and Elizabeth Oliver; husband of Evelyn Oliver, of West Hartlepool, Co. Durham.

SMITH, Boatswain, ERNEST, M.V. Shelbrit I. (Swansea) . Merchant Navy. 19th September 1940. Age 37. Husband of Nancy Vera Smith, of Spital Tongues, Newcastle-on-Tyne.

SMITH, Cook Steward, JOSEPH, M.V. Shelbrit I. (Swansea). Merchant Navy. 19th September 1940. Age 26.

TAYLOR, Second Officer, SAMUEL HERBERT, M.V. Shelbrit I. (Swansea). Merchant Navy. 19th September 1940. Age 56. Husband of I. S. Taylor, of Sunderland, Co. Durham.

WELLS, Assistant Cook Steward, SYDNEY BIRRELL, M.V. Shelbrit I. (Swansea). Merchant Navy. 19th September 1940. Age 17. DEMS Gunner Portsmouth Naval Memorial.

LAMPORT, Seaman, MAURICE, P/X 18710A. H.M.S. President III. Royal Naval Reserve. (lost in M.V. Shelbrit). 19th September 1940. Age 29. Son of Thomas and Alice Lamport, of South Shields, Co. Durham. Only one body was found from the Shelbrit I and is buried ashore.

STEWART, Fourth Engineer Officer, WALTER, S.S. Shelbrit I (Swansea). Merchant Navy. 19th September 1940. Age 34. Buried Carnmoney Cemetery, County Antrim. Section A.L. Grave 29.

Shelbrit II-(British Tanker Company). From 'The Times' Thu 7 Mar 1940 (p8): "AIR ATTACKS ON TANKER AND LIGHTSHIP" The Swansea tanker Shelbrit II *was attacked by bombs and machine-gun fire from two German aeroplanes off the North-East Coast of Scotland last night. The second officer, Mr. D. J. Thomas, was injured in the leg by a bullet."* The Second Officer was to die from his injuries sustained in the attack and is recorded on the Tower Memorial:

THOMAS, Second Officer, DAVID JOHN, M.V. Shelbrit II (Swansea). Merchant Navy. 6th May 1940. Age 36. Son of David and Hannah Thomas; husband of Ellen Josephine Thomas, of Borth. Buried Borth (St. Matthews) Churchyard South side of church.

Solon II-(Brockland of Liverpool, but its homeport was Swansea)-3.12.42. Torpedoed and sunk by U 508, carrying manganese ore and 2000 tons of copper, NE of Georgetown, British Guiana. The French ship Solon had been seized at Swansea and used as an MOWT. On voyage Turkey-Capetown-Pernambuco-Trinidad-Baltimore. 7 survivors, 75 dead.

Tafna-(F.C. Strick)- torpedoed and sunk by U 37, 80 miles W of Gibraltar, carrying iron ore Algeria-Gibraltar-London. 31 survivors, 2 dead.

Tunisia-(F.C. Strick)-4.8.41- bombed and sunk 300 miles W of Co. Mayo – see Captain Shute's report in Part Twelve. Only 5 survivors. 38 dead, of whom 19 were from Barry.

NEWPORT

Uskbridge-(Richard W. Jones)-17.10.40- torpedoed and sunk by U 93, NW of Rockall, carrying coal from Swansea to Montreal. 2 dead, 27 survivors.

Uskmouth-(Richard W. Jones)-25.11.39-torpedoed by U 43 WNW of Cape Farewell, and then shelled to sink her – 23 survivors, 2 dead.

FISHING VESSELS (steam trawlers varying between 140 and 340 tons)
Deaths recorded on the Merchant Navy Tower Hill Memorial
Cardiff trawlers
Naniwa – 16.2.41- bombed by aircraft - 5 dead
Oyama – 12.1.41 – unknown cause - 12 dead
Milford Haven trawlers
Charmouth – 14.11.46 – hit mine off Ireland - 9 dead
Craigewan – missing off S Irish coast after 12.10.45 – mined? - 10 dead
Cresswell – 12.11.39 – gunfire from submarine off Flannan Island - 6 dead
John Baptish – 9.9.40 - 13 dead
River Ythan – sailed out of Grimsby 12.44 - 12 dead
Thomas Deas – 16.2.41 – mined off Spurn Head - 13 dead
Westfield – 6.7.41 – aircraft, possibly gunfire off St Govan's Head - 10 dead
Whitby – 4.4.41 – sunk by aircraft off Blackwater LV
Ely – 14.1.45 – lost in collision
Milford Haven trawlers sailing from other ports
Aberdeen – 11.3.41 – bombed by aircraft off Cardigan Bay
Bass Rock – 24.9.41 – bombed by aircraft off Kinsale
Bianca – 20.3.41 – torpedo from aircraft
Exeter – 29.3.41 - bombed by aircraft off Ballycotton
Gozo – 27.7.45 – mined off Kinsale

Grenada – 3.10.45 – mined off Kinsale
Ressondo – 09.40 – lost with all hands off Kinsale
Tamura – 30.9.40 – mined off Falmouth
Togima – 11.2.40 – sunk by U37 off Ireland, 1 dead
Xania – 17.3.40 – sunk in collision
Milford Haven RN vessels (trawlers requisitioned along with crews, by Admiralty for the Royal Naval Patrol Service and as decoy vessels)
Aracari -3.10.43 – grounded on island off Sicily, total loss
Comet – 30.9.40 decoy vessel mined off Falmouth
Elk – 27.11.40 – mined off Cornwall
Elk(2) – 10.43 requisitioned by Admiralty 2.43
Manor – 9.7.42 OR 43?? – sunk by E-boat in English Channel
Milford Earl - ?.12.41 - bombed by aircraft at Lunan Bay, east coast of Scotland
Phineas Beard - ?.12.41 - bombed by aircraft at Lunas Bay, as above
Nogi – 23.6.41 - bombed by aircraft off Norfolk
Thomas Bartlett – 28.1.40 – hit British mine off Calais
Thomas Connolly – 17.12.40 – mined off Sheerness
Tranio – 26.6.41 – bombed by aircraft, North Sea
Swansea trawlers
Caerphilly Castle – 27.1.41 – bombed by aircraft - 3 dead

For the trawler John Baptish, of Milford Haven, we have the following remembrance from the 'West Wales Guardian', 27th September 1940:
Milford Haven has stood up to many blows in its time and come up smiling, but the past few days has filled the town's cup of sorrow to overflowing. The trawler left for the fishing grounds on Saturday, Sep 7th, and on a normal fortnight trip would have been in by the 21st. Meanwhile other trawlers reported that this boat had steamed for home with a big catch of herrings. It was hoped that all these stories were wrong and the boat was on a hake trip, but on Wednesday of this week Mr. O.W. Limbrick, a director of the company, issued the sad news that the vessel was now overdue and believed lost. She was in charge of Skipper W.J. McLean, 22, Shakespeare Avenue. The other twelve crew members were:
Mate - A.E. Pritchard, 50, Priory Road, Milford.
Bosun - J.H. Garton, 1, Canopus Avenue, Hessle Road, Hull.
Third Hand - J.R. Freeman, 21, Greville Road, Milford.
Deck Hand - Samuel Nelson, 35, Midway Grove, Gipsyville, Hull.
Spare Hand - H. Anson, 2, St. George's Grove, Gipsyville, Hull.
Spare Hand - H. Wordsworth, 10, Appleby Terrace, St. Paul Street, Hull.
Spare Hand - V.L. Bird, 64, Pharos Street, Fleetwood.
Cook - R. Jordan, The Strand, Rosslare, County Wexford.
Chief Engineer - W.H. Hughes, Hill Crescent, Merlin's Bridge, Haverfordwest.
Second Engineer - J.E. Thomas, 39, Portfield Avenue, Haverfordwest.
Fireman - A.L.G. Badham, 19, Merlin's Crescent, Haverfordwest.
Fireman - J.W. Eynon, Hillblock, Picton, Haverfordwest.
"Skipper McLean was an experienced fisherman, a hard working and conscientious man," said Mr Limbrick. Skipper McLean, who was 56 years of age, was one of the most popular Milford Skippers. A native of Brixham, he leaves a widow, five sons and one daughter.

Two of his sons are serving in the Navy and a third in the Royal Air Force. He came to Milford over forty years ago and had been one of the most successful skippers in the port, having sailed with most of the firms, including Brand and Curzon, and Mr Lawford's. During the last war (1914-1918) he served four and a half years in the minesweepers and was mentioned several times in despatches, the last on July 2nd, 1917. When this present war broke out he tried all he knew to join up but each time he was told to continue with his work of bringing in the food. Apart from his home and his work he had few interests, but his genial presence was always welcome at the Old Priory Lodge of Freemasons, of which he was a member.

A.E.Pritchard, his Mate, was a native of Hull. He leaves five children to mourn. Another Hull man, Garton, was a married man with family. Bob Freeman, the Third Hand, was a native of Milford. He was only twenty seven years old and was the sole support of his widowed mother. Little is known in the port about the Hull men who had just come round to the west to fish. It was the first trip out of the port for both Anson and Wordsworth, but Garton and Nelson were on their second trip. Little is known of Bird, a recent arrival at the port from Fleetwood. Jordan, an Irishman, was a married man with a family.

The four Haverfordwest men have all been going to sea for some time. Hughes was a married man and lived with his parents at Merlin's Bridge. There are no children. Badham was a native of Chepstow but has lived at Haverfordwest for some time. He was married but had no family. J. E. Thomas, Portfield Avenue, was a son of the late Mr Job Thomas, Haroldston Farm. He served in the last war and leaves a widow and grown-up family. James Eynon, Picton, was only twenty six and had been on Milford trawlers for some years. He was a single man and lived at home with his father, a widower.

There were approximately 105 Cardiff ships sunk in the war, 1198 men died. The sinkings were caused by Uboat (68), aircraft bombing (16), mines (8), Italian submarines (4), merchant raiders Orion and Atlantis (2), the warship Admiral Scheer (1), E-boat (1), manned torpedo (1), unknown (1), collision (1), used as a blockship (1) and scuttled (1). Of Swansea ships, 10 were sunk, 6 by U-boat, 2 bombed and 2 mines, for the loss of 271 men. Llanelli lost two ships, 1 grounded and 1 to aircraft bombing, with 10 dead, and Newport had 2 ships torpedoed, losing 4 crew. Trawler losses are incomplete.

Welsh merchant shipping losses = 119 ships and 33 fishing boats or converted trawlers
Men lost from Welsh ships = 1532 from ships and over 100 from boats
<u>Causes of Sinking of Merchant Ships</u> (not fishing trawlers)
Submarines and manned torpedoes – 81
Aircraft bombing - 22
Mines- 10
Surface craft – 4
Other – 6

PART FIFTEEN

The Atlantic Convoy System and U Boats

'The only thing that ever frightened me during the war was the U Boat peril.'
– Winston Churchill

With all the publicity about the capture of the Enigma machine and the wonderful work of the decoders at Bletchley Part, the failures of British intelligence in the War have been glossed over. In the time when we could not decipher German codes, they could decipher our, making Allied convoys 'sitting ducks' for wolf-packs of U boats. British intelligence also seriously underestimated the threat of U boats to this country's survival. Thankfully, so did Hitler until it was too late, after his failure to invade Britain. The fate of Britain had hung by a thread – the success of merchant shipping. Churchill understood this – it was his greatest, possibly his only, fear during the war years. With a little more foresight by the German High Command – if they had listened to Admiral Doenitz – the war would have been lost. That is the importance of the heroes of the Merchant Navy.

We also tend to think of the Merchant Navy bringing food and vital supplies to Britain, but equally it supplied our forces around the world with troops, food, fuel and equipment. Without it the nation would have starved, and our forces would not have been able to fight.

At the start of the war, both Britain and Germany saw the main threat as coming from Germany's big ships. These were meant to cut off all of Britain's oil, and most of its raw materials and food. U boats were considered complementary, operating in coastal waters. The plan may have worked, but Britain and France declared war on Germany before Hitler's building programme of battleships was completed. Poland had been invaded, and Hitler had not expected war so soon.

U boats were slow underwater, but faster on the surface than any convoy, and even their escorting corvettes. With a low silhouette, they could not be easily seen, even when on the surface, compared to the towering merchant ships. Doenitz had wanted 300 U boats to blockade Britain when the war started, but only had 57, most of them small coastal 250-tonners. Only 27 were able to operate in the Atlantic. Until France fell in summer 1940, and bases were built on its Atlantic coast, their voyage into the open waters of the Atlantic was difficult and dangerous, having to travel up the North Sea and around Britain.

Not until September 1940 was Doenitz able to properly deploy the wolf-pack system. He had conceived the idea of wolf-packs as early 1918, when he was captaining a submarine. The U boats received signals when a convoy was in progress, and assembled in a line across its route. The convoy was allowed to pass through while the U boats manoeuvred into favourable attacking positions. As soon as the first U boat was sighted, the U boats were free to attack. With the failure of Operation Sea Lion to invade England in 1940, Hitler agreed with Doenitz and switched resources into building more U boats. Doenitz developed the French ports of Brest, Lorient, St Nazaire, Bordeaux and La pallice to protect, refuel, repair and re-arm his fleets. At the same time Germany developed more powerful radio transmitters, enabling him to co-ordinate his U boats across the Atlantic.

The assembly point for faster North Atlantic convoys, capable of 10-15 knots was Halifax, Nova Scotia, and Sydney Nova Scotia was chosen for slower vessels. Many of the latter would not have been allowed to sail in peacetime, such was their condition, but Britain was running out of supplies and food, as were its armed forces overseas. From December 1941, with the entry of the USA into the war, New York was also used for slow convoys that could not maintain a steady speed of 10 knots. Bigger, faster ships such as the Queen Mary were often allowed to make their own way as they could outrun a U boat.

Britain simply did not have enough available resources to properly protect convoys – capital ships were required to guard against the threat of invasion, and the French surrender meant that the RN had to take the French navy's role in protecting the Mediterranean. It was thought that ASDIC would be sufficient to deal with the U boat threat. However, ASDIC only worked in locating submerged U boats, finding their range and bearing by using sound location. It only worked in 'good' conditions, which the Atlantic rarely offered. It only worked to a maximum range of 2000 yards. Only some destroyers were equipped with it at the start of the war, and few could be spared to protect convoys. And convoys were generally attacked by surface U boats, at night, on the surface. The commander of U 61 made the point that U boats were basically surface raiders 'that had the ability to dive.' Of the 20 ships U 61 sank, 19 were sunk from the surface… *'at night, if you were closer to your target than 3000-4000 metres, then from the bridge of a normal merchantman, the conning tower does not appear above the horizon. You only offer a small silhouette to your target, almost invisible.'*

Despite Doenitz having written a book, 'Die U-Bootswaffe', available on the open market, on U boat tactics and training, on using wolf-packs to attack on the surface at night, etc., British intelligence did not have a copy. There was no strategy to deal with wolf-pack attacks. The convoy would disperse, ships zigzagging madly away from a far quicker enemy (17 knots on the surface), which could see their targets, but be seen with difficulty.

A U boat spent 90% of its time on the surface. Underwater, it could only manage 7 knots, for a maximum of one hour. If travelling at 2 knots, it could stay underwater for only 36 hours. When it dived, the engines were shut down, and it was battery-propelled. On the surface, a 4-man watch was stationed on the conning tower. In one Atlantic storm, all 4 men on one U-boat were swept away, as the boat could not be controlled at periscope depth. She either had to ride it out on the surface, or descend to the depths. They trailed a target by day, just out of sight, listening to signals and spotting smoke trails from steam ships, and attacked on the surface at night.

Thus, at the start of the war, between July and October, U boats sank 144 unescorted Allied ships and 73 poorly escorted ships. Worse was to come, as wolf-packs formed, Germany read Allied convoy signals, and more U boats came into service. On September 21st, 1940, the fast convoy HX72 was attacked by U boats. 11 of the 41 ships were sunk, and the convoy commodore was certain that at least 2

U boats were involved. The slow convoy of 35 ships SC7 confirmed to the Admiralty that attacks were being co-ordinated, with the Cardiff ships Fiscus and Beatus being sunk. It left Sydney, Nova Scotia for the UK, hoping to make 8 knots, but there were soon stragglers. One of these, the Canadian SS Trevisa was lost on October 16th, 1940. She sent a distress signal but the lone escort, the sloop HMS Scarborough, could not leave its station.

On October 17th, the convoy was reinforced by the sloop Fowey and the new corvette Bluebell (which had picked up survivors from the Trevisa), but 3 ships were lost, including the oil tanker Languedoc. On the 18th, 7 ships went down, including the iron ore ship Creekirk bound for Cardiff, with all 31 hands being lost. On the 18th the sloop Leith and corvette Heartsease joined, but the convoy was still attacked as the escorts picked up survivors. On the 19th, 9 ships were lost, including the Empire Brigand, the commodore's ship SS Assyrian and the SS Fiscus.

Thankfully for the remnants of SC7, the U boats were alerted that a new and faster convoy, HX79, was approaching and they broke off the attack to sink another 14 ships from that convoy. In all, 34 ships were sunk in 48 hours. We must remember that in these early years of the war, there were rarely more than 12 U boats at sea at any one time. If Donitz had achieved his 300 U boat target, the war would have been over for Britain.

Ship SC7	Nation	Date	Cargo	Dest.	Hit by	Deaths & Survivors
Trevisa	Can	16.10	lumber	Aberdeen	U124	7d, 14s
Languedoc	UK	17.10	oil	Clyde	U48	0d, 41s
Scoresby	UK	17.10	pit props	Sunderland	U48	0d, 39s
Aenos	Greek	17.10	grain	Manchester	U38	4d, 25s
Convallaria	Swed	18.10	lumber	Glasgow	U46	0d
Gunborg	Swed	18.10	pulpwood	Medway	U46	0d, 23s
Fiscus	UK	18.10	steel	Clyde	U99	38d, 1s
Niritos	Greek	18.10	sulphur	Garston	U99	1d, 27s
Creekirk	UK	18.10	iron ore	Cardiff	U101	36d, 0s
Emp. Miniver	UK	18.10	steel/iron	Newport	U99	3d,
Beatus	UK	18.10	steel/wood	Tyne	U46	0d, 37s
Carsbreck	UK	18.10	lumber	Grimsby	U38	damaged
Shekatika	UK	18.10	steel/props	W. H'pool	U123	damaged
		18.10			U100	damaged
		19.10			U123	0d, 36s
Boekelo*	Dutch	18.10	lumber	London	U100	damaged
		19.10			U123	0d, 25s
Blairspey**	UK	18.10	lumber	G'mouth	U101	damaged
		19.10			U100	damaged
					U123	damaged
Clintonia	UK	19.10	pulpwood	Manchester	U99	damaged
					U123	1d, 34s
Thalia***	Greek	19.10	steel	Garston	U99	22d, 4s
Soesterberg	Dutch	19.10	pitprops	Hull	U101	6d
Sedgepool	UK	19.10	grain	Manchester	U123	3d, 36s
Emp. Brigade	UK	19.10	trucks	Tyne	U99	6d
Assyrian	UK	19.10	general	Liverpool	U101	19d, 29s

*Boekelo was hit rescuing survivors from Beatus.

**Blairspey was kept afloat by its cargo of timber, but not repaired until 1942.

***Thalia's 4 survivors and Fiscus' one survivor were picked up by the Snefjeld, which was then itself sunk.

Ship	Nation	Date	Cargo	Dest.	Hit by	Deaths &
HX79						Survivors
Wandby		19.10	lead, zinc	Middlesbro	U47	0d
Bilderdijk		19.10	grain		U47 or U38	0d
Ruperra	UK	19.10	aircraft	Glasgow	U46	30d
Matheran		19.10	zinc etc.	Liverpool	U38	9d
Uganda		19.10	steel/wood	Milford Hav	U38 or U47	0d
Shirak		19.10	kerosene	London	U47 U48	damaged 0d
Loch Lomond		20.10	steel/wood	Methil	U100	
Sitala		20.10	crude oil	Manchester	U100	1d
Caprella		20.10	fuel oil	Mersey	U100	1d
Whitford Point		20.10	steel	Liverpool	U47	37d
Janus		20.10	fuel oil	Clyde	U46	
La Estancia		20.10	sugar	Belfast	U47	1d
Athelmonarch		20.10	molasse	Liverpool	U47	damaged

Apart from intercepting convoy signals, and being linked by radio, U boats were assisted by Condor aircraft. These long-range reconnaissance bombers would report shipping movements. For some time the sinking of merchant ships, including neutral ones, was blamed upon mines, rather than U boats. The Condors were suspected. The Prize Regulations governing the Conduct of Nations at War at Sea were deliberately ignored, and British intelligence only realised what was happening when aircraft spotted surface U boats at sea. In fact, whereas the British, and later the Americans, ignored the use of their Sunderlands and Liberators for some time, Condors operated up to 800 miles out in the Atlantic from the Bay of Biscay, and sank 46 ships in January and February of 1941 alone, while U boats sank 60 ships in this period.

German intelligence, B-Dienst, informed U boat commanders of convoy destinations, and co-ordinated operation up until the moment of attack. The first U boat to make contact, 'the shadower', kept out of sight but recorded the convoy's strength, numbers, location, course and speed. While it was transmitting this information other U boats sped to a rendezvous. Condors sometimes assisted in gathering information, and reported back to B-Dienst. When enough U boats were assembled, an attack began, at night, simultaneously from 700-5000 metres. Overlapping targets were chosen, with the furthest being fired on first and the nearest last. This way, the explosions would be around the same time, not allowing ships warning time to divert their courses. Torpedoes with magnetic pistols were designed to impact beneath the target, breaking the hull in two. Early gas-powered torpedoes left a trail of bubbles, which could be spotted, but late electric torpedoes were wakeless.

For the first year of the war, Admiralty codes were easily decoded, until September 1940 when codes were changed to 'Naval Code Number One'. B-Dienst reacted by using Luftwaffe Gruppe 40, placed under the command of Doenitz. This force of Focke-Wulf Condors was used to gather convoy and shipping intelligence, and Churchill named them 'the scourge of the Atlantic.' The situation was grim for Britain, a fact not lost upon Roosevelt's government. It assisted the British war effort, principally because the fall of Britain would mean that it would be alone at the centre of the victorious Axis of Germany and Japan.

In fact, 1940 was known as 'The Happy Time' ('Die Gluckliche Zeit') by U boats crews. They were virtually invincible. But as defeat loomed for Britain, it urgently gave up overseas bases in return for 50 old World War I destroyers from America. However, these old Lease-Lend destroyers, if escorting, were too slow to be effective in defence against a pack of U boats, and their inefficient boilers gave off smoke which could be seen for miles, making convoy-spotting easier. Destroyers which had been kept in reserve to fight off the expected invasion were released for convoy escort duties. Corvettes were built, specifically for escort duties. Most importantly, radar was invented, allowing destroyers to detect surface U boats. Losses amongst U boats began to escalate.

There was a second 'Happy Time' when the USA entered the war. 'Lights Out' was not enforced along its Eastern seaboard, and ships passing Florida were outlined against its bright lights. The same was true off New York, and Donitz sent 21 U boats to operate in the area, sinking 505 ships. In 1941, Condors sank 371 ships and U boats sank 432 ships. With other causes such as mines, total Allied losses were 1299 ships, and they were being sunk more quickly than they could be replaced. In 1942, 1644 ships were sunk, and U boat strength was raised from a fleet of 94 to one of 212 by the end of that year.

However, at long last the tide turned. Huge numbers of American 'Liberty-ships' and Canadian 'Fort' and 'Park' ships were manufactured, more than replacing merchant losses. There were new developments in depth-charging. Previously the ship had to pass over a U boat and drop them over the stern. Now the 'hedgehog' could throw a pattern of 24 depth-charges in front of the corvette or destroyer, and the 'squid' did the same with three. More powerful depth-charges were available. There were more escorts, especially corvettes. Ideally, there would now be a destroyer leading a convoy, with one following up, and around 5 sloops, frigates or corvettes guarding its flanks. From 1941, some convoys had 'rescue ships' trailing behind to undertake the dangerous job of picking up survivors, allowing the destroyers to 'search and destroy.' Planes were also used to protect it within range of home and destination ports. As more plane cover was available, Doenitz moved his fleet out of their range, to an area 300 miles wide in the mid-Atlantic, known as the 'Atlantic Gap' or 'the black pit' because of Allied losses there. U boats there were supplied by specially equipped ships, 'milch-cows', which carried torpedoes and supplies.

An improved radar system was almost universally fitted, not only to ships but also to Coastal Command aircraft. The 'Huff-Duff' (HF/DF, or High Frequency Direction Finder) and an improved ASDIC were also employed. Admiral King, Commander-in-Chief of Eastern Seaboard, at last enforced a blackout and President

Roosevelt released Liberators to protect convoys.

Importantly, in May 1941, an Enigma machine was captured from U110. The Admiralty code had been known throughout the war, allowing U boats to pick off convoys at will when the resources were available. U boat commanders complained to Doenitz that their codes had been broken, and that their whereabouts were now known to convoys, but he refused to believe it. They knew that convoys were altering course to avoid waiting lines of U boats. British Intelligence at last was working for the merchant seamen. Great care seems to have been taken in Admiralty signals not to divulge the fact that Enigma had been broken. The cipher battle continued as B-Dienst broke 'Naval Code Number 3', and knew convoy routes well in advance, allowing the interception of no les than 10 convoys from August to October 1942. By 1943, U boat deployments were based upon the analysis of intercepted British messages. Also, by February 1942, Donitz (now head of the German Navy) had insisted on a 4th wheel being added to Enigma, and German messages were not able to be decoded until December of that year. Convoys again were under threat.

From September 1942, Commander Johnny Walker devised the new hunter-killer groups of destroyers, whose duty was not just to defend the convoy, but to exterminate attacking U boats. The 'Atlantic Gap' was closed by new long-range Liberators. The evidence of success is shown in unsustainable U boat losses:

>   1939 – 9
>   1940 – 24 (including one U boat sunk twice)
>   1941 – 31
>   1942 – 82 (most from September on)
>   1943 – 242 (41 in May alone)
>   1944 – 252
>   1945 – 120 (in 5 months)

As the USA entered the war, in the first 4 months of 1942, 2.6millions tons of shipping was lost. By November 1942, at last the Allies were building more ships than were being lost – Donitz was losing the battle, and morale was still high among merchant seamen despite the terrible causalties suffered. Donitz believed that Allied crews would have been pushed to the brink of mutiny. Indeed, over 1000 ships were lost in the Atlantic in 1942 – almost half the total – and it is a tribute to seamen that they kept turning up at their 'pools' after discharge. >From 1943, after three brutal years, the balance of power in the Battle of the Atlantic swung to the Allied Forces.

The critical year was 1943. In January, HX224 was attacked by 5 U boats in two attacks, and they were driven off with the loss of 3 ships out of 57. In February SC118 was attacked by 16 U boats. Although the convoy lost 11 of its 63 ships, with one damaged, the U boat losses were significant to Doenitz. He called it 'the hardest convoy battle of the entire war', losing 3 boats with 4 seriously damaged. In his analysis, his ace Commander Forstner had sunk 7 of the 11 boats, with another 3 U boats sinking 4 between them. This showed Donitz that the new convoy protection system could only be penetrated by very special commanders with fully trained crews. The rest of the fleet did not have the expertise or experience of Forstner, as training time had been reduced because of the rapid expansion of the U boat fleet.

There were 5 more convoy battles in February, with 63 Allied ships being lost, but also U boats regularly disappearing. Donitz now had 70 boats scattered across the seas, and Allied losses reached a climax. In the first 10 days of March, 41 Allied ships were sunk, before the greatest convoy battle of the war took place. Over a distance of 100 miles, 100 ships in convoys HX229 and SC122 were attacked by 42 U boats. 22 ships were lost, compared to 1 U boat sunk and 3 badly damaged. The Admiralty was shaken – was the convoy system feasible? In the first 3 weeks of March 1943, 97 ships and escorts totalling 500,000 tons had been lost. Two thirds had been in convoys. The losses were twice the ship-building capacity of the Allies at that time, and the Admiralty admitted that these 20 days almost cut the Old World off from the New World.

Even more strength was devoted at sea and in the air to protect convoys in April, halting attacks on 3 of the 4 convoys, and there were only 56 losses of 330,000 tons in the whole month. Allied ship-building capacity had gone up to 590,000 tons per month, and Doenitz could see the writing on the wall. On May 4th 1943 was the real turning-point of the battle. There were 4 packs totalling 60 U boats in the Atlantic, and 41 converged on convoy ONS5. Although 13 ships were sunk and one damaged, 7 U boats were lost and 3 severely damaged. On May 10th, the escorts of HX237 sank 3 U boats for no convoy losses. In 4 other May convoys, 3 ships and 5 U boats were lost. 41 U boats in total were lost in May, with around 1000 submariners, including Doenitz' son Peter on his maiden voyage. By May 24, Doenitz had admitted that wolf-pack operations against North Atlantic convoys were no longer possible. Attacks were stopped and the battle was won.

CONVOY BATTLES

	Date	U Boats attacking	Convoy Losses
		1939	
OB-4	15 Sept	1	1 ship 4.060 tons
		1940	
HX-65	24 Aug	3	1 ship 6.666 tons
HX-65A	24 Aug	3	4 ship 23.151 tons
HX-72	20 Sept	9	11 ships 72.727 tons
SC-7	16 Oct	7	20 ships 79.592 tons
HX-79	19 Oct	5	12 ships 75.069 tons
HX-90	1 Dec	7	11 ships 73.958 tons
		1941	
SC-26	1 Apr	8	10 ships 51.969 tons
OB-318	7 May	4	10 ships 55.347 tons
HX-126	19 May	11	9 ships 51.862 tons
OG-69	24 Jul	8	7 ships 11.303 tons
OG-71	17 Aug	8	10 ships 15.185 tons
SC-42	9 Sept	19	16 ships 68.259 tons
HG-73	19 Sept	5	10 ships 25.818 tons
SC-48	15 Oct	13	11 ships 49.835 tons

HG-76	16 Dec	10	4 ships 18.383 tons
		1942	
ONS-67	21 Feb	6	8 ships 54.750 tons
ONS-92	11 May	6	6 ships 31.813 tons
ONS-100	8 Jun	6	5 ships 20.478 tons
PQ-17	1 Jul	15 and Luftwaffe	16 ships 102.311 tons 8 ships 77,000 tons
ON-115	29 Jul	12	3 ships 21.456 tons
SC-94	5 Aug	17	11 ships 53.421 tons
ON-127	9 Sep	12	8 ships 51.619 tons
PQ-18	12 Sept	5	3 ships 19.689 tons
SC-100	18 Sept	17	5 ships 26.331 tons
QP-14	20 Sept	7	6 ships 23.474 tons
SC-104	12 Oct	17	8 ships 43.970 tons
HX-212	26 Oct	13	6 ships 51.918 tons
SL-125	27 Oct	10	12 ships 80.005 tons
SC-107	30 Oct	16	15 ships 82.817 tons
ONS-144	15 Nov	13	6 ships 26.321 tons
ON-153	15 Dec	13	4 ships 19.551 tons
ONS-154	26 Dec	19	14 ships 69.893 tons
		1943	
TM-1	3 Jan	14	7 ships 56.453 tons
SC-118	4 Feb	20	11 ships 59.765 tons
ON-166	21 Feb	19	14 ships 88.001 tons
UC-1	22 Feb	11	3 ships 26.682 tons
SC-121	6 Mar	26	12 ships 55.661 tons
HX-228	10 Mar	19	5 ships 25.515 tons
UGS-6	12 Mar	17	4 ships 28.018 tons
HX-229	16 Mar	43	13 ships 93.502 tons
SC-122	17 Mar	43	9 ships 53.094 tons
RS-3	27 Mar	7	3 ships 15.389 tons
TS-37	30 Apr	1	7 ships 43.255 tons
ONS-5	4 May onwards	41	13 ships 61.958 tons but 6 U boats sunk and 7 damaged – **the turning point.**

MAY 1943 – THE END OF THE NORTH ATLANTIC BATTLE

In April 1943, U-boat strength was up to 425 with 240 boats operational, with over half of them on passage through or on patrol throughout the North Atlantic. However, there was somewhat of a lull until the end of the month with the start of the ONS5 battle. A group also operated once again in the weakly defended Sierra Leone area. In just one night U-515 sank seven of the 18 ships in Takoradi/Sierra Leone convoy TS37. Changes were again made in the Allies' responsibility for the North Atlantic routes. With these organisational changes, the far more effective convoy Escort Groups, and the developments described in March, the scene was set for the decisive convoy battles of May 1943

At the start of May, Doenitz was shaken to the core by the U Boat losses when attacking ONS5. He had over 40 U-boats deployed in three patrol lines off Greenland and Newfoundland, with another group to the far west of the Bay of Biscay. Others were passing through the northern transit area and en route between their French bases and the North Atlantic. More were on patrol in the South Atlantic.

There were many Allied convoys crossing the North Atlantic, and the slow ONS5, consisting of 42, ships from was outward bound from Liverpool for North America. The convoy sailed on April 21st, and escort was provided by the British B7 group (Cdr P. W. Gretton) consisting of two destroyers, a frigate, four corvettes and two trawlers. At the end of April U 710 was sunk by an escorting RAF B-17 Flying Fortress south of Iceland. In early May, south of Greenland, all three U-boat patrol lines closed in. However, before the U boats arrived, the escort had been reinforced by the 3rd Escort Group from St John's, Newfoundland. Rough seas made refuelling difficult and some of the escorts had to leave, so the 1st Escort Group (EG) sailed from St John's to replace them.

Over the next few days 13 merchantmen were lost, but at a cost of a further six U-boats. All went down in often confused fighting to the south of Greenland or northeast of Newfoundland. More still were damaged. Type 271 radar played a large part in the escort's successes:

May 4th - U-630 sunk by a RCAF Canso (Catalina).

May 5th - B7 group corvette Pink sank U192, and sister ship Loosestrife sank U638.

May 6th - B7 group destroyer Vidette sank U125; Destroyer Oribi detached from convoy SC127, to join B7 together with corvette Snowflakeand sank U531. U-433 was sunk by the sloop Pelican of the 1st EG.

The surviving U-boats were regrouped for attacks on other convoys, but in the area south of Greenland/northeast of Newfoundland as well as throughout the North Atlantic, merchantmen sinkings went down as U-boat losses mounted alarmingly. Much of this was due to the way escort groups (EG) moved from one convoy to another to support the existing escorts. The number of convoys crossing the North Atlantic in both directions is truly impressive and the main movements in May, together with the U-boats sunk, is listed below:

North America/UK HX236 - 46 ships escorted by British B1 group and 2nd EG (Capt Walker); no merchant ships lost.

May 11th - U528 was damaged by US aircraft in an earlier attack on ONS5. Now southwest of Ireland, she was sunk by the sloop Fleetwood and RAF aircraft of No 58 Squadron.

Slow UK/North America ONS6 - 31 ships escorted by British B6 group and 4th EG with escort carrier "Archer"; no merchant ships lost.

North America/UK HX237 - 46 ships escorted by Canadian C2 group and 5th EG with escort carrier Biter. Three stragglers sunk in exchange for possibly three U-boats in mid-Atlantic.

May 12th - U-89sunk by destroyer Broadway and frigate Lagan, both of C2 group, assisted by Swordfish of 811 Squadron from Biter. RAF B-24 Liberator of No 120 Squadron damaged either U456 or U753, which may have been finished off by destroyer Pathfinder of the 5th EG.

May 13th - Either U456 or U753 was detected by RCAF Sunderlands of No 423 Squadron which brought up frigate Lagan and Canadian corvette Drumheller to sink the U-boat.

North America/UK SC129 - 26 ships escorted by British B2 group, with 5th EG transferred from HX237 on the 14th. Two merchant ships lost in mid-Atlantic for two U-boats: May 12th - U-136 sunk by destroyer Hesperus of B2 (Cdr Macintyre). May 14th - U-266 to a RAF B-24 Liberator of No 86 Squadron.

UK/North America ON182 - 56 ships escorted by Canadian C5 group, with 4th EG and carrier Archer transferred from ONS6; no merchant ships lost.

North America/UK HX238 - 45 ships escorted by Canadian C3 group; no merchant ships lost.

Slow UK/North America ONS7 - 40 ships escorted by British B5 group, with 3rd EG transferred from ONS5. One ship lost for two U-boats destroyed in the vicinity of the convoy to the southeast of Greenland and south of Iceland: 14th - "U-657" to a US Navy Catalina. May 17th - U-640 sunk by frigate Swale of B5. (

UK/NorthAmerica ON183 - 32 ships escorted by British B4 group, no merchant ships lost.

North America/UK SC130 - 38 ships escorted by British B7 group, with 1st EG transferred from ONS5. No merchant ships lost in exchange for four U-boats south of Greenland: May 19th - U954 to a RAF Liberator; U209 to frigates Jed and Sennen of 1st EG; and U-381 to destroyer Duncan and corvette Snowflake of B7. May 20th - U-258 sunk by another RAF Liberator.

UK/NorthAmerica ON184 - 39 ships escorted by Canadian C1 group and US 6th EG with escort carrier Bogu. No merchant ships lost in exchange for one U-boat: 22nd - U-569 in mid-Atlantic sunk by Avengers flying from Bogue.

North America/UK HX239 - 42 ships escorted by British B3 group and 4th EG and carrier Archer transferred from ON182 (and before that ONS6). No merchant ships lost in exchange for one more U-boat: 23rd - In the first success with aircraft rockets, U752 in mid-Atlantic was badly damaged by HMS Archer's Swordfish of 819 Squadron, and was scuttled as surface escorts approached.

May 23rd - Italian submarine Da Vinci, returning from a successful patrol off South Africa, was detected and sunk northeast of the Azores by destroyer Active and frigate Ness.

By May 24th, U-boat losses had been so heavy against these 12 convoys, and the attacks so fruitless, that Doenitz ordered his captains to leave the North Atlantic. They either returned home or concentrated on the US/Gibraltar routes. It was some time before the Allies realised the North Atlantic was almost free of U-boats. The air and sea escorts were winning.

May 26th - U436 was sunk west of Cape Ortegal, Spain by the frigate Test and Indian corvette Hyderabad.

The 13th may convoy North America/UK SC131 - 31 ships were escorted by British B6 group, 3rd and 40th EGs ; no merchant ships lost.

Slow UK/North America ONS8 - 52 ships escorted by Canadian C4 group and 2nd

U BOAT ATLANTIC LOSSES (Italian Submarine losses in brackets)
ALLIED ATLANTIC MERCHANT SHIPPING LOSSES (all causes, and tonnage)

	1939	1940	1941	1942	1943	1944	1945
Jan	'	**1**	**1(1)**	**1**	**4**	**13**	**1**
Ships		9	59	48	30	5	5
		36,000	273,000	277,000	189,000	36,000	29,000
Feb	'	**2**	**1(1)**	**2**	**15**	**13**	**2**
		17	69	73	50	2	6
		75,000	317,000	430,000	310,000	12,000	39,000
Mar	'	**1**	**5**	**3**	**12**	**13**	**1**
		2	63	98	90	8	4
		11,000	365,000	547,000	538,000	41,000	27,000
Apr	'	**1**	**2**	**2**	**14(1)**	**13**	**7**
		4	48	74	40	7	5
		25,000	282,000	439,000	242,000	48,000	32,000
May	'	'	**1**	**1**	**37(1)**	**11**	**2**
		10	60	122	40	3	1
		55,000	336,000	585,000	204,000	17,000	5,000
June	'	**2**	**4(1)**	**2**	**16(1)**	**13**	'
		53	70	126	7	3	'
		297,000	329,000	650,000	30,000	7,000	'
July	'	**1**	'	**11(1)**	**34**	**7**	'
		34	23	101	29	4	'
		173,000	98,000	511,000	188,000	29,000	'

Month							
Aug	-	1 / 39 / 190,000	3(1) / 25 / 84,000	9(1) / 106 / 544,000	20 / 4 / 25,000	1 / 1 / 6,000	-
Sep	2 / 20 / 110,000	- / 53 / 272,000	2(2) / 53 / 200,000	9 / 102 / 531,000	6 / 11 / 54,000	5 / 3 / 17,000	-
Oct	2 / 22 / 133,000	1 / 56 / 287,000	2(1) / 33 / 160,000	15 / 82 / 548,000	23 / 13 / 61,000	1 / - / -	-
Nov	1 / 6 / 16,000	2(1) / 38 / 201,000	1(1) / 11 / 55,000	7 / 94 / 567,000	16 / 7 / 28,000	- / 3 / 8,000	-
Dec	- / 7 / 36,000	1 / 42 / 239,000	7 / 11 / 57,000	5 / 54 / 305,000	5 / 7 / 48,000	1 / 1 / 5,000	-
U Boat Totals	5	13(1)	29(8)	67(2)	202(3)	91	13
Ships	55	357	525	1080	328	40	21
%	2%	15%	22%	45%	14%	2%	1%

NB From December 1943, the above figures include Russian Convoy losses. >From the table below, we can see that there were 2232 merchant shipping losses in the North Atlantic and 174 in the South Atlantic, making 2406 in total. In the terrible year of 1942, ships were being sunk faster than they could be replaced, as the Allies were losing around 90 ships with a g.r.t of c.500,000 tons per month. In the 'Happy Time' of May to September, there was an average of 111 ships, and 560,000 tons, lost per month

EG (Capt Walker) transferred from HX236 ; no merchant ships lost.

North America/UK HX240 - 56 ships escorted by Canadian C5 group and 2nd EG from ONS8. No merchant ships lost in exchange for one U-boat: May 28th - U-304 sunk by a RAF Liberator of No 120 Squadron south of Greenland.

May 1943 North Atlantic Convoy Actions

15 convoys of 622 merchantmen, supported by:

7 British B and 5 Canadian C convoy groups; 6 British and 1US supporting Escort Groups; and 3 escort carriers

There were in excess of 70 U-boats at sea, of which 23 were sunk.

11 convoys were unharmed, but 4 convoys lost 19 ships - a loss rate of just 3%.

Without the heavy losses of ONS5, the loss rate was 1%.

Without the U-boats sunk in the attacks on OSN5, 16 U-boats were lost in exchange for 6 merchantmen

In fact, in May 1943 alone, in the North Atlantic the Axis forces lost:

37 German and 1 Italian U-boats. In addition to those lost in or around the convoy battles: 3 were sunk by the RAF in North Atlantic; 6 by RAF and RAAF Bay of Biscay patrols; 4 by US forces in the North Atlantic, off Florida and Brazil; and 2 by collision in the North Atlantic.

At the end of World War II, U-Boats at sea were ordered to surface, signal their position, and flying a black flag, make for whatever port the Allies indicated. On April 30, 1945, the German Navy ordered all warships to be scuttled on receipt of the codeword, Regenbogen (Rainbow), but the codeword was never transmitted. Scuttling began spontaneously on the assumption that higher authority could not communicate due to Germany's capitulation, and also because of straightforward defiance by captains who balked at handing over their commands to the enemy. On May 4, 1945, in the port of Kiel U4712 became the 782nd U-Boat lost to hostile action in the Second World War. On the same day, Grand Admiral Karl Doenitz ordered his fleet of submarines to cease hostilities.

Despite a personnel loss rate approaching 70%, U-Boats had kept fighting. In WWII, submarine losses were highest in the navy of Imperial Japan, which suffered a loss rate of 72% (130 of 181). Italy lost 59% of its submarine fleet - 85 of 144, most in the Med. Among Allied navies, Britain lost 76 of 216 (35%) and the US lost 52 of 288 (18%), including accidental loss - the highest casualty rate of any US naval service. But in sheer numbers, Germany's losses outrun the others. Of about 1,160 submarines the Kriegsmarine commissioned that went to sea, 462 boats succeeded in damaging or sinking at least one ship. Most of the rest were lost to Allied attack very early on in their seagoing career, before any torpedoes were ever launched.

Breaking the Enigma code, air superiority, radar and effective anti-submarine tactics decisively turned the Battle of the Atlantic in the Allies' favour, from late 1942 to early 1943. U-Boats in the Second World War sank about 2,778 ships worldwide (2,450 of them in the Atlantic), killing over 30,200 Allied merchant seamen. Of about 39,000 men who entered U-Boat service, most of them volunteers, 27,491 perished. They were on average about 20 years old, and sank around 68% by tonnage of all merchant shipping.

TOTAL MERCHANT SHIP LOSSES 1939-45
(British, Allied and Neutral)

Location	Number of Ships	%	Gross Registered Tonnage	%
North Atlantic	2,232	43	11,900,000	55
UK Waters	1,431	28	3,768,000	17
Pacific Ocean	515	10	1,348,000	6
Mediterranean	413	8	1,740,000	8
Indian	385	7	1,790,000	8
South Atlantic	174	3	1,024,000	5
	5,150		21,570,000	

The British supply problem during the war is shown by the above table. Over 70% of ALL merchant losses, both by ships and tonnage were sunk in the North Atlantic and British waters, and around three-quarters if we include the South Atlantic. Around 300,000 tons of shipping were lost per month of the war at sea.

MERCHANT LOSSES BY CAUSE

Cause of Sinking	Number of Ships	%	G.R.T.	%
Submarines	2,828	55	14,686,000	68
Aircraft	820	16	2,890,000	13
Other Causes	632	12	1,030,000	5
Mines	534	10	1,406,000	7
Raiders	133	3	830,000	4
Warships	104	2	498,000	2
Coastal forces	99	2	230,000	1
	5150		21,570,000	

PART SIXTEEN

The Patrols and Sinking of the U515

EXCERPT FROM REPORT ON THE INTERROGATION OF SURVIVORS FROM U-515 - SUNK 9 APRIL 1944 dated17 June 1944

NAVY DEPARTMENT - OFFICE OF THE CHIEF OF NAVAL OPERATIONS - WASHINGTON

As the U 515 was responsible for the deaths of many Welshmen, it is instructive to realise the circumstances under which they operated and were eventually destroyed. U 515 was fortunate that so many of its crew survived the war, although Kapitanleutnant Henke committed suicide in a Virginia interrogation camp. The following consists of excerpts from the official report, released 2 days after Henke's suicide.

'U-515 and U-68, both 750-ton U-boats, were sunk on 9 and 10 April 1944, in a coordinated air-surface action. A third U-boat suspected in the vicinity was also attacked, but apparently escaped. The units involved were the U.S.S. GUADALCANAL, U.S.S. PILLSBURY, U.S.S. POPE, U.S.S. CHATELAIN and aircraft of VC-58.

U-515, commanded by one of Germany's U-boat aces, Kapitänleutnant Werner Henke, was sunk at 1512 GCT 9 April 1944 at 34.31 N - 19.29 W. U-515 was first sighted by VT-24 from U.S.S. GUADALCANAL at 2113 GCT 8 April 1944. At 0027 and 0735 two depth bomb attacks were delivered by VT-23 and VT-31 (or VT-30). Soon thereafter U.S.S. PILLSBURY, POPE and CHATELAIN made contacts and over a period of 3_ hours two hedgehog attacks were made and 82 depth-charges were dropped on the submerged U-boat. Direct hits were scored by the destroyers when U-515 was forced to surface; in addition VT-25 delivered a successful R.P. attack several minutes prior to the sinking.

Sixteen men, including the executive officer and a midshipman, were killed. Henke, the Engineer Officer, the second watch officer, the doctor and forty petty officers and men were rescued. U.S.S. GUADALCANAL landed the prisoners at Norfolk 26 April 1944. After preliminary interrogation seventeen prisoners were further questioned at a U.S. interrogation centre.

U-515 was the most successful active U-boat of the 10th Flotilla. Henke had been decorated with the Oal Leaves to the Knight's Cross after claiming the sinking of 28 ships totalling 177,000 tons. This total was divided among the various patrols, as follows:

1st Patrol: (8 August 1942 - about 20 October 1942) - 10 ships totalling 54,000 tons.

2nd Patrol: (7 November 1942 - 5/6 January 1943) - 2 ships totalling 29,000 tons.

3rd Patrol: (c.20 February 1943 – c. 23 June 1943) - 12 ships totalling 72,000 tons.

4th Patrol: (29 August 1943 - 12 September 1943) - No ships sunk.
5th Patrol: (1 November 1943 - 16 January 1944) - 3 ships totaling
22,000 tons.
6th Patrol: (30 March - 9 April 1944) - No ships sunk.
    The handling of prisoners aboard U.S.S. GUADALCANAL was outstanding
and the work of the interrogation officers at the interrogation centre was greatly
facilitated by it.

GREATEST DEPTH - About 200 metres.
DIVING TIME -   35 Seconds to periscope depth.
BRIDGE STRUCTURE AND ARMOUR -   New bridge including Platform
II fitted August 1943 at Lorient. Armour plate around forward part of bridge about
16-mm. thick. New structure incorporated so-called "air raid shelter".
UPPER DECK GUNS
(a) On first 3 patrols: One 105-mm. gun forward of conning tower; One single 20-
mm. cannon on Platform I; One 37-mm. gun on after deck.
 (b) On 4th patrol: One 37-mm. gun forward of bridge; Two single 20-mm cannons
on Platform I; One quadruple 20-mm. mount on Platform II.
 (c) On fifth patrol: One 37-mm. gun forward of bridge; Two twin 20-mm. cannons
on Platform I; One twin 20-mm. cannon on Platform II.
 (d) On 6th and last patrol: Two twin 20-mm. cannons on Platform I; One new
automatic 37-mm. gun on Platform II.
AMMUNITION
(a) 8/9,000 rounds for 20-mm. cannon.
(b) About 2200 rounds for 37-mm. automatic gun.
PRESSURE-PROOF AMMUNITION CONTAINERS
(a) One containing 20-mm. ammunition on the aft part of Platform I.
(b) Three on each side of Platform II, the forward 1 on each side containing 20-
mm. ammunition, the other 2 on each side 37-mm. ammunition.
TORPEDO TUBES
Four forward, two aft.
TORPEDOES
Seventeen carried on last patrol. For further details see Chapter V.
DIESELS
Two 9-cylinder 2200 horse-power M.A.N. Diesels.
U-BOAT PRESSURE HULLS THICKENED
    The Engineer officer believed that in the future the pressure hulls of U-boats will
be thickened to withstand either greater depth or closer depth-charge attacks.
    WALTERBOATSThe building program of Walterboats has been abandoned
according to U-515's Engineer officer. The lack of rare metals required to withstand
the extreme temperatures generated in internal combustion turbines was cited as
the main reason. This prisoner was also convinced that up to now German scientists
have failed to solve the problem of an underwater craft with relatively high
submerged speed and endurance

CREW OF U-515

U-515 carried a crew of 60 officers and men on her 6th and last patrol. Of this number 6 were officers, 17 were petty officers and 37 were enlisted men.

COMMANDING OFFICER

U-515 was commanded by Kapitänleutnant Werner Henke, of the 1933 Term, ace German U-boat commander. He claimed the sinking of 28 ships totaling 177,000 tons. Henke had been decorated with the Knight's Cross of the Iron Cross in December 1942 and the Oak Leaves to the Knight's Cross on 4 July 1943. Henke proved extremely security-conscious. He professed preference for American captivity rather than British but this fact made him no more accessible. His interrogating officers found him sullen and embittered. His conceit was limitless although he somewhat grudgingly gave some credit for his success to his crew. He stated that his crew had been the best U-boat crew anywhere, anytime but also said that this was due entirely to the training he had given them. Henke did not mention, however, that he had held up advancement for many of them in order not to lose them.

His ability to keep the crew intact is confirmed by the following figures. Of 40 petty officers and men who survived, 16 had made all 6 patrols on U-515 and 14 of these men had not served on any other U-boat; 8 men had made 3 or more patrols on U-515; 16 had made less than 3 patrols. Only for 5 of the 40 men was the 6th patrol the first U-boat patrol ever. Five prisoners interrogated had made more than 10 U-boat patrols in all. The feelings of U-515's crew toward their commander were mixed. Some admired his personality, others held his extreme strictness against him. The surviving officers, although admitting his ability, acknowledged his frightful conceit. It seems that ashore Henke was particularly disliked and few in the 10th Flotilla and on the staff of the Admiral U-boats could forgive his boundless ambition and egotism. Politically he had few convictions, but he attempted to pass off the present German situation as "only temporarily bad". Henke stated that new devices and weapons such as radar and the automatic 37-mm. gun would soon bring about more successful U-boat patrols.

OFFICERS ON 5TH PATROL

Oberleutnant Hans Schultz (of the 1939-B Term) replaced Leutnant Harmeln as second watch officer. Schultz was not available for interrogation because of a bone infection resulting from a wound inflicted at the sinking of U-515. His career previous to the joining of U-515 is unknown. Aboard, he was stated to have been on unfriendly terms with his commander.

Leutnant (Ing.) Günther Altenburger had made 10 patrols in U-43 under Korvettenkapitän Lüth and 2 patrols in U-652 commanded by Kapitänleutnant Fraatz as engine room rating and machinist. He was then promoted officer and in October 1943 was assigned to U-515 to relieve Mahnken. Altenburger made U-515's fifth patrol nominally as "Konfirmand" (engineer officer under instruction) but actually his ability and knowledge gave him at least an equal standing with Mahnken. It was because of his ability that U-515 was able to continue her fifth patrol after a long and precise depth-charge attack early on that patrol. Altenburger had been recommended for the award of the Knight's Cross of the Iron Cross. Had the sixth patrol of U-515 been completed successfully he most certainly would have received the decoration. The reasons for the award were said to have been twofold: (a) Altenburger had done a splendid job in effecting repairs to U-515 after severe damage on the fifth patrol; (b) he had more than 500 days of sea duty aboard U-boats and the award of the Knight's Cross to a lower deck promotion would have boosted morale particularly in engine room personnel.

OFFICERS ON SIXTH AND LAST PATROL

Oberleutnant Benz succeeded Oberleutnant Niemeyer on U-515's sixth and last patrol. He was a casualty at the sinking. The doctor, Marineoberassistenzarzt Jörg Jensen, was a pleasant type, well liked by the crew. He had made his first U-boat patrol in U- 33. He had been awarded the Iron Cross 1st class.

Oberfähnrich Dohrmann, a casualty, was the third watch officer aboard U-515. All of the petty officers on U-515 were experienced men. They were cooperative and greatly lacking in security.

ENLISTED MEN

Almost all men talked freely. They were glad to look forward to periods of less excitement than the always dangerous patrols under Henke.

TACTICAL EXERCISES

Early in July, U-515 sailed for Gotenhafen and was included in the next group of U-boats doing their tactical exercises. These lasted about 10 days. Upon completion of the exercises, U-515 returned to the Oder-Werke, Settin, for final overhaul and preparation for the first patrol.

FIRST PATROL OF U-515

DEPARTURE

U-515 left on her first patrol on 8 August 1942 from Stettin. She called at Kiel for three days, topping up with oil and water. U-515 left Kiel about 11 August 1942 in company with two other 750-ton U-boats.

SINKINGS

It is believed that U-515 sank her first ship soon after arrival in the operational area assigned to her, namely off Trinidad. During the next two weeks, she claimed the sinking of 10 ships, totaling about 54,000 tons. The 6 ships definitely identified as having been sunk by U-515 are the following:

STANVAC MELBOURNE, Panamanian tanker, 10,013 tons, torpedoed and sunk 12 September 1942, at 10.30 N. - 60.20 W.

WOENSDRECHT, Dutch tanker, 4,668 tons, torpedoed and sunk 12 September 1942, at 10.27 N. - 60.17 W.

OCEAN VANGUARD, British freighter, 7,174 tons, torpedoed and sunk 13 September 1942, at 10.43 N. - 60.11 W.

MAE, U.S. freighter, 5,607 tons, torpedoed, shelled and sunk 17 September 1942, at 08.03 N. - 58.13 W.

REEDPOOL, British freighter, 4,838 tons, torpedoed and sunk 20 September 1942, 08.58 N. - 57.34 W. The captain of REEDPOOL was taken prisoner aboard U-515.

LINDVANGEN, Norwegian freighter, 2,412 tons, torpedoed and sunk 23 September 1942, at 09.20 N. - 60.10 W.

Prisoners claimed the sinking of 4 other ships. One of them was said to have been SENTA, Norwegian freighter, of about 3,500 tons. Nine ships were sunk in approximate area 100 N - 600 W. during the period of 12 and 16 September 1942. In addition to those identified above there were HARBOROUGH, KIOTE, NIMBA, SORHOLT, WICHITA and COMMERCIAL TRADER

RETURN TO BASE

A prisoner stated that U-515 continued to range along the South American coast in search of shipping, reaching a latitude of about 060 N. After her initial successes, however, no further sinkings were claimed and U-515 returned to her assigned base at Lorient on about 20 October 1942. She was attached to the 10th Flotilla.

PREPARATIONS FOR SECOND PATROL

U-515 had not suffered any damage on her first patrol and consequently her layover at Lorient was of short duration and she was ready for her second patrol early in November 1942.

SECOND PATROL OF U-515

DEPARTURE

U-515 sailed from Lorient on her second patrol on 7 November 1942 for the African coast.

U-515 CLAIMS SINKING OF CRUISER AND DESTROYER

U-515 claimed to have sunk a cruiser of the BIRMINGHAM class, as well as a destroyer, during the night of 11 to 12 November 1942. Prisoners were quite certain that they had sunk the destroyer with one torpedo, and it was also their opinion that they had sunk the cruiser, although they did not actually see her sink. About 5 or 6 torpedoes were fired in all. During and after the attack, U-515 was depth-charged, but the damage was such that it could be repaired without much effort. (O.N.I. Note: The "cruiser" sunk by U-515 was in all probability H.M.S. HECLA, British depot ship, which was torpedoed first at 2315 G.M.T. 11 November 1942, and which sank at 0116 12 November 1942 in approximate position 35.41 N. - 09.54 W. Five torpedoes struck H.M.S. HECLA before she keeled over. H.M.S. MARNE, British destroyer, was torpedoed at 0105 12 November 1942, but was towed into Gibraltar. It is probable that depth charge attacks carried out by H.M.S. VENOMOUS during and after the attack on HECLA and MARNE were made on U-515.

SINKING OF CERAMIC

U-515 now set course for mid-North Atlantic, apparently operating independently. On the afternoon of 6 December 1942, she sighted a large passenger ship and after pursuing her for several hours fired 1 torpedo which hit. Although the ship was immediately abandoned U-515 rescued only 1 survivor; prisoners claimed the foul weather did not permit further rescue operations. The prisoner taken aboard U-515 stated that the ship was the S.S. CERAMIC, 18713 tons. After the passengers and crew had left the ship, U-515 fired another torpedo which quickly sank her. (O.N.I. Note: S.S. CERAMIC was torpedoed and sunk the night of 6/7 December 1942, at about 40.30 N. - 40.20 W.) The sinking of the CERAMIC brought the total tonnage claimed on this patrol to about 29,000 tons, and after reporting the sinking to Control, Henke was awarded the Knight's Cross of the Iron Cross.

RETURN TO BASE

U-515 continued to cruise west of the Azores for about a week. Thereafter she set course for Lorient where she arrived about 5 or 6 January 1943. The U-boat received a tumultuous welcome and her captain was well on his way to becoming the most successful U-boat commander of the 10th Flotilla.

PREPARATIONS FOR THIRD PATROL

By this time some repairs had become necessary and U-515 remained in dock until about mid-February 1943, when preparations for the next patrol had been completed.

THIRD PATROL OF U-515

DEPARTURE

U-515 sailed from Lorient about 20 February 1943. Prisoners generally spoke of her operational area as being off West Africa and the Gold Coast. But it is believed that she was first assigned an operational area in mid-North Atlantic and only from there proceeded to the above mentioned area.

SINKING OF CALIFORNIA STAR

The first ship sunk by U-515 on this patrol was S.S. CALIFORNIA STAR, British freighter, 8,300 tons, which was torpedoed and sunk 4 March 1943, at 42.32 N. - 37.44 W. The 2nd quartermaster of CALIFORNIA STAR was taken prisoner aboard U-515.

U-515 OPERATES IN GROUP

Prisoners knew that U-515 was operating with other U-boats while in the North Atlantic but were unable to identify any of the near-by U-boats. (O.N.I. Note: It is believed that U-515 belonged to a group which included U-513, U-410, U-172 and a boat commanded by Kapitänleutnant Keller. These boats are believed to have followed and attacked Convoy U.G.S.-6.)

SECOND SINKING

The next ship claimed sunk by U-515 could not be identified.

She was reportedly accompanied by corvette or destroyer escort. The attack probably took place on U-515's way from mid-North Atlantic to the West African Coast, about 20 March 1943.

MEETING WITH U-RASCH

Toward the end of March U-515 met a 750-ton U-boat commanded by Kapitänleutnant Rasch. The prisoner from CALIFORNIA STAR was transferred to U-Rasch which was returning from patrol and on her way to base. U-515 received about 30 cubic meters of oil and then continued her patrol.

U-515 IS ATTACKED BY AIRPLANES

U-515 was attacked off Freetown by airplanes identified by prisoners as Catalinas. Twelve bombs were counted in all and it was stated that the planes were fought off with the single-barrel 20-mm. cannon. Hits were obtained on a plane. No damage resulted from the bombs dropped by the airplanes, and U-515 submerged soon after the attack. (O.N.I. Note: Two R.A.F. Catalinas, D & B of Squadron 207, attacked a submarine 29 April 1943 in positions 08.51 N. - 14.35 W. and 08.34 N. - 14.24 W. A/A fire was experienced.)

U-515 ATTACKS CONVOY T.S. 37

Soon thereafter U-515 attacked a convoy off Freetown and nine ships were claimed sunk during a period of less than 12 hours. The prisoners were unable to identify the ships. (O.N.I. Note: Convoy T.S.37 was attacked during the night of 30 April to 1 May 1943 and the following 7 ships were sunk: KOTA TJANDI, Dutch freighter, 7,295 tons, torpedoed 2055 - 30 April 1943; BANDAR SHAPOUR, British freighter, 5,236 tons, torpedoed 2057 - 30 April 1943; CORABELLA, British freighter, 5,682 tons, torpedoed 2058 - 30 April 1943; NAGINA, British freighter, 6,551 tons, torpedoed 2100 - 30 April 1943; MOKAMBO, Belgian freighter, 4,996 tons, torpedoed 0328 - 1 May 1943; this ship was taken in tow 2 May 1943, but sank the following day in sight of Freetown; CITY OF SINGAPORE, British freighter, 6,555 tons, torpedoed 0330 - 1 May 1943; CLAN MAC PHERSON, British freighter, 6,940 tons, torpedoed 0345 - 1 May 1943. The 4 ships sunk 30 April 1943 were torpedoed at about 07.15 N. - 13.49 W; the three ships sunk 1 May 1943 were torpedoed in approximate position 07.50 N. - 14.14 W.)

During and after the attack on the convoy, some depth-charges were dropped, but none of them were close enough even to cause the crew any discomfort.

MEETING WITH U-460

A few days later, U-515 met a supply boat commanded by Oberleutnant Schnoor. (O.N.I. Note: Schnoor is believed to command U-460.) Fuel oil and four torpedoes were supplied by U-460 and as usual the doctor carried in the supply U-boat came aboard U-515. Henke, as well as his officers and some of the men visited aboard U-460. A machinist of U-515 who had been caught stealing provisions and coffee with the intention of selling them upon return to base was transferred to U-460. The crew later learned that he had been court-martialled and had received a long jail sentence.

SINKING OF CORNEVILLE

U-515 continued her south-easterly course and about a week later sank CORNEVILLE. (O.N.I. Note: CORNVILLE, Norwegian freighter, 4,544 tons, was torpedoed and sunk 9 May 1943 at 04.50 N. - 01.10 W.) This was the last sinking claimed by U-515 on her third patrol. The total tonnage reported to Control as sunk was 72,000 tons.

RETURN TO BASE

U-515 crossed the Equator and it was believed that her southernmost position had been about 040 South. She then shaped course for her base and after a leisurely trip, arrived at Lorient about 23 June 1943. All crew members were given liberal leaves and many of them were decorated with the Iron Cross, 2nd Class. Henke was awarded one Oak Leaves to the Knights Cross 4 July 1943.

PREPARATIONS FOR FORTH PATROL

Extended repairs were necessary after this patrol, which had lasted about eighteen weeks, and U-515 was not ready for her forth patrol until the end of August 1943.

FOURTH PATROL OF U-515

DEPARTURE

U-515 left on her fourth patrol 29 August 1943. Her operational area was to have been off West Africa.

ATTACK BY CONVOY ESCORT

When U-515 was off the Azores about one week after leaving Lorient she sighted a convoy and preparations to attack were made. However, before she could approach close enough the U-boat was detected and heavily depth-charged by one of the convoy's escorts. One of the diving tanks was torn, cells in both batteries were cracked and it was found that U-515 left an oil trace. The damage was sufficiently severe to necessitate return to base. (O.N.I. Note: This was probably the attack delivered by H.M.S. TAVY at 2147 5 September 1943 at 38.33 N. - 18.03 W.)

RETURN TO BASE

U-515 returned to Lorient without being attacked further and docked 12 September 1943.

PREPARATIONS FOR NEXT PATROL

The repairs took about six weeks and after the necessary trials U-515 was ready to leave on her next patrol by the end of October 1943.

FIFTH PATROL OF U-515

DEPARTURE FROM LORIENT

U-515 left Lorient 1 November 1943 in company with U-508, commanded by Kapitänleutnant Staats. Both U-boats put into St. Nazaire where two T-5 torpedoes were embarked by U-515. Presumably U-508 also took over some T-5 torpedoes.

DEPARTURE FROM ST. NAZAIRE

U-515 and U-508 left St. Nazaire 9 November 1943 and after passing through the Bay of Biscay joined a group of U-boats patrolling between the Azores and the Portuguese Coast. Prisoners from U-515 believed that this was one of the GROUPS SCHILL and identified several of the U-boats known to have belonged to these groups. It was stated that U-172 commanded by Kapitänleutnant Emmermann was a member of one of the groups. Prisoners reported that U-508, which occupied a position close to U-515 was sunk about one week after leaving St. Nazaire. (O.N.I. Note: This confirms information previously obtained from P/W sources.)

U-515 IS HEAVILY DEPTH-CHARGED

About eight days after sailing from St. Nazaire U-515 sighted a north-bound convoy. Before she could get into attacking position she sighted escorting aircraft and submerged. Surfacing shortly thereafter she sighted three destroyers. U-515 fired a T-5 torpedo from her stern tube. A second torpedo was fired soon after, but neither of the two apparently found its mark. Following the firing of the torpedo U-515 was heavily depth-charged over a period of several hours. One of the main ballast and reserve fuel oil tanks and the stern buoyancy tank were torn; several battery cells were cracked, the main switchboard was damaged as was the forward hydroplane motor. The clutches developed noises and many of the upper-deck oil connections were loose, causing oil traces to be left. Furthermore, the outboard valves of the Diesel air intake and outlet, as well as the exhaust valves, were damaged. The inner valves were still holding, but the depth to which U-515 could dive was limited. Also the water in the Diesel air intake and outlet valves made depth control difficult; this was aggravated by the fact that a pipeline through one or several regulating tanks was loosened and the tanks could not maintain pressure. (O.N.I. Note: On or about 18 November 1943 several attacks were made by destroyers escorting Convoy S.L.-139/M.K.S.30. One of the attacks on U-515 may have been made by H.M.S. EXE which dropped 4 depth-charge series and made one hedgehog attack starting at 1107 Z and continuing until 1209 Z, at 39.34 N. - 19.42 W. An oil patch was sighted between the third and forth attack and throughout the hunt the blowing of tanks was heard. The hedgehog attack was believed to have been made on S.B.T.)

REPAIRS

Within U-515 the situation was almost hopeless. The batteries were low and the air supply was almost exhausted. It was stated that if U-515 had been forced to remain under water for another one or two hours, she would have had to surface. Fortunately for the boat the depth-charge attacks stopped in time and she was able to surface well aft of the convoy. Henke consulted both of his engineer officers. Leutnant (Ing.) Altenburger, who was being broken in on this patrol, stated that in his opinion the damage could be repaired at sea. Although her regular engineer officer, Oberleutnant (Ing.) Mahnken advised return to base, U-515's commander, always willing to take a chance, ordered repairs to be effected. About two days later, when U-515 was in the neighbourhood of the Canary Islands, the crew rigged a tarpaulin under the protection of which the diving tank and the stern buoyancy tank were welded. At the same time repairs within the boat were continued and by about 22 November 1943 U-515 was again considered seaworthy. It was unanimously stated that the damage suffered on this patrol was by far greater than that which forced U-515 to return to her base on the proceeding patrol. The credit went mainly to the incoming engineer officer.

U-515 PROCEEDS TO OPERATIONAL AREA

U-515 now sailed along the West African Coast and proceeded into the Gulf of Guinea. On 17 December 1943 while surfaced at night she fired two torpedoes at a freighter which sank within about a quarter of an hour. (O.N.I. Note: KINGSWOOD, British freighter, 5,080 tons, was torpedoed and sunk 17 December 1943 at 05.57 N. - 01.43 E.)

Two days later, PHEMIUS was sunk with two torpedoes and her radioman was taken prisoner aboard U-515. (O.N.I. Note: PHEMIUS,

British freighter, 7,406 tons, was torpedoed and sunk 19 December 1943 at 05.01 N. - 00.17 W. She was in convoy S.T.- 77.)

U-515 was on her way to base when she again fired two torpedoes and sank another ship on Christmas Eve, 1943. (O.N.I. Note: DUMANA, British freighter, 8,327 tons, was torpedoed and sunk 24 December 1943 at 04.26 N. - 06.50 W. while in convoy S.T.L.-8.) One of the escorts dropped depth-charges, but they were nowhere near U-515 and no damage was suffered.

REPAIRS WHILE EN ROUTE TO BASE

The welded seam on the stern buoyancy tank broke when U-515 was on her way to base. It was stated that this had not come about through any counter-attacks but that the natural vibrations of the U-boat had loosened it. It was, therefore, decided to re-weld the seam. U-515 approached the southernmost island of the Cape Verde Islands, and within territorial waters re-welded the seam on New Year's Eve night. The stretch of coast along which U-515 was hove to was devoid of any houses. The repairs took about three to four hours.

RETURN TO BASE

U-515 then set course for Lorient where she arrived 16 January 1944 after an uneventful passage. Her escort into port consisted of two mine destructor vessels. However, just before entering the port of Lorient two Mosquito bombers were seen but were driven off by fire from the twin 20-mm. cannons. Henke claimed the sinking of 22,000 tons of Allied shipping on this patrol.

PREPARATIONS FOR NEXT PATROL

After extensive repairs and the fitting of new batteries U-515 was again ready to leave Lorient by the end of March 1944. The departure date had been set for 28 March, but at the last minute the rudder motor failed and had to be repaired. The sailing was delayed for one day.

SIXTH AND LAST PATROL OF U-515

DEPARTURE

U-515 left Lorient 30, March 1944, accompanied by several minesweepers. Her prospective operational area was not known and some prisoners thought that it might again be off the West African Coast, whereas others mentioned an area off Recife, Brazil. U-515 passed through the Bay of Biscay submerged, surfacing only at night for about 4 to 5 hours to charge her batteries.

USE OF RADAR DECOY BALLOONS

It was stated that radar decoy balloons were released every night while in the Bay of Biscay. Apparently no effort was made to use radar decoy balloons just before diving.

MESSAGE TO CONTROL

When U-515 passed 200 West she reported this as well as her fuel supply to Control. This was the only signal sent on U-515's last patrol.

EVENTS LEADING UP TO THE SINKING OF U-515

About midnight (German summer time) 8 April 1944. the bridge watch sighted a carrier based airplane, which however, dropped no bombs. As soon as the airplane was out of sight U-515 submerged.

U-515 surfaced about an hour later and soon after was attacked by another carrier-based airplane which dropped 2 bombs without causing any damage to the U-boat. U-515 used her new 37-mm. automatic gun for the first time without, however, claiming any hits. VT-23 dropped 2 depth bombs at 0027 GCT 9 April 1944 at 34.49 N. - 19.19 W. The pilot reported that the U-boat showed a white light.) The engineer officer of U-515 believed that the pilot may have seen light from the control room or a flashlight used in the conning tower.

SECOND AIRPLANE ATTACK

U-515 remained submerged until 0900 (German summer time) when her commander, for unexplained reasons, decided to surface. Shortly thereafter another carrier-based plane approached and dropped 2 depth-charges, which, although they were quite close to the stern, exploded without damaging the U-boat. U-515 promptly submerged after having again used her 37-mm. automatic gun. (O.N.I. Note: VT-31 dropped two depth bombs at 0735 GCT, 9 April 1944, at 34.38 N. - 19.39 W. A/A fire encountered.)

By now all within the U-boat were aware of the fact that it was the commander's intention to attack the carrier if at all possible.

SINKING OF U-515

About 1 hour after the airplane attack fast propeller beats were heard within U-515. Prisoners stated that they then heard noises similar to those made by a circular saw. The engineer officer said that he had the feeling as if the entire U-boat was made to vibrate and that this might have been the result of some new detection device. The hunting vessels were heard to reduce speed. The ping of sonar and "Knalloten" (possibly explosive sound ranging) was now heard. The latter was described as a dropping of some explosive charge onto the U-boat, thereby probably giving the exact depth to the hunting ships.

FIRST DEPTH CHARGE SERIES

Soon thereafter a destroyer was heard to make her run-in and a well placed series of about 8 depth-charges exploded near the U-boat. Lights failed temporarily, but the negligible damage caused by this series was easily repaired. Several more or less well-placed series of depth-charges followed, but so far the U-boat had not suffered badly. Destroyers were heard to stop, then start again. Finally the propeller noises vanished.

U-515's OIL TRACE BELIEVED DISCOVERED

The relief was only temporary, however, and about half an hour later the destroyers were heard directly over the U-boat. Again the sonar ping was clearly heard throughout the U-boat. The engineer officer was of the opinion that at this point the oil trace which U-515 was known to leave had been discovered, thus accounting for the closeness of the following depth-charge series. Ever since leaving Lorient attempts had been made to locate a small oil leak from a forward fuel oil bunker. Henke, counting on his habitual luck, had refused to turn around earlier, particularly as no one aboard was keen to pass through the Bay of Biscay any oftener than necessary. It was intended to use the oil from the suspected bunker until it was entirely empty thereby eliminating the oil trace.

WATER AND OIL ENTRY AFT

The next series of depth-charges caused a water entry of about a thumb's thickness in the stern torpedo compartment. At the same time a pipe carrying lubricating oil was torn off the pressure hull. The leak in the stern torpedo compartment could not be located immediately, but trim and buoyancy were maintained by pumping of the regulating tanks. The next depth-charge series caused entry of fuel oil into the stern torpedo compartment when a pipe line leading in from an outboard fuel oil bunker burst. Efforts were made to control both the water and the oil entry, but it was recognized that unless the depth-charging either stopped of became less accurate the counter-measures were in vain. The main ballast pump could not obtain suction as U-515 was too heavy by the stern; neither could the regulating tanks cope with the position of the boat which now was more than 200 down by the stern.

STERN TORPEDO COMPARTMENT CLOSED OFF

The next depth-charge series loosened the plugs which had at least partially controlled the water and oil entries. Water and oil rose above the floor plates. The U-boat's buoyancy could not be maintained as means of pumping were exhausted. All depth gages were broken and only the tendency of the boat either to rise or to fall could be observed. The engineer officer now decided to close off the stern torpedo compartment as the only means of saving the boat and the crew. This ended the use of the S.B.T. from which several series of pills had been spasmodically ejected.

ELECTRIC MOTOR COMPARTMENT FLOODED

Shaken by the preceding explosions a stuffing box bolt broke in the bulkhead between the stern torpedo compartment and the electric motor compartment. Water and oil entered. U-515 was now about 30⁰ down by the stern and could be held only by increasing to "Half Speed". All available crew members were sent forward. The depth of the boat was close to 200 meters. The engineer officer ordered main ballast tank No. 1 blown, thereby giving temporary relief. It soon was apparent, however, that the tank was ripped. U-515's stern sank again to a 30⁰ angle.

U-515 IS FORCED TO SURFACE

No more thought was given to evasive action. One after another the stern fuel oil bunkers were blown and slowly the U-boat returned to an even keel. Water continued to rise in the electric motor compartment and, flowing through the boat, made the U-boat

heavy by the bow. This was aggravated by the fact that the air in the rising aft part of the U-boat expanded. U-515 now rose and as the blown bunkers could not be vented, the ascent was rapid. She was about 45⁰ down by the bow. The main ballast tank amidships and the forward main ballast tank were blown and U-515 surfaced.

U-515 IS ABANDONED

Henke was the first to open the conning tower hatch. Observing 3 destroyers in the immediate vicinity, he accepted defeat and gave the final order to abandon ship.

U-515 SINKS IN FLAMES

Soon thereafter direct hits from destroyers set the bridge aflame and another direct hit forward accelerated the sinking of U-515 on which the vents had all been opened. Survivors felt 2 heavy underwater explosions several minutes after U-515 had sunk. Sixteen crew members were lost from the combined fire of destroyers and airplanes; 44 survivors were taken aboard by the attacking destroyers and later transferred to U.S.S. GUADALCANAL.

ACTION REPORT

At 0812 GCT 9 April 1944, U.S.S. CHATELAIN made contact. U.S.S. PILLSBURY AND FLAHERTY proceeded ahead of U.S.S. GUADALCANAL. At 0813 PILLSBURY fired hedgehog and 2 explosions were observed, bringing up debris. (O.N.I. Note: It is probably that this attack was made on a yet unidentified U-boat.) At 1133 U.S.S. POPE obtained sound contact and fired hedgehogs at 1157 and 1205. At 1214 POPE dropped 11 depth-charges followed by 13 depth-charges at 1234 and by 13 depth-charges at 1307. At 1310 U.S.S. CHATELAIN obtained contact. At 1320 U.S.S. POPE dropped 13 depth-charges followed by series of 7 depth-charges at 1343, 1357 and 1411. Thereafter contact was lost. At about 1455, after several questionable contacts, CHATELAIN regained contact and fired 11 depth-charges in 2 groups just as the U-boat was beginning to surface. At 1505, the U-boat surfaced within about 150 yards of CHATELAIN'S starboard quarter and CHATELAIN opened fire. At 1506 VT-25 made R.P. attack and VF-6 and VF-9 strafed the U-boat while the crew was abandoning her. At 1508 U.S.S. FLAHERTY opened fire. At 1509 CHATELAIN obtained a direct hit on the conning tower, starting a large fire. The U-boat sank bow first at 1512 GCT at 34.31 N. - 19.29 W.

REMARKS

None of the prisoners interrogated had any reaction to the firing of R.P.'s. Some stated that the airplanes dropped bombs, but apparently everyone was too busy abandoning ship to observe closely any hits on the U-boat. It was stated that the fire which broke out on the bridge was due to the ignition of the hydrogen bottles on Platform I.'

As noted previously in this book, Henke was responsible for the sinking of the Harborough, California Star and Reedpool which contained Barry men. His interrogation by the commander of the Guadalcanal, Daniel Gallery, is thought to have been responsible for his suicide.

According to uboat.net, Korvettenkapitan (posthumously awarded, March 18th, 1945) Werner Henke was born may 13th 1909 and died June 15th, 1944 at Fort Hunt, USA. He sank 25 ships and severely damaged 2 with U 515. From 1939, e had been awarded the Iron Class 2nd Class, Spanish Cross, U-Boat War Badge, Iron Cross 1st Class, Knights Cross and Knights Cross with Oak Leaves. Unlike the US records, U-boat.net records 7 patrols with U 515, for a total of 341 days at sea, from February 21st 1942-April 9th 1944. He had served on the warships Admiral Scheer and Schleswig-Holstein before joing U 124 under Kapitanleutnant Schulz. This was the famous 'Edelweissboot', and he completed his last 4 patrols with her under the renowned Jochen Mohr. Both the U 124 and Mohr are mentioned previously. His most venomous attack was on convoy TS37, south of Freetown, on 30th April to 1st May, 1943. On this, his 3rd patrol on U 515, he sank 8 ships in 8 hours.

PART SEVENTEEN

The Sinking of the Allende

The following story has been added at the last moment to this book, after it was discovered on a remarkable website run by Mike Kemble, who gave permission to reproduce the story of the Cardiff ship Allende and its mainly Welsh crew's imprisonment in a part of Africa controlled by the Vichy French. The interview of the cabin boy Wilf Williams was carried out by Professor Bernard de Neumann, and there are relevant photographs on the website, and more information from another survivor, Frank Brookes. The following is taken directly from Mike Kemble's website, www.mikekemble.com/ww2 , which details the Merchant Navy's exploits in World War II:

The good ship ss Allende began her life on the stocks in the year 1929, built to the specifications as required by Thomas Morel, ship-owner of Cardiff. Her duty in life was the transportation of general cargo to any part of the world as required by the Company. Sturdily built, of simple design, fitted with coal burning furnaces and a single triple expansion reciprocating engine, she was the typical tramp steamer of her day. Of 5081 tons, main superstructure amidships, with main holds fore and aft of it and central woodbine funnel, she represented, like a thousand others of her kind, the backbone of the British Mercantile Marine, created to fulfil the empire's trading on worldwide travel. In late 1939, with the advent of hostilities, Allende, like all other merchant ships of her class, was ill-fitted for war.

Decreed by My Lords of The Admiralty, her armament supplied at the outbreak was two First World War Lewis guns, a few rifles of ancient vintage, and a secret weapon, The Steam Projector. This weapon was almost useless in any sea or air action, and was presumably supplied mainly as a psychological boost to the crew. Some mention of the steam projector must now be made. The Steam Projector was a device dreamed up by some fertile imagination to act as a deterrent to low-flying enemy aircraft. Its barrel firmly fixed and pointing vertically upwards was muzzle-loaded with a projectile, to which a trailing wire was secured, with the other end of the wire being firmly secured to the deck. On attack by an enemy low-flying aircraft, at some precise moment, steam from the boiler room was injected into the bottom of the barrel, thus hurling a projectile and trailing wire to an undetermined height. Unsuspecting, the enemy aircraft became ensnared in the wire and theoretically was brought crashing down into the sea. Its inventor, even in his wildest dreams, never realised how beloved by the crew his invention would become. Soon the crew found the projector was just as efficient as a potato launcher. With much fun and hilarity, bets were laid and potatoes launched to great heights, providing the crew with many happy hours of joy when ploughing the monotonous seas.

Now homeward bound, on the 17th March 1942 the Allende had been almost constantly at sea for thirteen months. Earlier that day she had crossed the Equator, but no crossing the line ceremony was enacted. The captain was pushing her as fast as possible, hoping to reach the port of Freetown, Sierra Leone, in time to join an escorted, homeward bound convoy. Thrusting her blunt bow into an ever-rising swell, the ship became more alive. Her master cast a worried eye through the port side window of the bridge wing, seeing an ever thickening black wall of foul weather building up and swiftly advancing from the east. A further worry to the captain was the amount of thick, black, gritty smoke pouring from the tall salt encrusted funnel. Having coaled ship in Bombay, the bunkers were now filled with an inferior coal, much used in India, and, as such, it was impossible not to make smoke, an indicator to any prowling U-boat. At least, he knew that he could take on good Welsh steam coal at Freetown for the last leg home. Several old merchant ships were used as floating coaling stations at such gathering points, and Freetown was such a one. With the gathering storm and its accompanying loss in visibility, worry over making smoke dissipated, as did the smoke in the rising wind. Thus on the weatherworn Allende, with watch set, boats, rafts and weapons overhauled and ready for instant action, and all watertight doors shut, they were ready as could be for the coming storm. Girdling the earth and extending from the Equator to 10 degrees North of latitude lies that meteorological phenomenon called the Doldrums. This narrow belt, if viewed from space, is seen as a white belt surrounding the globe. From the earth's surface looking up, it is a canopy of cloud varying in intensity, but always there, especially during the winter months of the Northern hemisphere. High equatorial temperature, humidity, and low air pressure create a concoction of elements, making two human activities uncomfortable. Firstly, high temperatures and humidity give rise to an enervating physical and mental effect to one's body. Secondly, and much more frightening, weak pressure gradients, coupled to wildly fluctuating temperatures, create daily thunderstorms of such intensity that their appearance is sometimes awesome. These diurnal storms build up during daylight hours, and, presaged by a violent wind, break out into a combination of rain, lightning, and thunder. Lightning discharges are far more numerous and intense than ever seen in more temperate climes. These storms of daily periodicity almost always occur towards sunset.

The Cabin Boy

The crew of the Allende was comprised of thirty-nine souls. Being Cardiff owned, most of her crew came from Cardiff, Newport, or the Welsh valleys. The youngest member was the mess room boy, more commonly known as the cabin boy. His name was Wilfred Williams, born at Blackwood, Gwent, on the fifteenth of August 1925. Subsequently he had moved with his older sister Betty and parents, Wilfred and Maud, to another small mining town within the valleys of Gwent (then Monmouthshire) called Abersychan, his address being 105 Manor Road, Abersychan, Monmouth. Within the next few years, two more additions to the family were made, both boys, named Luther and Kenneth, Kenneth being the youngest and the author of this true narrative.

Leaving school at fourteen, Wilfred gained full employment at his father's place of work, Pontypool Town Forge, lying approximately three miles from his home. Being tall, well-built, and strong for his age, the arduous work within this extremely old-fashioned tin plate works suited him. Wilfred started work in early

August 1939, and so did the war. Wilfred was upset and despondent in that being so young, he could not volunteer for the armed services. Seeing older men from the works being called up or volunteering, he realised that no chance existed of getting into the war at his tender age. Almost a year had passed when one day whilst he was at work, a former workmate called in. He was wearing civilian clothes and sporting a Merchant Navy lapel badge. Their conversation resulted in Wilfred learning that he could get to sea at his age of fifteen as a cabin boy. Coming home from work he emphatically told his parents that he was going to sea, and, if they refused, he would run away. Down to the "Pool" at Newport he went. Signing the register he was informed to wait for a ship! Coming home, he sold off his pigeons (for a second, or third time, as they always flew back). Within a few more days, a letter arrived from the "Pool" requiring him to report and join a ship at Newport Docks the following week. No training was given or considered in those days.

Thus, on the eventful day of the twenty-fourth of February 1941, Wilfred joined the ss Allende, holding the rate of Mess Room Boy, ready to face all the dangers of modern sea war at the tender age of fifteen and six months for the princely sum of £4 per month. For this payment he was expected to carry out the following duties in general, from 0600 hours each morning. Firstly, take tea and toast to the bridge, and then below to the Second Engineer. Make up all the bunks, and wash the floors. Then, go to the galley, helping the Second Cook to peel potatoes, prepare food, and wash all the dirty pots and pans. Next, lay the table in the saloon, and serve the meals with the Steward, and then wash the dishes. Back to the cabins to polish the brass, and then take afternoon tea to the bridge and down to the engine room for the Third Engineer. On completion, make up sandwiches for the First Watch (8 – 12pm), trim all lamps, and clean all glasses. An additional task in wartime was the securing of deadlights over portholes to "darken ship" at night. If the ship was attacked by enemy aircraft, he also acted as loading number for the secret weapon, namely the Steam Projector. For doing all these duties, plus the very high chance of being killed (higher than the three armed services), he was rewarded a poor return of £1 per week.

Wilf was happy with his long hours of duty, also Allende was a happy ship. His shipmate and friend was a townie named Bill Haynes, who lived in Griffithstown, only a few miles from Wilfred's own village of Abersychan. Bill was a junior seaman, who, at the age of nineteen, was a grown man to Wilf, but, having both joined together, and now having served together for thirteen long, perilous months at sea, they were firm friends. On the evening of the seventeenth of March 1942, Wilfred, who was now an experienced cabin boy, had completed most of his duties. Having checked that all deadlights were down and screwed tight, he retired to his shared cabin to lie on his bunk and started reading a well-thumbed western magazine that was doing its rounds of the crew. Feeling the gradual increasing roll and pitch, Wilfred knew that the storm had arrived. Never being seasick, he had no concern for the weather. Lying on his bunk dressed in trousers, shirt and loosely tied life jacket, he slowly drifted off into sleep, drowsed by the tropical heat and closeness of the air. With the rhythmic thump of the ship's reciprocating engine giving an almost hypnotic effect, he sank ever deeper into sleep. Youth and innocence prevailed; young Wilfred was soon deep in the arms of Morpheus.

The U 68

In the same month that Wilfred joined the ss Allende as the youngest and lowliest in rank, another, and far more auspicious occasion was being re-enacted the other side of the English Channel. Korvettenkapit%on Karl-Friedrich Merten (transferred in early 1940 to the U-boat service) was given command of U68. Almost to the day, both joined their respective ships. Merten, born in Posen, Germany on the 15th August 1905, shared the same birthday as Wilfred, but exactly twenty years older to the day, joined the Reichmarine in 1926. On completion of his basic training as an officer, he received his commission as Leutnant zur See as Weapons Officer in the light cruiser K^nigsburg, a modern cruiser of 6,650 tons armed with nine 5.9" guns in three triple turrets. Subsequently he served in torpedo-boat T157 and the escort boat F7. Thereafter, with this experience behind him, he became a Cadet Training Officer in the training ship Schleswig Holstein, an old First World War battleship where he remained until the outbreak of war, thus, as previously mentioned, volunteering and transferring to the U-boat service.

Merten was to remain in command of U68 and to become one of the most successful U-boat commanders of the war. Before leaving the U68 in early 1943, Merten's achievements were recognised by the award of the Knights Cross of the Iron Cross (he was already the holder of the Iron Cross First and Second Class). Quickly following this distinction, came the coveted Oak leaves to the Knights Cross for the sinking of a total of 180,870 tons of Allied shipping.† Merten ended the war with the rank of Kapit%on zur See. The closing months of the war he spent in not destroying but saving lives. He assisted in organising the evacuation of over 50,000 refugees from the advancing Russians. When the war ended, Merten went into French captivity, where in 1948 attempts were made to try him on fabricated war crime charges. These allegations were totally unfounded, and he was released in March 1949. In the 1980s, he was still alive, living in retirement near Valdshut, Germany.

The Meeting

At approximately 5.30 p.m. local time, the storm broke over the area that the U-68 was prowling. Even at thirty metres, some movement was felt in the boat indicating a stormy surface. Still carrying out his sweep, the operator electrified the control room crew when, at 6.45 p.m., his report of a weak positive engine noise announced an approaching ship. Confirming the report, Merten ordered the crew to action stations. Grouping up on both motors, battery power was supplied to both electric motors and speed was increased, heading the U-boat on an interception bearing. On reaching his required position, Merten came once again to periscope depth. Now much closer to his intended victim, Merten picked up the dark shape of a ship sailing darkened out. This confirmed that the ship was not a neutral. Switching to high magnification his magnificent optics gave him a clearer picture. Plunging and rolling slowly due to her full cargo was a typical merchant freighter of roughly 5,000 tons. A quick all-round sweep of the periscope revealed no accompanying escort.

With some satisfaction, Merten realized the howling storm and darkness negated any chance of the periscope being seen by the oncoming ship, and being no escort meant a leisurely approach to the setting of the attack plot. After several minutes of intense periscope observation, Merten started the plot. Range, angle off the bow, relative bearings and speed, torpedo speed and angles were fed into the control calculator. From it came the new periscope bearing, torpedo gyro angle, and time of flight of torpedo to target. On Merten's orders, torpedo tubes Numbers 1 and 2 were flooded, and their bow caps opened. Seeing the freighter deep in the water, Merten set torpedo-running depth to 16 feet. Using impact type detonators, he did not intend the torpedoes to run under the ship, but to strike well below the water line.

With calculations made and set, Merten had only to wait until the cross-wires in his attack periscope centred amidships of his victim. He intended a single shot and hoped for a first hit. A comfortable range of 1200 metres against a slow moving target was reasonably simple, provided all went well.

Crouching at his periscope he saw first the blunt old bows come pushing into view, slowly rising and falling, crashing in a welter of foam in the raging sea. Next, following in succession, [he saw] forecastle, well-deck, derricks and bridge superstructure. With the bridge in the cross-wires of his attack periscope graticule, he gave the order: "Fire Number One."† Instantly, a jolt was felt in the boat as the torpedo was launched from its parent tube by compressed air. On leaving the forward tube, the torpedo, over a ton in weight, caused an upward movement of the bow. Quick, controlled flooding made up for the loss in weight and returned stability to the boat. Within seconds of the torpedo launch, a muttered report from the radio cubicle informed the control room that the torpedo was running true. Hydrophone effect used for finding targets also could be used to hear the receding propeller noise from the running torpedo.

The navigator, with his clipboard and stopwatch, was standing next to Merten, and timed the torpedo run. A simple calculation of range and speed gave the navigator the time of impact. If time ran out, a quick set-up for the next attack plot could be made. The whole crew were frozen in silence and anticipation during the torpedo run. Travelling at 30 knots, the launched torpedo quickly found its set depth of 16 feet, the efficient hydrostatic keeping it within inches of its setting. Guided by its gyro-controlled system, the rudders, offset by the calculation set prior to firing, guided the torpedo on a course to intercept the path of the target ship at a precise position. Whilst running, the flow of the water over the torpedo warhead turned the small propeller, winding off the safety range (for the safety of the U-boat) and unmasking the firing train of the detonator to its warhead. Once past its safety range, the fully-armed torpedo now sped towards its intended target.

The Explosion

At exactly 7.20 p.m. local time, on the wild stormy evening of 17th.March 1942, at the nautical position of 4∫ North 7∫, 44' West, only a few degrees above the Equator and approximately 18 miles from the coast of Liberia, the confrontation of U68 and ss Allende was enacted with tragic results. Another source, Alan S Pope, in Nov 1996 in a letter to Frank Brookes, puts this at 2153hrs local. The torpedo struck the ss Allende amidships, at the juncture of the Boiler and Engine Room bulkhead, at exactly 16 feet below the water line. With the impact, the primer fired its small charge into the detonator train, which, on exploding, lanced its energy into the 800-lb. warhead. This in sympathy detonated in one colossal explosion against the thin, unarmoured steel-plating of the ship's side.

Ever expanding, the gasses of this explosion, with its central core of a thousand or more degrees of heat, blew through the plating like it was paper. Preceding the noise, its catastrophic blast wave tore into the confined spaces of Boiler and Engine room alike, incinerating, blasting, and wrecking everything in its path. Mercifully those killed (which was the whole watch below) were killed instantaneously, saving them from a possible slow death of horrendous burns and scalds from escaping steam and scattered furnaces. The awful energy created by the high explosive still sought a pathway from the wrecked compartments, taking its easiest route. Rivets, plates and a thousand pieces of engine and boilers all blasted skywards, reducing the ventilation shafting and engine room deckhead to a shambles. From the single tall funnel shot a plume of coal dust, smoke and hot gasses 50 feet high, and jets of flame shot from the remaining boiler room and engine ventilator trunking in all directions, like giant flame-throwers. Seconds later, not only the tropical downpour hit the stricken ship, but debris rained from the sky, some still hot and smoking.

Young Wilfred never heard the roar of the exploding torpedo. Lying full length, sound asleep on his bunk, which luckily cushioned him from the whiplash effect many felt through the decks and superstructure. Wilfred was propelled vertically upwards with his mattress, his flight being arrested only when hitting the deckhead. Plunging back to the cabin floor, he lay there for several seconds, regaining his reeling senses and paralysed body. The freezing of one's body comes to all, usually followed by adrenaline charged mobility of sheer panic. Most overcome this in seconds, others in minutes. Wilfred being the former, rushed out the wreck of his shared cabin to be confronted by a scene that even his wildest nightmares could not envisage. Presented with an ever-tilting deck, in the pitch dark, intermittently lit by brilliant sheet lightning, Wilf struggled toward his lifeboat station, tightening his lifejacket as he staggered along.

Before taking two paces, he was saturated by the cold, heavy downpour, blown at terrifying force by the shrieking wind, [which was] slanting across the deck at a density that was difficult to penetrate. Compounding this horror was added clouds of condensing steam and coal dust, mixed with spent explosives, all combining to give a highly nauseous smell. Below decks, ominous rumbling of shifting cargo and broken machinery gave added impetus to the alarming tilt. Figures appeared from all directions, wraith-like apparitions appearing and disappearing in the steam cloud and darkness. Shrieks and shouts of frightened and hurt men filled the stormy evening. Some semblance [if order] followed the arrival of the captain, officers and bridge watch to the boat deck.

Most of the officers had torches, and by their fitful light, Wilfred could see his shipmate and friend, Bill Haynes. Bill, as a junior seaman, as is general in the

Merchant Navy, happened to be on the wheel during the second Dog Watch. The First Dog Watch (4 p.m. to 6 p.m.) and the Second Dog Watch (6 p.m. to 8 p.m.) were reserved for bridge watch-keeping instruction for junior seaman. Thus, on detonation of the torpedo, Bill, who was helmsman for the Second Dog Watch, was firmly holding the wheel. The sudden transmission of explosive energy through the steel hull, generated a whip-like shock to the superstructure, which was felt by all, most being flung off their feet with numbed ankles. In Bill's case, both his† ankles and wrists felt as if [they were] broken. Standing there on the boat deck, he was holding his hands in each armpit, trying to relieve the pain. [Added] to this, Bill had received a secondary shock, [because] debris, [having been] flung high by the explosion, had resulted in a large, heavy piece of the main engine plunging through the bridge deckhead and landing, smoking, between him and the Watch Officer.

With the destruction of engine and boiler room, the ship immediately lost way, gradually swinging broadside on to the heaving sea. Luckily, if such a term can be applied, the alarming tilt of the deck was to leeward, so assisting in the launching of the lifeboat. Quickly scrambling into the boat, the Bosun and Second Officer held the falls until the Master had made a quick round of the deck, ensuring that no survivors were abandoned. Coming back to the lifeboat, a hurried count was made. Added to the jolly boat and raft he counted nineteen, twelve, and two respectively. With thirty-three souls in the boats and raft and the knowledge of the watch below being five, all dead, the crew were accounted for.

Jumping down into the lifeboat, the Second Officer and Bosun let fly the falls, and, pushing off from the heavily listing ship, endeavoured to pull away, keeping to the leeside of the stricken vessel. The captain [was] still aboard, [and] lumbered off to join the survivors clustered in the jolly boat. Wilfred and Bill were sat on the thwarts in the centre of the boat. The horrors of the torpedoing and storm were now compounded by the rapid filling of the boat. Torrential downpour of rain, [along] with the weight of nineteen men and [a] boy, laid the boat heavy and almost unmanageable in the heaving sea. Freeboard was rapidly being lost, and the gunwales were hardly above the level of the sea. The Second Officer in charge of the boat ordered all to bail for their lives, with everything possible. A bucket, trilby hat, and even a fez were used in the frantic effort to lighten the lifeboat. As fast as they bailed, the ingress of water seemed greater in the wallowing darkness. After some minutes, someone in the boat shouted that the ship was not sinking. After some discussion, the Second Officer decided to re-board her to collect buckets for more efficient bailing. Giving the necessary order, they pulled back to the ship.

Korvettenkapitan Merten was slightly annoyed. Cruising around the hard-hit Allende at periscope depth, he observed the ship was not sinking. A tribute to her builders, the Allende, although almost torn apart, refused to sink. Her stout remaining bulkheads and riveted frame held together, giving her the necessary buoyancy to keep afloat. Now wallowing in a trough, then tossed high on the crest of high wave, she refused to sink. Merten realized that a gun action was not possible because the gun crew would hardly survive on the casing of the U-boat's narrow deck in such weather. Another precious torpedo would have to be used.

At point blank range, Merten fired his second torpedo, exactly sixteen minutes after his first. If he had waited, or, taken longer in his firing, he would undoubtedly have claimed the lives of all in the lifeboat.

The lifeboats' survivors redoubled their effort under the Second Officer in trying to pull back to the ship. The lifeboat, being waterlogged, was heavy and unmanageable and barely moving. This slowness was their salvation. [They were] still some distance from the ship [when] the second torpedo struck its after-end. An explosion that dwarfed the storm disintegrated the stern. The proximity of the lifeboat to the ship gave most survivors a feeling that their end had come. A bright orange flash that hurt the eyes was quickly followed by a blast of searing heat, that scorched and almost drove the lifeboat under. Again the acrid stench of burnt explosives swept over them. Wilfred in the centre of the lifeboat received less of the blast, being shielded by the bodies of the men around him. Looking back, he saw the Allende sinking by the stern, slowly at first, then rapidly, her blunt bows lifting higher and higher, until [the ship was] almost vertical to the sea, before finally disappearing.

Wilfred, in his thirteenth month at sea, and thirteen days from their last port of call, Durban, said a sad farewell to his thirteen-year-old ship. Thirteen was certainly an unlucky number. Merten had no need to watch the death throes of the Allende. Sound travels through the medium of water faster than air. Merten and crew heard the crashing detonation of the torpedo quickly followed by the screaming and rumbling of rupturing bulkheads, moving cargo and heavy machinery. Her insides torn loose and collapsing under the ever-increasing pressure, Allende plunged to her eternal watery grave in the ocean depths. Merten did not know what ship or what cargo his victim was or carried.

Taking a final sweep of his periscope, he decided to surface. Blowing main tanks, he surfaced in a flurry of foam and compressed air. With conning tower hatch opened. Electric motors were shut down and the diesels started, throwing plumes of water in the air from the main exhaust valves, as the boat slowly moved on the surface through the choppy sea. With the watch set on the U-boat's bridge they started a search for survivors. Aided by the lightning flashes they quickly saw the tossing boats. Closing on them, Merten, when in voice range addressed them through a megaphone. The question was standard: What ship, what cargo, what destination, and is the captain alive. All these demands were answered in some garbled form, which seemingly satisfied Merten. On completion Merten turned the U68 away from the survivors, increased speed and moved off into the wild darkness. Jagged shards of lightning silhouetted the sinister U-boat's shape against the inky backdrop of the sky, soon to disappear in the black tumbling seas.

With the U-boat gone the surviving crew turned to their immediate task, that of staying alive. In the darkness and heavy seas the boats and raft soon lost sight of each other. Within the lifeboat, waterlogged, and lying low in the water, the men and Wilfred bailed out with every available and conceivable item that would hold water. With sea anchor spread, the lifeboat's compliment found they were slightly gaining, and, with better buoyancy a higher freeboard was obtained. Now riding the waves better and taking in less water some semblance of order existed. A suggestion to complete the bailing by most going over the side and hanging on the lifelines, whilst a few remained to finish bailing was quickly killed with the Second Mate's reply of these were shark infested waters. Sharks for miles around would have been drawn in from the noise of the underwater explosions.

Some minutes later, shouts from the surrounding darkness, and the sudden pinpricks of lights attached to the lifejackets indicated someone was near. Rowing towards the sounds and winking lights, the lifeboat survivors made out the two men who had tied themselves to the raft. Securing the raft with a length of rope the two men transferred to the lifeboat. Now twenty men and one boy were in the lifeboat, facing all the perils of an open boat in an angry sea. All night they drifted, bailing continuously and keeping a lookout for the jolly boat and remainder of the crew.†

With the passing of the electric storm, its departure abrupt as its coming, the sea began easing off into long, high ocean swells. From the crest of the larger could be seen the coast, inhospitable and dark lay the coast of Liberia some 15 miles away. With dawn came light, and at first the welcome warmth of a new day. Having now bailed the boat comparatively dry the survivors under the direction of the Second Officer stepped the mast and raised the single sail. Wind and drift drove them sadly, in a southerly direction. With the sun rising ever higher from the eastern sky, so accordingly did the temperature. By noon the heat was almost unbearable, covering themselves with their meagre possessions, they crouched and sweated under the unrelenting sun. Another crisis now reared its ugly head, the emergency rations packed in watertight bags had all gone over the side during the first panic of foundering in the storm.

Worse was to come, the water held in a container jammed beneath the thwarts was found to be leaking and contaminated with sea water, the only remaining water being the small metal cask lashed to the raft. Small measures were dished out supervised by the Second Officer. 3:00 p.m. that afternoon once again the dark low-lying coast was visible, but by nightfall they were still unable to reach the coast. Another miserable night was spent in the overcrowded lifeboat. The following morning with a change in wind and spending some hours at the heavy, unwieldy oars, they approached the coast. Miles before they reached it the air changed to a heavy, dank, rotting wood smell typical of the mangrove swamp. This smell of primeval forest pervades the atmosphere along this coastline for a thousand miles, or more.

As the huge Atlantic rollers surge in towards the African coast, although hardly felt or noticed in an open sea, when hitting a shelving beach they begin building up. Gaining height and shortening in length, ever accelerating, they finally hit the beach like miniature tidal waves, superb for the expert surf rider but not compatible to the riding in an ungainly, strongly built, heavy lifeboat. Approaching the coast in the late afternoon of the second day, the lifeboat became livelier, the Second Officer finding difficulty to steer and keep the bows on to the beach, he could see and hear the heavy surf breaking on the beach with the ominous roar of a thousand guns. A decision was taken to beach the boat by the method of waiting for the passing of an huge roller, then rowing as fast as possible behind it so retaining control until safe on the beach. Unfortunately the weight of 21 beings and the heavy craft was much too slow and ungainly. Still some distance from the beach, the next incoming wave hit the stern and propelled them at ever increasing speed towards the beach.

The stern, ever rising with the lifting wave, pushed the bows deeper into the frothing sea, [and] within seconds control of the lifeboat was lost. Now completely out of control the boat turned broadside to the wave and immediately filling turned over and sank, depositing its contents in all directions.† Luckily all were wearing their lifebelts. Incredibly all were cast up on the beach--coughing, retching and spluttering--despite the deadly undertow. Gathering together in a bedraggled group, the Second Officer counted them off, being somewhat surprised to find all present. Young Wilfred being an excellent swimmer had been one of the first ashore and least affected. Standing there in only trousers, remnants of shirt and lifebelt, shifting his bare feet in the burning sands, he sought out his friend Bill.

Thankful now they were comparatively safe on dry land, the next priority was water followed by food. Water was imperative in importance in this furnace-like heat of an unshaded, equatorial beach. The thin, narrow beach of fine brown sand stretched away in both directions for hundreds of miles, with the ocean bordering one side and the thick, verdant rain forest to the other.† Holding a brief council, the decision was reached to keep to the beach and walk in the direction with the sea to their left, in this they hoped they were heading deeper into neutral territory. Having been torpedoed off the Liberian coast, they sincerely hoped they were travelling deeper into Liberia. After walking for a short time, many were suffering from swelling and abrasions to their feet. Pausing for a welcome rest, sitting beneath a Palm tree fringing the beach, Wilf with others cut and ripped up the bottoms of their trousers to wrap their throbbing feet.

Onward went the intrepid, ragged little band, when, after some seven miles they sighted smoke, closing with it they soon sighted a native fishing village. On entering they were greeted by the headman and village elders. Using sign language and halting French they found to their mortification they had landed in French Equatorial Africa, namely French Guinea to be exact. Unknowingly, the tide and winds had carried them only a matter of a few miles south, past the border with Liberia. The headman supplied them with much welcome water, then set them a large meal, to the natives a banquet. Having never seen so many white men in their lives this was an event unsurpassed in their village history, and probably spoken about now sixty years later.†The meal consisted of chicken, yams, plantains and rice, unfortunately all cooked and swimming in palm oil, almost inedible to most. Further sign language produced more vegetables which they cooked themselves. Whilst the meal was in progress, the headman sent off a runner to the nearest town to inform the authorities of his sudden guests.†

Later that evening, an old French government official arrived accompanied by some native gendarmes. The old Frenchman informed them they were the first Englishmen he had seen or spoken to since 1910, having spent most of his adult life in the colonial service. Further, they were to accompany him to the main town of that area, but a short distance away. Arriving at the town of Tabou the following day they were placed in semi-confinement, but told they would soon be released. Being so poorly dressed, each was issued with shirt, trousers and sandals. On the fourth day of their semi-confinement, the jolly boat survivors turned up. A joyful reunion was enacted, now all thirty-three of the crew were together. Later that same day, a French Navy sloop anchored off Tabou, sending an armed party ashore they quickly and not too gently rounded up the survivors and took them on board.

Prisoners

Keeping them under armed guard on deck the sloop weighed anchor and was soon steaming down the coast. Six hours later the sloop entered the mouth of the River Sassandra and was soon alongside the jetty there. Marched down the gangway they were transferred to an army guard and placed in a secure compound within the confines of Sassandra Town.† The once cheerful attitude of the crew saw some deterioration with the generally surly, and openly hostile French. French authority within this colony of French Guinea was Vichy French. Not openly at war with the Allies, but very pro-German and violently anti-British. This attitude was well portrayed in their treatment of, theoretically, non-combatant Merchant Seamen.

Some clarification of the short, inglorious history of Vichy France is required to realize the reason for the treatment meted out to the British Seamen. With the fall of France to the then victorious Nazi armed forces, in mid 1940 Marshal Petain former hero of Verdun, on the 11th July of that year assumed supreme power in defeated France. The new government under Petain, as president, and Laval as premier, formed its administration centred on the city of Vichy, in southern, or, as called in the war years Unoccupied France. Completely under the control politically and physically, they were mere a rubber stamp for Hitler's 'New Order' of Occupied Europe. Another faction the 'Free French', fighting under their political leader General De-Gaulle fought, when the occasion demanded with the Allies.† These two factions, Vichy and Free French, pro-German or pro-Allies was the complex problem set before all governors of the French Colonies. On the 26th August 1940, Chad, Cameroon and part of Equatorial Africa joined the Free French faction; the others accepted Petain's government. Doubly unfortunate the luckless survivors had landed, first only six to seven miles from Liberia, secondly on Vichy controlled soil namely the Ivory Coast Colony.

The French authorities in the colony were in an embarrassing position. Ivory Coast, like other surrounding colonies being Vichy, were holding British citizens classified as non-combatants, and refusing them repatriation, or, initially even informing British or friendly authorities of the seaman being alive. This withholding of information of their survival caused undue agonies to the families of these men and boy. Wilfred's mother applied almost daily to the Red Cross and the ship's agent at Morel's, Cardiff for news. Living in dread that he was missing, believed drowned. In war this was as much as one was ever told. Still agonising what to do with the prisoners, one can assume the French authorities carried out a system used by all bureaucracies, 'Pass the Buck', in other words pass them on to another authority. This policy seemed to be adopted thus causing most of their captivity to be spent in seemingly aimless travel through huge West African possessions, many times the size of Europe. Now sitting or wandering around in their cramped compound, they waited to know their eventual fate.

After a few days they were ordered to collect their meagre belongings and then marched out of the compound gate to awaiting lorries. Once loaded with their human freight, the small convoy moved off. Moving slowly through the town under the inquisitive gaze of the local natives they soon cleared the township of Sassandra. The first few miles of road paralleled the Sassandra River with unchanging scenery of long stretches of sandy soils interspersed with long, course grass and low lying thorn bush. Crossing the river some ten miles upstream from the town, the groaning trucks headed inland. After some hours of uncomfortable travel in the bare backs of these ancient military lorries under armed guard, mainly native, they reached the rain forest. The equatorial rain forest of West Africa, primeval in content, extends for hundreds of miles inland: Similar to its counterpart in Brazil. This was an area almost untrodden by man, consisting mainly of hardwood and softwood trees, growing in an almost impenetrable screen, each vying with one another for the life-giving sun. Some, many hundreds of years old and huge in size with their branches interlocked cast a perpetual gloom to the forest floor.†

Beneath this canopy, engines snorting and whining, the little convoy struggled on, keeping to the winding dirt road that scythed through the trees and undergrowth. With headlights almost constantly on day or night the survivors suffered severely from the hothouse conditions. Trapped by the leafy canopy, the almost airless, humid temperature was almost unbearable. Sweating profusely, almost all delirious with the heat, they clung on grimly to the lorries.† After the second day the forest noticeably thinned. Soon native habitation was sighted both sides of the road at ever increasing intervals, the land they now passed through was of low, rolling hills partially cultivated but mainly of tall coarse grass with scattered and stunted Acacia trees, Depressing and monotonous this scenery remained with them for the next three days.

Twice a day they stopped to eat, the food supplied was native, in the morning half boiled rice with a shred of meat, in the evening watery soup with a coarse black bread, all served up in a communal pot into which they and their guards fed themselves by the simple expedient of using fingers, some none too clean.† Portent of things to come was signified by an outbreak of dysentery a well-known scourge of the tropics. This disease affecting one's stomach and hence one's bowels needs little imagination to realize the suffering of one tossed hour after hour in an unsprung military truck. With armed guards under the command of an uncaring white, French sergeant to relieve oneself from a moving lorry was no mean feat. Security was lax, in his halting English the French sergeant explained the guard was provided not to much to stop escape, but to keep off marauding native lawless bands who would kill for the clothes they wore. Within this huge, sprawling French Equatorial Empire policing was very thin on the ground, leaving vast areas where law and order was almost unheard of.

At the end of their third day of travel they reached a large town. Passing through its outskirts the crew saw the road sign: Daloa. Unknown to them, having no maps or reference, they had reached the main town of West Central Ivory Coast, chiefly a collecting point for the forest region products of cocoa, kola nuts and timber.† Since 1903, it had become a French military post. Now showing signs of crumbling decay, a rapid, and seemingly natural process in the tropics, [the town† was] populated mainly by the Bete and Guro tribes. Many of these, along with a few inquisitive French civilians, flocked to the barracks to see the newly-incarcerated white prisoners.† Once again they were fed native-style, one bowl to four or five persons, and they ate using their hands. Knives, forks and spoons were never issued, although cheap enough to supply. Hygiene almost unknown to the native was never a forte of Colonial France. Now after some weeks in captivity, almost all were suffering in some degree or other from Bacillary Dysentery.†

On the morning of their second day of imprisonment in the filthy barrack-room of Daloa's military post, the door was flung open by a guard to admit a white-coated doctor.

A brief medical inspection ensured, but no words were spoken or exchanged; it ended with the issue of several white pills to everyone and a speedy departure of the doctor. Within minutes, a French officer appeared to inform them they were all fit to travel and [to] make ready to move. That afternoon, they boarded the same lorries, and, under the same guards, rumbled off through the dirty streets of Daloa, now empty in the enervating heat of the mid-day sun, bound for they knew not where.† With frequent stops for the sick, the caravan of lorries wended slowly, but ever moving farther into, and deeper, the African Continent. The monotony of the undulating Savannah gave one the feeling they were hardly moving. To this, their poor health and repetitive diet gave scope to a general feeling of melancholia, often felt by captives in such circumstances. The blasting, oppressive heat of the day drove all for cover under their makeshift sheets or blankets in the open trucks.

A welcome relief from the monotony was provided by the crossing, by ferry, of the Bandama River some 300 miles from Daloa. At the end of the second day of leaving Daloa, the township of Bouake was reached. Bouake as much the same as a thousand other African townships, had one outstanding quality, a railway terminus! On arrival at Bouake, the prisoners were driven straight to the small, dusty railway station and swiftly transferred to awaiting railway trucks normally reserved for natives. Within the hour, a small old-fashioned steam engine was connected up and was fussily steaming out of the town over its metre-gauge tracks. The trucks, although filthy and uncomfortable, were a welcome relief from the swaying and bumping of the open, unsprung lorries. For two days and nights, they remained on the train, ever travelling north westerly, but in more comfort than their previous mode of transport. One could lie and even stretch, remaining comparatively dry from the daily downpour. †On the third morning, the little train puffed its way into the first major town since leaving Bouake. Gradually slowing, it clanked its way to a stop at its rail end. Peering through the slats and narrow glassless windows, they saw the station board proudly announcing Bobo Dioulasso.

Detraining, they were mustered alongside the train, counted off, and handed over to a new guard, similar in size as the old, who, promptly on receipt of exchange, entrained for return to their parent unit. Standing with their few belongings, none too clean from lack of water, exuding the cloying stench prominent in all dysentery sufferers, the Allende crew presented a sorry sight. No pity, aid, or affection, was shown to them by the few white soldiers and civilians present [and] with their curiosity satisfied, they moved off without a word. After mustering, they were marched off, once again to the ever-present military barrack [that was] part of every French colonial town of any size.

Again they were visited by a military doctor who informed them they were now in the colony of Upper Volta, and now under a new administration. Like the colony of French Guinea, the Upper Volta administrators wanted to rid themselves of British non-combatant prisoners. Likewise, they were all pronounced fit for travel after another mockery of a medical examination.† On completion of the examination and with undue haste, the captive seamen were again marched out, some assisting others through the barrack gate and to awaiting lorries. This time, many required help in getting over the tailgates. Off again, hanging grimly on, similar in type to the previous lorries, poorly sprung, noisy, issuing clouds of noisome exhaust fumes, which tended to lessen their fly torment. A change in direction was now obvious to the mariners: for some hours they were travelling always due east. To converse with the guards was useless, not even they knew their eventual destination, happy to go along with their French superiors, their childlike confidence enough for their undeveloped mental capacities.† Late on the first evening on leaving Bobo Dioulasso, they reached another large town.

The fittest and more inquisitive stood up in the lorries in hope of reading any road signs. Soon they passed a road sign denoting the township of Sikasso. Stopping outside the main buildings, they disembarked and were locked up for the night in the town's jail compound, fed and told to rest until daybreak. Not knowing, they were now within the region of Sikasso, part of Southern French Sudan. They had now entered their third colony of the French African Empire. Some mention of the size of French Sudan (now Mali) must be made to give some indication of the distances travelled. French Sudan has been calculated to be 31 times the size of Switzerland, adding the other colonies surrounding French Sudan, some the size of major European countries, some idea of size can be grasped.† At daybreak they were fed again the same eternal meal of half-cooked rice and black bread. Having finished their meal and before the general daily rising of the townspeople, they were led, some half carried, to their waiting lorries. Within minutes, they had cleared the town still moving in a westerly direction. Moving once more through the Savannah-like countryside, now abounding in wildlife, whose proximity to the small caravan of lorries offered some break in the monotony. They spent their days in adapting themselves to the most comfortable position possible in the bouncing, swaying trucks.

An indication of their endless journey can best be illustrated in their routine for one day's travel: Starting at daybreak, after a meal of rice and bread washed down by weak coffee, they boarded their respective trucks; using the filled rice sacks, they positioned them for their own comfort. The first hours were the best of the day being reasonably cool and dry, the tropical sun only beginning to bite around 10 am. Rigging awnings and using their own ragged clothing, they sought some shade from the relentless sun. Late afternoon produced a build up of heavy, fetid heat and high humidity which although distressing was soon replaced by a bigger discomfort. The heavy diurnal (daily) rainstorm accompanied by thunder and sheet lightning descended upon them. Within minutes the lorries were flooded. The huge raindrops cold from rapid descent from great heights, blanked out visibility, stopping the lorries and leaving its human contents shivering in abject misery beneath their makeshift awnings. Collapsing awnings created a miniature Niagara over the tailgate. Luckily of short duration the storm passes and within the hour the heat and humidity returns rapidly drying them and their scraps of clothing.

On the passing of the rainstorm, once again the lorries move off if the road is passable; if not, a wait of some hour or so sufficed in this terrific heat to dry the track. Sometimes the lorries would bog down or leave the dirt road, requiring the occupants to exit the lorries and help push or pull them back to firmer terrain. This part of an almost daily routine, once welcome for the working of cramped muscle, was now a form of torture to weak, ill men. Late evening the welcome stop was made for the night. Fires were lit and they cooked their own rice, the hard black bread being supplied by the guards. After their frugal meal, some time was spent sat around their fires before retiring to sleep in their lorries. No guard was set for them [because] guarding them was of no importance; escape into the wilderness was death itself. Principally the guard, when set, was to ward off wild, dangerous animals and murderous bands of natives. All of French West Africa suffered from these brigands. Many unwary people travelling alone, or in small unarmed groups, had been killed by them.†

With troubled sleep, so ended a ënormal day' of their travel. An addition to this ënormal day', one must realize the needs of dysentery sufferers and other tropical diseases, now, symptoms accelerating in the torrid heat, gave further alarm, pain and suffering to the crew members. On their third day of leaving Bobo Dioulasso they crossed another large river. Brown and sluggish in appearance, the Volta Noire, one of the main rivers of the same named region was crossed by ferry without mishap. Travelling swiftly, within hours they reached the outskirts of the biggest township they had so far seen. Signs along the roadside way indicated they had reached Bamako. Unknown to the captive crew they were entering the chief town of the district similarly named within the colony of French Sudan. Occupied since 1880 and becoming capital town of French Sudan, Bamako extended some miles both sides of a huge, slow flowing river, of which they soon found to be the massive, and well-known Niger. Bamako although the premier town of French Sudan, was similar in appearance and smell as all the other towns they had passed through, the only difference being in size.† On entry they were assailed by the usual smells of open drains and rotting garbage. The garbage lying in huge rotting mounds gave off an overpowering smell, only equalled by the open town's sewage system. In this year of 1942, less than one in ten houses, including government buildings were attached to the crumbling, colonial sewage system emptying itself into the Niger.

Passing down its dusty, tree lined main street, the little convoy quickly drove through the market place, less than half-filled at this time of day, most market dwellers paying scant attention to the military transport. Passing through the market place, they observed its high enclosing walls and pink turrets, its design resembling a Medieval or French Foreign Legion fort. Closer inspection revealed time and lack of maintenance made one wonder how it was still standing. The captain, officers and crew now thought they had reached journey's end. Since the sinking of their ship, they had been almost continually on the move for two months, travelling hundreds of miles by lorry, train and foot, in one of the world's worst climates. Now through lack of food, ill health, hammered by a relentless sun and torrential rains, they were worn out, Walking, stumbling, and physically carrying some of their more supine comrades, the fittest helping the ill into their fourth native barracks, like all previous, filthy, damp, dark and alive with fleas and insects.† At each barrack or jail the captain and officers requested an interview with any senior French officer or administrator; none came.

Further entreaties were made for variation in diet, the regions they had passed through abounded in fresh meat, tropical fruits and vegetables, none was forthcoming. The refusal of cheap and plentiful supplies of this nature left the captain and crew with the nagging and frightening conclusion that the French authorities were hoping they would 'disappear' or die, hopefully whilst travelling between colonies relieving them of responsibility. Their hopes now centred on the investigations of the Red Cross. The Red Cross, efficient in time of war, seemed mainly designed in accordance with the Geneva Convention for the fighting services. The Merchant Marine classified derisively as Non-Combatants actually saw more 'front line' fighting in a continuous on going fighting than any of the Armed Services.

Some days after the sinking of the ss Allende a telegram arrived at the house of the parents of Wilfred. Dressed in his dark blue serge uniform with pillbox hat and pouched leather belt, the telegram boy knocked at the door. The telegram boy in wartime had become a figure of ultimate importance, far exceeding any other person in town or village. It was the practice of other children, on seeing the boy on his distinctive red bicycle, to follow him to his house of delivery, then run home to tell one's parents. In wartime, the contents of a telegram had only two meanings. Those few typed and pasted words covered the whole spectrum of human feeling: Utterly inexpressible joy, or, devastating grief.† Answering the knock on the door, Mrs. Williams, seeing the telegram, froze. In abject terror she received the proffered, small buff envelope. This was the second telegram in as many months, the first informing her that her nephew, Jack Gamboll, a regular Royal Navy Acting Petty Officer serving in the Submarine P33, had been lost with all its crew, believed sunk off Italy in an unknown minefield. Jack who was treated as a son having lost his mother (Mrs. Williams's sister} in childhood, presented a loss to the Williams family similar to loosing a son.† Mrs. Williams, still suffering and mourning Jack's memory, now held a second telegram in her quivering hands. Waiting patiently for a possible reply, the telegram boy, now used to such behaviour, watched Mrs. Williams slowly open the envelope, her reaction spelling the text of the telegram.

With no reply, the boy stole quietly away. Sitting at the kitchen table, the telegram held in both hands, she read it once again, the shock and grief making it almost unintelligible. The blurred words were as follows:

Morel's Ltd., of Cardiff has been informed by the Lordship's of the Admiralty, that the ss Allende of that company had been sunk by enemy action off the West African coast. NO KNOWLEDGE OF SURVIVORS HAD BEEN RECEIVED TO DATE.

Collapsing over the table, grief overwhelming, Mrs. Williams gave in to tears of despair. The arrival of the telegram, having been noted by the neighbours, resulted in Mrs. Hall from next door coming round. On seeing Mrs. Williams's condition, she offered some comfort and immediately had Mr. Williams, now a Ministry of Defence policeman, informed at his work at the local munitions factory.† Coming home immediately, Wilfred's father arrived coincidentally at the same time as the younger boys, Luther and Kenneth, from school. White and drawn, Wilfred's father, a veteran himself of the First War, twice wounded and having faced death a hundred times in the trenches, comforted the family in the knowledge that no deaths had been specified, and they could only wait and hope.† Access to information could only be obtained from two sources concerning Merchant Seamen lost or taken prisoner. Firstly the Red Cross, secondly the Shipping Line to which the ship belonged. Both sources were now constantly bombarded with letters and phone calls from Mrs. Williams requesting information.

Some months later another telegram arrived with all its mental trauma. With joy, this revealed that the Red Cross had received information that, on the sinking of the ss Allende, five of the engine and boiler crew had been killed, and the rest had been taken into captivity in Vichy-held territory within the French West African Colonies. With a mixed joy for her eldest son and grief for the families of those killed, Mrs. Williams, having obtained a list of the crew's addresses, wrote to every member's family, to those killed in sympathy and to the rest to pool any other information, also writing constantly to the Red Cross. Three sometimes four times a week she wrote, but month followed month with no added information. The Red Cross never received any signals other than they believed they were alive but not in receipt of Red Cross aid or treatment. So the torment of uncertainty was inflicted on Wilfred's family and the families and loved ones of the crew. Not knowing whether alive or dead, day followed day, and weeks then months passed. The agony and misery, like some malignant disease seemed eternal. Vichy French attitude to the prisoners was equalled only by the Japanese treatment meted out to theirs.

Lying now in their filthy barracks building, fitfully sleeping on the hard native mattresses supplied, incessantly tossing and turning, scratching countless insect and fleabites attracted by their body warmth they passed through the night. Daybreak brought the guards and their tasteless meal. A difference followed their general routine adopted so far; instead of a medical they were led out of the derelict building and led down to the river's edge. Passing over a rickety wooden pier, they embarked into a small flotilla of native canoes. These canoes, better known as pirogues, unbeknown to them were to be their transport and homes for the next eleven to twelve days. Their travel was to take them up one of the largest, but least known rivers in Central Africa, the River Niger.†

The Niger, third largest [river], being only inferior to the Nile and Congo in all Africa, rises within 150 miles of the sea in the mountainous regions on the North West borders of Sierra Leone and French Guinea. It flows through the interior in a vast curve. Firstly flowing northeast, then east, eventually turning southeast, finally entering the Gulf of Guinea through an immense delta: Its total length being some 2,600 miles. From its mouth to its limits of navigation from the sea, Niger was in British territory; above that point it flows through French territory.† Bundled into their waiting canoes, clutching their meagre belongings, the captives departed Bamako in first light, their departure witnessed by some beggars awakened from their sleep on the muddy riverbank. At this point, the Niger presents itself in all its majesty. Slow flowing, over 6 feet in depth and 1,300 feet in width, it provides the water and method of transportation for most of French West Africa, winding and curling like some gigantic python. Some comfort was gained by the small group of native craft, in that they moved slowly, paddling and poling when in shallows, always moving with the sluggish current as the ëdry season' which was about to end provided them with some ease. Some two months later in late May and early June the rains became continuous, bringing with it, insufferable heat and every conceivable disease prevalent in Equatorial Africa. Some 150 years previous, Mungo Park, a famous Scottish explorer, with some 43 European soldiers and fellow travellers had left the same town of Bamako.

Travelling downstream on a mission of discovery, sailing in exactly the same type of rudely constructed native pirogues as the Allende's crew, they were caught by the rains. Within two to three weeks, 40 of them were dead. Dying of diseases and fevers, some from apoplexy (thus recorded) brought on by the stultifying heat and humidity. Temperatures recorded by Parke at times were 120-135 degrees Fahrenheit.† The comfort of smooth journey was negated by the cramped conditions and appalling heat they suffered in the open, narrow canoes. Almost all, after some days, exercised their limbs when possible, by walking on the low river mud banks. Almost all wearing broken shoes or sandals unknowingly were subject to the immediate attack by the jigger flea.

On the third morning of river travel they reached the rapids of Tulimandio. Passing swiftly, and alarmingly through them, the high rocky banks with large granite outcrops opened out once more to low lying banks giving a vista of complete flatlands to the distant horizon, broken only by the occasional low-spreading Acacia tree. Heavily populated, much cultivation was in evidence. As they progressed these populated areas, many natives followed them for miles down the riverbanks, offering every conceivable item for sale. Unfortunately with no money and entirely ignored by the guards, they paddled on.† The morning of the fourth day, they reached the town of Segu. Segu like most towns on the Niger lay sprawled on both banks. Little change since Mungo Parke's a century or more earlier. Originally a Moorish slave trading centre, it now consisted mainly of clay, whitewashed houses, clustered around narrow streets and overshadowed by the inevitable Mosque. Without landing and with a change of native paddlers, they quickly proceeded on. For some hundreds of miles they slowly ventured on, passing, again without pausing, the small townships of Sansandig and Silla. Unchanging, the scenery was tiresome in its continuity of low banks and flatlands and occasionally broken by the herds of hippopotami and basking crocodiles, both given a wide berth by the paddlers and guards. The seventh day since leaving Bamako saw them enter the river township of Mopti. Situated at the junction of the main stream of the Niger, and, its breaking off into its several branches to pass for several hundreds of miles through a malarial, swampy, treeless region, possibly one of the most unhealthy, disease ridden areas of the tropics. Within its labyrinth of lakes, its largest lake Faguibini - 70 miles in length, 12 miles in breadth, and, at the height of the rainy season 160 feet deep - exists creeks, stagnant pools and stinking backwaters. Now being late April, the rains had not yet arrived, giving comfort and even life to the captive crew.

At Mopti, young Wilfred, assisted by his friend Bill, staggered ashore. Sitting on the mudflats, mindful of Chiggers, Wilfred noticed an occurrence he had seen several times before whilst descending the Niger. Into his view came a young Negro, similar in age to Wilfred, leading a chain of eight or more natives, all with their right or left hand alternately holding a loop in a length of rope. Its leading end [was] held by the boy, who, as he walked, chanted incessantly to the men stumbling on behind, not unlike a coffle of slaves being led to market. Having witnessed this scene before, sometimes with rope, other times a long stick. Wilfred with some difficulty asked a native guard, who or what were they? Pointing to the river then his eyes, he graphically explained the reason: River Blindness. (See base note) Within, and almost its whole length the Niger contained a parasitic worm, which, almost unique to this area, is carried by flies, breeding in the river and its tributaries, has caused an endemic, crippling disease, which, in some villages more than half its inhabitants are effected.† Millions of people in the region suffer from River Blindness, a horrifying and shocking disease, slow but inevitable. The parasitic worms burrow beneath the skin, laying their eggs which are carried by the blood stream eventually enter and grow behind the living eye. A tremor of apprehension felt by Wilfred and Bill was swiftly transmitted to their compatriots who now viewed every fly with mortal terror.

This region of Marcina, with its huge unhealthy marshlands, alive with Malaria and Blackwater Fever, being but two of the many killers, extend through the middle course of the Niger, forming channels and meandering waterways, causing a vast inland delta as large as Wales. Traversing this wild swampy marshland as quick as possible, even cooking their rice on board, their canoes paddled and poled onwards. Moving with the sluggish current their Fulani paddlers were only too happy to work hard to leave this God-Forsaken country behind.† Other diseases and tropical fevers were beginning to surface among the crew. Lack of mosquito netting, coupled to dietary and hygiene problems, left them weak and receptive to all ailments. Continuously bit by winged and other insects, some were beginning to signs of fever. Certain symptoms [like] hot sweating followed by extreme prostration was symptomatic of malaria, probably caught in the rainforests of French Guinea. Others were suffering from a form of tape worm found throughout Central Africa, caught usually by eating half-cooked food (mainly rice). The worm lived and grew at a phenomenal rate within the stomach, removing the goodness of the ingested food and giving immediate symptoms of loss of weight and a constant hunger. A native emetic was administered, vile, horribly smelling, and guaranteed to make one vomit.

Wilfred, a growing boy of sixteen, needing a wholesome diet to fuel his ever-growing frame, was much affected by the heat, lack of food and medical care. Through a never-changing diet, week after week, he was beginning to show the classic effects of pellagra, dietetic in origin [and] due mainly to vitamin B deficiency. The withholding of fresh meat, eggs, milk and fats, to which the body was conditioned, was having its effect. Its symptoms - dry tongue, pain when swallowing, and slight disorder of vision - was now being produced in the younger members, Both Wilfred and friend Bill were suffering in some degree these insidious symptoms.

On the evening of the eleventh day, they reached the river port of Kabara. After eleven days and nights of never-ending nightmarish travel in crude, open native pirogues, Wilfred and the remaining crew reached the upper-northern reaches of the Niger. At this bend of the Niger, where it flows eastwards before bearing south to eventually empty itself into the South Atlantic, lays the river settlement of Kabara. Kabara is the primary place of disembarkation from river traffic bound for Timbuktu. Lying on the muddy riverbanks, a mere huddle of low, mud brick buildings, it serves as a river port for Timbuktu a mere few miles away.

Now standing in a little, bedraggled, forlorn group, [they felt] the heat of the sun-baked mud flats through the soles of their broken shoes and sandals. The most seriously ill were laid gently down. [They used] what scraps of rags they could spare, covering themselves from the relentless Saharan sun. The ever-curious multitude of local natives was kept, by the guards, at a distance, which ensured speech or touch was not possible. †After a brief time, the Guard Commander, who undoubtedly had been enjoying his lunch in the town, appeared. With customary French efficiency, of shouts and blows with much swearing at the native soldiery, he formed the survivors up into some semblance of order for the march to Timbuktu. If Timbuktu had been more distant than a few miles, some of the seamen could well have died. The Lascar seamen, mainly stokers and trimmers, were beginning to lapse into a state of abject melancholia, accelerated by their physical condition, and they were giving up the will to live.

Wilfred was now finding difficulty to walk [but] never lost his spirit to live out this nightmare. Aided by Bill, he struggled and shambled along with the rest. Weak and unused to standing, alone walking, eleven days of crouching and sitting in cramped dugout canoes had left its mark.†With many stops for rest, they eventually passed through the crumbling town of Kabara. Clearing Kabara, they now entered a thick forest of low stunted and prickly scrub, impenetrable in its thickness. (This forest only fifty years later has entirely disappeared; only sand dunes exist now.) Passing slowly through this forest with even more frequent stops to revive their exhaustion, the guards grew increasingly worried. Even at mid-day the forest floor was dark and uninviting. The guards tried to quicken the pace; this short distance between Kabara and Timbuktu was bandit infested and the forest provided perfect ambush at any time. Even the guards feared this area. Their slowness, due to the prisoners' condition, caused some apprehension in that they may be caught by nightfall still some distance from Timbuktu. With trepidation and well-founded terror, the guards even physically helped the most incumbent along.

Towards evening, the forest edge was reached, and with apparent relief, the guards led their small caravan of scarecrow-like prisoners into the outskirts of Timbuktu. Entering the narrow alleyways and dirty streets, they passed firstly the mud brick hovels, [their] windows and doors heavily barred and barricaded. Often it seemed that these living on the outskirts suffered often from the hit and run raids of the dreaded Tuareg and their Negro helpers, who, after murder and pillage disappeared into the forest or the vast wastes of the Sahara. Advancing farther into the town, the dirt roads progressively widened with larger and better built houses, man-fitted with large front doors of incredible thickness, often carved and heavily studded with metal. Closer examination revealed the carving denoted some long past battle between Tuareg and Negro Kingdom, through the chequered history of Timbuktu. Like campaign medals of a modern age, these doors told the passer-by the wars or actions its original owner had partaken in. (These doors have become world renowned, many are worth much more than the house itself!). Onwards they struggled in the thickening gloom, passing down darkening alleys, wary of the open sewers, whose presence the smell gave warning of proximity sooner than sight.

Eventually they reached an area surrounded by barbed wire containing several mouldering mud brick huts. Through a heavily wired gate, entry was gained by the exhausted crew. Completely spent, some collapsed on the ground spending the whole night there, others staggered into the dark, dismal huts, windowless and stifling in the evening heat, only to find them infested with fleas, cockroaches and a myriad of other creeping crawling insects all intent on feeding off their new occupants. Uncaring through weariness in its extreme, they collapsed on the native beds provided, unsprung, unyielding and themselves uncaring. With daybreak those able and inquisitive enough rose and surveyed their new surroundings. Daylight revealed the depressing sight of a totally enclosed, heavily barbed wired, earth floored compound, within which a few dilapidated buildings represented their frugal living quarters. Outside their compound similar single storey hovels, some in even a worse state of repair lay huddled in little haphazard groups separated by narrow evil smelling alleys and garbage filled paths. The flat, brown vista was only broken by the remnants of an old Mosque, like some anthill, worn by the winds of time. To the prisoners it was now visibly obvious that their prison lay well within the poorer native section of Timbuktu. Rising early, seeking same small comfort from the cool of daybreak, their silence only broken by the call to pray of the Mezzuin atop the Mosque's minaret, the captives gained stock of their new confinement. Dressed now in rags, many having torn up their mattress covers converting them to crude skirts, worn to give cover from the burning sun, they sat around in the stifling, airless, desiccating heat of another day. Twice a day without fail, two huge bowls - one of rice and the other of weak soup with the inevitable black bread - were pushed into the compound, into which they plunged their hands and fed themselves native fashion.† Sixty-three days they remained in this hellhole, uncared for, unwanted and treated with complete indifference by the French authorities. By the second week most were lying down all day, conserving energy needed only for rising to their next meal. Sitting or lying in the shade when possible, with remnants of rags around their faces and exposed limbs, they desperately awaited the end of another day to the incinerating sun.† No cooling comfort came with the wind. When the unwelcome wind blew from the desert, it arrived like some furnace blast, drying every pore, and in seconds converting the mouth and lips to a dry swelling irritation, demanding instant relief found only in the brackish, bitter, sandy unfiltered water which grudgingly they were supplied. Seeking some shelter from the burning wind, they tottered into their mud hovels, flinging themselves down of their straw bundles, swooning with the intolerable airless heat within. After some two or more weeks living in these conditions, a parallel could be drawn to the French prisoners incarcerated in the infamous prison colony of French Guiana. Again situated in the tropics [and] suffering similar diseases, but probably fed better and at least under a penal institution, these French prisoners were hardly ever expected to live their sentence out. Undoubtedly the French wanted the crew to die.

They began to die. At the beginning of the fourth week of incarceration in Timbuktu, fevers compounded by dysentery and other unwelcome diseases had brought many of the crew to a new low. The Captain's entreaties for even the most basic medical treatment were now answered by a brief visit of a French military doctor. Entering the compound, the white-coated doctor, escorted by an armed NCO, gave a swift medical examination to the crew.† On his orders, one of the survivors - the worst ill - was removed from the compound and taken away. Their joy in receiving medical treatment was soon dampened; by nightfall of that day the Captain was tersely informed that the man taken away to the ëhospital' had died. A request by the Captain for a Christian burial in a predominantly Moslem country and town was granted. Buried the following day his shipmates, who could walk or stand, attended the funeral. Gathered in a forlorn, ragged little group around the open, wind swept graveside; they lowered their shipmate to his eternal rest within the barren soil of Timbuktu. Reading a short service the bare-headed Captain and crew were then hastily removed from the tiny Christian cemetery and unceremoniously bundled back to their compound.

After some two or more weeks, another crew member had reached crisis point. Weakened by continual neglect and lack of food, exacerbated by unknown fever he was rapidly reaching death's door. Again the Captain requested the doctor. Once again the doctor duly arrived, once again with an armed escort, and like before ordered the sick man to the ëhospital', a hospital that no crew member had ever seen. That night, as before, the Captain was informed the man had died. On both these occasions, although requested by the Captain, neither he nor an officer was allowed to accompany the sick men. The following day, once again a crew member was buried alongside his shipmate: Both laid to rest over 1000 miles from the sea and many more from home; both of the Christian faith - simple memorials were placed at the heads of each grave.† Once again back in the compound, the Captain gathered the survivors about him. In hushed silence the crew listened to the Captain's words. He informed them that he had now had the awful, frightening feeling that the French were deliberately killing the very sick, and no matter how ill they became they would remain together until death. All agreed, knowing that now it would be a matter of weeks or months before most would be dead. Some little comfort was felt in at least dying with friends.

Unbeknown to the prisoners, the French Colonial Authorities were having a change of mind. Pro-German and anti-Allies at the start, now with the recent loss of Madagascar to a British Free-French landing force, which in a matter of days destroyed part of their Navy and land forces firstly in Diego Suarez harbour then throughout the Colony, the French were now becoming rather frightened. Many Vichy Frenchmen were now beginning to 'turn their coats' as it became more obvious the Allies were going to win. This turncoat attitude was prevalent throughout the French Equatorial Colonies.

On the ending of the ninth week in captivity at Timbuktu almost half the crew could not stand, many, totally incumbent had taken to their straw bundles, having used their mattresses as crude body cover. Lying in the stupefying heat of their mud hovels, too weak to fend off the flies, lice and other insects, they lay in their abject misery. Lying on his straw bundle, now almost too weak to move, every day being an eternity, Wilfred was reaching the end. Being the youngest, there was a tendency of the crew to give him a little more food than they took from the communal bowl twice daily. His growing body required that extra sustenance; his stamina at the age of sixteen to withstand the rigours of this inhuman treatment was far less than a grown, older man. Now suffering from several open ulcers on his feet and legs, dysentery, mild fever and a low-grade Pellagra, his six foot slim frame was reduced to less that eight stone in weight, [and] he lay in an oven like heat of a sweltering native dwelling barely aware he was alive. At this time of the year, June, the Saharan sun rose daytime temperatures to a soaring 130 to 140 degrees Fahrenheit.† The word 'suffering' can, and often is passed over rather quickly. Wilfred's 'suffering' can be partially brought home to one if one remembers his age. Sixteen years old, when most were still in school Wilf was thousands of miles from home and family, treated worse than any German POW camp, and suffering from†multiple ailments, ailments hardly known in civilised countries:

Dysentery - A disease of the bowel, in its worst form a killer if not treated.

Ulcers - A superficial sore, discharging pus, becoming ever worse if not treated, giving incredible long lasting pain, and can result in loss of limbs.

Pellagra - An eruptive skin complaint, very similar to scurvy, caused mainly by the lack of vitamins, mainly vitamin Bl. This horrible disease leaves the skin, at least in Wilfred's case dry, scaly, almost fishlike.

Coupled to these mentioned above was the everlasting hunger, the knowing of no modern treatment, and the seemingly wish by the Vichy French Authority for them to die. All this combined needed an extra power to have the will to live. Helped by Bill Haynes, Wilfred was sitting outside in the shade awaiting the morning meal. The usual routine of the guards was interrupted by the entrance of the white-coated military doctor accompanied, startlingly, by senior uniformed French Army officers. Armed not with side-arms but with large oily smiles, they called the crew together.† Once mustered the French officers shook the hand of the old Captain and officers, professing with smarmy platitudes and much arm waving it must have been all a mistake, and was not their responsibility. Standing on a rickety, worm eaten bench, their sole furniture, the French doctor, the most-hated Frenchmen of all announced in broken English they would soon be going home.† Standing there on his precarious perch, he evinced his love and respect for the British people. Anyone of the crew given a rope would have gladly hanged him. With a further wave of his white-coated arm, more native guards entered the compound, each carrying armfuls of new clothing. Now told by the doctor to now discard their filthy rags, wash with unlimited water provided and dress in the lightweight, new socks, shirts, shorts and sandals provided. An extra shirt and shorts would also be issued to each man. Bemused by this the survivors were transported to limitless heights of happiness. At the beginning hardly able to believe it at first, this material gift gave reality to them going home. This news was better than any tonic; the will to live returned to all, even the Lascar element of the crew began showing signs of revival, their spirits raised by this glorious news.

Events moved swiftly. Told to collect their meagre belongings they were removed from their filthy and hated compound, and placed once again in waiting lorries. The French, now mindful of possibly a War Crimes Commission following up a victorious Allied conclusion to the war, treated them with the utmost kindness. Now the rainy season was well advanced, they were informed their return journey to the coast would not include the NIGER passage, during this mast dangerous of seasons.† Prior to leaving, a last request by the Captain was granted for those able to walk to visit the graves of their lost shipmates. Gathered in a little, sad group, they paid their last respects; A forlorn small party almost 1500 miles from the sea and over 3000 miles from home. Two British seamen laid to rest in a predominantly Moslem country under the blazing Saharan sun arid sterile soil. Of the remainder some half would have joined them within several short months, or even weeks! †

†After a brief service they returned to their awaiting trucks and quickly drove away due West into the desolate desert with never a backward glance. Once more on the move the crew adopted their well rehearsed and practiced mode of making do for lorry travel. Motoring due West, they travelled for two days and nights, moving swiftly over the compacted sands, steering by compass and stars, they traversed the trackless wastes of the Southern Sahara. Stopping near mid-day, they ate their rations, now varied and of much better quality. Using the lorries canopies, they spread them as awnings enabling them to sit in the shade,

panting in the awesome heat, now soaring to 130-140 degrees Fahrenheit at noon. Late afternoon they clambered back once again into their respective lorries. With the lessening heat they drove on, with the coming of sudden darkness, so swift in the desert, using headlights they carried on travelling at a reasonable high speed in these flat, arid wastes.† On the ending of the second night the lorries turned in a long South Westerly sweep. Skirting Lake Faguibine, they passed on well clear to the West of the Macina swamplands, now under constant heavy rain, and with it its attendant fevers as the rainy season was now well advanced. After six long days of driving through the sands and wild Savannah, they hit the dirt road to Segou. Progressing rapidly they soon reached the river town of Segou.

Once again they had reached the Niger, this time though purely for the crossing. Having crossed the Niger safely, the little convoy moved steadily on. Slower now in the heavy rains, heat and humidity that was now much higher than when they passed down the Niger in the 'dry season'. Weakened and ill, many were suffering terribly in the backs of the canopied lorries. Concern was now rising for the senior Wireless Operator and one seaman who were getting progressively worse. Struggling valiantly, grimly hanging on for dear life in the knowledge of soon being in friendly hands, they fought on. Wilfred too, was, with several others unable to stand. Spending all day lying under the rainproof awnings, they prayed for journey's end.† The eighth day of leaving Timbuktu, they crossed the Niger once again. Entering the township of Bamako once again, helped now by the 'friendly' French they were quickly transferred to the railway station. Knowing this station of old, the Captain and crew wondered if this was some elaborate trick being played on them, and were about to be sent back. Gathering on the station platform, they were informed that their journey would be by train on the Bamako to Dakar line. They would travel in the European section with accompanying guards and medical staff. Boarding the train they were separated from the French, placed into a carriage with upholstered and well-sprung seats, with comfortable mattresses for the incumbent. After open, poorly-suspensioned lorries, native rail trucks, mud brick hovels and bare earth, this luxury was beyond their wildest dreams.

For a further two days they travelled by train, by far the best mode of travel since captivity. Now in complete dryness and with some degree of comfort they traversed the Savannah landscape of the colony of Senegal. On the morning of the third day the train drew into a tiny station within the town of Tambacounda. In a heavy rainstorm they detrained and led to cover in a large, empty warehouse. Some minutes later a Civil Administrator complete with a retinue of junior officers appeared at the door. Re-enacting the performance of handshaking and crocodile tears of heartfelt sympathy and condolences of which the French have no equal, in perfect English he informed them they were now in the French colony of Senegal, but only a matter of two hours away from the British administered colony of The Gambia. Leaving with his retinue, he was quickly replaced by medical staff and military drivers. The French officer now conveyed to them they would now be driven to the border town of Brifu, within the colony of The Gambia, where a British delegation would meet them and the transfer would take place.

Within hours, most of them delirious with delight, some too far gone with fevers and dysentery to know what was happening, they arrived at Brifu. Brifu situated on the extreme tip of The Gambia was a nondescript native town lying within the unhealthy marshlands area of the upper reaches of the River Gambia. Helped from the lorries, some on stretchers, they were carried or tottered once again into a large open sided shed. On sight of fellow Britishers some broke down and sobbed. The transfer was quickly enacted without friendly overtures, the French leaving rapidly. A British doctor with native medical attendants now stepped forward, giving them a quick examination he declared their condition as deplorable, some not really being fit to move. Unfortunately local conditions could not allow them to stay in such inhospitable surroundings. Hurriedly moved to some small motor launches they were taken down the tortuous river Gambia. Reaching Georgetown that night they were taken ashore and given beds with clean sheets. Unused to them they spent a restless night. Next morning embarking on a single, but much larger craft they progressed downstream to the Capital town of Bathurst (now Benjal). On arrival they were taken immediately to the main hospital, many remaining there, the fitter and luckier taken to a convalescent area. Bureaucracy again reared its ugly head. No one it seems could decide whether the Allende crew were released Prisoners-of War, or, as non-combatants, merely released civilians. †If they had been a Royal Navy crew, undoubtedly they would have been feted; the officers lionized by the white authorities. If they had been civilians, they would have been treated as equals by their fellow colonials; but these were Merchant Seaman, bringing into play all the old racial, caste, and class position so remarkable among all British Colonials.

One common feeling felt between crew and administration was to leave The Gambia behind them as soon as possible. Within days the crew fragmented. Alone and almost unknown, the critically ill seaman died in hospital. Wilfred, with others too ill to walk or even stand, were transferred by ship to Freetown, Sierra Leone, just over one day's steaming away. Too ill to move, the Senior Wireless Operator stayed in Bathurst hospital. Bill Haynes, Wilf's friend and 'townie', accompanied by seaman Sidney Milroy worked their passage home in a merchant ship, luckily surviving their dangerous passage, although being attacked several times when in convoy. Being a 'slow convoy' they took some weeks before arriving home. Wilfred with the incumbent sailed home on a fast Hospital Ship, arriving home two or more weeks before Bill Haynes.† It is believed that nearly half the remaining crew, after suffering and surviving all this, went down on their way home. Torpedoed once again, but with no survivors.

Homecoming
Wilfred arrived at his home at 105, Manor Road, Abersychan, Monmouth (Now Gwent), on the afternoon of the 13th. August 1942 (another 13!). Two days before his seventeenth birthday. Six foot in height, weight eight stone! Hair still long, shoulder length (unusual then), covered in scars, wields and scabrous sores, he was a wreck of his former self. † Doted on by his mother, family and local

doctor (Dr Warren) he was still unable to eat normal meals. He was nursed with great love and devotion by his mother, who was a nurse many years ago. With passing months Wilfred grew stronger and fitter. What he had been through had earned him the right of a civilian job for the rest of the war, not that he could be 'Called Up', he was still one year under age, Feeling fit and ready for work, on a cold February day Wilfred disappeared from the house.

On returning he cheerfully announced he'd found a job. Further enquiry by his mother about the job reduced her to a flood of tears. He had been to Newport 'signed on the Pool'. No amount of persuasion or entreaties changed his mind. Some weeks later on the 3rd April 1943 young Wilfred joined his second ship, the ss Tortuguero at Cardiff, holding the rating of Assistant Steward, once again he went to war.† With infrequent leave, Wilfred spent the whole of the remaining war at sea. From ss Tortuguero he then served in ss Fort Norman followed by the ss Vermillion. Seeing many ships sank around him he was lucky to survive without another sinking. He saw service in the North and South Atlantic, Mediterranean, Indian and Pacific Oceans: The whole spectrum and theatres of the Second World War. When the war ended he wasn't even 21 years of age. His war service was longer and greater than many twice his age.

Bill Haynes, Wilfred's friend and 'Townie', like Wilf, was soon voluntary at sea again. Unlike Wilf, poor Bill paid the ultimate price at the tender age of 20 years. Joining the ss Empire Tower as a seaman he sailed from a Welsh port once again. On the 5th March 1943, only seven months after surviving his first adventure the Empire Tower was torpedoed and sunk. So rapidly did she sink that only four survived. Sadly Bill was not one of them. †The agony of war does not end with its declaration of peace. Until she died some twenty years or more later, Mrs. Haynes never locked her backdoor. Until her death she believed that one day, or night, he would return. Such is the awful finality of such a loss. Nothing is ever the same.

Wilfred stayed on in the Merchant Navy, serving in the following ships: ss Empire Prome until 1947. Then joining the Company of Charles Hill & Sons of Bristol, he served in: ss Boston City, ss New York City, ss Bristol City. He served in these ships for some eight years, eventually "swallowing the anchor" in September 1955. His last years were as Chief Ship's Cook.

Diary written by Thomas Williamson, Master of SS. Allende March 1942.
(provided by Audrey & John Williamson)
March 17th 1942 S.S. Allende torpedoed by German submarine, about 18 miles South of Cape Palmas, Liberia at 7 p.m. at ship. I had only just left the bridge, where Fullerton, the Chief Officer and I had been looking for Cape Palmas light, before altering course to the North. We had seen no sign of the light, and before leaving the bridge, I said to the Mate, "If you don't see the light before 8 o'clock, I'll alter course then."

I came down off the bridge and had just entered the saloon, switched on the light and shut the door, when she got it. A terrific explosion and instant darkness. The ship seemed to shudder and stop dead in her track, the engines were silent.

I rushed up the inside stairway and up to the bridge, the Chief Officer was not to be seen, but W. Haines, a deck boy was at the wheel and he said, "The Mate has gone down to get the boats away."

I rang half speed astern on the telegraph, but there was no answer. Looking over the side, the ship appeared stopped. and making no way at all. It was very dark and the sky moderately overcast. I sent the man away from the wheel to his boat, went down on the lower bridge with my binoculars, a pair of 7 X 50 prisms, and searched round for any sign of the submarine.

Lewis, W/T man transmitted S.O.S. about 20 times but afterwards in the boat he said that he thought someone was transmitting very powerfully close ship, possibly the sub. jamming. (Saw no sign of the sub.).

The Mate came up with the boat's crew of the Port Jolly boat. He said, "She's got it in the engine room, on the Port side, the port life boat's blown to bits and the 2nd Mate, P. McHugh is already away with your boat."

I said, "All right, get your boat in the water and I'll come in that when I've had a look around, I want to get everyone away if possible."

I gave one of the ABs. F.J. Meaker, my suit case to put in the boat. It contained all my papers, ship cash accounts, victualling bills, insurance etc., Rum, cigarettes, Brandy and some Liebigo Extract.

The Chief Engineer, Mr W. Soutter, came up to me and said, "The engine room's full of water. I'm afraid there's no hope for them down below." then he said, "You haven't got your life jacket on."

So I went back on the top bridge and got my life jacket from out the day room and put it on. The ship continued upright but well down by the stern, there was no panic or rush. The Mate said, "We'd better get a move on, Sir, before Jerry gives her the second one."

I said, "Carry on and stand near by for me when you've got the boat in the water."

I went down on deck with the ship's papers, confidential papers, with the intention of burning them in the galley stove, there usually being a good fire there about that time in the evening. I found the galley just about wrecked, with the stove blown to bits. I lashed up the bag and dropped it over the side. It sank at once.

The deck in the port alleyway seemed to be buckled, the hatch covers of the bunker pocket blown off. There was hot water ankle deep right away along to the engine room. Flashed my torch in the engine room but could make out nothing but heavily rushing water. Walked around house to starboard alleyway, deck was all right but nearly ankle deep in cinders. Climbed up on boat deck. Starboard boat away but not in sight. Port boat and davits blown to bits. Back on deck, Chief Engineer just going down sea ladder into starboard Jolly boat. The Mate and his crew already in the boat, he shouted out that the forward fall had jammed on the port Jolly boat, so they had abandoned it and lowered the starboard one. He said,

†"I've got all your papers safely in this boat, are you corning down now, she's settling rapidly by the stern, and I reckon she'll get a 2nd torpedo any minute now."

The Chief Engineer said, "I saw Sango (Trimmer) go along the fore deck just now, he's badly hurt in the face."

†I went along forward and into the f'ocsle saw Sango in the beam of my flash light, sitting on one of the benches. His face was very badly cut and. Burned. I went in and said, †"Come on my son, let's get amidships to the boat before the old ship goes."

He didn't want to leave, but I forced and dragged him out of the f'ocsle and along the fore deck and shouted down to the boat, "Here's Sango."

†I left him then and went back along the fore deck and let go the painter of the raft which had jammed. †Meaker and the Bosun, G.Emmerson were on the raft.

Came back along the deck, the Mate said, "You'd better come down now."

I said, "All right, I'm going in the saloon to get the kitten."

†Went in the saloon and found the kitten in the medicine chest, brought him out and threw him down to those in the (boat), caught him safely enough, called him Temoshenko because he was always ready to fight.

Steamer very low in the water aft, but still upright. Felt very reluctant to get in the boat and leave her. Went and looked down the X bunker, it was full of water, at least could see nothing but water, there was a good bit of coal there, went back to where Starboard Jolly boat was waiting under the bridge. Said "Goodbye" to the old ship. Climbed down the pilot ladder into the boat. The Mate said, "She'll go any minute now.'

Let go the painter and pushed off.

I said, "Stand by for a while, let's see what's going to happen to her."

Saw the 2nd Mate in the Starboard life boat, shouted to him to go alongside raft and pick up the Bosun and Meaker, saw him go alongside raft.

About 7.25 p.m. now, heard heavy explosion in Allende and, in a few seconds she seemed to collapse in the middle, the stern sank out of sight and the f'ocsle head rose up to the sky and then disappeared. The 2nd torpedo seemed to have been put in about No. 4 Hold, and that was the last of Allende. I felt like crying.

Noticed that our boat was making water badly. There was a little chop on the sea, but 12 men in her was too much. There remained only a few inches of free board. Carried on baling and commenced pulling away in a N. Westerly direction. Suddenly heard a noise and then a black shape came into view. The submarine had surfaced and was heading at good speed in our direction. I ordered "Vast pulling" and dead silence. The submarine at first sight looked like a trawler, her engines made considerable noise. I thought she might pass without seeing us, but suddenly she took on the appearance of trying to run us down. A voice from the Sub. hailed us, "Boat ahoy, come alongside, come quickly."

Answered "O.K." and commenced pulling in her direction. She got herself in good position to give us a lee and stopped her engines. We came up close alongside. She looked big and black. There appeared to be a 12 lb gun on her fore deck, and a heavier gun fairly close to the after side of her conning tower. Two men dressed in heavy weather clothing and sea boots were standing on the fore deck about half way along it and there was the glow of a cigar or cigarette in the conning tower. One of the men on the fore deck sang out, "What is the name of' your ship?"

All hands except myself answered, "Allende."

†"Is the Captain on board?" Milroy, O.S. answered yes, but I believe they must have taken that to mean that I had gone down with Allende for he asked no more questions about the Captain. He probably assumed, from the fact that everyone in the boat was answering his questions that quite possibly there was no senior officer present. I was content that he went on thinking it. He continued his questions with "What tonnage? Where from? What cargo?" and finally, "What is your port of Registry?"

Everyone roared out the answers to his questions and he replied "Oui".

Lightning flashes lighted up the submarine every minute or so. She showed light grey then, but although I looked carefully, waiting for the lightning flash, I could make out no mark or number on her conning tower. Saw the dim figure of the smoker there, probably the commander.

†He said "Carry on boat. Steer 008∞ ó 18 miles."

Everyone shouted ëThank you."

I was waiting for a burst of machine gun fire, but it never came, so I guess I thought an injustice on that commander.

Suddenly we noticed that the boat was filling up in spite of the baling. We were pulling away from the sub. and from the wash coming from her casing sides. The sea was a little more choppy now; the clouds were banking up, the lightning flashes became more frequent. The boat sank below the level of the water and capsized, turning everyone and everything into the sea of course. I grabbed an oar as it floated clear then as the boat rose above the surface again, bottom up now, we all managed to get back to her and cling to the keel, but we were not evenly spread out around her, so she just took another turn round and floated full of water. Then once more she capsized as we all made frantic attempts to hang on to her sides. This happened five times before we finally got ourselves evenly spread out around her. We were feeling very exhausted by this time. I should think we had been struggling in the water for about an hour.

Porpoises were leaping close by and some large multi-coloured fish glided past. Someone said afterwards that it was a Barracuda, I doubt it myself. If it had been, more than likely it would have attacked us there and then. However, it turned our thoughts to sharks and greatly increased our anxiety to be back in the comparative safety of the boat.

The Mate suggested that while the rest of us held the boat steady from the outside he would get in, make ?----plug and then bale the boat out again, and that is what we did. There were a couple of sheath knives amongst us and with it, the Mate cut down and shaped out a plug out of the wooden handle of one of the sea (?) lights, a tin of which still remained lashed to one of the thwarts, being not heavy enough to carry away when the boat turned over, I suppose. All this took us the best part of another hour I suppose, but with the help of the sea (?) light tin and a couple of soft felt hats the boat was baled out sufficiently for us all to get back in and give a hand with the rest of the baling. We were all mighty thankful to get back into the boat. The struggle with the capsizing boat in the first place had taken it out of us and we had all just about reached our limit.

For my own part, I would never have been able to climb back aboard but for the assistance of Mr Lewis, the Senior Wireless Operator, who very gallantly boosted me aboard before he himself climbed inboard. All my right side was paralysed, particularly my right shoulder and hand. The hand was grip-less and useless and the shoulder dead.

About now the sky was heavily overcast and it looked as if it might come on to blow. The lightning had ceased except for a faraway flash at long intervals. We took stock of our position. Most everything movable had been lost. The water was gone, all the oars except 3; buckets, baler, mast and sail all gone. The biscuits of course were all right, being secured to the thwart in an iron tank by iron bands. We also had the compass and. we settled down to gently pull through the night, just keeping a little way on the boat and her head in a N. Westerly direction. Too dark to see the compass, so as we kept getting a glimpse of the pole star, we steered by it, keeping it about 4 points on the starboard bow, hoping that we would make a little against the 2Ω knot current that was running to the Eastward.

Around about midnight it commenced to rain gently, the rain lasted about half an hour and was very cold. Everyone remained fairly cheerful. We spoke of the chances of being picked up when daylight and everyone agreed that the chances were rosy indeed. If our S.O.S. got through at all, someone would be looking for us, and the course we were steering across the current wouldn't take us far away from the position in which we were torpedoed by daylight. I lay aft close against the tiller trying to rest, my leg and my shoulder both being extremely painful by now. The Mate had the tiller while three men kept up a gentle pulling on the three oars, changing over about every half an hour. One or two of us were violently sick during the night, due most probably to the amount of sea water we had swallowed.

At last the dawn came with a morning sky away to the Eastward. As the light became stronger we could make out the land low down on the Northern horizon, too low down I thought, we were further off than I expected us to be as the current had evidently done better or worse than I had looked for. However, daylight and just the knowledge that land was in sight made most everyone cheerful, very hopeful of a quick delivery from an unenvious position.

About 6 a.m. smoke was sighted away to Starboard and we put on a spurt with the oars. Presently a steamer hove in sight, steering almost directly towards us. We were all very bucked now, thinking that in a very short while we should have reached succour in the shape of dry clothes, coffee and a bunk. As the steamer came closer it could be seen that she was about 9000 tons D.W. Buff topsides and we thought we could make out the shape of her 4 inch anti-submarine gun. British was in everyone's mind, but I thought without voicing the thought, "She's in a funny spot and steering in a peculiar manner if she is a British ship."

As we came closer together she altered her course more directly across our bow and appeared to be crossing ahead and that is what she actually did at increasing speed. We ceased pulling and tied the third Engineer's raincoat to an oar and hoisted it up in the air, a bit too difficult to wave about, but we tried even that. All to no purpose, she just kept her course and speed and left us to do the best we could for ourselves. If there had been an officer on the bridge at all, and it is most improbable that there was not, taking into account her close proximity to land and that she had altered her course only a few minutes before, if anyone at all had been on the bridge, we must have been seen, a pair of ëbinoculars should have done the rest.

However, if she was British or Allied maybe her master feared some submarine trick and wasn't having any, and thinking things over since that time, I'm inclined to think he was acting in the best interests of his ship, that is of course if he were a Britisher or an Allied Merchant ship. For my own part, I think his manoeuvring and position were suspicious. He could as easily have been a store ship for Subs. probably not long since having refuelled the fellow that sank us. However in about an hour she had disappeared to port which made me think that she had again reduced her speed after crossing ahead of us.

This incident of the passing steamer hit us where it hurt most, we all felt a little down in the mouth about it, yet when we had looked around and satisfied ourselves that the shore line was rising albeit all too slowly, we cheered up a bit, and put a little more vim into the pulling. I suggested a biscuit apiece and I also voiced the opinion that we would be landing on the beach just after midday, although I didn't believe it myself. We opened the tank and had a biscuit each. Chewing seemed to bring a little comfort and strangely enough no one complained about the absence of a drink, no one asked for water or protested that they were dying of thirst. For my own part I wasn't thirsty. No doubt, if water had been there I should have been glad of a drink, but just as it was I didn't miss it. Fullerton, later on in the day was the first to mention thirst. I wasn't very pleased about it but said nothing. He cut a button off his shirt and put it in his mouth. He said sucking a button was known to allay the pangs of thirst. After that most of the men complained of thirst.

Fullerton also had a ºlb. tin of tobacco which he had given Kenny to look after for him. After we had opened the biscuit tank and had chewed through a whole biscuit each, I mentioned about a smoke. He was very unwilling that we should do so. However I told Kenny to open the tin, and while he did so, we dried a packet of papers in the sun, which was pretty fierce by this time. All hands cheered up wonderfully when we had got our very ragged looking cigarettes under way. We commenced pulling again. It was very hot now and for the most part we had little or no protection from the sun. Here our life belts came in very useful and handy, we were able to cover our heads and necks with them. This must have saved us considerable subsequent suffering, for at the end, of the day we were all rather badly burned, mostly around the arms and. legs.

Slowly but surely the line of shore came up over the horizon. We could. make out the trees quite plainly now and about 2 points on the port bow, what we had taken for a tall palm tree gradually took on shape and towards noon we made it out to be a lighthouse. We steered directly for it. Fullerton thought it must be Cape Palmas Light, but didn't see how it could be, not if we had set with the east going stream. Of course there was the possibility of a counter current, but the chart had shown nothing of one, so I couldn't bring my hopes to a head there. Anyhow, it was something, it was a mark of civilisation. The sandy beach came into view now, one minute it was there, then the next it had disappeared. Some of us saw it for certain, the others said imagination, but in a little while there was no mistaking the white sandy appearance, and a little later still all uncertainty was swept away when we were able to make out the breakers.

Just on noon, the sun almost right overhead, we had our hopes raised to high pitch once again, this time by the unmistakable roar of an aeroplane engine. This time it was going to be a British plane sent out to look for us, an answer to our S.O.S. of the day before. We could hear the plane for some time before our eyes could pick it up in the brilliant sunlight. At last we found it, flying at about 6 or 7000 feet. We ceased pulling, sitting silently and hopefully, waiting for some signal from him that would let us know that we had been seen. No signal came though and in a little while the plane had disappeared to the Southeast. A French plane no doubt and not the least bit interested in a boat load, of ship wrecked seamen, of whatever nationality.

Some of them were getting a bit down now and Soutter made it worse by saying, "I don't think we are getting any closer."

I gave him a good mouthful, and they laid back on their oars again. It was a back breaking nerve racking strain all the time. We seemed to move with frightful slowness, the current carrying us out of the way all the time, and at a faster rate than we were able to approach the coast.

Suddenly though, the beach seemed to leap nearer and nearer at every pull of the sweeps. We were in smoother water now, we could make out two figures moving along the beach and. above the sandy line of the shore, some native huts stood silhouetted against the sky in a clearing surrounded by palm trees. The surf was roaring and curling along the entire stretch of beach, but away to port, some nasty looking rocks running out from the beach into the sea, made me think of a lee somewhere close to them, and with this in mind, I steered for the rocks.

†As we approached the lee could be seen as a small circular sweep of the beach close in behind the rocky promontory, a sort of tiny bay, where the breakers were falling short and running up the beach with tidal effect.

I told everyone to put on his lifebelt, and explained how the boat might probably capsize if the breakers were bigger than they looked to us. Glasgow, a native of Sierre Leone, one of Allendes' †firemen offered to take the tiller saying that he had done plenty of surf boating and knew just how to handle the lifeboat to make a safe landing. I let him hold the tiller, sitting close beside him as we approached the beach. The surf roared and foamed all around us rising up in the air like columns of solid steam, then curling back to show the black terrible looking jagged edges of the naked rocks. Pulling like mad, the water suddenly flattened out and the beach leapt to meet us, the boat stopped dead and in a split second had swung her stern up on to the sand. I jumped into the water and waded ashore with everyone close beside me. We were alive and safe ashore and at first I could hardly believe it possible that we were destitute and with no Allende to go back to. However, we were, and we had to do something about it.

Everyone felt a bit done in, but the elation at getting safely ashore made us forget how tired we were, but not how thirsty. With Roberts I set off along the beach to where we had seen the two natives, and after a couple of hundred yards came across a young fellow throwing a fishing net across a hidden pool, of what looked like stagnant fresh water. When he saw us he lifted his hand in the air, giving the peace sign.

I suppose I said, ëGood day" in English.

I told him we were a torpedoed crew, and were looking for water to drink an. if possible, something to eat. He understood the eating and drinking part, but not I think the torpedoing, although he knew that we were shipwrecked in some manner or other.

He led us by a narrow path through the trees, and presently we came upon a clearing where there stood about a dozen or so reed and bamboo huts, one or two of them were quite large, and there we were introduced to the head man of the village, an elderly gentleman with a ghastly open and running sore on the shin bone of his left leg. Again I explained about being torpedoed, meanwhile a tin bath of clean fresh water had been brought to us by a semi-naked native woman of big build. By this time the rest of the crowd had followed us up and were now all seated in a circle around the bathtub of fresh water, which now required several refillings.

Most of the villagers had gathered round, children and all, they were all eager and excited by us, but very sympathetic and extremely polite in a simple and. pleasantly unassuming way. Quite a number of the men could understand slowly spoken broken English, and so could some of the elderly women of whom there were quite a number gathered round us, all smoking short and black wooden pipes. Most of the men had worked as "kru-boys" loading the steamers of the Elder Dempster Company. They were all big strong and fine looking people, the women bare from the waist up. After we had satisfied our thirst we talked a great deal, during which time I was able to find out that we were on French soil, which of course was what we had expected, although there was always just the chance that we might have got above Cape Palmas and landed in Liberia.

Kapitan Merten

An overview of the life of Merten and his crew of U68, the U Boat responsible for the loss of the Allende.

Born in Posen on 15 August 1905, Merten joined the Reichsmarine in 1926. On completion of his basic training as an officer cadet 4pd his commissioning as Leutnant zur See, he served as weapons officer in the cruiser KONIGSBERG, a modern 6,650 ton vessel which was armed with nine 5.9 inch guns in three triple turrets. Subsequently, he served in T.157, a rather elderly torpedo boat, and in the escort boat F7. In the German Navy, a torpedo-boat was a fairly large vessel, more like a small destroyer and not at all comparable to what is known as a torpedo boat in the British or American Navies. Thereafter, Merten became a cadet training officer in the training ship, SCHLESWIG-HOLSTEIN, an old 13,000-ton battleship from the First World War, based in Wilhelmshaven before the outbreak of war. In early 1940, Merten transferred to the U-boat service and his rise to the status of a U-boat ace of the highest calibre began. His first posting was to U. 38 under the command of Heinrich Liebe. Having served his time as Wach Offizier, (Watch Officer) he was given his own command in February

1941. This was U.68, a large Type IXC built by Deschimag of Bremen. It was a powerful 1,200 ton ocean going boat, equipped with 22 torpedoes and a 4 inch gun.

During the summer of 1941, Merten began to build his score. On 28 July U68 made an attack on the ships of Convoy OG69, bound for Gibraltar from the United Kingdom. Although torpedoes were launched, no detonations were recorded though a vivid jet of flame was seen on the side of an escorting corvette. On 22 September It was the turn of Convoy SL87 from Sierra Leone to the U.K. The 5,300-ton British merchantman, SILVERBELLE was sunk. A tanker was also hit and was spotted again on the following day with a heavy list and under protective escort by two warships. On 22 October, the 5,300 ton British tanker DARKDALE was sunk of f St Helena and six days later the steamer HAZELSIDE of similar tonnage was also sent to the bottom. During November the last victim of that cruise, the 4,950-ton BRADFORD CITY was attacked and sunk.

U68 returned to port and after a welcome break began her next cruise, this time to the South Atlantic, off the coast of South Africa, and in the Caribbean. The first victim was the 7360 ton steamer HELENUS on 3 March 1942. Five days later the 7,000-ton BALUCHISTAN was sunk by a combination of torpedoes and gunfire. March was to be particularly successful month for Merten. On the 16th, the small 3380 ton steamer BARON NEWLANDS was added to the list of U. 68's victims. On the next day three more ships were sunk, these being the 5,750 ton ILE DE BATZ and the 4900 ton SCOTTISH PRINCE, sunk by a combination of torpedo and gunfire and the 5000 ton steamer ALLENDE was sunk by a torpedo later the same day. A quiet spell then ensued for almost two full weeks, broken on 30 March by the sinking of the 5850 ton MUNCASTER CASTLE.

Merten's next major success was the large Panamanian tanker C.O. STILLMAN of 13000 tons, sunk on 6 June 1942. On the previous day the tanker L.J. DRAKE of some 6690 tons was reported missing in the same area. Although not claimed as a kill, she was thought to bave been sunk by U.68. A particularly successful day was 10 June 1942 when the 5580 ton SURREY, the 5000 ton ARDENVOHR and the 5880 ton PORT MONTREAL were added to Merten's list of kills.. All were sunk by torpedo. On 13 June, Merten's achievements were rewarded by the Knight's Cross of the Iron Cross. Merten held the rank of Korvettenkapitan at this time. U.68 was still at sea when he learned of his award. On 15 June he celebrated his decoration with the sinking of the 9240 ton tanker FRIMAIRE in the Caribbean. The final success of this cruise was another tanker, the ARRIAGA,†2500 tons, sunk by a combination of torpedo and gunfire on 23 June. Merten's next cruise was to see several more sinkings. On 12 September 1942, the British TREVILLAY was sunk, followed three days later by the 6860 ton Dutch steamer BREEDIJK. On 8 October in the Indian Ocean, U68 destroyed four ships: the Greek KOUNOUNDOUROS of 3600 tons, the Dutch GAASTERKERK of 8700 tons, the US tanker SWIFTFIRE of 8200 tons and the British SARTHE of 5270 tons. All were sunk by torpedoes. On the following day the US EXAMELAI of 5000 tons and the

Belgian BELGIAN FIGHTER of 5400 tons were added to Merten's ever-growing score. This represented some 36000 tons in just two days. On 6 November the British CITY OF CAIRO, an 8000 tonner was also sent to the bottom, sunk by torpedo from U.68.

On 16 November, Merten's achievements were further recognised by the award of the coveted oakleaves to his Knight's Cross. After this, Merten was given command of 26th U Boat Flotilla in Pillau, and later on, the 24th Flotilla in Memel. Here his greatest achievements were not in sinking Ships but in saving lives.† In the closing stages of the war, Merten assisted in the evacuation of more than 50,000 refugees from the advancing Russians. Merten ended the war with the rank of Kapitan zur See under command of the Marine Oberkommando West. He had sunk a total of 180,870 tons of shipping. After the war he went into French captivity where, in 1948, attempts were made to try him on fabricated war crime charges. These allegations were totally unsubstantiated and he was released in March 1949. This accomplished U Boat ace died at his home near Waldshut in May 1993.

The following poem is a tribute to the men of the Merchant Navy, written by David Partridge of Botany Bay, Australia –

HEROES

Don't speak to me of heroes until you've heard this tale
Of British Merchant Seamen who sailed through storm and gale
To keep those lifelines open in our nation's hour of need,
When a tyrant cast a shadow across our island breed.
Captains, greasers, cabin boys, mates and engineers
Heard the call to duty and cast aside their fears.
They stoked those hungry boilers and stood behind the wheel
While cooks and stewards manned the guns on coffins made of steel.
They moved in icy convoys from Scapa to Murmansk,
They crossed the Western Ocean, never seeking thanks.
They sailed the South Atlantic where raiders lay in wait
And kept the food lines open from Malta to the Cape.
Tracked by silent U Boats which hunted from below,
Shelled by mighty cannons and fighters flying low,
They clung to burning lifeboats where the sea had turned to flame
And watched their shipmates disappear to everlasting fame.
I speak not of a handful but 30,000 plus,
Some whose names we'll never know, in whom we placed our trust.
They'll never know the honour of medals on their chests
Or marching bands and victory and glory and the rest.
The ocean is their resting place, their tombstone is the wind.
The seabirds cry their last goodbye to family and to friend.
Freighters, troopships, liners and tankers by the score,
Fishing boats and coasters, 2000 ships and more
Flew the proud Red Duster as they sank beneath the waves,
And took those countless heroes to lonely ocean graves.
To walk with clear horizons and never hide in fear.
So when you speak of heroes, remember those at sea
From Britain's Merchant Navy who died to keep us free.

MERCHANT SEAMEN

By Edward Carpenter
(from Voices from the Sea: Poems by Merchant Seamen, ed. Ronald Hope, 1977)

I've read about soldiers and sailors,
Of infantry, airmen and tanks,
Of battleships, corvettes and cruisers,
Of Anzacs and Froggies and Yanks:
But there's one other man to remember,
Who was present at many a fray;
He wears neither medals nor ribbons
And derides any show of display.

I'm talking of A.B.'s and firemen,
Of stewards and greasers and cooks,
Who manned the big steamers in convoy.
(You won't read about them in books).
No uniform gay were they dressed in,
Nor marched with their colours unfurled:
They steamed out across the wide oceans,
And travelled all over the world.

Their history goes back through the ages –
A record of which to be proud –
And the bones of their forefathers moulder
With naught but the deep for a shroud.
For armies have swept on to victory
O'er the bodies of those who have died;
'Tis thus that the nations do battle
For country, and freedom, and pride.

In thousands they sailed from the homeland.
From Liverpool, Hull and the Clyde;
To London, and Bristol, and Cardiff,
They came back again on the tide.
An old 'four-point-seven' their safeguard -
What nice easy prey for the Huns
Who trailed them with bombers and U-Boats
And sank them with 'tin-fish' and guns.

The epic of gallant 'Otaki',
That grim forlorn hope 'Jervis Bay',
Who fought to the last and were beaten,
But they joined the illustrious array
Whose skeletons lie 'neath the waters',

Whose deeds are remembered today,
And their glory will shine undiminished
Long after our flesh turns to clay.

They landed the Anzacs at Suvla
And stranded the old 'River Clyde',
Off Dunkirk they gathered the remnants
(And still they were not satisfied),
They battled their way through to Malta,
and rescued the troops from Malay;
They brought back the Eighth Army munitions
And took all their prisoners away.

And others 'signed on' in the tankers'
And loaded crude oil and octane -
The lifeblood of warships and engines,
Of mechanised transport and plane.
But these were the U-Boats' chief victims;
What death they were called to face
As men were engulfed by infernos
In ships that were 'sunk without trace'.

They were classed a non-combatant service -
Civilians who fought without guns -
And many's the time they'd have welcomed
A chance of a crack at the Huns.
But somehow in spite of this drawback
The steamers still sailed and arrived,
And they fed fifty millions of people
And right to the end we survived.

When the Master of Masters holds judgment
And the Devil's dark angles have flown,
When the clerk of the heavenly council
Decrees that the names shall be shown
They will stand out in glittering letters
Inscribed with the blood they have shed:
Names of ships – and the seamen who manned them:
Then the ocean can give up its dead.

CONCLUSION

The story of the Second World War at sea and, in particular, of the part played in that war by Welsh men and women, is one of indomitable courage and sheer dogged perseverance. Sometimes it was a war of high drama and great emotional tension. Sometimes it was a combination of sheer boredom, great discomfort and mind-wrenching home sickness. Always it was a time when men and women who might otherwise never have left their homes in places like the Welsh valleys and the tiny village communities of North Wales faced new experiences, saw sights they might only otherwise have dreamed about, on a daily basis.

Reading the stories so elegantly and so easily told by the men and women of the Royal and Merchant Navies, the one dominant characteristic, something that runs through them all, is a quiet and modest courage. The sailors did not think they were doing anything out of the ordinary. They still don't.

Courage is a hard characteristic to pin down or define. Who is to say that the man who charges, single handed, into certain death is braver than the one who goes quietly about his business, hoping and trusting that the ultimate victory will be his? But if a definition of courage is the ability to do your duty without complaint, never forgetting comrades, friends and family, then the men and women of the Royal and Merchant Navies had it in plenty.

The men and women whose stories are told in this book faced death on a daily basis. The threat of a sudden and violent end came from hidden submarines, from aircraft bombs and from the guns of the German navy. It also came from the elements, the wind and the very sea on which they sailed. The sailors faced them all with equanimity and a determination to see things through to the end.

All of us living in the 21st century owe a debt to the sailors of the Second World War, a debt that can never be repaid. The sailors probably would not want anything to be repaid – that has never been on the "agenda" - but they would also not want to be forgotten. If this book goes some way to remembering the men and women who made sacrifices – sometimes the ultimate sacrifice – so that we can all live in security, then it will have succeeded in its aim.

The war at sea, a vicious but vital combat that Britain had to win.

431

GLOSSARY

AB – Able Bodied seaman; a first-class or certificated deck rating.

Aft – towards the stern of the ship.

Aldis lamps – lamps designed to make signals in daylight.

ASDIC – underwater sound-ranging device for finding the position of a submerged submarine, known in the USA as sonar.

Boatswain, bosun – the senior deck rating on a merchant ship.

Bofors – Swedish anti-aircraft gun

Breaker – fresh water container on a lifeboat, usually holding 6-10 gallons, dependent on size of boat.

Bulkhead - one of the upright partitions dividing a ship into compartments and serving to add structural rigidity and to prevent the spread of leakage or fire.

Bulwark – steel plating around the deck, preventing personnel or cargo being washed overboard.

Chief Officer – the officer on a merchant ship ranking immediately below the captain. Usually they went on to become captains themselves.

Commodore – officer in charge of the organisation, tactics and progress of a convoy, often a retired naval officer.

Condensed milk - evaporated milk combined with sugar, and typically canned. It became very popular in wartime England as a preserved form of milk.

Conning tower – the raised, enclosed observation post in a submarine.

Corvette – small convoy escort vessel (based on the design of a pre-war Antarctic whaler).

Davits, radial davits – small cranes projecting over the side of the ship that can lower or raise boats, anchors, supplies etc.

DEMS – 'Defensively Equipped Merchant Ships'; a merchantman with some deck armoury, also the merchant ship's naval or army gunners were sometimes called DEMS.

Dipper: a container to dip into the breaker on a lifeboat for fresh water, about the size of a small coffee cup.

Donkeyman - a donkeyman looks after a donkey boiler, or engine and so serves in the engine room. In a merchant ship, a senior engine-room rating.

E-Boats - the British and American name for the German Schnellboot (S-boot), a small, fast torpedo boat a little larger than the American PT boat and the British MTB (Motor Torpedo Boat)..

Fireman and trimmer – on coal-burning ships, the stokers.

Forecastle, foc's'le – space below the deck in a ship's bows, used for stores and crew accommodation.

Forwards– towards the ship's bows.

Galley – ship's kitchen.

Gas oil – highly inflammable light diesel oil.

Gig – small open boat, usually used for shore contact when in harbour.

Greaser – engine room rating who oils and greases machinery.

Gunwales, gunnels, gunn'ls – the topmost planks on the side of a boat, or the point where the hull platform joins the main deck.

Heave to – to stop a ship at sea, e.g. to rescue survivors.

HX – fast Atlantic convoys, with a minimum speed of 9 knots.

Jolly boat – small ship's boat, like a gig.

Knot – a nautical mile per hour, of 6,080 feet (a land mile is 5280 feet).

Locker, as in forward locker – a lockable cupboard.

Maritime Regiment – British Army regiment which manned about half the guns on merchant ships. The others were staffed by the Royal Navy DEMS gunners.

Monkey Island – the ship's upper bridge; the enclosed deck directly above the wheelhouse, used for keeping watch.

Pemmican – pounded meat mixed with fat and sometimes berries, used by American Indians as survival food and adopted by the American then British forces.

Rod and chain – this system is referred to by Arthur Hellyar on the old Barrington Court. An old method of steering using a system of rods and chains driven by a steam engine.

T/T – radio/telephone.

Sea anchor – as explained in Philip Thomas 'A Narrow Escape' – a canvas drogue used by lifeboats to slow the boat and help it ride over high seas.

SC – slow North Atlantic convoy with a maximum speed of 9 knots.

Sparks – slang for wireless operator.

Stanchions – vertical posts or frameworks of vertical bars.

Starshell – these contained a pyrotechnic flare on a small parachute and were designed to illuminate the attack area.

Stokehold – the compartment containing the boiler furnaces.

Straggler – a ship which has fallen behind a convoy.

Swell – vertical movement of the sea, caused by a distant storm or wind.

Thwarts - side-benches on a small boat.

U Boat – short for Unterseebooten.

W/T – wireless/telegraphy, or a wireless/telegraphy operator.

BIBLIOGRAPHY

W D G Blundell "Royal Navy Warships 1939-45" Altmark Pubs, London, 1971
 "German Navy Warships 1939-45" Altmark Pubs, London, 1972
Ewart Brookes "Destroyer" Arrow, London, 1973
Phil Carradice "Wales at War" Gomer , Llandysul, 2004
 "Welsh Shipwrecks in Camera" Quotes, Buckingham, 1993
Edward Davidson and Dale Manning "Chronology of World War Two" Cassel and Co, London, 1999
Rear Admiral R K Dickson "Naval Broadcasts" Allen and Unwin, London, 1946
Jim Dwyer and Bernard Edwards (editors) "Death and Donkeys' Breakfasts: The War beyond Lundy" D&E Books, Newport, 1988
Bernard Edwards "Attack and Sink" New Guild, Dorset, 1995
 "They Sank the Red Dragon" GPC Books, Cardiff, 1987
 "The Road to Russia: Arctic Convoys 1942" Pen & Sword, 2002
 "Beware Raiders" German Surface Raiders - Second World War" Pen & Sword 2001
 "Blood and Bushido: Japanese Atrocities at Sea, 1941-1945" Self Publishing 1991
Ivor Wynne Jones "Shipwrecks of North Wales" Landmark Press, 2001
Reg Chambers Jones "Bless 'Em All" Bridge Books, Wrexham, undated
Donald Macintyre "The Battle of the Atlantic" Pan, London, 1969
David Masters "Up Periscope" Eyre and Spottiswoode, London, 1943
Martin Middlebrook "Convoy" Quill, New York, 1976
Marc Milner "Battle of the Atlantic" Tempus, 2005
Capt A B Sainsbury and Lt Cmdr F L Phillips "The Royal Navy Day by Day" Sutton, Stroud, 2005
Vernon Scott "An Experience Shared" Laleham Pubs, Pembroke Dock, 1992
Cmdr George Smith "Under Cunningham's Command" Allen and Unwin, London, 1944
David A. Thomas "The Atlantic Star: 1939-45" W.H. Allen & Co., 1990
Vernon Upton, GM "Upon Their Lawful Occasions" Matador, Leicester, 2004
Edward P Van der Porten "The German Navy in World War Two" Pan, London, 1970

OTHER BOOKS FROM GLYNDWR PUBLISHING

The Secret Vale of Glamorgan ISBN 190352900X 230pp (Terry Breverton 2000) Millennium Award – 'shows a local man's pride in the history and culture of his native patch, combined with a historian's delight in tracing the past and relating it to the present.' (OUT of PRINT) £13.99

The Book of Welsh Saints ISBN 1903529018 606pp hardback (Terry Breverton 2000) – 'this book is a really extraordinary achievement: a compilation of tradition, topography and literary detective work that can have few rivals. I have enjoyed browsing it immensely, and have picked up all sorts of new lines to follow up' – Rowan Williams, Archbishop of Canterbury; 'an enormous work of research'. £24.99

100 Great Welshmen ISBN 1903529034 376pp (Terry Breverton 2001) Welsh Books Council 'Book of the Month' – 'a revealing volume illustrating the great and good with Welsh connection... painstaking research'; 'a veritable goldmine of a book'. (OUT of PRINT) £17.99

The Dragon Entertains – 100 Welsh Stars ISBN 1903529026 230pp (Alan Roderick 2001)
' a celebration of Welsh talent in all its vibrany variety', 'this is the book to reach for the next time someone tells you that Wales has not nurtured any great talent in the worlds of entertainment or show-biz.' £5.99 (Special Offer, from £11.99)

A Rhondda Boy: The Memoirs of Ivor Howells edited by Owen Vernon Jones ISBN 1903529050 144pp (Ivor Howells 2001) 'a charming evocation of the childhood of a 93 year old Welshman. Son of a miner, Rhondda born and bred, Rhondda educated apart from his degree years at Aberystwyth, Ivor Howells spent all his professional life as teacher and headmaster in Rhondda schools.' £6.99

100 Great Welsh Women ISBN 1903529042 304pp (Terry Breverton 2001) – 'this book is an absolute must for all those who value their Welsh heritage, and for all those who wish to see women accorded their rightful place in history.' £16.99

The Welsh Almanac ISBN 1903529107 320pp hardback (Terry Breverton 2002) Welsh Books Council Book of the Month – 'a tremendous undertaking, and a very worthwhile and absolutely fascinating addition to the library of Welsh history'; 'It will take its place on the bookshelf with other works of reference.' £6.99 (special offer, from £16.99)

From Wales to Pennsylvania: The David Thomas Story ISBN 1903529085 112pp (Dr Peter N. Williams 2002) 'the story of the man who emigrated from Ystradgynlais, to transform the American iron industry and make America an economic superpower... Dr Peter Williams takes us back to the days of mass emigration to the United States. The terrible conditions at home, which sparked the Chartist Riots, are described, to put into context the reasons for this difficult transatlantic flight. Through Dr Thomas's correspondence with Wales, Dr Williams shows us the Welshman's immense contribution to the industrialisation and economic growth of America.' £8.99

Glyn Dwr's War: The Campaigns of the Last Prince of Wales 238pp ISBN 1903529069 (Gideon Brough 2002) 'The Great Liberation War is THE defining moment of our nation's history. Had it not been for Owain Glydwr and the men and women who stood at his side against overwhelming odds, there would be no Welsh nation today. You will find all the details here,' 'A massive undertaking indeed for a 30 year old, first-time author, but one which Brough, who himself boasts an impressive militart background, has tackled with immense confidence and success.' £13.99 (OUT OF PRINT)

The Path to Inexperience ISBN 1903529077 160pp (Terry Breverton 2002) – 'magnificent, compassionate and moving' Special offer £3.99

Glamorgan Seascape Pathways – 52 Walks in the Southern Vale of Glamorgan ISBN 1903529115 144pp (Terry Breverton 2003) ARWAIN Award - 'fascinating... useful to anybody interested in the topography, geography and history of the southern Vale of Glamorgan.' Special Offer £6.99

The Book of Welsh Pirates and Buccaneers ISBN 1903529093 388pp (Terry Breverton 2003) Welsh Books Council Book of the Month – 'an immense work of great scholarship... effectively, a study of the whole genre of piracy... exemplary, yet the writing is light and accessible... wonderful, fascinating detail and essential reading.' (OUT of PRINT) £17.99

The Man from the Alamo : Why the Welsh Chartist Uprising of 1839 Ended in a Massacre ISBN 190352914X 332pp (John Humphries 2004) 'one of the fastest-selling books in Welsh publishing history', 'the remarkable story of two men sentenced to hanging, drawing and quartering. Zephaniah Williams ended up a respectable businessman after being transported to hard labour in Tasmania. John Rees ('Jack the Fifer' escaped from the Alamo to probably fire the first shot at the Westgate Hotel, before escaping back to join the great California Gold Rush', 'an amazing story, full of meticulously researched new facts, from the former editor of the Western Mail.' W.H. Smith Welsh Book of the Month. £9.99

Black Bart Roberts – The Greatest Pirate of Them All ISBN1903529123 254pp (Terry Breverton 2004) 'a must read for anyone interested in pirates', 'the true story of John Robert, the most successful pirate of all time, who captured over 400 ships, and brought Atlantic shipping to a standstill', 'a fascinating story of piratical history on the High Seas', 'he basically declared war against the world.' £10.99

The Pirate Handbook- A Dictionary of PirateTerms and Places ISBN1903529131 388pp Welsh Books Council Book of the Month (Terry Breverton 2004) – 'this wonderful sourcebook is an absolute must for all those interested in nautical matters', 'the amount of detail and depth is phenomenal', 'a vitally important addition to the canon of literature about naval history'. £11.99

Heroic Science: Swansea and the Royal Institution of South Wales 1835-1865 ISBN1903529166 258pp – (Ron Rees 2005) – Who knows that at one time Swansea's scientists were at the centre of the Scientific Revolution, and the great men of the day made their way by carriage and boat to its Royal Institution? £9.99

Gringo Revolutionary: The Amazing Story of Carel ap Rhys Price ISBN1903529182 - John Humphries (2005) – 'the former editor of the Western Mail has done it again, following the amazing success of his The Man from the Alamo' – this is the true story of a Welsh anarchist who fought with Zapata and Pancho Villa, was Hollywood's first all-action hero, and a World War I hero. £9.99

100 Great Welshmen (New Edition) ISBN1903529157 432pp – (Terry Breverton 2005) 'a fascinating compendium', 'this book is great fun', 'a massive treasure-chest of facts and figures which no collector of books on Wales can overlook.'£14.99

Admiral Sir Henry Morgan: the Greatest Buccaneer of Them All ISBN1903529174 174pp Welsh Books Council Book of the Month – (Terry Breverton 2005) – what more is there to say? Breverton has recently given an academic paper at Gregynog to an international conference, pointing out the little-known fact that Morgan was one of the greatest 'generals' in history, a genius at defeating overwhelming odds. £11.99

FORTHCOMING BOOKS from GLYNDWR PUBLISHING

The Beggar's Legacy: William Williams and the First American Novel – Terry Breverton (2007) – Breverton went to Indiana to transcribe the original 'The Journal of Penrose, Seaman' and has appended a biography of its author, the amazing yet unknown William Williams, polymath, marooned buccaneer, artist, theatre-builder, poet, writer of America's first novel, who taught Benjamin West to paint. Williams has been called 'the first flower of American culture' and his factional novel, based upon his being marooned on the Miskito Coast, is the first American novel and probably the first anti-slavery book.

Cave of Heroes – Various Writers, edited by Terry Breverton with Rhys Parry (2007) – a children's book featuring all of Wales' greatest heroes, their stories told by the best Welsh writers of the day.

Welsh Airmen of the Second World War – Phil Carradice and Terry Breverton (2007)

Welsh Soldiers of the Second World War – Phil Carradice and Terry Breverton (2008)

Ramblings of a Patagonian: 'When You Going Back, Then?' – Rene Griffiths (2008) – if you like off-the-wall reminiscences, this is the biography of a Patagonian troubadour and film actor who spends half his life in Cardiff and half on his ranch in the foothills of the Andes. Very humorous, and utterly absorbing in his perspective of two vastly different cultures.

A Patagonian Diary – W.C. Rhys (2008) – the remarkable story of one of the first Welsh settlers in Patagonia, translated and updated from the previous Spanish edition.

Another 100 Great Welshmen – Terry Breverton (2008) – featuring many men who could have been in the original '100 Great Welshmen'

Other Books from Terry Breverton
An A to Z of Wales and the Welsh, 2000, Christopher Davies ('the first Welsh encyclopaedia!')
Contributions to A Song for Owain: Poems in Praise of Owain Glyndŵr, 2004 ed. Rhys Parry, Y Lolfa

Forthcoming books by Terry Breverton
A Historical Companion to Wales, 2007 Tempus Publishing

WHERE TO BUY

All of the Above Books are Available from The Welsh Books Council, Unit 16, Parc Menter Glanyrafon, Llanbadarn Fawr, Ceredigion SY23 3AQ, or from its website www.gwales.com, or from any good bookseller. If your bookseller states that it cannot get any of these books, they are on all the relevant ordering databases. Alternatively, send a cheque with order to Wales Books (Glyndŵr Publishing) at PO BOX 68, Cowbridge, Vale of Glamorgan CF71 9AY. There is no postage on orders in the British Isles, but £6 per book is charged for overseas orders. Visit our website www.walesbooks.com to download an order form, if you wish. The web pages feature a Welsh Quiz, addresses for over 400 Welsh Societies around the world, and reviews on all our books. Please let us know any additions or alterations to societies.

Our American Publishing Partners are Pelican Publishing Company, PO Box 3110, Gretna, New Orleans LA 70054, with the website www.pelicanpub.com. In 2004-5 Pelican published Terry Breverton's 'Black Bart Roberts' , 'The Pirate Dictionary', 'Admiral Sir Henry Morgan', and John Humphries' 'The Man from the Alamo' , and it is hoped that all of Glyndŵr Publishing's output will be available in the USA via Pelican over the forthcoming years.